W9-BSV-538

EGYPT

3rd Edition

Where to Stay and Eat
for All Budgets

Must-See Sights
and Local Secrets

Ratings You Can Trust

Fodor's Travel Publications   New York, Toronto, London, Sydney, Auckland
www.fodors.com

FODOR'S EGYPT
Editor: Doug Stallings

Editorial Contributors: Lindsay and Pete Bennett

Production Editor: Evangelos Vasilakis
Maps & Illustrations: David Lindroth, *cartographer*; Bob Blake, Rebecca Baer, *map editors;* William Wu, *information graphics*
Design: Fabrizio La Rocca, *creative director*; Guido Caroti, Siobhan O'Hare, *art directors;* Tina Malaney, Chie Ushio, Ann McBride, Jessica Walsh, *designers*; Melanie Marin, *senior picture editor*
Cover Photo (The Greco-Roman temple of Esna, Esna City) José Fuste Raga/age fotostock
Production Manager: Amanda Bullock

COPYRIGHT
Copyright © 2009 by Fodor's Travel, a division of Random House, Inc.

Fodor's is a registered trademark of Random House, Inc.

All rights reserved. Published in the United States by Fodor's Travel, a division of Random House, Inc., and simultaneously in Canada by Random House of Canada, Limited, Toronto. Distributed by Random House, Inc., New York.

No maps, illustrations, or other portions of this book may be reproduced in any form without written permission from the publisher.

3rd Edition

ISBN 978-1-4000-0730-1

ISSN 0147-8176

SPECIAL SALES
This book is available at special discounts for bulk purchases for sales promotions or premiums. Special editions, including personalized covers, excerpts of existing books, and corporate imprints, can be created in large quantities for special needs. For more information, write to Special Markets/Premium Sales, 1745 Broadway, MD 6-2, New York, New York 10019, or e-mail specialmarkets@randomhouse.com.

AN IMPORTANT TIP & AN INVITATION
Although all prices, opening times, and other details in this book are based on information supplied to us at press time, changes occur all the time in the travel world, and Fodor's cannot accept responsibility for facts that become outdated or for inadvertent errors or omissions. So **always confirm information when it matters,** especially if you're making a detour to visit a specific place. Your experiences—positive and negative—matter to us. If we have missed or misstated something, **please write to us.** We follow up on all suggestions. Contact the Egypt editor at editors@fodors.com or c/o Fodor's at 1745 Broadway, New York, NY 10019.

PRINTED IN THE UNITED STATES OF AMERICA

10 9 8 7 6 5 4 3 2

Be a Fodor's Correspondent

Your opinion matters. It matters to us. It matters to your fellow Fodor's travelers, too. And we'd like to hear it. In fact, we need to hear it.

When you share your experiences and opinions, you become an active member of the Fodor's community. That means we'll not only use your feedback to make our books better, but we'll publish your names and comments whenever possible. Throughout our guides, look for "Word of Mouth," excerpts of your unvarnished feedback.

Here's how you can help improve Fodor's for all of us.

Tell us when we're right. We rely on local writers to give you an insider's perspective. But our writers and staff editors—who are the best in the business—depend on you. Your positive feedback is a vote to renew our recommendations for the next edition.

Tell us when we're wrong. We're proud that we update most of our guides every year. But we're not perfect. Things change. Hotels cut services. Museums change hours. Charming cafés lose charm. If our writer didn't quite capture the essence of a place, tell us how you'd do it differently. If any of our descriptions are inaccurate or inadequate, we'll incorporate your changes in the next edition and will correct factual errors at fodors.com immediately.

Tell us what to include. You probably have had fantastic travel experiences that aren't yet in Fodor's. Why not share them with a community of like-minded travelers? Maybe you chanced upon a beach or bistro or B&B that you don't want to keep to yourself. Tell us why we should include it. And share your discoveries and experiences with everyone directly at fodors.com. Your input may lead us to add a new listing or highlight a place we cover with a "Highly Recommended" star or with our highest rating, "Fodor's Choice."

Give us your opinion instantly at our feedback center at www.fodors.com/feedback. You may also e-mail editors@fodors.com with the subject line "Egypt Editor." Or send your nominations, comments, and complaints by mail to Egypt Editor, Fodor's, 1745 Broadway, New York, NY 10019.

You and travelers like you are the heart of the Fodor's community. Make our community richer by sharing your experiences. Be a Fodor's correspondent.

Happy traveling!

Tim Jarrell, Publisher

CONTENTS

ABOUT
THIS BOOK

Our Ratings

Sometimes you find terrific travel experiences and sometimes they just find you. But usually the burden is on you to select the right combination of experiences. That's where our ratings come in.

As travelers we've all discovered a place so wonderful that its worthiness is obvious. And sometimes that place is so experiential that superlatives don't do it justice: you just have to be there to know. These sights, properties, and experiences get our highest rating, **Fodor's Choice**, indicated by orange stars throughout this book.

Black stars highlight sights and properties we deem **Highly Recommended**, places that our writers, editors, and readers praise again and again for consistency and excellence.

By default, there's another category: any place we include in this book is by definition worth your time, unless we say otherwise. And we will.

Disagree with any of our choices? Care to nominate a place or suggest that we rate one more highly? Visit our feedback center at www.fodors.com/feedback.

Budget Well

Hotel and restaurant price categories from ¢ to $$$$ are defined in the opening pages of each chapter. For attractions, we always give standard adult admission fees; reductions are usually available for children, students, and senior citizens. Want to pay with plastic? **AE, D, DC, MC, V** after restaurant and hotel listings indicate if American Express, Discover, Diners Club, MasterCard, and Visa are accepted.

Restaurants

Unless we state otherwise, restaurants are open for lunch and dinner daily. We mention dress only when there's a specific requirement and reservations only when they're essential or not accepted—it's always best to book ahead.

Hotels

Hotels have private bath, phone, TV, and air-conditioning and operate on the European Plan (aka EP, meaning without meals), unless we specify that they use the Continental Plan (CP, with a Continental breakfast), Breakfast Plan (BP, with a full breakfast), or Modified American Plan (MAP, with breakfast and dinner) or are all-inclusive (including all meals and most activities). We

always list facilities but not whether you'll be charged an extra fee to use them, so when pricing accommodations, find out what's included.

Many Listings

★	Fodor's Choice
★	Highly recommended
⊠	Physical address
✛	Directions
⌂	Mailing address
☎	Telephone
🖷	Fax
⊕	On the Web
✉	E-mail
🖃	Admission fee
☉	Open/closed times
Ⓜ	Metro stations
⊟	Credit cards

Hotels & Restaurants

🏨	Hotel
⤵	Number of rooms
⚖	Facilities
۞	Meal plans
✕	Restaurant
⌦	Reservations
↘	Smoking
♗	BYOB
✕🏨	Hotel with restaurant that warrants a visit

Outdoors

🏌	Golf
⛺	Camping

Other

☾	Family-friendly
⇨	See also
⊠	Branch address
☞	Take note

1

Experience Egypt

Consuegra, Toledo province

WORD OF MOUTH

"Egypt is a dynamic country, with friendly people, [an] exotic ambience, and the best historic sightseeing in the world. With the dollar falling worldwide, Egypt is still one of the best bargains around. I always felt safe, and the people seemed genuinely happy to have us."

—Rayner

"Go and enjoy Egypt. It is a spectacular place!"

—Grcxx

WHAT'S NEW IN EGYPT

A Revelation in the Valley of the Kings

Tutankhamun's mummy went on display to the public for the first time in November 2007 at his tomb in the Valley of the Kings. The mummy is enclosed in an air-conditioned glass casket that allows visitors to cast their eyes on the face of the boy king whose funereal treasures captured the world's imagination when they were discovered in 1922. The primary reason for the new display is to protect the remains. The mummy had previously lain inside the marble sarcophagus in the tomb, but the number of visitors has caused humidity levels inside to soar (through moisture given off in sweat and breath), which has damaged both the delicate fibers that wrap the king and the body itself. Ironically, the mummy is now better protected even though it is on daily public view.

Tut's Stuff to Get a New Home

In July 2007, Farouk Hosni, Egyptian Minister of Culture, made a first visit to the site of the Grand Egyptian Museum project in Giza. Designed by Shih-Fu Peng of the Dublin architects Heneghan, the building, which is close to the pyramids plateau, will house Tutankhamun's collection of artifacts (more than 120,000 will be on display), along with the ancient barque that is currently displayed at the foot of the Great Pyramid in the Solar Boat Museum. The new museum, which is expected to open in 2010, will be a major tourist attraction with as many as 3 million visitors a year heading through the doors, but it will also act as a world hub of Ancient Egyptian studies with a robust academic institution.

Cleopatra Returns?

The world of Egyptology may be on the brink of another great discovery. At the end of May 2008, Dr. Zahi Hawass—the big cheese in Egyptian studies in Egypt and head of the Council of Antiquities—announced that archaeologists uncovered a tomb at the temple of Taposiris Magna west of Alexandria, which he hopes is that of Cleopatra VII, Egypt's most famous queen.

Hatshepsut Identified

Egyptology continues to develop, and the application of DNA studies has led to the identification of Queen Hatshepsut's mummy. The cotton-bound body was found in tomb KV60 in the Valley of the Kings in 1903 along with many others, but it was only confirmed to be the queen—who was one of Egypt's most successful pharaohs, not to mention the only woman to hold that title—in June 2007, after a long series of state-of-the-art tests including DNA comparisons with a mummy known to be related to her.

A New Red Sea Resort

Tourism around the Red Sea continues to expand, with the new resort of Sahl Hasheesh being the latest megaproject along the coast. Long-term plans for the 12-square-mi community include eight golf courses, a coral reef and artificial submerged temple for divers, over 20 five-star hotels, and a downtown with 300 stores, multi-screen cinema, and casino, plus cafés, bars, and restaurants. The project will not be complete until 2020, but some hotels should be open by 2009.

Pyramid Access Is Improved

Visitors to the Great Pyramids in Giza will appreciate new improvements to the area. A new entry gate has been built and new perimeter fences better control the ever-present hawkers and picture-takers that have inundated travelers to the pyramids. The new enclosures will also increase security in the area and help protect both visitors and the monuments themselves. The bad news is that the new entry gate now includes metal detectors and X-ray machines (once used only for the Solar Boat Museum), which cause longer lines. When the project is complete, golf carts will ferry tourists around the massive site.

Fossil Field Opens

In February 2008, the Wadi al-Hitan (Whale Valley) in Egypt's Western Desert was inaugurated as one of Egypt's official tourist attractions. The site is of world importance for the volume and quality of rare whale fossils dating back 40 million years to the time when some land-based mammals are thought to have returned to live full-time in the oceans, begetting today's air-breathing whales, dolphins, and sirenians (dugongs and manatees). The fossils lie in unadulterated landscape that allows paleontologists to study their ecosystems and the skeletal evolution that took place over successive generations as they made the transition from land dwellers to ocean dwellers. Wadi al-Hitan became a UNESCO World Heritage Site in 2006.

New Cairo Airlift

In June 2008, Delta Airlines became the first U.S.-based airline to offer nonstop service to Cairo since TWA was dissolved in 2001 and its Cairo flight was discontinued by the new owner, American Airlines. The flight operates five days a week.

A Stroll Down Memory Lane

The heart of medieval Cairo becomes an open-air museum as Shar'a al-Mu'iz, with its 40 or so historical attractions, becomes a pedestrian-only zone. The street was named after a Fatimid caliph in the late 9th century. Since then it has seen the footfall of Mamluks, Ayyubids, and Ottomans and is replete with fine mosques, madrasas (religious schools), and fine family mansions. Almost £e850 million has been spent on archaeological renovations in the capital since 2000.

A New Luxury Nile Cruise

The Nile cruise is glamorous once again with the launch of the MS *Zahra* in November 2007. Managed by Oberoi Hotels—a company renowned for its high standard of luxury and service—this chic vessel has only 24 cabins and suites designed in cool contemporary style; the ship's seven-night standard routing adds at least three nights to the usual Nile itinerary, allowing a trip to Dendera, a less-visited temple north of Luxor. Guests dine on international cuisine at an à la carte, silver-service restaurant, and the ship even has a full spa on board. Since the ship has private moorings on the river in both Luxor and Aswan, guests need never mix with the hoi polloi.

WHAT'S WHERE

The following numbers refer to chapters.

2 Cairo. One of the world's great cosmopolitan cities for well over 1,000 years, Egypt's capital is infinite and inexhaustible. Just don't expect a city frozen in time: Cairo's current vitality is as seductive as its rich past.

3 Alexandria. Alexandria still embodies the Mediterranean side of Egypt's character: breezy, relaxed, oriented toward the sea. It is a city of cafés and late-night dinners, of horse-drawn carriages and long strolls along the Corniche. Since its founding by Alexander the Great in the 4th century BC, the city has constantly reinvented itself and remains vibrant.

4 The Nile Valley & Luxor. From the implacable nobility of its pharaonic monuments at Karnak to the towering stone walls of the Valley of the Kings, Luxor never fails to impress. Stark desert borders verdant fields and silvery palm groves, and the diamond gleam of the late-afternoon sun plays on the mighty river. Prepare yourself for a dose of pure iconography.

5 Aswan & Lake Nasser. Aswan, the gateway to Nubia, is much less hectic than either Luxor or Cairo, so it offers a chance to slow down and relax. To the south is the expansive Lake Nasser, where a cruise here is even more laid-back than one on the busier stretch of the Nile. But most people are happy with a day-trip to visit the magnificent temple of Ramesses II at Abu Simbel.

6 The Sinai & the Red Sea Coast. The Sinai Peninsula and the Red Sea Coast make up Egypt's holiday land, where great beaches and year-round sunshine attract thousands of vacationers. Visitors here worship at the temple of pleasure—the exceptional diving and water sports, plus great golf courses—while others seek spiritual strength at Christian monasteries hidden in the hills.

7 The Western Desert Oases. Far to the west of the Nile Valley, at the edge of the Great Sand Sea before Egypt gives way to Libya, lie a series of remote oases—refuges from an inhospitable desert landscape and fertile enclaves historically famed for their dates and olives. In the past, these oases were isolated, many days' caravan journey from civilization; today they are hot-spots for desert adventures and expeditions that push us beyond the boundaries created by our modern lives.

Sidi Barrani

Sallum

LIBYAN PLATEAU

Siwa Oasis

Siwa

LIBYA

GREAT SAND SEA

LIBYAN DESERT

0	100 miles
0	150 km

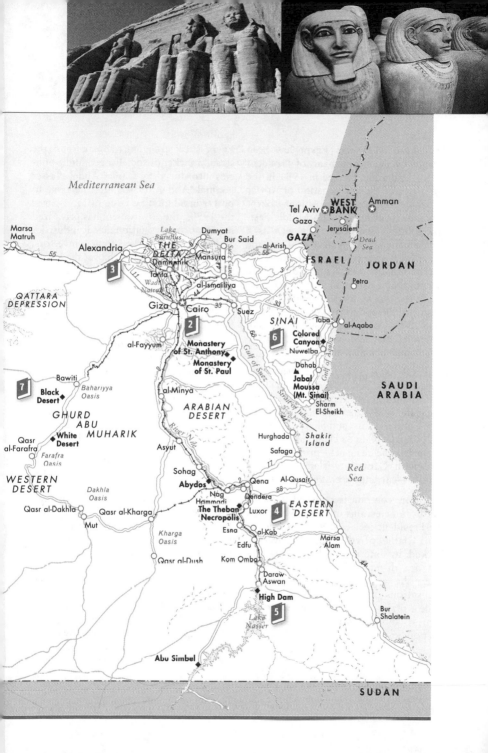

EGYPT TODAY

Politics

For almost 30 years Egypt has been steered by the strong hand of President Hosni Mubarak. Elected in 1981 in the aftermath of the assassination of Anwar Al Sadat, Mubarak has positioned Egypt at the heart of mainstream Middle Eastern politics. The country is seen as a bridge between the Arab world and the West, both as a geographical venue for international congresses and diplomatic meetings, and also as an active intermediary in the thorny Israeli-Palestinian situation. An Egyptian-brokered cease fire in June 2008 is only the latest of a series of initiatives that add weight to the country's role as a mediator.

Mubarak has had his own domestic problems, not least several terrorist incidents that killed foreign tourists in Cairo and along the Nile Valley between 1991 and 1997, and in Cairo and Sharm El-Sheikh in 2005. His regime's clampdown on dissident Islamic elements—primarily affiliated with Gama'a al-Islamiya (Islamic Group)—currently seems pretty tight.

Questions continue to be asked about the validity of elections in 2005, which saw the President reelected without opposition. Claims of vote-rigging have been backed by international organizations but are disputed by the government. The political system is also plagued by accusations of bribery and corruption. Still, a majority of the Egyptian people seem to support Mubarak and most of his policies.

Economics

Egypt is still struggling to break free of the straight jacket of socialist economic policies introduced by Gamal Abdel Nasser (Gamāl 'Abd an-Nasīr) after he came to power in a bloodless coup in 1952. Since the 1990s, the government has privatized many formerly nationalized industries and opened up markets to new investors, resulting in strong growth over the last 15 years. Although the economy is growing at a rate of 6% to 7% per year, the system is still hidebound by red tape, corruption, and a lack of entrepreneurial expertise in key industries.

The economy is supported by a base of four main sources: revenue from shipping on the Suez Canal; tourism; money sent to Egypt from expatriate workers; and oil and gas exports. Egyptian oil production is declining, but this has been balanced by the discovery of rich natural gas fields that are only now being tapped.

Four and a half million Egyptians (around 5% of the population) still work on the land and are dependent on crops like sugar cane, maize, and cotton for their livelihoods. With civil servants earning low salaries and no minimum wages in the private sector, large sections of the population are living on the bread line. Rises in the price of such staples as bread and rice led to riots in spring 2008, underlining the precarious economic situation of many families. While rising food prices should be helping farmers, the rising costs of fertilizer and fuel are currently eating into or surpassing increased profits.

Technology and Science

Groundbreaking engineering and design have kick-started periods of great growth and progress in Egypt. Starting with the pyramids at Giza and moving on to the temples and royal tombs of Upper Egypt through the mosques of Cairo to the building of Suez Canal, culminating in the erection of the Aswan High Dam in the 1960s, the country seems to be able to think outside the box every few generations to make giant leaps forward.

However, in many ways Egypt is still trying to maximize benefits made possible by damming the Nile. Plentiful electricity and the end of worrying about devastating floods were positives, but with them arrived negatives. Each year the flood brought precious nutrients in the form of black silt that replenished the fertility of the soil. What the Nile does not bring naturally, farmers must now add artificially, so fertilizer use has escalated dramatically. The annual flood also kept levels of salts in the soil at a low level, but no longer. Estimates are that one-third of Egyptian farmland was affected by high soil salinity levels since the 1970s.

Eight million acres of Egyptian soil is currently under agricultural production, but the country needs to keep producing more, so efficient irrigation is vital. A system of 50 main canals and more than 19,000 miles of smaller conduits now irrigate Egyptian farmland. Toshka Project in the western desert is yet another epic undertaking that will increase the area under irrigation by 33% when it comes fully online by 2020.

Although the Aswan High Dam still supplies electricity to the national grid, the maximum output is declining as a percentage of total needs in this energy-hungry country. In 2007, Egypt resurrected plans for a nuclear power program, which had been dropped after the Chernobyl incident. The government signed a deal with Russia in March 2008, beginning negotiations for the building of a nuclear power plant on the Mediterranean Coast, the first of four planned.

Sports

Soccer is the most popular sport in Egypt, and the national team—nicknamed The Pharaohs—is currently riding the crest of popularity after winning the African Cup of Nations in 2008. Domestic clubs have won several other pan-African championships, including the African Champions League Cup (12 times). Egypt's Premier League (the highest level) comprises 16 teams with Ahly (2008 champions) and Zamalek of Cairo, Ismaily of Ismailiya, Itihad of Alexandria, and Masry of Bur Said among the most successful. Egyptian players also play in big-league European teams in England, Germany, and Holland.

Golf has also exploded on the scene since the 1990s. Currently there are 16 courses in the country, but 14 more are in the pipeline, most by big-name course designers. Greg Norman has designed the upcoming Allegria course, while Nick Faldo is involved with Kateyama Dunes, and Nicklaus Design has entered the Egyptian market with Palm Hills—all near Cairo. Around the country, Ronald Fream is designing a course in Sharm El-Sheikh; Thomson, Perrett, and Lobb are working in El Ain Bay; and John Sanford is breaking ground on the Mediterranean Coast.

TOP EGYPT ATTRACTIONS

The Great Pyramids of Giza

(A) The only one of the Seven Wonders of the Ancient World to have made it into modern times, the Great Pyramids are truly worthy of the over-abused adjective "awesome." Everyone's got a theory as to their true purpose, but whatever you believe, your first glimpse will be truly breathtaking.

St. Catherine's Monastery

(B) Protector of the biblical burning bush and the approach to mystical Mount Sinai, St. Catherine's has been constantly inhabited for more than 1,600 years. The pilgrimage site is revered by Christians, Jews, and Muslims. The resident monks still live the simple life, but the monastery is an important reliquary for priceless art and rare ecumenical documents.

Cairo's Khan al-Khalili Bazaar

(C) enir-hunting spot in Egypt—if not the whole Middle East—this sprawling Cairo bazaar has been hawking since the late 14th century. Known locally as the Khan, Bloomingdale's it ain't. Haggling is compulsory, so go armed with a supply of cash and your sense of humor. When you're all shopped out, retreat to the El Fishawy café for a soothing glass of sweet tea.

The Karnak Temple

(D) The largest religious complex in Egypt—a kind of Vatican City meets Salt Lake City—Karnak gives up the secrets of the gods that sustained the ancient world and the human dynasties that built the ancient Empire. Whether you can understand the hieroglyphs or not, you'll marvel at the sheer scale and beauty of the temple here. Stroll around aimlessly to find a less busy corner for quiet reflection.

The Valley of the Kings

(E) You may feel a little Howard Carter-ish when you enter this arid cleft on the Nile's western bank. You'll be bowled over by the sheer beauty of the decoration and scale in some of the burial chambers of the pharaohs—true subterranean palaces, these were in effect waiting rooms for the start of the journey to the afterlife. New secrets are still giving themselves up.

The Red Sea Reefs

(F) Hundreds of miles of coral, a wealth of sea life, and crystal-clear waters put Egypt's Red Sea coast near the top spot on the list of the planet's best dive destinations. Whether you're a novice or you want to upgrade your diving skills, you'll find excellent instructors here.

The River Nile

(G) A serene journey along the Nile in Upper Egypt drops you on the doorstep of many of the country's finest temples and monuments—though you'll also pass equally fascinating glimpses of traditional rural life along the way. Your boat is your home for the duration, at once mode of transport, hotel, restaurant, and entertainment venue. Sitting on deck watching the ruby-red sunset across the river will be one of the magical moments of your trip.

The Egyptian Antiquities Museum

(H) Nowhere else on earth brings you so close to ancient Egypt in its multifarious guises—from the mundane chores punctuating daily life to the elaborate rituals surrounding death, from the smallest item of jewelry to monumental public statuary. Bask in the glow of Tutankhamun's golden funerary mask until it moves to its fancy new digs, or come face-to-face with the mummified remains of the great Pharaoh Ramesses II.

QUINTESSENTIAL EGYPT

Insha'Allah

Literally translated as "if Allah wills it" the phrase *Insha'Allah* invites a blessing on whatever arrangements are being made for the future—from the crops a farmer hopes to harvest when he plants in the spring to the bus ride you booked for next week. But the phrase also indicates that you're in a part of the world where arrangements can and do come unraveled, where time isn't counted to the exact second, and where life isn't as regimented as it is at home. Adapting your mindset to expect and accept the occasional delay or change in schedule will allow minor frustrations to flow over you and will certainly add to your enjoyment of the trip.

Tea

Tea oils the wheels of daily life at all levels of Egyptian society. It's served during business negotiations in executive office suites, and it warms the Bedouin as they sit around their campfires in the chill of the desert night. Egyptian tea is served strong and black; in glasses, not cups. Egyptians love it sweet. If the standard brew is not to your liking, then you may find hibiscus, mint, or apple tea to your taste. Do spend some quality time at a traditional café such as El Fishawy in Cairo's Khan al-Khalili bazaar, where sipping a glass or two over a newspaper or a game of backgammon is as authentic an experience as you can get.

If you want to get a sense of Egyptian culture and indulge in some of its pleasures, start by familiarizing yourself with the rituals of daily life. These are a few highlights—things you can take part in with relative ease.

Haggling

There's no such thing as a fixed price in Egyptian souks; haggling or bartering is a reality of daily life. So if you want to head home with a souvenir or two, you'll need to get with the program. First, remember that haggling isn't a battle; it's a time-honored method used to achieve a mutually suitable price. Negotiations should always be polite and good-humored. Express surprise at the vendor's first price. Smile and even chuckle. Then counter with a much lower offer. The vendor will certainly reject your bid, but he will also lower his own first offer, upon which you raise your first offer. This process continues until a compromise is reached. Tactics include acting nonchalant. Tell the vendor you've seen bigger or better at a shop around the corner—then throw in a lower counter offer. Keep smiling, and if the price isn't suitable, simply walk away. You'll live to haggle another day.

Shisha

When Egyptians get together to relax and while away a few hours with friends, they often do so over a *shisha*. This ornate, glass water pipe is ubiquitous everywhere from local street-corner joints to chic hangouts. It's enjoyed by young and old alike. You simply suck on the shisha's mouthpiece. This pressure draws smoke from the tobacco burning on the small bowl at the top of the pipe through a water-filled vessel and into the smoker's mouth. The regular sucking and consequent blowing of smoke out of the mouth over a period of an hour or so is meant to induce a state of relaxation. Shisha tobacco is sweeter then the cigarette variety and can be flavored with fruit or molasses, but that doesn't mean it's better for your health!

IF YOU LIKE

Ancient Monuments

Egypt's long and illustrious history has left a rich legacy in sandstone and granite. Nowhere else on earth is there such a wealth of fine ancient architecture. The major monuments listed here are simply the tip of a huge iceberg.

The Great Pyramid, Giza. Tomb of the Pharaoh Khufu (Cheops), this iconic monument constituted a design and engineering revolution and was the largest manmade structure on the planet for almost 4,000 years.

The Temple Complex of Ramesses II, Abu Simbel. The colossal statues of the pharaoh dominating the facade represent a high point in New Kingdom art and architecture. The relocation of the temple in the 1970s to save it from the rising waters of Lake Nasser was a triumph of engineering, and of international cooperation.

Deir al-Bahri, Luxor. She didn't manage to get a tomb plot in the Valley of the Kings, but the facade of Deir el-Bahri, the mortuary temple of Queen Hatshepsut, is one of the most graceful and elegant buildings in Egypt.

Valley of the Kings, Luxor. Burial ground of Egypt's ancient rulers, the tombs of the Middle and New Kingdom pharaohs are vividly decorated, and one—that of Tutankhamun—held a vast cache of treasures interred alongside the dead king for use in the afterlife.

Religious Edifices

Faith always has played an important role in daily life in Egypt, from the temples dedicated to the earliest ancient deities to the churches of Christianity and mosques of Islam still in use today.

Karnak Temple, Luxor. For centuries the most important place of worship in Egypt was Karnak, cult temple of Amun, which is really three temples in one. It charts the development of religion and power in this ancient realm.

Philae Temple, Aswan. Dedicated to Isis, the Queen of the Gods—or at least the leading Egyptian female deity—Philae's island setting helps make it the most romantic temple in Egypt. It was also in use most recently; offerings were still being made here in the 6th century AD.

St. Catherine's Monastery, Sinai. This 6th-century monastery at the foot of holy Mount Sinai was built to protect the site of the biblical burning bush. The site is considered holy by Christians, Jews, and Muslims, while the monastery guards a wealth of religious treasures and documents.

The Hanging Church, Cairo. Testament to the strength of the Coptic community even after the arrival of Islam, this 9th-century church is the most famous Christian place of worship in Cairo.

Mosque of Ibn Tulun, Cairo. Cairo's first mosque complex was completed in the late 9th century and is still the largest in the city. The center is also a fine example of early Islamic architecture.

The Natural World

The waters of the Nile and the sands of the desert are the two major natural combatants in the story of Egypt, but the country displays tremendous variety of topography both above and below the water.

The White Desert, the Western Desert. It seems as if icebergs have somehow been transported from the north here in Egypt's own Big Sky Country. Forests of white chalk towers fill the landscape, formed over many millennia by the action of the winds and the sand.

The Black Desert, the Western Desert. Scores of black-tipped conical hills rise from the desert floor in this uninhabited corner of the country.

Ras Mohammed National Park, Sinai. An arid cape at the top of the Sinai Peninsula on land, Ras Mohammed is one of the world's richest submarine environments and one of its top dive spots.

The Nile, the Nile Valley. The ancient Greek researcher and traveler Herodotus—the man who invented the notion of writing history—put it succinctly when he said, "Egypt is a gift of the Nile." This most mighty of rivers brings fertility and beauty to the land and was a conduit for trade and information from the dawn of civilization.

The Era of Grand Touring

The ancient history of Egypt fascinated the world in the years after the great temples were rediscovered and Champollion deciphered the hieroglyphs on the Rosetta Stone in the 1820s. This interest spawned Egypt's first tourist development—new museums, hotels, and restaurants, some of which have become tourist attractions in their own right.

Mena House Hotel, Giza. Originally the Khedive Ismail's hunting lodge in the shadow of the Great Pyramid, this mansion was built in 1869 and became a hotel early in the following century. Guests have included Franklin Roosevelt, Richard Nixon, Cecil B. DeMille, Randolph Hearst, and William Faulkner.

The Old Cataract Hotel, Aswan. Built in 1899 by Thomas Cook, the man who invented tourism in Egypt, the Cataract was *the* place to stay when the genteel arrived in Aswan on the new rail line. The setting, overlooking the boulder-strewn whitewater narrows that gives the hotel its name, couldn't be more dramatic.

Grand Trianon Café, Alexandria. The Grand Trianon has been a place to meet for afternoon tea since it opened in the 1920s. From the literary glitterati of that era to the academics of the present day, the period interior has been a party to many conversations.

The Old Winter Palace Hotel, Luxor. Completed in 1886 as a place for the Royal family to spend the cooler months, the Winter Palace adds an understated elegance to Luxor waterfront.

GREAT ITINERARIES

IN THE FOOTSTEPS OF THE PHARAOHS: THE CLASSIC TOUR OF EGYPT
7 days

This week-long itinerary is the whistle-stop tour of all whistle-stop tours, but it will give you the opportunity to see the most important locations relating to ancient Egypt in a limited period of time. Your days will be very full, but who wants to miss even one of these sites? If you are coming from the U.S., remember to figure in the travel time (more than 10 hours from New York), so this tour actually requires 9 full days away from home.

Cairo
1 day. Hit the ground running with an action-packed day. In the morning visit the Egyptian Museum, whose hallowed halls have the largest collection of artifacts of the Pharaonic era. The signage in this museum is abysmal, so you'll be at an advantage if you bring along a guide (or hire one once you arrive at the musem). Have lunch, either around the museum or in Giza, on the outskirts of the city. Then, in the afternoon, explore the mysteries of the Great Pyramid and the Sphinx. ⇨ Chapter 2, Cairo.

Memphis, Dahshur & Saqqara
1 day. Take a day to see these three Old and Middle Kingdom sites from your base in Cairo. Memphis was the first capital of Egypt, but there's little grandeur left on the ground. Saqqara is famous as the site of the first pyramid ever built, while Dahshur has five pyramids, including the Red Pyramid and the Bent Pyramid. Of the three areas, Dahshur is the less visited, and if you time your visit well, you may not encounter large crowds. ⇨ Chapter 2, Cairo.

Abu Simbel & Aswan
1 day. In the early morning, fly south from Cairo to Abu Simbel, site of two monumental temples commissioned by Ramesses II. As you head south along the Nile, you'll be able to see Lake Nasser as it snakes through the desert south of Aswan. A round-trip shuttle bus to the Temple of Ramesses II is included in the price of your airline ticket; flights are carefully timed (they leave Cairo very early, arriving at Aswan around 9:30 am) and will allow you just a couple of hours to view the temple. The colossal statues fronting the Great Temple are among the most photographed sites in the world, and rightly so, having been rescued through a heroic effort from the rising waters of Lake Nasser in the 1970s. Then fly to Aswan, which will get you to your hotel or cruise ship around lunch-time. In the afternoon tour the unfinished obelisk, Aswan High Dam, and Philae. Return to Philae in the evening for the Sound & Light show (depending on day and languages broadcast). ⇨ Chapter 5, Aswan & Lake Nasser.

Kom Ombo
½ day. The Ptolemaic Temple of Haroeris and Sobek combines worship of two gods: the crocodile-headed Sobek, protector of the earth, and Haroeris, a hawk-headed manifestation of Horus and god of medicine. The temple was also an ancient center for medicine and healing. If you are on a cruise, you'll probably arrive at the temple around sunset; if you are visiting on a day trip from Aswan, try to go in the morning to avoid the crowds disembarking from the dozens of ships in the afternoon. ⇨ Chapter 4, The Nile Valley & Luxor.

Giza · Cairo
Memphis
Dahshur · Saqqara

ISRAEL
JORDAN

SAUDI
ARABIA

LIBYA

River Nile

Asyut

Red
Sea

Dendera
Luxor · Karnak Temple

Edfu

Kom Ombo

Aswan
High Dam
Philae

Lake Nasser

Abu Simbel

Edfu

½ day. The Temple of Horus was built in the Ptolemaic era and completed in only 180 years; this is the best preserved temple on the Nile. On a cruise, you'll arrive in Edfu in the morning. You must take some kind of transportation from the cruise docks to the temple. The traditional method is by horse and carriage, but you can also take a taxi. ⇨ *Chapter 4, The Nile Valley & Luxor.*

Luxor

2 days. You have much to see in Luxor, on both sides of the river. Split your two days into a west-bank day and an east-bank day. Devote Day 1 to the west bank, spending the morning at the Valley of the Kings; have lunch, then tour Madinat Habu, the Valley of the Nobles, the Ramesseum, and the Colossi of Memnon. Tour the east bank on Day 2, hitting the sprawling Karnak Temple in the morning, then after lunch visit Luxor Temple, returning to Karnak for the Sound & Light show in the evening. ⇨ *Chapter 4, The Nile Valley & Luxor.*

Dendera and Luxor

1 day. One significant temple is on few one-week itineraries (and almost no cruise itineraries), but if you want to get a little off the beaten path, then book a tour to

TIPS

The least stressful way to see Upper Egypt is on a Nile cruise, which always includes shore excursions to the major temples. A four-night/five-day cruise from Luxor to Aswan will allow you to see most of the sights on this itinerary. You'll need to arrive in Luxor one day early to visit Dendera; and you can often add a post-cruise half-day visit to Abu Simbel.

If you only have limited time, then speed is very much your friend.

■ Use EgyptAir domestic flights to make the most of your visit.

■ Fly from Cairo to Upper Egypt and back.

visit the Temple of Hathor at Dendera, 40 km north of Luxor, especially noted for its Greco-Roman depictions of Queen Cleopatra presenting her son and heir Caesarion to the Egyptian gods. Return to Luxor, and shop in the *souk* for souvenirs on your final afternoon. ⇨ *Chapter 4, The Nile Valley & Luxor.*

GREAT ITINERARIES

THE BEST OF EGYPT
14 days

No visit to Egypt is complete without taking in some or all of the ancient sites in itinerary one, but you can certainly add a few important attractions to those already listed should you have a few more days in the country. More important, you can linger in each major destination for another day and experience some of the secondary sights and still have time to make a swing through the Sinai Peninsula.

Cairo
3 days. After spending your first two days exploring ancient Cairo (as described on the 7-day itinerary), it's time to immerse yourself in the post-Pharaonic era. On Day 3 explore the Islamic city and the attractions leading off Shar'a al-Mu'iz; the streets and alleys all still brim with life. Browse in Khan al-Khalili or the Tent Maker's bazaar for souvenirs, and stop for some tea or even lunch at El Fishawy or the Naguib Mahfouz Cafeé. Later, take a taxi to the Citadel to explore the mosques and museums here, and for wonderful views over the city. One night, have dinner in one of Cairo's floating restaurants or in one of the top hotels along the Nile. ⇨ *Chapter 2, Cairo.*

Aswan & Abu Simbel
2 days. A visit to Abu Simbel requires half-day, assuming you fly; spend the afternoon of Day 1 visiting the Philae Temple, and, if you have the time and energy, stop by the Nubian Museum for at least an hour or two either before or after your visit to Philae. On Day 2, cross to the west bank for the Tombs of the Nobles and the Tomb of the Aga Khan. If you still have time after your tour of the major sights, make for Kitchener's Island in the center of the river to explore the Botanical Gardens, then take a felucca ride in the late afternoon to enjoy the boulder-strewn cataracts of the Nile. Don't forget to leave some time for shopping; the souks of Aswan are less frenetic than those in Luxor or Cairo. ⇨ *Chapter 5, Aswan & Lake Nasser.*

Edfu & Kom Ombo
2 days. Don't forget these important temples between Aswan and Luxor. If you don't take a cruise, then Edfu is more easily seen on a full-day excursion from Luxor, and Kom Ombo on a half-day excursion from Aswan. ⇨ *Chapter 4, The Nile Valley & Luxor.*

Luxor, Dendera & Abydos
4 days. Spend two days seeing the highlights of Luxor, as outlined above. Spend a third day visiting Dendera. On your fourth day, book a trip to the Temple of Seti I at Abydos (93 miles north of Luxor), which is dedicated to the god Osiris. Cruises rarely stop here, and relatively few tourists make this trip, but the carvings on this temple are magnificent. After visiting the Osiris Temple, you can walk over to the Temple of Ramesses; though not as well preserved as Seti I's temple, the remaining walls still have some of their vibrant color. If you are traveling by land, because of the convoy system, you'll be allowed two hours at the site before you return to Luxor for an evening stroll or carriage ride along the riverside corniche. ⇨ *Chapter 4, The Nile Valley & Luxor.*

Sharm El-Sheikh
2 days. Early on Day 1, fly into Sharm El-Sheikh. Take an afternoon tour into the Sinai by camel or quad and then cool off in your hotel's pool or at the beach. Spend

Day two at Ras Mohammed National Park. Divers should book a dive on one of the famed sites offshore—perhaps Thistlegorm—while nondivers can take a snorkeling trip or glass-bottom boat ride. Nonswimmers can enjoy an overland tour of the terrestrial elements of the park with some beach time. If you plan to spend the night at the base of Mount Sinai, head there in the afternoon so you arrive before dark. ⇨ *Chapter 6, The Sinai & Red Sea Coast.*

St. Catherine's Monastery & Jabal Moussa

1 day. Stay overnight close to St. Catherine's Monastery, which is deep in the Sinai mountains. Wake before dawn to climb Jabal Moussa (Mount Sinai), reaching the summit just as dawn breaks. Retrace your steps and explore the monastery in the early morning. After returning to Sharm, you can fly back to Cairo that evening. ⇨ *Chapter 6, The Sinai & Red Sea Coast.*

TIPS

If you are taking the classic tour and adding these extra elements into the schedule, you'll save time by flying directly to Sharm El-Sheikh from Luxor. Egypt Air offers daily flights.

■ Tour companies in Cairo and Sharm El-Sheikh can arrange your trip to St. Catherine's Monastery with accommodation and transportation included. It's also possible to hire a car in Sharm El-Sheikh and make your own way to the monastery, but if you need to get back to Cairo for your return flight early on Day 14, it might be better to take a guided tour.

HISTORY YOU CAN SEE

Archaeologists divide Egyptian history into three major periods. The Old Kingdom, the Middle Kingdom, and New Kingdom. These eras encompass 30 pharaonic dynasties starting in approximately 2686 BC and lasting until 1213 BC.

The Early Pharaonic Era

Civilization in the Nile Valley began some 5,000 years ago, when Narmer united the kingdoms of Upper (southern) and Lower (northern) Egypt, establishing his capital at Memphis. Narmer's successors developed hieroglyphics and started building *mastabas* (burial mounds) from mud brick.

The **Old Kingdom** (approx. 2686–2134 BC) had a strong central government and efficient bureaucracy; technological innovations allowed Egypt to reach new political, economic, and artistic heights. Djoser, the first pharaoh to proclaim himself the gods' representative on Earth, and his advisor Imhotep designed and built the stone funerary complex at Saqqara that includes the Step Pyramid. Later dynasties constructed true pyramids at Dahshur, Fayyum, and Giza.

Records show that in the **Middle Kingdom** (approx. 2040–1640 BC), a stable and prosperous Egypt established diplomatic and commercial relations with the people of Libya, Sinai, Nubia, and Punt (present-day Somalia). The capital was moved to Thebes (now Luxor), and the great temples to Amun, Egypt's principal deity, began to rise at Karnak.

What to See: The **Great Sphinx** on the Giza Plateau is the world's earliest large-scale stone monument. **The Step Pyramid** at Saqqara represents the birth of architecture and building in stone. **The Bent Pyramid** at Dahshur perhaps represents the first architectural failure, as the design was flawed. **The Great Pyramid of Khufu** at Giza is the definitive pyramid and Egypt's largest. **Karnak Temple** in Luxor is the largest temple complex in Egypt. The **Egyptian Antiquities Museum** in Cairo is the only museum to include artifacts from all the pharaonic eras.

The New Kingdom

Thutmose I (1506–1493 BC) was the first important leader of the **New Kingdom** (approx. 1552–1070 BC), considered the high point of pharaonic history. The rulers of this period subdued and conquered surrounding lands, including Nubia to the south. Thutmose's daughter, Hatshepsut (the only female pharaoh), and her stepson, Thutmose III, made Egypt a regional superpower and Thebes the world's richest city.

King Akhenaten (1352–1338 BC) cut all ties with Thebes and established a new religion to one god, Aten, but monotheism died with the king. Akhenaten was succeeded by the child Tutankhaten (1336–1327 BC), who had a short, uneventful reign as Tutankhamun. Pharaoh Seti I (1294–1279 BC) was able to reconquer the lands lost during the reign of Akhenaten. His son Ramesses II (1279–1212 BC) reigned for 66 years, cementing Egypt's power.

What to See: The **Temple of Seti I**, at Abydos, has reliefs that are in exceptional condition. The colossal statues of Ramesses II at **Abu Simbel** show the pharaoh at his most powerful. **Deir al-Bahri**, Hatshepsut's Mortuary Temple, is a tour de force of New Kingdom architecture. The 62 royal tombs found in the **Valley of the Kings** represent a high point in art and engineering, with scenes depicting the royal journey into the afterlife. The **Hypostyle**

Hall at Karnak Temple contains 134 columns carved like papyrus. The **Tomb of Tutankhamun** is the only one to have been found with its contents intact. The ruins of **Akhetaten,** modern-day Tell al Amarna, are all that is left of the New Kingdom experiment that lasted one generation.

Greco-Roman Egypt

Alexander the Great established his capital at Alexandria and appointed Macedonian general Ptolemy Soter as governor. When Alexander died, the governor established the **Ptolemaic Dynasty** (332–30 BC); the Ptolemies made Alexandria their capital and built both the famous Pharos (lighthouse) and the Great Library. The infamous Cleopatra VII (51–30 BC) was the last of the Ptolemies and was defeated by the forces of Augustus.

With the **Roman occupation** (30 BC–AD 337), Egypt was relegated to provincial status. In AD 61, St. Mark arrived in Alexandria, and within 200 years Egypt had a significant Christian community. Responsibility for Egypt passed to the eastern Roman Empire in Constantinople in AD 337.

What to See: The cult **Temple of Hathor,** at Dendera shows New Kingdom style as embellished by the Ptolemies. **Philae** was the last pagan temple to operate in Egypt and has many Greco-Roman features. The **Temple of Horus** at Edfu, Egypt's finest completely Ptolemaic temple, was begun in 237 BC and finished in 57 BC. There's been a church on the site of el-Maollaqa, or **Hanging Church,** in Cairo since the 4th century AD, and it's still the spiritual center of Coptic worship in the city. **St. Catherine's Monastery** is the protector of more than 1,500 years' worth of Christian art manuscripts and liturgical objects.

Islamic Egypt

Arabs took control of Egypt in AD 642, bringing Islam with them. The Abbasid caliphate in Iraq ruled from 868 until the North African Fatimids took over in 969 and built al-Qahira (Arabic for Cairo) around the remains of an Abbasid mosque. During the Crusades, the Fatimids asked for protection from Salah al-Din al-Ayyubi, and this ushered in the 80-year Ayyubid era, beginning in 1168. By 1250, the slaves of the Ayyubids, the Mamluks, had usurped power from their masters. Under the Mamluks, Egypt grew rich on trade but was subject to constant political tensions.

The Ottomans put an end to Mamluk rule in 1517, and Egypt became an economic backwater of the Ottoman Empire, which ruled from Istanbul. Mohammed Ali, who ruled Egypt from 1805 until 1848, began modernizing the country, and his successors—known as Khedives—ushered in a final era of prosperity before the arrival of British colonial rule in 1882. The Khedive's crowning glory was the building of the Suez Canal.

What to See: Cairo is full of excellent Islamic architecture from every era. The **Mosque of Ibn Tulun,** built by the first Abbasid ruler in the 870s AD, is considered the foundation of modern Cairo. The **Mosque and University of Al Azhar,** founded in the late 900s by the Fatimids, is still one of the most important centers of learning in the Arab world. Completed in 1363 under the Mamluks, the **Mosque of Sultan Hasan,** is still one of the largest Islamic complexes in the world. The **Museum of Islamic Arts** in Cairo is the best place to see a full range of religious and domestic art from sites around Egypt.

KNOW YOUR EGYPTIAN
GODS & GODDESSES

Egyptian religion is immensely complex, and it is not well understood by scholars. Beliefs and practices changed, sometimes radically, over 3,000 years of Egyptian history, and few easily understandable texts were left behind. On the surface the religion was polytheistic, with many gods derived from nature and the natural elements that surrounded them, but the gods were all manifestations of aspects of one great divine force. During the course of Egyptian history several of the gods were syncretized.

The pharaoh was regarded as a living god closely identified with the falcon-headed god, Horus. People would also worship a major state god as well as local city gods or patron deities relevant to their employment. This might be likened to the Christian practice of having patron saints. The gods all had specific powers attributed to them, were associated with special animals, and had specific feast days. Gods were also often viewed in groups of trinities consisting of a father, a mother, and a child.

Ancient deities were worshipped in temples, in shrines in people's houses, and possibly on the wayside. Temples were of two types: cult and mortuary. Cult temples were located, for the most part, on the east bank of the Nile, and they were dedicated to the cult of a particular god. In addition to the temple proper, there were libraries—buildings where doctors, astronomers, and botanists did their research—housing for priests, and storage areas for grain and other items. Temples owned land that they farmed or rented out, and they functioned as administrative and religious centers. A temple's high priest had many ranks of priests below him.

Mortuary temples were similar to cult temples, save for the fact that they were built on the west bank of the Nile and were primarily dedicated to the cult of the deceased pharaoh.

For most of Egyptian history the chief among the major gods was **Amun,** or Amun-Ra, a solar deity who saw to the balance and functioning of the world. Karnak at Thebes (now Luxor) was his primary temple. He was usually depicted as a human with a tall crown, but when he took on the manifestation of Amun-Ra (the Sun God), he was sometimes depicted with a falcon head and the disc of the sun above his head, and would be seen holding an ankh.

Amun's wife was **Mut,** a goddess of queenship who is closely associated with the white vulture, the hieroglyph that signified her name. As a woman, she holds an ankh and usually wears the double crown, which symbolized the union of Upper and Lower Egypt.

The son of Amun and Mut was **Khonsu,** the moon god. Like Amun, Khonsu was often depicted as a hawk, but above his head was a crescent resting within the full disc of the moon. He was also depicted as a youth with the beard and flail of a pharaoh.

From the Middle Kingdom (2040–1640 BC) onward, **Osiris** was one of the most important Egyptian gods. He is depicted as a mummiform figure and was the ruler of the afterworld. His skin was often colored green to signify rebirth; he usually held a crook and flail and wore the white crown of Upper Egypt. His main sacred site is the fabulously elegant New Kingdom (1550–1070 BC) temple at Abydos, north of Luxor.

The wife of Osiris was **Isis,** goddess of magic and one of the most important figures in the Egyptian pantheon. She is usually depicted as a woman wearing a crown with the hieroglyph for *throne.* She usually holds a staff in one hand and an ankh in the other. Her greatest surviving temple is at Philae.

Their child was **Horus,** who became one of the greatest gods and is often shown as a falcon, the symbol of kingship, or with the head of a falcon. Reigning pharaohs were always associated with Horus.

Set was the brother of Osiris, and during the Late and Greco-Roman periods was regarded as Osiris's mortal enemy. He was god of storms and deserts. In art he had the head of an animal with a curved snout and square ears.

Set's wife was **Nephthys,** a goddess associated with funerary rituals. Her depictions are almost always of a woman with a hieroglyphic crown signifying her name.

Jackal-headed **Anubis** was in charge of embalming and mummification and the actual trip to the afterlife. In the Hellenic and Christian eras he was associated with Hermes, then with the now-decanonized St. Christopher.

Maat was the goddess of truth, justice, balance, and order—all very important concepts in the Egyptian view of the world. She usually holds a scepter and ankh and is crowned with an ostrich feather.

As well as being associated with kingship, **Hathor** was the goddess of love, music, beauty, and dancing. She was also goddess of remote places, such as turquoise mines. One of her sacred sites is Deir al-Bahri, Queen Hatshepsut's magnificent temple on Luxor's west bank, and her cult temple is at Dendera. She is almost always depicted with cow horns, or simply as a cow.

Ptah was a creator god, associated with Memphis; he is usually depicted in mummified form wearing a skullcap. **Sekhmet,** his wife, was goddess of plagues, revenge, and restitution and usually has the head of a lioness. Their child was **Nefertum,** associated with rebirth in the afterworld, depicted as wearing a water-lily crown.

Thoth was the ibis-headed god of writing and knowledge, and he was associated with the moon.

Ram-headed **Khnum** was associated with creation. His wife was **Anukis** (sometimes depicted as a gazelle or with a feathered headdress), and their daughter was **Satis.** They were all important in the region of the first cataract of the Nile, around Aswan, and therefore Khnum was associated with the river's annual inundation.

The crocodile-headed god **Sobek** was protector of the world from his watery home in the Nile. His main cult temple was at Kom Ombo.

It is interesting that there was no god identified specifically with the Nile, though the plump god depicted with the head of a baboon and pendulous breasts, **Hapi,** was the god of the inundation.

WHEN TO GO

It's best to visit Egypt in the cooler season, which begins in November and ends in March. Summers can be oppressive, especially in Cairo, Luxor, and Aswan. And forget about going to the desert oases in summer.

Generally speaking, it doesn't rain in Egypt. In cooler months, Alexandria and the Mediterranean coast can get cloudy, and a few wet days aren't uncommon. Considering how arid and relentlessly sunny the rest of the country is, these brief wet conditions can be a welcome relief.

Weather along the Mediterranean or Red Sea coast remains temperate throughout the year. The water does get a bit cold between December and March, but never frigid.

Climate

Egypt's climate is characterized by hot and dry summers in most of the country. The areas that are most humid are the Delta and along the Mediterranean coast. Summer lasts from the end of April until the beginning of October. Spring is very short, if not nonexistent. Winter is mild, but nights do get cool.

The most important time of year to keep in mind is the 50 days of the *khamaseen*. Between the end of March and mid-May, dust storms whip up occasionally and blot out the sky.

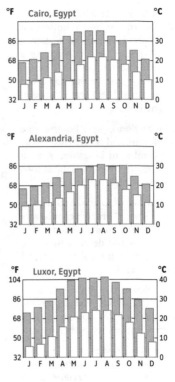

Cairo

INCLUDING MEMPHIS, SAQQARA, THE FAYYUM,
AND WADI NATRUN MONASTERIES

The Great Pyramids, Giza

WORD OF MOUTH

"I'm still fascinated by the way the traffic works [in Cairo]—and it does—lanes merge, cars cross each other's paths, people walk through (including children selling stuff), and you just sit back because you know that's how it is."

—Mazj

WELCOME TO CAIRO

TOP REASONS TO GO

★ **The First View of the Great Pyramids:** Stand at the viewing platform on the Pyramids plateau and gaze out over the only remaining wonder of the ancient world.

★ **King Tut:** Come face to face with Tutankhamun's golden funerary mask—and other treasures from his tomb—at the Egyptian Antiquities Museum.

★ **The Call to Prayer:** Stand in Islamic Cairo at sunset and enjoy the *muezzins* calling from hundreds of minarets in the district.

★ **Bettering Your Bargaining Skills:** Never pay the first asking price for that "must have" treasure at Cairo's famous Khan al-Khalili bazaar.

★ **The Nightlife:** Enjoy a cocktail while chilling out to cool vibes at Buddha Bar, one of Cairo's trendiest night spots in the Sofitel El-Gezirah Hotel.

1 Islamic Cairo North. The Khan al-Khalili bazaar is the heart of this district, surrounded by exceptional Islamic architecture.

2 Islamic Cairo South. Historic mosques, *madrasas*, and mansions lie in this tightly-knit district, where the Museum of Islamic Arts has an excellent collection reflecting Islamic traditions.

3 The Citadel. For several centuries Egypt was ruled from this fortress on a rocky boss overlooking the city. Several important mosques lie within or around its sturdy walls.

4 Mari Girgis. The Christian heartbeat of the city emanates from the Coptic churches and monasteries here. The Coptic Museum reveals the long history of Christianity in Egypt.

GETTING ORIENTED

Cairo is a large, sprawling city of some 15 million people. The oldest parts of the city are the Coptic quarter (Mari Girgis), the Islamic quarter, and the Citadel. The Downtown area along the river dates from the mid-19th century. Newer planned areas such as Heliopolis and Mohandiseen are more European in feel and scope. Giza is really a relatively new development, having been built between the pyramids and modern-day Cairo so that there is scarcely a gap now.

9 Ma'adi. A preplanned district laid out in the early 20th century, this is the least densely populated part of Cairo.

10 Giza. Location of the pyramids and the sphinx, the Giza plateau was once isolated from Cairo but is now caught in the embrace of its growing suburbs.

11 Heliopolis. A planned expansion northeast of the city center has modern shopping malls and hotels as well as the airport.

5 Downtown Cairo & Bulaq. The epicenter of the city with major hotels, shopping malls, and the not-to-be-missed Egyptian Antiquities Museum.

6 Rodah Island & Garden City. Home to a thriving expatexpat community in the 19th and early 20th centuries, these districts now have period mansions and a selection of upmarket hotels.

7 Zamalek & Gezira. Occupying the Nile's largest island, these two districts are relatively quiet enclaves in the heart of the city, home to elegant apartment blocks, independent boutiques, and neighborhood restaurants.

8 Mohandiseen. This modern commercial district is buzzing with offices, shops, and eateries for every budget.

CAIRO PLANNER

Transportation

By Air: Cairo is the main entry point for international flights and has the most international arrivals of any other destination in Egypt. You can also get flights to most major tourist destinations from here.

By Bus: Buses are an inexpensive means of traveling between cities, though they are hardly fast or comfortable. Most visitors to Cairo aren't likely to use the local city buses, but they are far and away the cheapest mode of transportation in the city; air-conditioned CTA buses in Cairo are a bit more expensive but much more comfortable than others.

By Subway: Cairo has a surprisingly efficient and certainly inexpensive Metro system that can get you to some of the oldest parts of the city in a fraction of the time it takes to drive. The Metro even goes to Giza, putting you within easy taxi distance of the pyramids themselves.

By Taxi: Though you must negotiate the fare, taxis are the best way of getting around. Hail them on the street, but be aware that many drivers will not speak English.

By Train: Trains connect Cairo with Alexandria, Luxor, and Aswan.

What's Great in Cairo

Ancient Monuments: *Homo sapiens* learned how to build their first big buildings in the Nile valley south of Cairo, and these monumental edifices still fascinate us. Visit the Great Pyramids, but don't neglect the monuments in Memphis, Abu Sir, Saqqara, and Dahshur.

Mosques and Madrasas: Islam's most important center of learning for many centuries, the city is heavy with historic and architecturally important mosques and madrasas. Ibn Tulun, the Sultan Hasan and Muhammad 'Ali Mosque high on the citadel are some of the best.

Museums: The Egyptian Antiquities Museum is the most comprehensive collection of ancient Egyptian artifacts in the world. The treasure of Tutankhamun is the highlight of this visit. Look a little further and you'll find the Museum of Islamic Art and the Coptic Museum, both adding greatly to the understanding and appreciation of the wider history of Egypt.

Shopping: You can spend, spend, spend here on arts and crafts still hand-produced as they have been for generations—plus Egypt produces some of the best kitsch anywhere. The Khan al-Khalili is *the* bazaar where you can find just about anything—antiques, gold, silver, carpets—but haggle you must! Cairo also has several modern retail palaces.

Nightlife: Cairo's buzzing social scene revolves around a selection of cool addresses frequented by the über-chic. Though most serve food, they are also chill-out lounges, *shisha* cafés, cocktail lounges, and clubs—depending on what time in the evening you arrive. The current crop include Absolute, Sequoia, and Buddha Bar, but a longtime favorite is the Cairo Jazz Club.

Café Society: Taking time out for a little refreshment is part of the Cairene way of life. Traditional *ahwas* (coffee shops) and grand cafés are being joined by a new generation of Seattle-style coffee bars, so it's easy to get your caffeine fix. Or why not try an Arabic tea? Fishawy Café in Khan al-Khalili is a must-visit for its atmosphere; Café Riche, Downtown, is another longtime favorite that's been open since the 1930s.

About the Restaurants

Egyptians eat late: lunch from 1 to 3 and dinner often starting at 9 or 10. Most restaurants are open daily for both lunch and dinner. Dress is generally smart casual. Local beers and wines are served in many restaurants, but expensive imported alcohol is limited to top-end establishments. Although fancier places levy a 12% service charge, it is customary to leave a tip in inverse relation to the size of the bill, ranging from, say, 8% at expensive places to 12% to 14% at cheaper places.

About the Hotels

Cairo's top hotels are all quite affordable by international standards, but few have any sense of Old World charm. Expect to pay a substantial premium for a Nile or pyramids view. While government authorities rate all hotels on a five-star scale, only a few really earn their stars. Outside the five-star range, Cairo's options quickly grow more limited. August and September are crowded with Gulf Arab arrivals, December and January and Easter are peaks for Europeans, and the major Islamic holidays see a lot of local and regional guests.

WHAT IT COSTS IN EGYPTIAN POUNDS,
U.S. DOLLARS, AND EUROS

$	$$	$$$	$$$$
Restaurants			
€15–€25	€25–€35	100 £e–150 £e	over 150 £e
Hotels in Dollars			
under $70	$70–$130	$130–$200	over $200
Hotels in Euros			
Under €45	€45–€80	€80–€130	Over €130

Restaurant prices are per person for a main course at dinner. Hotel prices are for a double room in high season, excluding 10% tax and service charges (usually 10%).

Planning Your Time

Although the pyramids are usually at the top of everyone's itinerary, it is more interesting to work your way back through the city's history and end with its pharaonic origins. So start with **Khan al-Khalili**, the great medieval marketplace, and wander the narrow alleys of nearby **Islamic Cairo** to get a feel for the texture of life in the city. In a full day you can explore the surface of Old Cairo, seeing both its Islamic and Coptic core. The **Great Pyramids** and **Sphinx** can be seen in a half-day, but also spend a half-day at Memphis and Saqqara or at the less-visited sights such as Abu Sir or Dahshur. Another day can be spent in either Fayyum or on a trip to the monasteries in Wadi Natrun.

When to Go

Cairo is only uncomfortable for a couple of months a year. Spring and autumn are both gorgeous, with warm days and cool nights, though spring brings the *khamaseen* dust storms that can turn the air yellow for a couple of days. Summer is *very* hot, but relatively dry. Winter is brief, eight weeks at most, and chillier than you might expect, though never truly cold. Cairo gets about 10 rainy days a year, mostly in winter. Ramadan, the holy month of fasting, brings both rewards and inconveniences for visitors.

By Sean
Rocha, Rami
al-Samahy,
Salima Ikram

Updated by
Lindsay and
Pete Bennett

ON FIRST IMPRESSION, THERE IS hardly a superlative too extreme to capture the epic scale of this city of some 15 million—or 14, or 16; no one really knows for sure—that sprawls in all directions. The traffic, the people, the chaotic rhythm of Cairo will all reinforce this impression, threatening to overwhelm you. So take your time, relax over a mint tea in a café, or wander the quiet back alleys, and a different world will be revealed to you. In many ways Cairo is the proverbial overgrown village, full of little districts and communities that feel much smaller and more intimate than the city of which they're part.

Like so much else in Egypt, Cairo's charm is a product of its history, its network of districts and communities the physical remains of a thousand years of being conquered and reconquered by different groups. The city didn't really begin, as you might expect, with the pharaohs; they quartered themselves in nearby Memphis and Heliopolis, areas only recently overtaken by Cairo's outward urban spread. The Pyramids at Giza, on the west bank of the Nile, mislead the eye in search of Cairo's origins because this has always been an east-bank city. It's only since the 1960s that the city has moved faster than the river, leaping the banks and drawing in the endless modern suburbs on the west bank.

No, Cairo's history begins with a Roman trading outpost called Babylon—now referred to as Old or Coptic Cairo—at the mouth of an ancient canal that once connected the Nile to the Red Sea. But it was the 7th-century AD Arab invaders who can be said to have founded the city we know today with their encampment at Fustat, just north of Old Cairo. Under their great leader 'Amr Ibn al-As, the Arabs took over a land that had already been occupied by the Greeks, the Persians, and the Romans. And in the millennium that followed 'Amr's conquest, the city was ruled by the Fatimids (969–1171), the Ayyubids (1171–1250), the Mamluks (1250–1517), the Ottomans (1517–1798), and then experienced 150 years of French and British colonial administration until the revolution of 1952 finally returned power to Egyptian hands.

But what makes Cairo unique is that each new set of rulers, rather than destroying what they had conquered, chose to build a new city upwind from the old one. Thus, from a bird's-eye view above the Nile, you can follow the progression of the historic center of Cairo cutting a question-mark-shaped path from Old Cairo in the south, curving north through Fustat, east to Islamic Cairo, and then west to the colonial Downtown district until you reach Maydan Tahrir (Liberation Square), where it has settled for the moment. But as the city continues to expand, the heart threatens to relocate again, perhaps to Maydan Sphinx, or Bulaq, or somewhere in Giza.

Cairo's districts have changed, of course, since the time when they were founded. Still, each district retains a distinct identity, not only in its buildings, but also among its residents and their way of life. Pre-Islamic Babylon is, to this day, a disproportionately Christian area, with more crosses visible than crescents. And the medieval precinct of Islamic Cairo is still where families traditionally go during Ramadan to spend the night eating and smoking after a day of abstinence. Indeed, one of the joys of Cairo is that its historic areas are still vibrant living spaces and not open-air museums. The past here is more a state of mind than a historical fact—and that, ultimately, is the way in which the city is truly overwhelming.

2

EXPLORING CAIRO

Cairo is big: just how big you'll see on the drive in from the airport, which sometimes takes so long you'll think you're driving to Aswan. And what you see on the way into town, amazingly, is only half of it—Cairo's west-bank sister city, Giza, stretches to the pyramids, miles from Downtown. But if you are the sort of person who instinctively navigates by compass points, exploring Cairo will be a breeze because the Nile works like a giant north–south needle running through the center of the city. If not, you might find the city bewildering at first.

Taxi drivers generally know only major streets and landmarks, and often pedestrians are unsure of the name of the street they stand on—when they do know, it's as often by the old names as the post-independence ones—but they'll gladly steer you in the wrong direction in an effort to be helpful. Just go with the flow and try to think of every wrong turn as a chance for discovery.

Thankfully, too, you don't have to conquer all of Cairo to get the most out of it. Much of the city was built in the 1960s, and the new areas hold relatively little of historical or cultural interest. The older districts, with the exception of Giza's pyramids, are all on the east bank and easily accessible by taxi or metro. These districts become relatively straightforward targets for a day's exploration on foot.

Old Cairo, on the east bank a couple miles south of most of current-day Cairo, was the city's first district. Just north of it is Fustat, the site of the 7th-century Arab settlement. East of that is the Citadel. North of the Citadel is the medieval walled district of al-Qahira that gave the city its name. It is better known as Islamic Cairo. West of that is the colonial district. Known as Downtown, it is one of several—including Ma'adi, Garden City, Heliopolis, and Zamalek—laid out by Europeans in the 19th and 20th centuries. (The west-bank districts of Mohandiseen and Doqqi, by comparison, have only sprouted up since the revolution in 1952.) The most interesting sights are in the older districts; the newer ones have the highest concentrations of hotels, restaurants, and shops.

ISLAMIC CAIRO NORTH: AL-HUSAYN MOSQUE TO BAB AL-FUTUH

If the Mamluks hadn't stopped the Mongols' furious advance at Ain Djalout (Palestine) in AD 1260, Cairo, like Baghdad and scores of other towns, might have been left in rubble. As it is, Misr al Mahrousa—a popular appellation that translates as "Egypt the Protected" offers one of the richest troves of Islamic architecture in the world. This is also because Cairo has been the capital of Islamic Egypt since its founding. Today the areas between Bab al-Futuh and Bab al-Nasr in the north and the Mosque of Amr in the south are still home to a rare concentration of buildings that represents a continuous, evolving architectural tradition.

Unfortunately, Islamic monuments don't attract as many visitors as pharaonic ones, and government funds for restoration haven't been so generous. A great many buildings were seriously damaged in the 1992 earthquake (some areas still lie in ruins), but much of the al-Azhar area has undergone a facelift since the start of the new millennium, and a visit to these historic neighborhoods should figure prominently on your agenda. A walk along these time-warped streets studded with monuments from different eras offers a rare taste of the extravagant beauty that once characterized the heart of the city. It is a visit to the past, light years away from the behemoth that modern Cairo has become.

You can get a very good feel for this area in a half-day, depending on how long you spend at each of the attractions. Leave enough time for a break and shopping afterward, if you wish. You can spend hours in the Khan al-Khalili, depending on how much browsing and haggling interests you. Keep in mind that most of the shops are closed on Sunday. Friday before noon is also a quieter time in the neighborhood.

MAIN ATTRACTIONS

⓬ **Bayt al-Suhaymi.** Considered the best example of domestic Islamic architecture in Cairo, this cooly luxurious 16th-century merchant's house is huge (more than 6,000 square feet), and with its gardens, well, and flour mill, it resembles a self-sufficient hamlet. As is the case with Islamic houses, the entrance passageway leads to a lush courtyard that is totally unexpected from the outside. On the ground floor are the *salamlik* (public reception rooms), and upstairs are the *haramlik* (private rooms). The house and adjacent alley have been restored, making this a charmingly evocative little corner of Cairo. ⊠ *19 Shar'a al-Darb al-Asfar, Islamic Cairo North* ☎ *No phone* ☎ *£e25* ⊘ *Daily 9–5.*

❷ **Khan al-Khalili.** The Khan has been a marketplace since the end of the
★ 14th century; commercial activity is its life blood. A maze of small streets and narrow alleys charts its way around the bazaar, and these passages are filled with scores of vendors hawking their wares and attempting to draw customers into their small shops. It is a chaotic mixture of Egyptians and tourists, smells of perfume and incense, fragments of age-old buildings next to modern amenities—and always noise and confusion. With a little determination, you can find just about anything you want to take home as proof of your trip to Cairo. Carpets, gold, silver, clothing, belly-dancing outfits, spices, perfumes, water pipes, woodwork, books, pottery, blown glass, leather, papyrus, pharaonic replicas—you name it, it's here. There are hundreds of little stores that will attract or repel.

A few words of advice: never take something at the first price; bargaining is the modus operandi in the Khan, and if you do not show interest,

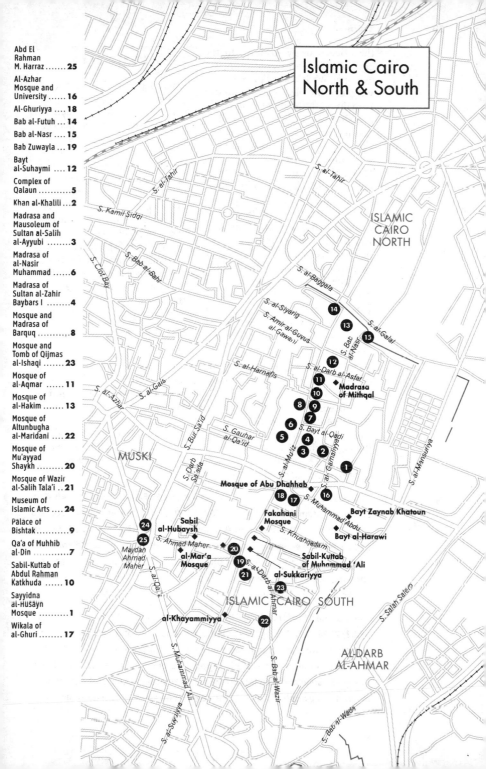

Islamic Cairo
North & South

ISLAMIC CAIRO NORTH

Madrasa of Mithqal

Mosque of Abu Dhahhab

Bayt Zaynab Khatoun

Fakahani Mosque

Bayt al-Harawi

Sabil al-Hubaysh

Sabil-Kuttab of Muhammad 'Ali

al-Mar'a Mosque

al-Sukkariyya

ISLAMIC CAIRO SOUTH

al-Khayammiyya

AL-DARB AL-AHMAR

MUSKI

Maydan Ahmad Maher

the price is likely to drop. In the case of a silver- or goldsmith, for example, while a fixed price for the weight of the piece exists, you can bargain on the quality of the workmanship. If a shopkeeper offers you tea or coffee and you take it, you are in no way obligated to buy something from his shop; it's just Middle Eastern hospitality. If someone offers to take you to his workshop on the second floor, accept if you have time; most of these crafts are fascinating to see in progress. If you pay by credit card, there may be a service charge of 3% to 6%; ask before handing over the plastic. The Khan has ATMs where you can take out Egyptian pounds. Finally, if someone offers to sell you marijuana or hashish, *do not* accept; you're likely to get oregano, compressed henna, or a stay in a dreadful local jail.

> ## THE ISLAMIC DAY
>
> Islamic sights are open from about 9 AM until 4 or 5 PM, depending on the custodian's whims. Muslims pray five times a day, and prayers usually last 15 minutes or so. Prayer times vary according to the season. The first of these is just before dawn (the *al-Fagr* prayer); the others are at noon or 1 PM (*al-Duhr*), midafternoon around 3 or 4 (*al-'Asr*), sunset (*al-Maghrib*), and evening (*al-'Esha*) at about 8 or 9 PM. If you happen to be visiting a mosque during prayer time, you may be asked to wait outside the main hall until prayers are completed.

The Khan has plenty of places to eat, including the grilled-meat restaurants on the corner of Maydan al-Husayn and Shar'a Muski and places that serve *fiteer*, Egyptian pancakes filled with everything from feta cheese to raisins. They form a row just outside the Khan, between Shar'a Muski and Shar'a al-Azhar. Most stores are closed on Sundays and during Friday prayers (the hour around noon, 1 PM from April through October, during daylight savings time). ⊠ *Main entrance on Shar'a al-Ahzar, near Sikkat Khan al-Khalili, Islamic Cairo North* ⊙ *Stores generally open Mon.–Sat., 10–9.*

NEED A BREAK?

Just past the Hotel el Hussein is the famous El Fishawy (⊠ *5 Sikkit Khan al-Khalili, Islamic Cairo North* ☎ *02/2590–6755*). The area has dozens of cafés, but this is the oldest, best-known, and most frequented by Egyptians and visitors alike. Here you can sip a Turkish coffee or mint tea; a *karkadeh*, a hibiscus drink served hot or cold; and *sahleb*, a warm milk-based drink sprinkled with coconut and nuts. You can also have your shoes shined or smoke a *shisha* (water pipe).

The **Naguib Mahfouz Café** (⊠ *5 al-Badestan Lane, Islamic Cairo North* ☎ *02/2590–3788*) is an air-conditioned, upscale coffee shop, and a perfect refuge from the clamor of the Khan. Have a drink, a light lunch, or—at the adjoining restaurant—a proper meal. To get here, face the Sayyidna al-Husayn Mosque and turn left into the passage that begins at the level of the minaret. Follow this through a couple of archways; the café is on the right.

⑭ Bab al-Futuh *(the Futuh Gate)*. To the left, inside the entrance to the ⇨ *Mosque of al-Hakim* is a small passageway that leads to a stairway up to the roof of the mosque. From here, you can get access to the Bab al-Futuh, one of the main gates of the Islamic city. Built in 1087 by Badr al-Gamali al-Gayushi, it was designed to protect al-Qahira from the Seljuk Turks who held Syria and were threatening Egypt. But the gate was never put to the test. ⊠ *Shar'a al-Mu'iz, Islamic Cairo North.*

⑮ Bab al-Nasr *(the Nasr Gate)*. This gate is similar to Bab al-Futuh, except that it is flanked by two square towers. On one of the towers is the inscription: TOUR CORBIN, a memento of the Napoleonic expedition, which renamed all the gates after French army officers during its occupation (Bab al-Futuh also has TOUR JUNOT and TOUR PERRAULT carved into its two rounded towers). The wall between the two gates is fun to explore. Tunnels with slit windows to provide light once connected the entire wall and its 60 gates with rooms and storehouses within the girth of the wall, making it possible for an army to defend the city without ever having to leave the wall. ⊠ *Shar'a Bab al-Nasr, Islamic Cairo North.*

❺ Complex of Qalaun. One of the early Mamluk rulers of Egypt, Mansur Qalaun was originally a Tartar (Mongol) brought to Egypt as a slave. Mamluks (literally, "those owned") were first imported from the Volga to Egypt by al-Salih Ayyubi, the man buried in the tomb across the street, who used them as his personal bodyguards. Aybak, the first Mamluk ruler, and his successor, Baybars al-Bunduqdari, both had been al-Salih's slaves. Qalaun was acquired by Baybars. In short, one's lot in life could be worse than being a slave to the Sultan in medieval Cairo.

Qalaun died at the ripe old age of 70, on his way to attack the Crusader fortress of Acre in 1290. The complex that he had built (it was begun in 1284) is noteworthy for its workmanship and the diverse styles that it displays.

A *bimaristan* (hospital and psychiatric ward) has existed on the site since Qalaun first saw the need for one. Only fragments of the original hospital remain, having been replaced by a modern (not necessarily better) one. In its heyday, Qalaun's bimaristan was famous for its care of the physically and mentally ill, and its staff was said to include musicians and storytellers as well as surgeons capable of performing delicate eye surgery.

The madrasa and mausoleum present the complex's impressive street facade, a series of pointed-arch recesses, almost Gothic in their proportions, each one pierced with groups of three windows, a much-seen feature of Islamic architecture. Look up at the 194-foot minaret with its horseshoe-shaped arched recesses and its corniced overhang, a device used since pharaonic times. The entrance is set slightly forward up a set of steps; its semicircular arch was the first of its kind in Egypt. Beyond the entrance is a long, tall corridor with the madrasa to the left and the tomb to the right. A door at the end of the corridor used to lead to the bimaristan but has been sealed off.

The gem of the complex, however, is the mausoleum, the burial place of Qalaun and his son al-Nasir Muhammad. The chamber is dark, cool, and mammoth. In its center is a wooden grille that encloses the tombs. There is much here to suggest that Qalaun was deeply influenced by what he saw on his exploits in Palestine. The plan of the mausoleum is similar to that of the Dome of the Rock in Jerusalem in that it contains an octagon fit within a square. The stained glass and tall proportions have a Gothic quality that are reminiscent of Crusader churches that he saw in the Levant. ⊠*Shar'a al-Mu'iz, Islamic Cairo North* ☎*No phone* ⊡*Free* ⊙*Daily 9–4.*

❶ Sayyidna al-Husayn Mosque. One of the holiest sites in Egypt, the mosque was originally built by the Fatimids in the 12th century as a shrine and is said to contain the head of Husayn, the Prophet's grandson. Al-Husayn is the spiritual heart of the Islamic city. It is here that the president and his ministers come to pray on important religious occasions. Many of the Sufi orders in the neighborhood perform Friday prayers at al-Husayn. During the *mulid* (celebration) of al-Husayn, held during the Muslim month of Rabi'a al-Akhiri (the fourth month in the Muslim calendar), the square in front of the mosque becomes a carnival. During Ramadan, the area is packed with people from sunset to dawn.

Not only was Husayn the grandson of the Prophet, but he was also the son of 'Ali, the fourth caliph and cousin of the Prophet. A group of followers who believed that 'Ali and his descendants should lead the faithful broke ranks with the majority (known as the Sunnis) when the Ummayads took control of the *umma* (the Islamic nation). This group became known as "the group of 'Ali" or Shi'a 'Ali, later Shi'a for short. Husayn is greatly revered by the Shi'a for his role as a martyr to the cause when, in 680, he and a band of his followers were massacred at the battle of Kerbala in Iraq.

If it seems strange that the head of a Shi'a martyr be given such importance in a country that is overwhelmingly Sunni, it should be noted that the Fatimids, the original builders of al-Qahira, were Shi'a. The 200 years in which they ruled the city left an impact on the traditions of the people. Not only did the Shi'a found the most prestigious Islamic university, al-Azhar, but they also were responsible for inculcating in the populace a veneration for saints, holy men, or relatives of the Prophet—a practice not at all in keeping with a strict interpretation of Sunni Islam. Thus, although the head of Husayn was brought to Cairo for safekeeping by a ruling minority, the Sunni majority quickly accepted the shrine as part of its heritage.

The mosque itself is a 19th-century stone building heavily influenced by the Gothic Revival; only elements of older structures remain. On the south end of the southeast facade stands a partial wall with a gate, known as Bab al-Akhdar (the Green Gate), which probably dates from the Fatimid dynasty. Inside the mosque, past the main prayer hall, is the tomb of Husayn, a domed chamber built by 'Abd al-Rahman Katkhuda in the 1760s. The grave is enclosed with a silver mashrabiyya screen.

The mosque is technically closed to non-Muslims. However, while large tour groups are not allowed to enter, there is more leeway for the individual traveler, provided that you avoid prayer times (the hour around noon; 1 PM between April and October during daylight saving time) and Fridays. ⊠ *Maydan al-Husayn, Islamic Cairo North* ☎ *No phone* ☜ *Free.*

ALSO WORTH SEEING

❸ Madrasa and Mausoleum of Sultan al-Salih al-Ayyubi. Although it does not appear to be very significant from the street, this building occupies an important place in Cairo's history as a point of architectural and political transition. The last descendant of Salah al-Din to rule Egypt, al-Salih Nejm al-Din al-Ayyubi, died in 1249 defending the country against the Crusader attack lead by Louis IX of France. Following his death, his wife, the famous Shagarat al-Dor, ruled for a brief time as queen and then as wife to Aybak, the first Mamluk ruler of Egypt.

This madrasa was the first in Cairo to have a *liwan* (a vaulted area) for more than one legal school. It was also the first to have a tomb attached. These two unique traits became standard features of a Mamluk madrasa. During Mamluk times, the madrasa of al-Salih was used by judges when hearing cases and issuing judgments. The street in front, the Bayn al-Qasrayn section of Shar'a al-Mu'iz, was used for meting out punishments to those deemed guilty. This was the city center for centuries.

Above the madrasa's minaret sits a top in the shape of an incense burner, in Arabic known as a *mabkhara*. It is the only one of its kind remaining from the Ayyubid period (1171–1250). Beneath the minaret, very little remains of this structure—part of an arched liwan in the courtyard, and the fragments of another arch opposite that suggest something of its former scale and importance. Some details, like the keel arch recess on the minaret with shell-like ornamentation and the shallow relieving arch over the doorway, deserve notice. ⊠ *Shar'a al-Mu'iz, Islamic Cairo North* ☎ *No phone* ☜ *Free* ☉ *Daily 9–4, except mosque during prayers.*

❻ Madrasa of al-Nasir Muhammad. Considered the greatest Mamluk sultan, al-Nasir ruled on three different occasions, for a total of 42 years (AD 1293–1340). It was during al-Nasir's reign that Egypt took advantage of its geographical location and gained control of the lucrative maritime trade routes that connected England with China. Al-Nasir built more than 30 mosques, the aqueduct from the Nile to the Citadel, and a canal from Cairo to Alexandria. Eight of his sons ruled Egypt in the 21 years following his death.

If Qalaun's complex has Gothic influences, all the more so his son's madrasa (built in 1304). In fact the entrance was literally lifted from a Crusader church in Acre. The minaret, with its delicate stucco work, is one of the finest in the city. Little of interest can be found inside. ⊠ *Shar'a al-Mu'iz, Islamic Cairo North* ☎ *No phone* ☜ *Free* ☉ *Daily 9–4.*

Madrasa of Mithqal. This beautifully restored Mamluk madrasa, which is built in a cruciform style, was built by Mithqal, chief eunuch to two Mamluk sultans, in 1361. To get here, start at the Palace of Bishtak and turn right, taking the little road that winds past the small mausoleum of Shaykh Sinan, instead of heading to Shar'a al-Mu'iz. The most interesting part of the complex is the tunnel that passes underneath it. Dare yourself to go through it and try to get to al-Mu'iz this way. (The tunnel takes you out to a small street that leads to the open Maydan Bayt al-Qadi. The last right off the square leads you down Shar'a Bayt al-Qadi to Muhhib al-Din, which in turn feeds onto al-Mu'iz.) ✉ *Darb al-Qirmiz, Islamic Cairo North* ☎ *No phone* 🎟 *Free* ☉ *Daily 9–4.*

❹ **Madrasa of Sultan al-Zahir Baybars I.** Al-Zahir Baybars' reign (1260–77) marked the real beginning of the Mamluk state, due in large part to his skills as a commander, administrator, and builder. It was he who halted the Mongols' western expansion by defeating them at Ayn Jalout in Palestine (1260), and he staged a series of successful campaigns against the Crusaders. All that survives of this once great madrasa is the restored corner across the street from Qalaun's mausoleum. Check out the leopards above the metal door; they were Baybars' insignia (*baybars* means "leopard lord" in Qipchaq, a Circassian language). ✉ *Shar'a al-Mu'iz, Islamic Cairo North* ☎ *No phone.*

❽ **Mosque and Madrasa of Barquq.** The first of the Circassian Mamluk Sultans, Barquq assumed power after a series of political intrigues that led to the downfall (and often deaths) of the Bahri (Tartar) Mamluks. Barquq (whose name means "the plum") took power in 1386 and rescued the country from the ravages of the Black Death and related famine and political unrest. His madrasa has an octagonal minaret with marble-inlaid carved stone. Notice the columns attached to the wall in the facade; one of them shows a stylized ram's head in the capital. The cruciform interior is spacious and austere, except for an ornate carved and gilded ceiling in the sanctuary (restored in modern times), and the *qibla* (the direction of Mecca) wall, decorated in marble dado. ✉ *Shar'a al-Mu'iz, Islamic Cairo North* ☎ *No phone* 🎟 *Free* ☉ *Daily 9–4, except mosque at prayer time.*

⓫ **Mosque of al-Aqmar.** The name of the mosque means "the moonlit" and refers to the way the stone catches the moon's reflection at night. Built in 1125, it is one of a few Fatimid buildings that have escaped major alterations. The shell-like recesses in the stone facade, later to become a common decorative element, were used here for the first time. This little mosque was also the first in Cairo to have an ornamented stone facade, and it was the first to alter its plan according to the existing urban structure, as the street existed before the mosque. ✉ *Shar'a al-Mu'iz, Islamic Cairo North* ☎ *No phone* 🎟 *Free* ☉ *Dawn–dusk, except during prayers.*

⓭ **Mosque of al-Hakim.** Originally built in AD 1010 by the Fatimid Khalifa (caliph) al-Hakim bi Amr Allah, this gigantic mosque was restored under the aegis of the Aga Khan, spiritual leader of the Isma'ili Shi'a sect.

Al-Hakim was, to put it nicely, an eccentric character. Some of the strangest edicts were declared during his caliphate, including a ban on *mulokhia*, a favorite Egyptian dish (he didn't care for it), and a ban on women's shoes, to prevent them from going out in public. Rumors began to circulate that he was claiming to be divine, creating extreme unrest among the populace. In order to quell the riots, he sent his main theologian, al-Darazi, to Syria (where he established the Druze religion), and then ordered his troops to attack Fustat, which at the time was the local town outside the royal city of al-Qahira. However, half his troops sided with the people, and the ensuing violence resulted in the burning of Fustat. He was given to riding around town on his donkey to ensure that his orders were being obeyed. One night after riding off into the Muquattam hills, he disappeared, never to be seen again, although the Druze claim that he has vanished only temporarily and will return to lead them to victory.

Built outside the original walls of Cairo (those standing now were constructed in 1087), the mosque has seen varied usage during its lifetime. During the Crusades, it held European prisoners of war who built a chapel inside it. Salah al-Din (1137–93) tore the chapel down when he used it as a stable. For Napoléon's troops it was a storehouse and fortress. Under Muhammad 'Ali in the 1800s, part of it was closed off and used as a *zawya* (small Sufi school). By the end of the 19th century, until the establishment of the **Museum of Islamic Arts** (⇨ *Islamic Cairo South, below*) in 1896, it was a repository for Islamic treasures.

Architecturally, the mosque does not compete among the finest in the city; the most significant element is its minarets, which were restored and reinforced by Baybars II in 1303, giving them that impressive trapezoidal base. Nevertheless, its scale and history are important, and its courtyard is large and breezy, making it a comfortable place to rest or meditate. ⊠*Shar'a al-Mu'iz, Islamic Cairo North* ☎*No phone* ☜*Free* ☉*Dawn–dusk, except during prayers.*

❾ **Palace of Bishtak.** Bishtak was a wealthy amir who married one of Sultan al-Nasir Muhammad's daughters. The original palace, completed in 1339, was purported to be five stories tall, with running water on each floor. The austere facade gives no hint of the lofty interior space. Only the women's quarters have survived the centuries, and even they are so impressive in scale as to give an idea of what the whole complex must have been like. See the mezzanine level with its *mashrabiyya* galleries, from which the sequestered ladies of the household watched events in the main hall below without being seen. The coffered wooden ceilings in these galleries are worth the climb, as is the view of the city from the roof. The palace entrance—the building itself fronts Shar'a al-Mu'iz— is around to the left side of the building as you face it. ■TIP➔ **Public bathrooms here are reasonably clean.** ⊠*Shar'a al-Mu'iz, Islamic Cairo North* ☎*No phone* ☜*Free* ☉*Daily 9–4.*

❼ **Qa'a of Muhhib al-Din.** Halfway up a street called Shar'a Bayt al-Qadi, on the west side of al-Mu'iz, this *qa'a* (great hall) has little to distinguish it save a small plaque (if the door isn't open, knock and the custodian will appear; otherwise just walk in and find him). Inside is one of the greatest spaces in Islamic Cairo: a hall that towers 50 feet, with exquisite wood and stone carving. Also known as the house of Uthman Kathkhuda, after the 18th-century Ottoman lieutenant who converted the original 14th-century Mamluk qa'a, the hall has superb features from both periods. The marble mosaic around the fountain is remarkable, and if you can get up to the roof, take a look at the *malqaf* (wind catcher) once used to ventilate Cairo houses. ✉ *Shar'a al-Mu'iz, Islamic Cairo North* ☎ *No phone* ✆ *Free, donation suggested* ✆ *Daily 9–4.*

🔟 **Sabil-Kuttab of Abdul Rahman Katkhuda.** *Katkhuda* is a Persian word meaning "master of the house." The powerful gentleman who endowed this building was a patron of the arts and architecture, as befitted his position. Before running water was available to the majority of Cairo's inhabitants, it was customary for wealthy patrons to build a *sabil* (a public fountain) to provide people with potable water. Often attached to a sabil was a *kuttab* (a basic school) for teaching children the Qur'an and other subjects. This 17th-century Ottoman monument is impressive for its ornate facade, tiled interior, and location at the head of a fork in the main road of medieval Cairo. ✉ *Shar'a al-Mu'iz, Islamic Cairo North* ☎ *No phone* ✆ *£e10* ✆ *Daily 10–6.*

▌ NEED A BREAK? On the roof of the **Hotel el Hussein** (✉ *Hussein Square, Khan al-Khalili, Islamic Cairo North* ☎ *02/2591–8479*) is a restaurant and café with a great view of the area—not to mention clean restrooms. The hotel is on the top floor of the large building on the left side of the square facing al-Sayyidna al-Husayn. To enter, take the arched passage (the hotel's name is written above it) on Shar'a al-Muski, just off the square. The hotel foyer is on the right side of the passage. Take the elevator up.

ISLAMIC CAIRO SOUTH: AL-AZHAR TO BAB ZUWAYLA

Here is a teeming, commercial area, more typically Egyptian and less geared toward tourism than the Khan area. But if you feel like shopping, you can find all sorts of postmodern "1,001 Nights" gear here, from pierced brass lanterns to Asian spices and teapots to pigeon-feather fans.

Anecdotes abound with regard to Bab Zuwayla, the southern gate of Fatimid Cairo: the severed heads of criminals were displayed there, warning of the perils of breaking the sultan's law; a troll was said to live behind the massive door; and the surrounding area was the center of activity for crafty ladies of the night who sometimes held their customers for ransom. On the way to Bab Zuwayla and beyond is a wealth of monuments. As in Islamic Cairo North, many buildings here are being restored, but there are a few gems that you shouldn't miss, culminating at the Museum of Islamic Arts, at the end of the walk.

There is much to capture the attention in this area, but relatively few monuments are open for visiting. Depending on how long you spend

A Feast of Fasting

The monthlong Ramadan holiday is a remarkable experience, exciting, and, yes, potentially frustrating. Fasting during Ramadan from sunrise to sunset is one of the five requirements of Islam and involves abstaining from food, water, cigarettes, sex, and impure thoughts. Visitors are not expected to fast, but you may find it is easier to fall into the natural rhythm of abstaining all day and then breaking the fast at *iftar* with everyone else. If you decide not to join in, it is polite to be discreet about it.

The somber mood only applies during the day. Ramadan nights are the liveliest of the year, with entire families trekking down to al-Hussayn in Islamic Cairo to eat or visit cafés until the wee hours. Concerts are given

throughout the city, and there are plenty of other performances. There are, as well, all-night feasts held in elaborately decorated tents that end with the *sohour*, the predawn meal that enables those fasting to get through the next day.

On a practical level, nothing meaningful gets done during Ramadan. Museum, restaurant, and business hours go haywire, and everyone claims to be delirious with hunger and thus unable to function. One great and unexpected pleasure reigns supreme: after the frenzied half-hour before iftar, a beautiful, almost eerie calm settles in, and the city appears to empty of its residents. You can walk through even the busiest square and not see a soul.

---

along the way and in the tent-makers' bazaar, this area is worth three or four hours, excluding lunch and the visit to the Museum of Islamic Arts; set aside about an hour for the latter. *For Islamic sights' hours and prayer times, see The Islamic Day in Islamic Cairo North, above.*

MAIN SIGHTS

16 Al-Azhar Mosque & University. Originally built in AD 970 by the conquering Fatimid caliph al-Mu'iz, al-Azhar is the oldest university in the world. Although the Fatimids were Shi'ite, the Sunni Mamluks who ousted them recognized the importance of the institution and replaced the Shi'ite doctrine with the Sunni orthodoxy. Today the university has faculties of medicine and engineering in addition to religion, and it has auxiliary campuses across the city.

Al-Azhar's primary significance remains as a school of religious learning. All Egyptian clerics must go through the program here before they are certified—a process that can take up to 15 years. Young men from all over the Islamic world come to study here, learning in the traditional Socratic method where students sit with a tutor until both agree that the student is ready to go on. The Shaykh of al-Azhar is not just the director of the university, but also the nation's supreme religious authority.

Built in pieces throughout the ages, al-Azhar is a mixture of architectural styles. The stucco ornamentation and the open courtyard represent early Islamic tastes; the solid stone madrasas and the ornate minarets are Mamluk; additions in the main sanctuary and its walls are Ottoman. The enclosure now measures just under 3 acres.

After you enter through the **Gates of the Barbers,** an Ottoman addition constructed under the auspices of Abd al-Rahman Katkhuda in 1752, remove your shoes. Then turn left to the **Madrasa and Tomb of Amir Atbugha.** Check out the recess in the qibla wall; an organic-shaped mosaic pattern rare to Islamic ornamentation can be found near the top.

Return to the ticketing and shoe-removal area and look up at the **Gates of Sultan Qayt Bay,** the second set on the way into the university. Built in 1483, they have a quality of ornamentation that verifies this Mamluk leader's patronage of architecture. The composition as a whole is masterful: from the recessed lintel to the multitier stalactite arch above the doorway, the grilles and medallions above the arch, and, finally, the finely carved minaret placed off center.

To the right of this lobby is the **Madrasa of Taybars.** Once ranked among the most spectacular madrasas in Mamluk Cairo, only its qibla wall remains. It is said that the ceiling was gold-plated and that Taybars, the patron, so wanted to glorify Allah that he specifically asked not to see any bills until it was completed, in 1309.

Sultan Qayt Bay's gateway opens to a spacious courtyard, quite typical of early Islamic design. Originally this court must have appeared similar to that of the Mosque of al-Hakim (➪ *Islamic Cairo North, above*), but changes over the centuries have diminished that effect. The keel arches of the arcades and the stucco decoration, however, remain true to that era. The raising of the arch that indicates entrance to the main sanctuary, while a common feature of Persian and Indian Islamic architecture, remains an oddity in Arab buildings.

The main sanctuary, which was traditionally a place to pray, learn, and sleep, is part Fatimid, part Ottoman. The Ottoman extension is distinguished by a set of steps that divides it from the original. Take some time to soak in the atmosphere, and look for the two qibla walls, the painted wooden roof, the old metal gates that used to open for prayer or the poor, and the ornate stuccowork of the Fatimid section. To the right of the Ottoman qibla wall is the **Tomb of 'Abdul Rahman Katkhuda,** the greatest builder of the Ottoman era and the man most responsible for the post-Mamluk extension of al-Azhar. To the extreme left along the Fatimid qibla wall is the small **Madrasa and Mausoleum of the Eunuch Gawhar al-Qunqubay,** treasurer to Sultan Barsbay. Although it is diminutive in size, the quality of the intricately inlaid wooden doors, the stained-glass windows, and the interlacing floral pattern on the dome make it a deserved detour.

Return to the courtyard. To the right of the **minaret of Qayt Bay** is the **minaret of al-Ghuri,** the tallest in the complex. Built in 1510, it is similar to, but not a copy of, Qayt Bay's: it is divided into three sections (the first two are octagonal) like its predecessor, but it is tiled rather than carved. The final section, consisting of two pierced rectangular blocks, is unusual, and not at all like Qayt Bay's plain cylinder.

A restoration project has left the complex shiny and clean and has made the custodians especially sensitive about its upkeep. But the beauty of al-Azhar, unlike many of the other monuments, stems in part from the fact that it is alive and very much in use. ⊠ *Gama' al-Azhar, Shar'a al-Azhar, Islamic Cairo South* 🕾 *No phone* 🎟 *Free* 🕙 *Daily dawn–dusk, except mosque at prayer times.*

⑲ Bab Zuwayla. Built in 1092, this is one of three remaining gates of

Fodor'sChoice Fatimid Cairo. It was named after members of the Fatimid army who

★ hailed from a North African Berber tribe called the Zuwayli.

The gate features a pair of minaret-topped semicircular towers. Notice the lobed-arch decoration on the inner flanks of the towers in the entrance. These arches were used earlier in North African architecture and were introduced here following the Fatimid conquest of Egypt. They are seen in later Fatimid and Mamluk buildings.

As you pass through the massive doorway, take into account that the street level has risen to such an extent that what you see as you walk would have been at eye level for a traveler entering the city on a camel. According to the great architectural historian K.A.C. Creswell, the loggia between the two towers on the outside of the wall once housed an orchestra that announced royal comings and goings.

However, Bab Zuwayla wasn't always such a lighthearted spot. It was here that public hangings and beheadings took place. The conquering Turks hanged the last independent Mamluk sultan, Tumanbay II, from this gate in 1517. The unlucky man's agony was prolonged because the rope broke three times. Finally, fed up, the Ottomans had him beheaded.

The views from the tower are some of the best in Cairo. Minarets galore and little glimpses of street life in the alleyways below mean you may spend more than a few minutes here.

Bab Zuwayla marks the southern end of the Fatimid city, as Bab al-Futuh marks the north. And al-Mu'iz, the central artery of medieval Cairo, runs from the latter through the former. Al-Mu'iz continues all the way to the Southern Cemeteries, but as is common with many older streets, the name keeps changing along the way, describing the area it passes through, as when it passes through the tent-makers' bazaar. ⊠ *Shar'a al-Mu'iz, Islamic Cairo South* 🎟 *£e15* 🕙 *Daily 8–5.*

㉔ Museum of Islamic Arts. Too often overlooked, this is one of the finest

★ museums in Cairo, with a rare and extensive collection of Islamic art. The collection comes mainly from Egypt, but there are pieces from elsewhere in the Islamic world as well.

Arranged according to medium, there are pieces from every era of development—from Ummayad to Abbasid, Fatimid, Ayyubid, and Mamluk works. You can see woodwork, stucco, intarsia, ceramics, glass, metalwork, textiles, and carpets.

Particularly notable items include one of the earliest Muslim tomb-stones, which dates from 652, only 31 years after the Prophet returned to Mecca victorious; a bronze ewer from the time of the Abbasid caliph Marwan II that has a spout in the shape of a rooster; a series of Abbasid stucco panels from both Egypt and Iraq displaying the varied styles of the time; frescoes from a Fatimid bathhouse; wooden panels from the Western Palace; carved rock crystal; a wooden piece from the Ayyubid era covered with exquisite carved inscriptions and foliage; an excellent brass-plated Mamluk door, which looks at first glance like a standard arabesque decoration but is in fact interspersed with tiny animals and foliage; and a series of mosaics from various Mamluk mosques, some made with marble and mother-of-pearl inlay.

The metalwork section contains the doors of the Mosque of al-Salih Tala'i. Metalwork inlaid with silver and gold includes incense burners, candlesticks, and vases, some with Christian symbols. There is also a set of astronomical instruments. The armor and arms hall is still impressive despite the fact that Selim, the conquering Ottoman sultan of 1517, had much of this type of booty carried off to Istanbul, where it is on display at Topkapi Palace. The ceramics display is excellent, particularly pieces from the Fatimid era and Iran. A hall of glassware merits particular attention, especially the Mamluk mosque lamps. The collection of rare manuscripts and books is also noteworthy. ⊠*Shar'a Bur Sa'id at Maydan Ahmad Maher, Islamic Cairo South* ☎*02/2390–9930* ⊡*£e40* ☉*Sat.–Thurs. 9–4, Fri. 9–11 and 2–4.*

ALSO WORTH SEEING

㉕ Abd El Rahman M. Harraz Seeds, Medicinal, and Medical Plants. Near the Museum of Islamic Arts is this fantastic shop (with Bab Zuwayla at your back, it's on the right); it has an incredible selection of medicinal herbs, traditional beauty aids, essential oils and cosmetics, and curiosities, including dried lizards. The bizarre window display features a stuffed gazelle. ⊠*1 Bab el-Kalq Sq., Islamic Cairo South* ☎*02/2511–5167* ☉*Sat.–Thurs. 9* AM–*10* PM.

⑱ Al-Ghuriyya *(al-Ghuri Cultural Palace).* This medieval landmark stands on either side of Shar'a al-Mu'iz where it crosses Shar'a al-Azhar. The surrounding area was the site of the Silk Bazaar, visible in David Robert's famous 1839 etching of the same name.

Built by Sultan al-Ghuri, who constructed the Wikala al-Ghuri three years later, al-Ghuriyya was the last great Mamluk architectural work before the Ottomans occupied Egypt. On the right side of the street (facing Shar'a al-Azhar) is the madrasa; opposite it stands the mausoleum. The former is a large-scale project, with almost Brutalist proportions (picture large, modern, exposed-concrete buildings). Note the unusual design of the minaret, its square base topped by five chimney pots.

The mausoleum was rebuilt several times during al-Ghuri's reign. After spending a reported 100,000 dinars on the complex, al-Ghuri was not buried here. He died outside Aleppo, and his body was never found. The bodies of a son, a concubine (both victims of a plague outbreak), a daughter, and Tumanbay II (his successor) are interred in the vault.

Al-Ghuriyya's official name today is the al-Ghuri Cultural Palace: a restoration converted the site for displays of art and other cultural events. Traditional musicians, singers, and dancers perform regularly in the madrasa. Sufi chanting and music performances take place on the second and fourth Friday of every month, while Nubian drum and instruments can be heard on the first and third Sunday of each month (show times are 9 PM in summer; 9:30 PM in winter). ⊠ *Qasr al-Ghuri, Shar'a al-Mu'iz, Islamic Cairo South* ☎*02/510–0823* ⊠*£e25* ⊙*Daily 9–5.*

OFF THE BEATEN PATH

House of Gamal al-Din al Dhahabbi. The second right after al-Ghuriyya along al-Mu'iz leads to a small alley named Shar'a Khushqadam. Fifty yards up on the right, look for the well-preserved, 16th-century, wealthy merchant's house. Enter through the massive wooden doors that feed into the courtyard. Of particular interest are the mashrabiyya and stained-glass windows, the stone Mamluk-style facia panels, the marble floors, and the reception room's wooden ceilings. ⊠ *6 Shar'a Khushqadam, Islamic Cairo South* ☎*No phone* ⊠*£e15* ⊙*Daily 9–4.*

㉓ **Mosque and Tomb of Qijmas al-Ishaqi.** Restored in the early part of the 20th century, this complex was one of the jewels of Mamluk architecture. Its decorated facade reflects the ornate style popular under the reign of Sultan Qayt Bay. Qijmas served in the sultan's court until he took an appointment as viceroy of Damascus, where he died peacefully and was buried in 1487. By the late 15th century, when this mosque was built, space was at a premium in this part of Cairo, and the careful and elegant orientation of the mosque on the small, irregular plot of land demonstrates the architect's creativity.

Despite its irregular footprint, the mosque is a perfect cruciform plan. And the quality of light is excellent, as it filters in through the *shukhshayhka* (lantern) of the central covered court and through the stained glass of the windows. Notice the prayer niche, with its inlaid white marble. The circle in the middle carries the name of the proud artist, written twice in mirror image—from left to right and vice versa. ⊠*Shar'a Darb al-Ahmar, Islamic Cairo South* ☎*No phone* ⊠*Free* ⊙*Daily 9–4.*

㉒ **Mosque of Altunbugha al-Maridani.** Built by a son-in-law of Sultan Nasir al-Muhammad who died at the tender age of 25, the mosque was completed under the supervision of the sultan's architect. It features fine examples of virtually every decorative art in vogue in the 14th century. Enter the sanctuary behind the fine mashrabiyya screen and notice the collection of pillars of pharaonic, Christian, and Roman origin The *mihrab* (prayer niche) is made of marble inlay and mother-of-pearl, and the wooden *minbar* (pulpit) is also beautifully carved and inlaid. Above the mihrab are excellent original stucco carvings, unique in Cairo for their naturalistically rendered tree motif. This wall also features dados of inlaid marble with square Kufic script.

Outside, be sure to admire the first example of a minaret in octagonal form from bottom to top; it is also the earliest extant example of just such a top. It is shaped like a pavilion, with eight columns carrying a pear-shaped bulb crown. The mosque caretaker is happy to allow you to climb up to enjoy the view—for a small tip, of course. Because this mosque is an active community center, its open hours tend to be longer than those of other monuments. ⊠ *Shar'a al-Tabbana, Islamic Cairo South* 🕾 *No phone* 🖆 *Free* ⊙ *Daily 9–8.*

⓴ **Mosque of Mu'ayyad Shaykh.** The Sultan Mu'ayyad chose this site because he was once imprisoned at this location. During his captivity, he swore that he would build a mosque here if he was ever freed. He made good on his promise in 1420 and tore down the infamous jails that once occupied the site.

The mosque's facade is remarkable only in that the *ablaq* (the striped wall) is black and white, less common than the usual red and white. The high portal is inspired by the famous entrance of the Sultan Hassan Mosque below the Citadel. The beautiful bronze-plated door was a little more than inspired; Mu'ayyad had it lifted from the mosque of his better-known predecessor. The two elegant **identical minarets** rest against the towers of Bab Zuwayla, which makes them appear to be a part of the gate and not the mosque.

The interior space is well insulated from the bustle of the surrounding district by high walls blanketed in marble panels. The wood and ivory *minbar* is flanked by a fine columned *mihrab* with marble marquetry of an exceptional level of quality. The gilt and blue ceilings are also noteworthy. ⊠ *Gam'a al-Mu'ayyad Shaykh, Shar'a al-Mu'iz at Bab Zuwayla, Islamic Cairo South* 🕾 *No phone* 🖆 *Free* ⊙ *Daily, dawn–dusk, except during prayers.*

㉑ **Mosque of Wazir al-Salih Tala'i.** Built in 1160, this is one of the last Fatimid structures constructed outside the city walls. It is also one of the most elegant mosques in Cairo, in part because of its simplicity. Like many mosques in Cairo, the ground floor housed several shops, which allowed the authorities to pay for the upkeep. Today these shops are underground, because the street level has risen considerably over time.

The mosque has a standard, early Islamic, rectangular courtyard plan. The main facade consists of five keel arches on Greco-Roman columns taken from an earlier building that are linked by wooden tie beams. Between each arch, a set of long panels is topped with Fatimid shell niches. The most distinctive architectural feature of this mosque is the porchlike area, underneath the arches of the main facade, that creates an open, airy interior court. Inside, the columns are also taken from elsewhere: no two of their capitals are alike. ⊠ *Gam'a al-Salih Tala'i, Shar'a al-Mu'iz at Bab Zuwayla, Islamic Cairo South* 🕾 *No phone* 🖆 *Free* ⊙ *Daily, dawn–dusk, except during prayers.*

⓱ **Wikala of al-Ghuri.** This handsome building with its strong, square lines seems almost modern, save for the ablaq masonry, a clear indicator of its Mamluk origin. Built in 1504–05 by Sultan Qansuh al-Ghuri, this classical Mamluk structure was constructed to accommodate visiting merchants. It went up, as fate would have it, at the end of a period of Mamluk prosperity, the result of their control of the spice trade

2

between Asia and Europe. When Vasco da Gama discovered a path around Africa in 1495, the decline in Cairo's importance began. Sadly, although al-Ghuri was a prolific builder and a courageous soldier, he was a decade behind the curve. He died in 1516 staving off the Ottomans in Aleppo, Syria. His successor, Tumanbay II, was destined to last only a year before succumbing to the might of Istanbul.

Nevertheless, the building is in fairly good shape, and it provides an indication of how medieval Cairene commerce operated. Merchants would bring their horses and carts into the main courtyard, where they would be stabled, while the merchants would retire to the upper floors with their goods.

Today the wikala's rooms are used as studios for traditional crafts, including carpet weaving, metalwork, and the making of mashrabiyya that are not so different from the ones that protrude from the upper floors into the courtyard. During the month of Ramadan, musical events are held here in the evenings. ⊠*Shar'a Muhammad 'Abdu, Islamic Cairo South* ☎*02/511–0472* ☲*£e15* ☉*Daily 9–4, studios Sat.–Wed. 9–4.*

DOWNTOWN & BULAQ

In the middle of the 19th century, the slavishly Francophile Khedive Isma'il laid out this district on a Parisian plan across the old canal from Islamic Cairo, which until then had been the heart of the city. It quickly became the most fashionable commercial and residential district, lined with cafés and jewelers and settled by all the major department stores. In time, as new residential districts such as Garden City and Zamalek opened up, Downtown lost favor as a place to live. But it was, above all else, a colonial city—standing in proximity to traditional Cairo but self-consciously apart from it.

With the rise of Egyptian nationalism in the early 20th century, that could not last. Much of Downtown was systematically torched in anti-foreign riots on Black Saturday in January 1952, in a spasm of violence that demonstrated how closely architecture was associated with colonial rule. The riots marked the beginning of the end for the foreign presence in Egypt: the revolution that overthrew the British-backed monarchy followed Black Saturday within months, and with it all the street names changed to reflect the new heroes. But it was the wave of nationalizations in the early 1960s that finally closed the colonial chapter Downtown, as those foreigners who had stayed on past the revolution lost their businesses, their way of life, and their place in a city that had never really belonged to them.

Downtown—called Wist al-Balad in Arabic—is still loved today, but more for its shoe stores and cinemas than for its architecture and the unique melding of cultures and influences that it once represented. Walking through the district gives you a sense of infinite discovery, of little fragments of a time and place now lost that haven't quite been swept away by the changing politics. Although all the shops at street

Inspiration

If you live in a city with an Arab neighborhood, you might have some luck tracking down the films of Egypt's best-known director, the recently deceased Youssef Chahine, who in 1997 was honored with a lifetime achievement award in Cannes. His film *Massir* (*Destiny*), is an antifundamentalist musical historical drama, if you can imagine such a thing. Much more impressive is a film Chahine made in the 1950s called *Bab al-Hadid* (translated in English as *Cairo Station*), an affecting story about people who sell drinks and newspapers on the platforms of the main train station. His *al-Arda* (*The Land*) expresses the intense attachment to the land of a society that is still largely agricultural.

The greatest Western film ever made about the region is *The Battle of Algiers*, by Italian director Gillo Pontecorvo. Shot in a documentary style in the 1960s, it focuses on the Algerian struggle for independence against the French. It so powerfully captures the feeling of the Arab streets that it reflects life in Cairo better than most films that are actually about Cairo. The most famous recent film involving Egypt is *The English Patient*, based on Michael Ondaatje's novel. Most of the Egypt scenes were filmed in Tunisia, however, and audiences burst out laughing at the way Egyptians were stereotyped on screen.

Egypt's most famous author is Nobel Prize–winner Naguib Mahfouz, although his work in translation is less nuanced than it is in Arabic. For a sense of the social and political changes in Egypt during the 20th century read his Cairo Trilogy—*Palace Walk, Palace of Desire,* and *Sugar Street*—which traces the transformation of a family from Mahfouz's native district in Islamic Cairo. More interesting are the works of Yusuf Idris, playwright Tawfiq al-Hakim, legendary man of letters Taha Hussein, and feminist writer Nawal al-Saadawi. The first half of Adhaf Soueif's lengthy *In the Eye of the Sun* gives an excellent feel for Nasser's Cairo. If you have a taste for mystery, look for Agatha Christie's *Death on the Nile*, best read on the terrace of the Old Cataract Hotel in Aswan. Perhaps best of all is Waguih Ghali's quirky, hard-to-find *Beer in the Snooker Club*, which subtly mocks all the sacred cows of the revolution.

For Alexandria, the standard reading is Lawrence Durrell's *Alexandria Quartet,* which defined the city for a generation of readers that came of age in the West in the late 1950s. Andre Aciman's story of his Alexandrian Jewish family, *Out of Egypt,* reveals little about the city but is exquisitely written. Much more relevant is the poetry of the melancholy Alexandrian Greek Constantine Cavafy. His most celebrated poems are "Ithaka," "The City," and "God Abandons Antony."

level have redecorated their own pieces of facade, look higher and the fin-de-siècle city comes alive. Sadly, most of the buildings are in an advanced state of decay, so you have to use a little imagination to re-create the neighborhood's former glory.

Quite apart from the experience of downtown Cairo, the Egyptian Antiquities Museum is a lens through which to see the ancient world. And it is essential to any trip to Egypt. Its vast stores of treasures from

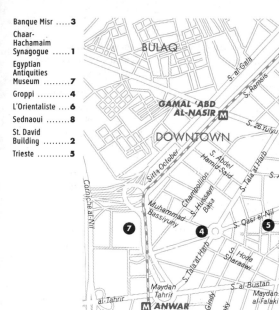

2

Downtown & Bulaq

ancient Egypt are as astonishing as they are daunting to take in. Tour the museum in conjunction with a day in Giza, or before you head upriver to Luxor, Aswan, and beyond for the Nile Valley monuments.

MAIN SIGHTS

① **Chaar-Hachamaim Synagogue.** This unusual concrete block with a subtle
★ art nouveau floral motif is easily overlooked from the outside. Arrive early, passport in hand, act unthreatening—the security guards can be touchy about letting people in—and one of Cairo's great hidden treasures awaits, with an interior of exquisite stained-glass windows and light fixtures rumored to be from Tiffany. Erected in 1899 by the Mosseri family, the synagogue is seldom used because there are too few remaining Jewish men to hold a service. This possible end masks a long and prosperous history for the Jewish community in Egypt. Over the past 500 years, whenever Europe went through its regular waves of persecution and expulsion, Jews sought refuge in Muslim lands such as Egypt, where they were protected as People of the Book. Only in the 20th century, with colonialism and the emergence of Israel, did local sentiment turn against them. The synagogue has no fixed hours, but mornings (Sunday through Friday) are the best time to visit. ■**TIP**➔ **Security is tight, so make sure you carry your passport as proof of identity** ⊠*Shar'a Adly (opposite Kodak Passage), Downtown.*

CLOSE UP

The Jewish Community in Cairo

The Chaar-Hachamaim Synagogue was paid for with contributions from some of the most powerful men in Cairo—a small coterie of Jewish families (including the Cattaui, Suares, Naggar, and Mosseri families) who owned and controlled many of Egypt's private banks, bus companies, and major department stores. Vita Mosseri was the main energizer behind the campaign for the new place of worship and Maurice Cattaui was the architect who produced the blueprint for the finished building.

The Jewish community lived in peace and security alongside the Muslim Arab and Christian peoples in Egypt for generations, but the founding of the state of Israel and the 1952 revolution in Egypt brought privatization and increased political tension that turned the world upside down for these families within a half a decade.

NEED A BREAK?

The **Windsor Hotel** (⊠ *19 Shar'a Alfi Bey, Downtown* ☎ *02/2591–5277*) has an atmospheric bar tucked away on its second floor. The Windsor opened in 1901 as the royal baths. Some years later it became an adjunct to the legendary Shepheard's. When Shepheard's burned, the Windsor survived, and the bar still retains a vaguely Anglicized air, with heavy colonial furniture that is ideal for reclining with a cold drink. The place draws a regular clientele that includes many aging members of Cairo's intellectual community. The sense of timelessness infects the staff as well, who appear to have worked here since the 1930s and will never rush you out the door.

⑦ The Egyptian Antiquities Museum. On the north end of Maydan Tahrir, this huge neoclassical building is home to the world's largest collection of ancient Egyptian artifacts. With more than 100,000 items in total, it is said that if you were to spend just one minute on each item, it would take over nine months to complete the tour. Needless to say, you need to be selective here, and it's a good idea to buy a museum guidebook or hire a museum guide. You can purchase a map of the museum (£e7), helpful in getting your bearings, but it doesn't include much in the way of historical description. *The Egyptian Museum in Cairo: Official Catalogue* (£e100) (available in the museum) is a far more comprehensive and practical guide. Official museum guides are available at £e40 an hour, but if you want a two- or three-hour tour, you can bargain for a lower rate. Five to six hours allow for a fair introduction to the museum.

Fodor'sChoice ★

Some of the museum's finest pieces are in the center of the ground floor, below the atrium and rotunda. The area makes a good place to start, acting as a preview for the rest of the museum. Among the prized possessions here are three colossi of the legendary New Kingdom pharaoh Ramesses II (1290–1224 BC); a limestone statue of Djoser (around 2600 BC), the 2nd Dynasty pharaoh who built the Step Pyramid in Saqqara; several sarcophagi; and a floor from the destroyed palace of Akhenaten (1353–1335 BC), the heretic monotheist king. The Narmer

Palette, a piece from about 3000 BC, is thought to document the first unification of northern and southern Egypt.

Rooms around the atrium are arranged chronologically, clockwise from the left (west) of the entrance: the Old Kingdom (2575–2134 BC) in Rooms 31, 32, 36, 37, 41, 42, 46, and 47; the Middle Kingdom (2040–1640 BC) in Rooms 11, 12, 16, 17, 21, 22, 26, and 27; the New Kingdom (1550–1070 BC) in Rooms 1–10, 14, 15, 19, and 20; Greco-Roman Egypt (332 BC–c. AD 395) in Rooms 34, 35, 39, and 40; and Nubian Exhibits in Rooms 44 and 45.

WORD OF MOUTH

"To do [the Egyptian Antiquities Museum] without a guide or a decent guidebook (which is not the same) would be near impossible . . . In fact, the whole museum looks and feels completely unchanged since it was built. This of course, adds to the charm . . . It is truly an amazing place to walk around, and all too soon did we have to leave.

—Mazj

Among the most important Old Kingdom items are a superbly crafted statue of Khafre (2551–2528 BC), builder of the second Great Pyramid at Giza (Room 42), and the delightful, lifelike dual statues of Rahotep and Nofret (2500 BC, Room 42). The Middle Kingdom display includes several statues of Senwosret I (1971–1926 BC), responsible for the first major temple to Amun at Karnak (Room 22). The rich collection of New Kingdom artifacts includes an exquisite statue of Thutmose III (1479–1425 BC), Egypt's greatest empire builder, suckling at the teat of the cow-goddess (Room 12); artwork from Akhenaten's reign, the realistic style of which is markedly different from anything that came before or after it (Room 3); and several statues and parts of colossi from the time of Ramesses II (Room 20). The works in the Greco-Roman exhibit are not as impressive as those on display in the Greco-Roman Museum in Alexandria, but they are interesting nonetheless in their attempts to weld Hellenistic and pharaonic cultures. Pieces in the Nubian section include saddles, weapons, and a mummified horse skeleton (Room 42)—again, of lesser quality than the Nubian Museum in Aswan but still of interest.

On the museum's upper floor is the famous Tutankhamun collection. Look for its beautiful gold funerary mask and sarcophagus (Room 3), ancient trumpet (Room 30), thrones (Rooms 20 and 25), the four huge gilded boxes that fit one inside the other (exhibits 7 and 8, located in the hallway just outside Room 30), and a royal toilet seat to boot (outside Room 30); it is one of the few air-conditioned rooms in the museum. (The collection is scheduled to be relocated to the new Grand Egyptian Museum in Giza as early as 2010.) Also upstairs is the royal Mummy Room, which houses 11 pharaonic dignitaries, including the body of Ramesses II (Room 52). If you are discouraged by the Mummy Room's steep entrance fee, don't miss the assortment of mummified animals and birds in the adjacent room (Room 53), which has no additional charge. Also on the upper floor is a series of specialized exhibits, including a collection of papyri and Middle Kingdom wooden models of daily life (Rooms 24 and 27).

In 2003, the museum unveiled "Hidden Treasures of the Egyptian Museum," more than 150 of the best objects that form part of the museum's vast stock of artifacts kept in storage. Fittingly, the new galleries sit in the museum basement, where the catalogued items used to lie on dark dusty shelves. ✉*al-Mathaf al-Masri, Maydan Tahrir, Downtown* ☎*02/2579–6948* 🎫*Museum £e60, Mummy Room £e100* 🕙*Daily 9–7.*

ALSO WORTH SEEING

 Banque Misr. Colonial Cairo emulated the French, was run by the British, and was built largely by Italians. Yet for all that colonial layering, its profoundly Middle Eastern cultural origins always won out in the end. Nothing symbolizes this strange synthesis better than the buildings of the Italian architect Antoine Lasciac, who worked in Cairo from 1882 to 1936 and served as the chief architect of the khedivial palaces. Lasciac set out to reflect Egypt's emergent nationalism in a new architectural style by updating the Mamluk decorative work so typical of Islamic Cairo and grafting it onto the technical innovations of his era. The result can be seen in this, his best-preserved building, which dates from 1927. Its mosaics, sculptural work, and decorations all draw on a range of Middle Eastern influences, while the core of the building, in plan and scale, is distinctly Western. ✉*Shar'a Muhammad Farid, south of Maydan Mustafa Kamil, Downtown.*

OFF THE BEATEN PATH

Old Red-Light District. Although the area around Shar'a Clot Bey is now rather conservative, at one time in the 20th century it was lined with brothels and bars, and you can still see the arched walkways and hidden nooks that once sheltered unspeakable vices. Prostitution was not made illegal in Cairo until 1949, but the trade had one last great boom period during World War II, when the nearby Shepheard's was commandeered as the British officers' base and the Ezbekiyya teemed with young men less interested in the pyramids than in more carnal pursuits. To them, this area was known simply as the Birka, after one of the adjoining alleys, and it offered them comforts of all sorts for just 10 piastres. The shuttered second-floor rooms see less traffic these days, reborn as cheap if largely respectable pensions, and the nearby St. Mark's Cathedral, once a source of succor for guilt-ridden consciences, now serves a more prosaic function for the local Christian community. Every once in a while the local newspapers run interviews with elderly women professing to have been madams in their youth, although few other Egyptians lament the passing of the trade.

④ Groppi. On the western edge of Maydan Tala'at Harb, recognizable by the gorgeous mosaic decorating the entrance, Groppi was once the chocolatier to royalty. Founded in the 1930s by a Swiss native, this café and dance hall (along with its older branch on nearby Shar'a Adly) was the favorite meeting place for everyone from celebrities and the local aristocracy to political activists and British soldiers. Ravaged by four decades of socialism and several tasteless renovations, Groppi now barely manages a good coffee, although the elaborate metal lights in the rotunda are worth a look. ✉ *Maydan Tala'at Harb, Downtown* ☎ *02/574–3244* ⊗ *Daily 7 AM–10 PM.*

6 **L'Orientaliste.** This small, unostentatious bookstore is one of the world's premier sources for antique maps and out-of-print books with Middle Eastern themes. The store smells appropriately musty, and you might easily while away an afternoon looking through the old postcards, photographs, and assembled treasures. Ask a clerk to show you what Downtown, particularly Opera Square, used to look like—it will aid your imagination as you walk around. Don't leave without seeing the map room, up the stairs in the back. ✉ *15 Shar'a Qasr al-Nil, Downtown* ☎ *02/575–3418* ⊗ *Mon.–Sat. 10–7:30.*

8 **Sednaoui.** A spectacular building modeled on a store in Paris, Sednaoui is on a back corner of Ezbekiyya near Ataba Square and is now largely forgotten by most Cairenes. It was built in 1913 as the main branch of a chain owned by a pair of Levantine brothers and has the sort of architectural flourishes rare in Cairo today: a large greenhouse atrium, a swirling central staircase, and two priceless copper elevators that are worth a quick ride. Sadly, since Egypt's department stores were nationalized in the early 1960s, the original owners have long since left and there is little of interest to buy. ✉ *3 Kazinder Sq., Downtown* ☎ *02/590–3613* ⊗ *Mon.–Sat. 10–8.*

2 **St. David Building.** Founded in the 1880s by a Welshman as the Davies Bryan department store—Cairo's largest at the time—this building has an odd, almost witty roofline reminiscent of a fortress. The facade retains the cursive *d* and *b* of its former owner who, patriot that he was, decorated it with Welsh symbols, to which later occupants have added about a hundred little Venus de Milos. The antique, ground-floor **Stephenson Pharmacy,** which is open Monday through Saturday 9:30–9, is not to be missed. It was once one of the best in the city (according to the 1929 Baedeker's guide) and still displays advertisements for ancient cure-alls. Also in the St. David is the beloved **Anglo-Egyptian Bookstore** (☎ *02/2391–4237*), which has a pleasant search-through-the-stacks ambience. The bookstore is open 9–1:30 and 4:30–8, except for Sunday, when it's closed. ✉ *Shar'a Muhammad Farid at Shar'a Khalek Sarwat, Downtown.*

5 **Trieste.** Designed by the architect of the Banque Misr but even more intriguing, this 1910 building is rich in Islamic sculptural elements. Long neglected, the Trieste was finally renovated as part of the Stock Exchange neighborhood renewal plan and is now disconcertingly tarted up in off-white and salmon. In compensation, the gorgeous mosaic work is easier to see now. ✉ *South side of Shar'a Qasr al-Nil, 1 block west of Shar'a Sherif, Downtown.*

THE CITADEL & SAYYIDA ZAYNAB

The view of the huge silver domes and needle-thin minarets of the Muhammad 'Ali Mosque against the stark backdrop of the desert cliffs of the Muquattam is one of Cairo's most striking visual icons. The mosque is just one feature of the Citadel, an immense fortified enclosure that housed the local power brokers from Salah al-Din, its 12th-century founder, to Napoléon in the 18th century and the British colonial governors and troops until their withdrawal in 1946. It served as the base of operations for Mamluk slave kings as well as for a series of sultans and pashas with their colorful retinues, including al-Nasir Muhammad's 1,200-concubine-strong harem.

The Citadel commands wonderful views of the city—smog permitting. From there, you can visit some impressive monuments, including the amazing Mosque and Madrasa of Sultan Hasan, one of the largest such structures in the world, and the remarkably calm, austere Mosque of Ibn Tulun, one of Cairo's oldest buildings.

The areas between these three mosques have been cut through with a series of main roads—including modern attempts to clear paths across the dense medieval urban fabric—and as a result, this part of the city lacks the coherence and charm of, say, Coptic Cairo or the area around Bab Zuwayla. Nevertheless, the scale and quality of these monuments is so impressive that if you have time to see only a few of Cairo's Islamic treasures, the Citadel and the Sultan Hasan and Ibn Tulun mosques should be among them.

For Islamic sights' hours and prayer times, see The Islamic Day in Islamic Cairo North, above.

MAIN SIGHTS

❶ The Citadel. Until Salah al-Din al-Ayyubi arrived in Cairo in 1168, local rulers had overlooked the strategic value of the hill above the city. Within a few years he began making plans for the defense of the city, with **al-Qala'a** (the fortress) the key element. He and his successors built an impenetrable bastion, using the most advanced construction techniques of the age. For the next 700 years, Egypt was ruled from this hill. Nothing remains of the original complex except a part of the walls and Bir Yusuf, the well that supplied the Citadel with water. The Ayyubid walls that circle the northern enclosure are 33 feet tall and 10 feet thick; they and their towers were built with the experience gleaned from the Crusader wars. Bir Yusuf is also an engineering marvel; dug 285 feet straight into solid rock to reach the water table, the well was powered by oxen who would walk in circles all day to draw water up to the level of the Citadel.

During the 1330s al-Nasir Muhammad tore down most of the Ayyubid buildings to make room for his own needs, which included several palaces and a mosque in addition to barracks for his army. These, too, were not to last, for when Muhammad 'Ali assumed power he had all the Mamluk buildings razed and the complex entirely rebuilt; only the green-domed mosque and a fragment of **al-Qasr al-Ablaq** (the striped

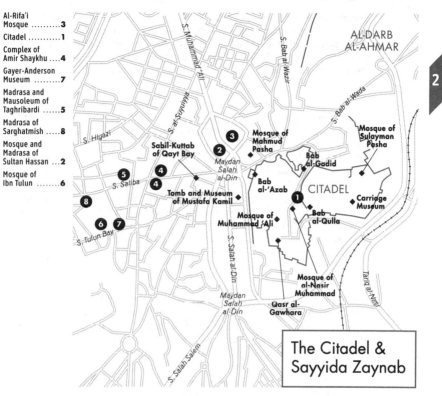

The Citadel &
Sayyida Zaynab

palace) remain. The Citadel's appearance today is really the vision of Muhammad 'Ali, particularly the mosque that bears his name.

The **Muhammad 'Ali Mosque** is the most noticeable in all of Cairo. For more than 150 years it has dominated the skyline, making it almost the symbol of the city. This is ironic because it is actually an imitation of the graceful Ottoman mosques in Istanbul. Notice the alabaster facing on the outside. The interior reflects a somewhat gaudy attempt to weld Middle Eastern and French rococo and is finished with ornate lines of red, green, and gold. Nevertheless, there are interesting aspects to the place. Ottoman law prohibited anyone but the sultan from building a mosque with more than one minaret, but this mosque has two. Indeed, this was one of Muhammad 'Ali's first indications that he did not intend to remain submissive to Istanbul.

The courtyard within the mosque is spacious and comfortable. It also has a gilded clock tower given to Muhammad 'Ali by King Louis Philippe in exchange for the obelisk that stands in the middle of Paris. It is fair to say that the French got the better end of the bargain: the clock has never worked.

Behind Muhammad 'Ali's gilded beast stands a far more elegant creature, the **Mosque of al-Nasir Muhammad**. The beautifully crafted masonry, the elegant proportions, the ornate but controlled work on the minarets—all indicate that the building is a Mamluk work of art. The conquering Ottomans carried much of the original interior decoration off to Istanbul, but the space is nevertheless impressive. The supporting columns around the courtyard were collected from various sources and several are pharaonic.

Directly across from the entrance of al-Nasir is the **National Police Museum.** A prison until 1985, this small structure is hardly worth the five minutes it will take to walk through it. Two things rescue it from complete dismissal: the exhibition on political assassinations in Egypt, and the spectacular view from the courtyard behind it. Directly below is the lower enclosure gated by the Bab al-'Azab, the site where Muhammad 'Ali decisively wrested control from the unruly Mamluk warlords, who, while they had submitted to Ottoman rule for 300 years, had not really accepted it. In his capacity as Ottoman governor, Muhammad 'Ali invited all the powerful Mamluks up to the Citadel where they ate, drank, and were merry. As they were making their way to the gate for their exit, the governor's men ambushed them, eliminating in a single stroke all internal opposition.

To the northwest of al-Nasir's mosque is the **Bab al-Qulla,** which leads to the **Qasr al-Harem** (the Harem Palace), now the site of the **National Military Museum.** The brainchild of King Faruq, the exhibit was intended to chronicle the glories of his family but has been extended by the post-Revolution administrations to include the military glories of presidents Jamal 'Abd al-Nasir (Nasser), Anwar Sadat, and Hosni Mubarak. The display of uniforms and weaponry may be of some interest to historians and military aficionados. For those less taken with martial affairs, the building itself is another example of the eclectic taste appreciated by Muhammad 'Ali and his descendants.

Farther west, the **Carriage Museum** was the dining hall of the British officers stationed at the Citadel in the early 20th century. It now houses eight carriages used by Egypt's last royal dynasty (1805–1952).

In the northwest part of the Citadel is a rarely visited site, the **Mosque of Sulayman Pasha.** Built in 1528 by Egypt's Ottoman governor for his crack Janissary troops, this is a small but graceful mosque. While its plan is entirely a product of Istanbul, the sparse stone decoration shows traces of Mamluk influence. The tomb contains the remains of several prominent Janissary officers, as well as a Fatimid saint.

Before leaving the Citadel, pass by the **Qasr al-Gawhara** (the Jewel Palace), where Muhammad 'Ali received guests. When the khedives moved their residence down to 'Abdin Palace in the city, it was opened to the public, and after the revolution it was turned into a museum displaying the royal family's extravagance. Heavily influenced by the early 19th-century French style, the building is similar in taste to the Harem Palace. The painted murals on the walls and ceiling of the main Meeting Hall are worth the visit, as is the furniture in the model royal bedroom.

There is a small gift shop in the complex that is well-stocked with books and CDs. If you stop in, you may want to pick up a copy of *The Citadel of Cairo: A History and Guide,* by William Lyster, a wonderfully detailed book and great companion for your visit, or a copy of the excellent SPARE (Society for the Preservation of the Architectural Resources of Egypt) Map, which covers the area. ⊠*Al-Qala'a, Shar'a Salih Salem, The Citadel* ☎*02/2591–3391* ⌨*£e50* ⊘*Daily 8–5.*

❼ **Gayer-Anderson Museum.** Also known as Bayt al-Kiritliya, the museum ★ consists of two Ottoman houses joined together, restored, and furnished by Major Gayer-Anderson, a British member of the Egyptian civil service in the 1930s and '40s. Gayer-Anderson was a talented collector and a sensitive, artistic gentleman, from the looks of the house's contents, which include lovely pieces of pharaonic, Islamic, and Central Asian art (though there are a few oddities). Spend some time in the reception room, where a mosaic fountain lies at the center of an ornate marble floor. In the courtyard of the east house is the "Well of Bats," the subject of much storytelling in the neighborhood. The house also inspired Gayer-Anderson's grandson, Theo, who illustrated a book on the subject and became an art conservationist, involved in the restoration of Bab Zuwayla. ⊠*4 Maydan Ibn Tulun, The Citadel* ☎*02/2364–7822* ⌨*£e35* ⊘*Daily 8–5.*

❷ **Mosque and Madrasa of Sultan Hassan.** Built between 1356 and 1363 by ★ the Mamluk ruler Sultan Hassan, this is one of the largest Islamic religious buildings in the world. Historians believe that its builders may have used stone from the pyramids at Giza. The scale of the masterpiece is so colossal that it nearly emptied the vast Mamluk Treasury.

You enter the complex at an angle, through a tall portal that is itself a work of art. Before going in, look at the carving on both sides of the entrance that culminates in a series of stalactites above. A dark and relatively low-ceilinged passageway to the left of the entrance leads to the brightly lit main area, a standard cruciform-plan open court.

What is different about this plan is the fact that between each of the four liwans is a madrasa, one for each of the four Sunni schools of jurisprudence, complete with its own courtyard and four stories of cells for students and teachers. Also unique is the location of the mausoleum behind the qibla liwan, which, in effect, forces people who are praying to bow before the tomb of the dead sultan—a fairly heretical idea to devout Muslims. Nevertheless, the mausoleum, facing the Maydan Salah al Din, is quite beautiful, particularly in the morning when the rising sun filters through grilled windows.

Only one of the two tall minarets is structurally sound, the one to the left of the qibla liwan. Have the custodian take you up inside of it to get a view of the city, especially of the Citadel. In fact, this roof was used by several armies to shell the mountain fortress, Bonaparte's expedition included. ⊠*Maydan Salah al-Din, The Citadel* ☎*No phone* ⌨*£e25* ⊘*Daily 8–5, except during Friday prayers.*

6 Mosque of Ibn Tulun. This huge congregational mosque was built in 879
Fodor's Choice by Ahmad Ibn Tulun with the intention of accommodating his entire
★ army during Friday prayers. Ahmad was sent to Egypt by the 'Abbasid
caliph in Samarra to serve as its governor, but it seems that he had his
own plans. Sensing weakness in Iraq, he declared his independence
and began to build a new city, al-Qata'i, northwest of al-Fustat and
al-'Askar, the Muslim towns that had grown up north of the Roman
fortress of Babylon. Replete with numerous palaces, gardens, and even
a hippodrome, al-Qata'i was not destined to survive. When the 'Abba-
sids conquered Egypt again, in 970, they razed the entire city as a lesson
to future rebels, sparing only the great Friday mosque but leaving it to
wither on the outskirts.

In 1293, the emir Lagin hid out in the derelict building for several
months while a fugitive from the Mamluk sultan, vowing to restore it
if he survived. Three years later, after being appointed sultan himself,
he kept his word, repairing the minaret and adding a fountain in the
courtyard, the mihrab, and the beautiful minbar. All of this background
is secondary to the building itself—you can delight in this masterpiece
without even the slightest knowledge of history. Its grandeur and simplicity set it apart from any other Islamic monument in Cairo.

The mosque is separated from the streets around it with a *ziyada* (a
walled-off space), in which the Friday market was once held and where
the famous minaret is located. At the top of the walls a strange crenel-
lation pattern almost resembles the cut-out figures that children make
with folded paper. Inside, the mosque covers an area of more than 6
acres. The vast courtyard is surrounded by four arcaded aisles. The
soffits of the arches are covered in beautifully carved stucco, the first
time this medium was used in Cairo. Look for the stucco grilles on the
windows, especially those in the qibla wall. The minaret, the only one
of its kind in Egypt, is modeled after the minarets of Samarra, with the
zigguratlike stairs spiraling on the outside of the tower. ⊠ *Shar'a Tulun
Bay, The Citadel* ☎ *No phone* ⊠ *Free* ☉ *Daily, dawn–dusk, except at
prayer time.*

ALSO WORTH SEEING

3 Al-Rifa'i Mosque. Although it appears neo-Mamluk in style, this mosque
was not commissioned until 1869 by the mother of Khedive Isma'il,
the Princess Khushyar. The project was completed in 1912, but, at least
from the outside, it seems more timeworn and less modern in style than
the 14th-century Sultan Hassan Mosque next to it.

True to the excessive khedivial tastes, the inside is markedly different
from the other mosque: where Sultan Hassan is relatively unadorned,
al-Rifa'i is lavishly decorated. Inside the mausoleum are the bodies of
Khashyar, King Fu'ad (father of Farouk, the last king of Egypt), other
members of the royal family, Sufi holy men of the Rifa'i order (hence
the establishment's name), and the last shah of Iran. ⊠ *Maydan Salah
al-Din, Sayyida Zaynab* ☎ *No phone* ⊠ *£e25* ☉ *Daily 9–4, except at
prayer time.*

❹ Complex of Amir Shaykhu. Flanking Shar'a Saliba, this mosque and khan-qah were built by the commander-in-chief of Sultan Hassan's forces and form a well-integrated whole. The mosque was badly damaged by shelling during the Ottoman takeover because Tumanbay, the last Mamluk sultan, hid here. Nevertheless, the qibla liwan still has the original marble inlay work. Today it is an active mosque frequented by people from the neighborhood.

The khanqah, with its central courtyard surrounded by three floors of 150 rooms, once housed 700 Sufi adherents. As in the mosque, classical pillars support the ground-floor arches. To the left of the qibla wall are the tombs of Shaykhu and the first director of the school. ⊠ *Shar'a Saliba (just east of Shar'a al-Suyuiyya), The Citadel* 🕾 *No phone* 🖼 *Free* 🕙 *Daily, dawn–dusk, except during prayers.*

❺ Madrasa and Mausoleum of Taghribardi. This small but impressive complex was built in 1440 by the executive secretary to Sultan Jaqmaq. Fitting the standard minaret, entrance portal, sabil-kuttab, and dome into a single ensemble required a talented architect. Much of the top part of the building is an Ottoman reconstruction, including the final tier of the minaret. The work is clearly of a lower standard, demonstrating architecturally the demotion in Cairo's status from the capital of an empire to that of a province within an empire. ⊠ *Saghri Wardi, Shar'a Saliba, The Citadel* 🕾 *No phone* 🖼 *£e8* 🕙 *Daily 9–4.*

❽ Madrasa of Sarghatmish. Completed in 1356 by the emir who succeeded Shaykhu, Sarghatmish was probably designed by the same architect who designed Sultan Hassan. The layout is a cruciform plan—its innovative placement of the madrasa in the corners is identical to that of the great mosque—although smaller in scale. But far from being a diminutive copy of a masterpiece, Sarghatmish has several features that make it interesting in its own right, the first being a tall arched entrance that rises slightly above the facade. Most significant are the two domes, which are very unusual for Cairo. One has unfortunately been renovated with concrete, the other is sublime. Built in brick, it has a slight bulge reminiscent of the Persian style domes of Iran and central Asia. The interior space is pleasing and replete with Islamic detail in marble and stone. ⊠ *Shar'a Saliba, just east of Shar'a Qadry, The Citadel* 🕾 *No phone* 🖼 *£e8* 🕙 *Daily 9–4.*

COPTIC CAIRO (MARI GIRGIS)

The area known as Mari Girgis (St. George) is centuries older than the Islamic city of Cairo. But even calling it Coptic Cairo isn't entirely accurate, because it includes an important synagogue and, nearby, some significant mosques. Known from the ancient historians as the town of Babylon, it was here that the Roman emperor Trajan (AD 88–117) decided to build a fortress around the settlement. At a time when the Nile flowed 1,300 feet east of its current course and was connected by way of canal to the Red Sea, the fortress occupied a strategic location.

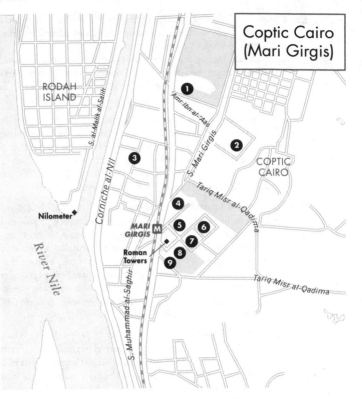

Tradition holds that St. Mark brought Christianity to Egypt in the first century. The Christians of Egypt became the first in Africa to embrace the new faith, and they were persecuted harshly for it. Many fled to the desert or south to the Upper Nile Valley. Later, under the Byzantine emperors, the local Christian population—known as Copts (an Arabic derivative of the Greek word for Egypt)—came out of hiding and began building several churches within and around the town walls.

But harmony within the church was not to last; serious theological disputes about the unity of God (the Coptic view) versus the trinity of God (the Byzantine) arose between the Egyptians and Constantinople, and once again the Copts were threatened with persecution. So when the Arabs arrived across the desert, local Copts initially welcomed them as liberators from the tyranny of Byzantium, despite their religious differences. Fustat, the encampment that the Arabs established just outside the walls of Babylon, quickly grew into a major city, leaving the older town as an enclave for Christians and Jews.

Thus Coptic Cairo encompasses elements from all these eras: portions of the Roman fortress survive; within the walled city stand four churches, a convent, a monastery, and a synagogue that was originally a church; and the oldest mosque in Africa is nearby. The Coptic

Museum has a collection of local Christian art that displays pharaonic, Hellenistic, and even Islamic influences. And there is a soothing quality to the neighborhood. In contrast to the big-city feel of downtown Cairo, or the hustle of the al-Husayn area, Coptic Cairo is relatively quiet and calm.

The sites are generally open to visitors daily from 9 to 4. However, places of worship are not open to tourists during services: no mosque visits during Friday prayers (around noon), no church visits during Sunday services (7–10 AM), and no temple visits Saturday. In churches it is customary to make a small contribution, either near the entrance or beside the votary candle stands.

MAIN SIGHTS

5 **Church of St. Sergius.** Known in Arabic as *Abu Serga*, this church is dedicated to two Roman officers, Sergius and Bacchus, who were martyred in Syria in 303. It was a major pilgrimage destination for 19th-century European travelers because it was built over a cave where the Holy Family was said to have stayed the night during their flight from King Herod—a special ceremony is still held every June 1 to commemorate the event. Originally constructed in the 5th century, the church has been destroyed and rebuilt several times, including a major restoration during the Fatimid era. Reconstructions aside, it is considered to be the oldest church in Cairo and a model of early Coptic church design.

The entrance is down a flight of steps that leads to the side of the narthex, at the end of which is a baptistry. Look up at the ceiling of the nave; a series of arched timbers is supported by 24 marble pillars that were taken from an earlier site, possibly from the Ptolemaic era (304–30 BC).

Most of the church furnishings are modern replicas of older pieces. The originals can be found in the Coptic Museum, including pieces from a rosewood pulpit and the sanctuary canopy, considered to be one of the museum's prized possessions. To the left of the sanctuary is the crypt in which the Holy Family is believed to have hidden. ⊠ *Hara al-Qadis 'Abu Serga, Mari Girgis* ☎ *No phone* ✉ *Free* ⊙ *Daily 9–4 (except during services).*

4 **Convent of St. George.** This convent's namesake holds a special place in the hearts of Copts. The remains of this Roman legionary who was martyred in Asia were brought to Egypt in the 12th century. Images of St. George abound in Egyptian Christianity, and the most common depicts the saint on a steed crushing a dragon beneath him. So it should come as no surprise that within the walls of Babylon are a church, a monastery, and a convent dedicated to the dragon slayer.

The convent, while less impressive in its present-day form than in the past—medieval historians describe a huge complex—is still worth the visit. Enter the courtyard and take the stairway on the left down to a structure that dates from the Fatimid era. Inside is a huge reception hall with a beautiful wooden door about 23 feet tall. Behind the door, a shrine contains the icon of St. George and a set of chains used for the chain-wrapping ritual (still practiced), said to represent the sufferings of St. George at the hands of the Romans. ⊠*Hara al-Qadis Girgis, Mari Girgis* ☎*No phone* ⊠*Free (donations welcome)* ☉*Daily 10–4, except during services.*

■ NEED A BREAK?

Orient Cafe (⊠*Shar'a Mari Girgis, Mari Girgis* ☎*012/2245–5136*) is a tiny hole in the wall that sits between a bookshop and an antique shop. Egyptian *mezze*-style snacks and *kofta* are available, but this is more the place for a cold soda, a beer, or a coffee.

❽ **Coptic Museum.** Housing the world's largest collection of Coptic Christian artwork, this museum provides a link between ancient and Islamic Egypt. Remember that Christianity was not just a flash in the Egyptian historical pan. St. Mark made his first convert in Alexandria in AD 61, and the majority of the city's population remained Christian until the 11th century, a full half-millennium after the Arabs brought Islam to Egypt. This link can be seen stylistically as well, because the collection includes pieces with a late-Pharaonic/Greco-Roman feel, as well as items identified as Islamic.

Fodor's Choice
★

The museum is classified by medium, more or less. The first floor has carved stone and stucco, frescoes, and woodwork. The second floor includes textiles, manuscripts, icons, and metalwork. In some cases, chronological divisions are made within each grouping to show the evolution of the art form.

The collection includes many exquisite pieces, but several are noteworthy first for their quirkiness or their syncretism, rather than their beauty. Look, for example, at carvings and paintings that trace the transformations of the ancient key of life, the ankh, to the cross; or Christian scenes with Egyptian gods. The depictions of the baby Jesus suckling at his mother's breast are striking in their resemblance to pharaonic suckling representations, including one at Karnak in which the god Horus is being nursed by Mut. Such characteristics are unique to Egyptian Christianity.

See the 4th-century bronze Roman eagle on the second floor, and a 4th-century hymnal (in the Coptic language) that was found beneath a young girl's head in her shallow grave near Beni Suef. For a detailed guide of the museum, look for Jill Kamil's *Coptic Egypt: History and Guide* (American University in Cairo Press). ⊠*Shar'a Mari Girgis, Mari Girgis* ☎*02/3362–8766* ⊠*£e50* ☉*Daily 9–5.*

❾ **The Hanging Church.** Known in Arabic as *al-Muallaqah* ("the suspended"), the church is consecrated to the Blessed Virgin. Originally built in the 9th century—and sitting on top of a gatehouse of the Roman fortress (hence, its name)—the Hanging Church has been rebuilt several times, like most of Cairo's churches. Only the section to the right of the sanctuary, above the southern bastion, is considered original. Nevertheless, it remains one of the most impressive churches in the city.

The entrance gates lead to a flight of stairs that opens onto a covered courtyard, the narthex, which is partially paved with glazed geometrical tiles that date from the 11th century. Beyond the narthex is the nave, the main section of the church, where services are held. This is divided into a central nave and two side aisles by eight Corinthian columns, a feature that suggests that they were taken from an earlier building. Most columns in Coptic churches were painted with pictures of saints, but few of the paintings survived. Those in the Hanging Church are no exception; only one column still has traces of a figure on it.

Perhaps the most impressive aspect of this space is the marble pulpit. Considered the oldest existing pulpit in the country, it was constructed in the 11th century, with some of its materials coming from earlier furniture. The pulpit is supported by a series of slender columns arranged in pairs of which no two are alike. Some say this represents the sacraments of the Church; others describe it as being symbolic of Christ and his disciples.

The sanctuary screen is also of exceptional quality. It is made of cedarwood and ivory cut in small segments, then inlaid in wood to form a Coptic cross, which has arms of equal length and three points at the end of each arm. The top of the screen is covered with icons depicting Christ in the center; the Virgin, the archangel Gabriel, and St. Peter on the right; and St. John the Baptist, St. Paul, and the archangel Michael on the left. Behind the screen is the sanctuary dedicated to the Virgin Mary. Two side sanctuaries are dedicated to St. John the Baptist (right) and St. George (left), a very popular saint in Egypt.

To the right of St. George's sanctuary is another beautiful screen dating from the 13th century. Made of wood and mother-of-pearl, it glows dark pink when a candle is held behind it. Behind the screen is a small chapel attached to the Ethiopian St. Takla Hamanout Church. This chapel is worth visiting for its two wall paintings, one depicting the 24 Elders of the Apocalypse and the other the Virgin and Child. A stairway leads from this chapel to one above it, dedicated to St. Mark. This area is probably the oldest part of the church, built in the 3rd century, when this was still a bastion of the old Roman fort. ⊠*Shar'a Mari Girgis, Mari Girgis* ☎*No phone* ✉*Free* ☉*Daily 9–4, except during services.*

2 **Mosque of 'Amr Ibn al-'Aas.** Built in 642 following the conquest of Egypt, this was the first mosque on the African continent. Because the original structure probably had mud-brick walls and a palm-thatch roof, it did not survive for long. It was restored and expanded in 673 and again in 698, 710, 750, and 791. In 827, it was expanded to its current size. It has since been renovated at least five times, most recently in the late 1980s, in an attempt to restore its interior to its 827 appearance. ⊠*Shar'a Mari Girgis, Mari Girgis* ☎*No phone* ✉*Free* ☉*Daily 9–4, except during prayer.*

ALSO WORTH SEEING

7 **Ben Ezra Synagogue.** Originally the Church of St. Michael, the synagogue is named after the 12th-century rabbi of Jerusalem who obtained permission to build a temple of worship on this location. According to the local Jewish community, now numbering about 50 families, this was the site of the temple built by the prophet Jeremiah. Some claim that Jeremiah is actually buried here beneath a miracle rock. Another legend associated with the area is that this was the location of a spring where the pharaoh's daughter found the baby Moses.

Little differentiates the synagogue's outside appearance from a church, save, of course, signs like the Star of David on the gate. Inside, a fine 12th-century *bimah* (pulpit in a synagogue), made of wood and mother-of-pearl, remains.

During the last restoration in the 1890s, it was discovered that the site was used by medieval Jews as a *genizah* (storage) for any documents on which the name of God was written (it is against Jewish law to destroy any such papers). Thus, all contracts, bills of sale, marriage licenses, and the like were placed in the genizah. Needless to say, this find was a treasure trove for medieval Middle Eastern historians. ⊠ *Hara al-Qadisa Burbara, Mari Girgis* 🕾 *No phone* 🎟 *Free* ⊙ *Daily 9–4, except during services.*

6 **Church of St. Barbara.** Named for a young Nicodemian woman who was killed by her pagan father for converting, the church was originally dedicated to Sts. Cyrus and John (in Arabic, Abu Qir and Yuhanna, respectively), two martyrs from the city of Damanhour. It is said that when they refused to renounce their Christianity, they were shot with arrows, burned, and drawn and quartered, but would not die until they were beheaded.

The church was first built in 684, destroyed in the great fire of Fustat in 750, and then restored in the 11th century. Additions were made when the relics of St. Barbara were brought here. The church is one of the largest in Cairo. Replete with the standard division of narthex, nave, side aisles, and three sanctuaries, the church is also considered one of the city's finest.

The sanctuary screen currently in place is a 13th-century wooded piece inlaid with ivory—the original screen is in the Coptic Museum. The icons above the church's screen include a newly restored Child Enthroned and a rare icon of St. Barbara. A domed apse behind the main altar has seven steps decorated in bands of black, red, and white marble. To the left of the sanctuary is the chapel dedicated to Sts. Cyrus and John, a square structure with a nave, transept, two sanctuaries (one for each saint), and a baptistry.

Access to Coptic Cairo's cemetery is through an iron gate to the left of the church. ⊠ *Hara al-Qadisa Burbara, Mari Girgis* 🕾 *No phone* 🎟 *Free* ⊙ *Daily 9–4, except during services.*

1 **Church of St. Mercurius.** Yet another Roman legionary, Mercurius, or Abu Sayfayn ("of the two swords"), dreamed one night that an angel gave him a glowing sword and ordered him to use it to fight paganism. He converted to Christianity and was martyred in Palestine. His remains were brought to Cairo in the 15th century.

This site is of great importance to Coptic Christians. It was the cathedral church of Cairo, and when the seat of the Coptic Patriarch moved from Alexandria to Cairo, St. Mercurius was the chosen location. The complex actually contains a monastery, a convent, and three churches: Abu Sayfayn, Abna Shenouda, and a church of the Virgin. At this writing, all three were being restored but remained open to visitors. ⊠*Shar'a 'Ali Salem, Mari Girgis* ☎*No phone* ☞*Free* ☽*Daily 9–4, except during services.*

❸ **Tomb of Sulayman al-Faransawi.** Sulayman, a Frenchman, was born Octave de Sèves in Lyons, France. An officer in Napoléon's army, he came to Egypt when Muhammad 'Ali was in need of European trainers for his army. After facing dissent among the ranks, he converted to Islam and took the name Sulayman. Popular with the khedive Ibrahim for his role in victories in Arabia, Crete, Syria, and Anatolia, he died in 1860 a rich man. His tomb was designed by Karl von Diebitsch, the architect responsible for the palace that is now the Marriott Hotel in the suburb of Zamalek. Like the hotel, the cast-iron pavilion manages to combine orientalist kitsch and elegance. ⊠*Off Shar'a Muhammad al-Saghir, Mari Girgis* ☎*No phone* ☞*£e8* ☽*Daily 9–4.*

RODAH ISLAND & GARDEN CITY

Nilometer. At the southern end of Rodah Island, *al-miqyas* (the nilometer) was used from pharaonic times until the completion of the Aswan Dam in the late 1950s to measure the height of the flood. If the Nile rose above 16 cubits (a cubit is about 2 feet), no flood tax would be levied that year. Needless to say, this was a ceremony that the populace followed with great interest—and if the floods were plentiful, with great celebration.

Built in 861 on the site of an earlier nilometer, the present structure is considered to be the oldest extant Islamic building (the conical dome is an 1895 restoration). Inside is a shaft that houses the graduated column that served as the measuring device. Outside the structure is a model explaining how it worked. ⊠*Southern tip of Rodah Island, Rodah Island* ☞*£e15* ☽*Daily 9–4.*

HELIOPOLIS

In 1905, the Belgian industrialist Édouard Louis Joseph bought a swath of land northwest of Cairo. His plan was to build a new self-sustaining community in the desert with housing, shops, and recreation facilities, which came complete with luxuries like street lighting, water, and drainage plus a tram link to the capital. The town he called Heliopolis became a hit with upper-class Egyptians and expat movers and shakers. It remained an oasis of well-manicured mansions, of weekends at the country clubs, and of cocktail parties with the social elite until the coup d'état of 1952.

By the 1990s, Heliopolis had been swallowed by the massive growth of Cairo and was decaying under decades of neglect. However, Suzanne Mubarak, wife of President Hosni Mubarak and a native

Baron Empain

Édouard Louis Joseph, Baron Empain, was born in 1852 in a small town in Belgium. His first career was as a draughtsman, but during his work on railway construction in Belgium, he realized that this was the way forward for transport. He founded a company with his brother to build a short line from Liège to Jemeppe, which proved a great success. So he began building lines in countries across the world. The brothers later founded their own bank and diversified into electricity production, beginning a business empire that turned them into multimillionaires.

It was the construction of an electric tram line in Cairo that first brought Empain to Egypt. Although his bid failed, the industrialist was captivated by this land and, rumor had it, by a certain Egyptian socialite, Yvette Boghdadli. He founded his Egyptian enterprise, the Cairo Electric Railways and Heliopolis Oases Company, in 1906.

In 1905, Empain secured an ancient Egyptian mastaba for the Royal Museum in Brussels that helped earn him his title. As his interest in Egyptology developed, he provided funding for the first excavation of ancient Heliopolis by Belgian archaeologist Jean Capart.

Empain died during a trip back to Belgium in 1929, but his body was returned to Heliopolis, and he is interred in the Basilica of Notre Dame.

of Heliopolis, pledged to save her home neighborhood, a campaign which has revived the heart of Heliopolis. It's now one of Cairo's most charming districts.

There are no particular attractions here. The early 20th-century palace modeled on Angkor Wat Temple that Empain built for himself now stands empty and isn't open to the public. The grand Heliopolis Palace Hotel is now the presidential palace, set behind well-guarded walls. However, the downtown core—the Korba—a diminutive quarter of ornate colonnaded streets in neo-Renaissance style, is now gentrified with a smart coat of paint and is a lovely place to relax. The colonnades now house cafés, boutiques, and jewelry shops where the well-to-do families of the area stroll in the evenings.

GIZA

It used to be that you approached Giza through green fields. Cairo's expansion means that now you have to run a gauntlet of raucously noisy city streets clogged with buses, vans, taxis, and the odd donkey cart, not to mention a busy four-lane bypass. Unfortunately, the large concrete towers lining the road obscure the view of the Giza pyramids that loom at the desert's edge.

Although Giza is technically a suburb, it's one of the more popular places for tourists to stay when they visit Cairo. If you are staying in Central Cairo, you can get to the pyramids by taking the metro to Giza station (£e1), then the public bus that plies a route along pyramids road

(£e0.50). To get to the pyramids by bus from central Cairo, take a CTA bus from Abdel Meneim Riyadh Station on Tahrir Square for £e2; it will bring you to the foot of the Giza Plateau opposite the Mena House Hotel. Hiring a taxi for the day to take you to the pyramids and other ancient sites is by far the most convenient way to get to and from the site. Your hotel can arrange a taxi, or you can hail one in the street. A reasonable daylong taxi hire should cost £e30–£e40 per hour—if you bargain well.

Fodor's Choice   **Pyramid Plateau.** The three pyramids of Khufu (Greek name: Cheops),
★   Khafre (Chephren), and Menkaure (Mycerinus) dominate the Giza Plateau. Surrounding the father-son-grandson trio are smaller pyramids belonging to their female dependents, and the *mastabas* (large, trapezoid-shaped tombs) of their courtiers and relatives. The word *mastaba* comes from the Arabic word for bench, which these tombs resemble in shape, if not in scale, and the mastabas were often painted and/or decorated with reliefs inside, with the actual burial sites placed in shafts cut into the bedrock. The great Sphinx crouches at the eastern edge of the plateau, guarding the necropolis; admission to the Sphinx is included in the Pyramid Plateau admission, but it is accessible only from a separate entrance. A museum south of the Great Pyramid contains one of the most extraordinary artifacts from ancient Egypt, Khufu's own royal boat. The pyramids, Sphinx, and some of the mastabas date from the 4th Dynasty, while other mastabas date to the 5th and 6th Dynasties. South of the Sphinx and its adjacent temples are the living and eating areas of the workmen who built the pyramids, as well as their cemeteries. To the north, the walls of the soon to be state-of-the-art Grand Egyptian Museum are beginning to take discernable shape (the museum may open as early as 2010, but any estimate on the actual opening is considered very premature at this writing).

Several monuments on the plateau are open to visitors: a combination of pyramids, a mastaba, the Solar Boat Museum, and the Sphinx will give you a taste of the site. Generally, two of the three pyramids can be entered on any given day (this varies depending on restoration and conservation work). If you are able to choose one pyramid to go into, make it the Great Pyramid of Khufu. The sheer mass of it, pierced by the elegant Grand Gallery leading to the burial chamber, is one of the wonders of the world—ancient and modern. △ **Anyone suffering from heart disease, claustrophobia, and back strain should not enter *any* of the pyramids.) The Egyptian government restricts the number of visitors allowed to actually enter the pyramids.** Only 300 tickets are sold for each of the pyramids daily, 150 starting at 8 AM, and 150 staring at 1 PM. To make sure you get a ticket, you must go early, especially during high season and especially if you are not part of a group. Friday is the most crowded. Still and video cameras are not allowed into any of the pyramids.

Before you see the monuments, you may wish to drive out to the viewing area beyond the third pyramid for a commanding view of the entire site—nine pyramids, one view, as the camel drivers will tell you. It is possible to ride around part of the site on rented horses and camels,

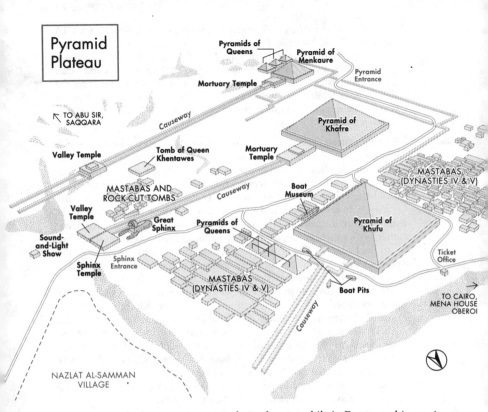

Pyramid Plateau

TO ABU SIR, SAQQARA

Pyramids of Queens

Pyramid of Menkaure

Pyramid Entrance

Mortuary Temple

Causeway

Valley Temple

Tomb of Queen Khentawes

Mortuary Temple

Pyramid of Khafre

MASTABAS (DYNASTIES IV & V)

MASTABAS AND ROCK-CUT TOMBS

Causeway

Boat Museum

Valley Temple

Great Sphinx

Pyramids of Queens

Pyramid of Khufu

Sound-and-Light Show

Sphinx Temple

Sphinx Entrance

Ticket Office

Boat Pits

TO CAIRO, MENA HOUSE OBEROI

MASTABAS (DYNASTIES IV & V)

Causeway

NAZLAT AL-SAMMAN VILLAGE

which is picturesque and worth a try while in Egypt, and in carriages, which are ungainly. These are slowly being restricted to certain areas, the viewing area and environs remaining unrestricted areas. If you choose to use any of these modes of transportation, the cost should be £e30 to £e50, depending on your bargaining skills. If you're not interested, be prepared to firmly refuse several times over, as you will be accosted with offers as you wander around the site.

Several thousand mastabas and tombs are located on the Giza Plateau, and there has been a great deal of archaeological discovery around these sites in the last decade. Ask at the ticket booth for information and directions to the open ones. Most mastabas are decorated with scenes of daily life and offerings. The most beautiful mastabas are found at Saqqara, so it is not absolutely necessary to see the ones at Giza if you plan to continue to Saqqara.

Drinks and light snacks are available at the Sphinx, and young boys sell bottles of soda and water all over the site. For a real break, go for lunch or coffee to the Mena House Hotel at the foot of the pyramids, at the end of Shar'a al-Haram (Pyramids Road). Built in the 19th century as an opulent palace to celebrate the opening of the Suez Canal, it is now a five-star hotel. The coffee shop and the garden terrace both have views of the pyramids. Otherwise, try lunching at Barry's, near the entrance to the Sound & Light Show; the restaurant serves grilled chicken, pigeons, kebabs, and mezze on a pleasant terrace. ⊠ *Pyramids Rd., Giza* ☎ *No phone* ✉ *General admission £e60, Great Pyramid £e100, Khafre's Pyramid £e30, Mankaure's Pyramid £e25, Solar Boat Museum £e50* ⊙ *Site daily 8–6:30, pyramid and tomb interiors daily 9–4 (but the openings are staggered, so not all pyramid interiors are open every day).*

2

★ The oldest and largest monument at the Giza site, **Khufu's Pyramid** *(the Great Pyramid)* measures 753 feet square and 478 feet high, and it is the only remaining wonder of the seven wonders of the ancient world. Its casing stones, once covered by graffiti dating from pharaonic times, were systematically stripped in the Middle Ages for a variety of Cairene building projects, leaving the structure as you see it. The pyramid took some 20 years to build for the Pharaoh Khufu, and it is one of two pyramids that contain the burial chamber within their bodies.

The surprisingly modest north entrance—this is not the ancient entrance but one made in the 9th century when the Caliph Ma'mun blasted his way into the pyramid in search of buried treasure—leads through a curving passage and up to a long corridor that opens onto a small landing. From here, another passage leads to the so-called **Queen's Chamber,** which was probably for the pharaoh's grave goods rather than for the actual burial of a queen. The next stage from the landing is the magnificent **Grand Gallery** that soars up to the king's burial chamber. This contains a sarcophagus that was found empty because it had been robbed in antiquity. Narrow air passages lead out of the burial chamber. Remains of the mortuary temple are on the east side, with the Queens' pyramids beyond.

★ Khufu's Pyramid, more than any other, is the focus of several fanciful beliefs that hold that the pyramids are either the site for the initiation for a secret priesthood; an ancient observatory or a landing device for extraterrestrials; or even a way of projecting oneself into space. In a similar vein are the ideas that, within the pyramid, dulled razor blades are sharpened, food and drink are preserved, people are healed, and meditation is enhanced. Experiments with foods, blades, and the rest have shown no supporting evidence for these beliefs, yet neither have the believers shown much interest in the experiments. New Age devotees continue to come to the Great Pyramid to meditate and seek miracles. ✉ *£e100 to enter the Great Pyramid.* Five boat pits surround Khufu's Pyramid on the south and the east. Two of these, the southern ones, contain cedar boats that the pharaoh probably used during his lifetime. One of these is in the **Solar Boat Museum,** and it may even have been used on the pharaoh's last voyage from the capital of Memphis to his tomb at Giza. When found in the 1960s, it lay dismantled in its limestone pit, in 1,200 pieces. It was painstakingly restored by the late conservationist Hajj Ahmed Yusif over the course of 14 years. ✉ *£e50.* **Khafre's Pyramid,** that of Khufu's son, is the second-largest pyramid on the Giza site. It measures 702 feet square and stands 470 feet tall. It looks taller than Khufu's Pyramid because it stands on a slightly higher part of the plateau, and it still retains part of its fine limestone casing—brought from the quarries at Tura in the cliffs on the eastern bank of the Nile—at its summit. Like Khufu's complex, Khafre's includes five boat pits (empty of boats), together with mortuary and valley temples and a connecting causeway some 430 yards long carved out of the living rock. The burial chamber, which is underground, contains a red granite sarcophagus with its lid. Next to this is a square cavity that presumably once contained the canopic chest with the pharaoh's viscera.

The pyramid has two entrances: one in the north face of the pyramid and another in the pavement on the north side. The latter is currently in use. Before reaching the burial chamber, the two entrance passages connect beneath the pyramid.

The pyramid was first entered in modern times by Giovanni Battista Belzoni—a colorful circus strongman, engineer, and archaeologist—in March 1818, an event he commemorated by scrawling his name in soot along the length of the burial chamber. The **valley temple**, near the Sphinx, is a massive building made of red granite, Egyptian alabaster, and limestone. It contains spaces for several statues—some of which are now in the Egyptian Antiquities Museum, notably the diorite piece showing a seated Khafre with a Horus falcon enfolding his head in its wings—and an area from which to view the Sphinx. 🖼£e30.
Menkaure's Pyramid is the smallest of the kings' pyramids at the Giza site, measuring 215 feet square and 215 feet tall. It is probable that Menkaure (2490–2472 BC) intended to cover his entire pyramid with a red granite casing, but only the bottom 16 courses of this were in place when he died. The completion of the casing in limestone may have been undertaken subsequently only to be plundered. His successor, Shepseskaf, was responsible for finishing his **mortuary temple**, a very pleasant place to wander about in, in mud brick.

On the left side, as you climb the ladder to enter the pyramid, is a carved inscription concerning the restoration and care of the pyramid subsequent to its construction. The subterranean granite burial chamber contained a sarcophagus that was lost at sea in the 19th century as it was being shipped to Britain. The pyramid and mortuary temple were refurbished in the 26th Dynasty (664–525 BC), when the king's cult enjoyed a renaissance. There are two queen's pyramids and a subsidiary pyramid associated with Menkaure's pyramid complex. 🖼£e25.

★ **Great Sphinx.** The enigmatic Sphinx is attached to Khafre's Pyramid complex, just north of his valley temple, with a separate temple (now very much destroyed) of its own. The Egyptian Sphinx is related to the Greek Sphinx only in that both types are compound animals, part human and part feline. The figure of a recumbent lion with a man's face wearing the *nemes* (traditional headdress of the pharaoh), is thought to be Khafre in the guise of Ra-Harakhte, a manifestation of the sun god, and, in this case, a guardian of the necropolis.

The Sphinx was carved from living rock, with additional details and the final casing made of limestone blocks. The monument used to sport a *uraeus* (the royal cobra) on its forehead and had a beard that has fallen off, bit by bit, through the ages. It is possible that the entire statue was painted; only some traces of red ocher remain on the upper part of the cheeks. A stela stands between the Sphinx's paws, erected by Pharaoh Tuthmose IV (1401–1391 BC) to commemorate his coming to the throne and his clearing the Sphinx of encroaching desert sand.

The Sphinx is viewed by some as a guardian of hidden knowledge, with claims that an underground chamber beneath the Sphinx's paws contains these secrets. Various resistivity tests have been made, and there is no evidence of any cavities. The Sphinx does have three openings in it: one behind its head, which contained nothing; the second, in the north side, which contained a pair of old sandals; and the third, most fittingly, behind its tail. This opening led down to an area that contained some Late Period and Ptolemaic (712–30 BC) burials, but nothing else. ✉ *Al-Haram, Giza* 🚹*Sphinx £e60 (includes general admission to Pyramids Plateau), Sound & Light Show £e75* ⊙ *Daily 8–6:30; Sound and Light Show (in English) Oct.–Apr., Mon.–Wed. and Fri.–Sat. 6:30 PM, Thurs. 7:30 PM, Sun. 9.30 PM; May–Sept., Mon.–Wed. and Fri.–Sat. 8.30 PM, Thurs. 9.30 PM, Sun. 11.30 PM.*

OFF THE BEATEN PATH

Harraniyya. Intricate, handwoven carpets are the big draw in this small village, but you can see all kinds of textiles and pottery as well. The Wissa Wassef center—named after the family largely responsible for developing the town's crafts into an industry—is the best place to see them. Bring lunch and enjoy the lavish gardens between touring the workshops. Saturday through Wednesday are the best days to come. ✉ *4 km (2½ mi) south of Giza on Saqqara Rd., Giza* 🕿*02/385–0746.*

WHERE TO EAT

Cairo's restaurant scene has really developed over the last decade, breaking out of the five-star hotels and onto the streets. Eating out is now a regular form of entertainment, affordable to the growing upper and middle classes in Egypt. Naturally, Egyptian food remains the local favorite, and Cairo is the place to find the best of the country's specialties. Restaurants compete mainly on quality of ingredients rather than refinement of preparations. However, the range of cuisine options has expanded dramatically to include Indian, Thai, French, Italian, and even Japanese.

Local beers (including Stella Premium, Luxor, and Sakara) are common, and you can usually find a range of drinkable, if unremarkable, local wines (the top-rate Grand Marquis label, then the passable Omar Khayyam, Sheherazade, and Obelisque, and a much less wonderful Rubis).

ISLAMIC CAIRO NORTH

$$

MIDDLE EASTERN

✕**Naguib Mahfouz Café.** Named after Egypt's most famous novelist and run by the Oberoi Hotel Group, this is a haven of air-conditioned tranquility in the midst of the sometimes chaotic Khan al-Khalili. The restaurant serves variations on the usual Egyptian dishes, dressed up in historically resonant names to justify what, by the standards of the area, constitute exorbitant prices. That said, the food and service are also of higher quality than you'll find in most of the nearby restaurants. The adjoining café serves lighter fare, consisting mostly of sandwiches, at a fraction of the price of the main dishes. ⊠ *5 al-Badestan Ln., Khan al-Khalili, Islamic Cairo North* ☎ *02/2590–3788* ⊟ *AE, MC, V.*

MA'ADI

$$ ✕ **Bua Khao.** Run by a Thai woman who uses ingredients flown in from
THAI Bangkok, this restaurant manages mouthwateringly authentic food that has saved many an expatriate longing for *massaman* or *penang* curries. Start with a soup, perhaps *tom kar gai* (chicken in a coconut-milk broth), then move on to a delicious glass-noodle salad with shrimp, and end with a curry or two. ⊠ *9 Road 151, Ma'adi* ☎ *02/2358–0126* ⌕ *Reservations essential* ⊟ *MC, V.*

$ ✕ **Lucille's Mermaid Columbus.** Despite the arrival in Cairo of internation-
AMERICAN ally recognized American fast food chains, expats still flock to Lucille's
CASUAL for tasty authentic burgers—hand-crafted patties that are cooked to
★ order—and Tex-Mex dishes. Lucille's also serves up great American breakfasts with all-day breakfasts Friday and Saturday. Fill up on fresh OJ, pancakes, and syrup. Authentic diner decor keeps homesick Americans happy. ⊠ *54 Shar'a 9, Ma'adi* ☎ *02/2359–2778* ⊟ *MC, V.*

DOWNTOWN & BULAQ

$$ ✕ **Alfi Bey Restaurant & Grill.** A mainstay of the old theater district since
MIDDLE 1938, this restaurant, with its wood-paneled dining room, white table-
EASTERN cloths, and marble floors, is a step above the standard local eatery. Slow-cooked mutton and beef stews served with rice predominate, though the ribs (sold by the kilo) and grilled meats are especially good. No alcohol is served. ⊠ *3 Shar'a El Alfi, Downtown* ☎ *02/2577–1888* ⊟ *No credit cards.*

$–$$ ✕ **Cafe Riche.** Founded in 1908, Cafe Riche was the social headquarters
MIDDLE of much of Cairo's theater and literary communities and once had a
EASTERN cabaret where Umm Koulthum got her start in 1922. The food has not changed much since then and features such standard French-influenced Egyptian grill dishes as entrecôte in wine sauce with fries. The steak with pistachios is more innovative (and quite good), while there are all the usual local options, including *fatta* (a meat or vegetable casserole) and tahini. You can also get a good breakfast here. ⊠ *17 Shar'a Talaat Harb, Downtown* ☎ *02/2392–9793* ⊟ *AE, MC, V.*

$–$$ ✕ **Caspar & Gambini's.** This popular casual coffee bar and eatery is one
CAFÉ of a chain around the Middle East. The Corniche branch opens out onto the mezzanine of the Towers Mall, and the clientele is a mixture of expats and young trendy Cairenes who work in the corporate office blocks around the area. The menu is a good mix of snacks (including sandwiches and wraps), salads, plus international entrees (including pastas and chili). The coffee is excellent, and there's Wi-Fi. ⊠ *Towers Mall at Nile City, Corniche al-Nil, Downtown* ☎ *02/2461–9201* ⊕ *www.casparandgambinis.com* ⊟ *AE, MC, V.*

2

$ **✕Felfela.** This Cairo institution is popular with both Egyptians and
MIDDLE visitors for good Egyptian food at inexpensive prices. Felfela is a good
EASTERN place to introduce yourself to such Egyptian staples as *shorbat 'ads*
(lentil soup), which is tasty with a squeeze of lemon in it; *taamiya* (the
local version of falafel); and *ful* (stewed fava beans). Felfela serves beer.
There's also another downtown branch on Maydan Ramsis and others
around the city. ✉*15 Shar'a Hoda Sharaawi, Downtown* ☎*02/2392–
2833* 🖃*No credit cards.*

$$$ **✕Pane Vino.** An ultra contemporary and fashionable open kitchen–style
ITALIAN Italian restaurant puts a modern twist on the traditional trattoria. Pane
Vino has Italian chefs who cook with authentic Italian ingredients. Sig-
nature dishes include crispy fried calamari or deep-fried carpaccio with
rocket salad and Parmesan cheese. You can eat light or enjoy a meal of
several courses, just like mama used to serve. ✉*Semiramis InterConti-
nental, Corniche al-Nil, Downtown* ☎*02/2795–7171* ⚖*Reservations
essential* 🖃*AE, MC, V.*

$$$$ **✕The Semiramis Grill.** This top-notch restaurant concentrates on sim-
CONTINENTAL ple, classic Continental dishes. Starters include lightly cooked scallops.
For main courses, the menu divides evenly between seafood and meat;
highlights include lobster with cheese ravioli and a delectable beef au
poivre. The extensive dessert menu is supplemented with a dozen or
so daily specials, all of them enticing. The restaurant's contemporary
gentleman's-club atmosphere is enhanced by waiters in tails who are
engaged in a sedate bustle. ✉*Semiramis InterContinental, Corniche
al-Nil, Downtown* ☎*02/2795–7171* ⚖*Reservations essential* 🖃*AE,
DC, MC, V* ⊙*No lunch.*

$$$$ **✕Villa d'Este.** This restaurant manages a nice balance between for-
ITALIAN mal elegance (with brocade tapestries on the wall and heavy, carved-
wood chairs) and relaxed comfort (largely due to the friendly service).
The *bresaola* (air-cured beef) comes thinly sliced with basil pesto and
arranged around a honeydew melon, suggesting the rays from a sun.
There are vegetarian dishes, and others billed as "healthy food" (iden-
tified by a little heart icon on the menu). But this is not spa cuisine—
everything here is rich and filling, so why not just have the roast rack of
lamb with polenta or the grilled king prawns? ✉*Conrad International
Hotel, 1191 Corniche al-Nil, Downtown* ☎*02/2580–8000* ⚖*Reser-
vations essential* 🖃*AE, MC, V* ⊙*No lunch.*

ZAMALEK & GEZIRA

$$ **✕Abou el Sid.** You'll feel as though you're walking into an Arabian
MIDDLE palace when you pass through the portal of this restaurant—the decor
EASTERN might be a touch kitschy, but the food definitely isn't. This is the place
Fodor's Choice to immerse yourself in the full works, Egyptian style, and it serves just
★ about the best Egyptian cuisine in Cairo. The choice of mezze—both
hot and cold—is impressive. For main courses you'll have a choice
of grilled meats, stuffed pigeon, and slow-cooked meat stews. There's
also a branch at City Stars Mall. ✉*157 Shar'a 26th Yulyu, Zamalek*
☎*02/2735–9640* ⚖*Reservations essential* 🖃*AE, MC, V.*

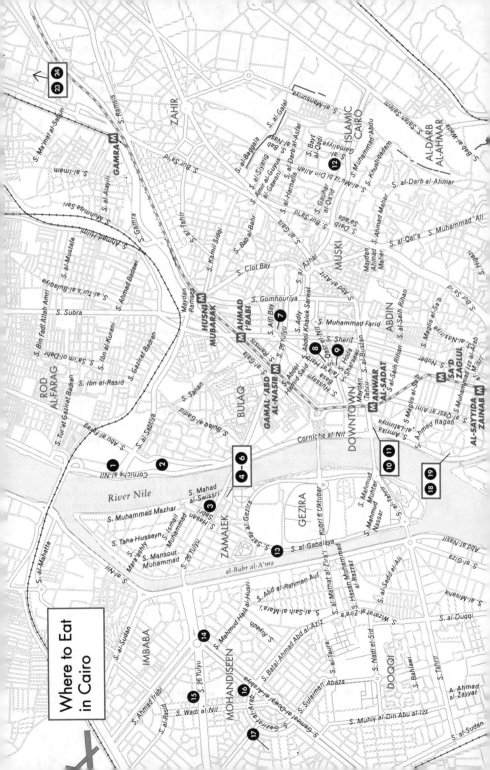

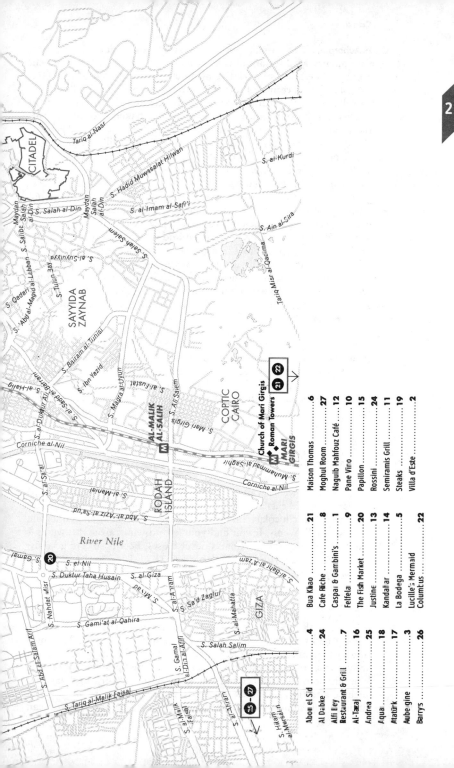

2

CITADEL

Tariq al-Nasr

S. al-Kurdi

S. Hadid Muwasalat Hilwan

Maydan Salah al-Din

S. Salah al-Din

Maydan Salah al-Din

S. al-Imam al-Safi'i

S. Ain al-Sira

S. al-Suyufiyya

S. Salah Salem

Tariq Misr al-Qadima

S. Tulun 3dy

S. Qadari al-Labban

S. Abd al-Magid al-Labban

SAYYIDA ZAYNAB

S. Bairam al-Tunisi

S. Ibn Yazid

S. Magra al-Uyun

S. al-Fustat

S. al-Saff al-Barrani

S. al-Duktur Ali Ibrahim

S. al-Halig

AL-MALIK AL-SALIH

S. Ali Salem

S. Mari Girgis

COPTIC CAIRO

Church of Mari Girgis

21 22

Roman Towers

Corniche al-Nil

S. al-Salat

S. al-Manial

S. Muhammad al-Sahir

MARI GIRGIS

RODAH ISLAND

S. Abd al-'Aziz al-Sa'ud

Corniche al-Nil

River Nile

S. Gamal

S. el-Nil

20

S. Duktur Taha Husain

S. al-Giza

S. al-Bahr al-A'zam

S. Nahdat Misr

S. Misr

S. al-Ayam

S. Sad Zaglul

S. Gami'at al-Qahira

GIZA

S. al-Mahatta

S. Salah Salim

S. Abd el-Salam Aril

S. Gamal al-Din al-Afifi

S. Gamal

S. Tariq al-Malik Faisal

25 27

S. al-Malik

S. al-Arian

S. Hitam al-Mursala

$$ ╳**Aubergine.** This casual, mostly vegetarian, restaurant is a rare find,
VEGETARIAN with an airy Mediterranean-style ground floor and a darker, candlelit upstairs. The always innovative menu changes daily but usually consists of a soup, a couple of salads, baked vegetable dishes, and pastas—as well as meat and seafood specials. Favorites include green salad with sautéed mushrooms and Parmesan shavings; baked avocado, mushroom, and eggplant lasagna; pan-fried halloumi cheese with grilled cherry tomatoes; and salmon ravioli in a creamy dill sauce. There's Wi-Fi here. ⊠*5 Shar'a Sayed al-Bakry, Zamalek* ☎*02/2738–0080* ⚐*Reservations essential* ▤*AE, MC.*

$$$$ ╳**Justine.** Established in the mid-1980s as Egypt's premier French res-
FRENCH taurant, Justine has only improved with age. The daily specials are
★ always great choices. Perhaps a shipment of fresh mussels from Alexandria is given a light, delicious broth and placed over pasta; asparagus, harvested in the morning, is steamed and on your plate by evening; duck- and goose-liver paté is transformed into an array of delights. The à la carte menu is equally inspired. At the end of your meal, prepare yourself for one last indulgence, because Justine is in a league of its own when it comes to dessert. Service is flawless. ⊠*4 Shar'a Hassan Sabri, Zamalek* ☎*02/2736–2961* ⚐*Reservations essential* ▤*AE, MC, V.*

$$$ ╳**La Bodega.** This expansive restaurant, bar, and lounge is one of the
ECLECTIC hottest spots in town and one of the hardest reservations to get. The dining area is a series of elegant high-ceilinged rooms, which, with their dark wood and seductive lighting, evoke Casablanca as much as Europe. The see-and-be-seen crowd is as hip as Cairo gets. The kitchen produces a number of specialties hard to find anywhere else, including homemade focaccia with rosemary or olives, gazpacho, honey-glazed duck, and tuna carpaccio. The bar is at least as popular as the restaurant. Be prepared to eat early (by Cairo standards) if you want a shot at getting a table. ⊠*Balmoral Hotel, 157 Shar'a 26 Yulyu, Zamalek* ☎*02/2735–0543* ⚐*Reservations essential* ▤*AE, MC, V.*

$ ╳**Maison Thomas.** Famous among Cairenes for its pizza, Thomas also
ITALIAN prepares smaller dishes to eat in or take out, including squid or mushroom salad, as well as various sandwiches based on local and imported cheeses and cold cuts available in the deli section. The real treat is dessert: the plain chocolate cake (ask to have it warmed) and chocolate mousse are heavenly. If you find yourself prowling around town at 4 AM, steer yourself here; Thomas never closes. Beer is sold to go only. ⊠*157 Shar'a 26 Yulyu, Zamalek* ☎*02/2735–7057* ⚐*Reservations not accepted* ▤*No credit cards.*

RODAH ISLAND & GARDEN CITY

$$$$ ╳**Aqua.** With a dining room lined by wall-size aquariums, this is the
SEAFOOD coolest and most expensive seafood restaurant in the city. The sushi and sashimi are incredibly fresh and varied, but the fusion-style menu moves from the simplest dishes such as pan-fried prawns, to unusual combinations like sea eel and foie gras, to great extravaganzas that include a terribly indulgent lobster served four ways. This is a grand dining opportunity with service to match. For surf and turf you can

also order from the menu of neighboring Steaks restaurant. ⊠*Four Seasons Nile Plaza, Corniche al-Nil, Garden City* ☎*02/2791–7000* ⚐*Reservations essential* ▤*AE, DC, MC, V* ⊗*No lunch.*

$$$$ ✕**Steaks.** The sepia-tone photographs of proud owners and their cattle
STEAK from around the world tell you what's on the menu, if the name of the restaurant isn't obvious enough. The steaks served here are not just any old slabs of flesh. Choice cuts from the finest beef-producing countries vie for attention, including Wagyu beef from Australia and prime or Black Angus meat from the U.S. You can combine menus with Aqua, the hotel's seafood restaurant next door. ⊠*Four Seasons Nile Plaza, Corniche al-Nil, Garden City* ☎*02/2791–7000* ⚐*Reservations essential.* ▤*AE, DC, MC, V* ⊗*No lunch.*

MOHANDISEEN

$ ✕**Al-Tazaj.** When it comes to speedy service, McDonald's could learn
MIDDLE a thing or two from the Saudis who own al-Tazaj. They claim to get
EASTERN their produce from farm to grill in fewer than four hours, which is why (despite the fast-food decor) this joint turns out some of Cairo's tastiest grilled chicken—and little else. The birds are small, so you might want two; and while you're at it, ask for an extra container of the deliciously garlicky tahini to use as a dip. ⊠*13–14 Sour Nadi el Zamalek, Mohandiseen* ☎*09018 in Egypt only* ⊠*30 Talaat Harb, Downtown* ⚐*Reservations not accepted* ▤*No credit cards.*

$–$$ ✕**Atatürk.** More Levantine than Turkish—despite the name and kitsch
MIDDLE Ottoman decor—this restaurant serves delicious food that is a bit of
EASTERN a change from the routine. The *manakish* (flatbread) comes in a long flat loaf covered in black cumin and sesame seeds rather than the usual *zaatar* (sesame seeds mixed with powdered sumac and thyme); and the *börek peynir* (phyllo pastries stuffed with cheese) are spiced with a hint of nutmeg. You are likely to feel stuffed even before the heavy main dishes arrive, but try to leave room for the *sharkassia* (half a chicken in a mild walnut sauce). ⊠*20 Shar'a Riyadh, Mohandiseen* ☎*02/3347–5135* ▤*No credit cards.*

$$$ ✕**Kandahar.** Overlooking Maydan Sphinx (Sphinx Square), Kanda-
INDIAN har serves superb North Indian food. Because all dishes are excellent, consider ordering one of the set menus that include the highly seasoned mulligatawny soup, appetizers, a delicious stewed dal, a lamb or chicken curry, and rice and bread, as well as dessert. This will give you a chance to try a bit of everything. If you like your food heavily spiced, make this known—the heat has been turned down for local tastes. This is not a sign of a lack of authenticity—chili pepper is only one of the spices in the Indian culinary palette. The service is some of the best in town. ⊠*3 Shar'a Gameat al-Dowal al-Arabiya, Mohandiseen* ☎*02/3303–0615* ▤*AE, MC, V.*

$$ ✕**Papillon.** Beautifully remodeled to resemble a stone mansion, complete
MIDDLE with a grand staircase at the entrance and a dining area that feels like
EASTERN a drawing room, Papillon serves superb Lebanese food. Although the menu is inevitably biased toward meat, including delicious lamb kebabs and *kofta* (ground meat shaped as kebabs), you can fashion a vege-

tarian meal out of the substantial appetizers. Be sure to try *fattoush* (a salad with fried-pita croutons) and the hummus, which comes with warm *'aish shami* (a puffy bread). ⊠ *Tirsana Shopping Center (across from the Zamalek Sporting Club), Shar'a 26 Yulyu, Mohandiseen* ☎ *02/3347–1672* ⚑ *Reservations essential* ⊟ *AE, MC, V.*

NILE DINNER CRUISES

For a different type of meal, try one of the many Nile cruise boats. Most offer a buffet dinner followed by a folk or belly-dancing show with live music. The Marriott-operated **Maxim** (⊠ *Shar'a Saraya El Gezirah, Zamalek* ☎ *02/2738–8888*) offers an à la carte menu as well as the buffet. The **Nile Peking** (⊠ *Corniche al-Nil, Coptic Cairo* ☎ *02/2531–3755*) offers dinner cruises with a Chinese menu but no entertainment—though you may prefer to enjoy the views on deck to watching a show.

HELIOPOLIS

$$ ✕ **Al Dabke.** The décor is pure
MIDDLE Arabian and the cuisine authentic
EASTERN Middle Eastern, though you're in the heart of a modern 5-star hotel. You can watch the bread being cooked in the open oven, so you know it's the genuine article. From soups and hot and cold mezze through the grilled meat and chicken and the stews, the food is delicious. ⊠ *Fairmont Heliopolis, Shar'a Uruba, Heliopolis* ☎ *02/2267–7730* ⊟ *AE, DC, MC, V.*

$$$ ✕ **Rossini.** Rossini is in a renovated villa in Heliopolis, but you'll thank
SEAFOOD yourself if you forgo the pleasant (if generic) interior and sit in the garden for one of Cairo's only alfresco dining experiences, with tables scattered among spotlit palm trees. Rossini is best known for its Italian-influenced seafood, including tender stuffed crab and a delicious shrimp and linguine. For a more local touch, whole fish baked in a casing of salt is a Coptic favorite, especially during the holidays. For dessert, have an authentic tiramisu—Rossini is one of the few places in town that does this dessert right. Service is excellent. ⊠ *66 Shar'a Omar Ibn al-Khattab, Heliopolis* ☎ *02/2291–8282* ⚑ *Reservations essential* ⊟ *AE, DC, MC, V.*

GIZA

$–$$ ✕ **Andrea.** Out by the pyramids and down an unmarked canal off Shar'a
MIDDLE King Faisal, Andrea is hard to find—your taxi driver might know it,
EASTERN or ask pedestrians once you get out there—but it is absolutely worth the effort. Friday lunch in the gardens is an Egyptian family tradition. Chicken is grilled on beds of charcoal, and *warak einab* (stuffed grape leaves and chicken livers) are unequaled. At night, the Byzantine interior becomes Cairo's most sophisticated nightclub (only November through March)—and getting in is almost as hard as finding the place. ⊠ *60 Maryotteya Canal, Shar'a Kerdessa, al-Haram, Giza* ☎ *02/383–1133* ⚑ *Reservations essential* ⊟ *AE, MC, V.*

2

$$ ✕**Barry's.** The magnificent views of the pyramids would be reason
MIDDLE   enough to take the trip to Barry's, but this restaurant gilds the lily. You'll
EASTERN   eat on a wide terrace furnished with local antiques—from the tables and
Fodor's Choice   chairs to the ornate lighting fixtures and eclectic mixture of grand oil
★   paintings of pashas and belly dancers on the walls. The menu is typi-
cal local cuisine served in ample portions. Stay into the evening for the
Sound & Light show—you'll be able to watch the full performance from
your table. ⊠2 *Shar'a Abu Aziza, extension of Shar'a Abul Houl, Giza
(close to the entrance to the Sound and Light Show)* ☎02/3388–9540
⊕*www.barry1.com* ⚑*Reservations essential* ☰*AE, MC, V.*

$$ ✕**The Fish Market.** On the upper deck of a boat permanently moored on
SEAFOOD   the west bank of the Nile, the scene here is decidedly simple: there's no
menu, just a display of unbelievably fresh fish, shrimp, crabs, calamari,
and shellfish on ice. Pick what appeals, pay by weight, and the kitchen
will prepare it however you like, with a slew of Middle Eastern salads
on the side. The delicious bread is baked on the premises in a *baladi*
(country) oven. ⊠*26 Shar'a al-Nil, Giza* ☎02/3570–9691 ⚑*Reservations essential* ☰*AE, MC, V.*

$$$$ ✕**Moghul Room.** The Mohgul Room is a temple to the grandeur and
INDIAN   refinement of Indian cuisine. The setting in the arches-and-romance
Fodor's Choice   splendor of the Mena House could hardly be more sublime, and Indian
★   musicians create a seductive aural backdrop. Try luscious, yogurt-mari-
nated tandoori; rich, buttery *masala* (a classic blend of spices); or tender dal cooked slowly over a flame—all accompanied by delicious,
fresh-baked breads. The best of the desserts are *kulfi* (a slightly grainy
ice cream infused with pistachio and cardamom) and *gulab jamun*
(fried milk balls). ⊠*Mena House Oberoi Hotel, Shar'a al-Haram, Giza*
☎02/3377–3222 ⚑*Reservations essential* ☰*AE, DC, MC, V.*

WHERE TO STAY

Cairo has a growing number of five-star hotels (as rated by the Egyptian Hotel Association) scattered across the city, but many of Cairo's
big business hotels disappoint. This may be because they are too char-
acterless and modern (distinctive Egyptian atmosphere is lacking in
almost all cases) or because they simply fail to measure up to international standards, most often in terms of service. There are certainly
exceptions, and the general quality of the top hotels is on the rise at
this writing. Regardless, the top-end hotels will offer all the facilities
and modern conveniences you need to recuperate after a long day of
sightseeing and shopping. Outside the five-star range, Cairo's options
quickly grow limited, though there are still a few more budget-oriented
hotels that fit the bill.

DOWNTOWN & BULAQ

$$$$ 🏨**Conrad International.** A rather boxy-looking building, the Conrad
rather disappoints when compared to other corniche hotels, but it is
a comfortable place to retreat at the end of a long day. The lobby is a
reassuring field of marble graced by palm trees, while the rooms are

spacious and pleasant, albeit with a slightly generic international-chain feel. The 24-hour Felucca Café, with tables out on a terrace overlooking the Nile, is a great place to relax. **Pros:** The staff are friendly; the hotel offers the occasional homey touch, such as the apples in the giant glass vase that are available at check-in. **Cons:** This is a big hotel and won't suit those who want a more personalized experience; three restaurants doesn't seem like much of a choice for such a large hotel; although all the rooms technically have Nile views, only the rooms in the front of the building on the high floors live up to the billing. ✉*1113 Corniche al-Nil, Downtown* ☎*02/2580–8000* ⊕*conradhotels1.hilton. com* ↩*565 rooms, 56 suites* ⌂*In-room: safe, Internet, Wi-Fi. In-hotel: 3 restaurants, room service, bars, pool, gym, spa, laundry service, no-smoking rooms* ⊟*AE, MC, V* �⊙ì*EP.*

$$$$
Fodor's Choice
★

⌨**Fairmont Nile City.** Set between two towering office blocks overlooking the Nile, this luxury hotel will appeal to both business and leisure travelers. The decor looks to the early 20th century for its inspiration; to balance the yin and yang, there are two different color schemes for the room decor—a rich black and gold, contrasting with cool ivories and natural tones. **Pros:** Most rooms have Nile views; shopping mall with cinema is part of the complex; the roof terrace is a great place to chill out. **Cons:** It's downtown but not really within walking distance to the downtown attractions. ✉*Nile City Tower, 2005 Corniche al-Nil, Bulaq* ☎*02/2461–9356* ⊕*www.fairmont.com* ↩*567 rooms* ⌂*In-room: safe, Wi-Fi. In-hotel: 5 restaurants, room service, bars, pool, gym, spa, laundry service, parking (paid), no-smoking rooms* ⊟*AE, DC, MC, V* �⊙ì*EP.*

$

⌨**Pension Roma.** Hidden away above the Gattegno department store, this small, shoestring-budget pension is adored by students and backpackers. The high-ceiling rooms are large—a few even have balconies—and beautifully appointed with 1930s-style furniture. The toilets and showers are communal for the most part but well kept, and the staff are more friendly and helpful than at many five-star hotels. The sunlit breakfast room is a great place to pick up tips from fellow guests on travel far afield. **Pros:** There's a real home-away-from-home feeling here. **Cons:** The elevator is old and a little shaky; it's a long climb up the stairs; not all rooms have a private bathroom. ✉*169 Shar'a Muhammad Farid, Downtown* ☎*02/391–1088* ↩*32 rooms, 5 with bath* ⌂*In-room: no phone, no TV* ⊟*No credit cards* �⊙ì*BP.*

$$$$

⌨**Ramses Hilton.** This large hotel is geared toward the needs of tour groups and business travelers (largely Japanese), and it's one of the most recognizable high-rises along the corniche. Rooms are quite large at 387 square feet and better decorated than most comparable rooms in Cairo, in the kind of generic international style Hilton uses everywhere. **Pros:** A good choice of eateries on-site. **Cons:** The hotel is surrounded by major roads that make it difficult to wander around on foot; small pool and pool terrace, especially when many guests want to use it at the same time; balconies are small. ✉*1115 Corniche al-Nil, Downtown* ☎*02/2577–7444* ⊕*www.hilton.com* ↩*900 rooms, 152 suites* ⌂*In-room: safe, Internet. In-hotel: 7 restaurants, room service, bars, pool, gym, laundry service, parking (paid), some pets allowed, no-smoking rooms* ⊟*AE, DC, MC, V* �⊙ì*EP.*

2

$$$-$$$$ ⊞**Semiramis InterContinental.** This modern high-rise was, for many years, the center of the city's hotel life. Today it's got more vigorous competition but stands up well when compared with newer properties. Rooms are spacious, with full-length windows that make the most of the city views. All rooms have balconies. The clientele are predomi-nantly businesspeople, and the crisp service and quality of the facilities reflect their needs. **Pros:** The hotel is a little less expensive than many of the same quality; it's in the heart of downtown. **Cons:** Could be a little too large and impersonal for some visitors. ⊠ *Corniche al-Nil, at Maydan Tahrir, Downtown* ☎*02/2795-7171* ⊕*www.ichotelsgroup. com* ⊅*728 rooms, 79 suites* ⌂*In-room: safe, Internet. In-hotel: 6 restaurants, room service, bars, pool, gym, spa, laundry service, Wi-Fi, parking (paid), no-smoking rooms* ⊟*AE, DC, MC, V* ⫣*EP.*

$$$ ⊞**Talisman Hotel de Charme.** The approach through dusty alleyways and
Fodor's Choice the climb through floors of nondescript grey offices could be a little off-
★ putting, but misgivings vanish as soon as you enter the Talisman's inviting reception area. A one-floor B&B filled with antique furnishings, Egyp-tian art, and hand-woven Persian carpets on traditional Cairene marble floors, this is an oasis of calm in the middle of downtown. Rooms vary in size but are well furnished and brightly painted. Rooms are interspersed with Arabic-style lounges for relaxing. **Pros:** Surrounding area has a range of inexpensive local cafés and bars, plus hundreds of shops; the design and decor are excellent; well-stocked library. **Cons:** A small, old, and creaky elevator serves the whole building; no restaurant on-site; no outside space. ⊠ *39 Shar'a Talaat Harb, Downtown* ☎*02/2393-9431* ⊕*www.talisman-hotel.com* ⊅*24 rooms* ⌂*In-room: safe, refrigerator. In-hotel: laundry service, Internet terminal* ⊟*No credit cards* ⫣*BP.*

$ ⊞**The Windsor Hotel.** Opened in the early 1900s as the khedivial bath-house and converted to a hotel in the 1930s, the Windsor oozes atmo-sphere. The original fixtures have all been carefully preserved, including an antique elevator. Rooms are comfortably fitted with heavy wooden period-style furniture that gives the place the breezy, slightly creaky feel of a Somerset Maugham story about life in the colonies. Each room is different, so ask to see a couple before you settle on one you like. Ten of the rooms have showers only. **Pros:** Wonderful period history—the atmosphere is palpable; your fellow guests will be a cosmopolitan and interesting crowd of all ages. **Cons:** Rooms are in need of some TLC; communal landings don't have modern soundproofing. ⊠ *19 Shar'a Alfi Bay, Downtown* ☎*02/2591-5277* ⊕*www.windsorcairo.com* ⊅*55 rooms* ⌂*In-room: refrigerator. In-hotel: restaurant, bar, laun-dry service, Wi-Fi, parking (free)* ⊟*AE, MC, V* ⫣*EP.*

ZAMALEK & GEZIRA

$$$$ ⊞**Cairo Marriott.** The centerpiece of this large hotel is a breathtaking
★ palace built by Khedive Isma'il to give French Empress Eugénie a suit-able place to stay on her visit for the opening of the Suez Canal in 1869. Unfortunately, you can't stay in the palace itself, because the Marriott's bright but comparatively indistinctive rooms are in two adjoining mod-ern blocks. Room decor is rich but conservative, with dark woods

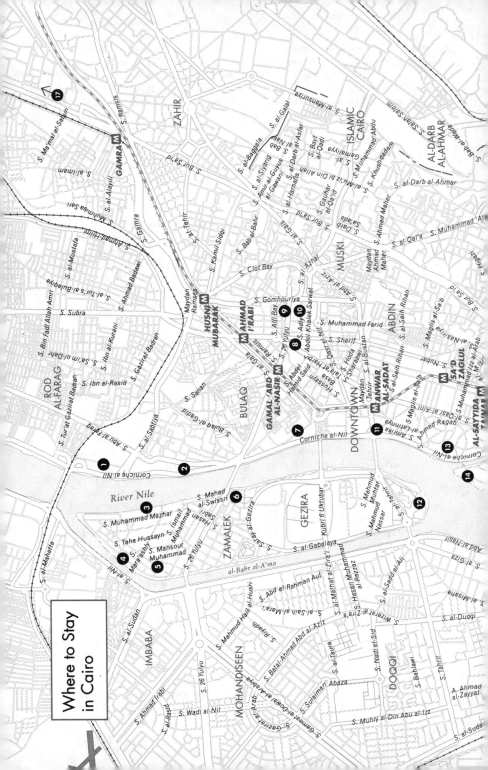

CITADEL

Tariq al-Nasr

S. al-Kurdi

S. Hadid Muwasalat Hilwan

Maydan
Salah
al-Din
S. Salah al-Din
Maydan
Salah
al-Din
S. al-Imam al-Safi'i

S. Ain al-Sira

Maydan
S. al-Din
S. al-Suyuwiya

S. Salah Salem

Tariq Misr al-Qadima

Jadari al-Magid al-Labban

SAYYIDA
ZAYNAB

S. 'Abd al-Magid al-Labban
S. Tulun Bay

S. Bairam al-Tunisi

S. al-Hai
S. ar-Sadd al-Barrani

S. al-Barrani
S. ad-Duktur Ali

S. Ibn Yazid

S. Magra al-Uyun

S. al-Fustat

AL-MALIK
AL-SALIH
M

S. Mari Girgis

COPTIC
CAIRO

Church of Mari Girgis
◆ Roman Towers

MARI
GIRGIS
M

S. Muhammad al-Sahir

Corniche al-Nil

S. al-Saral

S. al-Saral

Tariq al-Manial

RODAH
ISLAND

S. al-Manial

S. 'Abd al-'Aziz al-Sa'ud

River Nile

S. Gama
15
S. el-Nil
S. Duktur Taha Husain
S. al-Giza

S. Nahdat Misr
S. Murad
S. al-Atram
S. Sa'd Zaglul
S. al-Mahatta

GIZA
16

S. Gami'at al-Qahira

S. Salah Salim

S. Abd al-Salam Arif
S. Gamal
al-Din al-Afifi

S. Tariq al-Malik Faisal
18
S. al-Malik
S. al-Malik
S. Faisal
S. Hilmi
S. al-Saff
S. al-Ahram

complemented by deep blues and golds, and the same styling carries on through the public areas. **Pros:** The gardens of the hotel make a peaceful retreat from the city; the restaurants at the Marriott attract lots of Cairenes and expats, so it's a great place to feel the authentic atmosphere of the modern city. **Cons:** It's the biggest hotel in Cairo, so not for those who want more personal service. ⊠ *16 Shar'a Saray al-Gezira, Zamalek* ☎ *02/2728–3000* ⊕ *www.marriott.com* ↝ *978 rooms, 115 suites* ᐸ *In-room: safe, Internet. In-hotel: 12 restaurants, room service, bars, pool, gym, spa, laundry service, Wi-Fi, parking (paid), some pets allowed, no-smoking rooms* ⊟ *AE, DC, MC, V* ❢ *EP.*

$$$ ⌖ **Golden Tulip Flamenco Hotel.** Cairo has very few hotels that bridge the gap between the luxury properties and the more basic budget options, but this one—part of a European chain—makes a good attempt. Rooms are rather dated in style, with clashing green and red in the decor. However, they are spacious and clean, and there's a good range of facilities on-site. Rooms at the back of the hotel are quieter and offer water views. The hotel is particularly popular with Western Europeans. **Pros:** Good value for the money. **Cons:** Some rooms need a coat of paint; some staff are more helpful than others. ⊠ *Shar'a El Gezira El Wosta, Zamalek* ☎ *02/735–0815* ⊕ *www.goldentulipflamenco.com* ↝ *174 rooms* ᐸ *In-room: safe (some), refrigerator, Wi-Fi (some). In-hotel: 2 restaurants, room service, bar, laundry service, Internet terminal* ⊟ *AE, MC, V* ❢ *BP.*

$$ ⌖ **Hotel Longchamps.** This lovely little B&B-style hotel is on the upper
★ floors of a medium-sized tower block, offering a quiet refuge from the city. Rooms are individually furnished. Superior rooms have modern styling, and the bathrooms are modern and well tiled; standard rooms are slightly smaller and the fittings older, but they are still wearing well. The Longchamps has a small restaurant open for a couple of hours in the evening. There's a cozy lounge and two large terraces replete with well-tended plants and a decent library of books if you want to read and relax. This is a popular hotel, so book as far in advance as possible. **Pros:** Excellent value for money; friendly, welcoming staff; superior rooms have free tea and coffee. **Cons:** The old elevator is a touch creaky; lots of repeat guests mean it can be difficult to get a room. ⊠ *Shar'a Ismail Mohammed, Zamalek* ☎ *02/2735–2311* ⊕ *www. hotellongchamps.com* ↝ *22 rooms* ᐸ *In-room: refrigerator, Wi-Fi. In-hotel: restaurant, laundry facilities* ⊟ *MC, V* ❢ *BP.*

$$$$ ⌖ **Safir Hotel–Zamalek.** This all-suites hotel is popular with long-staying guests, but short-term visitors can also rent suites. The Safiri suites (two bedrooms) and the Emiri (three bedrooms) are both quite large, with full kitchens and late-1970s-style white furniture. In the Emiri suites, the master bedroom has a walk-around balcony with views of the Nile. Somehow, these suites come to feel like home: You find yourself swearing that one day you'll get around to remodeling the kitchen and living room. **Pros:** An excellent option for families; Zamalek is a quiet, leafy neighborhood with lots of independent boutiques for browsing. **Cons:** It's a taxi ride to any of the attractions, and taxis don't pass on this street as a matter of course. ⊠ *21 Shar'a Muhammad Mazhar, Zamalek* ☎ *02/2737–0055* ⊕ *www.safirhotels.com* ↝ *104 suites* ᐸ *In-room:*

kitchen. In-hotel: 2 restaurants, room service, laundry facilities ⊟*AE, MC, V* †○†*EP.*

$$$$ ⚃ **Sofitel El-Gezirah Cairo.** The circular tower has been gracing the Cairo skyline for well over two decades, but the interiors here have been brought up to date after a takeover by Sofitel in 2006 (it was formerly a Sheraton), and the hotel has re-emerged as a must-visit place for expats and visitors for its bars and restaurants. Contemporary luxury and understated style are the watchwords for the public areas. Rooms are decorated with cool neutral shades and pale pastels. The hotel sits on the southern tip of Gezira Island surrounded by parks and residential districts. **Pros:** Quiet (for Cairo) location surrounded by greenery; all rooms have a view of the city and the Nile; cool Buddha Bar on-site. **Cons:** Despite the central location, you're dependent on the hotel's taxi fleet to get anywhere because nothing is in easy walking distance. ⊠*3 Shar'a El Thawra Council, Gezira* ⌂*Box 732, al-Orman, Giza* ☎*02/2737–3737* ⊕*www.sofitel.com* ⬅*383 rooms, 50 suites* ♿*In-room: safe, Internet, Wi-Fi. In-hotel: 4 restaurants, room service, bars, pools, gym, spa, laundry service, parking (paid), no-smoking rooms* ⊟*AE, DC, MC, V* †○†*EP.*

RODAH ISLAND & GARDEN CITY

$$$$ ⚃ **Four Seasons Hotel Cairo at Nile Plaza.** The most sophisticated address in the city, this Four Seasons is the top place to see and be seen. The attention to detail is evident everywhere, from the proliferation of marble in the vast double-height lobby to the expensive gourmet ingredients used in the restaurants. The overall design draws on several eras, but it all seems to come together. The outdoor spaces, with their blue-and-white striped cotton furnishings, have a very Mediterranean resort feel, while the bar's decor is inspired by the art deco movement. Rooms are luxurious but conservative. **Pros:** You'll be surrounded by the Cairo glitterati here; standard rooms have 500 square feet of space; the spa is excellent. **Cons:** Public spaces could be viewed as gaudy by some; atmosphere is more corporate than resortlike; not all rooms have terraces or balconies. ⊠*1089 Corniche al-Nil, Maglis El Shaab, Garden City* ☎*02/2791–7000* ⊕*www.fourseasons.com* ⬅*288 rooms, 77 suites* ♿*In-room: safe, Internet. In-hotel: 6 restaurants, room service, bars, pool, gym, spa, laundry service, parking (paid), no-smoking rooms* ⊟*AE, DC, MC, V* †○†*EP.*

$$$$ ⚃ **Grand Hyatt Cairo.** Occupying the very northern tip of Rodah Island, this high-rise hotel offers exceptional views of the river and the city. Rooms are simply furnished with warm wood and neutral tones; perhaps they don't want to compete with the amazing views through the full-length windows that lead to a balcony. Bathrooms are spacious and lavishly decorated with marble. The Grand Hyatt has an excellent variety of restaurants on-site plus more offerings in an adjacent shopping mall. This is a very popular property with visitors from the Middle East and Gulf States. **Pros:** Nile-side eateries offer lovely views by day and romantic views by night; the gym and spa facilities are excellent. **Cons:** Alcohol is not available in all bars and restaurants (only on the

41st-floor panorama restaurant and if ordered through room service). ⊠*Corniche al-Nil, Rodah Island* ☎*02/2356–1234* ⊕*www.cairo. grand.hyatt.com* ⇆*633 rooms, 83 suites* ♿*In-room: safe, Internet. In-hotel: 12 restaurants, room service, bar, pool, gym, spa, laundry service, parking (paid), no-smoking rooms* ☰*AE, DC, MC, V* ⦿*EP.*

HELIOPOLIS

$$$$ ⊡ **Fairmont Towers Heliopolis.** Cairo's most stunning new hotel, the six-story building is designed to mimic the eye of Horus. Rooms are in a curved stone edifice, while the public spaces are in a vast glass atrium that hugs the inner curve of the main block. The interior is über-cool with full-size palm trees and fountains plus several open-plan bars and restaurant areas. The rooms, too, are very contemporary, with hardwood floors, flat-screen TVs, and more than 450 square feet of space. The spa is by Willow Stream. **Pros:** Only 10 minutes from the international airport, so it's excellent for onward travel and early morning flights; there's a wide range of amenities shared with the neighboring Fairmont Heliopolis. **Cons:** It's a 45-minute drive to downtown. ⊠*Shar'a El Shaheed Sayed Zakaria, off Shar'a Uruba, Heliopolis* ☎*02/2696–0000* ⊕*www.fairmont.com* ⇆*247 rooms* ♿*In-room: safe, Wi-Fi. In-hotel: 4 restaurants, room service, bar, pool, gym, spa, laundry service, Wi-Fi, parking (paid), no-smoking rooms* ☰*AE, DC, MC, V* ⦿*EP.*

GIZA

$$$$ ⊡ **Four Seasons Hotel Cairo at The First Residence.** In a word, this hotel is
★ superb. Once through the portal you'll feel like you're entering a modern Venetian palace. Service is smoothly efficient, attentive to the smallest detail and seemingly never more than a whisper away, waiting to meet your needs. The rooms, too, are a marvel of luxury, with marble bathrooms standard. The best rooms face west (be sure to request a balcony), with the lush green tapestry of the zoo just below and the haunting form of the pyramids hovering in the distance. **Pros:** Spacious rooms (standard rooms start at 452 square feet); there's a shopping mall attached to the hotel. **Cons:** The eastward Nile-view rooms face a residential tower; the swimming pool is in shade for all but a few hours a day, so don't come here for a tan. ⊠*35 Giza St., Giza* ☎*02/3568– 1212* ⊕*www.fourseasons.com* ⇆*226 rooms, 43 suites* ♿*In-room: safe, Internet. In-hotel: 3 restaurants, room service, bars, pool, gym, spa, laundry service, Wi-Fi, no-smoking rooms* ☰*AE, MC, V* ⦿*EP.*

$$$$ ⊡ **Mena House Oberoi.** This is *the* great colonial-era hotel in Cairo and
★ has hosted almost every politician, celebrity, and member of royalty to visit Egypt. It began life in the mid-19th century as a khedivial hunting lodge, but there have been a number of expansions over the years. Of course, it is the view of the pyramids—they are so close you can almost touch them—that will leave you gasping, and rooms with a view are in high demand. The old section is a thousandfold more atmospheric than the newer garden wing. There is a clear hierarchy of rooms here,

2

and the best of them go fast, so book six months or more in advance. In truth, group bookings keep the hotel sold-out virtually year-round, so it's easier to book through a connected travel agent if you are traveling independently. **Pros:** Proximity to the pyramids cannot be beaten; the main building oozes period charm. **Cons:** It's at least 45 minutes from Downtown Cairo, so you might consider a one-night stay only for the day you visit the pyramids; some rooms need to be renovated; only the suites in the main building have period furniture. ⊠ *Shar'a al-Haram, Giza* ☎*02/3377–3222* ⊕*www.oberoihotels.com* ⟿*498 rooms, 25 suites* ⚷*In-room: DVD, Internet. In-hotel: 5 restaurants, room service, bars, golf course, pool, gym, spa, laundry service, parking (free)* ☰*AE, DC, MC, V* ⦿*EP.*

$$ ⚏**Swiss Inn.** This 14-story hotel opened in 2008. Everything is clean and modern, with tile and marble in the public spaces and the rooms, but the atmosphere is more appropriate to an up-market motel rather than a full-service hotel. There's a kitschy roof pool in the shape of a boat plus a shisha café and seating area. **Pros:** Equidistant between downtown and the pyramids (about 20 minutes to either by taxi); views of the city and of the pyramids from the roof terrace. **Cons:** Music around the pool can be too loud; there's little around the hotel beyond the Pharaonic Village theme park, so it's a taxi ride to anywhere; beds are narrow and won't suit tall or wide travelers; only one dedicated no-smoking room per floor. ⊠ *110 Shar'a El Bahr El Aazzam, Corniche al-Nil, Giza* ☎*02/3776–6501* ⊕*www.swissinn.net* ⟿*90 rooms, 9 suites* ⚷*In-room: safe, Internet. In-hotel: restaurant, room service, bars, pool, laundry service, Internet terminal, no-smoking rooms.* ☰*AE, DC, MC, V* ⦿*BP.*

NIGHTLIFE & THE ARTS

The Cairo cultural scene defies preconceptions. You can go to a concert of classical Arabic music in a restored medieval house, watch dervishes whirl in an old palace, then take in a performance of *La Bohème* by the Cairo Opera Company, and end the night on a club's dance floor. Layered around this traditional cultural season is a thriving and hip nightlife scene that's one of the best in the Middle East, with bars and clubs that attract vacationing Gulf Arabs as well as Western visitors and expats. Occasionally the two meet in a fusion style—a jazz concert of trumpet and *oud* (an Arabic stringed instrument), for example—that is unique to this city. For the latest listings and movies, check the English-language *al-Ahram Weekly, Middle East Times,* the weekly *Cairo Times,* or the monthly *Egypt Today.* Always call ahead to double-check performances because arrangements can and do go awry.

THE ARTS

ART GALLERIES

Centre des Arts (✉1 *Mahad al-Swissri, Zamalek* ☎02/2340–8211) is a state-run gallery in an old villa that hosts the annual Youth Salon, which gives a good survey (the work can be of mixed quality) of what is happening in the local art scene.

Duroub Gallery (✉4 *Shar'a Latin America, Garden City* ☎02/2794–7951) offers a variety of thematic exhibitions throughout the year.

El Sakia (✉*Shar'a 26 Yulyu, Zamalek* ☎02/2736–6178 ⊕*www.culturewheel.org*), which can be translated as "The Waterwheel," is the legacy of writer and novelist Adel-Moneim El Sawy. It's a cultural center offering writing workshops, literary seminars, film screenings, musical performances, and art exhibitions. The programs cut across all genres.

Mashrabia Gallery (✉8 *Shar'a Champollion, Downtown* ☎02/2578–4494 ⊕*www.mashrabiagallery.com*) shows all the best contemporary artists in Egypt—including Adel al-Siwi, Muhammad Abla, Rehab al-Sadek, Hamdi Atteya, and Awad al-Shimy. The exhibits change monthly, and there is a small shop in the back. The gallery is generally open Saturday through Thursday from 11 to 8.

The Townhouse Gallery (✉10 *Shara'a Nawbawy, off Shar'a Champollion, Downtown* ☎02/2576–8086 ⊕*www.thetownhousegallery.com*) is an eclectic space showcasing the work of contemporary artists. Part of it is a converted factory space that hosts live performances, film screenings, and lectures in addition to art exhibitions.

The World of Art Gallery (✉6 *Shar'a 77C, Gold Area, Ma'adi* ☎02/2351–4362) offers a mixed program of exhibitions by local and regional artists.

FILM

Multiscreen cinema complexes are springing up all over the city, usually linked to major malls. Foreign films are subtitled in Arabic and usually start 30 minutes after the scheduled time (arriving 15 minutes after that time is usually fine). All theaters have reserved seating. Also note that most embassies have cultural centers that show original-language (and uncensored) movies—these are well worth looking into if you're in the mood to see a film.

Good News Cinema (✉*Galleria Mall, Grand Hyatt Hotel, Corniche al-Nil, Rodah Island* ☎02/2362–8400) is a small cinema with a program of popular hits. **Golden Stars Cinema** (✉*Citystars Mall, Shar'a Ibn El Khattab, Heliopolis* ☎02/2480–0533 ⊕*www.citystars.com.eg*) is a multiscreen movie house showing Arabic- and English-language films. **Metro Theatre** (✉35 *Shar'a Talaat Harb, Downtown* ☎02/2393–7566) is a downtown, streetside movie theater. The top floor of the **Ramses Hilton Annex** (✉1115 *Corniche al-Nil, Downtown* ☎02/2461–9102), a shopping mall next to the hotel, has long been a popular choice for the latest English-language films. **Renaissance Cinemas** (✉*Nile Towers Mall* *at Nile City, Corniche al-Nil, Downtown* ☎*02/2461–9000* ⊕*www. nilecitytowers.com*) is a multiscreen complex with the latest hits.

DANCE, OPERA & MUSIC

Al-Ghuri Cultural Palace (✉*Qasr al-Ghuri, Shar'a al-Mu'iz, Islamic Cairo South* ☎*02/2510–0823*) offers regular whirling dervish and Arabic music performances in a medieval mansion setting.

Al-Hanager (✉*Shar'a Tahrir, Gezira* ☎*02/2735–6861*), part of the Opera House complex—but intended as a space for experimental performing arts—hosts some of Cairo's most interesting music and dance. The complex is currently undergoing a renovation, but some elements always remain open. There are also a café and gallery on-site.

Gomhouriya Theater (✉*12 Shar'a Gomhouriya, Abdin* ☎*02/2739–0114*) hosts many good visiting artists, who perform at this surprisingly elegant theater near Abdin Palace.

Cairo's **Opera House** (✉*Shar'a Tahrir, Gezira* ☎*02/2739–0114 for ticket office* ⊕*www.cairoopera.org*) is the home hall for the Cairo Opera Company. Although not quite of international standard, the opera has an excellent soprano in Italian-trained Iman Mustafa. And the collection of performing arts companies housed here is unparalleled in Africa. There are also resident Western and Arabic orchestras in addition to a constant stream of visiting artists. Pick an event from the newspaper and go. Note that jacket and tie are compulsory in the Main Hall but not in the others.

NIGHTLIFE

Cairo's nightlife scene is certainly cool, but most locations defy easy definition, moving seamlessly from early evening cocktail lounge to mid-evening eatery to late-night dance venue. The clientele is a cosmopolitan mix of wealthy Egyptians, foreign residents and workers, and a mix of international visitors. In summer, Cairo is a great playground for visitors from Gulf countries, many of whom come to enjoy the city's clubs and bars. Popular clubs usually close around 2 AM, though some close earlier.

BARS

Absolute (✉*8 Maydan Amman, Mohandiseen* ☎*02/2579–6512*) has an in-house DJ concentrating on Arabic techno music. Absolute attracts wealthy Egyptians in their twenties and thirties. It's one of the city's exclusive venues, so dress up, and if you're coming with a group, reserve a table. It generally closes around 2 AM.

★ **Buddha Bar** (✉*Sofitel El-Gezirah, 3 Shar'a El Thawra Council, Zamalek* ☎*02/2737–3737*) is one of the world's coolest brands and has found a home on the banks of the Nile, where its Asian-influenced decor gets a few pharaonic additions. There's a contemporary fusion menu, great cocktails, and chill-out sounds mixed under the Buddha Bar label.

Hard Rock Café (⊠ *Grand Hyatt, Corniche al-Nil,, Rodah Island* ☎ *02/2532–1277*) has a great staff, who do a creditable job with their dance routines, so the place is full of energy by 10 PM. It's no different than any other Hard Rock, but don't forget the souvenir T-shirt before you leave.

Jazz Club (⊠ *197 Shar'a 26 Yulyu, next to 15th of May Bridge, Mohandiseen* ☎ *02/3345–9939*) has dark, scruffy decor that isn't much to look at, but this is far and away the best place to hear live music in the city—not that there is much competition. Regular bands play a fusion of Western and Arab styles that always has the twenty-something crowd on its feet.

Le Tabasco (⊠ *8 Amman Sq., Mohandiseen* ☎ *02/3336–5583*), which has no sign or windows, is hard to find—look for the bouncer standing outside—but this seductively lit subterranean nightclub is easily Cairo's coolest bar scene. Look hip and go early if you want to eat dinner, because by 10 it starts to fill up with funky twenty-something Egyptians, and it doesn't empty until late.

The rooftop **Odeon Palace Bar** (⊠ *Odeon Palace Hotel, 6 Shar'a Abdel Hamid, Downtown* ☎ *02/2577–6637*) continues to attract crowds for its laid-back ambiance despite the fact that the hotel has passed its prime. Relax on the low couches and enjoy *shisha* and views across the Downtown skyline.

Pub 28 (⊠ *Shar'a Shagaret El Dorr, Zamalek* ☎ *02/2735–9200*)is the perfect destination if you just want a few beers in a neighborhood bar with a friendly bunch of expats.

Sangria (⊠ *Casino El-Shagara, Corniche al-Nil, Downtown* ☎ *02/2579–6511*) is part restaurant, part lounge, and definitely one of the "in" places in Cairo for its relaxed ambiance.

Fodor'sChoice
★ **Sequoia** (⊠ *Shar'a Abdul Feda, Zamalek* ☎ *02/2735–0014*), an atmospheric tented venue on the banks of the Nile, offers a contemporary menu that attracts as many people for dinner as for the laid-back ambiance and great music. Come for a meal, and you can stay till the place closes.

Windows on the World (⊠ *Ramses Hilton, 1115 Corniche al-Nil, Downtown* ☎ *02/2577–7444*), which is on the top floor of the Ramses Hilton, draws a forties-plus crowd for the late-night views and musicians playing softly in the background.

The downtown **Windsor Hotel** (⊠ *19 Shar'a Alfi Bey, Downtown* ☎ *02/2591–5277*) has a quiet and comfortable bar with a pre-revolutionary style that is better for a relaxing over an early-evening beer than for late-night reveling (it closes at 1 AM).

BELLY DANCING

What was once a favorite performing art is falling out of favor with both Egyptians and visitors. Your best bet if you want to see tame versions of these once risqué performances is to visit one of the major hotels in the city. Belly dancers will normally gyrate for 15 or 30 minutes nightly at their signature Middle Eastern/Lebanese restaurants. At this writing, only a couple of hotels still offer dancers.

Abu Nawass Nightclub (⊠ *Oberoi Mena House Hotel, Pyramids Rd., Giza* ☎ *02/3377–3222*) has nightly performances from 10 PM. **Empress Lounge** (⊠ *Cairo Marriott Hotel, Shar'a Saray al-Gezira, Zamalek* ☎ *02/2728–3000*) has nightly shows along with singing performances.

CAFÉS

International coffee chains have arrived in Egypt, so there's no need to miss out on your favorite caffeine hit. However, Cairo has its own café culture, where you can be assured of a freshly brewed espresso or cappuccino, though you'll find that Egyptians will more often take tea.

Fodor's Choice
★ **El Fishawy** (⊠ *5 Sikkit Khan al-Khalili, Khan al-Khalili, Islamic Cairo North*) is right in the heart of the medieval marketplace; this is *the* great café in Cairo, open around the clock and beloved by tourists and locals alike. The chairs spill out into the alley, and the walls are hung with thick, old-style mirrors decorated with elaborate woodwork. Tea with fresh mint is the house specialty.

The Promenade (⊠ *Cairo Marriott, Shar'a Saray al-Gezira, Zamalek* ☎ *02/2340–8888*), which is in the gardens flanked by the restored palace that serves as the lobby of the Cairo Marriott, is the best place to spend a summer night. The place is immensely popular with Gulf Arabs; it serves food and alcohol. It's open until 2 AM from May through October, until 6 PM from November through April.

Trianon (⊠ *Arkadia Mall, Corniche al-Nil, Downtown* ☎ *19020 (in Egypt only)*) is one of a chain of cafés with branches throughout Egypt. It serves delicious coffee and mouthwatering pastries and cakes.

CASINOS

Most major five-star hotels have casinos that are open until sunrise, with all the usual games (roulette, blackjack, slot machines, and so forth), and horrifically poor odds. The best of them is the **Omar Khayyam** (⊠ *Cairo Marriott, Shar'a Saray al-Gezira, Zamalek* ☎ *02/2728–3000*), which is open 24 hours and plies gamblers with free drinks as long as they're playing.

DANCE CLUBS

After Eight (⊠ *6 Shar'a Qasr al-Nil, Downtown* ☎ *02/2574–0855*) has been on the scene for many years and gone through many reincarnations, but this night-spot still pulls in the crowds. There's a resident DJ as well as a program of live bands.

Bliss (⊠ *Imperial Boat, Shar'a Saray al-Gezira, Zamalek* ☎ *02/2736–5796*) will probably have either full-on house or techno music playing, but it's always right up to date with the current club music trends and attracts a predominately younger crowd.

Morocco (⊠ *Blue Nile Boat, Shar'a Saray al-Gezira, Zamalek* ☎ *02/2735–3314*) occupies part of a stationary Nile cruise ship. Morocco has a resident DJ who flips between 1980s disco and contemporary dance, trance, and techno. For this reason it attracts cosmopolitan crowds that span the age range from teens to 40s.

SHOPPING

Cairo has always been a great place to shop for traditional items because of its spectacular medieval marketplace, the Khan al-Khalili, where browsing and bargaining are half the fun. There is no tried-and-true bargaining strategy; just shop around, decide how much something is worth to you, and start bargaining lower than that in order to end up at that point. In the Khan, the opening price is *never* the final price.

In the last decade Cairo has embraced the shopping mall. These enclosed, air-conditioned spaces stacked with international brands have revolutionized shopping for residents. Most malls also have shops selling a range of the same kinds of souvenirs that you'd find in the Khan al-Khalili, though at higher, nonnegotiable prices.

Wealthy and upwardly mobile Cairenes not only have the wherewithal to fund their lifestyles, but they also have great taste, so you'll find a wide selection of art galleries, designer shops, and fashion boutiques to indulge your need for retail therapy.

SHOPPING CENTERS & MARKETS

MARKETS

Fodor'sChoice
★
Cairo shopping starts at the **Khan al-Khalili** (⊠ *Islamic Cairo North*), the great medieval souk. Although it has been on every tourist's itinerary for centuries, and some of its more visible wares can seem awfully tacky, the Khan is where everyone—newcomer and age-old Cairene alike—goes to find traditional items: jewelry, lamps, spices, clothes, textiles, handicrafts, water pipes, metalwork, you name it. Whatever it is, you can find it somewhere in this skein of alleys or the streets around them. Every Khan veteran has the shops he or she swears by—usually because of the fact (or illusion) she or he is known there personally and is thus less likely to be overcharged. Go, browse, and bargain hard. Once you buy something, don't ask how much it costs at the next shop; you'll be happier that way. Many shops close Sunday.

SHOPPING MALLS

Arkadia Mall (⊠ *Corniche al-Nil,, Downtown* ☎ *02/2575–5578*) is the largest downtown mall, with more than 500 shops plus an arcade with games to keep the kids happy. **City Stars** (⊠ *Shar'a Hashad, Heliopolis* ☎ *02/2480–0500* ⊕ *www.citystars.com.eg*), Cairo's mega mall, is huge, with more than 500 stores. There are also three hotels and a variety of restaurants and cafés plus two food courts. The **Galleria** (⊠ *Grand Hyatt, Corniche al-Nil, Rodah Island* ☎ *02/2356–1234*), which is attached to the Grand Hyatt, has a small selection of individual boutiques, but it's anchored by a 12-screen cinema complex. **Towers Mall** (⊠ *Nile City Towers, Corniche al-Nil, Bulaq* ☎ *02/2461–9000*), underpinning two vast office blocks (plus the new Fairmont

Nile Towers hotel), caters to upwardly mobile executives and office workers. There's also a multi-screen cinema on-site. **Maadi City Centre** (✉ *Maadi/Katyama Ring Road, Ma'adi* ☎ *02/2520–4000* ⊕ *www. maadicitycentre.com*) is a small mall that's a resource for the many families in this residential district; there are few designer names but lots of mainstream brands. The mall is anchored by a major supermarket.

Mall at First Residence (✉ *First Residence Complex, 35 Shar'a al-Giza, Giza* ☎ *02/3571–7806*) is a series of up-market boutiques selling jewelry, designer clothing, and elegant housewares in a series of galleries around an open atrium. There's a café on the ground floor.

SPECIALTY STORES

ANTIQUES & AUCTION HOUSES

Although most of what you see are reproductions of varying quality, there is a long local tradition in Egypt of connoisseurship in collectibles, which means that there is always the possibility of finding a real gem. Be prepared, however, for local tastes that favor ornate French-style furniture and antiques, not the Middle Eastern pieces you might be longing for. There are several nameless antiques shops in downtown Cairo along Shar'a Hoda Sharaawi that are worth looking into. Lots are shown for several days in advance of a two-day auction, which usually operates on a cash-only basis. Check the *Egyptian Gazette* for the latest auction schedules.

One of the best auction houses in town is **Catsaros** (✉ *22 Shar'a Gawad Hosni, Downtown* ☎ *02/2392–6123*), in an unmarked alley off Shar'a Qasr al-Nil.

To get to **Osiris** (✉ *17 Shar'a Sherif, Downtown*), a good auction house, look for a small blue sign on the building's second floor.

Ahmed Mostafa Hassan (✉ *4 Shar'a El Kadi El Fadil, off Qasr al-Nil, Downtown* ☎ *02/2392–5095*) is a source for antiques and collectibles of all kinds—from wooden doors taken from old palaces to colonial-era metal advertising hoardings. There are several rooms here full of stuff.

ART GALLERIES

Mashrabia Gallery (✉ *8 Shar'a Champollion, Downtown* ☎ *02/2578–4494*) is on the tree-lined Shar'a Champollion (the street named after the Frenchman who broke the hieroglyphic code), and it's Cairo's best contemporary-art gallery. The space itself is not much to look at, but the quality of work is sometimes exceptional. Be on the lookout for exhibitions by Adel al-Siwi, Muhammad Abla, Rehab al-Sadek, Hamdi Atteya, or Awad al-Shimy. The gallery is open Saturday through Thursday from 11 to 8.

ARTS & CRAFTS

Al Khatoun (✉ *3 Shar'a Mohamed Abdou (behind Al-Azhar Mosque), Old Cairo Islamic Cairo South* ☎ *02/2514–7164*) is in a renovated yet still run-down workshop and is an outlet for varied local artists and artisans including weavers, potters, and woodworkers. Styles vary from the traditional to the contemporary. **Fair Trade Egypt** (✉ *27 Shar'*

Yahia Ibrahim, First floor, Apt. 8, Zamalek ☎*02/2736–5123*) sells an interesting selection of handmade items from more than 40 artisans and cooperatives around Egypt, including crafts from the Western desert oases, Fayyum, and Upper Egypt. Prices are fixed and, as the name suggests, fair for the producers. **Nomad** (✉*Cairo Marriott, Shar'a Saray al-Gezira, Zamalek* ☎*02/2736–1917*) offers relatively inexpensive, vaguely Bedouin-style jewelry, along with some interesting textiles from Siwa Oasis and the Sinai. There is another branch at the Grand Hyatt Hotel.

BOOKSTORES & NEWSSTANDS

For a surprisingly extensive selection of foreign-language newspapers and magazines, try any major hotel bookshop or the cluster of stands at the corner of Shar'a Hassan Sabri and Shar'a 26 Yulyu in Zamalek. Alternatively, try the one near the McDonald's across from the entrance to the American University in Cairo.

The **Anglo-Egyptian Bookstore** (✉*165 Shar'a Muhammad Farid, Downtown* ☎*02/2391–4237*) has an excellent selection of books, especially the nonfiction offerings. It's open Monday through Saturday from 9 to 1:30 and 4:30 to 8.

L'Orientaliste (✉*15 Shar'a Qasr al-Nil, Downtown* ☎*02/2575–3418*) is the best source in Cairo for old books, antique maps, and postcards. It's open Monday through Saturday from 10 to 7:30.

The **Virgin Megastore** (✉*City Stars Mall, Heliopolis* ☎*02/2480–2244*) offers a good choice of English-language reading from magazines to hardcover books, as well as music, films, and games.

FURNITURE

Mit Rehan (✉*13 Shar'a Mara'ashly, Zamalek* ☎*02/2735–4578*) is the best source for modern Egyptian furniture—which means Islamic or pharaonic motifs applied to traditional pieces, like mashrabiyya screens, or to Western-style pieces, like sofas. It's open Monday through Saturday from 10 to 8.

JEWELRY

Azza Fahmy (✉*73 Shar'a El Hussein, Dokki* ☎*02/3338–1342*), Egypt's leading jewelry designer, has become an international brand in the last five years with her traditional motif-inspired pieces. A purchase here is a genuine designed-in-Egypt souvenir. Other branches are at First Mall and Beyman Store at Four Seasons Hotel at Nile Plaza.

SIDE TRIPS FROM CAIRO

In order that the living could view the grandeur of the dead god–kings—and, in many cases, be buried alongside them—ancient Egyptians used the sites in the desert west of Memphis, one of the most enduring of ancient capitals, for their royal necropolises. These sites are filled with tombs from all periods of Egyptian history. Just beyond Cairo proper on the Nile's west bank, stand the monuments most closely identified with Egypt: the timeless Sphinx and the Pyramids of Giza. But slightly farther away lie the pyramids of Abu Sir, Saqqara, Dahshur, and the site of Memphis. Most of the visitable pharaonic sites in the environs of Cairo date from the Old Kingdom (2575–2134 BC), although these sites also contain monuments and statuary from the Middle and New Kingdoms and later.

Driving to the various Memphite cemeteries from central Cairo takes one to two hours, depending on which places you decide to visit. Part of the road to Abu Sir, Saqqara, Dahshur, and Memphis follows a canal and passes through small villages, fields, and palm orchards, which is soothing compared to the drive to Giza. Seeing Abu Sir should take a leisurely 1½ hours; Saqqara can take from four hours to an entire day. For Memphis an hour is more than enough, but allow two for Dahshur. Taking in a combination of sites in one day can be very pleasant—Giza and Saqqara; Abu Sir, Saqqara, and Memphis; Dahshur and Saqqara, and so forth. The Fayyum, Egypt's largest oasis, is farther south of Cairo, and the Wadi Natrun monasteries are northwest of Cairo; both require more travel time but can still be visited on day trips.

MEMPHIS

29 km (18 mi) southeast of Cairo.

Memphis was the first capital of unified Egypt, founded in 3100 BC by King Narmer. Little is visible of the grandeur of ancient Memphis, save for what is found in the museum and some excavated areas (not open to the public as yet), that include the sites of temples to various gods and a curious embalming area used to mummify the sacred Apis bulls. Most of the monuments of Memphis were robbed throughout history for their stone. This stone, together with that stripped from the casings of various pyramids, was used to build Cairo. Most of the other remains of the ancient city are covered by the modern village of Badrasheen, noted for its palm-rib furniture industry.

The **museum** enclosure encompasses all of what is viewable in Memphis. The most dramatic object is the colossal limestone statue of Ramesses II (1290–1224 BC) that lies within the museum proper. There is a viewing balcony that runs around the statue and provides good views of it from above. The statue shows fine details like a very elaborately carved dagger at the pharaoh's waist. Outside the museum building, a sculpture garden contains a scattered assortment of statuary, coffins, and architectural fragments recovered from the area of Memphis. The Egyptian alabaster sphinx is one of the larger sphinxes found in Egypt, and there are several statues of Ramesses II in granite and limestone. A curious sarcophagus carved upside down also lies in the garden, as well as columns decorated with textile motifs, dating to the later periods of Egyptian history. A series of stalls selling replicas of Egyptian artifacts is set up on one side of the garden. Quality varies, but on the whole you can find some attractive items here. ⊠ *Mit Rahineh Rd., Mit Rahineh, 3 km (2 mi) west of Badrasheen* 🕾 *No phone* ⊠ *£e35* ⊘ *Daily 8–4.*

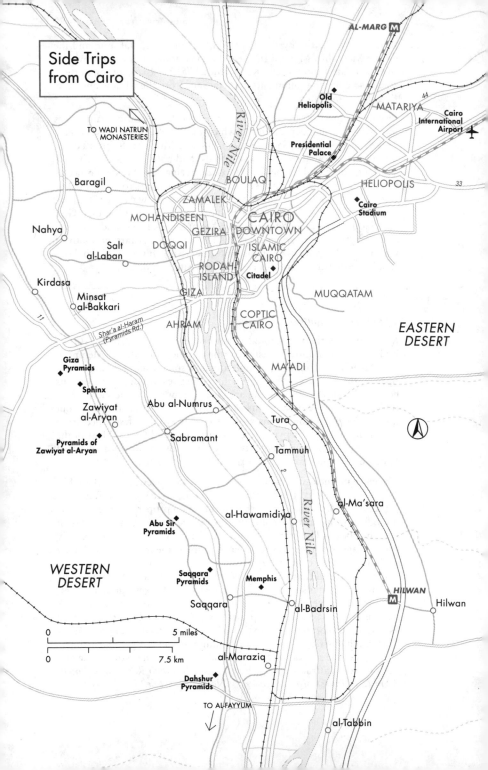

Side Trips from Cairo

AL-MARG Ⓜ

Old Heliopolis

44

MATARIYA

Cairo International Airport ✈

TO WADI NATRUN MONASTERIES

River Nile

Presidential Palace

33

HELIOPOLIS

BOULAQ

Baragil

ZAMALEK

Cairo Stadium

MOHANDISEEN

GEZIRA

CAIRO DOWNTOWN

Nahya

DOQQI

Salt al-Laban

ISLAMIC CAIRO

RODAH ISLAND

Kirdasa

GIZA

Citadel

MUQQATAM

Minsat al-Bakkari

AHRAM

COPTIC CAIRO

11

Shar'a al-Haram (Pyramids Rd.)

EASTERN DESERT

Giza Pyramids

MA'ADI

Sphinx

Abu al-Numrus

Zawiyat al-Aryan

Tura

Sabramant

Pyramids of Zawiyat al-Aryan

Tammuh

2

al-Ma'sara

al-Hawamidiya

River Nile

Abu Sir Pyramids

WESTERN DESERT

Saqqara Pyramids

Memphis

HILWAN Ⓜ

Hilwan

Saqqara

al-Badrsin

0   5 miles

0   7.5 km

al-Maraziq

Dahshur Pyramids

TO AL-FAYYUM
↓

al-Tabbin

GETTING THERE & AROUND

The site of ancient Memphis is traversable by foot. The best way to get here is by hired car or with a tour. Combine it with Saqqara, or Giza and Saqqara—you needn't stop here for more than a half hour.

ABU SIR

23 km (14 mi) southwest of Cairo.

Abu Sir is the site of four pyramids—three of which are obvious, the fourth one less so—all dating to the 5th Dynasty (2465–2323 BC), as well as several mastabas and shaft tombs. The area has been the scene of much excitement because, in 1997–98, a Czech team of archaeologists came upon an intact shaft tomb of an official who lived sometime between 525 and 340 BC. This tomb is not open to the public at this writing; plans to make it visitable have been delayed. Abu Sir itself has been open to the public only sporadically, which means that the rather beautiful site nestled at the edge of the desert is rarely visited and free of tourists and touts. You can wander around the ruins, but the pyramids and other intact structures are closed to visitors at this writing.

The three pyramids that greet you when you arrive at Abu Sir are those of Sahure, Nyuserre, and Neferirkare. These—especially the pyramid of Sahure—are excellent pyramids to visit, because the whole complex of mortuary temples, valley temples, and a causeway are close together and easily visible.

Sahure's Pyramid, the northernmost of the three, is 257 feet square; its original height was 154 feet. This pyramid complex is typical of royal funerary complexes of the 5th Dynasty (Sahure ruled from 2458 to 2446 BC), and it contains all the elements of a pyramid complex, save boat pits. The pyramid itself is not too impressive, as its poor-quality core masonry collapsed after the Tura limestone casing stones were removed. Its interior has been closed to visitors since a 1992 earthquake rendered its internal structure unstable.

The mortuary temple is very pleasant to wander through, with its granite pillars, stairs leading to a now nonexistent second floor, and fine basalt pavement. It is one of the few mortuary temples found in Egypt that retains a sense of its ancient grandeur. The causeway was decorated with finely carved scenes (now removed from the site) showing archery and fighting. There is much less left of the valley temple: a pavement, some doorways, and a scattering of fallen blocks. The area of the valley temple is wet, because it is close to the water table.

Nyuserre's Pyramid is 265 feet square, and it was originally 169 feet tall. Not much is left of this pyramid because the casing stones and part of the limestone core were removed and burned for lime in the 19th century. The builder of this pyramid complex, Nyuserre (2416–2392 BC), usurped the valley temple and causeway of Neferirkare Kakai's Pyramid, which are therefore not directly aligned to the east of this pyramid but are at an angle out toward their original owner's pyramid.

Neferirkare's Pyramid is the largest on the Abu Sir site—344 feet square and originally 229 feet tall. The pyramid complex was meant to be larger than that of Sahure, but the pharaoh died prior to its completion. The pyramid itself, however, does dominate the site. Nyuserre usurped the causeway and valley temple, completed them, and appended them to his pyramid complex, leaving Neferirkare (2446–2426 BC) with only a pyramid and a mortuary temple that was completed after his death in cheap mud brick rather than limestone or granite.

The very large **Mastaba of Ptahshepses** lies between Sahure and Nyuserre's pyramids. The tomb is noted more for its size than for any remains of decoration. To the southwest is a double room that might have held boats, an unusual feature for a private tomb. The entire tomb is now completely inaccessible. ✉ *Off the Abu Sir village road* ☎ *No phone* 🎫 *£e20* ⊙ *Daily 8–4.*

GETTING THERE & AROUND
It is best to visit Abu Sir in conjunction with some combination of Giza, Memphis, Saqqara, and Dahshur. Either go with a tour or hire a taxi from your hotel or on the street (in the latter case, remember to bargain). To reach the site, go on the Saqqara Road, turn off for Saqqara, then turn right at the canal before reaching the Saqqara ticket booth, which is marked with a large blue-and-white sign. Continue down the road through the village, then follow the sign pointing left over a bridge that spans the canal. If you get lost, ask villagers for the Athar wa Haram Abu Sir. Walking is the best way to see the site itself.

SAQQARA

25 km (16 mi) southwest of Cairo.

Approached through orchards of waving palm trees, Saqqara is best known for being the site of the earliest stone pyramid constructed in Egypt, the Step Pyramid of Djoser. The site encompasses at least four other pyramid complexes of different dates, countless tombs from all eras of Egyptian history, as well as several animal necropolises, the most notable of which is the Serapeum. Much active archaeological work is being done at Saqqara by both Egyptian and foreign teams. In the 1990s, a French team found the rock-cut tomb of Maya, the wet-nurse of Tutankhamun, at the edge of the plateau. This find complements the earlier finds of the tombs of Maya (the treasurer), Horemheb, and Aparel, all of whom were active during the reign of Tutankhamun.

Saqqara is large, sprawling, and best covered on foot and by car. A suggested route, which depends somewhat on which tombs are open to the public when you visit, is to start at the Step Pyramid complex and the Imhotep Museum; from there visit the Pyramid of Unas, which you can reach on foot. Then return to the car, drive to the Mastaba of Mereruka and the Pyramid of Teti, then drive to the Serapeum if it is open. If you have more time, visit the Tomb of Ti near the Serapeum. There are other mastabas open near the Step Pyramid, as well as the Mastaba of Ptahhotep near the Serapeum. See these if you have time,

2

energy, and interest. The ticket booth is at the main entrance to the site, and a ticket covering the majority of the sites in Saqqara is £e60.

One of the best places to really feel the energy of the pyramid-building era, the **Imhotep Museum** brings together a collection of artifacts and state-of-the-art educational aids to add background to this pivotal era in the development of civilization. Highlights of the seven-room museum, which was opened in 2006, include a set of the blue and turquoise tiles that decorated the interior of Djoser's pyramid, remains of a seated Djoser, and the feet of Imhotep on a monumental base. ⊠*At the ticket office for the Saqqara Monuments* ☎*No phone* ᐧ*£e60, as*

★ *part of the Saqqara general admission* ☉*Daily 9–4.* **Kagemni's Mastaba** adjoins the mastaba of Mereruka and is also well decorated. Presumably the artist or atelier responsible for decorating the mastabas in this area was the same, because certain scenes keep reappearing, such as the force-feeding, the poultry yards, and the tomb owner being carried about on a chair. ᐧ*£e60, as part of the Saqqara general admis-*

★ *sion* ☉*Daily 8–4.* **Mereruka's Mastaba,** shared by his son and his wife, is the largest mastaba tomb in Saqqara. It dates to the 6th Dynasty (2323–2150 BC) and shows some of the finest scenes of fishing, hunting, metalworking (note the dwarfs), sailing, and force-feeding of animals, including a hyena in the statue chamber. A statue of Mereruka emerging from a niche marks the main offering spot for his cult. ᐧ*£e60, as*

★ *part of the Saqqara general admission* ☉*Daily 8–4.* The **Niankhkhnum & Khnumhotep's Mastaba** is considered one of the "new tombs" that have been excavated in Saqqara since the late 1990s and shares a separate admission with seven other tombs (the others are not terribly noteworthy but can be visited if you have extra time). This one dates from the 5th Dynasty and is also known as the Tomb of Two Brothers, or the Tomb of the Hairdressers. It's noted for its fine colors, as well as the unusually intimate poses of the two tomb owners. Niankhkhnum and Khnumhotep worked as the pharaoh's body servants, and they were buried together in this exquisitely decorated joint tomb. The scenes in the mastaba are fairly standard, showing everyday activities such as fishing, cooking, hunting, and the processing of foodstuffs. An unusual scene of the tomb owners on donkey back is carved on the second set of door jambs. ᐧ*£e30 as part of the New Tombs ticket* ☉*Daily 8–4.* **The Serapeum** is the site of the burials of the Apis Bulls. The Apis was a bull that was regarded as a manifestation of Ptah, a creator god. During its lifetime, the bull was worshiped, fed, washed, brushed, sung to, and generally made much of. When it died, it was elaborately mummified and buried, with golden grave goods, in a large basalt or granite sarcophagus that was placed in a chamber of the Serapeum. Then the priests embarked on a quest for a new bull, who took up the position of Apis. The dusty and gloomy Serapeum galleries stretch for miles under the bedrock. The Serapeum is closed to the public at this writing. The

★ **Step Pyramid** complex was built in the 3rd Dynasty (2649–2575 BC) for the pharaoh Djoser by his architect Imhotep, and it has been undergoing study and restoration since 1927. This monument has earned Djoser, and more importantly Imhotep, everlasting fame—Imhotep was later deified and regarded as the patron god of architects and doctors.

The base of the pyramid measures 459 feet by 386 feet, and the structure was originally 197 feet tall.

The pyramid complex is completely unlike those of the 4th and 5th Dynasties. It is the first stone pyramid (and complex) to have been built in Egypt, and its form imitates wood, papyrus, mud brick, and matting in limestone. The Step Pyramid itself was begun as a mastaba tomb, but its design was modified six times before the final, six-stepped pyramid emerged. The structure was enlarged by accreting vertical faces, visible on the east side as you walk around the pyramid rather than by stacking mastabas on top of one another.

You enter the complex from a small doorway that leads through a long passage flanked by columns that in turn leads to the vast open Heb-Sed court. The Heb-Sed was a race that the pharaoh had to run every 30 years, theoretically, in order to reaffirm his strength, power, and ability to rule—and to renew the favor of the gods. After he successfully completed the race, the pharaoh would officiate and participate in religious rituals that emphasized the support of the gods for his reign and the fealty of his nobles and governors. These ceremonies took place in the adjoining courtyard, which is flanked by shrines.

The simple mortuary temple attached to the pyramid is to the north rather than to the east. Just before reaching it is a small structure, the *serdab* (a small room containing the statue of the deceased). It contains a statue of the pharaoh—a plaster cast, as the original is in the Egyptian Antiquities Museum—that was placed there to receive offerings. The substructure is closed to the public because it is unstable, but you can view it from a window that has been constructed.

The site of Djoser's Pyramid was a great attraction in antiquity: As the graffiti attests, people came here as tourists and seekers of blessings from as early as the Middle Kingdom (2040–1640 BC), if not earlier. Portions of the pyramid were restored in the 26th Dynasty. 🖾 *£e60, as part of the Saqqara general admission* ☉ *Daily 8–4.* **Teti's Pyramid** measures 257 feet square and originally rose to 172 feet. Recognizing this as a pyramid is quite difficult, because the casing stones were stolen and the structure has been reduced to a pile of rubble. The site has two queens' pyramids to the east and north, which are virtually indistinguishable from the sand, and a mortuary temple to the east. The burial chamber, with its pointed roof, is decorated with pyramid texts and contains a basalt sarcophagus. Teti ruled from 2323–2291 BC. 🖾 *£e60, as part of the Saqqara general admission* ☉ *Daily 8–4.* **Ti's Mastaba** is architecturally different from the mastabas of Mereruka and Kagemni in that it has a large courtyard that contains a stairway leading to Ti's burial chamber, which still contains his sarcophagus. The rest of the tomb is exquisitely decorated and painted, with the original roof preserved throughout much of the tomb. A statue—it is a reproduction—of Ti is visible in the serdab. ⊠ *Athar Saqqara* ☎ *no phone* 🖾 *£e60, as part of the Saqqara general admission* ☉ *Daily 8–4.* **Unas' Pyramid** was the last pyramid built in the 5th Dynasty, and it was the first to contain a burial chamber decorated with the pyramid texts, a set of spells to ensure that the pharaoh had a successful afterlife. The pyramid occupies an area 188 feet square; its original height was 141 feet. The mortuary temple, on the east side, is ruined, save for the pavement, some column fragments, and a doorway leading to the causeway. The causeway is decorated in places with scenes of markets, transporting columns, wild animals, and so forth. To the south lie two empty boat pits. At the end of the causeway stand the remains of the valley temple. ✉️ *£e60, as part of the Saqqara general admission ⊙ Daily 8–4.*

GETTING THERE & AROUND

You can get to Saqqara either by signing up for an organized tour or by hiring a taxi for the day from your hotel or the street (bargain hard). It is best to combine Saqqara with one or more sites, such as Memphis and Abu Sir, or with Giza. One of the more adventurous ways to combine Saqqara and Giza is to join one of the many horseback-riding tours offered by the stables near the Giza pyramids. These lead you around the Giza Plateau, through the desert, on to Saqqara and back, for about the same price as taking a taxi. Saqqara is best seen via a combination of walking and driving or on horseback.

DAHSHUR

33 km (21 mi) southeast of Cairo.

Dahshur is one of the most tranquil and awe-inspiring pyramid sites. It contains five pyramids dating from the Old and Middle Kingdoms, of which three are obvious; only one—the Red Pyramid—can be entered. A suggested itinerary for the site is to drive to the first pyramid on the left of the entrance. After you take it in, drive over to the Bent Pyramid. You can walk around this, then over to the Black Pyramid (this is optional and takes about half an hour or so), and then return to the car.

The **North Pyramid** *(Red Pyramid)*—named for the pinkish limestone of which it is made—belonged to the 4th-Dynasty pharaoh Sneferu (2575–2551 BC), father of Khufu. It is 721 square feet and was originally 341 feet tall—just a little smaller than Khufu's Great Pyramid. It marks the first successful attempt at building a true pyramid. This is the second of Sneferu's two pyramids. The other is the Bent Pyramid. Why he commissioned two pyramids is unknown; some scholars believe that Sneferu built this pyramid after the Bent Pyramid because he feared the latter would collapse. The North Pyramid contains three chambers with corbeled roofs and a plethora of 19th-century graffiti. The floor of the topmost chamber was battered by tomb robbers in search of treasure they never found. The **Bent Pyramid,** built for Sneferu, is obviously ★ named for its unique shape, which seems to demonstrate the transition between the step and the true pyramid. It is 599 feet square, and its original height was 344 feet, although it was intended to be 421 feet. It retains much of its limestone cladding.

This was the first pyramid to have been planned as a true pyramid, as opposed to a step pyramid. Its unusual bent angle seems to have occurred because the builders felt that the initial angle was too steep, and that the pyramid would collapse if they did not adjust it. This pyramid is also unusual in that it has two entrances: the typical north-face entrance, and a second in the west face that is just visible above the change in the angle.

Although the pyramid itself was undecorated, its valley temple is among the earliest to be adorned. (None of the decorated portions are at the site; the temple is a bit of a walk to the northeast, and it isn't very rewarding to visit.) The pyramid contains two chambers with corbeled ceilings. A passage from the north entrance leads to the chambers. To the south stands a subsidiary pyramid built of limestone, and on the east are the very ruined remains of a stone and mud-brick mortuary temple.

★ The **Black Pyramid,** which was built for Amenemhet III (1844–1797 BC), was constructed out of mud brick and faced with limestone. The limestone was plundered, leaving only the black mud brick that gives the pyramid its modern name. The pyramid measures 344 feet square and originally rose to 265 feet. The entrance to the burial chamber was not in the north face but outside the pyramid, in a courtyard opposite the southern corner of the east face. The top of the pyramid was crowned by a black basalt pyramidion, now in the Cairo Museum. Amenemhet, like Sneferu, had two pyramids; the other one is in Hawara in the Fayyum. The Black Pyramid is the southernmost of the Dahshur group of pyramids. ⊠ *Al-Haram Dahshur, Menshat Dahshur* ☎ *No phone* ⌕ *£e30 for site and North Pyramid entry* ☉ *Daily 8–4.*

GETTING THERE & AROUND
Combine a trip to Dahshur with Saqqara and Memphis. A taxi or an organized tour are the best ways to get here. Drive down the Saqqara Road, past Saqqara and Memphis, and turn right at the sign for the Dahshur Antiquities. The road goes through the mainly mud-brick village of Dahshur straight into the site. You need to drive around the site, as it is very large.

THE FAYYUM

100 km (62 mi) southwest of Cairo.

The Fayyum is one of the largest and most fertile of all Egyptian oases, with an overall population of about 2 million people. Unlike the Western Desert oases, which are watered by artesian wells, the Fayyum is fed by a small river, the Bahr Yusuf (Joseph's River), which connects with the Nile. The rural Fayyum measures about 65 km (40 mi) from east to west, and the lake, Birket Qarun (which classical writers called Lake Moeris), is located in the northwest. The lake was much larger and richer in wildlife in antiquity, and it was the site of some of the earliest settlements (c. 6000 BC) in Egypt.

Sights in the Fayyum include the pyramids of al-Lahun and Hawara, the Greco-Roman site of Karanis, the large singing waterwheels, and some fine agricultural countryside that includes the lake, which is pleasant to visit on a warm day. The Fayyum was especially important during two periods of Egyptian history: the Middle Kingdom, when it

2

began to be intensively exploited for agriculture, and the Greco-Roman Period (332 BC–AD 395), when it provided most of the grain for the Roman Empire.

There are two centers of activity in the area: one is the very salty Birket Qarun, the other Medinet Fayyum, the major city. The site of old Karanis is on the way in from Cairo, as is the lake. Medinet Fayyum is 20 km (12 mi) south of the lake, and the Hawara and Lahun pyramids are south of the city. The Fayyum is a day trip on its own from Cairo, because there are several things to see here in addition to the pharaonic antiquities.

Kom Aushim, the Greco-Roman town site of Karanis, is on the desert road on the way into the Fayyum, and it feels like a ghost town. It includes a temple dedicated to the local gods Petesuchs and Pnepheros, as well as the remains of houses, cooking installations, and bathrooms. Some of the latter are decorated with frescoes. A small **museum** at the entrance to the site contains some objects unearthed here and others found elsewhere in the Fayyum and around Egypt: mummies, statuary, relief fragments, a few objects of daily life, as well as Coptic and Islamic textiles and ceramics. It has a separate admission price. ⊠ *Fayyum Desert Rd.* ☎ *No phone* 🎫 *Site £e25, museum £e10* ⊗ *Daily 9–4.*

Medinet Fayyum, the center city of the oasis, is built around **waterwheels.** They are an icon of the Fayyum, and you can hear them—the sound resembles the moaning of humpback whales—amid the honking of horns and the rush of traffic. There are four waterwheels in Medinet Fayyum, and many others are scattered throughout the oasis.

Al-Hawara Pyramid, 393 feet square and originally 190 feet tall, is one of Amenemhet III's two pyramids; the other is at Dahshur. Both are built of mud brick with a limestone casing. The interior structure, entered from the south, is full of dead ends and false passages and shafts, inaccessible now because of the high water table. In Classical times this pyramid was most famous for its **mortuary temple,** then known as the Labyrinth. It was located to the south rather than the east of the temple and was a very elaborate mazelike structure filled with riches, of which little remains. To the east lies a Greco-Roman cemetery, where many of the celebrated Fayyum mummy portraits were found. There was also a cemetery of sacred crocodiles revered in this area. ⊠ *Haram al-Hawara, about 12 km (8 mi) southeast of Medinet Fayyum* ☎ *No phone* 🎫 *£e35* ⊗ *Daily 9–4.*

Al-Lahun Pyramid, built by the Middle Kingdom pharaoh Senwosret II (1897–1878 BC, also called Sesostris II), is a mud-brick pyramid whose outer casing was stolen in antiquity. (The pyramid is 347 feet square, and the original height was 157 feet.) A natural knoll of rock was used as a central core for the pyramid, and stone walls were built radiating out from it; the interstices were filled with mud brick before finally being cased with fine limestone. This gives the illusion that this was a true pyramid completely built of stone. Lahun was the first pyramid to abandon a single northern entrance in favor of two entrances on the south side. Its underground chambers (inaccessible) contain dead ends and twists and turns to disguise the whereabouts of the granite burial chamber, which when discovered in modern times contained an empty red granite sarcophagus and an alabaster offering table. The devious layout of the substructure, along with the transfer of the entrance from north to south, was perhaps the result of a quest for greater security for the place of burial. ⊠ *On outskirts of al-Lahun village, about 21 km (13 mi) southeast of Medinet Fayyum* ☎*No phone* ☑*£e35* ☉*Daily 9–4.*

OFF THE BEATEN PATH

Nazla. The precariously perched kilns that dot the ravine at the edge of this village are a spectacular sight (note that some locals aggressively seek tips for pointing you in the right direction). Specialized pots, such as the *bukla*, a squat vessel with a skewed mouth, are made here, but all are sold at the Tuesday market in Medinet Fayyum. ✛ *From Medinet Fayyum take main rode west about 20 km (12 mi) into Nazla; turn onto road next to mosque.*

WHERE TO EAT

$

MIDDLE EASTERN

✕ **Cafeteria al-Medina.** The location is lovely: the restaurant was built in a green spot around the waterwheels at the center of town. The wheels' eerie whining and the cool splashing of water make a lovely accompaniment to a relatively unexceptional meal. The fare is basic: shish-kebab, roast chicken, and the regular mezze. Service is not exactly speedy. Beer is generally available, except during Ramadan. ⊠ *Off Shar'a al-Gomhurriya, Medinet Fayyum* ☎*No phone* ⊟*No credit cards.*

GETTING THERE & AROUND

The best way to get to the Fayyum is by hiring a car (a taxi should cost around £e40 per hour) or by taking a tour—a car is absolutely necessary to get around the area and between the sights. An organized tour might be better, because most Cairene taxi drivers don't know the geography of the Fayyum or its antiquities, and it can be difficult to navigate between sights. To get to the area, take Shar'a al-Haram and turn left just before the Mena House on the Alexandria road, which is marked for Alexandria and the Fayyum. Then follow signs to the Fayyum. There are a few police checkpoints along the way, so bring your passport. If you are not part of a tour group, you may be provided with an armed security guard for your trip. The more adventurous can take a bus to Medinat Fayyum from Munib Station (every half hour, £e4). Once you get to the city, hire one of the ubiquitous pickup-truck taxis to take you to the various sites.

THE WADI NATRUN MONASTERIES

100 km (62 mi) northwest of Cairo and 160 km (100 mi) southeast of Alexandria, just off the Desert Road near the dreary planned satellite town of Sadat City.

One of the many Egyptian contributions to Christianity was the idea of going off into the wilderness to subject yourself to all manner of deprivation as a means of devoting yourself to God. Monastic life began on the coast of the Red Sea with St. Anthony in the 4th century. Some of his earliest disciples migrated to the desert just west of the Delta and established monasteries in Wadi Natrun. At its peak in the centuries after the death of St. Anthony, the Natrun Valley hosted 50 monasteries and more than 5,000 monks. Afterward, however, it suffered almost uninterrupted decline until the 1970s, when the monasteries began to see something of a rebirth as educated, worldly Copts started taking their vows in record numbers.

Although the modern world encroaches on Wadi Natrun's earlier isolation, the monasteries still feel remote, huddled behind the high walls the monks built a millennium ago to protect themselves from Bedouin attacks. But make no mistake: these are some very hip monks. They speak countless foreign languages, run several successful businesses that include a large fruit and vegetable farm, and are more clued in to the ways of the world than most young Cairenes. They are, as well, profoundly devout, and the monasteries maintain an air of spiritual calm no matter how many pilgrims are visiting. And when the winds sweep off the desert, rustling the tall, graceful tamarind trees that shade the sand-hue domes and smooth walls of the churches, you feel a long, long way from Cairo.

There are now four active monasteries: Deir Anba Bishoi, Deir al-Sourian, Deir Anba Baramus, and Deir Abu Maqar. Deir Abu Maqar has long been one of the most important Christian institutions in Egypt; as a result, permission to visit is rarely granted without a very compelling devotional reason—even Copts find it almost impossible to get in. The monasteries are administered by the **Coptic Patriarchate of Cairo.** The first three are open to visitors—mostly Coptic pilgrims come here to pay their respects or to baptize children. It isn't necessary, as it has been in the past, to get advance permission from the patriarchate in Cairo; however, it is still worth calling ahead to verify opening hours, because they vary based on the fasting schedule (devout Copts fast the majority of the year). ⏏*222 Shar'a Ramses, Abbasiya, Cairo* ✣ *Next to the Cathedral of St. Mark* ☎*02/682–5374, 02/682–5375, or 02/682–5376 for information from the patriarchate* ☉ *Roughly 9 AM to 8 PM (6 PM in winter).*

THE MONASTERIES

If only by virtue of its accessibility, **Deir Anba Bishoi** has become the busiest monastery in Wadi Natrun, but it remains one of the most charming. The monastery dates from the 4th century, as does its oldest church (one of five), which was built with domes and irregular stone-and-silt-mortar walls covered in smooth sand-hue plaster. The interior consists of a high triple-vaulted main hall. Tiny apertures pierce the ceiling, admitting streams of brilliant sunlight that catch the plumes of incense that fill the air. To the left, through a spectacular 14th-century door, is the *haykal* (sanctuary), where contemporary frescoes depict John the Baptist, St. Mark, and the 12 apostles, along with early monastic fathers. The carved wooden door (hidden behind a velvet curtain) was donated in the 7th century by the last Byzantine pope, just before the Arab invasion marked the emergence of Islam in Egypt. The coffin is that of St. Bishoi.

Monastic Life

Copts may elect to join a monastery after they have fulfilled some surprisingly unspiritual requirements. They need to be at least 25 years old, and they have to have finished university and national military service and held a job, because professional skills are needed to run the monastery. The primary criterion for entry, of course, is devotion to God, and monks must take vows of poverty and obedience.

The monastic day begins at 4 AM, when the monks gather in the church to pray and chant. At 6 AM the liturgy is recited, although monks may elect to pray privately. Then the work day begins: on the farm, in construction, guiding tourists, and so forth, until 4 PM (in winter) or 8 PM (in summer), with a break at 1 PM to eat in the refectory. A half-hour of prayer follows, and the monks are free to pray on their own until morning.

Fasting is an integral part of Coptic devotion, and it fills roughly two-thirds of the year. The comparison with Muslim fasting during Ramadan is interesting: Muslims do not eat, drink, smoke, or have sex during daylight hours, but Copts give up all animal products day and night for the duration of their fast. During fasts they eat nothing until early afternoon, when they eat a vegetarian meal. The fasting periods are usually broken with major holidays, such as Christmas or Easter.

Although Coptic monks may have retreated to the monasteries to forsake the world, they are very accustomed to having the world come to them. They run arguably the smoothest tour-guide systems in Egypt, with a knowledgeable *abuna* (father) to walk you through the compound and tell you genuinely useful information about what you are seeing—even if their claims about the age of the buildings or the achievements of the Coptic community at times sound a bit grandiose. They do not charge admission, and the baksheesh customary elsewhere in Egypt is inappropriate here. The monasteries do welcome donations, for which there is usually a box near the reception areas.

Dress modestly—no shorts, and the less skin showing the better—but you needn't expect any fanaticism on the part of the monks. Copts can seem remarkably casual in their devotion: pilgrims sleep on the floors of the church, and children run and play in the middle of Sunday mass (the same is true in mosques, except at prayer time). Of course, you would do well not to take similar license. Be sure to remove your shoes before entering any of the churches.

Elsewhere in the monastery, there is a workable (though unused) grain mill that looks every bit as old as the church itself. The monks live in cells known as *lauras,* and a cell is exactly what they are: small boxes with a single window and few comforts. Near the entrance gate is the keep, a defensive tower with a drawbridge into which the monks could retreat in the event of attack. The Coptic Pope Shenouda III maintains a residence within the monastery, but it is not open to the public.

If you exit the grounds by a small door in the back wall, you will see the rolling fields of farmland that the monks reclaimed from the desert and now use to grow dates, grapes, olives, and vegetables for sale in markets throughout the country. If that's not worldly enough, the monks even have their own gas station and car-repair shop. They employ impoverished Egyptians, mostly from the Upper Nile Valley, and teach them skills for use when they return to their home villages.

When you exit Deir Anba Bishoi, turn left, and a 10-minute walk brings you to **Deir al-Sourian.** Even if you have a car, it is worth walking: the approach gives you a powerful sense of the desert's small dunes with the lush foliage of the monastery just peeking over the high walls that shimmer in the haze of heat off the sands.

Deir al-Sourian was founded by a breakaway faction from Deir Anba Bishoi and dedicated to Theotokos (God's Mother). A later reconciliation made the new monastery redundant, so it was taken over by monks from Syria—hence its name al-Sourian, the Syrian. There is a tamarind tree in the rear of the monastery that supposedly grew out of the walking stick of the 4th-century Syrian St. Ephraem. Challenged by younger monks, who thought he carried the staff to look authoritative, Ephraem announced: "Were it used due to weakness, it will bud out," and he stuck his staff in the ground.

Many sections of Deir al-Sourian, including the 9th-century Roman-style keep, are not open to the public, but the main church has a number of interesting sights. The most impressive is the ebony Door of Symbols, inlaid with ivory, in the haykal. Its seven panels represent what were thought of locally as the seven epochs of the Christian era. An inscription shows that it was installed in the church in the 10th century, when Gabriel I was the patriarch of Alexandria. On either side of the haykal are two half-domes decorated with frescoes, one showing the Annunciation to the Virgin and the other the Virgin's Dormition. Many other frescoes have been discovered throughout the church including, most recently, several 7th-century renditions of as yet unknown Coptic martyrs. The monks are inordinately proud of these discoveries.

In the rear of the church is the Refectory, with a kitschy display of monastic eating habits, complete with plaster figures dressed up like monks. If you duck through a narrow passage to the left of the Refectory, you can find a stone cave that was St. Bishoi's private laura. According to legend, St. Bishoi tied his hair to a chain (now a rope) that hung from the ceiling to prevent himself from falling asleep during his marathon prayer sessions.

Deir Anba Baramus is thought to be the oldest monastic settlement in the wadi. Its Arabic name is derived from the Coptic word *Romeos* (meaning Roman), used in honor of Maximus and Domitius, sons of Emperor Valentinus who lived as monks in this area. It is impossible to access except by car and, despite its age, it is probably the least interesting of the three monasteries, because many of the buildings are of quite recent construction. The oldest church on the grounds is the restored 9th-century Church of al-'Adhra' (the Virgin). Work on the church in 1987 uncovered frescoes, in rather poor condition, long hidden by plaster. The coffins in the haykal are of St. Isadore and St. Moses the

Black (a convert from Nubia). Adjacent to the coffins is a photograph of a T-shirt supposedly scrawled in blood during an exorcism. In the back corner of the church is a column, easily missed next to a wall, that is from the 4th century. It is the oldest part of the monastery, marking the spot where St. Arsenius, the one-time tutor to the sons of Roman emperor Theodosius the Great, is said to have sat regularly in prayer.

WHERE TO STAY & EAT

While the monastery complexes don't boast much in terms of food and drink, the area around them is building up so quickly that it might not be long before the golden arches rise up out of the sand. For now, you can find sandwiches, snacks, continental dinners, and a full bar at the **Rest House,** 9 km (5½ mi) from Deir Anba Bishoi on the Desert Road. Just across from the Rest House, a service area catering to travelers on their way to Alexandria and the Mediterranean Coast features more refined and comfortable dining, serving everything from pizza to fast food to sit-down, Egyptian-style, full-course meals.

It's best to see Wadi Natrun as a day trip, but if you want to stay overnight, you can do so at the El-Hammra Eco Lodge (⊕www. elhammraeco-lodge.com), a charming little rustic backwater. Permission to stay overnight at the monasteries is granted only in writing to theological students or groups traveling with their priest.

GETTING THERE & AROUND

You have two options when traveling to the monastery. The most painless one is to book a tour with an approved travel agent and a guide. Altenatively, negotiate with a taxi driver from Ramses Square in Cairo to take you to each of the monasteries and back to the capital for around £e250–£e300, depending on your haggling skills and the number of people in your group. Be sure that the driver knows the way and understands the amount of waiting time involved—plan for an hour per monastery—and pay once you're safely back in Cairo. The ride should take 1½ to 2 hours each way.

Otherwise, West Delta air-conditioned buses leave every half-hour between 6 AM and 8 PM from Targoman Station, behind the *al-Ahram* newspaper offices; one-way tickets cost £e4.50. The trip takes two hours to meander its way to the Wadi Natrun Rest House along the Desert Road, and from there on to the village. From the village, you can catch a service taxi with other people (50pt to £e1.25 per person) to Deir Anba Bishoi. It's an easy walk from there to Deir al-Sourian, but if you want to go on to Deir Anba Baramus, you have to rely on the kindness of those fellow pilgrims (with a vehicle), because there is no established transportation system between the monasteries. You can also hire a driver from the village to take you to the three monasteries, wait for you, and then bring you back to the village; depending on your bargaining skills, it should run no more than £e40.

The last West Delta bus back to Cairo leaves at 5:30 PM from the village, but if you're feeling brave you can always flag down one of the frequent minibuses heading that way, from either the village or the Rest House.

CAIRO ESSENTIALS

TRANSPORTATION

BY AIR

Cairo is the main entry point for international flights and has the most international arrivals of any other destination in Egypt. The airport is divided into three terminals: Terminal 1 for domestic flights only, Terminal 2 for most international flights, and the brand-new Terminal 3 for Egyptair and its Star Alliance partners.

AIRPORT TRANSFERS If you are traveling independently, taxis and limousines are the best option for getting to and from the airport. The minute you exit the arrivals hall, you will be inundated with offers from taxi drivers. This will be your first opportunity to test out your bargaining skills—you should be able to bring the price down to around £e50. Keep in mind that most taxis will not use their meters. If you are too tired to go through the hassle, opt for one of the limousine companies located in the arrivals hall for a flat fee of £e80 to £e100 for central Cairo hotels. Cairo taxis are black and white or black and yellow; limousines are black, usually old-model Mercedes sedans. Going to the airport from the city is much easier, because you can have your hotel arrange your transportation.

The airport also has a fleet of modern shuttle buses that travel to and from the airport to Downtown, Giza, Heliopolis, Mohandeseen, Ma'adi, Nasr City, and Zamalek. Buses depart every 30 minutes, and single tickets cost £e25 to Heliopolis and £e35 to Downtown.

BY BUS

TO & FROM CAIRO Buses are an inexpensive means of traveling between cities. Generally they are safe, if not always relaxing. Most companies have installed videos to play Arabic and Indian movies at top volume, even on night buses. If this counts as local color rather than an annoyance, take a bus. It's wise to buy your ticket a day in advance, especially when traveling during peak periods. However, be aware that currently the security authorities do not encourage independent bus travel on routes down the Nile Valley, preferring visitors to travel by train or by plane, modes of travel that can more easily be kept under surveillance by relatively small numbers of officers.

Popular bus companies include the East Delta Bus Company, El Gouna Bus Company, Super Jet, and Upper Egyptian Bus Company. All buses in Cairo depart from Targoman Station off Gala' Street, Downtown. *For more specific information about bus lines and bus travel in Egypt, see By Bus, under Transportation in Egypt Essentials.*

WITHIN CAIRO Most visitors to Cairo aren't likely to use the local city buses, but they are far and away the cheapest mode of transportation in the city, with tickets costing a mere 25pt to £e2. Buses arrive at and depart from stations at Maydan Tahrir, Maydan Ataba, Opera Square, Pyramids Road, Ramses Station, and the Citadel. Route numbers are sometimes missing from the buses, so it is always best to ask where a bus is going before it lurches off with you on board.

Much less of an experience, and more reliable, are the orange-trimmed minibuses. They charge slightly more than the larger buses (£e1–£e2) and are usually much less crowded. ⚠ **If you decide to use either type of bus service, be very cautious. Especially on large buses, pickpockets are known to look for potential victims.**

The Cairo Transport Authority operates a fleet of comfortable air-conditioned buses that are surprisingly convenient and affordable. Marked with a large CTA logo on the side, for £e2 the bus will take you from the airport, through the city's northeastern suburbs and Downtown, eventually passing through Giza to deposit you at the foot of the pyramids. Route 356 stops at Abdel Meneim Riyadh Station in Maydan Tahrir, and route 799 runs via Shubra to Maydan Ramses, but you can flag them down or ask the driver to let you off at any point along the routes.

MAJOR BUS
ROUTES

To and from Maydan Tahrir: No. 400 for Heliopolis and Cairo International Airport (all terminals) and 27 to the airport via Maydan Roxi; 268 and 63 for the Khan al-Khalili; 951 and 154 for Ibn Tulun Mosque and the Citadel; 997 for the pyramids in Giza; all lines except 154, 951, and 268 for Ramses Station.

To and from Maydan Ataba and Opera Square: 948 for Cairo International Airport; 950 and 80 for Khan al-Khalili; 104, 17, and 202 for Maydan Tahrir and Mohandiseen; 94 for Fustat and the Mosque of 'Amr; 50 and 150 for the Shrine of Imam Sahfe'i; 48 for Zamalek.

To and from the pyramids: 804 for Ramses Square and the Citadel; 905 for Maydan Tahrir and the Citadel.

To and from Ramses Station: 971 for the airport, 65 for Khan al-Khalili, 174 for the Citadel.

To and from the Citadel: 840 for Maydan Ataba and Maydan Tahrir; 905 for Rodah Island, Shar'a al-Haram, and the pyramids.

Another option is the microbus, or service taxis. These privately owned 12-seaters, painted blue and white, cost 60 pt–£e1 and go from all the major terminals to just about anywhere you want to go. They are unnumbered, however, so ask the driver where he's headed.

BY CAR

Attempting to rent a car and drive oneself around Cairo is something we would discourage in the strongest terms. If you manage to find (and fend) your way driving through the aggressive streets of Cairo, parking will prove to be an even greater challenge. Either you will spend half your day looking for a parking place or you will be ripped off by a *monadi* (one of the self-employed valet parking boys). Just do yourself a favor and forget about driving.

If you simply must rent a car and drive it yourself, you must be at least 25 years old, possess an international license, and have nerves of steel. *For more information, see By Car, under Transportation in Egypt Essentials.*

CAR RENTALS Major car-rental agencies have offices in Cairo; cars come with or without chauffeurs.

2

Contacts Budget Rent-a-Car (✉ *22 Shar'a El Mathaf El Ziraee, Dokki* ☎ *02/3726-0518* ✉ *Cairo International Airport* ☎ *02/2265-2395*) **Europcar** (✉ *6m Maydan 1226, Heliopolis Sheraton Buildings, Heliopolis* ☎ *02/2267-1815* ✉ *Cairo International Airport* ☎ *02/2267-2439*). **Hertz** (☎ *02/347-2238 for central reservations office* ✉ *Ramses Hilton, 1115 Corniche al-Nil* ☎ *02/2575-8914* ✉ *Cairo International Airport* ☎ *02/2265-2430* ✉ *Le Méridien Pyramids Hotel, Giza* ☎ *02/3377-3388* ✉ *InterContinental Pyramids Hotel & Resort, Giza* ☎ *02/3838-8300*).

BY SUBWAY

By far the most efficient mode of public transportation in Cairo, the Metro is clean, reliable, and cheap. Tickets cost from £e1; there are no multiday passes. Trains run from South Cairo (Helwan) to North Cairo (Heliopolis), with sublines to Shubra, Ataba, and Abdin. One of the most useful lines is the cross-Nile line from Giza to Shubra. The metro runs from 5:30 AM to midnight in winter (to 1 AM in summer), with trains arriving every 5 to 10 minutes. Each train has cars in the middle reserved for women and children. Women traveling alone are advised to sit here, especially during rush-hour travel, to avoid being hassled or groped.

BY TAXI

The fact that meters are rarely used by Cairo taxi drivers makes life a bit more difficult for visitors, who are considered to be the best prey for the exorbitant fares that some drivers try to charge. The first rule is that you should not take any taxi parked in front of a hotel unless you bargain the price down before getting in. It is always cheaper to hail a taxi off the street after walking a few meters away from the hotel.

Fares vary according to the time you are in the taxi and the distance you cover. Early in the morning and very late at night, fares are about 40% to 50% higher than during daylight. During normal daylight hours and in the evening, a 20-minute cab ride from Maydan Tahrir to the pyramids should cost about £e50 one way; a 5- to 10-minute ride should cost no more than £e10. If you are going a long distance, such as all the way to Saqqara, the ride should be about £e80 one way, and you should have the driver wait—it is extremely difficult to get a cab back to the city from there. With waiting this may push the price up to around £e200.

Some drivers are extremely stubborn, so you must set a price before embarking on your ride to avoid unpleasant scenes once you arrive at your destination. When giving directions, name a major landmark near your destination (rather than a street address), such as Maydan Tahrir, or al-Azhar University. As you get closer to the destination, give more specifics; this will avoid confusion.

Most taxis are independently operated—the blue-and-white fleet—so they can't be called. Just go hail one on the street. There are always taxis in the streets of Cairo; however, the condition of some of these taxis is dire, with mechanical defects and poor conditions inside. City Cabs operates a fleet of better-serviced vehicles with a distinctive yellow livery. Though City Cabs is more expensive than the blue-and-white taxi fleet, the cabs should have working meters, and they run on natural gas, so they're better for the environment. City Cab drivers are not allowed to smoke in the vehicles.

Information City Cabs (☎ *16516 or 19195*).

BY TRAIN
All railway lines from Cairo depart from and arrive at Ramses Station, 3 km (2 mi) northeast of Maydan Tahrir. Trains traveling to and from Alexandria, the Nile Delta towns, and Suez Canal cities use Tracks 1–7 in the station's main hall. Trains to al-Minya, Luxor, and Aswan depart from Platforms 8, 9, 10, and 11 outside the main hall.

Cairo and Alexandria have several convenient daily connections, with a travel time of 2 to 3¼ hours depending on the type of service. Tickets cost between £e19 and £e46 depending on the class of service.

Abela Egypt operates the long-distance and sleeper trains that connect Cairo, Luxor, and Aswan. Tickets for these trains should be purchased at least 10 days in advance, either in person at the station or from a travel agent or tour company.

For more information, see Train Travel under Transportation in Egypt Essentials.

Contacts Abela Egypt (☎ *02/2574–9474 for reservations* ⊕ *www.sleepingtrains. com*).

CONTACTS & RESOURCES

BANKS & EXCHANGE SERVICES
Banking hours are Sunday through Thursday, from 8 AM to 2 PM. The travel offices of American Express and Thomas Cook offer currency exchange, and there are numerous commercial exchange offices. Commercial exchange offices open later into the evening than banks and are, therefore, more convenient. Many larger hotels have bank branches within. Your hotel will also change currency directly, but may offer a poor rate of exchange.

You'll find lots of ATMs across the city, at bank branches, in shopping malls, and in hotel lobbies. You can rely on getting access to Egyptian pounds from ATMs in Cairo—though not so much in the rest of the country as machines are not filled up as regularly outside the capital.

Keep any receipts from currency exchange of ATM withdrawals as you may need to show these to customs officials.

Information Credit Agricole Egypt (⊠ *2-6 Shar'a Hassan Sabry, Zamalek*). **BNP Paribas** (⊠ *Nile Towers, Downtown*). **Egyptian Exchange** (⊠ *6 Shar'a El Bostan, Maydan Tahrir, Downtown* ⊠ *171 Shar'a 26th Yulyu, Zamalek*). **HSBC** (⊠ *Maydan Roxy, Downtown*). **National Bank of Egypt** (⊠ *201 Shar'a 26th Yulyu, Giza*).

2

EMERGENCIES

In case of any emergency, contact your embassy first for a referral; general hospital emergency rooms leave much to be desired.

General Emergencies Ambulance (☎123). **Fire** (☎125). **Police** (☎122). **Tourist Police** (☎126).

Dentists The Dental Group (✉13 Shar'a 207 Degla, Ma'adi ☎02/2521–3170 ⊕ www.dentalgroup.com.eg). **Egyptian German Dental Clinic** (✉9 Shar'a Gameat El Dawal El Arabia, Mohandiseen ☎02/3303–0059). **Dr. Lamisse Mahkyoun** (✉29 Shar'a El Batel Ahmed Azis, Mohandiseen ☎012/671–1257 for emergencies). **Dr. Nabil Moawad** (✉22 Shar'a Wadi El Nil, Mohandiseen ☎02/3346–9050 ⊕ www.cdc.com.eg).

Hospitals Ain Shams Specialised Hospital (✉Shar'a Khalifa El Maamoun, Abbasiya ☎02/2402–4111). **Anglo-American Hospital** (✉Shar'a al-Burg, Zamalek ☎02/2735–6162 or 02/735–6165). **Misr International Hospital** (✉12 Shar'a al-Saraya, Finny Square, Doqqi ☎02/3760–8261 ⊕ www.misrinternational.com).

LATE-NIGHT PHARMACIES By law, every neighborhood is required to have at least one pharmacy open all night. Often pharmacies take turns. Check with your hotel staff about the open one nearest you.

Contacts El Rehan First Pharmacy (✉Specialised Medical Centre, Shar'a Ahmed Shawky, New Cairo ☎02/2607–7779). **El Safa Hospital** (✉79 Shar'a Iraq, Mohandiseen ☎02/3336–1010). **Grand Hyatt Pharmacy** (✉Galleria Mall, Corniche al-Nil, Rodah Island ☎010/537–1689). **Seif** (✉76 Shar'a Qasr Al-'Ainy, Downtown ☎02/794–2678 or 19199 (within Egypt)).

INTERNET, MAIL & SHIPPING

The number of Wi-Fi hotspots have exploded in the city over the last couple of years. Look for café chains like Starbucks, Costa, Cilantro, and Beano's, as well as fast food outlets such as Pizza Hut and McDonalds, which usually have free access. Internet cafés are usually dusty back-street affairs, but they stay open until around midnight, and access is cheap—around £e4 to £e10 per hour. Cafés open and close with great regularity. Your hotel will also probably offer Internet service, but at a higher price.

The mail service Egyptpost is both slow and unreliable. Postcards can take more than two weeks to reach the United States, and a good percentage fail to reach their destination. If you need any letters or packages to arrive at their destination, it is far better to use a courier service.

If you go overboard on souvenirs, think about shipping some home. Bona fide retailers are used to shipping to the U.S. and are happy to organize this. However, FedEx courier services offer a reliable service that allows you to fill a 10 kg or a 25 kg box with a mixed shipment and send it home for a set price. DHL offers a 10 kg Junior Jumbo Box and a 25 kg Jumbo Box shipped worldwide for a set price.

Internet Cafés St@rnet Cyber Café (✉Bustan Centre, 18 Shar'a Bindi, Downtown ☎02/2735–3739). **Netsonic** (✉10 Shar'a El Nouwari (behind the Military Academy), Heliopolis ☎02/2620–7967). **Just Click C@fé** (✉16 Shar'a El Kawsar, Mohandiseen ☎02/335–4870).

Wi-Fi Hotspots Caspar & Gambini's (✉*Towers Mall at Nile City, Downtown* ☎*02/2461–9201*). **Cilantro** (✉*157 Shar'a 26th Yulyu, Zamalek* ☎*02/2736–1115*). **Coffee Roastery** (✉*3 Shar'a Mecca, Mohandiseen* ☎*02/3761–0995*). **Grand Café** (✉*Americana Boat, 26 Shar'a al-Nil, Giza* ☎*02/3570–9695*). **McDonalds** (✉*Ramses Hilton Annex, Downtown* ☎*19991 (only in Egypt)*).

Post Offices Bulaq Post Office (✉*79 Shar'a 26th Yulyu, Bulaq* ☎*02/2574–6835*). **Giza Post Office** (✉*Shar'a Morad, Giza* ☎*02/3572–1383*). **Ministry of Tourism Post Office** (✉*Shar'a Adli, Downtown* ☎*02/2393–2799*). **Ramses Post Office** (✉*29 Shar'a Ramses, Downtown* ☎*02/2575–0713*).

Shipping Companies DHL (✉*1 Shar'a Gawad Hosni, Garden City* ☎*02/3302–9810*). **FedEx** (✉*1079 Corniche al-Nil, Garden City* ☎*02/2795–2083*).

TOUR OPTIONS

Cairo is awash with companies offering tours and guides, but the quality varies greatly. Official tour guides have to be licensed by the Egyptian authorities and must undergo a strict program of training and examination before they receive their accreditation. This is your assurance of quality, so always make sure that any guide you engage is licensed. If you intend to visit the sites at Dahshur, Wadi Natrun, or Fayyum, booking a guided tour with a well-respected company or an accredited personal guide is your best option because you'll have travel and navigation taken care of, plus an expert on hand to answer questions you have during the tour. Booking through a company will also take care of any security issues with police escorts. If you are looking for a guided tour, your best bet is to try to set it up with a travel agent.

One well-respected American tour guide based in Cairo is Debbie Senters of Casual Cairo Detours. She organizes bespoke tours of any length and is happy to create a personal program for you. These tours are not cheap, but her guides are licensed, and tours include all transportation.

Information Casual Cairo Detours (☎*02/2417–8718* ⊕*www.casualcairodetours.pyramids.net*).

TRAVEL AGENCIES

Information American Express Travel (✉*15 Shar'a Qasr al-Nil, Downtown* ☎*02/2574–7991*). **Misr Travel** (✉*1 Shar'a Tala'at Harb, Downtown* ☎*02/2393–0010*). **Thomas Cook** (✉*12 Shar'a Mahmoud Bassiouny, Downtown* ☎*02/2576–6982* ✉*Cairo International Airport* ☎*02/2265–4447*).

VISITOR INFORMATION

Information Egyptian Tourist Authority (☎*126 for Tourist Information Hotline* ✉*Misr Travel Tower, Abbasia* ☎*02/2285–4509* ✉*Ramses Station, Maydan Ramses, Downtown* ☎*02/2579–0767* ✉*5 Shar'a al-Adli, Downtown* ☎*02/2391–3454* ✉*Manyal Palace, Rodah Island* ☎*02/2363–3006* ✉*Pyramids Village, Pyramids Rd., Giza* ☎*02/3385–0259*).

Alexandria

Fort Qayt Bay

WORD OF MOUTH

"I enjoyed Alexandria. It has a feeling much different than the rest of the country. I did it in a day and felt very rushed."

—Diane60030

"I do agree that if you aren't very interested in WWII history, you don't need to go all the way out to [El Alamein], but if you are, it is a good site to visit . . . especially the museum."

—Casual_Cairo

WELCOME TO ALEXANDRIA

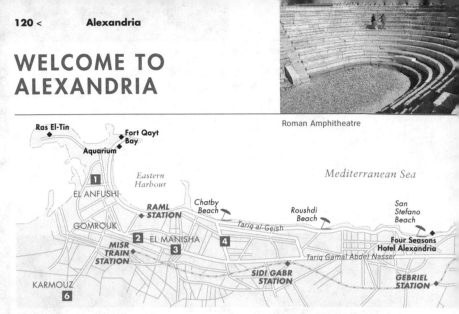

Roman Amphitheatre

Ras El-Tin
Fort Qayt Bay
Aquarium
Eastern Harbour
1 EL ANFUSHI
GOMROUK
RAML STATION
Chatby Beach
Tariq al-Geish
Roushdi Beach
San Stefano Beach
Mediterranean Sea
MISR TRAIN STATION
2 EL MANISHA
3
4
Four Seasons Hotel Alexandria
Tariq Gamal Abdel Nasser
SIDI GABR STATION
KARMOUZ
6
GEBRIEL STATION

TOP REASONS TO GO

★ **Café Culture:** Linger over coffee and pastry at the famous Grand Trianon Café.

★ **The Seaside Promenade:** Stroll or take a carriage ride along the seafront Corniche, taking in the faded glory of the turn-of-the-20th-century architecture.

★ **A Seafood Meal:** Order fresh seafood from the tantalizing choices on ice at Fish Market or Kadoura.

★ **The Remains of an Ancient Wonder:** Climb the parapet of Qayt Bay Fort, site of the famed ancient Pharos (lighthouse), for magnificent panoramas of the seafront.

★ **Antiquities on Display:** Visit the Greco-Roman Museum to explore artifacts excavated from ancient Alexandria.

1 **El Anfushi.** The westernmost tip of the main bay at the end of the Corniche, this colorful district is home of the fishermen, El Anfushi tombs, and Qayt Bay Fort. This was the city's core in ancient and medieval times. Some of the city's best seafood restaurants can be found here.

Alexandria

2 **Raml Station.** The heart of modern Alexandria has its main tram station on a square surrounded by early 20th-century buildings. The district is cut by major shopping streets that are always bustling with people. Nowhere else in the city is its cosmopolitan past more alive. Most of the major sights are within a short taxi ride from Raml Station.

3 **El Manisha.** The center of colonial Alexandria has fine squares and monumental buildings, colonnades, statues, and churches.

Custodians El Bosery Mosque

3

4 El Chatby. Location of the iconic modern Bibliotheca Alexandrina and the closest public beach to downtown.

5 Montazah. The once-royal domain has always been an upmarket district marking the traditional eastern limit of Alexandria. Visit the gardens and enjoy the facade of the old palace. Montazah marks the easternmost edge of the main tourist development in Alexandria.

Alexandria

6 Karmouz. Inland, and bounded by the canal El Mahmoudeya, this district has Alexandria's best known Roman-era ruins—the Catacombs of Koum Al Shukafa and Pompey's Pillar.

GETTING ORIENTED

As a rule, addresses are rarely used, and everyone navigates by names and landmarks, but with breezes almost always coming off the sea, orientation is fairly easy—when in doubt, head into the wind. Unfortunately, several of the city's best hotels are inconveniently located in or near Montazah. But it's a relatively painless drive into downtown—about 15 minutes from downtown to Montazah, less from other districts—past a string of neighborhoods with such evocative names as Chatby, Roushdi, and Sidi Gabr.

ALEXANDRIA PLANNER

Transportation

By Air: Alexandria has a domestic airport (30 minutes from Cairo), but few people choose to fly there since the trip from Cairo by train takes only a bit over 2 hours.

By Bus: Depending on traffic, the trip from Cairo to Alexandria by air-conditioned bus takes about 3 hours. Buses drop you off in an Alexandria suburb, so you will have to take a taxi on arrival.

By Train: A comfortable fast train will get you to Alexandria in a little over 2 hours at about double the price of a bus. Tickets are best purchased a day in advance but are often available on the same day. Don't get off at Sidi Gabr but continue to Misr Station.

Taxis: Taxis in Alexandria are cheap and convenient, but don't be surprised if you are charged double what locals might pay. Short trips may be as little as £e10, or you may pay about £e30 to get to Montazah. Taxi drivers will usually pick up more than one fare; single men should sit in the front.

What's Great in Alexandria

Café Society: Alexandria's multicultural and literary set made café life de rigeur, and the most famous venues, including the Grand Trianon, Pastroudis, and Vienous, still offer a slice of gentility and a snapshot of a time gone by with their period interiors.

20th-Century Literary Echoes: The city was a hotbed of literary excellence in the prerevolutionary era (from the turn of the 20th century until 1952), and you can follow in the footsteps of Constantine Cavafy, Laurence Durrell, and E. M. Forster as you stroll the streets.

Fresh Seafood: You've only to try and count the number of colorful fishing boats bobbing in the bay to realize that Alexandria has a well-deserved reputation for seafood. Fish Market is a current favorite with locals and an air-conditioned restaurant with fantastic views, but Kadoura is another long-standing choice with an excellent reputation—even if the dining room is less impressive.

Touring Alexandria

There's little reason to take a guided tour in Alexandria, given the limited number of historical sights and easy transportation. If you do want a guide, make arrangements through your hotel (or arrange a guide through any top-end hotel, if you're just coming for the day). This should offer a modest guarantee of quality in a market saturated with imposters. Use taxis to get around; Alexandria is not nearly as intimidating or busy as Cairo.

Money Matters

If you need to change currency, you'll need to use a bank or facilities at your hotel—four- and five-star hotels should have exchange facilities on-site; some have a small bank office open at set hours every day. ATMs are growing in number, and most major bank branches will have an ATM that accepts international cards for use 24 hours a day, though they are not always in service.

About the Restaurants

Because the focus is on fresh seafood, restaurants in Alexandria (especially the good ones) tend to be informal and quite inexpensive for the quality of what they serve. Naturally, many are near the water, some of them appropriately weathered, while others consist of no more than a few tables in an alley. A few places will levy a service charge, but most will not. In all places a tip of 10% is appropriate. Do not expect alcohol to be served in most restaurants.

Off-season, Alexandrians eat meals at standard times: 1 to 3 for lunch and 8 to 11 for dinner. But in summer dinner often begins much later. There is nothing more Mediterranean about Alexandria than the pace of dinner in the summer: after an evening siesta, have a *shisha* (water pipe) around 11, arrive at a waterfront restaurant after midnight, then wrap up the meal with an early morning espresso at an outdoor café nearby. You don't have to eat so late, of course, but you might be surprised how seductive it is.

About the Hotels

In truth, with the exception of the Salamlek Palace and the Four Seasons, the luxury hotels in Alexandria are drab, generic places not worth what they charge. Fortunately, a couple of mid-range hotels, including the surprisingly elegant Metropole, make attractive alternatives in the city center. Summer is a busy season, when advance reservations are essential. In spring and fall you may find hotels fully booked on weekends (Friday through Sunday), when residents of Cairo head to Alexandria for some downtime. Outside peak summer season, most hotels discount their prices by 30% to 40%.

WHAT IT COSTS IN EGYPTIAN POUNDS, U.S. DOLLARS, AND EUROS			
$$$$	$$$	$$	$
Restaurants			
over 150 £e	100 £e –150 £e	50 £e –100 £e	under 50 £e
Hotels in Dollars			
over $200	$130–$200	$70–$130	under $70
Hotels in Euros			
Over €130	€80–€130	€45–€80	Under €45

Restaurant prices are per person for a main course at dinner. Hotel prices are for a double room in high season, excluding 10% tax and service charges (usually 10%).

Planning Your Time

Three days in Alexandria is ample time to see the main sights. A visit to the Greco-Roman Museum will give you some historical context; the ruins of the original Pharos were incorporated into Fort Qayt Bay; the great Library of Alexandria was destroyed, but its modern replacement is one of the world's most ambitious collections of printed and electronic media. Leave time to browse in the Attarine market and to walk along the Corniche. Be sure not to miss the wild European/Middle Eastern palace of the former khedive in Montazah; the gardens are also beautiful.

If you have any extra time, take a day trip and head west along the coast to explore the memorials on the El Alamein battlefields—reminding us of sacrifices made during World War II; you can do this by taxi or with a car and driver hired through your hotel.

When to Go

Alexandria's peak season is summer, when Egyptians flee here for the refreshing Mediterranean breezes. Hotels are also busy on weekends. Off-season, Alex is spectacular, as the city settles back into its natural, relaxed rhythm. It rains more here than anywhere in Egypt. Winter is chilly and sometimes windy, which can be a pleasant break from Cairo's annual 360 days of sunshine.

By Sean
Rocha
Updated by
Lindsay and
Pete Bennett

THERE IS A WONDERFUL ITALO Calvino story about a city so removed from its own history that it is as if the modern metropolis sits on the site of an unrelated ancient city that just happens to bear the same name. At times Alexandria, which Alexander the Great founded in the 4th century BC, feels like that. Yet the fallen Alexandria of the ancient Greeks, of Ptolemy, Cleopatra, Julius Caesar, and the Romans, and of pagan cults and the Great Library is underfoot, quite literally, as all of modern Alexandria has been built on the ruins of the old, a city that was capital of Egypt from the third century BC until AD 642, when the Arabs first arrived.

Overlay a map of the contemporary city with one from antiquity, and you see that many of the streets have remained the same: Shar'a al-Horreya runs along the route of the ancient Canopic Way, and Shar'a Nabi Daniel follows the route of the ancient Street of the Soma. Near their intersection once stood the Mouseion, a Greek philosophic and scientific center that had at its heart the collection of the Great Library. Yet only fleeting glimpses of this ancient city peak through the modern crust.

By the early 20th century, Alexandria was a wealthy trading port. The merchants were fantastically rich—cosmopolitan without being intellectual—and they enjoyed the sort of idle existence that is born of privilege, a privilege not of high birth but rather of colonial rule, which shielded foreigners from Egyptian law. They lived in villas with extravagant gardens, frequented luxurious shops, gossiped over tea in grand cafés, and lounged on the beach in private resorts along the coast. The population was a multicultural mix of Greeks and Arabs, Turks and Armenians, French and Levantines, Jews and Christians, and this spawned a unique atmosphere. It was this city that belonged to Constantine Cavafy, now regarded as the greatest Greek poet of his era. It was this city to which the novelist E. M. Forster, author of *A Passage to India,* was posted during World War I. And it was this city that gave birth to Lawrence Durrell's *Alexandria Quartet,* which captivated a generation of American readers when the books were published in the late 1950s.

Then quite suddenly everything changed. The intellectuals and merchants fled, driven out of Egypt by the nationalist revolution of the 1950s, the wars with Israel, and the nationalization of their businesses.

It's been five decades since most of the foreigners left—some Greeks and Armenians remained. But if you take the city as it is today and not as a faded version of what it once was, you will find that Alex (as it's affectionately known) remains an utterly charming place to visit. The Mediterranean laps at the seawall along the Corniche, and gentle sea breezes cool and refresh even in the dead of summer. Graceful old cafés continue to draw lovers and friends—Egyptians now, rather than foreigners—while the streets remain as lively and intriguing as ever. Alexandria is still a great city, even now, shorn of its many pasts.

EXPLORING ALEXANDRIA

Alexandria has grown so rapidly in the last 50 years that it now runs along the coastline from the Western Harbor all the way to Montazah, a distance of more than 16 km (10 mi). It is, nonetheless, a great walking city because the historic downtown occupies a compact area near the Eastern Harbor, while the ancient sights are a short taxi ride away.

DOWNTOWN & RAML STATION

Nowhere is Alexandria's cosmopolitan past more evident than downtown, where its Italianate buildings house French cafés, Armenian jewelers, and Greek restaurants. Because so few buildings survived the British bombardment in 1882, it is no surprise that what stands today reflects the late-19th-century European city that rose from the rubble of the city's past. There are a few historical and cultural sights downtown, including the Roman Theater, the Greco-Roman Museum, and the resurrected Great Library and Montazah Gardens, which are a bit of a side trip from the heart of downtown.

MAIN ATTRACTIONS

❹ **Attarine Market.** This area acquired its reputation in the 1960s as the place where the high-quality antiques sold by fleeing foreigners resurfaced. Those days are long gone. There are now only a few true antiques stores left in the area, but it's fascinating nonetheless to see the tiny workshops where the reproduction French-style furniture so popular in Egypt originates. Almost all the workshops will be happy to sell direct if you find a piece that appeals to you, but consider the challenge of shipping it back home before you give in to temptation. The market actually consists of a series of alleyways, the sum of which feels less established—and far less touristy—than Cairo's Khan al-Khalili. ✢ To find the market, walk one block west of the Attarine Mosque and cross Shar'a al-Horreya to the alley between the café and the parts store, El Attarine.

❿ **Bibliotheca Alexandrina.** This monumental, $190 million, UNESCO-sponsored project began with an instinctively appealing idea: to resurrect the Great Library of ancient Alexandria, once one of the world's major centers of learning. Its location near the Silsileh Peninsula on the edge of the Eastern Harbor has tremendous symbolic resonance, having been the royal quarters in ancient times and one of several possible locations of the original library.

The modernist Norwegian-designed building is in the form of an enormous multitiered cylinder tilted to face the sea, with a roof of diamond-shape windows that allow controlled light into the seven cascading interior floors. The most impressive feature, however, is the curving exterior wall covered in rough-hewn granite blocks from Aswan that have been engraved with letters from ancient languages.

With an aim to promote intellectual excellence, the library is a repository for the printed word—it holds millions of books including rare manuscripts—but is also a facility to store knowledge in all its forms, from tape recordings of the spoken word to electronic media. It is a robust academic organization with seven specialist research centers and has the Virtual Immersive Science and Technology Appplications (VISTA) system, which transforms 2-D data into 3-D simulations so researchers can study the projected behavior of theoretical models. The library also acts as a forum for academic cross-cultural discussion and is home to more than 10 institutes. Membership allows you to explore the archive and use the Internet for research, but don't expect to be able to use the facility like an Internet café. Personal emails are not allowed.

> **DID YOU KNOW?**
>
> Modern Alexandria started with an architecturally clean slate, when much of downtown was destroyed in 1882 by British warships in an effort to put down an Egyptian nationalist rebellion. The enclave of elegant boulevards and neo-classical mansions that constitute the heart of the city all date from a building boom in the final years of the 19th century.

Once you've enjoyed the view of the vast interior from the mezzanine gallery, there's little to hold you in the main hall, but the library has several small museums and exhibitions that are of more interest. The **Manuscripts Museum** has a large collection of rare documents, parchments, and early printed books. The **Impressions of Alexandria** exhibition features paintings and sketches of the city dating from the 15th to the 19th centuries and photographs taken in the late 19th and early 20th centuries. The **Antiquities Museum** on the basement level has a collection of finds from the Pharaonic, Roman, and Islamic Alexandria. Examples of monumental Roman statuary include "Huge Forearm Holding a Ball" (nothing else remains of the immense piece), and a finely chiseled bust of the Emperor Octavian (Augustus). Egypto-Roman artifacts include the mummy of Anhk Hor, governor of Upper Egypt, and several 2nd-century funerary masks showing the prevalent cross-styling between the classical Egyptian and Roman Egyptian styles. ⊠ *63 Shar'a Soter, Chatby* ☎ *03/483–9999* ⊕ *www.bibalex. org* 🖅 *Library £e10, Antiquities Museum £e20, Manuscripts Museum £e20* ⊘ *Sat.–Thurs. 11–7, Fri. 3–7.* .

❷ ★ Catacombs of Kom al-Shoqafa. This is the most impressive of Alexandria's ancient remains, dating from the 2nd century AD. Excavation started in 1892, and the catacombs were discovered accidentally eight years later when a donkey fell through a chamber ceiling. A long spiral staircase leads to the main hall. The stairs run down the outside of a shaft, which excavators used to transport the bodies of the dead. The staircase leads to the rotunda, which, like all but the lowest chamber, is undecorated but striking for the sheer scale of the underground space, supported by giant columns carved out of the bedrock.

A few rooms branch off from the rotunda: the Triclinium was a banquet hall where relatives and friends toasted the deceased, and the Caracalla Hall has four lightly painted tombs and a case of bones. The next level down contains a labyrinth of smaller nooks for storing bodies and leads to the lowest excavated room, which is framed by columns and sculpted snakes. Casts of two statues stand here—the originals are in the Greco-Roman Museum—and three tombs are of interest for their mix of pharaonic and Greek imagery. ⊠*Shar' El Shenity Abu Mandour, Karmouz* ☎*03/482–5800* ☎*£e35* ⏱*Daily 9–4:30.*

NEED A BREAK?

Even if your body can't handle any more caffeine, it's worth stopping at Baudrot (⊠ **23 Shar'a Sa'd Zaghlul, Mahatet El Raml** ☎ **no phone), one of downtown's easily overlooked oases, for a soda. The plain white facade and empty display cases in the window seem purpose-built to put off customers, but if you walk straight through the drab patisserie, there's a peaceful vine-covered garden café in back. The plastic chairs and tables aren't exactly luxurious, but in this little sliver of tranquility the only noises are made by birds chirping in the trees overhead. The café is open daily from 9 AM to midnight.**

❾ ★ **Grand Trianon.** One of Alexandria's most stylish institutions since it opened in the 1920s, the Grand Trianon remains a forum for courtship, gossip, and rediscovery. Its most popular area is the café, which has a certain old-world grandeur, despite being the least decorated part of the place. The adjacent restaurant is an extravagant art nouveau jewel, with colorful murals on the wall and a spectacular stained-glass window over the entrance to the kitchen. But the pièce de résistance is in the patisserie around the corner. There, behind elaborately carved wooden cabinets, a series of Venetian wood-panel paintings of sensual water nymphs will take your breath away. The colors are muted, but as your eyes adjust the images will start to shimmer like a Gustav Klimt kiss. The café and restaurant close at midnight, the patisserie at 8 PM. ⊠*Maydan Sa'd Zaghlul, Mahatet El Raml* ☎*03/486–8539.*

❼ **Greco-Roman Museum.** This museum was founded in 1895 and contains the best of the pieces found at Pompey's Pillar—including a statue of the Apis Bull—and two statues from the catacombs at Kom al-Shoqafa (⇨*Historical Alexandria, below*). In spite of some uninteresting pieces, this is Egypt's finest museum covering the period of Egyptian history from Alexander the Great's conquest in 332 BC to the third Persian occupation in AD 619. There are a great many pharaonic pieces here as well; indeed, the most impressive thing about the museum is that it shows the scale of cross-fertilization between pharaonic culture and the Greek and Roman cultures that followed. Highlights of the collection include its early Christian mummies, remnants of a temple to the crocodile god Sobek, and a courtyard full of sun-drenched statuary. ⊠*5 Shar'a al-Mathaf, Raml Station* ☎*03/483–6434* ☎*£e10* ⏱*Daily 9–4:30.*

❺ **Kom al-Dikka** *(Roman Theater).* The focal point of this excavated section of the ancient city is a well-preserved amphitheater—the only one of its kind in Egypt—originally constructed in the 4th century AD, then rebuilt in the 6th century, following an earthquake. At that time a large dome was added (only its supporting columns still stand), and the theater went from being a cultural venue to a forum for public meetings of the City Council—a change deduced from ancient graffiti promoting various political parties.

The Ancient Library of Alexandria

Relatively little is known about the ancient library itself, beyond its reputation for scholarship. It was founded by Ptolemy I in the 4th century BC and is said to have held a collection of 500,000 volumes—at a time when books were rare, costly commodities and all written by hand. Succeeding pharaohs gathered existing knowledge from around the Greek world but also invited scientists and scholars to contribute current research, ensuring that Alexandria was at the cutting edge of learning.

Theories about its destruction abound, but most assume it stood for roughly 500 years before being consumed by fire. What is known is that the Great Library—and the complex of lecture halls, laboratories, and observatories called the Mouseion, of which it was part—was a source of literary and scientific wisdom that changed the world. It was here, for example, that Euclid set forth the elements of geometry still taught in schools today, and Eratosthenes measured the circumference of the Earth. And it was here that the conqueror Julius Caesar had a new, more accurate calendar drawn up—the Julian calendar—that became the framework for the measurement of time throughout the Western world.

The other half of the site is the ancient baths and living quarters, although much of this area is, in fact, best seen through the fence from the side near Pastroudis Café, where the cisterns and walls are clearly visible. The red bricks mark the location of the heated baths—warmed by an elaborate underground system—which complemented the adjacent cold and steam baths. The whole area fell into disuse after the 7th-century Persian conquest of Egypt. One noteworthy site in the residential section is a Roman house known as the **Villa of the Birds**, so named for its colorful floor mosaics depicting birds in several forms. The colorful and detailed craftsmanship shows a high level of sophistication. The mosaics, now restored, are protected by a modern structure. ⊠ *Off Maydan El Shohada, opposite the Misr train station, Kon al-Dikka* ☎ *03/490–2904* ▱ *£e20, £e15 for Villa of the Birds* ⊙ *Daily 9–4:30.*

⑪ **Montazah Gardens.** When the descendents of Mohammed Ali became *khedives* (princes) of Egypt in the mid-18th century, they began to surround themselves with the trappings of a royal lifestyle, and one of these rewards was the lavish El Montazah palace, built outside Alexandria in the 1890s by Khedive Abbas Hilmi Pasha. During the era of Egyptian Royalty (1922–1952) the palace, enlarged in ornate Italianate style by King Faoud and surrounded by acres of lush gardens, played host to lavish parties. It was from here that Faoud's son King Farouk made his last journey on Egyptian soil after his abdication in 1952. He went into exile in Rome, Italy, and died there in 1965. Today the palace (under renovation at this writing) is part of the presidential property portfolio. The formal gardens, with their flower beds, lawns, and beaches, offer a shady place to stroll or picnic and are very popular with local fami-

Café Life

The cafés in Alexandria are unlike any others in the rest of Egypt: grand, atmospheric, rich with history, with much more in common with Europe than the Middle East. Their heyday was at the beginning of the 20th century, when the city's diverse cocktail of nationalities—Greek, British, and French among others—used the cafés as common ground on which to meet. Some, like Pastroudis, became associated with literary figures; others, like Athineos, with a particular community. There are, as well, small stand-up espresso bars like the Brazilian Coffee Stores, where regulars stop in on their way to work. But the most majestic of all is the Grand Trianon, where young lovers court and old women gather in groups to keep up their French.

lies. ⊠ *Corniche al-Nil, Montazah* ☎ *No phone* ▭ *£e5 (unless you are checking into a hotel in the park)* ⊙ *Daily 7* AM*–11* PM.

❶ **Pompey's Pillar** (*Serapium Oracle*). Despite being Alexandria's most famous tourist sight, Pompey's Pillar is a disappointment. After all, it's just a granite pillar—albeit at 88 feet, a very tall one—placed on a hill surrounded by ruins. Known in Arabic as *al-'Amud al-Sawiri* (Column of the Horseman), the pillar was misnamed after Pompeius (106–48 BC) by the Crusaders. In fact, it dates to the 3rd century AD, when it was erected in honor of the emperor Diocletian on the site of a Ptolemaic temple to Serapis.

Helpful signs on the ruins name each virtually empty spot as a "pool" or "bath," which to the untrained eye look like indistinguishable rocks. The late-model sphinxes lying around on pedestals add a little character. The most interesting element, ironically, is that from the hill you can get a glimpse inside the walled cemetery next door, as well as a view of a long and busy market street. ⊠ *Corner of Amoud El Sawary and El Shenity Abou Mandour, Karmouz* ☎ *03/482-5800* ▭ *£e20* ⊙ *Daily 9–4.*

ALSO WORTH SEEING

❸ **Anglican Church of St. Mark.** After St. Mark visited Alexandria in AD 49, the city became an early Christian outpost, building its first cathedral by AD 282. This church, constructed in 1855, was one of the few buildings undamaged during the shelling of the city by British warships in 1882. It exhibits an odd mix of Western, Moorish, and Byzantine design elements that somehow manage to blend together harmoniously. The soft yellow stone and colorful stained-glass windows are particularly exquisite in the early morning sun. The walls are lined with plaques, some of which date back almost a century, commemorating members of the Anglican community for their years of long service to the church. ⊠ *Maydan Ahmed Orabi, Manshia* ☎ *03/486-7103* ⊙ *Daily 9–4 except during services.*

8 **Brazilian Coffee Stores.** Little has changed since this stand-up espresso bar opened in 1929, as you can see from the foot-traffic patterns worn into the tile floor. The ancient roasters are visible to the right—if you're lucky they'll be roasting beans when you walk in, and the café will be filled with plumes of aromatic smoke. Lining the walls are the original stunningly painted mirrors showing a map of South America, along with population and coffee-production statistics for Brazil, now endearingly out of date. There's even an enormous Brazilian flag painted on the ceiling. ⊠ *44 Shar'a Sa'd Zaghlul, Mahatet El Raml* ☎ *03/482–5059* ⊙ *Daily 7 AM–11 PM.* .

6 **The Cavafy Museum.** The writer Constantine Cavafy was ignored during his lifetime but has received international recognition since his death in 1933. His poetry, which focused on such themes as one's moral dilemmas and uncertainty about the future, spoke to the Greek-speaking community around the Eastern Mediterranean and has been translated into all major languages.

The small flat where Cavafy spent the last years of his life has been turned into a museum. Half of it is given over to a re-creation of his home, with a period-piece brass bed and a case of reputedly genuine Christian icons. On the walls is an endless collection of portraits and sketches of Cavafy that only the most vain of men could have hung in his own apartment. The other half of the museum houses newspaper clippings about the poet's life and a library of his works, in the many languages and permutations in which they were published after his death—a remarkable legacy for a man who lived so quietly. There is, as well, a room dedicated to a student of Cavafy named Stratis Tsirkas, who lived in Upper Egypt and wrote a massive trilogy set in the Middle East. And there is one last curiosity: a cast of Cavafy's death mask, serene but disfigured, lying cushioned on a purple pillow. ⊠ *4 Shar'a Sharm al-Sheikh, Mahatet El Raml* ☎ *03/468–1598* ⊠ *£e10* ⊙ *Tues.–Sun. 10–3.*

EL ANFUSHI

Somewhere—really, everywhere—under Alexandria lies a wealth of archaeological remains, but little of it has been excavated. As a result, the city's ancient and medieval remnants exist in scattered pockets. The most central sights are the Greco-Roman Museum and the Roman Theater (⇨ *Downtown & Raml Station, above*), but none of the rest are more than a 15-minute taxi ride from Raml Station in the El Anfushi, Karmouz, and Koum El Dakka districts.

MAIN SIGHTS

2 **Anfushi Tombs.** You need to have a fairly serious death fetish to make the effort to see these 3rd century BC Ptolemaic tombs. Although built on a smaller scale than the Catacombs at Kom al-Shoqafa, this necropolis has more extant decoration, including paintings on the limestone walls that simulate marble and include various images from the pantheon of pharaonic gods. The tombs are on the spit of land (which at one time was an island) separating the Western and Eastern harbors, roughly

CLOSE UP

Constantine Cavafy

Constantine Cavafy (Konstantinos Kavafis) was born in Alexandria to Greek parents in 1863 and began writing poetry at age 19. It wasn't until much later, as a result of the exposure given to him in the novelist E. M. Forster's celebrated guidebook to Alexandria that Cavafy came to be regarded as the most accomplished Greek poet of our age. Cavafy's poems—including "God Abandons Antony," and, most famously, "The City"—are suffused with melancholy, and with a sense of his alienation from the society around him. Ironically, considering his rejection during his lifetime, they give such a strong evocation of place that they define the cultural memory of Alexandria in his time. Jacqueline Kennedy Onassis left a request that Cavafy's poem "Ithaka," which describes life's beauty being in the journey and not in the destination, be read at her funeral.

a third of the way between the Palace of Ras al-Tin on the western point and Fort Qayt Bay on the eastern point. ⊠ *Shar'a Ras El Tin, El Anfushi* ☏ *No phone* ▱ *£e20* ⊘ *Daily 9–4:30.*

❶ **Fort Qayt Bay.** This sandstone fort lies on the very tip of the Corniche, dominating the view of the Eastern Harbor. It was built on the site of Alexandria's Pharos lighthouse, one of the seven wonders of the ancient world and incorporates its remains—much of which are still visible—into the foundation. The lighthouse was constructed under the Ptolemies by a Greek named Sostratus in the 3rd century BC. Standing about 400 feet high and capable of projecting a light that could be seen 53 km (35 mi) out to sea, it was one of the most awesome structures created by ancients. The base of the four-tiered Pharos was thought to have contained some 300 rooms, as well as a hydraulic system for lifting fuel to the top of the tower.

In the centuries that followed, the Pharos was damaged and rebuilt several times, until it was finally destroyed in the great earthquake of 1307. It lay in ruins for two centuries until the Mamluk Sultan Qayt Bay had the current fortress constructed in 1479. Recently, a French team found what are thought to be parts of the Pharos in shallow waters just offshore, rekindling local interest in the ancient monument—there is even talk of an underwater museum, although that is unlikely to materialize anytime soon.

The outer walls of the fort enclose a large open space, and the ramparts' walk affords magnificent views of miles and miles of coastline. The fort also encourages romance—the arrow slits built into the ramparts that were once used to defend the fort now shelter Egyptian couples enjoying the chance to court each other in semiprivacy. The interior of the building within the fort, by comparison, is exceptionally dull, housing an undecorated mosque, a patriotic mural of President Jamal 'Abd al-Nasir (Nasser) reviewing a fantastically outfitted Egyptian navy, and a kitsch historical model of "the fleet of Senefroo." Upstairs are the iron bullets, swords, bombs, and shards of pottery recovered from

CLOSE UP

Ptolemaic Egypt

After the sudden death of Alexander the Great in 323 BC, the Macedonian general Ptolemy was appointed *satrap* (protector or governor) of Egypt but declared himself Pharaoh Ptolemy I in 305 BC, starting the Ptolemaic dynasty. His descendents had a 300-year tenure as Egyptian rulers, during which time the political focus of the country shifted to the north coast. The Ptolemies were more concerned with events in the Mediterranean basin (the area encompassing the modern countries of Greece, Turkey, Syria, Lebanon, Israel and Libya) than with Memphis or Thebes.

They were leaders in a Greek world that had Alexandria at its epicenter—being educated in Greek style, upholding the Greek rule of law, and using the Greek language in the court. However, at his inauguration Ptolemy I proclaimed that the lands of Egypt would be restored to Horus during his reign and that of his descendants, a message that got the Egyptians on his side immediately. The new regime spent considerable funds renovating the old temples and even building new ones; and they were mummified with wrappings bearing images of the "Book of the Dead," just as pharaohs in the New Kingdom era had been.

Initially, the Ptolemies were a positive force in Egypt. Astute businesspeople, their investment in good agricultural practices and improved transport

systems allowed Egypt to become a regional economic powerhouse. They also had a passion for learning, inviting scientists from around the known world and collecting knowledge that made the country a hotbed of innovation. It was during this period that the Great Library was founded in Alexandria.

However, as the generations passed, problems surfaced that would eventually lead to their downfall. The Ptolemies kept a tight hold on power—perhaps a little too tight. Brothers married sisters, weakening the royal bloodline. Sibling rivalry was rife. Egypt's famous last queen Cleopatra was in conflict with her co-ruler, husband and brother Ptolemy XIV, and she was exiled from her country when she made a house call on Julius Caesar wrapped up in a carpet. The ensuing love affair between the two put an end to the Ptolemaic Dynasty's chances of keeping the throne and melded Egypt's future with Rome. Cleopatra produced an heir for Julius Caesar—but was no doubt genuinely shocked by his assassination. However, her later love affair with Mark Antony plunged Egypt into the maelstrom of an epic Roman power struggle. Mark Antony and Cleopatra lost in battle to Octavian, who became Roman Emperor Augustus, and *realpolitik* dictated that Ptolemaic Egypt had to succumb to Roman rule.

Napoléon's ship *l'Orient,* which the British sank off Abu Qir, several miles east. ⊠ *Corniche (far western end), El Anfushi* ☎ *03/480–9144* ☎ *£e25* ⏷ *Daily 9–5:30.*

NEED A BREAK?

El Koubeze (⊠ 50 26th of July St., the Corniche, Gomrouk ☎ 03/486-7860), a small palace of marble decorated with piles of colorful fresh fruit, is one of the most incongruous places in Alexandria. Though a casual juice bar—the juice is pressed when you order, so it's mouth-wateringly fresh—El Koubeze's

crisp uniformed staff look as if they could grace a fine-dining establishment. The only letdown is the cheap plastic seats and tables and the roadside setting. But it's great for a refreshing pit stop.

OFF THE BEATEN PATH

The Battlefield and Monuments of El Alamein. The desert west of Alexandria was the field of one of the decisive battles of World War II. In 1942, the British Eighth Army led by General Montgomery attacked the German Afrika Corps led by Fieldmarshall Rommel (the famous "Desert Fox") and sent them into a retreat, which would eventually clear Axis troops from the whole of North Africa.

Three carefully tended military grave sites hold the remains of Allied, Italian, and German soldiers—each with a suitably somber monument. The gardens of El Alamein museum display an array of military hardware used in the battle. Inside, the galleries offer background information on the forces involved and explain how the campaign in North Africa developed and how the decisive battle played out. However, the museum has collected a wealth of personal items, including letters and photographs from soldiers on all sides that layer a compelling human story on top of the military records. The sites are around an hour west of Alexandria along the coastal road. Renting a taxi for the morning would be the most convenient way to see the museum, monuments, and graveyards. Local tour companies also organize guides and transportation. ⊠ *El Alamein, 96 km (60 mi) west of Alexandria* ☎ *046/410–0031* ✆ *£e10* ☉ *May–Sept., daily 9:30–3:30; Oct.–Apr., daily 9:30–2:30.*

ALSO WORTH SEEING

❸ **Abu al-Abbas al-Mursi Mosque.** This attractive mosque was built during World War II over the tomb of a 13th-century holy man, who is the patron saint of the city's fishermen. The area surrounding it has been turned into Egypt's largest and most bizarre religious/retail complex, with a cluster of mosques sharing a terrace that hides an underground shopping center. Intruding on the space is a horrific modernism-on-the-cheap office building (with yet more shops) that is as pointed and angular as the mosques are smooth and curved. If you are dressed modestly and the mosque is open, you should be able to get inside. If so, remove your shoes and refrain from taking photos. ⊠ *Corniche, al-Anfushi, El Anfushi.*

WHERE TO EAT

Alexandria's culinary gift is extraordinary seafood, drawing on the best of the Mediterranean and the Red Sea. The preparation tends to be simple: grilled or fried, perhaps laced with garlic, herbs, or butter, and typically served with *tahini* (sesame paste) and a couple of salads on the side. The ingredients are so fresh that anything more elaborate would obscure their flavors. Most places display their offerings of fish, shrimp, crab, calamari, and mussels on ice, and you pay by weight or per serving. The price includes preparation and everything else—there are no

CLOSE UP

Laurence Durrell

Laurence George Durrell was born in 1912 in northern India to expat parents of English and Irish descent. At the age of 11, Durrell was sent to England for his education, but he hated his time there and didn't complete his formal schooling. Instead, he resolved to make a living as a writer.

In 1935 he moved to Corfu, an island off Greece, with his wife, mother, and brothers and sisters. He thrived there but was forced to leave when German troops invaded in 1941. He settled in Cairo with his wife and small daughter, then moved to Alexandria alone to take up a position as press attaché at the British Information Office.

After the war, Durrell returned to Greece for two years before taking up a post in Argentina, then in Yugoslavia. In 1952 he bought a cottage close to the coast in the north of Cyprus and took a job as an English teacher to fund his literary career. He wrote the first volume of *The Alexandria Quartet* in Cyprus. But peace was elusive as Cyprus had become the focus of an independence struggle. Durrell moved one more time, to Sommières in the south of France, where he spent the final 35 years of his life, completing *The Alexandria Quartet* and two more cycles of novels. He died in 1990.

hidden costs. If you need help choosing, there will always be someone on hand to guide your selection.

DOWNTOWN & RAML STATION

$ ✕**China House.** There are Indian, Chinese, and Thai chefs working here, so although the menu seems a little wide-ranging, you do get pretty authentic cuisine. Having said that, the choice in each cuisine type is limited, and chefs concentrate on what they can do easily given the limitation on some ingredients. The rooftop setting with views along the Corniche makes this one of the best places to enjoy the sunset and take a respite from the bustle of the city. ⊠ *Sofitel Cecil Hotel, Maydan Sa'd Zaghlul, Raml Station* ☎03/487–7173 ext.782 ▤*AE, MC, V.*

$$ ✕**Grand Trianon.** This is Alexandria's most gorgeous restaurant, with high ceilings, elaborate carved wooden chandeliers, and swirling art nouveau murals decorating the walls. People have always said that some day the kitchen will be taken over by a chef equal to the decor, but for now the food remains enjoyable but unspectacular. If you stick close to the Egyptian or French basics, you'll play to their strengths. As appetizers the *sambousik* (phyllo pastries stuffed with cheese or meat) and French onion soup are quite good, and the entrecôte of beef makes an excellent main course. For dessert, you can linger at your table or relocate to the adjoining café. ⊠*Maydan Sa'd Zaghlul, Raml Station* ☎03/482–0986 ▤*AE, MC, V.*

$ ✕**Taverna.** This is more a pizzeria than a real Greek taverna, but the pizza is delicious, assembled in front of you and baked in an oven to the left of the entrance. The baladi oven to the right is used for *fatir,* a kind of Egyptian pizza than can be sweet or savory; it's also often fairly oily—ask them to go light on the *ghee* (clarified butter). The menu also includes some fish and shrimp dishes. The proper seating area is upstairs, but it's even cheaper if you eat at the informal area downstairs, where a *shwarma* (pressed lamb carved from a vertical rotisserie) sandwich makes a nice midday snack. ⊠*1 Maydan Sa'd Zaghlul, Raml Station* ☏*03/482–8189* ⊟*AE, MC, V.*

EL ANFUSHI

$$–$$$ ✕**Fish Market.** On the waterfront side of Alexandria Corniche, this is
★   probably the biggest fish restaurant in the city and sees a regular crowd of locals who know they'll get excellent but simply cooked seafood plus a great view out across the harbor. The catch is priced by kilogram, and the rice and salads are included. Choose your fish and ask them to price it, so you know how much you'll be paying. There's also a decent wine list featuring local labels. ⊠*Corniche (near the Abu al-Abbas al-Mursi Mosque), Gomrouk* ☏*03/480–5114* ⊟*MC, V* ⊘*No lunch.*

$ ✕**Grand Café.** Adjacent to the Tikka Grill and under the same management, this outdoor restaurant is one of the coziest, most romantic places in Alexandria. Tables are scattered throughout a lush garden, amid palm fronds lit against the night sky and small wooden bridges leading to private corners. The menu offers the standard Egyptian dishes—kebabs, including *shish taouk* (chicken kebabs) and *kofta* (minced lamb on a skewer), and so forth—but it's the setting that should bring you here. ⊠*Corniche (near the Abu al-Abbas al-Mursi Mosque), Gomrouk* ☏*03/480–5114* ⊟*MC, V* ⊘*No lunch.*

$$ ✕**Kadoura.** Granted, it looks unpromising: not shabby enough to feel authentic, not stylish enough to feel elegant. So close your eyes. Kadoura is famous throughout Egypt, and it's every bit as good as its reputation. Fish is grilled with a delicious fresh tomato, garlic, and herb purée; calamari come lightly fried, tender, and tasty. Pick your seafood downstairs, grab a wood-block number, and sit upstairs. Everything else that comes to you—salads, tahini, drinks—is included in the price. It's very popular for lunch, especially on Fridays, when space is at a premium. ⊠*47 26th of July St. (the Corniche), Gomrouk* ☏*03/480–0967* ⌂*Reservations not accepted* ⊟*No credit cards.*

$$ ✕**Samakmak.** This seafood restaurant is located in a suitably rundown area near the port where the fishing boats dock, and it is so close to the landing stage you could throw the fish straight from the dock to the restaurant grill. Inside, the place has a slightly more formal atmosphere than most and serves exquisitely fresh seafood that benefits from the short walk from boat to plate. The staff is friendly and helpful. ⊠*42 Shar'a Ras al-Tin, El Anfushi* ☏*03/481–1560* ⌂*Reservations essential* ⊟*No credit cards.*

$ ✕**Tikka Grill.** Alexandrians swear by this place, and it's packed with families in the early evenings and an older crowd later on. It has surprisingly elegant decor and a magnificent setting next to the water—the only Eastern Harbor restaurant to have one, though the atmosphere can be a little manic as waiters rush around with trays full of food. The menu is wide-ranging, but you'd be best to stick with the Egyptian dishes. The roasted meats make good choices, as do the cold mezze. Try to get a table by the window for fantastic views across the har-

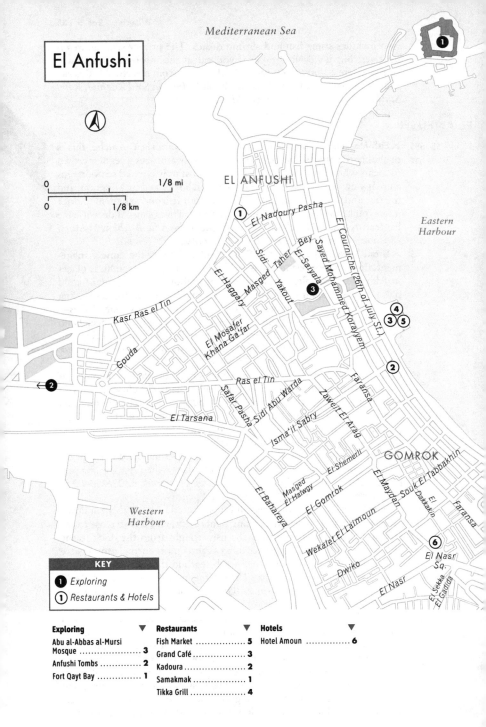

El Anfushi

Mediterranean Sea

EL ANFUSHI

Eastern Harbour

El Nadoury Pasha

El Corniche (26th of July St.)

Sidi Taher Bey

El Haggary

Masged

El-Saiyala

Sayed Mohammed Korayyem

Yakout

Kasr Ras el Tin

El Mosafer Khana Ga'far

Gouda

Ras el Tin

Faransa

Safar Pasha

Sidi Abu Warda

El Tarsana

Isma'il Sabry

Zaweit El Arag

GOMROK

El Shemerli

El Maydan

Souk El Tabbakhin

El Dakkakin

Masged El Halwgy

El Gomrok

El Bahareya

Wekalet El Laimoun

Faransa

Hotel Amoun

El Nasr Sq.

Dwiko

El Sekka El Gadida

El Nasr

Western Harbour

KEY

- **1** *Exploring*
- **①** *Restaurants & Hotels*

0 — 1/8 mi
0 — 1/8 km

bor. ⊠*Corniche (near Abu al-Abbas al-Mursi Mosque), Gomrouk* ☎*03/480–5114* 🖃*MC, V.*

EASTERN SHORELINE

$$$$ ✕**Al Farouk.** Named for King Farouk (who ruled from 1936 to 1952), this restaurant used to be his summer office. The decor is definitely fit for a king: alabaster columns, china, and stained-glass windows. The gorgeously printed menu mixes old photos of royal weddings and affairs of state with dishes on an internationally regal theme. Look for tender foie gras Louis XV (foie gras in a port-wine sauce) or decadent Caviar Raspoutine (caviar selection with blinis) served on a bed of ice. The best entrées are the *sharkesseya d'Istanbul* (chicken stewed in a subtle walnut sauce) and the filet blanc et noir Ras el-Tin (veal and beef steaks with foie gras and mushrooms). ⊠*El-Salamlek Palace, Montazah Palace grounds, Montazah* ☎*03/547–7999* 🖃*AE, DC, MC, V.*

$$$ ✕**Byblos.** The signature restaurant of the Four Seasons, Byblos serves excellent Lebanese dishes and brasserie-style French cuisine—you can mix and match depending on your mood. Start with a selection of hot and cold *mezze*, then try *sheikh al manshee* (eggplant stuffed with minced beef and tomato sauce) or *kebbeh bel laban* (lamb meatballs smothered with yogurt sauce and mint). The French dishes steer clear of heavy sauces, concentrating instead on fine meat and fish, such as rack of lamb or roasted sea bass. ⊠*Four Seasons Hotel, 399 El Geish Rd., San Stefano* ☎*03/581–8000* 🖃*AE, DC, MC, V* ⊙*No lunch. Dec.–Apr., closed Mon.*

$$ ✕**Zephyrion.** Established in 1929 in the dusty village of Abu Qir east of Montazah, Zephyrion has been synonymous with good seafood for three generations. The restaurant could seat 400 without effort—more in the summer when the veranda is open—so it never feels crowded, and the seafood is as fresh as it gets. The restaurant is at its most peaceful in the late afternoon sun. It has no address, but everyone in Abu Qir knows where it is, so just ask. Since it's 20 minutes from Montazah (and 40 minutes from downtown), the big question is whether it's worth the trip. The answer: yes, if you see the trip itself as part of your adventure. ⊠*Abu Qir* ☎*03/562–1319* 🖃*No credit cards.*

WHERE TO STAY

Hotels in Alexandria are located in two clusters that are roughly 30 minutes apart. Upscale resort hotels are all out along the eastern shoreline in Montazah, close to or even within the manicured khedivial palace gardens—but not convenient to the city or the historic sights. Lower-budget hotels are almost all downtown, much more convenient but less tranquil.

EL ANFUSHI

$ ⊡ **Hotel Amoun.** The Amoun curves around one side of Maydan Nasser. The functional rooms here are reasonably large, with funky green velour curtains and very basic furniture. All overlook the square, which makes street noise less of an issue on higher floors. The main drawback is the late-night "disco," which, given the proximity to the port, is more active as a front for prostitution than as a dance club. The hotel's clientele is almost exclusively Russian. **Pros:** Good-size rooms. **Cons:** Communal access means the elevator is dirty and unkempt; bathrooms are small. ⊠ *32 Shar'a al-Nasr, Manshiya* ☏ *03/481–8239* ⥤ *86 rooms* ⚭ *In-room: refrigerator. In-hotel: restaurant* ⊟ *No credit cards* ⦿ *EP.*

DOWNTOWN & RAML STATION

$ ⊡ **Hotel Union.** Don't be misled by the dingy entrance and modest common area: this is the best inexpensive hotel in the city. The upstairs rooms with baths all have white walls, hand-blown glass lamps suspended in the middle of the room, and decent bathrooms. But it is the balconies, which appear to hang over the Mediterranean, that make the place feel like such a steal at this price—be sure to request one. The rooms without bath (downstairs) are in much worse shape. **Pros:** Excellent value for money, especially those rooms with sea views. **Cons:** Some facilities in need of a little TLC; noise from the Corniche won't please light sleepers. ⊠ *164 Corniche, Raml Station* ☏ *03/480–7312* ⥤ *37 rooms, 26 with bath* ⚭ *In room: no a/c (some), safe (some), refrigerator, no TV (some)* ⊟ *No credit cards* ⦿ *EP.*

$$$ ⊡ **Paradise Inn–Metropole.** The best value in Alexandria, the turn-of-the-
★ 20th-century Metropole has an elegance few others can match. The lavishly overdone lobby has gilt mirrors, Flemish tapestries, and bas-relief moldings that cry out for a restraining hand, but the large rooms come as a pleasant surprise. The 20-foot ceilings, simple antique furnishings, and flowing velvet drapes project a feeling of luxury. Though some of the fixtures could benefit from a little TLC, the overall feel is of a grand mansion that you've been lucky enough to stumble upon. **Pros:** A delightful period atmosphere; friendly and helpful staff; excellent location for exploring downtown on foot. **Cons:** Rooms sizes can vary dramatically; some traffic noise in rooms overlooking the main street. ⊠ *52 Shar'a Sa'd Zaghlul, Raml Station* ☏ *03/486–1467* ⊕ *www. paradiseinnegypt.com* ⥤ *66 rooms* ⚭ *In-room: safe, refrigerator. In-hotel: restaurant, room service, laundry service, Wi-Fi* ⊟ *AE, MC, V* ⦿ *BP.*

$ ⊡ **Petit Coin.** The name ("Little Corner" in French) fits this cozy hotel, just off Maydan Ahmed Orabi. There's nothing complicated about the Petit Coin—the spare rooms are clean, comfy, and air-conditioned, which makes it an inviting choice if you want a convenient place to stay right in the city. Rooms look out over the busy square and down to the water; for rooms on high floors, the noise is not an issue, but on lower floors you will hear traffic noise even with your windows closed. The best views are at the hotel's café, which is a fine place to watch the

Downtown & Raml Station

KEY

1 *Exploring*

① *Restaurants & Hotels*

3

Exploring ▶

Anglican Church of St. Mark	3
Attarine Market	4
Bibliotheca Alexandrina	10
Brazilian Coffee Stores	8
Catacombs of Kom al-Shaqafa	2
The Cavalry Museum	6
Grand Trianon	9
Greco-Roman Museum	7
Kom al-Dikka	5
Montazah Gardens	11
Pompey's Pillar	1

Restaurants ▶

Al Farouk	16
Byblos	15
China House	3
Grand Trianon	7
Taverna	6
Zephyrion	14

Hotels ▶

El-Salamek Palace	11
Four Seasons Hotel Alexandria at San Stefano	10
Helnan Palestine	12
Hotel Union	8
Paradise Inn–Metropole	5
Petit Coin	1
Renaissance Alexandria Hotel	13
Sea Star	9
Sofitel Alexandria Cecil	4
Windsor Palace	2

sun set over the rooftops. The hotel serves no alcohol, and it's a good idea to pass on the restaurant. **Pros:** Views from the roof terrace, which is a good place to relax; friendly staff. **Cons:** Street noise is a problem on lower floors; restaurant not recommendable. ⊠*5 Shar'a Ahmed Orabi, Manshiya* ☎*03/487–1503* ↵*52 rooms* ♿*In room: refrigerator. In hotel: restaurant, laundry service* ⊟*No credit cards.*

$ 🎦 **Sea Star.** A rather basic hotel, Sea Star's greatest appeal is its location. If you are on a budget it's a clean if uninspiring option that's close to the tram station and within walking distance of downtown, the museum, and the library. Decor is minimalist 1980s kitsch against a backdrop of plain whitewashed walls, but the rooms are spacious. The Sea Star restaurant offers Egyptian and European dishes and claims 24-hour room service, but it seems little used. Head into the city for better eating options. **Pros:** Clean option for the price; location means you're in the heart of the action but on a quieter side street. **Cons:** Very ordinary decor; disinterested front desk staff. ⊠*24 Shar'a Amin Fikhry, Raml Station* ☎*03/483–1787* ↵*49 rooms, 14 suites* ♿*In-room: no a/c (some). In-hotel: restaurant, room service* ⊟*No credit cards* ⦿*EP.*

$$$$ 🎦 **Sofitel Alexandria Cecil.** With the Cecil, you're paying for history. Built in 1930 and immortalized as one of Justine's haunts in Lawrence Durrell's *Alexandria Quartet*, it actually retains few reminders of that era—just its elegant revolving door, two gorgeous old wooden elevators, and a dusty bar that's changed little since World War II. The rooms have high ceilings and large shuttered windows, and there's a richness in the burgundy and gold drapes and soft furnishings that decorate the space, which give a classical French feel. **Pros:** excellent location for exploring downtown on foot; cozy historic hotel. **Cons:** rooms are overpriced for the size (hotel is priced partly because of its history); small bathrooms. ⊠*16 Maydan Sa'd Zaghlul, Mahatet El Raml* ☎*03/487–7173* ⊕*www.sofitel.com* ↵*83 rooms, 6 suites* ♿*In-room: safe, Internet. In-hotel: 2 restaurants, room service, bars, gym, laundry services, concierge, Wi-Fi, no-smoking rooms* ⊟*AE, DC, MC, V* ⦿*BP.*

$$–$$$ 🎦 **Windsor Palace.** Erected on the Alexandria Corniche in 1906, the Windsor Palace retains a period look and feel thanks to its furnishings, tapestries, and oil paintings. The rooms have been modernized but have not lost their character, with high ceilings and tall windows; the front rooms have elegant iron balconies. The hotel serves no alcohol. **Pros:** Excellent location on the downtown Corniche; period atmosphere harks back to the early-20th-century heyday of Alexandria. **Cons:** Although grand in scale, the lobby has a souless quality; on-site facilities are limited when compared to the competition. ⊠*17 Shar'a al-Shohada, Raml Station* ☎*03/480–8700* ⊕*www.paradiseinnegypt. com* ↵*71 rooms* ♿*In-room: Internet. In-hotel: restaurant, laundry service* ⊟*AE, MC, V* ⦿*BP.*

EASTERN SHORELINE

$$$$ 🎦 **El-Salamlek Palace.** Built in the late 19th century by the khedive as
★   a lodge for his Austrian mistress, the Salamlek is Alexandria's most unusual luxurious hotel. Each suite is a unique, charming space, with

sloping wood ceilings or arched windows, though the canopy beds and glittering gold furnishings can sometimes feel a touch nouveau riche. The heart-stoppers are the gorgeous tiled terraces in three of the suites—overlooking the royal gardens and the nearby cove, they have wicker furniture practically begging you to lounge, drink in hand, in the late-afternoon sun. You'll feel like you're part of a royal house party. **Pros:** Small, intimate hotel with antique furnishings; exceptional restaurant on-site. **Cons:** No resort-style facilities in the house, so in some ways it feels like a glorified B&B, albeit with a restaurant. ⊠ *Montazah Palace grounds, Montazah* ☎ *03/547–7999* ⊕ *www.sangiovanni.com* ⟿ *14 suites, 4 rooms, 2 studios* ⟡ *In-room: safe (some), Wi-Fi. In-hotel: 3 restaurants, room service, bar, tennis courts, spa, beachfront, diving, water sports, bicycles, laundry service, Wi-Fi, parking (fee), no-smoking rooms.* ☰ *AE, DC, MC, V* ⦿| *AE, BP.*

$$$$ ⊞ **Four Seasons Hotel Alexandria at San Stefano.** The opening of the Four Seasons in 2007 has at last given Alexandria a world-class five-star property. Rooms are sumptuous and chic, styled with a hint of Louis XVI, yet with strong emphasis of classical Egypt, by Frenchman Pierre Yves Rochon. The hotel has excellent service, and its restaurants and bars form a focus for well-heeled Alexandrians and also Cairenes who weekend in the city. The hotel's sheltered sandy beach is private and well tended. The spa is one of the best in Egypt. **Pros:** High-quality appointments throughout; a good choice of restaurants and cafés; spectacular two-story spa. **Cons:** You must traverse a tunnel under the Corniche road to get to the beach; it's a 10-minute taxi ride to downtown. ⊠ *399 El Geish Rd., San Stefano* ☎ *03/581–8000* ⊕ *www.fourseasons. com* ⟿ *118 rooms* ⟡ *In-room: safe, Internet. In-hotel: 6 restaurants, room service, bars, pool, gym, spa, diving, water sports, children's programs (ages 5–12), laundry service, Wi-Fi, no-smoking rooms.* ☰ *AE, DC, MC, V* ⦿| *EP.*

$$$$ ⊞ **Helnan Palestine.** In a magnificent setting in the royal gardens between the old palace and a private cove, the fan-shaped concrete dreariness of the Palestine is an example of modernism gone very wrong. Built in 1964 to house visiting heads of state attending an Arab summit, the architectural styling has now fallen from fashion, though the interior space has been brought into the 21st century. North-facing rooms have excellent sea views, while others overlook the gardens. The small cove and its artificial beach have an Italian Lido feel. **Pros:** The hotel setting offers peace and tranquility. **Cons:** Far from the energy of downtown Alexandria; some staff members are indifferent. ⊠ *Montazah Palace grounds, Montazah* ☎ *03/547–3500* ⊕ *www.helnan.com* ⟿ *203 rooms, 27 suites* ⟡ *In-room: safe. In-hotel: 4 restaurants, room service, bars, pool, spa, gym, beachfront, water sports, laundry service, parking (free).* ☰ *AE, DC, MC, V* ⦿| *EP.*

$$$–$$$$ ⊞ **Renaissance Alexandria Hotel.** The Renaissance will never win any design rewards; in fact, those with a love of period buildings or an eye for ultracontemporary architecture will find this late-20th-century tower rather dreary. The interior, however, is a different story, as it has received a face-lift since the hotel opened and has kept pace with current trends. Gold and terracotta highlights against ivory walls make for a soothing color scheme in rooms. The hotel is especially popular with weekending Cairenes and business travelers. **Pros:** Good range of resort-style facilities on-site; sea-view rooms are the most recently renovated, so they offer the best value for money. **Cons:** Service can be patchy for this caliber hotel. ⊠ *544 Tariq al-Geish, Sidi Bishr* ☎ *03/549–0935* ⊕ *www.marriott.com* ➪ *115 rooms, 43 suites* ⚭ *In-room: safe, Internet (some). In-hotel: 3 restaurants, room service, bars, pool, gym, spa, diving, water sports, laundry service, Wi-Fi.* ⊟ *AE, DC, MC, V* ⦿ *EP.*

NIGHTLIFE & THE ARTS

The arts scene in Alex lags way behind Cairo, but there are some beacons of interest to explore. Although Alexandria has a couple of annual and biennial festivals, none would warrant a special trip to Alexandria in itself; however, several events are worth attending if you're in town when they're on.

The **Alexandria Biennial** is a festival of international and local artists held in October in even-numbered years at the Museum of Fine Arts (⊠ *18 Shar'a Menasce, Moharrem Bay* ☎ *03/493–6616*), which has been renamed in honor of Husayn Sobhi. The **Alexandria International Film Festival** is held every September at local theaters. Chaotically organized, it is regarded mainly as a chance for Egyptians to see fleeting nudity on screen (there's censorship the rest of the year). The festival occasionally brings interesting art films.

The **Alexandria Song Festival** is a competition for international and local singers, songwriters, and composers held in late July.

THE ARTS

In Alexandria, the main venues for music, theater, and exhibitions are the cultural centers attached to foreign consulates. Their programs are often very interesting, particularly those at the Cervantes Institute and the French Cultural Center, and they connect you with the cosmopolitan side of Alex that is often invisible in the city at large. To find out what's happening, call the individual consulates for their schedules; pick up *Egypt Today,* which occasionally lists events; or look for advertisements at expatriate hangouts, such as the restaurant **Elite** (⊠ *43 Shar'a Safiya Zaghlul, Mahatet El Raml* ☎ *03/482–3592*).

FOREIGN CULTURAL CENTERS
American Cultural Center (⊠ *3 Shar'a Pharana* ☎ *03/486–1009*).
British Cultural Center (⊠ *9 Shar'a Batalsa* ☎ *03/486–0199*).
Cervantes Institute (⊠ *101 Shar'a al-Horreya* ☎ *03/492–0214*).
French Cultural Center (⊠ *30 Shar'a Nabi Daniel* ☎ *03/492–0804*).
German Cultural Center (⊠ *10 Shar'a Batalsa* ☎ *03/483–9870*).
Greek Cultural Center (⊠ *18 Shar'a Sidi al-Metwalli* ☎ *03/482–1598*).
Italian Cultural Center (⊠ *52 Shar'a al-Horreya* ☎ *03/482–0258*).
Russian Cultural Center (⊠ *5 Shar'a Batalsa* ☎ *03/482–5645*).

OTHER PERFORMANCE VENUES

Alexandria Creativity Centre (⊠ *1 Shar'a al-Horreya* ☎*03/495–6745*) has a theater plus galleries and workshop space, running a varied program of arts performances, films, and exhibitions throughout the year.

MUSIC & OPERA

Alexandria Opera House (⊠*22 Shar'a al-Horreya* ☎*03/486–5106*) is also known as the Sayed Darwish Theatre. The 1921 edifice reopened after a full renovation project early in the new millennium. It offers a season of eclectic performances plus the occasional visiting company.

NIGHTLIFE

The joke among foreign residents in Alex is that if you want nightlife, go to Cairo. Things aren't quite that dire, but you'll still find that your nocturnal activities lean toward the wholesome rather than the iniquitous. Some top-end hotels have what pass for discos, and the Salamlek has a casino, but the city as a whole is definitely quieter than the capital.

BARS

Alexandria is a conservative town, so there's no bar scene to speak of, and most restaurants don't serve alcohol. If you want to enjoy a drink in convivial surroundings, head to the five-star hotels, which have a selection of international and local brands.

Bleu (⊠ *Four Seasons Hotel, 399 El Geish Rd.* ☎*03/581–8000*) is Alexandria's coolest venue. You can enjoy the shisha along with your cocktail. With a contemporary decor and a marble-floored terrace overlooking the north coast beaches and Corniche (open May through November only), the bar offers a venue for the trendy in-crowd.

Cap d'Or *(Sheikh 'Ali)* (⊠*4 Shar'a Adib, Manshiya* ☎*03/487–5177*), a modest place blessed with a gorgeous old art nouveau bar, serves a range of Stellas (the primary Egypt beer brand) along with some cognacs. Drinks will arrive with snacks that may be charged for—ask before you tuck in. The bar is on the small street that runs south from Sa'd Zaghlul; it is usually open until 3 AM.

Centro do Portugal (⊠*42 Shar'a Abdel Kader, next to Dr. Ragab's Papyrus Museum, Roushdi* ☎*03/452–7599*) feels more like the British Isles than Iberia. No matter, it's a central element in the local expatriate life and a great source of information about what's happening in the city. It's more like a social club than a commercial bar, but you're sure to make friends. The bar is usually open from 1 PM to midnight, later on Thursday night.

Monty Bar (⊠ *Sofitel Cecil Hotel, Maydan Sa'd Zaghlul* ☎*03/487–7173*) was named after General Montgomery, who commanded the Allied troops in the Battle of El Alamein. Monty Bar is a suitably conservative, wood-paneled venue. The clientele is a mixture of expat workers and sophisticated Cairenes. There's regular live music, but Monty's is too small to take the volume levels, so conversation can become impossible.

Spitfire Bar (✉7 *Shar'a Ancienne Bourse, Manshiya* ☎03/480–6503 ▭*No credit cards*) is a real sailor's bar: banknotes and bumper stickers from all over the world cover the walls, and among the other decorations are a yellowing advertisement for the Marines by the cash register, a fairly tame poster of a woman in a wet T-shirt, and the inevitable dogs-playing-pool carpet. But the atmosphere couldn't be more congenial—it's almost sedate—and there isn't a hint of sleaze to be found anywhere. The Spitfire is just north of Shar'a Sa'd Zaghlul on Shar'a Ancienne Bourse. It's closed on Sunday, and open until midnight all other nights.

CASINOS

El Salamlek Casino (✉ *El Salamlek Palace Hotel, Montazah* ☎03/547–7999), a small property, offers black jack, stud poker, and American roulette. It is Alexandria's only casino.

FILM

Movies are a mixture of Arab-produced films in Arabic (Egypt has its own production facilities), as well as Hollywood and other English-language films—usually with original soundtrack with Arabic subtitles.

Alexandria City Centre (✉*City Centre Mall, Cairo Desert Rd.* ☎03/397–0009) is a six-screen venue. **San Stefano Cinema** (✉*San Stefano Mall, 388 Shar'a El Geish* ☎03/582–3589) has 10screens with the latest blockbusters.

SHOPPING

Alexandria isn't a shopping city. There's little to buy here that you can't do better finding in Cairo, where the selection is much greater. If you're looking for chain stores, try Shar'a Suriya in Roushdi, Alexandria's most upscale neighborhood (15 minutes east of downtown by taxi), or one of the new shopping malls that have opened up in the past few years. But even there the options are limited.

MARKETS

The **Attarine Market** is the best, if slightly informal, source for reproduction furniture and antiques (⇨*Downtown Alexandria, in Exploring Alexandria, above*). Used books are sold at the street market on Nabi Daniel near al-Horreya, although mostly they are school textbooks. The other markets in Alexandria tend to be more basic and practical, selling kitchen items or cheap clothing and are aimed almost exclusively at locals. There's a **flea market** at the back end of the Attarine Market, and clothes are sold in the streets west of Maydan Orabi. Perhaps the most visually interesting market in Alexandria is the **produce market,** which begins at Maydan al-Gumhorreya in front of the Misr Train Station and runs west for a mile.

MALLS

Alexandria City Centre (⊠ *Alexandria International Park, Cairo Desert Rd.* ☎ *03/397–0009* ⊕ *www.alexandriacitycentre.com*), the city's largest mall, is anchored by a huge Carrefour supermarket and includes such well-known names as Timberland, La Senza, and Sony stores. **Green Plaza Mall** (⊠ *Cairo Desert Rd.* ☎ *03/420–9141*) is just 10 minutes from downtown by taxi; this mall is anchored by a modern Hilton Green Plaza Hotel, and there are almost 400 shops on site. **San Stefano Mall** (⊠ *388 Shar'a El Geish* ☎ *03/582–3589*), with Alexandria's most upscale shopping, sits underneath and around the new Four Seasons Hotel. You can buy designer sunglasses, jewelry, and formal and casual fashion clothing here.

SHOES

Downtown has a large number of shoe stores, but most of the shoes are of poor quality. The best are on Falaki Street (try the Armenian-owned Gregoire or Fortis), where, given enough time, the *chaussuriers* can produce custom-made shoes at a fraction of the price they would be in Europe or the United States.

SPORTS & THE OUTDOORS

BEACHES

The beaches along Egypt's Mediterranean coast differ greatly in character from those along the Red Sea and in the Sinai. Waves can be strong and persistent in fall, winter, and spring, helped by stiff offshore prevailing breezes. This wave action and water movement affects underwater visibility, making diving less enjoyable here than in the Red Sea.

The beaches along the Corniche in Alexandria are narrow but composed of fine sand. Many are formed from shallow coves interspersed with rocky outlets. The character of the public beaches in the city is much less cosmopolitan than at, say, Sharm El-Sheikh or Hurghada, and they are frequented far more by local and Cairene families than international visitors. For this reason you should dress modestly (no skimpy bikinis), though it must be stressed that the atmosphere is not oppressive. On hotel beaches, such as at the Four Seasons, there is no problem with beachwear, and you will be able to sunbathe without attention.

SPAS

The **Fours Seasons Hotel Spa & Wellness Center** (⊠ *Four Seasons Hotel, 399 El Geish Rd., San Stefano* ☎ *03/581-8000* ⊕ *www.fourseasons. com*) is one of the biggest spas in Egypt; this facility has excellent fitness rooms and rooms for massage and body treatments in addition to separate sauna, Jacuzzi, and steam-room facilities for men and women.

ALEXANDRIA ESSENTIALS

TRANSPORTATION

BY AIR

There is an airport in Alexandria, but flying to Alex from Cairo will end up taking longer than catching a train, which is why so few people do it. Taking into account ground transport to and from the airports, frequent delays of flights, and having to get to the airport an hour before your flight, the half-hour flight doesn't save any time. However, EgyptAir offers at least one flight per day to Alexandria Nozha Airport, and tickets currently cost around £e430 round-trip.

Contacts EgyptAir (☎ *03/427–1989*).

BY BUS

If you want to travel between Cairo and Alexandria by bus, Super Jet and the West Delta Bus Company run air-conditioned deluxe buses every half-hour from around 5 AM to midnight. Tickets cost £e21. Buses depart Cairo from Maydan Abdel Monem Riyad under the overpasses in front of the Ramses Hilton and take up to three hours, depending on traffic. Or you can depart from Almaza Station in Heliopolis or the station in Giza. They drop you off behind Sidi Gabr railway station in an Alexandria suburb, where they in turn depart for Cairo. The railway station is between downtown and Montazah, so you need to take a taxi from the station to get to either place.

Contacts Super Jet (☎ *02/2575–1313 in Cairo, 03/543–5222 in Alexandria*). **West Delta Bus Company** (☎ *02/2579–9739 in Cairo, 03/480–9685 in Alexandria*).

BY MINIBUS

Although most local bus routes are too convoluted to bother with, a constant stream of minibuses makes the Corniche run night and day. Flag them down anywhere, using a hand signal to point the direction you want to go, then pile in. They are shockingly cheap (£e1 to Stanley, say, and £e1.50 to Montazah) and, if anything, too fast. There are two catches to minibus travel: first, you have to know the name of the district to which you are traveling (Manshiya, Sporting, Montazah, and so forth), because you need to shout it in the window to the driver, who lets you know if he goes there. Second, you have to know what your destination looks like so you can tell the driver to stop. It's easier than it sounds, and your fellow passengers always help out.

BY CAR

Unless you plan to continue on to remote areas of the Mediterranean coast west of Alexandria, there is little reason to come by car. Taxis within the city are inexpensive, and parking is so difficult that a car is more trouble than it's worth. On top of that, the two highways connecting Cairo and Alexandria—the Delta and Desert roads—are both plagued by fatal car crashes. If you still want to come by car, the Desert Road, which starts near the pyramids in Giza, is the faster route, taking roughly three hours. If you do come by car, avoid driving at night.

If you are brave enough to elect to drive to Alex, you'll find traffic relatively orderly compared to that of Cairo. Streets are less crowded, and drivers are better about obeying traffic regulations. The governor has even instituted a no-horns policy, complete with wooden cut-out policemen at intersections to remind drivers. Although it's not totally effective, you'll notice far less horn noise than in Cairo.

The main road in Alexandria is the Corniche—technically 26th of July Street, but no one calls it that—which runs along the waterfront from Fort Qayt Bay all the way to Montazah. East of Eastern Harbor, the Corniche is mostly called Tariq al-Geish. Unless you park on a hill, be sure to leave your car in neutral, because people will push it around a bit to maximize parking space.

CAR RENTALS

You can rent a car (without a driver) from Avis, Alex Car, or Target Limousine; the latter can also provide you a car with a driver.

Contacts Alex Car (⊠ *El Bekpashi El Esawy, Abd El Aziz Ahmed, Sidi Besher* ☎ *03/555–4808* ⊕ *www.alexcar.com*). **Avis** (⊠ *Cecil Hotel, Maydan Sa'd Zaghlul, Raml Station* ☎ *03/485–7400*). **Target Limousine** (⊠ *Helnan Palestine Hotel, Montazah Gardens* ☎ *03/547–4033*).

BY TAXI

Taxis are the best way to get around Alexandria. They are very inexpensive, and you can flag them down almost anywhere. If you're alone and male, you're generally expected to sit in the front; women and couples can sit in the back. The reason for the men-in-front rule is that the driver might try to pick up another passenger en route—it's standard practice, so don't be surprised.

Drivers don't use their meters, so you have to guess at the appropriate fare. A ride within downtown should be £e10 to £e15; from downtown to Montazah (15–30 minutes), roughly 6 km (10 mi), about £e30. If you look rich, expect to pay a bit more—this is a progressive system: elderly widows often pay little, whereas prices double, at a minimum, if a driver picks you up at a five-star hotel. There are no radio taxis in Alexandria, but major hotels always have taxis waiting.

BY TRAIN

Trains are by far the most comfortable and convenient option for getting to and from Alexandria, and the travel time and ticket prices are the same in either direction. Turbo trains are the fastest (average journey time a little over 2 hours), and tickets for these services cost £e46 for first class and £e29 for second class. Speed trains take a few minutes longer, and tickets cost £e41 for first class and £e25 for second class. Tickets for the slower Express train services (average journey times 3¼ hours) are £e35 for first class and £e19 for second class.

Currently Turbo trains depart Cairo at 8 AM, 9 AM, 12 noon, 2 PM, 6 PM, and 7 PM. Returning Turbo trains depart Alexandria at 7 AM, 8 AM, 2 PM, 3 PM, 7 PM, and 7:30 PM.

Speed trains depart Cairo at 9:15 AM, 5 PM, and 10:20 PM. Returning Speed trains depart Alexandria at 8:15 AM, 11 AM, 4:30 PM, and 10:15 PM.

Express trains depart Cairo at 6 AM, 8:15 AM, 11 AM, 2:10 PM, 3:10 PM, 4 PM, 5 PM, 7:15 PM and 8:10 PM. Returning Express trains depart Alexandria at 5:50 AM, 7:15 AM, 10 AM, 12:30 PM, 1 PM, 3:30 PM, and 8 PM.

Be sure to confirm the scheduled departure times in advance. Seats are reserved, and tickets are best bought a day in advance—a laborious process that requires a trip to the station. If you take your chances, there are almost always seats available for same-day travel (except on the morning Turbo services), though summer Fridays out of Cairo and Sundays out of Alexandria can be booked up. When arriving in Alex, do not get off at the first station in the city, Sidi Gabr, as many of the passengers will; the main station is Misr Station, one stop further, which is the end of the line.

BY TRAM
Picturesque and cheap, Alexandria's trams are likely to take four to five times longer to get where you're going than a taxi would. The main station is Raml, near Maydan Sa'd Zaghlul. Buy tickets on board.

Blue trams (25 pt) run east: numbers 1, 2, 6, and 8 terminate at al-Nasser (formerly Victoria) College, Tram 3 at Sidi Gabr (by the sea; a two-hour trip), Tram 4 at Sidi Gabr Station, and Tram 5 at San Stefano. Yellow trams (15 pt) run west: Tram 16 goes to Pompey's Pillar (a 40-minute trip), Tram 11 to the Nouzha Gardens, and Tram 15 to Ras al-Tin. Numbers are marked—only in Arabic—on cards in the front windows, but the newer trams now have maps inside.

CONTACTS & RESOURCES

BANKS & EXCHANGE SERVICES
Credit Agricole has ATMs in Saleh, Salem, at 69 Shar'a El Sultan Hussein, and at 545 Shar'a al-Horreya. In addition to its main branch, HSBC has ATMs in the Alexandria City Centre Mall, at 47 Shar'a El Sultan Hussein, in Green Plaza Mall, in San Stefano Mall.

Contacts **Credit Agricole** (⊠ *14 Shar'a Salah Salem, Alexandria*). **HSBC** (⊠ *47 Shar'a El Sultan Hussein, Alexandria*). **NSGB** (⊠ *33 Shar'a Safia Zaghoul, Alexandria*).

EMERGENCIES
All four- and five-star hotels should have a doctor on call, and should you feel unwell at your hotel your concierge should be your first call. If you are taken ill or have an accident while touring, the emergency numbers below will link you to the appropriate services. There are several general and specialist hospitals in Alexandria that will be able to treat a wide variety of health problems. For specialist treatment, you may need to transfer to facilities in Cairo. Most doctors and dentists will speak English. Qualified pharmacists will be able to offer advice on remedies for common ailments such as stomach bugs or sunburn.

Emergency Services Ambulance (☎123). **Fire** (☎180). **Police** (☎122).

Dentists Dr. Adham Mohammed Aly Faramawry (✉275 Shar'a Abdul Salam Aref, Sidi Bishr, Alexandria ☎03/358–3330).

Doctors Dr. Hassab (✉47 Shar'a Menasha, Moharram Bey, Alexandria ☎03/493–5788). **Dr. Shalaby** (✉5 Shar'a Abdel Kader El Aswa, Moharram Bey, Alexandria ☎03/493–1433).

Hospitals German Hospital (✉56 Shar'a Abdel Salam Aref, Saba Basha ☎03/584–1806). **Smouha Medical Centre** (✉14 Shar'a May, Smouha ☎03/427–2652).

Late-night Pharmacies Ashraf (✉693 Shar'a al-Horreya, Roushdi ☎03/572–1675). **Oxford (24 hours)** (✉10 Kuliat al-Teb, Raml Station ☎03/487–6720). **Roushdi** (✉423 Shar'a al-Horreya, Roushdi ☎03/542–8018).

ENGLISH-LANGUAGE BOOKSTORES

El-Maaref, the best of a limited set of options, has a small selection of foreign-language (particularly French) novels and guidebooks and maps in the back. For newspapers and magazines, there's a very good newsstand in front of the post office at Raml Station and a smaller one near the entrance to the Metropole Hotel.

Contacts El-Maaref (✉44 Shar'a Sa'd Zaghlul, Raml Station ☎03/487–3303)

INTERNET, MAIL & SHIPPING

There's been a great expansion of Internet services in the city, but Internet cafés open and close with great regularity. Some hotels offer Wi-Fi in the lobby, and some cafés offer the same service.

Postal services are slow, taking two weeks to reach the U.S., if they arrive at all. If you simply want to send postcards; deposit them at your hotel concierge desk rather than seeking out a post office. International shipping companies operate in Egypt, and their service is reliable. Many Egyptian companies operate shipping services for bulky items such as carpets or antiques. Be aware that because Alexandria is a large port, many companies will quote only for large commercially viable quantities rather than for items of a personal nature.

Internet Cafés Micro Media Center for Internet (✉8 Shar'a El Ghazaly, Al Laban, ☎03/393–9425).

Wi-Fi Hot Spots Caffé Cino (✉Bibliotheca Alexandrina Plaza ☎03/483–9999).

Starbucks (✉San Stefano Mall ☎03/489–0216 ✉ Alexandria City Centre Mall, Cairo Desert Rd. ☎03/397–0181).

Post Offices Al Raml Station (✉Al Raml Station tunnel ☎03/483–6693). **Main Post Office** (✉2 Shar'a Mahmoud Salema ☎03/496–0088).

Shipping Companies DHL (✉9 Shar'a Saleh Salem, Manshiya ☎19633 (within Egypt only) or 03/487–3603). **FedEx (Egypt Express)** (✉314 Shar'a al-Horreya ☎03/545–3572).

TRAVEL AGENCIES

Contacts **Alex Tours** (✉ *2 Shar'a El Horreya* ☎ *03/486–1840*). **Annie Travel** (✉ *30 Shar'a Ahmed Orabi,* ☎ *03/487–0007*). **Thomas Cook** (✉ *15 Maydan Sa'd Zaghlul, Raml Station* ☎ *03/484–7830*).

VISITOR INFORMATION

The maps and brochures at the Tourist Information Center are of poor quality, but the multilingual staff is easily one of the most helpful of any government office in the country.

Contacts **Tourist Information Center** (✉ *Maydan Sa'd Zaghlul, Raml Station* ☎ *03/485–1556*).

The Nile Valley and Luxor

Reliefs in the tomb of Ramose. Tombs of the Nobles

WORD OF MOUTH

"The incredible feat of building these things—and particularly the tombs—boggles the mind."

— Mazj

"[W]e visited the Temple of Luxor and the Temple of Karnak. They are both very impressive sights and rank among our favorites. It's hard to imagine that the temples once were linked to each other. What an awesome sight it must have been! Allow some time to enjoy them."

—AZEBS

WELCOME TO THE NILE VALLEY & LUXOR

TOP REASONS TO GO

★ **The Valley of the Kings:** Follow the storyline of the pharaoh's journey into the afterlife in the images from the *Book of the Dead* on the walls of a royal tomb.

★ **The Temple of Karnak:** Stroll amongst the columns in the petrified "forest" of the hypostyle hall, which was built as a garden for the gods.

★ **Deir El-Medina:** Step back and absorb the panorama of the multitiered facade at the mortuary temple of Queen Hatshepsut.

★ **A Trip on the Nile:** Make the Nile your home for a few days, either on the deck of a traditional wind-powered *felucca* or in the more comfortable cabin of a luxury river cruiser.

★ **The Temple of Edfu:** Admire the architectural perfection of the temple dedicated to Horus; it's the finest surviving Ptolemaic-era building in Egypt.

1 **The Middle Nile Valley: Al-Minya to Tell al-Amarna.** Tomb complexes from several dynasties lie around Al-Minya. Farther south in Tell al-Amarna, the Pharaoh Akhenaten's capital city, the epicenter of a move to monotheism, lasted just a single generation.

2 **The Upper Nile Valley: Abydos to Luxor.** Powerful pharaohs stamped their marks on the Nile with magnificent temple complexes. Seti I and Ramesses II ordered the building at Abydos at the start of the New Kingdom, while the Ptolemies and Romans funded the Temple of Hathor, at Dendera.

Valley of the Kings, Painting in King Horemheb's Tomb, Luxor

3 **Luxor.** The capital of ancient Egypt in the late Middle Kingdom and New Kingdom eras—and home to two massive temple complexes—Luxor is now one of Egypt's busiest tourist centers and has the widest selection of hotels and restaurants in the Nile Valley.

4 **The Theban Necropolis.** The burial place of the pharaohs, the landscape on the Nile's West Bank is dotted with vast mortuary temples and extensive rock-cut tombs that constitute a high point in human art and architecture. The most famous of these mortuary temples are in the Valley of the Kings, but standing apart is the Deir El-Medina, the mortuary temple for Queen Hatshepsut.

5 **The Upper Nile Valley: South of Luxor.** A rash of temples grace the Nile south of Luxor, including the finest Ptolemaic-era edifice at Edfu and Egypt's only dual-deity temple at Kom Ombo. Most can be visited on land excursions if you are not on a cruise.

Karnak

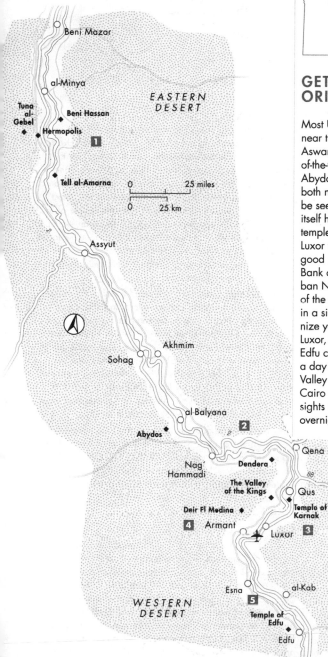

Beni Mazar

al-Minya

EASTERN DESERT

Tuna al-Gebel

Beni Hassan

Hermopolis

1

Tell al-Amarna

0   25 miles

0   25 km

Assyut

Akhmim

Sohag

al-Balyana

2

Abydos

Nag' Hammadi

Dendera

Qena

The Valley of the Kings

Qus

Deir El Medina

Temple of Karnak

4 Armant

Luxor **3**

Esna **5**

al-Kab

WESTERN DESERT

Temple of Edfu

Edfu

GETTING ORIENTED

Most Upper Nile sights lie near the towns of Luxor and Aswan. Two of the more out-of-the-way monuments, at Abydos and Dendera, are both north of Luxor and can be seen on day trips. Luxor itself has two magnificent temples (the Karnak and Luxor temples) as well as a good museum. On the West Bank of the Nile is the Theban Necropolis, and many of the tombs can be visited in a single day if you organize your time well. South of Luxor, the temple of Horus at Edfu can also be visited on a day trip. The Middle Nile Valley is actually closer to Cairo than to Luxor, so those sights are often visited as an overnight trip from Cairo.

THE NILE VALLEY & LUXOR PLANNER

Transportation

By Air: Luxor is linked to Cairo by several EgyptAir flights a day, as well as to Alexandria, Aswan, and Sharm El-Sheik. There are also many nonstop flights from European destinations.

By Boat: Nile cruises depart from Luxor to Aswan, as well as end here. You can also take a local *felucca* sailboat around the city.

By Bus: It's difficult for foreign travelers to travel by bus in Upper Egypt (authorities strongly discourage it). If you can get a ticket, it's definitely the cheapest way to move around, though not terribly comfortable.

By Car: The convoy system makes a private car-rental less than ideal in Upper Egypt. It's easier, and usually no more expensive, to hire a taxi.

By Train: One easy way to get to Luxor from Cairo is on the overnight trains operated by Abela. A compartment is fairly reasonably priced and allows you to travel overnight, arriving in Luxor early the next morning. Regular seats are cheaper, and a more inexpensive way still is the first-class section of a regular train.

What's Great in the Nile Valley & Luxor

Temples: The Nile Valley, particularly the section in Upper Egypt, is the heartland of ancient Egyptian religion. Karnak Temple in Luxor is considered the "headquarters" for the main triumvirate of deities, Amun, Mut, and Montu, and is renowned for the immense hypostyle hall in the main complex. But more than a dozen other temples vie for "finest" or "best," depending on the criteria—see the temple of Seti I in Abydos for its excellent carvings or Edfu as an example of the "Greek style." Each temple has a story to tell—stories of battles won and gods worshipped and of how, whatever was going on here on earth, the gods were the one constant in the lives of the people.

Tombs: Life after death was an integral belief of the ancient Egyptians, and the complicated and ornate tombs carved for the ruling dynasty display the engineering prowess and the dazzling wealth of artistic talent found in Thebes (Luxor) during the New Kingdom era. Art in the royal tombs depicts scenes from the *Book of the Dead,* while those in the Valleys of the Nobles and tombs of the workers have scenes of home, family, and everyday life in pharaonic Egypt. And, of course, one mustn't forget the tomb of Tutankhamun—the only tomb yet found with its royal treasure intact.

River Trips: The languorous waters of the Nile have an almost magnetic appeal. Spend several days aboard a Nile cruise and your floating hotel will carry you close to all the major monuments. Luxor has no river islands but still has wonderful waterside landscapes to explore, plus, the sunset over the West Bank here is exceptional.

Logistics

As part of increased security measures, travel between Abydos and Aswan by road is done in police-accompanied convoys. This limits your freedom of movement, but it also provides for your safety. Always travel with your passport; you may need to present it at checkpoints. Aside from these understandable inconveniences, it must be said that Egypt is a remarkably safe country, with one of the lowest crime rates in the world.

About the Restaurants

Luxor is a busy tourist destination and has a wide range of restaurants; outside of Luxor, your choices are more limited, particularly in al-Minya. Alcohol is not served everywhere.

The variable city tax on restaurants, combined with service charges, can total as much as 26%. Check menus to verify how each restaurant operates. Unless you are in a major hotel, consider tipping even if a service charge is included in the bill: waiters are not well paid, and the courtesy will be appreciated. If service is not charged, 10% to 15% is a reasonable tip. As a rule, most hotel restaurants are open to the general public. Reservations are recommended at all hotel restaurants.

About the Hotels

Remember that rates are less expensive in summer—late April to the end of September—though Luxor has less dramatic variations than Aswan since tourism is strong year-round.

Almost all hotels include breakfast in their rates, and some offer meal plans. Most hotels arrange transportation from airport to hotel if requested.

If you choose to stay at a place that doesn't have a pool, be aware that many hotels open their pools to nonguests for a small fee (around £e50). In Luxor, the splendid Club Med includes a beverage in its pool fee, the Sheraton is on a peninsula extending into the Nile, and the Hilton has a peaceful Nile-side garden and pool.

DINING & LODGING PRICE CATEGORIES IN EUROS, POUNDS, AND DOLLARS

$	$$	$$$	$$$$
Restaurants			
under £e50	£e50–£e100	£e100–£e150	over £e150
Hotels in dollars			
under $70	$70–$130	$130–$200	over $200
Hotels in Euros			
under €45	€45–€80	€80–€130	over €130

Restaurant prices are per person for a main course at dinner. Hotel prices are for a double room in high season, excluding 10% tax and service charges (usually 10%).

Planning Your Time

Are you taking a cruise? If yes, remember that cruises typically devote only a single day to Luxor, and this major city deserves more time. You'll need at least a day to visit the Valley of the Kings, another to visit Karnak and the Luxor temples, and a third day if you want to explore Abydos or Dendera, which cruises generally omit. If you want to visit the Middle Nile Valley to see the sights around al-Minya, that trip alone requires two or three days, whether you are doing it as a side trip from Cairo or as a stopover on the trip between Cairo and Luxor.

When to Go

Traditionally, high season begins at the end of September, peaks around Christmas, and lasts until April. The heat kicks in as early as March in Upper Egypt—a dry, pollution-free heat that you can get used to. Evenings are always cool in the desert. And Luxor is typically cooler than Aswan, though the sun beats down on the Nile's West Bank, and the Valley of the Kings can seem like a furnace on hot, sunny summer days. A season of *mulids* (religious feasts) occurs about a month before Ramadan, the Islamic month of fasting. Life slows down (but never stops) during Ramadan.

By Maria
Golia,
Salima Ikram,
Nathalie
Walschaerts

Updated by
Lindsay and
Pete Bennett

THE ULTIMATE PROOF OF HERODOTUS'S claim that "Egypt is a gift of the Nile" is visible on a flight from Cairo to Upper Egypt. From the air the Nile is a thin blue line, fringed with green, wending its way through a limitless horizon of sand. You realize that this is the Sahara, and that here, on the edge of the world's harshest desert, Africa's greatest city and Egypt's 80 million souls rely on one river's undiminished bounty.

From antiquity until modern times, the Nile was a principal trade route between the interior and the Mediterranean. And Upper Egypt, the Nile Valley south of Abydos, was a gateway to Africa. Because of the ease of access it afforded, the river shaped destinies: Nubia, Sudan, and Ethiopia alternately benefited from trade and suffered the predations of pharaohs.

Luxor, originally called Thebes, was the capital of Egypt during the New Kingdom and the center of religion, which was focused on the enormous temple devoted to Amun-Ra at Karnak. The city's importance continued even into the Ptolemaic period and, later, the Roman period, interrupted only briefly during the reign of Akhenaten, who moved the capital to the Middle Egypt city of Akhetaten; when he died, his capital died with him.

Today, Luxor is one of the most-visited destinations in Egypt. With its range of archaeological sights and temples, it provides a wide, if not completely comprehensive, introduction to life in ancient Egypt. Many travelers either join or disembark from a Nile River cruise in Luxor. It's possible to visit the sights downriver (Abydos and Dendera) on a day trip, and the temple of Horus at Edfu upriver on another day trip.

A more extensive trip is necessary to visit al-Minya, which is between Cairo and Luxor. Usually overlooked by tourists, it offers a fascinating glimpse into Egypt's Middle Kingdom as well as the 18th-Dynasty ruler Akhenaten.

THE MIDDLE NILE VALLEY: AL-MINYA TO TELL AL-AMARNA

Middle Egypt has a slew of extremely interesting monuments dating from all periods of Egyptian history. The major sites in the area that are easily accessible are the Middle Kingdom tombs of Beni Hasan, the New Kingdom town-site and tombs at Tell al-Amarna, the Greco-Roman tombs and catacombs at Tuna al-Gebel, and the Greco-Roman remains of al-Ashmunayn. Beni Hasan, al-Amarna, and Tuna al-Gebel are the most worthwhile sites, though al-Ashmunayn is intriguing if you are interested in more Classical-style remains.

You can visit almost all the Middle Valley sites in one to two days. Al-Amarna is best done on its own, and Beni Hasan and Tuna al-Gebel are easily combined if you rent a taxi for the day. You could also combine al-Amarna and Beni Hasan in a day if pressed for time. Take plenty of food and water with you, as, for the most part, there is none at the sites.

AL-MINYA

260 km (160 mi) south of Cairo; 450 km (280 mi) north of Luxor.

The best place for a base in Middle Egypt is the bustling town of al-Minya, which the Italians developed. The town has several pleasant piazzas, gardens, and fine buildings, which, alas, are rapidly being knocked down and replaced by modern Egyptian concrete boxes.

WHERE TO STAY

There's not much choice of accommodation in al-Minya, and none of the hotels can be classed as luxurious. Just expect a basic room and bathroom and a restaurant on-site that serves such Egyptian staples as roasted chickens or kebabs with bread and salad, *ful* (fava beans stewed with tomatoes), *ta'amiya* (falafel), and *koshary* (a meal of rice, lentils, and pasta served with browned onions and tomato sauce).

4

$–$$ **Nefertiti and Aton Hotel.** Certainly the best of a small selection of hotels in the region, the Nefertiti is a comfortable downtown hotel with some nice facilities that include a pool and a choice of restaurants—though the bulk of the clientele are Egyptian businesspeople so there's no resort or vacation atmosphere. Rooms are a reasonable size with modern furnishings and balconies. Some have good river views. **Pros:** The hotel that comes closest to international standards in this area; good river views from the terrace. **Cons:** The hotel has three restaurants, but they aren't always in operation if the hotel is quiet; alcohol isn't easily available. ⊠*Corniche al-Nil, al-Minya* ☎*086/234–1515* ⤶*96 rooms* ⚭*In-room: refrigerator, Internet. In-hotel: 3 restaurants, bar, tennis court, pool, gym, laundry service, parking (free)* ⊟*AE, MC, V* ⏹*BP.*

BENI HASAN

25 km (15 mi) south of al-Minya.

This magnificent cemetery site is on the East Bank of the Nile. Beni Hasan is generally approached from the West Bank by ferry, which shows the site to its best advantage: a narrow, vibrant strip of green bordering the river that suddenly ends in dramatically sloping limestone cliffs that stand out starkly against an intense blue sky. The cliffs are pierced by tombs (39) of local rulers that date to the Middle Kingdom (c. 2040–1640 BC). Generally only four or five are open to visitors at any time.

Take a taxi from al-Minya to the ferry (be sure to bargain); you may be assigned an armed security officer for the trip. This is a routine security procedure for travelers in this part of Egypt. If you are traveling as part of a prebooked tour, your guide will make any necessary arrangements. Then cross the Nile to the site. From the ferry landing proceed by microbus (note that service is erratic) or walk (a 10-minute walk at a slow pace) to the base of the cliffs and the ticket booth. From here it is a stiff climb up modern concrete stairs to the top of the cliff and the tombs. (Have your taxi wait while you visit the site and then take you on to other sites in the area.)

On the climb up the stairs you pass shaft tombs (closed) for the less important people. The tombs of the wealthy and more important folk are in the upper portions of the cliff. There are three basic tomb types on the cliff, aside from the shaft tombs. The first has a plain facade and is single-chambered (11th Dynasty); the second (11th and 12th Dynasties) is plain on the outside, but its chamber is columned; and the third type (12th Dynasty) has a portico in front and a columned chamber.

You can never be sure of which tombs will be open, but the ones listed here usually are accessible. The lighting in the tombs varies greatly, so bring a flashlight. A café at the base of the cliff offers cold drinks, but you should bring your own packed lunch.

Tomb of Amenemhat (No. 2), 12th Dynasty. Not only was the tomb-owner a nomarch, or governor, but he also was the military commander-in-chief of the area. This tomb has some entertaining scenes of musicians, knifemakers, and leather workers in addition to the usual daily-life scenes.

Tomb of Bakht III (No. 15), 11th Dynasty. Built for a governor of the Oryx Nome, this tomb contains seven shafts, which suggests that members of his family were buried with him. The wall paintings show hunting in the marshes and desert, weavers, counting livestock, potters, metalworkers, wrestlers, and offerings bearers. The desert hunt scenes are particularly interesting because they show some very bizarre mythological animals.

Tomb of Kheti (No. 17), 11th Dynasty. Kheti was the governor of the Oryx Nome. Scenes on the walls show hunting, offerings, daily activities, and the wrestlers that are typical of Beni Hasan. An attack on a fortress is also depicted.

Tomb of Khnumhotep (No. 3), 12th Dynasty. This large tomb, entered between two proto-Doric columns, belonged to Khnumhotep, a governor of the Oryx Nome as well as a prince. It is famous for its hunt scenes and depictions of foreign visitors to Egypt. Carved in the back wall is a statue of the deceased, and the color of the paintings is much better preserved in this tomb than in any of the others. ⊠ *Beni Hasan* ☎ *No phone* ⊠ *£e30* ☉ *Daily 7–5.*

TELL AL-AMARNA

40 km (25 mi) south of Beni Hasan.

Little remains of the magnificent town of Akhetaten, which was founded by the apparently monotheist pharaoh Akhenaten in the late 18th Dynasty. Akhetaten was quite an impressive city, with a population of 10,000 in its short heyday, but it has almost completely vanished. Indeed, it is hard to imagine this large expanse of barren desert as a bustling town busy with government workers, commerce, and artisans. The few visible remains include the foundations of the North Palace and the Small Aten Temple with its single restored pillar.

The northern tombs are more easily visited than their southern counterparts and are quite interesting, although somewhat ruined. Not all the tombs are open, but they are all relatively similar in design and decoration. Most of the tombs consist of an outer court, a long hall and a broad hall, sometimes columned, and a statue niche. The tombs are decorated in the typical "Amarna" style, with depictions of the town and architecture and depictions of the pharaoh and his family rather than the tomb's owner. (The tomb owner generally is shown only in the doorway, hands raised in praise of Aten.) People tend to be shown with sharp chins, slightly distended bellies, and large hips and thighs. Some tombs show evidence of being reused in the Coptic period, so watch for crosses, niches, and fonts (Tomb 6, for example).

To get here, hire a taxi and either cross the river at al-Minya and take the desert road to the site (not always easy), or drive down to Deir Mawass and cross over by ferry, which is the more traditional way to go. At the ferry, you can hire a hardy vehicle (a tractor or pickup) to get around the site, as walking would take all day. On the East Bank, purchase tickets for the site and pay for the vehicle. You may be assigned an armed security officer at the nearest police checkpoint to al-Minya, and this officer may accompany you to the site. This is a routine security procedure for travelers in this part of Egypt. If you are traveling as part of a prebooked tour, your guide will liaise with the police and make arrangements for your trip. ⊠*Tell al-Amarna* ☎*No phone* ⊴*£e30* ⊘*Daily 8–5.*

AL-ASHMUNAYN (HERMOPOLIS)

30 km (19 mi) south of al-Minya.

The site features a late-Roman basilica, the only surviving large building of its kind in Egypt, as well as a giant statue (one of a pair) of the god Thoth in the guise of a baboon. A large New Kingdom temple to Thoth, god of Ashmunayn, used to stand at the site but is pretty much invisible today. ☎*No phone* ⊴*£e20* ⊘*Daily 8–5.*

TUNA AL-GEBEL

10 km (6 mi) southwest of al-Ashmunayn.

Tuna al-Gebel was the necropolis of Hermopolis—a large and scattered site, its focal point being a cluster of Greco-Roman tombs. These tombs, built literally as houses for the dead, show an entertaining blending of Classical and Egyptian styles of art. The **tomb of Petosiris** is one of the best preserved and is open to the public.

The **mummy of Isadora,** a woman drowned in the Nile in the second century AD, is on display in a nearby building; be sure to tip the guard. The other major attraction of the site is the elaborate **catacombs** containing burials of ibis and baboons, animals sacred to the god Thoth.

CLOSE UP

The Amarna Era

Akhenaten turned ancient Egypt upside down. When he came to the throne around 1353 BC, he took the name Amenhotep IV, but in the fifth year of his reign he underwent an epiphany. He declared that all the Egyptian gods—including Amun—were to be usurped by Aten (a minor God once worshipped in the Old Kingdom era), represented by a sun disk with rays emanating from it and an ankh symbol depicting the gift of life. The reason for this major religious change is unclear. The pharaoh was the only person allowed to have close contact with the god, a regulation that highlighted the pharaoh's divinity and reduced the power of the priesthood. Akhenaten moved the royal residence and capital of Egypt to the brand-new city al-Amarna (Akhetaten), thus effectively crippling the towns of Memphis and Thebes and putting distance between the seat of power and the priests at Karnak.

Akhenaten revolutionized art in this era by introducing the so-called real style—with scenes of the royal family in very relaxed poses with the pharaoh kissing his children and sharing affection. Statues and carvings show the pharaoh as a long-skulled, long-chinned individual with an androgenous body form—wide hips, drooping belly, protruding breasts, and long fingers. Modern scientists have theorized that Ahkenaten suffered from Marfan

Syndrome (a genetic disorder of the connective tissue), but his mummy has never been found so it's impossible to be certain about this.

As pharaoh, Ahkenaten had little concern for the well-being of his lands. Sensing weakness, Egypt's neighbors raided the borders, taking territory and instilling fear in the Egyptian people. Ahkenaten reigned for 18 years, and immediately upon his death the priests of Amun moved to reinstate Thebes and its temple to Amun as the true heart of Egypt. In addition, they systematically wiped Ahkenaten's reign from the history books. His capital was destroyed, and not only Akhenaten but also his successors Smenkhkare, Tutankhamun, and Ay, were excised from the official records (this is one of the reasons the tomb of Tutankhamun lay untouched throughout history, because there was so little evidence of his rule).

It wasn't until the 19th century that archaeologists began to piece together this missing segment in the Egyptian timeline, though many details are mysteries that still await answers—including the vexing question of Tutankhamun's relationship to Ahkenaten. The last of the Amarna bloodline, Tutankhamun was christened Tutankhaten. His change of name indicates a final victory of Amun over Aten and a return to the old ways for the people of Egypt.

These date to the late Persian and Greco-Roman periods, and you can see some animal burials in situ. An embalming workshop is also visible at the entrance. Approaching the site, you can see on the right side, cut into the cliffs, the best surviving stela (now protected by glass) erected by Akhenaten; this one was to mark the western boundary of his capital, Akhetaten. ☎No phone ✉£e20 ⊙Daily 8–5.

THE UPPER NILE VALLEY: ABYDOS TO LUXOR

Traveling along the Nile takes you through both space and time. Ancient Egyptian civilization as we know it came alive around 3100 BC, when Narmer united Lower and Upper Egypt, and breathed its last breath in the 4th century AD during the simultaneous rise of Christianity and collapse of both paganism and the Roman empire. The monuments you see are the accretions of centuries of dynastic power, ritual practice, artistic expression, and foreign interference that continually adapted and renewed an inspiring system of beliefs.

You don't need to know any of this to appreciate the beauty and refinement of the paintings in Seti I's temple at Abydos or the majesty of the temples at Karnak. Just consider the high level of societal organization that it took to conceive and create what the ancient Egyptians left behind. Looking back at their civilization from the third millennium of the Christian era, we are gazing eye-to-eye with our equals in ambition, achievement, and, in many ways, technology.

4

ABYDOS

150 km (93 mi) north of Luxor.

The drive from Luxor to Abydos (as part of a convoy) takes you through lush fields of sugarcane, swaying palm trees, and picturesque mud-brick villages dotted with pigeon towers. At the end of the trip, the temple appears rather surprisingly amid a cluster of houses and shops, the desert stretching out behind them. Groups are not allowed to visit the temples here, so Abydos is a good place to break away from whatever crowds there might be farther upriver.

Abydos was one of the most sacred sites in ancient Egypt, because it was the supposed burial place of Osiris, god of the netherworld. The complex here includes several temples, tombs, and sacred animal burials dating from the predynastic period onward. Now the only parts of the site accessible to visitors are the Osireion—the temple to Osiris—erected by Seti I (19th Dynasty, 1290–1279 BC) and the temple erected by his son, Ramesses II.

★ **Seti I's Temple to Osiris.** This low-lying temple (1306–1290 BC), modestly stretching across the desert nestled amid a group of shops and houses, is one of the jewels of ancient Egypt. It is filled with exquisitely carved and colored reliefs that delight the eye and stir the soul. Seti I had initiated construction of the temple complex but he died before its completion, which left Ramesses II to finish it.

After passing the ticket booth, walk up to the ruined first pylon, which leads into the almost completely destroyed first courtyard built by Ramesses II. This first court contains two wells, and only the lower level of the court's enclosure wall survives. These remaining walls are decorated with scenes of Ramesses killing the enemies of Egypt and making offerings to the gods. A ramp leads to the second court, which is similarly decorated. Beyond this are a portico and the entrance to

Abydos

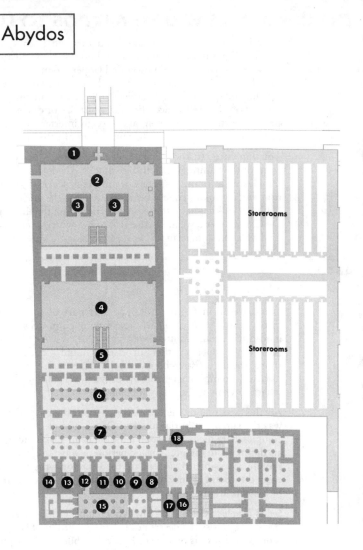

the temple proper. The portico is carved and painted with scenes of Ramesses II making offerings to the gods and being granted a very long and prosperous reign in exchange.

From the portico, enter the **First Hypostyle Hall,** which was begun by Seti I and completed by Ramesses II. (A hypostyle hall is one in which interior columns support a roof; in most temples the ancient roofs caved in long ago.) The hall consists of 12 pairs of papyrus-style columns aligned to create seven aisles that lead to seven chapels set in the back wall of the Second Hypostyle Hall. The walls are decorated with scenes showing the pharaoh offering to Amun-Ra (the sun god), preparing and dedicating the temple building and making offerings to Thoth (god of writing and knowledge).

The next room, the **Second Hypostyle Hall,** was built and decorated—with its decoration scheme *almost* completed—by Seti I. The exquisite quality of the relief carvings here stands in stark contrast to the cruder work commissioned by Ramesses II. Scenes include dedicatory texts of Seti I and show the pharaoh making offerings before various gods and receiving their blessings. A continuous row of fertility figures with *nome* (provinces of ancient Egypt) standards above their heads runs along below the main scenes.

The seven **chapels** off the rear wall are dedicated to various deities and are a rare feature in Egyptian temples. From left to right (east to west), they are dedicated to Seti I, Ptah (a creator god), Ra Harakhte, Amun-Ra, Osiris, Isis (goddess of magic), and Horus (the god associated with kingship). Each chapel is decorated with scenes showing the daily temple ritual, which involved offerings, libations, and censing. The Osiris chapel leads to the Osiris complex, which has depictions of Seti making offerings of wine, bread, incense, vases, and so forth to various deities. The last rooms in the Osiris complex are mostly reconstructed. This is where the mysteries of Osiris were performed; their exact nature remains, of course, mysterious—in other words, unknown to modern scholarship.

Beyond the chapels, to the east, is a **hall** with two back rooms dedicated to Nefertum and Ptah-Sokar. The one on the right (west) is remarkable for its scenes showing the conception of Horus: as the story goes, Seth (who became the god of storms and deserts) had his brother Osiris, the king, killed and chopped up into pieces. Isis, Osiris's wife and a great magician, traveled throughout Egypt gathering the bits of her husband to remake him with magic. She found and reconstructed all of him, save his genitalia. These she fashioned out of mud, stuck them onto him, made them viable with magic, and, changing herself into a kite (a small hawk)—no one is absolutely certain why this bird is her animal counterpart—placed herself on his member and thus conceived Horus. Later, Horus avenged his father's death and became king, and Osiris became king of the netherworld. (Seth was exiled to distant places.)

The **Gallery of Lists** leads left from the portico before the seven chapels out to the Osireion. On its walls is a list of gods and kings that is one of the cornerstones of Egyptian history. This king list notes the divine and semidivine (i.e., pharaonic) Egyptian rulers in the order of their reigns. The list, though incomplete, has been of great importance in helping to retrace the chronology of the pharaohs. Other rooms (a sacrificial butchery court, a hall of ritual barques), all of which are closed, lead off this passage. Another corridor, known as the corridor of the bulls, was named for a scene showing Ramesses II and one of his sons lassoing a bull before a god. A curious boat associated with Sokar, a god of the dead, is also carved on the wall.

Directly behind the temple lies the **Osireion.** Built of sandstone and granite, the monument was considered to be the tomb of Osiris. The architectural style and massive quality of the building is reminiscent of Old Kingdom (2625–2134 BC) constructions, and it was rebuilt during the reign of Seti I, who left the only decoration. The Osireion includes built-in pools of different shapes—an unusual feature—that might represent the primeval chaotic ocean of Nun. Most of the chambers off the central room are inaccessible because they are filled with water (a little poetic irony). At the far end of the central room is a transversal chamber, its ceiling adorned with a representation of the god Shu upholding the goddess Mut, the nocturnal journey of the sun, and a list of the constellations. South of the Osireion is an extension, the **long passage**, added by Merneptah, Ramesses II's successor. This is decorated with scenes from various books, such as the *Book of Gates,* the *Book of Caverns,* and the *Book of What Is in the Underworld,* containing spells to ensure a safe passage to the afterworld. ⊠ *Mabed Seti* ☎ *No phone* ✆ *£e30 (includes Temple of Ramesses II)* ☉ *Oct.–May, daily 7–5; June–Sept., daily 7–6.*

Temple of Ramesses II. Some 300 yards northwest of the Seti I temple lies the Temple of Ramesses II (1290–1224 BC). Its roof and most of the upper portions of its walls are missing, but enough of it remains to give you a feeling for its layout and decoration. What is left of the decoration shows that this temple—unlike the inferior work that Ramesses commissioned to complete Seti I's temple—is close in style and quality to what was done during the reign of Seti I. And the vibrant reds, yellows, and bright green here are a joy to behold.

The first pylon and court are no longer in existence; instead, the entrance is through the semipreserved second pylon, which leads to a court surrounded by pillars decorated with the figure of Ramesses in an Osirid pose (as a mummy with arms crossed in front of his breast). The walls are carved and painted with scenes of Ramesses making offerings to various deities, animals being taken for sacrifice, and prisoners of war.

From the court, walk up to the portico leading to two hypostyle halls with chapels off of them. Scenes of captives, religious processions, and offerings made by the king to the various gods adorn the walls. ⊠ *Mabed Seti* ☎ *No phone* ✆ *£e30 (includes Temple of Seti I)* ☉ *Oct.–May, daily 7–5; June–Sept., daily 7–6.*

DENDERA

65 km (40 mi) north of Luxor.

The prime point of interest in Dendera, a small village north of Luxor, is the Temple of Hathor. The area is pleasantly green, and the ride provides an agreeable view of rural life in Egypt. The site of Dendera was occupied at least from the Old Kingdom onward, but it is the remains of the Late Period and Greco-Roman structures that are of interest here. The site includes the main temple, two *mammisis* (gods' birth houses), a Coptic church, a sanitorium, the remains of a sacred lake, and a small temple to Isis, as well as some other less visible monuments.

Seti I

Son of Ramesses I, founder of the 19th Dynasty, Seti's main role during his rule (c. 1290 BC–1279 BC or c. 1294 BC–1279 BC) was to build up the cult of Amun and expunge the last memories of the Amarna era (i.e., the rule of Akhenaten and his successors), and also to strengthen the borders of an Egypt that was seen as vulnerable by its neighbors during the reign of Ahkenaten. Seti opened a new quarry in Aswan and commissioned several monuments to aggrandize existing temples. He also started work at Abydos.

Militarily, Seti had several confrontations with the Hittites, the main threat to his empire, and regained lands lost under Ahkenaten's rule. He sent forces to Nubia and Libya, and his forces marched up the "Ways of Horus," the road that ran along the Mediterranean coast to what is now the Gaza Strip, pushing the Hittites back north. Seti's tomb is the longest in the Valley of the Kings, and his mummy rests in the Cairo Museum.

Dendera is reached by daily convoy from Luxor; you can book a private taxi or a tour with a local tour operator.

Temple of Hathor. Hathor of Dendera was the goddess of love, beauty, music, and birth. She was often depicted as a cow, and in later periods of Egyptian history was syncretized with Isis. She was married to Horus of Edfu, and the two temples celebrated an annual festival, lasting about two weeks, when the statue of Hathor would sail upriver to Edfu to celebrate the divine marriage. This temple was built between the 4th century BC and 1st century AD.

As you enter the temple grounds through stone portals, there is a dramatic view of the temple facade fronted by a row of Hathor-head columns (their capitals carved with reliefs of the face of the goddess) and a decorated screen wall. The exterior of the temple is carved in relief with scenes of the pharaoh and divinities being suckled by goddesses and of the pharaoh making offerings to various gods.

The portal leads into the **Outer Hypostyle Hall,** which consists of 24 tall columns (including the facade columns), all with Hathor-head capitals. The ceiling is carved and painted with a depiction of the night sky. The columns themselves are densely decorated with scenes of the pharaoh making offerings to the gods and receiving their blessings in return. This very crowded, *horror vacui* (fear of blank spaces) decoration is typical of the Greco-Roman period.

The next room is the **Inner Hypostyle Hall,** with its six columns. Six small rooms open off this hall. These rooms are decorated with different scenes that supposedly illustrate what went on in them, or, more likely, what was stored in them. The first room on the left is the most interesting. Known as the **Laboratory,** it is where ritual perfumes and essences were prepared. The other rooms include a **Harvest Room,** the **Room of Libations,** and the **Treasury,** which is illustrated with carvings of jewelry and boxes containing precious metals.

The hall leads to the **First Vestibule**, where many of the daily offerings to Hathor would have been placed. Gifts included all kinds of food and drink: breads, fresh vegetables, joints of meat and poultry, beer, and wine. Staircases lead up to the roof from either side of the First Vestibule.

The **Second Vestibule** follows the first as a transitional area between the sanctuary and the rest of the temple. The **Sanctuary** was the most sacred spot in the temple and in antiquity would have had an altar and a plinth supporting a *naos* (shrine) containing the sacred image of the goddess, probably either gilded or made of gold. The sanctuary is surrounded by a corridor, and several chapels are off of it. The best chapel is the one immediately behind the sanctuary, because it contains a raised shrine that is reached by a ladder.

Dendera also has at least 32 **crypts** built into the walls and under the floor of the temple—hiding places for temple plates, jewelry, and statues. Some of the wall crypts would have permitted priests to hide behind different images of the gods and act as oracles. One of these, behind and to the right of the sanctuary, is open to the public. It is beautifully carved with scenes showing divinities. Look for the exquisite relief showing the god Horus in his falcon form.

On the right side of the temple's ground floor is another small and beautifully carved **chapel,** called Wabet (the pure one). The ceiling shows the sky goddess, Nut, swallowing the sun and giving birth to it the next day, with Hathor emerging from the horizon.

The stairways that lead from both sides of the First Vestibule to the roof are carved with priestly processions wending their way up the sides. There are three chapels on the roof. The open chapel with Hathor-head columns was used for solar rituals; the two closed chapels were used for the cult of Osiris. The eastern one of these, on the right as you face the temple, contains the cast of a famous zodiac ceiling—the most complete early zodiac, the original of which is in the Louvre in Paris. A metal staircase leads to the highest part of the roof, which offers a wonderful panorama of the temple precincts and the surrounding landscape. Note the sacred-lake enclosure (now dry) on the west side of the temple.

The **temple exterior** is decorated with scenes of pharaohs and gods. The rear wall is particularly interesting, because it shows Queen Cleopatra VII—yes, the famous one, who was involved with Julius Caesar and Mark Antony and was Egypt's last pharaoh—presenting her son Caesarion to the gods as the next ruler of Egypt.

In the context of ancient Egyptian temples, mammisis depict the birth of a god and are often concerned with the divinity of the king. The mammisi on the right side of the Temple of Hathor entrance is of the Roman period (built mainly by Trajan, who ruled from AD 98 to 117). It celebrates the birth of the god Ihi, son of Horus and Isis, as well as the divinity of the pharaoh. Ascend a short flight of stairs into a court; beyond it lies another courtyard with columns at the side. Two rooms then lead to the mammisi's **sanctuary**, which is illustrated with scenes of the divine birth and the suckling of the divine child by various divinities. The sanctuary is surrounded by an ambulatory, the outer portion of which is partially decorated.

Next to the Roman mammisi at the entrance to the Temple of Hathor lies a **Christian basilica** that probably dates from the 5th century AD, making it one of the earliest intact Coptic buildings in Egypt. There is no roof, but the trefoil apse and basilical hall and several shell niches are still visible.

Next to the Coptic basilica are the ruins of an earlier mammisi—founded by Nectanebo I (381–362 BC). Its decorative scheme is similar to that of the later, more intact mammisi.

4

Next in line stand the mud-brick remains of the temple's **sanitorium**, consisting of several small rooms and bathing areas for pilgrims. The pilgrims came to be healed by what today would be called dream therapy. They would sleep in the temple precincts and have dreams in which the gods came to them and cured them or told them what to do to be cured. The sanitorium contained several bathing areas lined with stones that were carved with spells and incantations. The water would run over the stones, taking the magic of the texts with it, and into the baths where pilgrims sat and received the magical waters' cures.

Behind the main temple is a small **Temple of Isis**, which has a strange, dual orientation: east–west as well as north–south. It contains scenes of Isis's divine birth and consists of a court, a small hypostyle hall, another columned hall, two chapels, and the sanctuary. Here, as in the main temple, a number of the images of the "pagan" gods were methodically defaced by the pious Copts. ✉ *Mabed Dendera* 📧 *No phone* 💰 *£e35* 🕐 *Oct.–May, daily 7–5; June–Sept., daily 7–6.*

LUXOR

670 km (415 mi) south of Cairo; 210 km (130 mi) north of Aswan.

Known in antiquity as Thebes, Luxor takes its name from the Arabic al-Uqsur (the palaces). It is a town that merits both poetry and a grain of pragmatism. One of the world's most popular destinations, Luxor lives (or dies) from tourism. But if a well-worn path has been trod to every sight you see, Luxor's universal value in terms of art, natural beauty, and historic monuments is undeniable.

Sunset in Luxor has a transcendent beauty. As the red orb returns to the Western Lands, setting the land-

DID YOU KNOW?

In ancient Egypt, settlements tended to be built on the East Bank of the Nile while tombs were located on the West Bank. This is because the sun rises, or is born, in the east. The sun gives life, so the east became associated with the living. The sun sets in the west signaling an end to the sun's energy, which became associated with death, so Egyptians buried their dead on the West Bank.

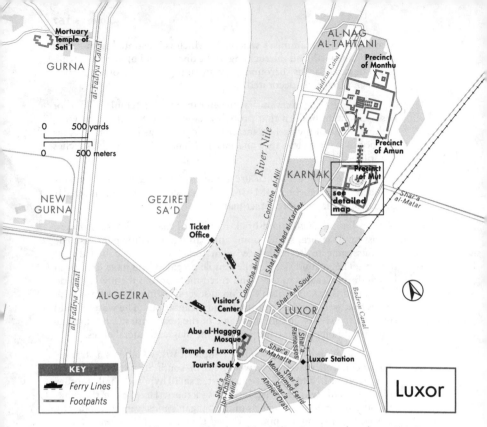

Luxor

KEY
- Ferry Lines
- Footpahts

scape ablaze, consider that this civilization was already ancient in antiquity. Egyptians who witnessed the erection of Abu Simbel, for example, knew even then that the pyramids were at least 2,000 years old.

EXPLORING LUXOR

On the East Bank of the Nile, the modern town thrives amongst the temples to the living. Across the river, the western Theban hills, with their tomb and temple openings gaping black in the beige stone, are dedicated to the dead. They are a constant presence in Luxor, as are the clip-clop and jangle of horse-drawn calèches and the twittering of birds. Along the tree-lined Corniche, clusters of tall felucca masts hem the shore, and the boat captains approach and ask: "Other side?" When you cross the Nile to the West Bank you enter another world, where against a background of modest mud-brick dwellings and pastoral calm lie the Valley of the Kings and Valley of the Queens—awesome rock-hewn demonstrations of political muscle.

★ **Karnak Temple.** Karnak is, without a doubt, the most complex and impressive assemblage of ancient Egyptian religious monuments. The site is divided into three major precincts, dedicated respectively to the divinities Amun-Ra (the central complex), Mut (south of the central complex), and Montu (north). Inside the temple precinct, as in the Temple of Luxor, the Theban Triad of Amun-Ra, Mut, and Khonsu were the deities worshiped. The enclosure also includes smaller sanctuaries dedicated to Khonsu, Ptah, and Opet. The various temples were continuously enlarged and restored from at least the time of the Middle Kingdom down to the Roman period. We owe the most immense and enduring structures to the pharaohs of the New Kingdom.

The 660-yard-long **main axis** of Karnak proceeds from west to east, oriented toward the Nile. Another axis extends south toward Luxor from the midpoint of the main axis.

An **avenue of ram-headed sphinxes,** protecting statuettes of Pinudjem I between their front legs, opens the way to the entrance of the **First Pylon.** This pylon was left unfinished by the kings of the 30th Dynasty. It is the most recent of all the pylons of Karnak, as well as being the most monumental on-site. Against the pylon, on the right side of Karnak's first **forecourt,** are the remains of ancient mud-brick scaffolding, used for the erection of the pylon. In the center of the court, a single open-papyrus column remains of what once was the 10-columned kiosk of Taharqa (690–664 BC), an Ethiopian pharaoh of the 25th Dynasty.

The small temple on the left side of the forecourt entrance is the **Shrine of Seti II** (19th Dynasty), some 1,000 years older than the First Pylon. Seti II built this building, with its three small chapels, to receive the sacred barques of the Theban Triad (Amun-Ra in the center, Mut on the left, and Khonsu on the right) during the Opet processions. The barques are depicted on the walls of each chapel.

In the southeast portion of the forecourt, the **Temple of Ramesses III** (20th Dynasty) is fronted by two colossi representing the king. It has the same structure as most New Kingdom temples: a pylon, a court with 20 Osirid statues of the king (Ramesses III in the form of Osiris), and a hypostyle hall. Like others, the sanctuary is divided into three parts for the cult of the Theban Triad.

Next along the compound's main axis, the **Second Pylon** was built during the reign of Horemheb (18th Dynasty). Most of the pylon was filled with blocks dismantled from buildings of the heretic pharaoh Akhenaten.

The second pylon opens onto the **Hypostyle Hall.** Before you plunge into this fantastical court, the statue of Amun-Ra, in the company of a king, is on the left. Then wander into what seems like a stone forest—with its breathtaking 134 columns. Not only are the dimensions gigantic, but the colors and hieroglyphs are remarkable. The 12 columns alongside the processional way have open-papyrus capitals, while the remaining 122 columns have papyrus-bud capitals and are smaller. New Kingdom pharaohs built the elaborate hall: Ramesses I began the decoration in the 19th Dynasty; Ramesses III completed it some 120 years later in the 20th Dynasty.

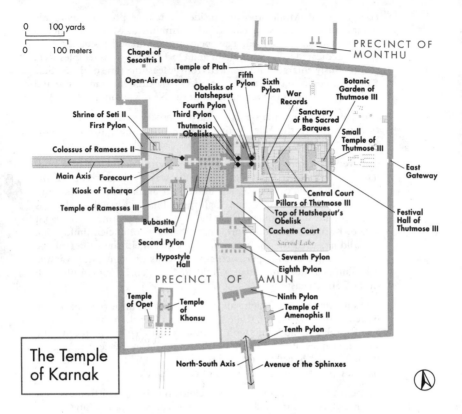

The Temple of Karnak

0 100 yards
0 100 meters

PRECINCT OF MONTHU

Chapel of Sesostris I
Temple of Ptah
Open-Air Museum
Fifth Pylon
Sixth Pylon
Obelisks of Hatshepsut
War Records
Botanic Garden of Thutmose III
Fourth Pylon
Sanctuary of the Sacred Barques
Shrine of Seti II
Third Pylon
First Pylon
Thutmosid Obelisks
Small Temple of Thutmose III
Colossus of Ramesses II
East Gateway
Main Axis   Forecourt
Kiosk of Taharqa
Central Court
Temple of Ramesses III
Pillars of Thutmose III
Top of Hatshepsut's Obelisk
Festival Hall of Thutmose III
Bubastite Portal
Cachette Court
Second Pylon
Sacred Lake
Hypostyle Hall
Seventh Pylon
Eighth Pylon
PRECINCT OF AMUN
Temple of Opet
Temple of Khonsu
Ninth Pylon
Temple of Amenophis II
Tenth Pylon
North-South Axis   Avenue of the Sphinxes

Amenhotep III (18th Dynasty) constructed the **Third Pylon,** which leads to the **Obelisk of Thutmose I** (18th Dynasty), inside the **Court of Amenhotep III.** The **Fourth Pylon,** erected by Thutmose I, gives access to the colonnade of Thutmose I, where an **Obelisk of Hatshepsut** (18th Dynasty), one of two, still stands. The lower part of the obelisk is well preserved because Thutmose III, Hatshepsut's successor, encased it with a brick wall—probably not to preserve it, however, because in other places he usurped her monuments and tried to erase her name from history. Perhaps the intention here was to mask its presence within the temple proper.

Pass through the Fifth and Sixth pylons. In the vestibule that follows, look for the two **Pillars of Thutmose III,** before the sanctuary, representing the union of Egypt. The papyrus (left) signifies Lower Egypt, and the lotus (right) represents Upper Egypt. There is also an elegant statue of the gods Amun-Ra and Amunet, carved during the reign of Tutankhamun. The **Sanctuary of the Sacred Barques,** behind the vestibule, was built by Philip III Arrhidaeus, brother and successor of Alexander the Great. It is made of red granite.

At the end of the main axis rises, transversely, the **Festival Hall of Thutmose III**, also called the Akhmenu. This unusual building was erected to commemorate the king's military campaigns in Asia. The columns are exceptional—massive representations of tent poles used during those campaigns. On the main axis behind the hall is the famous **Botanic Garden of Thutmose III**. The reliefs on the walls show exotic plants and animals that the pharaoh brought back from his expeditions. The hall was later reused as a Christian church. At the end of the west–east axis is one of the eight monumental gates that gave access to the complex of the Temple of Karnak. This one was erected by Nectanebo.

Southeast of the temple lies the **Sacred Lake**, which is fed by the Nile. The morning rituals of the priests included purifying themselves in this lake. At the northeast side of the lake, a large scarab dates from the reign of Amenhotep III and symbolizes the newborn sun. Legend has it that a woman who runs around it three times, clockwise, will become pregnant in the near future (at this writing, the southernmost sectors are not open to the public, so it's not possible to prove the theory). Farther on the left lie the remains of the other obelisk of Hatshepsut (its partner is back between the Fourth and Fifth pylons).

The **north–south axis** begins from an entrance between the Third and Fourth pylons and continues outside of the Precinct of Amun with a southbound avenue of sphinxes. The **Cachette Court,** at the top of the axis, was so named because thousands of statues were found in it in 1903. South lie the Seventh through Tenth pylons, each pair separated by a court. All elements of this axis date from the 18th Dynasty but are not accessible at this writing due to active archaeological research work.

Besides fragments of temples and statues recovered from the Temple of Karnak itself, the **Open-Air Museum** contains the small, white, well-preserved **Chapel of Senwosret I,** dating from the Middle Kingdom 12th Dynasty (1938–1759 BC). It was used during Senwosret I's reign to receive the sacred barques. Its new location and reconstructed state are due to the fact that Amenhotep III dismantled the chapel and used it to fill his Third Pylon. Two other small chapels lie beside it, also found inside the pylon. One of these is the Red Chapel of Hatshepsut. The museum is rather small, and its chapels and fragments are totally swallowed up in the gigantic complex of Karnak, which by its size detracts from the beauty of the museum's elements.

Karnak's **Sound & Light Show** includes a walk through the temple, with several monuments illuminated successively, and ends at the Sacred Lake, where the second part begins. From a tribune, the entire complex can be seen, with different temples lighted, music, and a narrated history of the site. On a rotating schedule throughout the week, shows are conducted in Arabic, English, French, German, Italian, Japanese, and Spanish. English shows run each night, the other languages less frequently.

It is best to visit the Temple of Karnak early in the morning for a few reasons: massive groups of people begin arriving around 9 AM; the slanting light calls relief carvings into better focus; and later in the day the heat can be overwhelming. ✛ *From the Temple of Luxor, follow the Corniche north 2 km (1 mi), then turn right and proceed 100 yards* 📞 *No phone* 🖼 *Temple £e65, Open-Air Museum £e25, Sound & Light Show £e75 (video camera £e35)* 🕙 *Temple Oct.–May, daily 6 AM–5 PM; June–Sept., daily 6–6. Sound & Light Show (in English) Oct.–May, Thurs.–Fri. and Mon. 6:30 PM, Tues.–Wed. and Sat.–Sun. 7:45 PM; June–Sept., Thurs.–Fri. and Mon. 8 PM, Tues.–Wed. and Sat.– Sun. 9:15 PM.*

★ **Luxor Museum.** The Luxor Museum contains, without a doubt, the crème de la crème of New Kingdom sculpture. On three floors, objects ranging from the Predynastic to Coptic periods are displayed in a soothing atmosphere. Each object has its own space, affording it the attention it deserves. Descriptions of artifacts are thorough and accurate.

The ground floor has several masterpieces. The statue of Thutmose III (18th Dynasty) in green schist of rare quality emits pharaonic inner peace and transcendence. The calcite statue of Sobek with Amenhotep III is also exceptional, both for its workmanship and its rather unusual subject—there are very few representations of the god Sobek offering life to a pharaoh. Colored reliefs, a sphinx, a scribe, and other royal statues are also superb.

On the first floor are Greco-Roman bronzes, a wooden maquette of a boat of Tutankhamun (18th Dynasty), papyri, royal statues, a sarcophagus, and other objects. At the end of the hall, in the first part of the first floor, is a statue of the famous architect Amenhotep, son of Hapu, who served under Amenhotep III and had his own funerary temple in the West Bank. A little variation in style is offered with the two sculptures representing the head of the heretic pharaoh Akhenaten (18th Dynasty); they are a good example of the Amarna style (Akhenaten ruled from Tell al-Amarna).

Back on the ground floor, a room to the left of the entrance is dedicated to the 16 New Kingdom statues found in 1989 in the cachette of the Solar Court of Amenhotep III in Luxor Temple. These were hidden to protect them from destruction by later rulers. ✉ *Corniche al-Nil, 1 km (½ mi) north of the Luxor Temple* 📞 *No phone* 🖼 *£e80* 🕙 *Oct.–May, daily 9–1 (last ticket at 12:30) and 4–9 (last ticket at 8:30); June–Sept., daily 9–1 (last ticket at 12:30) and 5–10 (last ticket at 9:30).*

Mummification Museum. The Egyptian Antiquities Museum in Cairo has an entire section devoted to mummification, but a visit to this museum is worth the detour if you didn't have the opportunity to see the exhibits in Cairo. The exhibits here are intelligently designed and include the most important elements of the mummification rituals. And the slightly macabre atmosphere is perfect for the subject. The museum is divided into two parts: the first explains, with modern drawings based on ancient Egyptian reliefs and wall paintings, the stages the deceased goes through during mummification, as well as his journey toward heaven. To complement the scenes, a mummy is exposed at the end of the first section. After this introduction, the actual display of artifacts begins. There are tools, canopic jars, painted sarcophagi, and products used during the mummification process. There are also mummified animals, among them a baboon, a crocodile, a ram, a cat, and an ibis. The thrill here comes from the mummified animals—and the split human head, post-mummification. The museum is 200 yards north of the Temple of Luxor, on the opposite side of the road. ⊠ *Corniche al-Nil* 🕾 *No phone* 🖃 *£e50* ☉ *Oct.–May, daily 9–1; June–Sept., daily 9–1 and 5–10.*

NEED A BREAK? The venerable Victorian lounge at the **Sofitel Old Winter Palace** (⊠ *Corniche al-Nil* 🕾 *095/2238–0422*), lined with richly upholstered divans and armchairs and hung with Oriental-style paintings of turbaned men wielding sabers, is a wonderful place to decompress with a spot of tea after a day of temple stomping. Afternoon light filters through tall windows, and birds twitter in the garden, while you whittle away at a plateful of sandwiches, pastries, and fresh-baked scones in the Royal Bar or on the terrace. Tea is served (daily 4–7) in heavy silver pots and poured into porcelain cups. Note: Casual attire is not permitted; jacket requested for men.

Temple of Luxor. Far easier to explore and digest than the sprawling Temple of Karnak just downriver, the Luxor temple (built between 1390 and 323 BC) stands near the edge of the Nile surrounded by modern buildings in the city center. The temple was dedicated to the Theban Triad—the gods Amun-Ra, Mut (goddess of queenship), and Khonsu (moon god)—as well as to the cult of Ka (the royal spirit). The ancient name of the 285-yard-long temple was Ipet-resyt (Southern Harem), the southern partner of Karnak, which was the starting point of the late-summer Opet festival. This feast involved a great procession of priests bringing the ceremonial barque of Amun-Ra from Karnak to Luxor, where the god would be united with the Mother of the King to allow her to give birth to the royal Ka.

It is likely that the largely 18th Dynasty (1539–1292 BC) temple was built over a Middle Kingdom predecessor. Amenhotep III (1390–1353 BC) started to develop the temple, then Ramesses II added to it a century later. Ruins from later periods also surround the main temple. The Avenue of Sphinxes was the creation of Nectanebo I (381–362 BC), almost 1,000 years later. The next considerable work was accomplished relatively soon thereafter, during the reign of Alexander the Great, who built, in the heart of the temple, a sanctuary for Amun-Ra's sacred barque.

During the Roman period, the temple was transformed into a fortified camp. Following the 4th-century AD (i.e., Christian) ban on pagan cults, several churches were built inside the temple. One of them, in the northeast corner of the court of Ramesses II (19th Dynasty), was superseded by the Abu al-Haggag mosque during the 12th century AD, and locals refused to allow it to be torn down to complete the excavation of the Luxor temple.

Enter the temple compound through the modern gate on the Corniche, north of the Winter Palace Hotel. Go down the stairs, which lead to the temple esplanade and the south end of the 3-km (2-mi) **Avenue of Sphinxes,** which is lined with 70 human-headed sphinxes, 34 on the west side and 36 on the east. The 6-yard-wide avenue at one time connected the Luxor and Karnak temples. Only part of the Luxor end of it has been fully cleared, but the Egyptian government has issued plans to re-create as much of the avenue as possible—notwithstanding any mosques that have been built along the route—and have demolished buildings for several hundreds yards north of the temple site to begin excavation for what remain of the original statues.

The Temple of Luxor's massive **First Pylon** (58 yards wide) is the work of that tireless builder Ramesses II—ample evidence of whom you can see in the scenes of the Battle of Qadesh (a campaign that Ramesses II waged against the Hittites in Syria) that adorn the outer face of the pylon. Two obelisks and six colossi representing the king used to stand in front of the pylon. One of the obelisks was given to France as a present by Muhammed 'Ali Pasha; it graces the Place de la Concorde in Paris. Of the six colossi (two seated and four standing), only three are still on-site. France was also given two of these, and they are in the Louvre.

Beyond the pylon lies the **Peristyle Court of Ramesses II,** a double row of papyrus-bud columns interspersed with a series of standing colossi representing the king. To the right of the entrance is a triple shrine, also called a way station, originally built by the queen Hatshepsut. Her successor, Thutmose III, usurped it—a relatively common practice by which a later ruler took credit for a monument by excising the original builder's cartouches and writing in his own. The shrines here are dedicated to the Theban Triad: Amun-Ra in the middle, Mut on the left, and Khonsu on the right. The shrines' purpose was to receive their sacred barques during the Opet processions. To the left of the entrance to the court is the **Mosque of Abu al-Haggag,** built atop a Christian church. Al-Haggag was a holy man, originally from Baghdad, who died in Luxor in 1244 AD.

To the right of the entrance leading to the colonnade, on the western half of the southern wall, a relief scene shows the dedication of Ramesses II's **Second Pylon.** It provides a view of what the pylon must have looked like after its construction. In front of the colonnade, two colossal statues represent Ramesses II seated on a throne, with his wife Nefertari, as the goddess Hathor, standing at his side.

The **Colonnade of Amenhotep III** consists of two rows of seven columns with papyrus-bud capitals. The wall decoration, completed by Amenhotep's successors, illustrates the voyage of the statue of the god Amun-Ra from Karnak to Luxor Temple during the Opet festival. On each side of the central alley are statues of Amun-Ra and Mut, carved during the reign of Tutankhamun, which Ramesses II later usurped.

The Colonnade of Amenhotep III leads to the **Solar Court of Amenhotep III,** where 25 superbly executed 18th-Dynasty statues of gods and kings were found in 1989. This peristyle court is surrounded on three sides with a double row of columns with papyrus-bud capitals of remarkable elegance. At the far side of the solar court is a direct access to the **Hypostyle Hall of Amenhotep III,** which consisted of eight rows of four papyrus-bud columns. Between the last two columns on the left as you keep walking into the temple is a Roman altar dedicated to the emperor Constantine.

South of the Hypostyle Hall are **three chapels:** one dedicated to Mut (directly on the east side of the central doorway) and two to Khonsu (on each side of the central doorway). The first antechamber originally had eight columns; they were removed during the 4th century AD to convert the chamber into a Christian church, with an aspidal recess flanked on both sides by granite columns in the Corinthian style. The ancient Egyptian scenes were covered with Christian paintings, which have been almost completely destroyed.

WORD OF MOUTH

We decided to buy the Antinal [our guide in Egypt] recommended . . . (It's a pill that is described on the package as an anti-bacterial and one Web site describes it as an antibiotic [a trade name for Nifuroxazide]—it's not just a super form of Immodium). It was a good decision and it works. It's not available in the U.S. [but we bought it in] a local pharmacy . . . for $1 over the counter without a prescription. Take it on the first indication of problems.—AZEBS.

The second antechamber, known as the **Offering Chapel,** has four columns and leads to the inner sanctuary of the sacred barques. The chamber had the same divisions as the previous chapels, but Alexander the Great removed the four columns and replaced them with a chapel. This sanctuary received the sacred barque of Amun-Ra during the Opet celebrations.

On the east side of the Offering Chapel, a doorway leads to the **Birth Chamber,** dedicated to the divine conception of the pharaoh. The purpose of the scenes in the Birth Chamber was to prove that Amenhotep III was, indeed, the son of the god Amun Ra, to strengthen the pharaoh's position as absolute ruler. On the left wall, birth scenes spread over three registers. In the first one, look for the goddess Selkis, the Queen Mutemwia (mother of Amenhotep III), and two goddesses suckling children, with two cows suckling children below it. In the second register, the third scene is the pharaoh's actual birth, in front of several divinities. In the fourth scene, Hathor presents the infant to Amun Ra. The third register's fourth scene represents the conception of the royal child. The queen and Amun-Ra face each other, supported by Selkis and Neith. ⊠ *Corniche al-Nil, Luxor center, north of the Winter Palace Hotel* ☎ *No phone* ▦ *£e50* ✆ *Oct.–May, daily 6 AM–9 PM; June–Sept., daily 6 AM–10 PM.*

WHERE TO EAT

Upper Egypt may not be an epicurean paradise, but the standard fare of soups, salads, *mezze* (hot and cold appetizers), grilled meats, and *tagines* (earthenware-baked vegetables, meat, or chicken in a tomato-based sauce, variously spiced) can be perfectly satisfying when well prepared.

Luxor is one of the most popular destinations in Egypt, so there are many restaurants that appeal particularly to the tourist trade. Most of the nicest establishments are in hotels, but you'll also find a wide range of restaurants (especially those serving Egyptian food) around town.

$$$
FRENCH
✕ **The 1886.** Play lord or lady of the manor beneath the Venetian crystal chandeliers of this dining room. Candlelight is reflected on the heavy silver plates and thick linens. Twenty-three-foot-tall windows open onto a garden. In massive gilt mirrors you can observe yourself or the other diners struggling with a gigantic menu bearing complicated French names that sound terribly pedestrian in their English translations. White-gloved waiters are a bit over the top, but the food is fine, if overpriced. Dress and go for the ambience. ⊠ *Sofitel Old Winter Palace, Corniche al-Nil* ☎ *095/2238–0422* ⚑ *Reservations essential. Jacket and tie* ⊟ *AE, MC, V* ⊘ *No lunch.*

$
MIDDLE
EASTERN
✕ **El Hussein.** One of the best values in Luxor caters to both Egyptians and foreigners. This no-frills restaurant is clean, the service is friendly, and the location is ideal for a break from shopping or sightseeing. Choose from grilled meats, vegetarian and meat tagines, soups, salads, pizzas, and sandwiches, all competently prepared and served in large portions for remarkably low prices. The air-conditioned dining room is a little cafeteria-like. No alcohol is served. ⊠ *Savoy Market, Corniche al-Nil, just south of the Etap Mercure Luxor* ☎ *095/237–6166* ⊟ No credit cards.

$$
MIDDLE
EASTERN
✕ **El Tarboush.** This restaurant in the gardens of the Winter Palace Hotel sits under the canopy of mature palm fronds, serving excellent Egyptian food in a lovely, quiet setting with views of the beautifully lit hotel. There's a full range of hot and cold *mezze* for starters; main courses include a decadent stuffed pigeon, *shish tawouk* (chicken kebab), or a tender mixed grill. There's a full bar service and wine list. ⊠ *Sofitel Old Winter Palace, Corniche al-Nil* ☎ *095/2238–0422* ⚑ *Reservations essential. Jacket and tie* ⊟ *AE, MC, V* ⊘ *Closed Oct.–Mar. No lunch.*

$$
CONTINENTAL
✕ **The Flamboyant.** Despite the constant stream of large tour groups at the modern Hotel Etap Mercure, the hotel restaurant, with a large bay window overlooking the Corniche, is an intimate place for dining by candlelight. A Continental menu includes the tasty *soupe des pecheurs,* a creamy fish and shrimp bisque accompanied by croutons, grated cheese, and aioli (garlic mayonnaise); ravioli stuffed with Red Sea lobster served in a peppery sauce; a thick, tender beef fillet; and an excellent roasted rack of lamb. Several French wines are available. ⊠ *Mercure Luxor, Corniche al-Nil* ☎ *095/237–4944* ⊟ *AE, DC, MC, V* ⊘ *No lunch.*

$–$$
MIDDLE
EASTERN
✗**Jamboree.** A popular restaurant with visitors of all nationalities, Jamboree is only a minute or so from Luxor Temple. The menu concentrates on Egyptian staples of roast chicken, grilled meat, and stuffed pigeon accompanied by rice and salad. But you can also order steak in red-wine sauce, cottage pie, or even chili con carne, and it's all very good. There's seating on three levels, including an open-air terrace on the upper floor. Beer is served. ⊠*29 Shar'a El Montazah* ☎*095/235–5827* ⊟*No credit cards.*

$$
JAPANESE
✗**Miyako.** Miyako is Luxor's finest Asian restaurant. The room is sedately but luxuriously decorated in a Far Eastern style, with teals, golds, and deep green marble. There is a formal tea area and a sequestered alcove for romance or business. A variety of Asian specialties are available, including excellent sushi and sashimi, which is prepared before your eyes at the sushi bar; however, the *teppan-yaki* (Japanese grill), prepared in flamboyant, percussive style, is a signature. ⊠*Sonesta St. George, Corniche al-Nil* ☎*095/238–2575* ⊟*AE, MC, V* ⊗*No lunch.*

$
MIDDLE
EASTERN
✗**Nubian Village.** A re-created Nubian village on the banks of the Nile, this leisure facility has open-air, low-level seating, a *shisha* area, an open grill, and a bread oven. The food is standard Egyptian, with mostly grilled meats and mezze, but the setting is delightful—you are surrounded by trees and away from the traffic in town. You'll need a taxi to drop you off and pick you up after your meal. ⊠*7 mi south of Luxor at the eastern end of the south bridge* ☎*010/355–2330* ⊟*No credit cards* ⊗*No lunch.*

$
CAFÉ
✗**Oasis Café.** In one of the few remaining 19th-century mansions in town, this relaxed eatery decorated in period style lives up to its name. American-owned, it's an informal place with old photographs on the walls and a lively crowd of travelers around the globe. Drop in for a coffee or light lunch of soups, sandwiches, or salads. Main dishes include pastas, curry, or mixed grill, and there's a wicked chocolate cake to finish. ⊠*Shar'a Lahib Habashi* ☎*095/237–2914* ⊟*No credit cards.*

$
FAST FOOD
✗**Snack Time.** One of a new generation of modern Egyptian fast-food style cafés, this spot serves a combination of traditional street food such as *swarma* (thin-cut meat and salad wrapped in unleaved bread—like a gyro), along with burgers, paninis, and salads. There's a good choice of sodas, and the coffee is excellent. You'll find it's frequented by tourists in search of familiar fill-me-ups and teenage Egyptians out with their friends. There is both an air-conditioned dining room and an open-terrace eating area. There's also free Wi-Fi. ⊠*Shar'a Luxor Temple* ☎*095/237–5407* ⊟*No credit cards.*

$$
INDIAN
✗**A Taste of India.** An English restaurateur has plugged a gap in the market with a menu of Bangladeshi and northern Indian dishes including excellent full-flavored curries. If the Indian food is too hot for your palate, he's also added a few European staples including spaghetti Bolognese and chicken *panne* (a thin cutlet covered in breadcrumbs then sautéed). The dining room has an Italian trattoria feel with heavy wooden and wrought-iron furniture and a tile floor. ⊠*Shar'a Joseph Hotel* ☎*010/214–8079* ⊟*MC, V.*

4

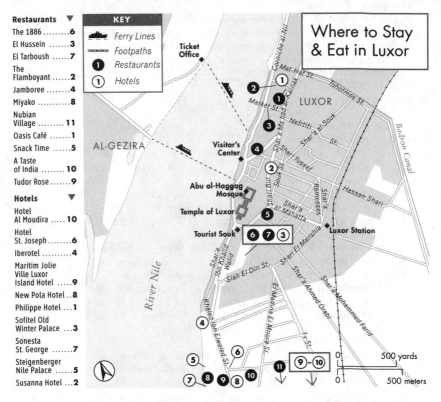

$ ✕ **Tudor Rose.** This small dining room overlooks a tree-lined street,
MIDDLE and the standard Upper Egyptian and Western fare comes at reason-
EASTERN able prices. Try the *kobbeba,* fried balls of crushed wheat stuffed with
spiced minced meat; ask for lime to squeeze on top. The moussaka is
a tasty and filling eggplant-and-ground-meat dish smothered in béchamel sauce. ⊠ *Shar'a Khaled Ibn El Waleed, beside St. Joseph Hotel*
☎ *095/381–707* ⊟ *AE, MC, V.*

WHERE TO STAY

In Luxor, hotel standards have little to do with the star rating you see
in the lobbies. They usually fall into three categories, which rise and fall
according to room rates: the luxurious, the mediocre, and the decrepit.
It's best to ask for a Nile view, slightly more pricey than a garden
view, and to specify the bed size you want when making reservations,
because many double rooms come with twin beds.

Most hotels in Luxor are located on the East Bank of the Nile along the
Corniche. A handful of others can be found on islands in the river and
on the West Bank. Prices at the large five-star hotels can be high, but
you will rarely pay the rack rate if you book a package or tour.

Hotels in Luxor can help you arrange tours and felucca cruises, but there is also a collection of travel and tour agencies around the Winter Palace Hotel's shopping arcade.

$$$$ ⊞ **Hotel Al Moudira.** A beautifully designed Arabian palace complete
★ with ornate Islamic arches and domes is set in 8 hectares of gardens. This is a true oasis, where you can completely relax after sightseeing. The owner is a polyglot photographer and jewelry designer who's stamped a very personal mark on the property in its design and furnishings. The individually decorated rooms, with their hand-painted frescoes, silk and satin drapes, and antique furniture, are linked by colonnaded courtyards graced by fountains that lead to a pool and pavilion with a bar and restaurant. You probably won't want to leave. The hotel can be reached by taxi or ferry. **Pros:** Exceptional attention to detail; you'll think you've walked into a photo shoot for a decorating magazine. **Cons:** The hotel is on the West Bank, quite far from town and a 20-minute taxi ride from downtown Luxor and its restaurants. ⊠ *West Bank ✢ From the ferry travel inland and then turn left at the junction; the hotel is a 5-minute drive along this road* ☎*012/325–1307* ⊕*www.moudira.com* ◥*54 rooms* ⟁*In-hotel: restaurant, bars, pool, spa, parking (free), no-smoking rooms.* ⊟*AE, DC, MC, V* ⦁⊙*BP.*

$ ⊞ **Hotel St. Joseph.** This cozy hotel is one of the preferred stopovers
★ for demanding, budget-minded British travelers. Low-key decor, a high standard of cleanliness, very decent food, and a friendly staff are among the advantages. The small pool on the roof has one of the best views on this end of Luxor. Rooms have spacious balconies and full baths, though they could use some updating. Still, this is both a reliable and attractive low-cost lodging option. **Pros:** Clean and spacious rooms; pool on-site (rare for a hotel in this price range). **Cons:** Rooms are rather dated and worn compared to newer budget options in Luxor. ⊠*Shar'a Khaled Ibn El Waleed* ☎*095/238–1707* ◥*75 rooms* ⟁*In-room: refrigerator. In-hotel: restaurant, bar, pool* ⊟*AE, MC, V* ⦁⊙*BP.*

$$ ⊞ **Iberotel.** Ideally situated at the southern end of the Luxor Corniche, this rather uninspiring tower-block building offers an excellent, modern mid-range option. The hotel is well-appointed but has no frills. Rooms, accessed from an atrium, are compact but well furnished, decorated in warm reds and creams. Rooms overlooking the street or the atrium are much cheaper (you pay a €30 premium for a Nile view). The swimming pool floating on the Nile makes the most of the outside space under the Nile-view rooms. The hotel is popular with European tour groups. **Pros:** Iberotel has the least expensive direct Nile views in Luxor; good position for strolling to Luxor temple and the downtown area. **Cons:** Arguably the ugliest hotel along the riverfront; public areas and bar are smoking areas and popular with smoking tourists. ⊠*Shar'a Khaled Ibn El Waleed* ☎*095/238–0925* ⊕*www.iberotel-eg. com* ◥*185 rooms* ⟁*In-room: safe, refrigerator, Internet (some). In-hotel: 5 restaurants, bars, pool, bicycles, laundry service, no-smoking rooms* ⊟*AE, MC, V* ⦁⊙*BP.*

$$$$ ⊞ **Maritim Jolie Ville Luxor Island Hotel.** Mother Nature reigns supreme
★ at this garden-of-paradise resort, whose timeless, unsullied Nile vistas are 4 km (2½ mi) from Luxor's bustling center (there's free shuttle ser-

vice). Occupying 60 acres on pastoral King's Island, the Maritim's exotic plants and flowering trees are filled with a multitude of migrating and local birds. The low, vine-covered clusters of bungalow-style rooms dispersed about the property are spacious and immaculate with blue and turquoise highlights. There is a good program of activities for children, which is rare in hotels on the Nile. **Pros:** Restful and natural surroundings; island location puts you at one with the river. **Cons:** About 30 minutes by free shuttle bus or taxi to reach the city center; some of the furnishings are showing a little wear and tear. ⊠ *King's Island* ☎ *095/227–4855* ⊕ *www.maritim.de* ↩ *322 rooms, 4 suites* ⟳ *In-room: safe, refrigerator, Internet. In-hotel: 3 restaurants, room service, bars, pool, tennis courts, gym, children's programs (ages 5–12), laundry service, parking (free), no-smoking rooms* ⊟ *AE, MC, V* ❙⊚❙ *BP.*

$ ⊡ **New Pola Hotel.** On the southern hotel strip—though one block inland from the river—this is a excellent budget option with a good range of facilities. Rooms are well-furnished with clean, bright bathrooms, and those at the front have good-size balconies, though views of the Nile are blocked by trees. The best attraction at the New Pola is the roof pool with its wooden sundeck offering views out over the Nile. **Pros:** Quite modern facilities for the price; large enough that you can sometimes find a room if you arrive without a reservation. **Cons:** Breakfast is a spartan affair. ⊠ *Shar'a Khaled Ibn El Waleed* ☎ *095/236–5081* ⊕ *www.newpolahotel.com* ↩ *81 rooms* ⟳ *In-room: refrigerator. In-hotel: 2 restaurants, bar, pool* ⊟ *MC, V* ❙⊚❙ *BP.*

$ ⊡ **Philippe Hotel.** Leave the clamor of a shop-filled downtown street and enter what appears to be a miniature palace: the Philippe has definitely succumbed to the local predilection for gleaming marble lobbies. Everything from the elevators on up adheres to the same Lilliputian—albeit pristine—standard. Superior rooms are more modern with a higher standard of furnishings and fittings. The Philippe's major asset, aside from value for money, is a swimming pool on the remarkably spacious sixth-floor roof. The basement restaurant, with its Tiffany-style glass panels, is a lovely bonus. **Pros:** Good location and price; superior rooms are well furnished, and superior bathrooms are small but well appointed with the most professionally tiled walls and floors in Egypt. **Cons:** Rooms vary in size and in the amount of light (some have windows out into a communal shaft); cheaper standard rooms aren't as nice. ⊠ *Shar'a Labib Habashi, just off the Corniche al-Nil near the Hotel Etap Mercure* ☎ *095/237–2284* ⊕ *www.philippeluxorhotel.com* ↩ *64 rooms* ⟳ *In room: refrigerator. In hotel: Restaurant, room service, bar, pool, spa, laundry service* ⊟ *V.*

$$$$ ⊡ **Sofitel Old Winter Palace.** This noble Victorian-style edifice, built in
★   1886, exudes the heady scent of colonial luxury. Designed for the Egyptian monarchy, the Winter Palace has seen many an august personage pass through its revolving doors, including Russian tsars, the Shah of Iran, and Hollywood stars. The interiors are grandiose. Each room is slightly different in decor and form, but all are large and elegant, and all contain a scattering of antiques. The entire hotel and grounds seem suspended in time, a fugitive from some more gracious era. Rooms in the modern Pavilion annex, which has a separate reception but shares

4

the gardens and other facilities, are actually larger, more luxurious, and have garden views, though they lack the period atmosphere. **Pros:** One of Egypt's most iconic hotels; surroundings are luxurious yet still of their period; the gardens are a cool and quiet respite from the hubbub of the town. **Cons:** The dress code in bars and restaurants (jacket and tie for men) may be too restrictive for some travelers; the atmosphere may be too formal for families with young children. ⊠ *Corniche al-Nil* ☎ *095/2238–0422 or 800/515–5679* ⊕ *www.sofitel.com* ↪ *92 rooms* & *In-room: safe. In-hotel: 3 restaurants, room service, bars, 2 tennis courts, pool, gym, bicycles, laundry services, Internet terminal, no-smoking rooms* ⊟ *AE, MC, V* ⧫ *BP.*

$$$$ 🏨 **Sonesta St. George.** Neo-pharaonic ostentation is squeezed into a small parcel of Nile real estate that has been developed to within an inch of its life—that's the St. George. The Sonesta is known throughout the region for its excellent cuisine and the profusion of colored-marble in the lobby. It's exceedingly popular with Asian tour groups because of the high standard of the facilities and service. Rooms are well appointed but small, but those with Nile views have balconies and graceful lotus-motif wrought-iron railings. **Pros:** Excellent river views from Nile View rooms; there's an excellent range of amenities on-site; restaurants are uniformly good. **Cons:** There isn't much outside space in which to relax; service can be a little lax for a five-star property. ⊠ *Corniche al-Nil South* ☎ *095/238–2575 or 800/700–3782* ⊕ *www. sonesta.com* ↪ *224 rooms* & *In-room: safe. In-hotel: 6 restaurants, room service, bars, pool, gym, spa, laundry service, no-smoking rooms.* ⊟ *AE, DC, MC, V* ⧫ *BP.*

$$$–$$$$ 🏨 **Steigenberger Nile Palace.** The Nile Palace's imposing salmon-colored facade is easily the most visible hotel on the strip south of the Corniche. This is a hotel designed and furnished with attention to detail, both in the public areas and restaurants as well as in the rooms; the details can be seen at their best in the Casa de Napoli trattoria. Many rooms have Nile views. **Pros:** Excellent design and decor throughout; good choice of eateries on-site. **Cons:** Standard rooms are on the small side; limited outside space; poolside can get crowded if the hotel is busy. ⊠ *Shar'a Khaled Ibn El Waleed* ☎ *095/236–6999 or 866/991–1299* ⊕ *www. steigenberger.com* ↪ *256 rooms, 48 suites* & *In-room: safe, Internet. In hotel: 6 restaurants, room service, bars, pool, gym, spa, laundry facilities, no-smoking rooms* ⊟ *AE, MC, V* ⧫ *BP.*

$ 🏨 **Susanna Hotel.** The best value in Luxor, the Susanna is a well-★ appointed, clean budget hotel with views overlooking Luxor Temple in the heart of town. Rooms are small but well furnished, and some at the front have small balconies. The hotel has a roof terrace with a pool plus a restaurant on the mezzanine below with great views of the temple and the evening Sound and Light Show. **Pros:** Inexpensive but well furnished; double-glazed windows cut down on outside noise; great location for access to the Luxor temple, the souk, and the Corniche. **Cons:** Rooms are small, but that is typical of hotels at this price point; cash only. ⊠ *Shar'a Mabed El Karnak* ☎ *095/236–9915* ↪ *45 rooms* & *In-room: refrigerator. In-hotel: restaurant, bar, pool* ⊟ *No credit cards* ⧫ *BP.*

CLOSE UP

The Scarab

One of the least expensive souvenirs you can bring back from your trip is a small scarab beetle carved from stone. The scarab, or dung beetle, isn't the prettiest insect, but it had a special place in ancient Egyptian religion. The beetle pushes a ball of dung from east to west just as the god Khepri rolled the earth from east to west, so it's a symbol of a cycle of renewal that's central to ancient beliefs. The dung beetle also rises out of the earth when it hatches in the same way that ancient Egyptians hoped to emerge into the afterlife. That's why the image of this humble beetle is seen in royal tombs, and why replicas are bought every day by tourists all across Egypt.

SHOPPING

The **New Tourist Souk** (⊠ *Shar'a al-Karnak*), a shopping area, runs parallel to the Old Souk but lacks its charm. You'll find the full gamut of souvenirs and spices minus the fruit, vegetables, and animal and car traffic of the Old Souk—which makes for more contemplative bargaining. It's open daily from 8 AM until midnight.

Early morning is the best time to hit the **Old Souk** (⊠ *Shar'a al-Souk, from Abu Haggar Sq.*), a fairly calm, provincial market, and mingle with the locals doing their grocery shopping. It's a long, narrow street running between concrete dwellings and lined with shops, carts, and turbaned men and black-robed women hawking their wares. You'll find brass trays, alabaster vases and bowls, leather poufs, jewelry shops, and racks of brightly colored cotton scarves (around £e30) and *galabeyyas* (cotton shifts, around £e70)—mixed with hardware stores, displays of cow heads, and great piles of fruits and vegetables in hemp baskets. Donkeys bray, chickens cackle (sold live or with their necks wrung for a small additional charge), and people shuffle along calling greetings. All is redolent of pungent spices, incense, tangy mint, and the occasional whiff of offal and freshly butchered meat. The souk is open daily from 7 AM until midnight.

The Queen Nefertari Museum (⊠ *Corniche al-Nil, corner just north of Hotel Etap Mercure* ☎ *095/237–4702*) has a collection of fabulous fake antiquities. The small and midsize statuary crafted in the last century looks so real you must take a certificate to the airport so you won't be accused of smuggling artifacts. The shop's hours, however, are erratic.

NIGHTLIFE

King's Head Pub (⊠ *Corniche al-Nil, above Naf Naf Shop* ☎ *095/238–0489*), like its logo—a portrait of English King Henry VIII with the face of the pharaoh Akhenaten—is an anomaly, with an eclectic pub

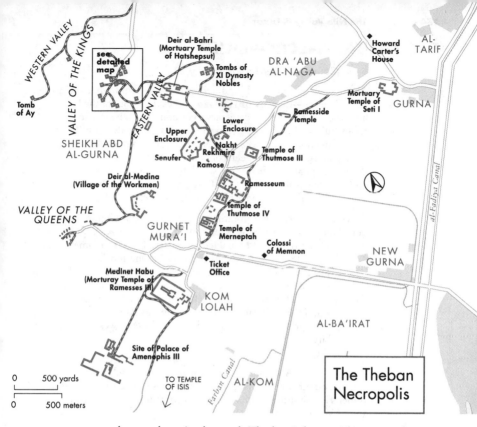

The Theban Necropolis

atmosphere and a mixed crowd. The bar is hung with coasters from around the world, pewter mugs, mosque lamps, and an Australian flag, and Bob Marley posters abound. A small blackboard announces the cocktail of the week.

The Royal Bar (⊠ *Sofitel Old Winter Palace, Corniche al-Nil* ☎ *095/238–0422*) is hardly a jumpin' joint, but it's worth a visit for its colonial panache—burgundy walls, mahogany woodwork, beamed ceilings, lavish drapery, and bookshelves stocked with such oddities as *Who's Who of 1938* and a hardbound Tom Clancy novel. Enjoy good mixed drinks in the lounge or at the semicircular brass-and-black-granite bar. Complimentary canapés and nuts are available.

Subil Disco (⊠ *Hotel Etap Mercure, Corniche al-Nil* ☎ *095/237–4944*) is catacomb-dark and nondescript, except for the illuminated tiled arch that encloses the dance floor and looks like something out of a very old *Star Trek* episode. It's frequented by a volatile mixture of vacationing Britons, hopeful Egyptians, and a smattering of insomniacs. Sometimes there is a belly dancer: Oriental posturing accompanied by a shiver of beads.

THE THEBAN NECROPOLIS

4 km (2½ mi) west of Luxor.

At the edge of cultivated land across the Nile from what the ancients called Thebes—the City of 100 Gates—lies their City of the Dead, arguably the most extensive cemetery ever conceived. New Kingdom pharaohs built their tombs here, in the secrecy of the desert hills, with the goal of making them less accessible than the Old and Middle Kingdom royal tombs, which had been robbed even by the time of the New Kingdom. The pharaohs had their sepulchres hollowed out underground, and workers isolated from the East Bank decorated them. These artisans had their own village, temples, and cemetery at Deir al-Medina.

To celebrate their own greatness, as well as the magnificence of the god Amun-Ra, most New Kingdom rulers constructed huge mortuary temples surrounded by palace granaries. These monuments spread across the edge of the fields, as if to buffer the fertile land from the desert. The choice of the West Bank was based on its rugged landscape (which should have kept robbers away), but the overall rationale came from ancient Egyptian religious beliefs. Every night, the old sun set in the west and was reborn the next morning as Khepri, the young sun. By the same principle, the dead were buried in the west to prepare for their rebirth.

The West Bank is not only a royal necropolis, reserved for the sovereign and his family. A considerable number of tombs belonged to Egyptian nobles and other preeminent courtiers. Their sepulchres were of smaller dimensions, but the quality of their decoration was comparable to that found in the tombs of the kings.

Because the tombs of the nobles were dug into the limestone hills at the edge of an open plain, numerous objects were robbed over the centuries. The same destiny was reserved for most of the graves of the Valley of the Kings and the Valley of the Queens, despite the extreme measures that were taken to avoid it. The remarkable exception to this, of course, is the tomb of Tutankhamun, which archaeologist Howard Carter discovered with its treasures nearly intact in 1922.

To do a full circuit of the various tombs, start making your way around the West Bank at the Valley of the Kings, then move on to the Temple of Hatshepsut at Deir al-Bahri, the Temple of Seti I, the Valleys of the Nobles, the Ramesseum, the Valley of the Queens, and Deir al-Medina. End with the splendid mortuary temple of Ramesses III at Medinet Habu.

June through September are only for the brave—come then if you thrive on high heat and sweat. In these months, bringing a large bottle of water is even more essential than at other times. October, November, April, and May are the nicest months. From December through March, you might want to carry a sweater with you.

■TIP→ The best times of day to see the monuments, especially in summer, are in the early morning or in late afternoon—to avoid the high heat of midday and, likewise the waves of sightseers who begin to arrive between 8:30 and 9 AM. In winter, the weather is perfectly bearable, and the main obstacle to seeing the monuments is other tourists. Again, early-morning and late-afternoon forays are best for avoiding crowds. At sunset, the mortuary temple of Ramesses III at Medinet Habu is extremely pleasant—there is nothing better than relaxing on one of its terraces after a long day of monument hopping.

There are several ways to cross the Nile from Luxor. The least expensive is by local ferry (£e1; tickets are available from the kiosk in front of the East Bank launch), which leaves from in front of the Luxor Temple. The ferry runs from early morning until about midnight, but the boat leaves only when it is fully occupied. For a quicker crossing, special boats can take you across the Nile for £e5. The most hassle-free way is to rent a private taxi in town £e50 per hour or better if you haggle hard, and this will take you across the bridge, which is 12 km (7½ mi) south of Luxor to reach the West Bank.

If you take the ferry, once on the West Bank, there are a few ways to get around. The easiest, fastest, and most expensive is by private taxi, but there are fewer taxis here than in downtown on the East Bank. Service taxis (group taxis) are a very cheap way (£e1) to get to the middle of the tourist area, but they only take main roads and skirt the monuments. To get a service taxi to stop and let you out, knock on the little window in the front.

Alternatively, bicycles (rentals cost £e15) are always an option, as are donkeys. You can hire both at the West Bank docks or by the ticket offices. Cycling, or even walking, is definitely doable in winter, but either is exhausting in summer. As for the donkeys, they bring you through the local village to the sites, and they're an evocative form of transportation if time is not such a concern.

DEIR AL-MEDINA

Take the main road from the ferry landing for 4 km (2½ mi).

Between the Valleys of the Nobles and the Valley of the Queens, in its own small valley, lies Deir al-Medina, the Village of the Workmen. Artisans who inhabited the village were in charge of building and decorating the royal tombs of the Valley of the Kings between the 18th and 20th Dynasties. The site includes their houses, the tombs of many of the workmen, and a small temple dedicated to several gods. The temple was founded during the reign of Amenhotep III (18th Dynasty) and was rebuilt more than 1,100 years later during the reign of Ptolemy IV. Coptic Christians later turned the temple into a monastery.

The village is made up of houses of small dimensions, built against each other. They have similar plans, consisting of three or four rooms, some of which are decorated. Some have basements, and all, probably, had second floors, or used their roof space. Hygiene in the village is believed to have been good—there was a village doctor—and the villagers likely

How to Make a Mummy

Mummification is indelibly linked with ancient Egypt, and mummies continue to fascinate us. However, the earliest mummies were likely made by accident, when bodies were placed in the dry desert sand. These mummies were probably accidentally found by the ancient Egyptians (after being disturbed by robbers or animals) and gave birth to the idea of mummification. The ancient Egyptian word for mummy was *saah*. The present-day word is derived from the Persian/Arabic word *mum*, which means pitch or bitumen, which was thought to have been used in making mummies. It was believed that the preserved body would provide a permanent home for the soul in the afterlife. The process of mummification changed throughout Egyptian history, reaching an acme in the 21st Dynasty.

The classic method of mummification was as follows: a slit was made in the left side of the body, and the lungs, liver, stomach, and intestines were removed. The heart, believed to be necessary for rebirth, was left in place. The viscera were mummified separately, wrapped, and placed either in canopic jars or back in the body cavity prior to burial, depending on the period. Then a chisel was inserted up the nose and through the ethmoid bone. A long, slim metal instrument was then used to poke, prod, and punch the brain before it was teased out of the nostril. The brain cavity was then filled with resin to purify it.

The body was first washed with palm wine, then packed with natron (a mixture of salt and carbonate found in the Wadi Natrun, northwest of Cairo), incense, and herbs. This process was repeated a few times over the course of 40 days. Then the body cavity was emptied, packed with resinous bandages and herbs, and sewn up.

After it was clean, the body was adorned with amulets and jewelry, wrapped elaborately in bandages while being prayed over by priests, annointed with oils, and enshrouded. The wrapping and annointing took another 30 days—a total of 70 days were required to make a good-quality mummy. During certain periods of Egyptian history a mask made of cartonnage (linen, papyrus, and plaster prepared like papier-mâché) or gold (like that of Tutankhamun) was placed over the head and shoulders of the mummy.

The body package was then put into a wooden coffin, which, in turn, was placed in a sarcophagus (like a coffin, but larger and generally of stone), before being placed in the tomb. The canopic jars with the viscera were buried next to the body. Sometimes a funerary text containing spells to help the deceased in the afterlife was written on papyrus and placed within the coffin.

lived much as local people do today. Long lists of clothing items and the foods the residents ate have been found but have yet to be translated.

Although the tombs are small, they are jewel-like, with vibrant colors and beautifully detailed images—in other words, the workers applied the technical and artistic skill that they used on their employers' projects to their own as well. On the outside of many tombs stood small pyramids, where offerings were brought for the deceased. Since the artisans worked on the royal tombs, it is natural that there would be certain similarities between the decoration of the tombs of the Valley of the Kings and the decoration of their own sepulchres.

One of the most astonishing workers' tombs is that of **Senedjem** (No. 1), who was an artist during the reigns of Seti I and Ramesses II. The paintings on the walls of the burial chamber are extremely fresh looking. Notice on the opposite

> ## TOMB NUMBERING
>
> All tombs on the West Bank are numbered according to their positions in their respective valleys— the Valley of the Kings, the Valley of the Queens, and the Valleys of the Nobles—and the dates when they was discovered. The higher numbers indicate the most recent discoveries.

4

wall, left of the entrance, the god Anubis tending a mummy on a couch, surrounded with texts from the *Book of the Dead.* On the ceilings are several scenes showing the deceased kneeling in adoration before the gods. ⊠£e30 *(access to two tombs)* ☉6 AM–5 PM.

VALLEYS OF THE NOBLES

Abd al-Gurna, 4½ km (2 ¾ mi) from the ferry landing.

★ The Valleys of the Nobles are divided into several necropolises distributed over the West Bank at Luxor. More than 1,000 private tombs have been found and numbered. Most of them can be dated to the 18th through 20th Dynasties, although some were reused during the 25th and 26th Dynasties (760–525 BC).

As the name of the valley indicates, the necropolises were occupied mostly by nobles, but priests and officials were buried here as well. Funerary scenes appear in the tombs, but so do scenes of the daily life of the time; it is not unusual in these tombs to admire the joy of a banquet, discover the leisure-time activities, and analyze the professional lives of the deceased.

Sheikh Abd al-Gurna is the largest and most attractive necropolis. A present-day village was built on top of the cemetery. To protect the site, the government tried to relocate the local population to another village, made especially for them. The attempt was all in vain. The advantage of this is that you have the opportunity to get acquainted with the daily life of modern Egyptians even as you're looking back at how the ancients lived 3,500 to 2,500 years ago. ■TIP→ Local villagers offer themselves as guides to lead you to the tomb entrances. They can be very useful, but of course you'll be expected to contribute a little baksheesh (a little pocket money, something like £e5–£e10) for their efforts.

The **Tomb of Nakht** (⊠ *Tomb 52, Abd al-Gurna*), the second on the left opposite the Ramesseum, is somewhat small, and only the vestibule is decorated with vivid colors. Before the vestibule is a small display of the finds inside the tomb. Nakht was a royal scribe and astronomer of Amun (high priest) during the reign of Thutmose IV (18th Dynasty). Start with the first scene on the left of the entrance which shows the deceased with his wife, who pours ointments on the offerings—and keep moving right scene by scene. Underneath the first is a butchery scene. Then three registers represent agricultural scenes in which Nakht himself supervises. The wall to the right of the agricultural scenes has a false door. The offerings bearers kneel, two tree goddesses carry a bouquet, and other offerings bearers stand before the gifts.

The wall opposite the harvest depictions presents a famous banquet scene with dancers and musicians—look for the blind harpist. The first scene on the right of the entrance represents, once again, the deceased and his wife pouring ointments on the offerings. To the right of the banquet scene, offerings bearers present gifts to Nakht and his wife. Farther right still, the wall shows hunting and fishing scenes in the Delta with the deceased and his family.

The **Tomb of Ramose** (✉ *Tomb 55, Abd al-Gurna* 📧 *£e30*) is one of the finest tombs of Abd al-Gurna. Ramose was a vizier during the reign of Akhenaten. His tomb is unusual for having both reliefs executed within the traditional norms of ancient Egyptian art, as well as reliefs done in the elongated Amarna style that the heretical pharaoh Akhenaten adopted. The tomb was left unfinished. It has a court with a central doorway that leads into a hypostyle hall with 32 papyrus-bud columns, most of which were destroyed, though others were reconstructed in modern times (full-height columns are all reconstructions). The inner hall that follows has eight columns and a shrine.

On the left side of the entrance to the hypostyle hall is a representation of the funerary banquet. The guests are seated in couples before the deceased. Their wigs are all different, and the eyes of the figures are accentuated with black contours. On the wall opposite, in an unfinished scene, Ramose presents the Theban Triad and Ra-Harakhte to the king, Akhenaten, who is accompanied by Maat. To the right of this traditional scene, another scene bears the telltale Amarna influence: Ramose stands in front of Akhenaten and his wife, Nefertiti, adoring the sun disc Aten. From the parking area, the tomb is 100 yards ahead, on the right side. This is the only tomb that has a separate admission fee.

The **Tomb of Rekhmire** (✉ *Tomb 100, Abd al-Gurna*), governor of Thebes and vizier during the reigns of Thutmose III, Hatshepsut, and Amenhotep II (18th Dynasty), is well preserved, and the scenes are almost complete. The texts on the walls explain the installation, the duties, and the moral obligations of the vizier. The right wall of the hall to the left of the entrance shows the deceased inspecting and recording foreign tributes. Within this scene, you may recognize people of Punt bringing animals and incense trees; the Kheftiu with vases and heads of animals; the Nubians with animals; and Syrians bringing vases, a chariot, horses, a bear, an elephant, and human captives. The second scene, on the left inside the chapel, represents several stages of various crafts. The depictions of jewelry-making and sculpting here helped archaeologists to understand the techniques used during the pharaonic period. The focus of the last group of scenes in the tomb is mainly on funerary rituals, such as the Opening of the Mouth Ceremony. To get to the tomb, you must make your way from the parking area to the top of the valley. The **Tomb of Sennefer** (✉ *Tomb 96, Abd al-Gurna*) held the body of the mayor of Thebes during the reign of Amenhotep II (c. 1439–1313 BC). He was the overseer of many daily activities in the city, responsible to the vizier for the smooth running of Nile commercial ports, collecting taxes on the grain harvest, and for the day-to-day maintenance of the temples. This was a position of great trust and responsibility.

In the antechamber are scenes of Sennefer receiving offerings presented by priests and family members. He sits under a fruit-laden vine—leading this tomb to be named Tomb of the Vineyards in earlier eras. The right-hand or eastern walls depicts a funerary procession with Sennefer's possessions being carried into the tomb for his use in the afterlife. The burial chamber itself has colorful scenes of Sennefer's journey after death, the rituals he must perform during his journey and his rebirth into the afterlife, including a vivid image of Sennefer and his family making a pilgrimage to Abydos where the deceased has his heart weighed to ensure he is worthy of entrance in the afterlife.

The **Tomb of Userhat** (✉ *Tomb 56, Abd al-Gurna*) was that of a public servant during the reign of Amenhotep II. Userhat was "the scribe who counts the bread in Upper and Lower Egypt." His tomb is a fine example of an inverted T-style, with a wide antechamber leading directly to a long, slender burial chamber. Scenes in the antechamber depict Userhat's earthly responsibilities—his counting boxes of grain and overseeing the distribution of bread rations to the Egyptian army. In the main chamber there are vivid scenes of Userhat hunting and fishing. 🎫 *Ticket for two tombs £e25, Tomb of Ramose £e30* ⊙ *Daily* 6 AM–5 PM.

VALLEY OF THE KINGS

10½ km (6½ mi) from the ferry landing: take the main road 3½ km (2 mi), then turn right. After 3 km (2 mi), turn left into the limestone hills. The valley is 4 km (2½ mi) farther.

Encircled by majestic hills, the New Kingdom royal necropolis is slightly isolated from the other West Bank monuments. A mountain overlooks the valley. This was the domain of the goddess Meretseger: "She who loves the silence." Meretseger was honored mostly during the New Kingdom as one who punished criminals. Her cult began to decline after the Valley of the Kings fell out of use as a burial site.

The valley's 62 tombs can be dated between the reigns of Thutmose I (18th Dynasty) and Ramesses XI (20th Dynasty). For most of the royal tombs, the internal structure is the same: a long corridor sloping downward and leading to a burial chamber. There are exceptions, of course, such as the tomb of Tutankhamun, which is smaller because it was not designed to be a royal tomb.

The texts and decoration inside royal tombs are very different from those inside private tombs. The royal tombs contain illustrations of complex spiritual texts—the *Book of the Dead* among them—intended

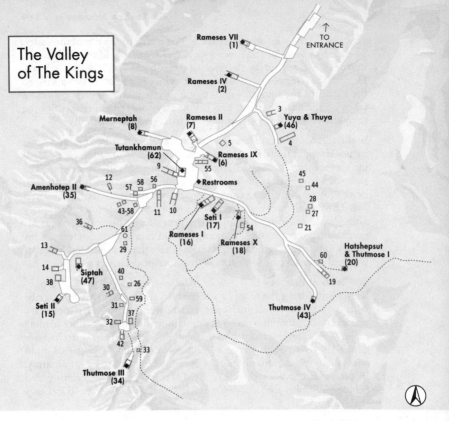

The Valley of The Kings

Rameses VII (1)

TO ENTRANCE

Rameses IV (2)

3

Yuya & Thuya (46)

4

Merneptah (8)

Rameses II (7)

5

Tutankhamun (62)

Rameses IX (6)

55

9

Restrooms

45

44

Amenhotep II (35)

12

58 56

57

28

27

43-58

11 10

Seti I (17)

54

21

36

61

29

Rameses I (16)

Rameses X (18)

60

Hatshepsut & Thutmose I (20)

13

14

Siptah (47)

40

38

30

26

19

31 59

Seti II (15)

37

Thutmose IV (43)

32

42

33

Thutmose III (34)

to accompany the deceased during the journey through the netherworld and to aid with the long-term expectation of rebirth. Private tombs, by contrast, were decorated with meaningful scenes from daily life.

Cameras can be used in the valley to take the exterior landscapes, but not in the tombs. Video cameras are not allowed past the ticket checkpoint, and you'll need to leave them in the small security office during your visit.

Valley of the Kings Welcome Centre (⊠ *Near the main entrance and ticket booth*) has a fascinating 3-D Plexiglas scale model of the tombs cut into the hillside, which shows how the tombs sit and sometimes collide with one another. Take some time to explore the model to get a feel of how immense this whole complex is. The center also has videos about the Valley of the Kings. This room is quickly bypassed by most tour groups but offers interesting background information about discoveries and archaeological techniques. The **Tomb of Ramesses IV** (⊠ *Tomb No. 2*)was built for the son and successor of Ramesses III. Ramesses IV (20th Dynasty) is considered the first of a series of weak pharaohs whose declining power brought about the end of native kingship in Egypt. Ramesses IV's tomb (the second tomb on the right, off the main path) was robbed in antiquity and must have been accessible during the Ptolemaic and Coptic periods, because graffiti from those times are found on the walls at the entrance of the tomb.

The tomb's first striking scene is the sun disk containing a scarab and Amun-Ra (represented with a ram's head). Both are adored by the divine sisters Isis and Nephthys. The first two corridors contain several parts of the *Litany of Re*—a celebration of the god Ra identified as Osiris. The third corridor is dedicated to the *Book of Caverns,* which relates the journey of the sun god Ra through the 12 hours of night before he is reborn in the morning, and which was to instruct the deceased on his own passage to rebirth. The fourth corridor includes passages from the *Book of the Dead*—a better title for which would be "Spell for Coming Forth by Day"—and parts of the *Negative Confession,* the purpose of which was to prove to the gods that the deceased was pure of heart. The walls of the sarcophagus room are decorated with passages of the *Book of the Gates,* similar to the *Book of Caverns.* The goddess Nut is represented two times on the ceiling. On the left side, she is supported by Shu: this half relates parts of the *Book of Nut.* The other half is called the *Book of the Night.* Both narrate the night-time journey of Ra through the netherworld (again, like the *Book of Caverns*). Ramesses IV's sarcophagus is still inside the tomb. The **Tomb of Ramesses IX** (⊠ *Tomb No. 6*)held the body of one of the last great pharaohs of the 20th Dynasty and the New Kingdom. As with the tomb of Ramesses IV, the outer lintel (here badly preserved) is decorated with a sun disk, inside of which is a scarab, adored by the king and surrounded by the goddesses Isis and Nephthys. The first corridor has four undecorated side rooms, but on its left wall are scenes from the *Book of the Dead*—composed of a series of spells supposed to aid the deceased in getting into the next world—and parts of the *Book of Caverns* on the right side. The same divisions apply in the second corridor. Two niches border the corridor, and inside the niches are representations of different divinities. The third corridor, on the left, contains passages of the *Am-duat* (*The Book of What Is in the Duat, duat* meaning netherworld) and images of rows of kneeling captives, some of whom are shown with their heads cut off. The third corridor is followed by three largely undecorated halls, the last of which is the burial chamber. Nut is represented on the ceiling as part of the *Book of the Night.* The tomb (on the main path, near the beginning of the court on the left side) does not contain a sarcophagus. The **Tomb of Merneptah** (⊠ *Tomb No. 8*)was built for the successor of Ramesses II and fourth king (1213–1204 BC) of the 19th Dynasty, who is called by some scholars the Pharaoh of the Exodus. His tomb (from the main path, take the first small path on the right off the central court) is composed of five corridors, three halls, and several side rooms. On the left wall, in the first corridor, are three scenes. The first shows the king before the god Ra-Harakhte. It is followed by three columns of the *Litany of Re,* and it ends with a disk surrounded by a crocodile and a serpent, adjoining the rest of the *Litany.* The wall opposite is completely devoted to the *Litany.*

On both sides of the second corridor are figures of gods with texts from the *Book of the Gates* and the *Am-duat.* The jackal god Anubis

4

is in the company of Isis on the left side, Nephthys on the right side. Most of the following chambers are decorated with passages from the *Am-duat.* The sarcophagus chamber has eight pillars. The inner lid of the sarcophagus, which is made of red granite and is decorated with scenes from the *Book of the Gates,* is still preserved. The **Tomb of Thutmose III** (⊠ *Tomb No. 34*) was built for the 18th-Dynasty successor of the pharaoh queen Hatshepsut; he was one of the great warrior kings of Egypt. During his reign, he reestablished Egypt's authority over Syria and Palestine. Before climbing the stairs leading to his tomb, ask one of the guards if it is open.

Several undecorated corridors lead to the pillared antechamber that has a sudden 90° change of axis to the left before you reach the burial chamber itself. On the walls is a list of divinities described in the *Am-duat,* scenes from which decorate the sarcophagus chamber. Note the curviness of the decorations—a remarkable feature of 18th-Dynasty royal burial chambers. The chamber is atypically shaped like a cartouche. The sarcophagus and lid, made of red sandstone, are still in the tomb. To get to the tomb, start at the central court and go straight ahead; after 50 yards, turn left at the first fork. At the second fork, after another 100 yards, take the left path; the stairs are about 150 yards ahead. Why the **Tomb of Tutankhamun** (⊠ *Tomb No. 62* ▨£e100) went undiscovered and unraided for some 3,200 years might forever remain a mystery, but there's no doubt that the treasures that Howard Carter pulled out of it in 1922—after digging in vain for six seasons—made it the most famous tomb of the valley during the 20th century. The artifacts found inside, now housed in a large section of the Egyptian Antiquities Museum (and will eventually move to the new Egyptian museum probably in 2010), are so astonishing that it is hard to imagine the luxury of the tombs of more important kings.

What is known about Tutankhamun's reign is so vague that retracing the life of this young king is almost impossible. He was enthroned at the age of eight, and died under suspicious circumstances around the age of 18. Tutankhamun was buried in a hurry, in a smaller-than-average sepulchre for a pharaoh, because his original tomb (No. 23) was not completed by the time of his death. (Tomb 23 was usurped by his successor, Ay.)

In late 2007, the mummy of Tutankhamun was removed from the marble sarcophagus where it had rested since the tomb opened to the public. The body—minus its mummy wrappings—is now on display inside an air-conditioned glass case in the main chamber of the tomb. The tomb (off the main path, on the west side of the court) has four small rooms, and only the burial chamber is decorated. One of the scenes, from the *Am-duat,* represents the god Khepri in a sacred barque, followed by three registers each with four baboons, which among other functions "scream" to announce the sunrise. Inside the burial chamber is one of the gilded coffins where the mummy of Tutankhamun originally rested.

Kent Weeks and Tomb KV5

Recent archaeological work on the West Bank has concentrated on attempts by Dr. Kent Weeks to create a comprehensive database of tombs, temples, and archaeological sites across the Theban Necropolis. This venture, called the Theban Mapping Project (⊕ *www.thebanmappingproject.com*), was begun in 1978 and continues to this day. But something that happened in 1987 has overshadowed the progress of this worthy and necessary work.

While mapping the extant tombs in the Valley of the Kings, attention was turned to a small tomb at the very bottom of the valley, a tomb used as storage for the spoils unearthed by Howard Carter when he was excavating Tutankhamun's tomb. Kent and his team cleared this space and discov-ered a whole complex of tombs, the like of which had not been seen on the West Bank before. Long corridors leading off the initial antechamber revealed at least 150 separate carved rooms—a veritable underground palace. Weeks proposed that this tomb was built by Ramesses II for his many children, and fragments of human bones found in one of the chambers proved to be those of Amun-ker-khepeshef, eldest son of Ramesses II, who died during his father's reign.

The tomb, called KV5, remains closed to the public as excavation work continues, partly because much of it lay under the old Valley of the Kings parking lot and the structure was weakened by the regular comings and goings of the tourist traffic above.

In order to avoid too much damage to the delicate paintings by the moisture from sweat and breath emitted by visitors, tombs in the Valley of the Kings are opened and closed in rotation, so there's no guarantee that you'll be able to enter a particular tomb during your visit. Tutankhamun's tomb is not currently part of this rotation system and remains open for the foreseeable future; it is the only tomb that carries a separate admission charge. ⊠ *Tomb No. 62* ▥ *£e100.* ☎ *No phone* ✆ *Ticket for three tombs £e50, Tutankhamun's Tomb £e100* ☉ *Daily 6–5.*

VALLEY OF THE QUEENS

5½ km (3½ mi) from the ferry landing: take the main road 3½ km (2 mi), then turn left and climb into the limestone hills. The valley is 2 km (1¼ mi) farther.

The Valley of the Queens was also known as *Ta Set Neferu*, the Place of the Beautiful Ones. Although some 17th- and 18th-Dynasty members of the royal family were buried here, the valley was more widely used for royal burials during the Ramesside period of the following two dynasties.

About 100 tombs were cut into the valley rock. A great number are anonymous and uninscribed; others have extremely delicate and well-preserved paintings. The tombs of Nefertari, Amun-her-Khepshef, Thyti, and Khaemwaset are at various points on the path through the

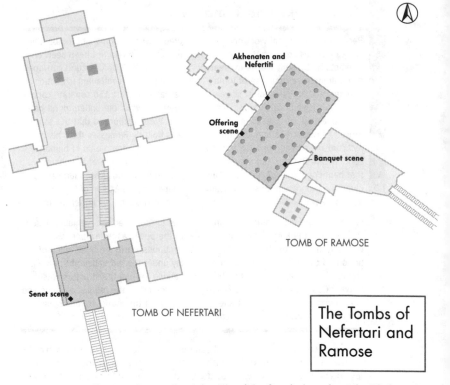

Akhenaten and
Nefertiti

Offering
scene

Banquet scene

TOMB OF RAMOSE

Senet scene

TOMB OF NEFERTARI

The Tombs of Nefertari and Ramose

valley, starting on the right side of the first fork to the right (Nefertari). That fork continues around a loop to Amun-her-Khepshef, and then to Thyti's tombs. Another path leads right before the loop returns to the first fork; at the end of that path is Khaemwaset's tomb. ■TIP→ **Carry a small flashlight with you, as the lighting in some tombs is not good.**

★ The famous **Tomb of Nefertari** (✉ *Tomb 66*), wife of Ramesses II, is generally closed to the public, which is regrettable since it has some of the most vivid surviving decorations of any tomb in the Theban Necropolis, as the postcards you will no doubt be offered will attest. Permission for a private viewing can be sought from the Egyptian Supreme Council for Antiquities for a substantial extra fee that is out of the reach of the typical traveler. Like most tombs in the Valley of the Queens, Nefertari's consists of an antechamber, a corridor, various side chambers, and a tomb chapel. The walls of the antechamber are decorated with scenes showing Nefertari adoring several deities. One remarkable scene shows the queen herself seated playing *senet,* a popular backgammon-like game. The **Tomb of Amun-her-Khepshef** (✉ *Tomb No. 55*) is that of a prince who was a son of Ramesses III (20th Dynasty). His tomb's wall paintings have very bright and lively colors and show scenes of the young prince, in the company of his father or alone, with a variety of gods. The anthropomorphic, uninscribed sarcophagus remains in the undecorated burial chamber. The tomb (it's the last one on the main road) contains an unusual item inside a glass case: the mummified remains of a fetus (not the prince himself). The cruciform **Tomb of Thyti** (✉ *Tomb No. 52*) is well preserved. Her sepulchre dates to the Ramesside period, but it is not known to whom she was married. The corridor is decorated on both sides with a kneeling, winged figure of the goddess Maat (who represented truth, justice, balance, and order) and the queen standing in front of different divinities. In the chamber on the right is a double representation of Hathor (goddess of love, music, beauty, and dancing), first depicted as a sacred cow coming out of the mountain to receive the queen, then as a woman, accepting offerings from Thyti. This tomb is on the main path, the second one on the left after the little resting place. Wall paintings in the **Tomb of Khaemwaset** (✉ *Tomb No. 44*), who was the young son of Ramesses III, are one example of the fine workmanship of the Valley of the Queens tombs. The scenes represent the prince, either with his father or alone, making offerings to the gods. Texts from the *Book of the Dead* accompany the paintings. To get to the tomb from the main path, take the left fork and continue left to the path's end. ✉ *Ticket for three tombs £e35* ☉ *Daily 6–5.*

OTHER TOMBS AND MOMUMENTS

In addition to the four major clusters of tombs, there are other mortuary temples in the Theban Necropolis. Each pharaoh worked to assure his eternal life in the netherworld, as well as in the world of the living. One way of achieving it was to introduce a royal cult among the living. Offerings and rituals guaranteed the survival of the royal *ka* (the individual life force). For this purpose, several kings, from the 18th Dynasty to the 20th Dynasty, had mortuary temples built on the West Bank at Thebes. In these temples, deceased kings were adored as gods. Most of the mortuary temples are seriously damaged or utterly lost. Those that still stand demonstrate once again the ancient Egyptian mastery of architecture.

Colossi of Memnon. Standing (sitting, actually) over 50 feet tall, these seated statues of the great Amenhotep III are the most significant vestiges of his mortuary temple. The missing pieces were taken away for use in other buildings as early as the end of the New Kingdom. Alongside the legs of the colossi are standing figures of the king's mother and his queen, Tiyi. Relief carvings on the bases of the colossi depict the uniting of Upper and Lower Egypt. Ancient graffiti also covers the ruined giants.

The poetry of these colossi is the sound that the northern statue emitted in earlier days. After an earthquake fractured the colossus in 27 BC, it was said to sing softly at dawn. That sound recalled for Greeks the myth of Memnon, who was meeting his mother Eos (Dawn) outside the walls of Troy when Achilles slew him. In the 3rd century AD, Roman Emperor Septimus Severus had the statue mended. After this the colossus was silent. There is currently active archeological work taking place around the statues, but the viewing areas are still open to the public at this writing. ✛*3 km (2 mi) west of the ferry landing, on the main road* 🖼*Free* 🕐*Dawn–dusk.*

★ **Deir al-Bahri.** The Mortuary Temple of Hatshepsut (1465–1458 BC), built by the architect Senenmut, is a sublime piece of architecture—some say the finest on the planet for its harmony with its surroundings. It consists of three double colonnades rising on terraces that melt into the foot of towering limestone cliffs.

Hatshepsut (18th Dynasty) was the most important woman ever to rule over Egypt as pharaoh. Instead of waging war to expand Egyptian territory like her predecessors, she chose to consolidate the country, build monuments, and organize expeditions to the land of Punt to bring myrrh, incense, and offerings for the gods. Prior to acting as pharaoh, she served as regent for her (then-young) successor, Thutmose III. As soon as Thutmose III came of age to rule over Egypt, he began a program of selectively eradicating her names and images from the monuments of Egypt. Curiously, he didn't erase all of her names, and in some cases the defaced and the intact cartouches are quite near each other.

The reliefs inside the first colonnade are damaged. They included a detailed scene of how the queen's granite obelisks were transported on boats from Aswan to Karnak. Take the large ramp that leads to the second court. The chapel on the left is dedicated to the goddess Hathor. The capitals of the columns are carved in the shape of the face of Hathor as a woman, with cow's ears surmounted by a sistrum. To the right of the chapel starts the second colonnade. Its first half is consecrated to the famous expeditions to Punt—modern scholars have yet to determine where Punt actually was—and shows the variety of products brought from Punt. The colonnade on the right of the second ramp is devoted to the divine birth of Hatshepsut, with Hatshepsut's mother seated with the god Amun-Ra, between the first and second columns. By showing that she was of divine origin, Hatshepsut proved she was able to rule over Egypt as pharaoh. The better preserved chapel to the right is dedicated to Anubis.

The Third—upper—terrace is reached by a ramp flanked by twin representations of Horus. The hypostyle hall on the terrace has carvings depicting two different scenes. On the north side are celebrations for the "Beautiful Feast of the Valley," which observed the connection between the living and the dead. The carvings show priests carrying barques with statues of the gods and the Pharaohs followed by musicians and dancers. On the south side scenes of royal statues carried in barques with their associated coterie—depicting the mortuary cult of ancestor worship—in this instance for Hatshepsut. Beyond the wall and cut into the rock is the sanctuary of Amun, the Holy of Holies where the barque of Amun would rest in preparation for its next day of festivities.

The temple is not open at night, but it is floodlit and makes a marvelous spectacle. The temple is not included on all guided tours, so be sure to verify its inclusion if you would like to see it. Otherwise, you can easily arrange private transportation. ✣ *From the ferry landing, take the main road; after 3½ km (2 mi), turn right; after 1½ km (1 mi), turn left; the temple lies ahead* 🖃£e30 ⊘ *Daily 6–5.*

Medinet Habu. The mortuary temple of Ramesses III (1550–332 BC) is an impressive complex that was successively enlarged from the New Kingdom down to the Ptolemaic period. Hatshepsut built the oldest chapel. Ramesses III built the temple itself, which functioned as a temple to the deceased pharaoh.

The second king of the 20th Dynasty, Ramesses III had a certain admiration for his ancestor Ramesses II, so he copied the architectural style and decorative scheme of his predecessor. Following Ramesses II's example a century before him, Ramesses III consolidated the frontiers of Egypt. He also led successful campaigns against the Libyans and their allies, and against the Sea Peoples (the Phoenicians).

Enter the complex through the Migdol (Syrian Gate). Two statues of Sekhmet (goddess of plagues, revenge, and restitution) flank the entrance. The path leads directly to the first pylon of the mortuary temple. The reliefs on this building, as well as in the first court, relate the king's military campaigns. On the back of the pylon, on the right side, a scene shows how the hands and tongues of the enemies were cut off and thrown in front of the king. At the Window of Appearances, on the south side of the first court, the living pharaoh received visitors or gave rewards to his subordinates. The second court, through the second pylon, is dedicated to religious scenes, and the colors and reliefs in the court are well preserved. The remains of the hypostyle hall and the smaller chapels that surround the second court are less complete. On the left flank of the temple, inside the enclosure, are several mud-brick palaces that have been in need of restoration. ✣ *Take the main road from the ferry landing for 4 km (2½ mi) and turn left; the temple is 500 yards ahead* 🖃£e30 ⊘ *Daily 6–5.*

The Ramesseum. The mortuary temple of Ramesses II (19th Dynasty) is one of the many monuments built by the king who so prolifically used architecture to show his greatness and to celebrate his divinity. The temple is a typical New Kingdom construction, which means that it includes two pylons, two courtyards, and a hypostyle hall, followed by the usual chapels and a sanctuary. The numerous surrounding granaries are made of mud brick. A huge quantity of potsherds, from amphorae that contained food and offerings, was found in situ. It shows that the temple had religious—as well as economic—importance.

Note the 55½-foot-tall (when it stood) broken colossus of Ramesses II, between the first and the second courts. It was brought here in one piece from quarries in Aswan. A Roman historian's flawed description of the colossus is supposed have inspired Percy Bysshe Shelley's poem "Ozymandias"—its title was the Hellenic name for Ramesses:

I met a traveller from an antique land Who said: Two vast and trunkless legs of stone Stand in the desert. Near them, on the sand, Half sunk, a shattered visage lies, whose frown, And wrinkled lip, and sneer of cold command, *Tell that its sculptor well those passions read Which yet survive, stamped on these lifeless things, The hand that mocked them, and the heart that fed. And on the pedestal these words appear: "My name is Ozymandias, king of kings; Look on my works, ye Mighty, and despair!" Nothing beside remains. Round the decay Of that colossal wreck, boundless and bare, The lone and level sands stretch far away.*

Shelley got the facial expressions (if not the sculptors' talents), the fictitious inscription, and the desert location all wrong, but the poetic evocations of ancient political might and its wreck do have their power. ✤ *From the ferry landing, take the main road; after 3½ km (2 mi), turn right, then turn right again after 700 yards* ⌂ *£e30* ⊘ *Daily 6–5.*

Temple of Seti I. Seti I's 19th-Dynasty temple is the northernmost of the New Kingdom mortuary temples. Son of Ramesses I and father of Ramesses II, Seti I was one of the great kings who guaranteed safety inside the country and repelled the attempts of enemies to upset the balance of Egyptian supremacy.

The temple, which is extremely damaged, is dedicated to Amun-Ra, Ramesses I, Seti I, and Ramesses II (who finished parts of it). Much restoration work has been accomplished, but the remains of the buildings are so poor that only lower parts of the walls were rebuilt. Nine impressive papyrus-bud columns of the peristyle hall, the hypostyle hall, and the sanctuary are the only massive parts of the temple still standing. ✤ *Take the main road from the ferry landing for 3½ km (2 mi), turn right and follow that road for 3 km (2 mi); turn left; the temple is 400 yards ahead* ⌂ *£e30* ⊘ *Daily 6–5.*

THE UPPER NILE VALLEY: SOUTH OF LUXOR

There are three noteworthy stops south of Luxor: Esna, where two locks in the Nile require the cruise ships to line up and navigate their way; al-Kab, which has a little-visited temple; and Edfu, where the Temple of Horus is the most impressive and intact temple on the shores of the Nile. Esna and al-Kab are normally bypassed by the Nile cruisers (and even by the tourist convoys plying the land route between Luxor and Aswan), though it's possible to book private tours from Luxor. Edfu is included on all Nile cruise itineraries, but the temple can also be seen on overland day trips from Luxor.

ESNA

54 km (33 mi) south of Luxor.

The town of Esna enjoyed some notoriety in the 19th century, when quite a number of singers, dancers, prostitutes, and other similar folk were exiled from Cairo and resettled here. French novelist Gustave Flaubert visited Esna expressly to see the performances of the artists and professionals. He wound up becoming somewhat obsessed with a prostitute–dancer, and he spent a good deal of time describing her (and his opium-induced visions) in letters to his long-suffering wife.

The **Temple of Khnum,** which is one of the most truncated and least attractively sited Egyptian temples that you are likely to see, was constructed between the 2nd century BC and the 2nd century AD. It sits in a 30-foot-deep pit in the middle of Esna, and to get to it, you have to run the gauntlet down a short street from the river that's lined with souvenir sellers anxious to peddle their wares. Resist all temptation to go into a shop here, because salespeople are known to be unpleasantly aggressive. The temple is in a pit because the level of the town has risen over time, sinking the partly excavated temple below the level of the modern houses. There is some fine stratigraphy, made visible from the excavations, in the soil behind the temple. The ticket booth is at the iron entrance gate that leads to a staircase descending into the pit.

Composed of 24 columns, only the hypostyle hall of this Ptolemaic/Roman temple dedicated to Khnum (the god associated with creating people) is visible. There is a question as to what happened to the rest of it—was it never built, or was it robbed for its stone in antiquity? The portion of the temple that remains is completely decorated and has some very unusual cryptographic inscriptions that are hymns to Khnum. One is written almost entirely with hieroglyphs of crocodiles, another with rams. The columns are also inscribed with significant texts that provide an outline of different festivals held at the temple throughout the year. The ceiling is decorated with zodiacal motifs, and fragments of paint are still visible. In the forecourt and around the temple lie picturesquely scattered fragments primarily of Roman and Coptic date, including a particularly charming lion-faced basin. At this writing, Esna is not a stop on the cruise-ship schedules (the ships usually just clear the locks and sail on into Luxor), and the convoy system also bypasses the town. If you want to visit the site, you'll need a security escort. Book a private taxi or inquire with a tour operator such as Thomas Cook in Luxor about current arrangements when you are there. ⊠ *Mabed Esna* 🖼 *£e20* ⊗ *Oct.–May, daily 7–5; June–Sept., daily 7–6.*

AL-KAB

32 km (20 mi) south of Esna.

Al-Kab, on the East Bank of the Nile, is the site of an impressive though imperfectly preserved town, temple area, and tombs. The site was first inhabited around 6,000 BC and occupied thereafter. It was sacred to the vulture goddess of Upper Egypt, Nekhbet—the ancient name of al-Kab is Nekheb. Nekheb was allied with the town of Nekhen on the West Bank of the Nile (modern Kom al-Ahmar).

The only way to get to the ancient site is by private taxi. You may need police permission and should visit the tourist office in Luxor before making the trip to find out what you need to do. Tour operators may also offer the trip, though it isn't a standard program. Service taxis go to the village but not to the antiquities, and they may be reluctant to carry tourists because this might mean them being caught up in the convoy system.

Egyptian Hieroglyphics

Egyptian writing, known popularly as hieroglyphs, was first developed in about 3,000 BC; the symbolic form of discourse consists of a series of signs derived from nature and common utensils. Hieroglyphics are read left to right, right to left, or top to bottom: You read into the beaks of the birds or into the faces of the animals.

There are two main types of signs: phonograms, which signify sounds, and determinatives, which signify what type of word it is. Phonograms have different sounds attached to them: single-letter sounds, biliteral, and triliteral sounds. Thus, a hoe has the sound *mr*, and depending on its determinative can mean "hoe" or "love," or be part of another word. Determinatives come at the end of words and help define what the word is or means. For example, a pair of legs at the end of a word indicates that it is a motion word meaning (depending on the spelling of the word itself) walk, move forward, or run.

Egyptian grammar and vocabulary changed throughout ancient history, with Middle Kingdom Egyptian being the most classic and widely used. Hieroglyphs (sacred images) were generally used only for important inscriptions on monuments or on papyri. Everyday accounts, letters, and even many religious texts were written in hieratic, a cursive form of hieroglyphs.

Jean-François Champollion deciphered ancient hierogylphics in 1822. Other scholars had come close to accomplishing this, but Champollion was the first one to publish his results. He managed to do this by using the Rosetta Stone, a large granite stone carved with hieroglyphs, demotic (everyday script of the Late and Greco-Roman periods), and Greek, that is now housed in the British Museum. The stone was discovered in the port city of Rosetta on Egypt's Mediterranean coast. The ancient Greek, still a known, if not spoken, language, provided Champollion with a clue as to how to break the code. When he broke it, Egyptology became a literate discipline.

The town of Nekheb is enclosed by a massive mud-brick wall and includes houses, the principal **Temple of Nekhbet,** smaller temples, a **sacred lake,** and some early cemeteries, which are rather difficult to make out. About 400 yards north of the town are several **rock-cut tombs** that date primarily from the New Kingdom, although there are some earlier tombs as well. The most famous are those of **Ahmose Pennekhbet, Ahmose son of Ibana,** and **Paheri.** The first two are noted for their historical texts, which discuss the capture of the Hyksos capital Avaris and various military campaigns of the pharaohs of the early New Kingdom. The tomb of Paheri is noted for its scenes, especially the small scene of a herd of pigs. Some distance into the wadis are the rock-cut **Sanctuary of Shesmetet,** a chapel, and a small **Temple of Hathor and Nekhbet** (these are not always open). ⊠ *Athar al-Kab* ☎ *No phone* 🎫 *£e30* ⊙ *Oct.–May, daily 6–5; June–Sept., daily 6–6.*

EDFU

115 km (71 mi) south of Luxor; 105 km (665 mi) north of Aswan.

Although the town itself is somewhat dull, Edfu's temple, dedicated to Horus, would make even Cecil B. De Mille gasp. It is the most intact of Egyptian temples you are likely to see, and it is a most unexpected and breathtaking sight. Visiting Edfu's temple, set at the edge of the modern town of Edfu—portions of which peer over the temple enclosure wall—is the closest you can get to being an ancient Egyptian going on a pilgrimage. To get the full effect of this marvel, buy your tickets and walk along the exterior of the temple, around the pylon, to the end of the courtyard toward the birth house, without turning around. At the end of the courtyard, turn suddenly to face the great Temple of Horus at Edfu.

4

Visit Edfu either on a Nile cruise (all cruises include tours to this temple), or by hiring a private taxi in Luxor or Aswan for a set price. The taxi driver will know what time you'll need to be ready at the convoy departure point. If you are coming from Aswan, you will probably also want to stop at Kom Ombo (➪ *North of Aswan: Kom Ombo and Draw Camel Market, Chapter 5*). Regular buses and service taxis also run from Luxor and Aswan, but they may be reluctatant to carry tourists because they may get caught up in the convoy system (thus ruining their schedules). If you can get a service taxi, be prepared to hire another taxi to get from the bus or service taxi stop to the temple.

★ The **Temple of Horus** is mainly from the Ptolemaic period. The temple does, however, rest on earlier foundations, which may date from the Old Kingdom (2625–2130 BC). The exterior walls are covered with texts that give details of the temple's construction. It was started in 237 BC by Ptolemy III, and the entire building was completely finished and decorated in 57 BC. Access to the temple originally would have been from the south, but because of the growth of the town, it is now entered from the north.

The enormous **pylon,** fronted by a pair of statues of Horus as a falcon, leads into a columned courtyard at the end of which stands another, better-preserved statue of Horus as a falcon. The doorway behind this leads to the **Hypostyle Hall.** The columns in this temple are typical of the Ptolemaic period, which means that they have varied capitals: palm-leaf capitals, lotus capitals, papyrus capitals, and a large variety of elaborate composite capitals. The bottoms of the column shafts, above the bases, are carved to show the leaves found at the bases of various plants.

Following the central axis, the Hypostyle Hall is succeeded by a series of rooms. The last in the series is the temple's sanctuary, which contains a finely polished monolithic *naos,* or shrine, of syenite (an igneous rock) that would have housed the statue of the god set in another smaller shrine made of gilded wood. An altar stands before the naos; originally the naos would have been fronted by gilded wooden doors, the sockets for which are visible in the jamb area.

Rooms off of the central axis are thought to have been storerooms for various ceremonial items, such as perfume, wine, incense, gold, and vessels made of precious metals. A series of rooms in the rear of the sanctuary contains access, now blocked for the most part, to crypts made to store the most precious of the temple's possessions. The central room at the back includes a model barque (a modern reproduction) that is very probably identical to the one used in antiquity to transport the golden statue of the god in religious processions around town and on boats north to Dendera.

The inner rooms of the temple are dark, lit by shafts of light entering from narrow slits at ceiling level. Originally the temple would have been lit thus, with additional light coming from flickering torches. The richly colored walls would have shone and glimmered like jewels in the half-light; it is easy to imagine priestly processions passing through the temple on sandaled feet, chanting and praying amid clouds of incense.

The interior of the temple is decorated with scenes of divinities and pharaohs making offerings to one another, as well as some scenes of the founding of the temple. Elements of a celestial ceiling are visible in the hypostyle hall. A **side chapel** to the east with its own tiny courtyard contains a beautiful ceiling showing the course of the sun as it is swallowed by the sky goddess, Nut, and then born from her the following morning.

The inside of the temple's stone enclosure wall shows scenes of Horus fighting with and defeating his enemy, the god Seth. This is one of the few places where an illustrated version of the Horus and Seth myth is visible. There are several variations on the tale in which Seth killed his brother Osiris and set himself up as ruler in his stead. Isis, Osiris's wife, used her magic to bring Osiris back to life and to become pregnant. The result was Horus, who sought to avenge his father's murder and to rule, as was his right. He and Seth engaged in a series of battles using both strength and magic. Ultimately Horus was the victor, and he was rewarded with rule over Egypt—hence the living pharaoh's identification with Horus—and Osiris ruled over the afterworld. Seth became god of deserts and distant lands.

The reliefs show Horus defeating Seth in his different guises (hippos, crocodiles, and so forth) and are quite entertaining. It is believed that a mystery play illustrating this struggle took place at a Horus–Seth festival at Edfu. Another amusing fact to note about this temple (and other Ptolemaic temples) is that many of the cartouches are left empty. This is because the Ptolemies overthrew one another so frequently and so speedily that the architects, contractors, and priests decided to leave blank cartouches that could be painted in with the ruling Ptolemy's name whenever the appropriate time arose.

On one side of the temple, between the outer and inner stone walls, is a Nilometer, a gauge used to measure the height of the Nile—and to calculate taxes. The expectation was that the higher the river, the better the harvest was going to be and, therefore, the higher the taxes.

✉ *Mabed Edfu* ☎ *No phone* ✉ *£e50; additional £e30 if you bring a camera with a tripod* ☉ *Daily 7* AM–9 PM.

NILE VALLEY & LUXOR ESSENTIALS

TRANSPORTATION

BY AIR

EgyptAir flies daily to Luxor from Cairo, Alexandria, Aswan, and Sharm El-Sheikh, offering the only domestic air service. There are usually at least two 1-hour flights daily from Cairo; reconfirming tickets (in person or through your hotel) two days in advance is an absolute must. The Luxor office is open daily 8–8. EgyptAir also has scheduled international flights direct to Luxor from London, Brussels, Paris, and Rome. Many European discount carriers—including Transavia (from Paris and Amsterdam), Air Berlin (destinations in Germany and Austria), FlyThomasCook (from several cities in the UK), and Condor (from several cities in Germany)—have nonstop flights to Luxor; however, they don't support offices in town. *For contact information on European airlines, see By Air under Transportation in Egypt Essentials.*

Contacts EgyptAir (✉ *Corniche al-Nil, Luxor* ☎ *095/238–0580 up to 83* ⊕ *www.egyptair.com*).

AIRPORTS Luxor Airport is approximately 7 mi (11 km) northeast of town; travel time from central Luxor is about 15 to 20 minutes.

Contacts Luxor Airport (☎ *095/237–4655* ⊕ *www.luxor-airport.com*).

BY BOAT

You can still take the public pedestrian ferry in front of the Luxor Temple for £e1. It plies back and forth every 15 minutes or so from early morning until about midnight. Powerboats take you across the river a bit faster, for about £e5. They leave from in front of the Winter Palace and at the car-ferry landing near the Novotel.

Feluccas have fixed rates that tend to be highly negotiable and start at around £e50 an hour. You can find out these rates at the Tourist Information Office, hotels, and Thomas Cook and American Express offices.

BY BUS

Twelve-seater minibuses run services around town, and locals pay around £e1 to £e3 per trip. However, drivers don't always stop for visitors and will try to charge more if they do stop. Know the fares (ask at the tourist office) and refuse to be intimidated into paying more.

Government buses to Upper Egypt can be a very rough ride, because of the condition of the seats, the sporadic functioning of the air-conditioning, and the blaring of the onboard videos. However, they are by far the cheapest way to go—about £e90 one-way to Luxor. At this writing, the authorities discourage foreign visitors from traveling down the Nile Valley by bus because public transport does not fall under the jurisdiction of the convoy system—you may be dissuaded from buying a ticket. If you insist on traveling by bus, purchase tickets from the Targoman Station in central Cairo.

Contacts **Targoman Bus Station** (✉ *Gala' St., Downtown, Cairo* ☎ *02/2431–6723*).

BY CAR

A rental car would free up your time when visiting the monuments of the West Bank. It would allow you to spend as much time as you need at the Valley of the Kings, Valley of the Queens, and Tombs of the Nobles. But having said that, you could haggle a good hourly rate with a taxi driver and not have to deal with hassle of organizing the car rental or having the responsibility of navigating the West Bank monuments. Furthermore, there's no other advantage in renting and self-driving because you won't be free to explore the Nile Valley on your own schedule—you'll be locked into the timetable of the convoy system if you travel north or south of the town.

BY CARRAIGE

In Luxor, support the local calèche drivers (and their horses) and take a Nile-side ramble in a horse-drawn carriage. The entire 45-minute Corniche promenade sets you back around £e30.

BY TAXI

Luxor is rife with taxis, usually six-seater Peugeot station wagons, but prices are the highest in Egypt. You can travel the length of the Corniche for about £e20; shorter trips cost £e10. In practice, prices can fluctuate from driver to driver, but check with the tourist office or at your hotel to find out what the theoretically fixed rates are to all destinations. Everyone knows the rates, especially the taxi drivers, but it's a good idea to agree to a price before you set out. Tipping just a couple of extra pounds depending on the length of the journey is customary.

If you decide to take a taxi to the West Bank, the ride plus up to four hours of touring and waiting time on the West Bank costs about £e40 per hour.

BY TRAIN

Train travel in Egypt is inexpensive. The lights are always on and the air-conditioning functions sporadically, but the trains otherwise are comfortable enough. From Cairo to Luxor, a one-way ticket is £e90 in first class and £e46 in second class. First class offers you more space, and you have a choice of traveling during the day or at night. You can also take the train from Luxor to Aswan; fares are £e41 first class, £e25 second class.

Comfortable sleeper cars run by private company Abela make the daily trip to Luxor from the cavernous Ramses Station in central Cairo. Buy tickets at least 10 days in advance at the Abela office in the station. At this writing, there are four trains daily, two heading south and two heading north. Train 84 leaves Cairo at 8 PM, reaching Luxor at 5:05 AM; Train 86 departs Cairo at 9:10 PM, arriving in Luxor at 6:10 AM. For the return trip, Train 85 departs Luxor at 9:40 PM, reaching Cairo

CLOSE UP

The Convoy System

Since the late 1990s, all tourist traffic along the Nile Valley has been controlled by the police. This means that tourists (whether in tour buses, taxis, or private cars) must all travel together in a convoy with an armed escort. These convoys depart at the same time each day and they must stay within the scheduled timetables, and they have put an end to real independent exploration.

For destinations such as al-Kab—where tour groups do not regularly visit—you must have police permission to travel and you may be allocated an armed vehicle or an armed officer in the vehicle for your trip. It will usually be granted, but you should make these arrangements at least 24 hours before your departure.

If you book a trip to these destinations with a tour company, it is this company's responsibility to inform the security authorities about the trip. The tour company may ask for your passport, but it will be returned to you when the formalities have been completed. All this may sound quite disconcerting and even frightening, but in reality it is just the way things are done in Egypt at the moment and shouldn't be taken as an indication that you will encounter danger on your travels.

Of course, the regimentation of vehicular travel in this area negates one of the prime advantages of travel by private car, which is to organize your own timetable—and to spend as much or little time at any particular site, according to your own interests. Given this circumstance, the next-best scenario would be to book a guide and transport for your party to offer you a personal service so you can make the best of your short time at the sites rather than booking a trip with a large group.

There are no set convoy timetables for the region around **al-Minya** because there are far fewer tourists in this region. If there are enough vehicles carrying tourists, then one will be organized and you'll be told of the time and place to meet. When there's only one vehicle, security procedures are more bespoke, with an armed officer or armed truck being assigned to each traveling party or group. This security officer will act as your escort during your sightseeing trip.

From Luxor, convoys north to **Dendera** and **Abydos** and east to **Hurghada** on the Red Sea Coast depart from outside the Catholic Cathedral at 8 AM, with stops at the temples, and 2 PM and 5 PM direct to Hurghada. Convoys south to **Aswan** depart from outside the Catholic Cathedral at 7 AM, with stops at Edfu and Kom Ombo, and 11 AM and 3 PM direct to Aswan.

4

at 6:45 AM; Train 87 leaves Luxor at 12:40 AM and arrives in Cairo at 9:30 AM. The cost (per journey) of a single couchette with dinner and breakfast is $80 per person; a double with dinner and breakfast costs $60 per person. These fares must be paid in a foreign currency, not Egyptian pounds.

Contacts Abela (⊠ *Ramses Train Station* ☎ *02/2574-9474* ⊕ *www.sleeping trains.com*).

CONTACTS & RESOURCES

BANKS & EXCHANGE SERVICES

Luxor has a good supply of banks, exchange offices, and ATMs. Exchange offices tend to be open long hours, usually daily and until 10 PM or 11 PM. Banks open shorter hours and may not be open on weekends. American Express and Thomas Cook also change money. Most hotels have cashier desks to change money. Exchange offices generally offer better rates than either banks or hotel desks. Don't rely solely on ATMs as these may not be replenished regularly. Have a range of options including foreign currency and travelers checks in addition to credit cards and cash withdrawal cards. Banks are usually closed on Friday and Saturday but are open on Sunday.

Information **Bank of Alexandria** (⊠ *Corniche al-Nil, near the Hotel Etap Mercure, Luxor* ☎ *095/238-0282)*. **Egyptian Exchange** (⊠ *86 Shar'a Maabad El Karnak, Luxor* ☎ *095/238-8258)*.

EMERGENCIES

All major hotels will have an emergency doctor and dentist on call at all times, so if you fall ill or suffer an accident in your room call the front desk for help. All senior medical staff will speak English, so you will be able to explain your symptoms or your concerns. Pharmacies are plentiful and easy to find, though 24-hour pharmacies are less common. Hospitals are generally clean and well kept; however, medical facilities are not comprehensive.

Emergency Services **Ambulance** (☎ *123)*. **Fire** (☎ *180)*. **Police** (☎ *122)*. **Tourist Police** (☎ *095/237-6620 in Luxor)*.

Dentists **Dr. Nehad Harby** (⊠ *In front of El Qurna Hospital, Luxor* ☎ *095/238-5044 or 010/513-1283)*.

Doctors **Dr. Magis Abd El Azis Magid** (⊠ *Near the central hospital, El Qurna, Luxor* ☎ *010/560-2207)*.

Hospitals **New International Hospital** (⊠ *Shar'a Moustafa, end of Television St., Luxor* ☎ *095/238-7192)*.

24-hour Pharmacies **Dr. Amier Marriee** (⊠ *Next door to the Philippe Hotel, Luxor* ☎ *095/238-3432)*.

INTERNET, MAIL & SHIPPING

Most major hotels offer some form of Internet connection, though not all have connectivity in the rooms. Internet cafés are numerous but open and close with great regularity. Access is cheap (around £e10 per hour), but connections are not always fast. There are an increasing number of Wi-Fi hot-spots for travelers with their own laptops.

The mail service in Egypt is slow and unreliable. If you need to make sure that any letter or package gets to its destination it's advisable to use a courier service, which is very expensive.

Internet Cafés **GBC Internet Café** (⊠ *Corniche al-Nil (on the waterfront walkway close to the Tourist Office), Luxor* ☎ *011/229-9677)*.

Wi-Fi Hotspots Snack Time (✉ *Shar'a Luxor Temple, Luxor* ☎ *095/237-5407*).

Post Offices Main Post Office (✉ *Shar'a Saad Zaghloul (at the western entrance to the souk), Luxor* ☎ *095/237-3158*).

Shipping Companies DHL (✉ *Corniche al-Nil, Luxor* ☎ *02/302-9810 (Cairo but active nationwide)*). **FedEx** (✉ *Corniche al-Nil, Luxor* ☎ *095/236-1752*).

TOUR OPTIONS

If you are not taking a cruise, you can arrange land-based tours to visit the sights along the Nile between Luxor and Aswan, the most important of which are Edfu and Kom Ombo (*for information on Kom Ombo, see South of Aswan: Kom Ombo and Daraw in Chapter 5, "Aswan & Lake Nasser"*). You can also easily travel to the less-visited sights of Abydos and Dendera, both north of Luxor, on a daylong guided tour. Since the development of the convoy system, independent travel has been made extremely difficult, and booking a tour is an easy, stress-free way of getting to the sites. Since most companies have to travel to the ancient sites at the same time, look for tour companies offering services for small groups to allow you to get the best out of the visit.

If you haven't prearranged tours, your best options for guided tours in Luxor are Thomas Cook and American Express. The first two are particularly flexible in arranging tours to suit a variety of desires and budgets, even arranging last-minute Nile cruises, but any of the offices can arrange day trips. Most of the tour companies have conveniently located offices at the shopping center attached to the Winter Palace Hotel.

Tour Companies Thomas Cook (✉ *Winter Palace Hotel Mall, Corniche al-Nil, Luxor* ☎ *095/237-2402* ⊕ *www.thomascook.com.eg*). **American Express** (✉ *Winter Palace Hotel Mall, Corniche al-Nil, Luxor* ☎ *095/237-8333*). **Noble Tours** (✉ *Corniche al-Nil, at the far southern end, Luxor* ☎ *095/237-3155*). **Karnak Tours** (✉ *Winter Palace Hotel Mall, Corniche al-Nil, Luxor* ☎ *095/237-2360* ⊕ *www.karnak-egypt.com*).

HOT-AIR BALLOON RIDES Balloon flights make for a very serene and peaceful way of viewing the Valley of the Kings and are a favorite activity among tourists. The balloons take off from the West Bank just after dawn and spend an hour or so gliding over the temples and tombs (exact route depends on the prevailing breezes). If you don't want to take to the air in a balloon, you can take off from the river in a seven-seater seaplane and take in the vistas of the east and West Bank of Luxor under powered flight.

Contacts Sindbad Balloons (✉ *37 Shar'a Adb El Hamid El Omda, Luxor* ☎ *095/227-2960* ⊕ *www.sindbadballoons.com*). **Viking Air** (✉ *3 Shar'a Ahmed Orubi, Luxor* ☎ *095/227-7212* ⊕ *www.vikingairegypt.com*). **Magic Horizons** (✉ *Shar'a Ohed, off Television Street Luxor* ☎ *095/236-5060* ⊕ *www.magic-horizon.com*).

VISITOR INFORMATION

Open daily 8 AM to 8 PM, the tourist office in Luxor has a good range of information about opening times, taxi and felucca fares, and train timetables.

Contacts Luxor Tourist Information Center (✉ *Corniche al-Nil, in front of Luxor Museum* ☎ *095/372-215*).

Aswan & Lake Nasser

Temple of Nefertari at Abu Simbel

WORD OF MOUTH

"We were told to use one of the guides at entrance to [Abu Simbel], which we and a few other English speakers did (we were a group of about 8). [Our g]uide was very good, [with an] excellent command of English, thorough, [and] willing to answer questions. After touring the two temples and inside of the mountain on which the temple is built, we had time to wander about and take photos.

—Sandi

WELCOME TO ASWAN & LAKE NASSER

Souk in Aswan

TOP REASONS TO GO

★ **Abu Simbel:** Study the powerful yet serene face of the pharaoh on the monumental statuary on the facade of the Temple of Ramesses II.

★ **Philae:** Soak in the atmosphere at the island-bound temple dedicated to the goddess Isis, which was still welcoming worshippers in the 5th century AD.

★ **A Felucca Sail:** Take to the Nile on a traditional sail around the Cataracts—the colossal mounds of granite that are scattered across the path of the river.

★ **A Nile Cruise:** Immerse yourself in Agatha Christie's novel *Death on the Nile* while relaxing on the upper deck of a luxury cruise boat.

★ **Nubian Culture:** Turn amateur anthropologist as you explore the long history and rich culture of the Nubian people at the Nubia Museum.

1 North of Aswan: Kom Ombo & Daraw. Kom Ombo is a popular archaeological site that is on all Nile cruise itineraries and reachable overland from Aswan. Daraw's camel market is less visited and less tourist-oriented.

2 Aswan. A jumping-off point for Egypt's south, Aswan is a much more laid-back destination than either Luxor or Cairo. The center for felucca sails on the Nile and cruises on Lake Nasser; it's also a focus for exploration of Egyptian Nubian culture.

Tea time on deck

3 South of Aswan: Philae and the Aswan Dams. The Temple of Isis at Philae and the Old and High Aswan dams are popular destinations within a few minutes of Aswan.

4 Lake Nasser. While New Kalabsha is reachable on a day trip from Aswan, other sights require either a flight (Abu Simbel) or a cruise (all other sights along the lake).

Qasr Ibrim ◆

◆ Abu Simbel

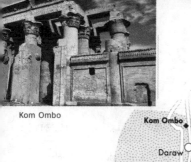

Kom Ombo

Kom Ombo

Daraw

Aswan

Philae

New Kalabsha

Beit al-Wali

Gerf Hussein

Lake Nasser

WESTERN DESERT

Wadi al-Sebua

al-Derr

al-Dakka

Amada

```
0          25 miles
0          25 km
```

GETTING ORIENTED

For sights near Aswan, private taxis are by far the easiest way to get around. You can take a prebooked day trip to Kom Ombo and the camel market. The Aswan High Dam and the point of departure for Lake Nasser cruises is a short distance from town, as are the docks for boats going to the island temples of Philae and Kalabsha. Abu Simbel, south of Aswan on Lake Nasser, is a 30-minute flight from Aswan or a three-hour road trip.

Temple of Philae, Aswan

5

ASWAN & LAKE NASSER PLANNER

Transportation

By Air: Aswan is linked to Cairo by several EgyptAir flights a day, as well as to Alexandria, Luxor, Abu Simbel, and Hurghada. There are no nonstop international flights that go directly to Aswan.

By Boat: Nile cruises depart from Aswan to Luxor or Lake Nasser. Aswan is also the main center where you can arrange a felucca sail up or down the Nile, though few feluccas will take you as far as Luxor.

By Bus: It's difficult for foreigners to travel by bus in Upper Egypt (authorities strongly discourage it). If you can get a ticket, it's definitely the cheapest way to move around, though not terribly comfortable.

By Car: The convoy system makes private car-rental less than ideal in Upper Egypt. It's easier and usually not much more expensive to hire a taxi.

By Train One easy way to get to Aswan from Cairo is on overnight trains operated by Abela. Sleeping compartments are fairly reasonably priced; overnight trains arrive in Aswan early the next morning. Regular seats are cheaper, and a more inexpensive way still is the first-class section of a regular train.

What's Great in Aswan & Lake Nasser

Temples: Kalabsha is known for its vivid color, Abu Simbel for its monumental statues of Ramesses II, and Philae for its Roman influences. Most of the Nubian temples are rarely visited, since they are visible only on a Lake Nasser cruise.

Tombs: Although much less visited than those in the Theban Necropolis, the tombs of the nobles on Aswan's west bank can be visited on an easy day trip across the river and combined with St. Simeon's Monastery and a short camel trek.

Nubian Culture: During ancient times, Egypt's southern neighbor, Nubia, was sometimes friend, sometimes foe. In modern times, the Nubian people who lived along the Nile valley south of Aswan developed a culture independent of Arab Egypt, and it lives on in the households of 50,000 Nubians in and around Aswan. This culture is best celebrated at the Nubia Museum.

River Trips: Popular Nile cruises begin and end in Aswan. For shorter trips in Aswan, the monumental rose-red granite boulders of the cataracts and their associated river islands make for wonderful late-afternoon felucca rides. Aswan is also the jumping-off point for the relaxing trip down Lake Nasser to Abu Simbel.

Birding: The Nile valley offers a wealth of opportunities for bird-watching. Cattle egrets follow the farmers and herds, but they roost in the riverside trees at night. Heron species are abundant. Pied kingfishers and moorhens make a living on the water; various species of hirundines (swallows and martins) swoop for insects just above the surface, and black kites and ospreys—common raptors—circle the skies above. Along with endemic species, the Nile acts as a major pit stop during the spring and fall journeys of millions of migratory birds.

Relaxation: The pace in Aswan is simply slower than in the rest of the country, and the atmosphere less pushy. Part of Aswan's strong appeal is the chance to simply relax and explore at a less breakneck pace. The smart traveler uses his or her time in Aswan to enjoy the sunset with a drink or have a relaxing sail on a Nile felucca or a camel trip along the western bank.

About the Restaurants

The variable city tax on restaurants, combined with service charges, can total as much as 26%. Check menus to verify how each restaurant operates. Unless you are in a major hotel, consider tipping even if a service charge is included in the bill: waiters are not well paid, and the courtesy will be appreciated. If service is not charged, 10%–15% is a reasonable tip. As a rule, most hotel restaurants are open to the general public. Reservations are recommended at all hotel restaurants.

About the Hotels

In Aswan, rates are less expensive in summer—late April to the end of September—sometimes dramatically so, and many hotels will offer discounted rates in times of low occupancy regardless of the season. Aswan in particular has a lot of large groups that stay for only one or two nights to see Philae and the local sights and then move on. Several Aswan hotels are on islands with regular ferry services to the town.

WHAT IT COSTS IN EGYPTIAN POUNDS, U.S. DOLLARS, AND EUROS

$$$$	$$$	$$	$
Restaurants			
over £e150	£e100–150	£e50–£100	under £e50
Hotels in dollars			
over $200	$130–$200	$70–$130	under $70
Hotels in Euros			
Over €130	€80–€130	€45–€80	Under €45

Restaurant prices are per person for a main course at dinner. Hotel prices are for a double room in high season, excluding 10% tax and service charges (usually 10%).

Planning Your Time

Most travelers spend only one night in Aswan to see the temple at Philae and the Nubia Museum, and perhaps take a short felucca sailing trip around the cataracts. Add another day if you want to do the trip to Abu Simbel by air before joining a Nile cruise, which will take three or four nights. If you have more time, see St. Simeon's monastery and the tombs of the nobles on Aswan's west bank, and definitely reserve a day to see Kom Ombo if you are not taking a Nile cruise. You can also see the temples on New Kalabsha as a day excursion from Aswan.

When to Go

Traditionally, high season begins at the end of September, peaks around Christmas, and lasts until April. To avoid crowds, stay away at these times. The heat kicks in as early as March in Upper Egypt—a dry, pollution-free heat that you can get used to. Evenings are always cooler in the desert. However, life slows down even more in Aswan in summer, when it is noticeably hotter here than in Luxor. Ramadan is much quieter still, especially in Upper Egypt.

5

Updated by
Lindsay and
Pete Bennett

CAIRENES TAKE FOR GRANTED MODERN control of the Nile: they open their faucets complacently, even if they don't always obtain the desired results. But in antiquity the river and its capricious annual floods were endowed with divinity and honored with all the force of the empire. The floodwaters acted as god and teacher, as the ancients learned the movements of the stars and devised calendars in order to predict the arrival of the inundation.

The Nile was the pharaohs' vehicle for empire building. It was the carriage road for troops, trade, and the massive granite blocks quarried in Aswan—the temples that line its banks from al-Minya to Abu Simbel glorify both the ancient gods and the Egyptians' ingenuity in putting the river's power and wealth to work. The river also made agriculture and the feeding of the population—the workforce—so easy: Herodotus noted in 460 BC that the Egyptians "gather in the fruits of the earth with less labor than any other people." Having mastered several straightforward irrigation techniques still in use today, farmers sowed their seeds and harvested two annual crops from the rich silt that the floods left behind.

No other river and no other ancient civilization have so fired the imagination of the modern West. But, aside from the works of ancient Greek, Roman, and Arab historians, and an antagonistic contact during the Crusades, the West remained essentially ignorant of Islamic culture and the marvels of the pharaohs until the late 1700s. And the people of the Upper Nile lived in relative isolation, working the land as they had for millennia.

In 1902 the British built the first Aswan dam to conserve late-summer floodwaters for the low-water season and increase agricultural output. As the population grew, these reserves became insufficient. The building of the Aswan High Dam in the 1960s altered the river's character dramatically, putting an end to the seemingly eternal and sometimes devastating annual floods. But the dams are just technological updates on what men have been doing for ages: tapping the river's power.

Today, the river remains the lifeblood of the country, but for most visitors it is first and foremost a leisure facility, the now benign waters allowing easy access to Egypt's most magnificent ancient monuments.

NORTH OF ASWAN: KOM OMBO AND DARAW CAMEL MARKET

The temple of Sobek at Kom Ombo is the first stop on many Nile cruise itineraries; it's a widely visited and popular temple. For those not on Nile cruises, it's also possible to see it on a day trip from Aswan, or as a stopover on the way from Luxor to Aswan on the overland route. Lesser known is the camel market at Daraw, which remains a more local institution, having not turned into merely a tourist destination.

KOM OMBO

65 km (40 mi) south of Edfu; 40 km (25 mi) north of Aswan.

Kom Ombo, a fertile area, is interesting because it supports not only its original Egyptian inhabitants, but also a large Nubian community that was resettled here after the construction of the Aswan High Dam and the flooding of Lower Nubia. As a result, the town has grown considerably in the past 25 years. Kom Ombo was an important town strategically, because it was one of the places where the trade routes to the Nile Valley, the Red Sea, and Nubia converged. It is also the site of a very unusual double temple dedicated to the gods Sobek, depicted as a crocodile or a crocodile-headed man, and Haroeris, a manifestation of Horus represented as a falcon or a falcon-headed man.

You can visit Kom Ombo either as part of a Nile cruise, an organized tour, or by private taxi hired in Aswan for a set price, which can include a stop in Edfu. Buses, minibuses, and service taxis also run from Aswan, but they may be reluctant to take independent travelers because this may mean they (and the rest of their passengers) must travel in the tourist convoy system. *(For further information, see The Nile Valley & Luxor Essentials in Chapter 4.)*

★ The **Temple of Haroeris and Sobek** (built between the 2nd century BC and 1st century AD) stands on a bend in the Nile. It is especially romantic to approach the temple in the moonlight, if you arrive on a cruise at the right time of the month. Virtually all the remains of the temple date to the Ptolemaic period and later, although evidence of earlier structures has been found, most notably an 18th-Dynasty gateway.

The temple is remarkable for its duality: it has two of almost everything, enabling its priests to conduct equal services for two deities simultaneously. The southern part of the temple, on the right when you face the entrance, is dedicated to Sobek, the northern part to Haroeris.

Immediately across the courtyard to the right after you enter the compound is a small shrine, dedicated to Hathor, which now houses some mummified crocodiles. Crocodiles, sacred to Sobek, were worshiped at Kom Ombo. The crocodiles were regarded as semidivine, and they were fed the finest foods, provided with golden earrings, and given elaborate manicures, which involved gilding their nails. Areas in the northwestern parts of the enclosure are thought to have been the place where the sacred crocodiles were kept when alive.

The double entrance to the temple proper is from the southwest, leading into a large courtyard—the structure was oriented with its entrance to the river, rather than having a true east–west axis. This courtyard is the only shared space in the temple proper; from here, the building is divided in two. There are two doorways that lead to **outer hypostyle halls, inner hypostyle halls,** a series of **offering halls,** and twin **sanctuaries.** The sanctuaries contain a set of crypts from which priests provided oracular advice and the respective god "spoke" whenever necessary. Behind the sanctuaries is a series of storerooms now inhabited by bats.

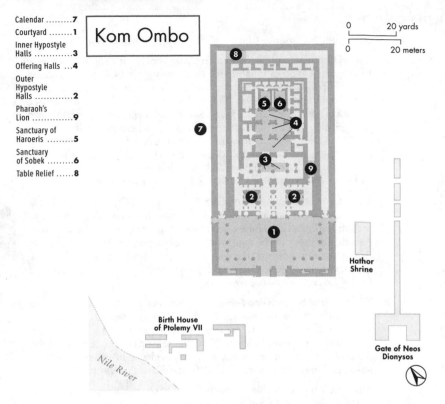

Kom Ombo

The decoration of the walls is the usual type found in temples: pharaohs making offerings to divinities and divinities blessing pharaohs. The different gods being honored show to whom the temple is dedicated. Look for a calendar on the southwest wall of the offering hall, and a table laden with surgical implements on the back (northeast) wall of the outer stone enclosure. Surgical implements found at archaeological sites (and used worldwide until quite recently) can clearly be identified on the table as a clear reference to the fact that the temple was a center of healing for many centuries during pharaonic times. A rather charming relief of a pharaoh's pet lion nibbling on the unwillingly proffered hands of the king's enemies is carved on the exterior of the southeastern wall.

A large, deep well and a Nilometer are within the mud-brick enclosure west of the main building. This is also the area where the sacred crocodiles were supposed to have been kept. Fragmentary remains of a birth house stand at the temple's western corner (in front). Behind the temple is a yet-to-be-excavated area that was probably the site of priestly houses and a very modest town, built of mud bricks. ☏No phone ✉£e30 ☉Daily 7 AM–9 PM.

DARAW CAMEL MARKET

5 km (3 mi) south of Kom Ombo; 35 km (22 mi) north of Aswan.

Known for its Tuesday camel market—the largest camel market in the Middle East—Daraw is otherwise a hot, dusty, and flyblown place. The camels come up from Sudan along the 40 Days Road. Traditionally, they made the trek on foot, but now more and more of them arrive in the backs of Toyota pickup trucks, which the camel drivers rent at Abu Simbel for the final leg of their trip. Merchants from Cairo, mostly, make their way to Daraw to take the camels back to Cairo. The camels are sold to farmers or for slaughter—sadly not for the more romantic options of riding or racing.

The Daraw market sells, in addition to camels, livestock: sheep, goats, cows, bulls, and poultry. Full of dust, tumult, and herders with whips, market days are nothing if not colorful and crowded with people and animals. However, while it's an exciting experience to push your way through the crowds, if you have a soft spot for four-legged creatures, you should brace yourself for the occasional upsetting sight. After you inspect the varieties of livestock and exchange views with Sudanese, Egyptians, and Beshari tribesmen about the animals, saunter over to the produce section before moving on to inspect the different sticks, staves, fly swatters, whips, and harness bits on sale here. Trading usually ends by noon. In summer, the market is very hot and very odorous.

The round-trip from Aswan by private taxi costs about £e50 per hour riding in a standard Peugeot cab. Make sure to tell the driver that you expect him to wait a couple of hours while you take in the sights. You'll need to travel north with the morning convoy. Some tour operators in Aswan have the market on their itineraries.

ASWAN

880 km (546 mi) south of Cairo; 210 km (130 mi) south of Luxor.

For thousands of years Aswan was the "Southern Gate," the last outpost of the Egyptian empire. Its name comes from the ancient Egyptian *swenet* ("making business"), and its reputation as a frontier emporium dates from the colonial era of the ivory trade and commerce in ebony, gold, slaves, spices, gum arabic, ostrich feathers, and, at least until 1929, panther skins. In today's souk, various hoofed animals mingle freely with Sudanese in high white turbans, Bedouin camel traders, and black-clad women balancing impossible packages on their heads. The sound of singing and the beating of drums reminds you that this is a gateway to Africa, and that the Tropic of Cancer lies just a few miles to the south.

As seen in the climate-adapted architecture and gaily painted houses of the Nubian areas, Aswan town and its gracious inhabitants have an aesthetic sense rarely found in modern Egypt. This is a desert city, austerely clean, full of trees and gardens, the scents of baking sand and the Nile, oleander and frangipani.

CLOSE UP

Gamel Abdel Nasser

Lake Nasser is named after Egypt's most important modern-day politician, Gamel Abdel Nasser (Gamal 'Abd al-Nasir). Nasser broke the ties of colonialism and rocked the European powers during the 1950s, leading Egypt after independence and becoming a leading light in the pan-Arab movement.

Born in Alexandria in 1918, he graduated from the Military Academy in 1938 but had a deep desire for Egyptian autonomy and founded a group called the Free Officer's Movement. In 1952 the movement staged a military coup, ousting the Egyptian royal family. Nasser left the military and became Prime Minister in 1954.

The 1950s saw the rise in tensions between the Communist bloc and the West. Nasser tried to tread a middle path, joining the nonaligned movement in 1955. But Egypt couldn't avoid making choices between the capitalists and the Soviets. The United States pulled out of a deal to fund the Aswan High Dam in 1956, so Nasser nationalized the Suez Canal to pay for the project, prompting military action by the Israelis, the British, and the French, which petered out after pressure from the U.S. The Arab world saw this as a victory for Nasser, and he became a regional hero.

In 1956, Egypt officially became a socialist state. There was nationalization of key industries and land reform, but it never reached the amount of state control that it needed to truly live up to the title. But Nasser also announced Russian funding for the Aswan High Dam, and this further alienated the West. Pan-Arab relations took a step forward in 1958, when Egypt entered a political union with Syria under the banner Arab United Republic, but this wasn't a success and only lasted until 1961.

Throughout the 1960s, pressure in the region was building, and Nasser used his rhetoric against Israel in an attempt to drum up help from other Arab nations to crush the Jewish state. But the Israelis didn't wait and launched a pre-emptive action in 1967 that became known as the Six Day War. It brought a massive defeat for Egypt and a personal loss of face for its president. Nasser offered his resignation, but in a massive show of popular support his people took to the streets to call on him to reconsider. Although he remained president, the defeat had dampened his spirits. His health suffered, and he died of a heart attack in 1970 at the age of 52.

Nasser was not universally popular at home. After an assassination attempt in 1954, he clamped down on all domestic opposition, putting his main rival, Mohammed Naguib, under house arrest and replacing a judiciary that suggested rule of law ought to prevail. However, he is still viewed as a hero by many.

It wasn't quite so shady when French troops arrived in 1799 on Napoléon's orders to capture or kill Mamluk leader Mourad Bey. By the time the exhausted regiment reached Aswan, the nimbler Mamluk cavalry had disappeared into the Nubian Desert. That gave the French time to take stock of the pharaonic and Greco-Roman monuments that even now seem strangely remote.

Although Aswan was a winter resort popular with Greeks, Romans, and Egyptians in antiquity, Europeans didn't come until Thomas Cook sent down his luxuriously outfitted and provisioned *dahabiyyas* (large feluccas) in 1869. Credited by some as having created the travel industry in Egypt, Cook provided the means for wealthy Victorians to comfortably explore one of the outreaches of their realm while enjoying Aswan's excellent, dry climate.

> **WORD OF MOUTH**
>
> "We really liked Aswan. It's a manageable size, it's prosperous, and there is plenty to do."
>
> —AZEBS

Rich in granite, this area was quarried by Egyptians and Romans, the evidence of which stands in monuments up and down the Nile Valley. It continues to yield mineral wealth to this day—in addition to the distinctive pink-and-black-flecked Aswan granite, there are iron foundries, aluminum mines, and important talc deposits that help fuel Egypt's development. South of Aswan, the High Dam testifies to Egypt's modern determination and its unparalleled ability to renew itself, even to the extent that Egypt no longer ends at Aswan. The use of Lake Nasser for tourism—and its open-air museum of salvaged monuments—extends the grand tour well into what is appropriately, and poignantly, called the New Nubia.

Aswan, like Luxor, is laid out along the Nile Corniche, but the West Bank here is undeveloped desert, accessible only by water. This means that you must make short river crossings by felucca—which are wonderful preludes to visiting Elephantine Island and Kitchener's Island, and the Tombs of the Nobles and St. Simeon's Monastery on the West Bank.

THE EAST BANK

Aswan Souk. You won't find fresh elephant tusks here these days, as in the past, but this is still a lively, colorful marketplace filled with Nubian music.

Enter the souk beside the Benzion department store, or start from the train station. Walking along the wide, traffic-free thoroughfare, you can find better cotton fabrics here than in Cairo—either plain white or printed with African or pharaonic designs (about £e11 per meter, which is a bit longer than a yard). Ready-made buys include galabeyyas (£e70), tablecloths (£e100), and simple, fine white cotton scarves that come in handy in the heat of the day (£e25–£e40). Antiquarians should be on the lookout for antique tribal items, such as daggers, jewelry, and household items. Carpets are also a good option, as many Bedouin and Nubian handmade carpets find their way to Aswan. Unfortunately, most vendors have their most kitsch patterns at the front of house (decorated with camels or village scenes), and you need to ask for the genuine article—giving away one of your bargaining chips by declaring an interest. Stop in a café for tea and watch the traffic flow. ✉ *Souk St. (parallel to the Corniche)* ⊙ *Daily 8 AM–midnight.*

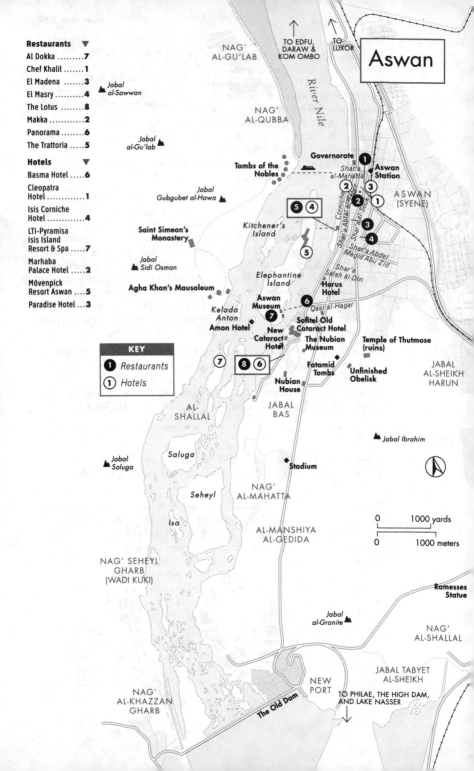

Nubia Museum. The Nubia Museum is the triumphant capstone of the effort to preserve Nubian culture and folk heritage in the wake of the building of the Aswan High Dam. It was financed by the Egyptian government with technical assistance from UNESCO. Arranged chronologically, it takes you through Nubia's prehistory; the pharaonic dynasties, including the Kingdom of Kush, when Nubian kings ruled Egypt; and onward through its Christian and Islamic periods. The selection of statuary is extraordinary for its range and eclecticism. There is also a diorama with scenes of Nubian village life. There is a lot to take in—allow about two hours for the well-curated displays.

The museum's harmonious architecture incorporates a Fatamid tomb. It comes from a group of poorly preserved monuments believed to date from the 8th to 12th centuries AD, located in the adjacent Fatamid Cemetery. The museum is a five-minute walk south of the Old Cataract Hotel. ⊠ *Shar'a Abtal al-Tahrir* ☎ *097/231-9111* ⊠ *£e50; additional £e100 to use a video camera* ⊙ *Oct.–May, daily 9–1 and 5–9; June–Sept., daily 10–1 and 6–10.*

Unfinished Obelisk. This site is an abandoned workshop, in which balls of greenish dolorite are still lying about. Dolorite is an extremely hard stone that was attached to rammers and used to pound and dress the surfaces of the quarried granite. Note the rows of slots where wooden wedges were driven in, then soaked in water to expand and split the rock. The ancient techniques were so precise that once a stone was hewn, it needed only finishing touches to ready it for its place in a temple wall.

In this case, a flaw was discovered in the massive obelisk-to-be, and it was left imprisoned in the bedrock. Had it been raised, it would have stood 137 feet tall—taller than any other obelisk—and weighed 1,162 tons. But the stone's supine potential makes it no less impressive and takes little away from the scale of the ambition of the builders of old. Note that the site is a 20-minute walk from the Nubia Museum. ⊠ *East of the Fatamid Cemetery* ⊠ *£e30* ⊙ *Daily 7–5.*

THE ISLANDS IN THE NILE

Unlike the stretch of the Nile that passes through Luxor, this section has several islands as it approaches the cataracts. Many of these are worth exploring.

ELEPHANTINE ISLAND

Sources attribute the name Elephantine to three possibilities: the elephant cult symbol of a predynastic Egyptian tribe; the ancient Greek name Abu (Elephant Land); and, more prosaically, to the presence of gargantuan granite boulders that resemble the animals' rumps. The island was the site of a sanctuary to the gods of the flood and the home of noblemen whose tombs lie farther north on the West Bank. These days Elephantine is, in large part, an open-air museum, brilliantly excavated and restored by German and Swiss archaeological institutes; the island also is home to a few Nubian villages.

Start with the **Aswan Museum**, built in 1912 to house the British engineer of the first dam. It is small and rather dingy, but you can pay your respects to the mummy of "the bearded man," whose horny toes peek out of the linen binding. A more modern **Museum Annex** is even smaller, but it is a revelation. Maps inside show the areas you are visiting as they appeared from 3000 bc to AD 300, along with some unusual finds, such as a papyrus marriage contract—accompanied by its translation—and a hefty hoard of Ptolemaic coins.

The archaeological area is so jam-packed with debris of the island's ancient town that every time you move, you crunch pottery shards beneath your feet. Highlights include the **Temple of Satis** (the goddess who "let fly the current with the force of an arrow"), a fine example of modern restoration techniques. The **Temple of Khnum** (a ram-headed god of the flood and the whole locality) was the center of the ancient town and was recently cleared of rubble in the 1990s. On the southern tip of the island is a small Ptolemaic shrine dedicated to the Nubian god Mandolis. Beside it is a statue of an elephant. Back near the dock is the **Nilometer,** built by the Romans on the site of an older one and reused again in the 19th century to gauge the annual floods. Close by are a flight of metal stairs and a platform erected by the German archaeological team, from which you can take in a panoramic view of the island and its neighbors.

North of the archaeological area is a Nubian village, where you can go for a stroll and imbibe in the traditional rhythms of village life. Children are likely to approach you, and you might receive an invitation for a cup of tea. ✛ *To get to the island, take a felucca from anywhere in Aswan, or the public ferry from the south end of the Corniche (£e1)* ▣ *£e30* ☉ *Oct.–May, daily 8:30–6; June–Sept., daily 8–5.*

KITCHENER'S ISLAND
Also known as the Island of Plants, Kitchener's Island is named after Lord Horatio Kitchener, famed for his campaigns in the Sudan at the start of the 20th century, his role as Consul General in Egypt, and his love of exotic trees and plants. The island's enchanting **botanical garden,** which he endowed, is proof of the latter, and the birds just love it. A public ferry will take you here for 50 piastras, but you should also be able to hire a felucca for about £e10—just be sure to negotiate a price in advance and make sure the felucca captain knows to come back and pick you up at an agreed-upon time. ✛ *West of Elephantine Island, 15 min by felucca* ▣ *£e25* ☉ *Daily 8 AM–dusk.*

SEHEYL ISLAND
Seheyl Island is one of many islets (some of which are game preserves) in the cataract, or rapids, where the Nile narrows in the midst of dramatic outcroppings of pink-and-black granite—the trip here by felucca (£e60) through the cataract is half the reason to come. Seheyl was sacred to the goddess Anukis, who was entrusted with channeling the floodwaters upriver. A mountain of crumbling rock on Seheyl's southeast corner is covered with 250 inscriptions, the graffiti of several thousand years' worth of travelers. The **archaeological area** is gated, but

the ticket kiosk is seldom manned. If the guardian isn't in, go to one of the nearby houses and someone will serve you tea (offer baksheesh in return for the courtesy) while you wait for him to return. ✛40 min. south of Aswan by felucca. By taxi, it's 15 minutes south and over the Old Dam to Gharb Seheyl, where you can catch a public rowboat–ferry to the island ▨£e25.

TAKE YOUR CAMERA

If you don't want to take a felucca ride, you'll find the best views of the Nile cataracts are from the landscaped waterside Fryal Gardens at the southern end of the Corniche. The entry fee is £e5, and you can sit and enjoy the vistas for hours.

THE WEST BANK

You can take in the West Bank sights in a half-day trip. Just sail to the West Bank dock for nearby Gubgubet al-Hawa, and tell your felucca captain to pick you up at the Mausoleum of the Aga Khan (to the south) about four hours later. After visiting the Tombs of the Nobles, you can ride a camel through the desert (£e35 is the going rate) to the Monastery of St. Simeon and onward, past the Aga Khan Mausoleum to the felucca landing at its feet. Bring a bottle of water with you (one per person) at all times of the year.

Mausoleum of the Aga Khan. The Fatimid-style tomb of Sultan Muhammed Aga Khan III (d. 1957), leader of the Shi'a Isma'ili (Shi'ite) sect, stands sentry over Aswan on a cliff of the West Bank. The tomb is closed to the public, but you can pass the outer walls on your way to or from St. Simeon's Monastery.

St. Simeon's Monastery. This brooding mass dates from approximately the 7th century AD, and it is one of the largest and best-preserved Coptic monasteries in Egypt. Little is known of its origins, and although St. Simeon is said to have lived here in the 5th century, findings suggest that the monastery may have been originally dedicated to someone else. The place feels like an abandoned town, full of vaulted passages and crumbling arches. Some poorly preserved frescoes remain in the basilica on the lower level. A stroll through this austere and mysterious romantic ruin, with its awesome desert vistas, is memorable.

The monastery is 4 km (2½ mi) through the desert from the Tombs of the Nobles; by camel the trip takes 40 minutes and costs £e35. From the Aga Khan Mausoleum, you can hike uphill to a footpath that leads from behind the mausoleum to the monastery, about a 30-minute walk. This is a strenuous and hot walk even in winter, so take plenty of water and wear sturdy shoes. ▨£e25 ☉Daily 7–5.

Tombs of the Nobles and Gubgubet al-Hawa (Tomb of the Wind). The West Bank is the final resting place of the Keepers of the Southern Gate, the adventuresome ancient Egyptian noblemen of Elephantine who were entrusted with securing caravan routes, monitoring the granite quarries, and supervising trade shipments to the capital of Memphis. Take a camel or walk up the slope to the necropolis and enjoy a sense of discovery that you rarely achieve when perusing Egyptian antiquities. Many tombs are closed or undergoing excavation, but there is a great deal to see nevertheless. The view as you make your way south along the cliff is stunning.

Start with the north-end **Tomb of Serenput I** (No. 36, 12th Dynasty, 1938–1759 BC), which is noted for its lovely forecourt, with six columns inscribed with male figures, and its 28-yard-long inner passageway, forged through bedrock. (Ask the people at the kiosk if this tomb is open; if not, they can send someone who has a key with you). Move on to the **Tomb of Khounes** (No. 34, 6th Dynasty, 2323–2150 BC), located beneath the ruins of a Roman wall; traces remain of its conversion into a Coptic monastery. Look for the graffiti left by French soldiers in 1799. Continue south along the cliff to one of the best-preserved tombs of this era, that of **Serenput II** (No. 31, Middle Kingdom, 1980–1630 BC), grandson of Serenput I. Allow your eyes to adjust to the dim interior and watch the brilliantly colored reliefs (showing the deceased and his family) at the end of the 32-yard passage come to life. The last tombs are those of **Mekhu** and **Sabni** (No. 25 and No. 26, 6th Dynasty, 2350–2170 BC). These impressive rock-pillared chambers contain some frescoes—and the occasional bat. Mekhu died in equatorial Africa on an expedition. His son Sabni went to punish the tribe who killed him and to carry his father's body back home. Pharaoh Pepi II sent along mummification paraphernalia as a sign of appreciation for these exploits.

On your way back from the Tombs of the Nobles take a short hike up to the domed **Gubgubet al-Hawa,** the tomb of a sheikh, for the best view in Aswan and a cooling breeze year-round. ▢£e30; additional £e30 if you bring a camera with a tripod ☉Daily 7–5.

WHERE TO EAT

Upper Egypt may not be an epicurean paradise, and Aswan is a much smaller town than Luxor, but the standard fare of soups, salads, *mezze* (hot and cold appetizers), grilled meats, and *tagines* (earthenware-baked vegetables, meat, or chicken in a tomato-based sauce, variously spiced) is available in a variety of local restaurants and can be perfectly satisfying when well prepared.

Alcohol is not served everywhere; for drinks, look primarily to the large hotels along the Corniche and on the islands in the Nile. Upscale restaurants are not as prevalent in Aswan, nor is the variety found in Luxor and Cairo.

$$
MIDDLE
EASTERN

✕**Al-Dokka.** This Nubian-style restaurant sits on one of the several small islands around the cataracts of the Nile. It is surrounded by the river and the gargantuan boulders of the adjacent Elephantine Island, and has a view of the desert beyond. Try the tandoori chicken, which is uncharacteristically tumeric-yellow but wonderfully spiced, marinated in yogurt, and baked to a crisp. A selection of Western and Middle Eastern items is also available. Live Nubian music adds extra spice to your dinner, but if you prefer silence, you can dine on the outdoor patio. Call to have the restaurant's boat pick you up. ⊠ *On small island directly in front of the Sofitel Old Cataract Hotel* 🕾 *097/231–8293* 🖃 *AE, MC, V.*

$ **✕ Chef Khalil.** Ask any local which is the best fish restaurant in town,
SEAFOOD and they'll point you to Chef Khalil, which has a small, marble-covered dining room. The fish sits in small cases under ice, so choose what you want, and they'll tell you the price. You can also get a delicious paella-style dish with rice and mixed seafood. There's a small outer terrace for al fresco dining. ⊠ *Shar'a Saad Zahgloul, next door to the Paradise Hotel* 🕾 *097/231–0142* 🖃 *No credit cards.*

$ **✕ El Madena.** In the heart of the souk, you can dine out on the small
MIDDLE terrace and watch the world go by as you eat. There's nothing surpris-
EASTERN ing on the menu, but large portions of grilled meats, chicken, or stews served with rice and the trimmings are all delicious and fresh. The small interior dining room looks rather like a careworn diner. ⊠ *Shar'a Saad Zahgloul* 🕾 *097/230–5696* 🖃 *No credit cards.*

$ **✕ El Masry.** Frequented by Egyptians and foreigners, the well-known
MIDDLE Masry is a cool refuge from the rigors of the souk. The restaurant's
EASTERN been running since 1958 and has an American-diner-meets-French-café appeal. Charcoal-grilled meats are preceded by a broth of lamb and beef, a plate of rice, a dish of veggies, and a basket of whole-wheat flatbread. Service is quick. No alcohol is served. ⊠ *Shar'a Matar, just off Shar'a al-Souk* 🕾 *097/230–2576* 🖃 *No credit cards.*

$$–$$$ **✕ The Lotus.** Whether you choose the apricot-color dining room, the
CONTINENTAL outdoor terrace with its nighttime view of the lights of Aswan, or a table by the attractively lighted pool, the Lotus is nothing if not atmospheric. A pan-European menu includes a creamy veal Zurich, served with Swiss-style hash browns; an *escalope cordon bleu*, stuffed with cheese and beef-ham (the local alternative to taboo pork); and a Hungarian goulash full of fresh mushrooms, with homemade noodles on the side. Breakfast, lunch, and dinner buffets are also served. ⊠ *Basma Hotel, Shar'a Abtal al-Tahrir (road running parallel to and between the Corniche al-Nil and the souk)* 🕾 *097/231–0191* 🖃 *AE, MC, V. .*

$ **✕ Makka.** If you want to try Egyptian street food in a more upmarket
MIDDLE setting, then Makka is ideal. A small eatery bathed in red and green
EASTERN marble and complete with welcoming air-conditioning, the restaurant serves staples like grilled meats and stuffed pigeon complete with rice, salads, and bread. There's no outdoor seating area, however. ⊠ *Shar'a Abtal al-Tahrir* 🕾 *010/287–6754* 🖃 *No credit cards.*

$ **✕ Panorama.** Sit outside or in at this sparkling-clean Nile-side restau-
MIDDLE rant, which has a shady terrace and a plant-filled and Nubian-deco-
EASTERN rated dining room. The walls are filled with beaded amulets, brass
★ fetishes, basketry, and camel saddlebags. The simple menu proposes Egyptian tagines and charcoal-grilled *kofta* (ground-beef meatballs), kebabs, pigeon, and chicken. There is no alcohol, so instead try one of the herbal teas, fresh fruit juice, or one of Aswan's unusual ice-cold libations: *karkadey* (hibiscus tea), tamarind, carob, or *dom* (a drink made from the fruit of Sudanese palms). After the meal, don't miss the

CLOSE UP

The Old Cataract Hotel

The Old Cataract, which opened in 1900, is a living monument to the age of imperialism. Rising out of a granite bluff overlooking the temples of Elephantine Island and the stark mountains of the West Bank, it belongs to the Nile. The orderly sprawl of the brick Victorian facade is dotted with wooden balconies and terraces where one could imagine Agatha Christie enjoy a gin and tonic while watching the sunset. This was the preferred winter resort of the blue bloods of the early 20th century. Howard Carter stayed here after his discovery of

Tutankhamun's tomb downriver. Later, Winston Churchill passed through, and the late French president Mitterand was a frequent guest. The hotel's fame was revived in 1978 with the filming of Agatha Christie's *Death on the Nile*, starring Peter Ustinov, and modern visitors flocked to stay in this little piece of history. In 2008, Sofitel closed the Old Cataract Hotel in order to undertake a comprehensive renovation of the Grand Dame. At this writing, it's not due to open its doors again until late 2010.

Bedouin coffee. ⊠ *Corniche al-Nil (just south of the EgyptAir office)* ☎ *097/230–6169* ▭ *No credit cards.*

$–$$
ITALIAN

✕ **The Trattoria.** The pasta and main dishes on the basic Italian menu are appetizing alternatives to Aswan's ubiquitous kebabs and tagines. Tagliatelle served with a fresh tomato sauce and a remote relative of Parmesan cheese is fresh and surprisingly light. Although it's home-made, the lasagna is not always spinach-based, as advertised; this Upper Egyptian version is a hot, hearty tagine of spiced ground meat, pasta, and cheese topped with béchamel sauce. Breaded veal cutlets served in tomato sauce and cheese are tasty and substantial. ⊠ *Isis Corniche Hotel, Corniche al-Nil* ☎ *097/231–5100* ▭ *AE, MC, V.*

WHERE TO STAY

While Aswan's grand dame, the Old Cataract Hotel, is closed for a massive renovation until 2010, there are still several five-star properties that cater to upscale tourists, the best of which is probably the Mövenpick on Elphantine Island. Like Luxor, Aswan has relatively few good mid-range hotels.

If you choose to stay at a place that doesn't have a pool, be aware that many hotels open their pools to nonguests for a small fee (around £e50). In Aswan, the Basma Hotel and the Isis have good pools.

You can consult hotel staff on taxi and felucca rates, which are fixed either by the hour or the length of your trip. Most hotels can also arrange sightseeing excursions.

$$$
🏨 **Basma Hotel.** Occupying the highest point in Aswan, the Basma is an example of something seldom seen in Egypt: tasteful contemporary architecture. Several local artists helped to decorate it, and throughout the grounds and the interior are sculptures, murals, fountains, and mosaics. The large swimming pool has ample deck space. Standard

rooms are quiet, relatively spacious, and unpretentiously decorated. All have semi-enclosed balconies, some of which overlook the pool and gardens and offer a glimpse of the Nile. Others have a great view of the Nubia Museum, the Fatamid Cemetery, and the city. The staff is friendly and helpful. **Pros:** Large pool (heated in winter) and deck; there are no main thoroughfares passing close to the hotel, so it's relatively quiet. **Cons:** The small hill you need to climb to reach the entrance is really tiring in the heat, so it's best take a taxi from central Aswan (or the hourly hotel shuttle) if you're not in shape; a small number of rooms on the lower floors sit next to the driveway and therefore, can be noisy and smelly from the fumes of arriving tour buses. ⊠ *Shar'a Abtal al-Tahrir* ☎ *097/231–0901* ⇱ *188 rooms, 21 suites* ⚒ *In-room: safe, refrigerator. In hotel: 3 restaurants, room service, bars, pool, laundry facilities, Internet terminal, no-smoking rooms* ☱ *AE, MC, V* ⦿ *BP.*

$ ⛶ **Cleopatra Hotel.** The big plus at this pleasant, modern, low-rise hotel is the rooftop swimming pool with beautiful panoramic views. Otherwise, the Cleopatra doesn't offer Nile views from any of its rooms, but it does allow you to experience the rhythms of Aswan from the heart of the souk. The lobby is decorated with low arches and small domes, and it houses a 24-hour restaurant. The rooms are disappointing and need to be updated, but they are clean. Some rooms are housed in an adjacent building. **Pros:** Probably the best budget hotel with a pool in Aswan. **Cons:** rooms are careworn (though clean). ⊠ *Shar'a Saad Zaghloul (near the train station and souk)* ☎ *097/231–4001 (all others have 7-digit phone numbers)* ⇱ *100 rooms, 25 suites* ⚒ *In-room: no a/c (some), refrigerator. In-hotel: restaurant, room service, bar, pool, laundry service* ☱ *AE, V* ⦿ *BP.*

$$ ⛶ **Isis Corniche Hotel.** This well-located bungalow-style hotel on the river resembles a cruise ship—its terraced areas are connected by staircases, and the Nile-side rooms have water-level views. Rooms are small, but the decor is bright and modern and the bathrooms quite comfortable; each room has a terrace. The bungalows are interspersed with gardens, and multicolor flowering trees surround the large pool area. **Pros:** Full renovation in 2008 means rooms are fresh; pool is open 24 hours, affording the possibility of a late-night dip. **Cons:** Nile-view bungalows can have views obscured by cruise vessels; rooms are small for the price. ⊠ *Corniche al-Nil* ☎ *097/231–5100 or 097/231–0200* ⇱ *100 rooms, 2 suites* ⚒ *In-room: refrigerator. In-hotel: 2 restaurants, room service, bar, pool, laundry service* ☱ *MC, V* ⦿ *EP.* .

$$$ $$$$ ⛶ **LTI Pyramisa Isis Island Resort & Spa.** This sprawling, low-rise concrete structure occupies what used to be a nature preserve. Except for the hotel, the island is still deserted, and the greenery and gardens surrounding it are undoubtedly the hotel's most attractive feature. The decor throughout is indistinctive and contemporary. Rooms are quiet and have semi-enclosed balconies with Nile views. Separate chalets, some with their own pools, are available for families or larger parties. A boat is available around the clock to ferry guests to the East Bank or other islands. **Pros:** Verdant surroundings with plenty of birdlife; the boat transfer to town takes you through the most beautiful part of the cataracts. **Cons:** Rooms are now in need of some renovation; guests are

often large groups staying only one or two nights, so the lobby has the atmosphere of a an airport check-in area. ✉ *Isis Island* ☎ *097/231–7400* ⊕ *www.pyramisaegypt.com* ⤴ *457 rooms and 2 chalets* ⚬ *In-room: safe, refrigerator. In-hotel: 3 restaurants, room service, bars, tennis courts, pools, gym, spa, laundry service, Internet terminal* ▭ *AE, MC, V* ⦿ *EP, BP, MAP.*

$$ ⊞ **Marhaba Palace Hotel.** Separated from the Nile and the Corniche by a small green space called Al Salaam Gardens, this hotel does have Nile views from a few of its room—mainly the front-facing rooms on the upper floors. The lobby makes a grand statement with a lot of marble, but rooms are more sober—spacious, light, and reasonably furnished, with tile floors. The hotel has a nicely kept roof garden and terrace with excellent panoramic views. The pool on the first floor is modern and well maintained. **Pros:** Well positioned for visits to the Corniche and souk; prices are quite reasonable given the facilities. **Cons:** There's an 80% price premium for Nile views, which is too much; the pool loses sunlight in the afternoon, making it cool in winter. ✉ *Corniche al-Nil* ☎ *097/233–0102* ⊕ *www.marhaba-aswan.com* ⤴ *78 rooms* ⚬ *In-room: refrigerator, Internet. In-hotel: restaurant, room service, bar, pool, gym, spa, laundry service, Internet terminal* ▭ *MC, V* ⦿ *BP.*

$$$–$$$$ ⊞ **Mövenpick Resort Aswan.** A free 24-hour boat shuttle whisks you from the Aswan Corniche in two or three minutes across the Nile to this modern concrete low-rise hotel. The property is in many ways an architectural eyesore with its 10-story tower—at odds with the Nubian villages on its boundary—but it's currently Aswan's most luxurious option. The interiors feature vast open spaces furnished with Scandinavian-style low-level furniture (imagine scenes from the original *Thomas Crown Affair*). Rooms are bright and well furnished, and most have good Nile views. **Pros:** The pool is the nicest in Aswan, having been totally redone in 2005; the hotel is a retreat from the town, yet it's only a couple of minutes across the water. **Cons:** Noisy Nubian wedding celebrations in the adjoining village start at midnight and end at sunrise, and these can disrupt sleep in the villas and south-facing rooms; attracts some large tour groups. ✉ *Elephantine Island* ☎ *097/230–3455* ⊕ *www. moevenpick-aswan.com* ⤴ *196 rooms, 38 suites, 8 villas* ⚬ *In-room: safe, Internet (some). In-hotel: 3 restaurants, room service, bars, pool, laundry service, no-smoking rooms* ▭ *AE, DC, MC, V* ⦿ *BP. .*

$ ⊞ **Paradise Hotel.** Set on pedestrian-only Saad Zaghloul, this is a clean budget hotel with fixtures and fittings in good condition. Rooms vary in size, but even the triple-bed rooms are spacious. Bathrooms have modern shower/tub combos and are freshly painted. There are a rooftop restaurant and terrace but no pool—though the owner has an agreement with a nearby hotel where you can take a dip. There's no bar, but you're allowed to bring in your own supplies. **Pros:** In the heart of the vibrant souk; little vehicular traffic noise. **Cons:** Street noise can be an issue in rooms on lower floors, and there is some background train noise; some rooms are dimly lit by light shafts; some rooms have colored glass in the windows; elevator has no inner door. ✉ *373 Shar'a Saad Zaghloul (50 yards from the train station).* ☎ *097/232–9690* ⊕ *www.paradisehotel-aswan.com* ⤴ *66 rooms* ⚬ *In-room: No a/c* *(some), refrigerator. In-hotel: 2 restaurants, room service, laundry service, Internet terminal* ▤*MC, V* ⦿|*BP.*

NIGHTLIFE & THE ARTS

Aswan doesn't have a buzzing nightlife scene. Most of the large hotels will have some kind of Nubian folk dance performance or can arrange for you to see one at a neighboring village. The most popular pastime in the town is finding somewhere to have a cocktail on a terrace while watching the sun set. Now that the Old Cataract Hotel bar has closed until 2010, there are a few more places to enjoy this Aswan ritual.

BARS

Blue River Terrace (✉*Basma Hotel, Shar'a Abtal al-Tahrir* ☎*097/231–0901*) has a lovely setting with shaded tables, where you can sit and enjoy a drink with views of the cataracts, and the sunset. **El Pasha Coffee Shop** (✉*Isis Corniche Hotel* ☎*097/231–5100*) has tables directly on the water's edge, which are at a premium in Aswan; therefore, this narrow café, with its coffee and *shisha* services, is an increasingly popular place to relax in the evening. **Tower Bar on 12th** (✉*Mövenpick Hotel, Elephantine Island* ☎*097/230–3455*) offers the best panoramic views across the city from its full-length windows. It's a very contemporary bar that doesn't have the atmosphere of the Old Cataract, but seats on four sides give you a choice of views—up- or downriver, out to the Tombs of the Nobles, or across to the Corniche.

SOUTH OF ASWAN: PHILAE AND THE ASWAN DAMS

Within a few miles of Aswan, between town and the northern shores of Lake Nasser, are a few popular sights, the most impressive of which are the High Dam or the Philae Temple, depending on how many pharaonic sights you've visited during your trip.

PHILAE: THE TEMPLE OF ISIS

★ *Agilqiyya (Philae) Island, 8 km (5 mi) south of Aswan.*

The consequences of building the first dam on the Nile south of Aswan were alarming. In the case of Philae Island, water partially submerged the Temple of Isis when floods filled the dam as a result of seasonal rains upriver. Archaeologists feared that this periodic flooding would soften the monument's foundations, causing it to collapse. It was not until 1960, with the construction of the second dam, that UNESCO and the Egyptian Antiquities Service decided to preserve Philae and other important Upper Egyptian temples. The dismantling of the Philae complex started in the early 1970s, when a huge coffer dam was erected around the island. Then nearby Agilqiyya Island was carved so that the Temple of Isis would stand just as it had on Philae, and the whole complex was moved and meticulously reinstalled on Agilqiyya.

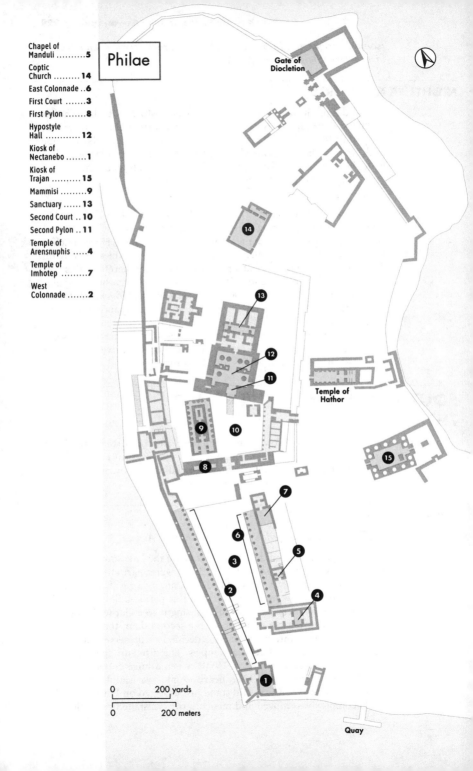

Philae

Gate of
Diocletion

Temple of
Hathor

0   200 yards

0   200 meters

Quay

The process took until 1980, when authorities reopened the site to the public.

The oldest physical evidence, from blocks found on-site, of the worship of Isis dates back to the reign of the 25th-Dynasty Ethiopian pharaoh Taharqa (690–664 bc). During the 30th Dynasty, Nectanebo I built the temple's more imposing structures. The major part of the temple complex is the legacy of the pharaohs who ruled over Egypt between the reigns of Ptolemy II Philadelphos (285–246 bc) and the Roman emperor Diocletian (284–305 AD). The cult of Isis was upheld until the first half of the 6th century AD, when Justinian abolished the ancient Egyptian beliefs of the temple, by force.

Whereas most ancient temples are surrounded by modern habitations, the temple of Philae stands alone on an island. The boat to the monument takes you past islands of rock, among which rises, as an image of order amid the natural randomness, the magnificent Temple of Isis. The approach can be chaotic, as many boats jostle for space; expect that you may have to climb over other boats to get onto the dock.

The first sight that strikes you, once on the island, is the long **First Court,** surrounded by a series of refined columns, all unique. The first building on the left is the **Kiosk of Nectanebo I.** The **West Colonnade,** built during the Roman period, leads up the west side of the island. In the First Court, turn east to admire, from right to left, the **Temple of Arensnuphis,** the **Chapel of Mandulis** (both are Nubian gods), the first **East Colonnade** (Roman period), and Ptolemy V Epiphanes's small **Temple of Imhotep.**

The First Court leads to the **First Pylon of Ptolemy XIII Neos Dionysos.** Both of the obelisks erected in front of the pylon are now at Kingston Lacy, in Dorset, England, taken there by Giovanni Battista Belzoni in 1819. Belzoni (1778–1823) was an Italian explorer, adventurer, and excavator. His methods destroyed a lot of valuable material, but considering the techniques used in his day, he was no worse than other archaeologists.

The small *mammisi* on the left side of the **Second Court** was erected in honor of the birth of Horus. Earlier New Kingdom (1539–1075 bc) counterparts of Greco-Roman mammisi are reliefs depicting the divine birth of the king, as in Hatshepsut's temple at Deir al-Bahri (Luxor West Bank) and Thutmose III's shrine in the Temple of Luxor (East Bank).

At the north end of the Second Court, through the **Second Pylon,** the **Hypostyle Hall** is the actual entrance to the temple of Isis. It consists of 10 columns and is mainly the work of Ptolemy VIII (Euergetes II). The majority of the reliefs on the walls are offering scenes: the king, by himself or accompanied by his wife, donates incense, vases, and wine to the gods to please them.

It is not uncommon to hear scholars call the art of the Greco-Roman period decadent and coarse. Although it is less classically Egyptian than the art of preceding periods, it nevertheless is an interesting mixture of Hellenistic and Egyptian traditions. At the same time, the religious beliefs—the most important part of the functioning of the temples—remained the same throughout the centuries, because the temples gained a degree of independence inside Egypt.

As with every temple, the **sanctuary** is the focal point in the complex. The **Pronaos,** behind the Hypostyle Hall, was converted into a Coptic church, with an altar visible on the right—which also explains the crosses on the walls. To the east of the Temple of Isis, close to the river bank, the unfinished **Kiosk of Trajan** is a small open temple with supporting columns. Inside are offering scenes.

The **Sound & Light Show,** like the one at the Temple of Karnak, has two parts. The first is a walk through the partly illuminated temple, and the second delivers a brief history of the site combined with music and the light show. It is a pleasant spectacle, less showy than that at Karnak.

Agilqiyya Island is in the basin between the Old Dam and the High Dam. Boats leave for Philae from the docks of Shellal, south of the Old Aswan Dam. The easiest but also the most expensive way to get to the docks is by private taxi or with a group tour, which you can arrange at your hotel. If you visit as part of a group, your guide will negotiate for the boat passage out to the island; if you go on your own, you'll have to negotiate with the boatman yourself. Buy tickets for the temple before you board the boat at Shellal. ☎*No phone* ✉*Temple £e50, boat (cost is divided among passengers) £e50, entry to High Dam area £e20, Sound & Light Show £e75* ☉*Temple Oct.–May, daily 7–5; June–Sept. 7–6. Sound & Light Show (in English) Oct.–May, Mon. and Fri–Sat at 6:30* PM, *Tue.–Wed. at 7:30* PM, *Thurs. and Sun. at 8:30* PM; *June–Sept., Mon. and Fri.–Sat. at 8* PM, *Tues.–Wed. at 9:15* PM, *Thurs. and Sun at 10:30* PM.

THE ASWAN DAMS

Two large dams have been built to control the flow of the Nile and to preserve its flow for later irrigation of crops. One dates to the turn of the 20th century; the other (a much more massive undertaking) was built in the 1960s. The latter dam created Lake Nasser, the largest man-made lake in the world.

The Old Dam. The British built the first Aswan Dam between 1898 and 1902 using blocks of local granite. The structure stands 130 feet tall, 8,000 feet long, and has a capacity of 7 billion cubic yards of water. In its day, it was one of the world's largest dams, and one of the sights to see in Aswan. These days the High Dam dwarfs it, and you can only drive over the Old Dam, because no stopping is allowed. The Old Dam is five minutes south of town, on the way in from the airport.

The Fisherman's Port. Just before you get to the High Dam, on the way out from Aswan, turn left down the road to the water to get to this ramshackle port, with its jumble of *African Queen*–style fishing boats and launches for the **Temple of Kalabsha.** The launch to New Kalabsha Island costs £e45.

CLOSE UP

The Cult of Isis

Isis is a central figure in the Egyptian pantheon. Wife of Osiris, she was responsible for bringing her husband back to life after he was killed by his jealous brother Seth. After his reincarnation, Osiris impregnated Isis who gave birth to Horus. Through these activities Isis is identified as "life giver" and "nourisher"; she was a protective force for the Pharaoh in life and in death—often seen on temple carvings carrying the ankh (which symbolizes the life force). The role of Isis in the resurrection of her husband also imbued her with power over magic, healing, and miracles.

In the Hellenic and Roman eras, worship of Isis spread far beyond the boundaries of Egypt. Temples to the goddess were built in Delos and Delphi in Greece, Pompeii and Rome in Italy, and also in Spain, Germany, and along the Black Sea coast. The Cult of Isis was even an early rival to Christianity. Worship of the goddess died out when pagan cults were outlawed throughout the Roman Empire by Emperor Constantine in the early 4th century; however, the core temple at Philae remained active into the 5th century because many of its worshippers came from Nubia, well beyond the reach of Rome.

5

Aswan High Dam. Jamal 'Abd al-Nasir's (Nasser's) vision of a modern Egypt rose and fell on the construction of the dam, which began in 1960. It took Soviet financing, plus the sweat of 30,000 Egyptians working around the clock, to complete the work by 1971. The volume of the dam itself is 17 times that of the Great Pyramid.

Lake Nasser is the world's largest man-made lake, 500 km (310 mi) long—150 km (93 mi) of which is in Sudan—and it has a storage capacity of 210,000 billion cubic yards of water. The dam doubled Egypt's power-generating capabilities, and it ensures a net surplus of 26 billion cubic yards of water as a reserve against low annual floods upriver.

The disadvantages of damming the Nile included the loss of fertile silt that the floods brought, which has made the use of chemical fertilizers a necessity. An incalculable loss is Nubia, which now lies beneath so many cubic yards of water that its 100,000 inhabitants relocated along the river valley. As one Nubian elder put it, "we cut off the arm to save the body."

Visit the stylized lotus monument commemorating the Russian–Egyptian collaboration, and try to convince the guard to take you up the tiny elevator for a view of unsurpassed splendor. The lake and Nubian desert stretch out to one side; on the other stretches the now-tamed Nile.

The High Dam is 15 minutes south of town by taxi. Allow 1 to 1½ hours to take in the spectacle. £e20 ☉ Oct.–May, daily 6–5; June–Sept., daily 6–6.

LAKE NASSER

Until a few decades ago, Lower Nubia, the area south of Aswan below the First Cataract, was much like the Nile Valley north of Aswan—save for the fact that the primary inhabitants were Nubian Egyptians, rather than Egyptians of Arab, Turkish, or Bedouin descent. As in Upper Egypt, Nubia's thin ribbon of green, fed by the Nile, was hemmed in by desert. Nubians cultivated their fields, and massive pharaonic monuments line the riverbanks.

The Aswan High Dam and Lake Nasser put an end to that, of course, forcing the Egyptian Nubian population inhabiting the flooded areas to move downriver to areas around, and to the north of, Aswan. Many of the monuments from antediluvian Nubia were also relocated to higher ground, or salvaged and removed to foreign countries. Unfortunately, others could not be saved, and they were swallowed up by the waters of Lake Nasser—some were hastily excavated first, while the rest were submerged without a trace.

Except for Abu Simbel and Philae, the temples along the shores of Lake Nasser are less visited than those along the lower reaches of the Nile. It's possible to take a cruise on Lake Nasser to see many of these, and Kalabsha is reachable by boat from Aswan. *For information on Lake Nasser cruises, see Chapter 8.*

NEW KALABSHA

30 minutes south of Aswan by taxi (or bus) and ferry.

The temples from the sites of Kalabsha and Beit al-Wali were moved to the island of New Kalabsha near Aswan. This rocky island, redolent of fish, is uninhabited save for a few dogs, foxes, and the Antiquities guards that care for the temple and monitor the ticket booth. The view of the lake and the dam is very fine from the island, and especially charming from the landing dock.

The largest freestanding Egyptian temple in Nubia, **Kalabsha** was built by Augustus Caesar (who reigned from 27 bc to AD 14) and dedicated to Osiris, Isis, and Mandulis, the latter a Nubian fertility god with a very elaborate headdress. Although the temple building was almost completed in antiquity, its decoration was never finished. Only three inner rooms, as well as portions of the exterior, are completely decorated with reliefs. Kalabsha's half-finished column capitals and fragments of relief decoration do, however, provide a great deal of information about ancient construction and carving techniques. And the view from the pylon and the roof area is wonderful and well worth the climb.

The temple complex includes a birth house, in the southwest corner, and a small chapel in the northeast corner, dating to the Ptolemaic period. A large rock stela dating to the reign of Seti I has also been erected at this site. Its original location was Qasr Ibrim.

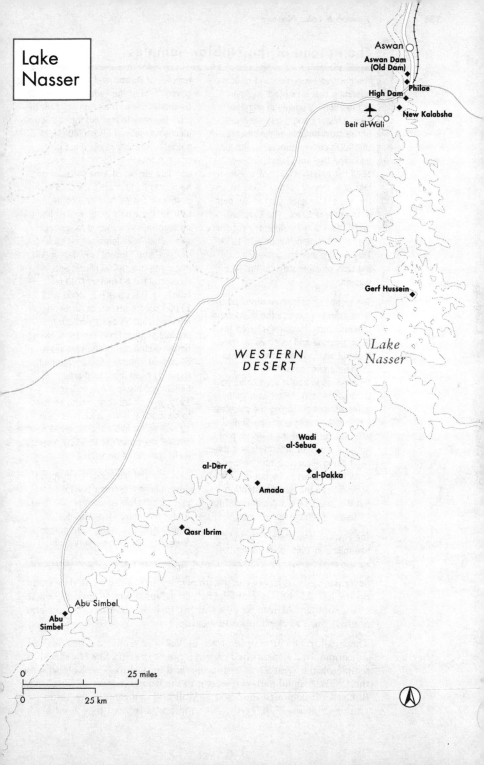

The Rescue of the Nubian Temples

The massive excavation and relocation operation that took place in Egypt in the 1960s is unique in archaeological history, and it has been one of the most notable achievements of UNESCO's cultural programs. Rubles and expertise from Russia helped build the Aswan High Dam, but there was little money in the coffers to save the ancient temples lying in the path of the new reservoir. The Egyptian and Sudanese governments called on the United Nations for help in 1959. Fifty nations answered the call, offering cash or expertise, and the race was on.

The campaign presented many problems: how to prioritize the many monuments, since it was clear given the tight deadline and rising water levels that not all could be saved; how to dismantle and reassemble monumental carvings in fragile sandstone; how to move painted plaster over many miles without damaging the priceless frescoes. The temple at Abu Simbel was without doubt the flagship project, and the sight of Ramesses' carved head being separated from his body and hoisted away to be put into storage captured the world's attention. But the "must-save" list amounted to 21 temples, a huge undertaking.

The Egyptian government started the ball rolling in 1960, dismantling the temples of **Debod** and **Taffa**. The government of the Federal Republic of Germany funded the saving of **Kalabsha**. The temple was cut into 13,000 pieces and moved 60 km (40 mi) by barge, before the whole giant puzzle was put together again at its new site. The temple of **Amada** could not be dismantled because it would have destroyed the painted images inside. Instead, the whole building was lifted up onto rails and moved to a new site—a half-mile journey that took six months. **Abu Simbel** was dismantled into more than 8,000 pieces and reconstructed 60 meters (200 feet) higher up the same hill, along with 12,000 square meters of surrounding landscape to exactly match the original setting. Finally, in 1969, work began on the last of the temples to be moved—**Philae**. The temple had regularly been inundated after the building of the first Aswan Dam in 1902, so a coffer dam had to be used to surround the site, and more than 12 feet of silt had to be removed from around the base. The UNESCO projects were completed by 1979.

As a token of gratitude, the Egyptian government presented several temples as gifts to the countries involved. It's for this reason that **Dendur** temple now sits in the Metropolitan Museum of Art in New York City.

Several large boulders covered with petroglyphs of uncertain date stand on the left side of the temple. The petroglyphs, which resemble those of the southern African San (Bushmen), include carvings of people and animals, such as elephants and antelopes.

The small, rock-cut temple of **Beit al-Wali** was removed from its cliff-side home—the ancients had carved it out of the cliff, like Hatshepsut's temple on the West Bank at Luxor—and moved to New Kalabsha in the 1960s. A small path connects it to the Roman temple of Kalabsha. Ramesses II commissioned Beit al-Wali and dedicated it to Amun-Ra and other deities. Originally, the temple was fronted by a mud-brick pylon, which was not moved, and consisted of an entrance hall, a hypostyle hall, and a sanctuary. This small, jewel-like temple is a delight, because its painted decorations—its reds, blues, and greens—still look very fresh. The entrance hall contains scenes of Ramesses II quelling various enemies of Egypt, often accompanied by a pet lion. The columned hall shows the pharaoh interacting with different deities, chief among them being Amun-Ra. The sanctuary contains carved seated statues of Ramesses II and deities, such as Horus, Isis, and Khnum.

The site is a stop on Lake Nasser cruises, and it is accessible from Aswan—by taxi to the fisherman's port east of the High Dam, then by boat (£e35) to the island. 🕿 *No phone* 🖂 *£e35* ☾ *Daily 7–5.*

INTERIOR LAKE NASSER MONUMENTS

All of Lake Nasser's interior monuments—those located apart from Aswan and Abu Simbel—can only be visited on a multiday lake cruise. They are set in rather bleak landscapes relieved only by the odd reed and bird. You don't need entry tickets, because admission is included with your cruise (*For more information on Lake Nasser cruises, see* ⇨ *Chapter 8*).

The remains of the temple at **Gerf Hussein** are fragmentary. Built by Setau, a viceroy of Kush during the reign of Ramesses II, it was originally a combination rock-cut and freestanding temple, similar in plan to the temple of Abu Simbel. It was dedicated to the deified Ramesses II, Ptah (a creator god), Hathor (goddess of love, beauty, and music), and Ptah-tanen (a Nubian–Egyptian creator god). Seated statues of the four were carved out of the rock in the sanctuary. Unfortunately, the portion of the temple that now remains is badly preserved, and it retains little of its former grandeur. (For that, you must travel to its counterpart at Abu Simbel.)

Wadi al-Sebua is famous for being the site of two New Kingdom temples. The earlier temple, which had both freestanding and rock-cut elements, was constructed by Amenhotep III and added to by Ramesses II. It consists of a sanctuary, a court, a hall, and pylons. The temple was originally dedicated to a Nubian form of Horus but was later rededicated to the god Amun-Ra.

The more dramatic and larger site at al-Sebua is the temple of Ramesses II, Ra-Harakhte (a sun god), and Amun-Ra. It is yet another of Ramesses II's projects, and it once stood about 150 yards northeast of the Amenhotep III temple; it was moved about 3 km (2 mi) to the west. This temple has both freestanding and rock-cut sections.

The Ptolemaic and Roman temple of **al-Dakka** has been moved from its original site to a new one not far from Wadi al-Sebua. Dakka was originally built by reusing fragments of an older temple dating from the 18th Dynasty.

The main part of the temple of **Amada**, dedicated to Amun-Ra and Ra-Harakhte, was constructed in the 18th Dynasty. Various 19th-Dynasty pharaohs repaired it and added to it. Between 1964 and 1975 it was moved to its current spot, about 2 km (1 mi) away from its original location.

Amada is noted for two important historical inscriptions. One dates to the reign of Amenhotep II; it appears on a round-topped stela on the eastern wall of the sanctuary. The inscription describes a definitive military victory over rebellious chiefs in Syria. The other is on a stela carved from the northern thickness of the entryway and dates to the reign of King Merneptah (1212–1202 BC). It describes how the king successfully repelled a Libyan invasion of Egypt in the early years of his reign.

The temple of **al-Derr** was moved near the site of Amada in 1964. It is a rock-cut temple built by Ramesses II and dedicated to himself, Amun-Ra, Ra-Harakhte, and Ptah. The temple is well decorated, and its bright colors are still visible—particularly in the area before the sanctuary.

Qasr Ibrim is a large site on what is now an island. Not too many years ago the area was attached to the mainland by a spit of land. Because of the rise in the level of water in the lake, it is now impossible to land and walk around Qasr Ibrim, although archaeological work here continues. The fortress is interesting because it encompasses several periods of history: pharaonic, Roman, Christian, and Arab/Nubian, up to the mid-20th century.

The island houses the remains of temples from the 18th and 25th dynasties, as well as rock-cut shrines dedicated to different pharaohs and assorted gods dating to the 18th and 19th dynasties. Remains of a sizable fortress of the Augustan period are also visible, as are portions of a large basilica and foundations and standing sections of dwellings. Archaeologists working at the site have found much well-preserved evidence—leather, manuscripts, pottery, and animal and botanical remains—that sheds light on daily life during the various periods of occupation at Qasr Ibrim.

ABU SIMBEL: THE TEMPLES OF RAMESSES II AND NEFERTARI

★ *280 km (174 mi) south of Aswan.*

Abu Simbel began as a small village of a few houses clustered at some distance from the temples of Abu Simbel. Now it is a lush oasis with hotels and a sizable settlement. Arriving by plane or bus steals some of the drama that is so much a part of Ramesses II's monument of monuments. The lake approach, on the other hand, fulfills every fantasy you might have about the grandeur of ancient Egypt.

Ramesses II's two enormous temples at Abu Simbel are among the most awe-inspiring monuments in Egypt. The pharaoh had his artisans carve the temples out of a rock cliff to display his might as the Egyptian god king and to strike dread into the Nubians—and the temples are most effective as such. They originally stood at the bottom of the cliff that they now crown (they're some 200 feet above the water level and 1/3 mi back from the lake shore).

The first of the two temples of Abu Simbel, the **Great Temple,** was dedicated to Ramesses II (as a god) and to Ra-Harakhte, Amun-Ra, and Ptah. The second was dedicated to the goddess Hathor and Nefertari, Ramesses II's wife and chief queen. The Great Temple is fronted by four seated colossi, about 65 feet tall, of Ramesses II wearing the double crown of Upper and Lower Egypt (one crown is broken). Around the legs of the statues stand smaller figures of Ramesses II's wives and offspring. The top of the temple facade is covered by a row of rampant baboons praising the sun as it rises. Between the two pairs of statues is a carved figure of Ra-Harakhte that stands over the door to the temple.

The doorway between the colossi leads to the **first hall,** which contains columns decorated with figures of Ramesses II. The hall itself is carved on the right (north) with reliefs showing events from Ramesses II's reign, most notably his self-proclaimed victory at the Battle of Kadesh in Syria (his opponent might beg to differ). It shows the besieged city, the attack, and the counting of body parts of the defeated enemies. The left (south) side shows Ramesses' battles with Syrians, Libyans, and Nubians, and it has some fine scenes showing Ramesses on a chariot. Vultures with outstretched wings decorate the ceiling. Several side chambers are accessible from this hall. These were probably used as storerooms for the temple furniture, vessels, linen, and priestly costumes.

The **second hall** contains four square columns and is decorated with scenes of Ramesses II and Queen Nefertari making offerings to various deities, including the deified Ramesses himself. This hall leads into a narrow room that was probably where the king made offerings to the gods of the temple.

Three chapels branch off the narrow offering room. The two side chapels are undecorated, but the central chapel, the **main sanctuary,** is decorated not only with scenes of the pharaoh making offerings and conducting temple rituals, but also with four rock-carved statues of the deities to whom the temple is dedicated. They are, from left to right, Ptah, Amun-Ra, Ramesses II, and Ra-Horakhte. These were originally painted and gilded, but the paint and the gold have long since gone. The temple was originally constructed so that twice each year the first rays of the rising sun would pierce the dark interior of the temple and strike these four statues, bathing them in light. When the temple was moved, this was taken into consideration and still happens, albeit a day late, on February 21 and October 21.

The smaller temple at Abu Simbel is the **Temple of Queen Nefertari,** dedicated to Hathor. The temple is fronted by six colossal standing rock-cut statues of Queen Nefertari and Ramesses II. Each statue is flanked by some of their children. The temple doorway opens into a **pillared hall** that contains six Hathor-head columns much larger than those in Deir al-Bahri. The ceiling contains a dedicatory inscription from Ramesses II to Queen Nefertari. The hall itself is decorated with scenes of the royal couple, either together or singly, making offerings to or worshiping the gods. A narrow vestibule, decorated with scenes of offerings, follows the pillared hall, and the **main sanctuary** leads off of this vestibule. The sanctuary contains a niche with a statue of Hathor as a cow, protecting Ramesses.

EgyptAir flies to Abu Simbel from Cairo (2½ hours) and makes the journey from Aswan (½ hour) several times a day. The flight is structured to allow you only two hours on the ground, including the transfer between Abu Simbel and the airport; these flights book up far in advance, and independent travelers would be well-advised to work with a travel agent or tour operator to book this portion of their trip. If you want more time to explore, it's possible to arrange your return on a different day (but making this arrangement is out of the norm, so it's best to use a travel agent to book your ticket). It's also possible to visit Abu Simbel in the daily convoy via the desert road. ⊠ *Mabed Abu Simbel* ☎ *No phone* ✑ *Site £e80, Sound & Light Show £e75* ⊙ *Temple daily 8–5. Sound & Light Show Apr.–Sept., nightly at 8 PM, 9 PM, and 10 PM; Oct.–Mar., nightly at 7 PM, 8 PM, and 9 PM (show will only go on if at least 30 people have made a booking).*

WHERE TO EAT & STAY

Abu Simbel is a small, rural town. There are no international-style restaurants in the town; however, small street stalls and basic cafés offer a seemingly never-ending supply of grilled meats and chicken, rice, and soup to keep hunger pangs at bay. Look for roadside stalls selling seasonal fresh fruits. Alternatively, if you travel by land convoy or are staying over, you can carry supplies with you from Aswan and have a picnic. Even if you fly in, you may have time for a snack, coffee, or cold drink at the small café next to the monument entrance.

If you can make the time, it's well worth staying overnight at Abu Simbel. You can visit the temples when the hoards of day-trippers have departed, take in the Sound & Light show, and enjoy the bucolic atmosphere of the town.

$$$ ⊞ **Seti Abu Simbel Lake Resort.** The most comfortable hotel in the town is right on the lakeshore. Nubian-style two-story buildings are scattered around a verdant garden replete with waterfalls and a swimming pool. The whitewashed interiors have terracotta-tile floors and fauxstone detail. Domes and arches are major features of the public areas. The resort has a choice of eateries, including a seafood restaurant that serves lake-caught fish in season. **Pros:** A stylish place to relax after a day of sightseeing; panoramic lake views from the pool and terrace. **Cons:** Not all facilities are available in the off-season or if the hotel has few guests (laundry service and restaurants may not be operating, for example). ⊠ *Abu Simbel* ☎ *097/340–0720* ⊕ *www.setifirst. com* ✑ *138 rooms* ⚘ *In-room: refrigerator (some). In hotel: 3 restaurants, bar, tennis courts, pool, laundry service, parking (free)* ☐ *MC, V* ⏇ *MAP.*

Abu Simbel

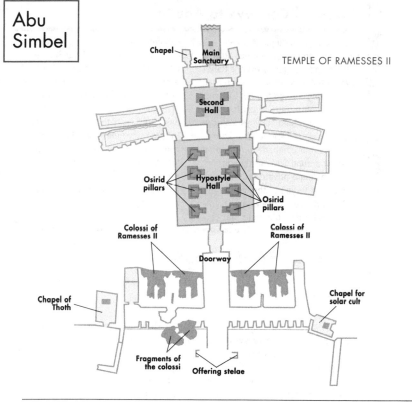

TEMPLE OF RAMESSES II

Chapel — Main Sanctuary

Second Hall

Osirid pillars — Hypostyle Hall

Osirid pillars

Colossi of Ramesses II

Colossi of Ramesses II

Doorway

Chapel of Thoth

Chapel for solar cult

Fragments of the colossi

Offering stelae

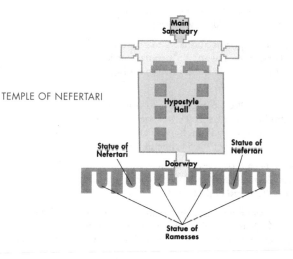

TEMPLE OF NEFERTARI

Main Sanctuary

Hypostyle Hall

Statue of Nefertari

Statue of Nefertari

Doorway

Statue of Ramesses

Overland Convoys to Abu Simbel

As is the case throughout Upper Egypt, foreign tourists are not allowed to travel independently even if they have rented cars. All taxis and rental cars carrying foreign tourists—as well as larger tour groups—must travel in regularly scheduled convoys. You can book an overland trip to Abu Simbel through a tour company in Aswan (at a cost of around $90 per person) or by contracting a private taxi in Aswan to transport to you to the temple and back. If you use a private taxi, haggle hard to get a day rate; note that you should offer to pay for the driver's lunch while you are in Abu Simbel, which will cost you an extra £e10–20. These arrangements should be made at least one day in advance, as tour operators may need to take your passport details to the police so that they know you are traveling in the convoy on a given date. The convoy for Abu Simbel departs from behind the Nubia Museum in Aswan at 4 AM and 11 AM daily. The journey takes around 3½ hours.

ASWAN & LAKE NASSER ESSENTIALS

TRANSPORTATION

BY AIR

EgyptAir, your only option for domestic flights, operates several flights a day from Cairo to Aswan and to Abu Simbel (usually direct). There are also regular flights linking Aswan with Alexandria, Abu Simbel, Luxor, and Hurghada. From Cairo to Aswan, the journey takes about two hours one-way (often with a stop in Luxor); flights from Luxor to Aswan, or from Aswan to Abu Simbel, take 30 minutes one way.

Contacts **EgyptAir** (✉ *1 Shar'a Abtal al-Tahrir (at the south end of the Corniche), Aswan* ☎ *097/231–5000* ⊕ *www.egyptair.com).*

AIRPORT TRANSFERS   The Aswan airport is about 15 to 20 minutes from town, a taxi ride of about £e50 from Aswan. An airport shuttle bus linking Abu Simbel airport with the temple is included in all EgyptAir tickets to Abu Simbel.

BY BOAT

Aswan has no West Bank roads, so you have to travel by felucca to visit the sights across the river. Powerboats also run between sights, but they are less romantic and much more expensive, at about twice the cost to cut the already short travel time in half.

Public felucca ferries cross regularly to Elephantine Island for a couple of pounds from early morning to midnight. Catch them by the public park on the south end of the Corniche.

Feluccas have fixed rates that tend to be highly negotiable and start at around £e30 an hour. You can find out these rates at the Tourist Information Office, hotels, and the offices of local travel and tour agencies.

For longer felucca trips from Aswan, consult the Tourist Information Office for help in arranging tours to Kom Ombo (a full day and night); to Edfu (two days and nights); and to Esna (three days and nights). Prices for these trips are reasonable, from about £e50 per person per night (minimum 6 people, maximum 8, or you can rent the whole boat). Captains can be reluctant to sail all the way to Luxor, because the return trip upriver takes longer; if you are going to end the trip south of Luxor, be sure to arrange to be picked up.) You need a group of six people for one of these rustic, camp-out-style journeys. *(For information on arranging multiday felucca trips, see Chapter 8, Nile & Lake Nasser Cruises.)*

Powerboats leave for New Kalabsha Island (its temples are Kalabsha and Beit al-Wali) from beside the entry to the High Dam; the £e45 fare allows for a visit of about an hour. Philae has its own dock about a 15-minute drive from town, on the east side of the basin between the Old Dam and the High Dam. Powerboats make the trip for about £e50, but they will offer to wait for only two hours. It's advisable to allow three hours to see Philae's Temple of Isis, so mention this in advance; if you are traveling independently, make sure that the price you have agreed upon includes extra waiting time and the return journey.

BY BUS

Government buses to Upper Egypt can be uncomfortable but cheap. The one-way fare to Aswan from Cairo is about £e90, but foreign travelers may be dissuaded from booking regular public bus transport because of security concerns. *(For more information on the convoy system, see Luxor Essentials in Chapter 4.)* If you must go by bus, purchase tickets in advance from Targoman Station in central Cairo.

Contacts Targoman Bus Station (⊠ *off Gala' Street, Downtown, Cairo* ☎ *02/2431-6723).*

BY CAR

Car rental isn't a practical option in Aswan since you can walk between downtown attractions, and most other sights (Philae Temple, Kalabsha Temple, Elephantine Island, West Bank attractions) involve a boat transfer. You'll be able to negotiate a taxi rate that's not much more than a car-rental rate and have someone who knows their way around the town.

All foreigners traveling out of Aswan are required to join the daily convoys. For destinations that are not on the well-worn tourist route—such as Daraw camel market—where tour groups do not regularly visit, you must have police permission to travel, and you may be allocated an armored vehicle or an armed officer for your trip. This does not mean that you will not be allowed to travel. This should be done at least 24 hours before your departure. A tour company will make these arrangements for you.

Convoys north to Luxor depart from the Coca-Cola plant on the north Corniche at 8 AM, with stops at Kom Ombo and Edfu en route, and at 2 PM, direct to Luxor with no stops.

Convoys south to Abu Simbel depart from behind the Nubia Museum at 4 AM and 11 AM.

BY TAXI

You'll find plenty of taxis in Aswan, the same six-seater Peugeot station wagons as in Luxor. You can travel the length of the Corniche for about £e20; shorter trips cost £e10.

You can also use taxis to travel outside of Aswan. Approximate costs for Peugeot taxi service from Aswan—as quoted by the Tourist Information Office—and covering up to four passengers in the same vehicle are as follows: £e90 round-trip for the half-day, 90-km (56-mi) journey to Kom Ombo; £e250 one way for the full-day, 225-km (140-mi) trip to Luxor, including stops at the temples at Edfu and Kom Ombo. However, some drivers may be reluctant to undertake this journey because of the convoy system. You should expect to pay £e100 round-trip to Philae, including the driver's three-hour wait while you visit the temple (you'll also have to hire your own boatman if you go independently); and £e50 to the High Dam, including a stop at the rest area.

BY TRAIN

From Cairo to Aswan, the regular train costs £e109 for first class and £e55 for second class. First class offers you more space, and you have a choice of traveling during the day or at night. The fares for the journey between Luxor and Aswan are £e41 first class and £e25 second class. Travel time between Luxor and Aswan is about 3 hours.

Most tourists traveling to Aswan by train will prefer the comfortable sleeper cars run by Abela, which make the daily trip to Aswan from the cavernous Ramses Station in central Cairo. Tickets should be purchased at least 10 days in advance at the Abela office in the station. There are two daily departures in each direction. Train 84 leaves Cairo at 8 PM, reaching Aswan at 8:15 AM; Train 86 departs Cairo at 9:10 PM, arriving in Aswan at 9:30 AM. For the return journey, Train 85 departs Aswan at 6:30 PM, arriving in Cairo at 6:45 AM; Train 87 leaves Aswan at 9:20 PM, arriving at Cairo 9:30 AM. A single couchette with meals costs $80 one-way; a double couchette costs $60 per person. These fares must be paid in foreign currency, not Egyptian pounds.

Contacts Abela (✉ *Ramses Station, Cairo* ☎ *02/2574-9474* ⊕ *www.sleeping trains.com*).

CONTACTS & RESOURCES

BANKS & EXCHANGE SERVICES

Aswan has a good supply of banks, exchange offices, and ATMs where you can exchange or withdraw money. Exchange offices tend to be open long hours, usually daily and until 10 PM or 11 PM. Banks open shorter hours and may not be open on weekends. American Express and Thomas Cook also change money. You can almost always change money at your hotel, but exchange offices generally offer better rates than either banks or hotel desks. Don't rely solely on ATMs as these may not be replenished regularly. Have a range of options, including Egyptian currency, in addition to credit cards and an ATM card.

Information Bank of Alexandria (✉ *Corniche al-Nil, across from the Isis Hotel, Aswan* ☎ *097/230-2765*). **Egyptian Exchange** (✉ *83 Corniche a-Nil, Aswan* ☎ *097/235-5122*).

EMERGENCIES

All major hotels and cruise ships will have an emergency doctor and dentist on call at all times, so if you become ill or suffer an accident in your room, call the front desk for help. All senior medical staff will speak English, so you will be able to explain your symptoms or your concerns. Hospitals are generally clean and well kept; however, medical facilities are not comprehensive.

Emergency Services Ambulance (☎ *123*). **Fire** (☎ *180*). **Police** (☎ *122*). **Tourist Police** (✉ *Aswan* ☎ *097/231-4393*).

Dentists Dr. Adel Soliman (✉ *By Sarwat Pharmacy, Aswan* ☎ *097/231-1155*).

Doctors Dr. Medhat Romano (✉ *By Sarwat Pharmacy, Aswan* ☎ *012/356-3927*).

Hospitals The German Hospital (✉ *Corniche al-Nil (south), Aswan* ☎ *097/230-2176*).

24-hour Pharmacies Dr. Said Saber Pharmacy (✉ *Shar'a Abtal al-Tahrir (off the main souk street), Aswan* ☎ *097/233-3399*).

INTERNET, MAIL & SHIPPING

Most major hotels offer some form of Internet connection, though not all have in-room service. Internet cafés are numerous but open and close with great regularity. Access is cheap (around £e10 per hour) but connections are not always fast. There is an increasing number of Wi-Fi hot-spots for travelers with their own laptops.

The mail service in Egypt is slow and unreliable. If you need to make sure that any letter or package gets to its destination, it's advisable to use a courier service. Courier companies will also ship excess baggage (i.e., if you've bought a lot of souvenirs or a large or heavy object), but the cost is very high.

Internet Cafés Philae Net (✉ *Corniche al-Nil, Aswan* ☎ *097/233-2452*).

Post Offices Post Office (✉ *Corniche al-Nil (next door to the Rowing Club), Aswan* ☎ *097/2305-5042*).

Shipping Companies FedEx (✉ *Corniche al-Nil, Aswan* ☎ *010/341-8147*).

TOUR OPTIONS

Aswan has a wide range of tour companies that can help you arrange travel to all the surrounding tourist sights. Since the development of the convoy system, independent travel has been made extremely difficult, whereas booking a tour is an easy, stress-free way of getting to the sights. Since most companies have to travel to the ancient sites at the same time, look for tour companies offering services for small groups to allow you to get the best out of the visit.

Information **American Express** (✉ *Corniche al-Nil, Aswan* ☎ *097/230–6983*). **Thomas Cook** (✉ *Corniche al-Nil, Aswan* ☎ *097/230–6839* ⊕ *www.thomascook. com.eg*).

VISITOR INFORMATION

The tourist information office is open daily 9 to 2 and 6 to 9 and has a very helpful, multilingual staff that can tell you about fixed taxi and felucca rates for short and long trips. The staff can also recommend guides and provide most any other information about Aswan.

Information **Aswan Tourist Information Office** (✉ *Next to train station* ☎ *097/231–2811*).

The Sinai Peninsula & Red Sea Coast

Beach resort, Hurghada

WORD OF MOUTH

"Dahab is a wonderful and exotic-looking town on the Red Sea. Hurghada is glittery and modern like Cancun or Miami Beach, and it feels nothing like being in Egypt."

—P_M

"Sharm [El-Sheikh] is the nightclub of Egypt with snorkleing and scuba. It is also the gateway to St. Catherine's [Monastery]."

—Diane60030

WELCOME TO THE SINAI PENINSULA & THE RED SEA COAST

TOP REASONS TO GO

★ **St. Catherine's Monastery:** See the chapel that purports to hold the burning bush that appeared to Moses.

★ **Scuba Diving:** Dive to the wreck of the *Thistlegorm* in the protected waters of Ras Mohammed National Park.

★ **Climbing Mount Sinai:** Rise before dawn and climb up the mountainside to welcome the sunrise over the Sinai mountain range.

★ **Kite-Surfing:** The tides and winds are perfect along the Red Sea Coast; catch some air while kite-surfing off Mangroovy Beach at El-Gouna.

★ **Dancing the Night Away:** Sinai resorts are magnets for young club-goers from all over Europe; strut your stuff on the dance floor in one of the top spots—Pacha Club in Sharm El-Sheikh.

1 **The Sinai Peninsula.** Come here for spectacular desert mountainscapes, the natural home of the Bedouin peoples, and St. Catherine's Monastery. Around the fringes, the growing resorts of the coast offer excellent R&R, including some of the world's best diving and for Egypt's best beaches, especially near Sharm El-Sheikh. From Taba it's possible to take a day-trip to fabled Petra in Jordan.

2 **The Red Sea Coast.** Excellent diving, great beaches, and a wealth of water sports are the major draws of this coast, which is popular with European vacationers for its year-round sunshine. The main destination is Hurghada. Beaches here are not quite as good as those on the Sinai Peninsula, but the diving is even better.

3 **The Suez Canal.** Visit the canal region if you like 19th-century architecture and an authentic small-town Egyptian atmosphere. Don't visit if you're seeking ancient monuments or great beach resorts. Most people visit on a day-trip from Cairo, but those who appreciate a slower pace may wish to spend the night.

Sharm el-Sheikh seaside resort.

Bur Sa'id
Suez Canal
3
al-Quantara
al-Ismailiya
Lake Timsah
Great Bitter Lake
Suez
Ash-Shatt
Suez Bay
Gulf of Suez
Za'farana

| 0 | | 25 mi |
| 0 | | 50 km |

Snorkeling on the Red Sea

A camel train winds its way around the Sinai shoreline near Dahab.

Mediterranean
Sea
al-Arish

55

NEGEV
DESERT

Quseima

3

Bir Hasana

33

Nakhl

al-Thamad

Eilat
Taba

SINAI

Colored
Canyon

Abu Zneima

Nuweiba

Gulf of Aqaba

Monastery of
St. Catherine

Dahab

Ras Gharib

al-Tur

Nabq

Strait of Jubal

Sharm
El-Sheikh

Na'ama
Bay

EASTERN
DESERT

Shakir
Island

El-Gouna

Hurghada

Red
Sea

Jabal
Shaib

1

2

GETTING ORIENTED

Because the Sinai Peninsula and Red Sea Coast both have seaside activities and ancient monasteries—the most impressive mountain scenery is in the Sinai—you don't need to go to both areas. Air connections are limited and unreliable. To avoid long desert drives, you can fly from Cairo, Luxor, or Alexandria to your beach resort of choice. The resorts on the Red Sea Coast are also best reached by plane (or by road from Luxor). Bur Sa'id is best seen as a day trip from Cairo or as a stopover on the way to the Sinai if you are going by road.

6

Red Sea windsurfing

THE SINAI PENINSULA & THE RED SEA COAST PLANNER

Transportation

By Air: The main airport in the Sinai is in Sharm El-Sheikh. The main airport on the Red Sea Coast is in Hurghada, but a new international airport has been opened at Marsa Alam, 132 km (82 mi) south of al-Quseir. Both Hurghada and Sharm have frequent flights both from within Egypt and from Europe, the latter primarily serving European tourists on all-inclusive beach holidays.

By Bus: Buses are inexpensive but time-consuming, but most bus lines do offer some service to the Red Sea Coast, Sinai, and Suez. Direct lines connect Cairo to Bur Sa'id (3 hours), Hurghada (6 hours), al-Quseir (11 hours), Sharm El-Sheikh (6 hours), Dahab (9 hours), Nuweiba (6 hours), and Taba (6 hours).

By Car: Although it's not recommended, you can drive from Cairo to Sharm El-Sheikh or one of the other Sinai resorts; however, foreign travelers will be expected to join a traveler's convoy.

By Ferry: High-speed ferries connect Hurghada and Sharm El-Sheikh except on Friday and Sunday. The trip takes between 2 and 3 hours and is the easiest way to travel from the Sinai to the Red Sea Coast since flights are much less frequent.

What's Great in the Sinai and Red Sea Coast

Beaches: The best beaches are near Sharm El-Sheikh, where there are several large resorts. Along the Red Sea Coast, the beaches are not as good; the best ones are around El-Gouna, though beach access is limited to the guests of the area's resorts.

Diving: The waters of the Red Sea hold some of the world's finest dive sites. Weather conditions and sea temperatures are good year-round, and the waters offer excellent visibility. In addition to coral, there are several wrecks to explore. The diving, however, is better along the Red Sea Coast than in Sinai.

Early Christian Monasteries: Two of Christianity's most revered hermit saints, St. Anthony and St. Paul of Thebes, made their home on the Red Sea Coast in the early centuries of the first millennium, becoming the first monks; monasteries were built on the sites of their respective hermitages. In the 5th century, a monumental monastery dedicated to St. Catherine was built in the Sinai to protect the site where many people believe Moses received the Ten Commandments.

Kite-Surfing: Acres of coastal shallows and onshore winds mean the area along the Red Sea Coast is ideal for windsurfing and kite-surfing, particularly around El-Gouna. Several high-quality schools and international competitions have made this a hot-spot for these two sports.

Mountains: The serrated peaks of the Sinai mountain range are unique in Egypt. This arid land offers opportunity for adrenaline adventure—trekking, climbing, quad biking—or a quieter camel safari with the Bedouin who have lived here for generations. Many travelers choose to make a dawn climb to the top of Mt. Sinai to watch the sun rise.

Nightlife: Both Sharm El-Sheikh and Hurghada are on Europe's clubbing trail—house and chill-out sounds launched here by the pantheon of celebrity DJs resonate around the world. Both resorts are very popular with young partiers (mostly Europeans) from their late teens to early twenties. El-Gouna, which draws wealthier Cairenes and tourists, has a more mature crowd.

About the Restaurants

The Sinai and the Red Sea Coast resorts cater primarily to European tastes, so resort food tends to be Continental and Italian fare and buffet breakfasts. Fresh seafood can be very good. Typical Egyptian food is most readily available in the cities of Bur Sa'id and Ismailiya along the Suez Canal. A few words of caution: Water is not always potable, so stick to bottled water to be safe. Likewise, vegetables are not always washed properly, so stay away from uncooked greens, especially lettuce and cucumbers. Oil, ghee, and butter, along with anything fatty, is very popular. A dish that you would expect to be light, like sautéed vegetables, may come dripping with oil.

About the Hotels

Around the Sinai and the Red Sea you'll find everything from luxury resorts to motels and seedy camping areas. Prices are considerably higher in peak seasons (September through November and April through June). European tour operators generally buy these rooms in bulk and sell them only as part of holiday packages; therefore, independent travelers may find it diiffuclt too book upscale resort rooms. Hotel rates are almost always charged in either U.S. dollars or euros. In Suez, lodging options are much more limited; the Sonesta in Bur Sa'id and the Mercure Hotel in Ismailiya are the best hotels, and both are comfortable and have waterfront views. Bear in mind that, like elsewhere in Egypt, there is a precipitous drop in quality between high- and low-end hotels, with very few options in the middle.

WHAT IT COSTS IN EGYPTIAN POUNDS, U.S. DOLLARS, AND EUROS

$$$$	$$$	$$	$
Restaurants			
over £e150	£e100–£e150	£e50–£e100	under £e50
Hotels in dollars			
over $200	$130–$200	$70–$130	under $70
Hotels in Euros			
over €130	€80–€130	€45–€80	under €45

Restaurant prices are per person for a main course at dinner. Hotel prices are for a double room in high season, excluding 10% tax and service charges (usually 10%).

Planning Your Time

If time is short, the Sinai is a better choice; St. Catherine's Monastery, with its proximity to Mt. Sinai, is a greater draw than the monasteries of St. Anthony and St. Paul. Sharm's golf course is one of the best in Egypt. Diving and kite-surfing are better on Egypt's mainland Red Sea Coast, but the beaches are inferior to those in the Sinai. The Suez Canal is best seen on a day trip from Cairo, but you can also stay overnight in Bur Sa'id or Ismailiya and continue the next day to Sharm El-Sheikh or the Red Sea Coast if you are traveling overland.

6

When to Go

April through October are the hot months, when temperatures climb as high as 113°F. It's a great time to come for diving, because the visibility is at its best. November through March is cooler, with temperatures as low as 46°F. The desert gets very cold at night, and temperatures may even drop below freezing, so bring warm layers in winter. The Sinai's high season is during the hotter months, but July and August are considered low season, as the heat is oppressive during this time. The Red Sea, on the other hand, is great in winter, which is its most popular time. Except in March, during the khamaseen (sandstorm) season, the sun shines here almost every day of the year.

Updated by
Lindsay and
Pete Bennett

FOR CENTURIES, EUROPEAN TRADERS AND Arab merchants had to sail around the Cape of Good Hope to travel east to Asia from Europe and the Mediterranean. However, 2,000 years earlier, ancient Egyptians had that problem licked. The records of the Greek historian Herodotus speak of a canal begun around 600 BC that connected the Nile to the Gulf of Suez. The canal was used during the time of Alexander the Great, left to ruin, then reopened during the Arab domination that began around AD 645. The canal was the primary route between the Nile Valley and the Arab world's trading center in Mecca, on the west coast of Saudi Arabia. Then the ancient canal was abandoned, and traders returned to the desert, risking their goods and their camels. Aside from the accounts of historians, all traces of that canal have vanished. The Suez Canal—an effort of thousands of Egyptian men who manually shoveled tons of sand between 1859 and 1869 to create a 110-km (66-mi) trench through the desert—follows a different course.

Since the dawn of human culture in Africa and the Middle East, the Sinai and Red Sea region has been an important crossroads—then a land bridge, now a sea bridge—connecting East and West, North and South. Enormous container ships and fancy ocean liners line up to pass through the Suez Canal. Canal towns such as Ismailiya and Bur Sa'id (Port Said) make interesting day trips from Cairo, if you have the time. But the novelty of passing ships can wear off rather quickly, leaving little else to do.

Not so the Sinai Peninsula and the Red Sea Coast, where relaxing on the beach, trekking through the desert, and diving amidst a wealth of marine life are probably the opposite of what you'd expect from a trip to Egypt. The desert itself, inland Sinai, has changed little since the times when Bedouins moved from one watering hole to the next. It remains awe-inspiring, especially if you get up for sunrise and catch the mountains changing from purple to red, then orange to yellow. The Red Sea continues to be an underwater haven, a living aquarium, in spite of the impact that a rush of divers has had on the reefs. Since the mid-1990s this coastline has undergone a multimillion-dollar makeover and has been transformed into the so-called Red Sea Riviera and marketed successfully to vacationers across northern Europe and the newly emerging countries of the old Soviet bloc. If you want resort amenities and the option of escaping to virgin desert spotted with shady acacia trees and lazy camels, this is the place for you. If you want to see ancient monasteries and biblical sites, or follow Moses' path from Egypt to Jordan, you can do that here, too.

Although Egypt is conservative when it comes to everyday attire, guests in the resort areas of the Sinai and the Red Sea often walk around in shorts and tank tops. Some people choose to dress up for dinner, although it is not mandatory. If you plan to visit any of the monasteries, dress modestly. The Suez is not a resort area, so don't walk around in shorts, women especially; long, loose clothing is a better idea. If you are driving around the area, and definitely if you are taking buses, wear long pants and short sleeves (nothing sleeveless).

Remember that you will be in a desert, and prices will necessarily be higher than elsewhere in the country because so many things have to be imported. If you plan to shop, plan to haggle. Always carry identification as you may be stopped for security checks, and if you visit a Bedouin village, take along some candy to give to Bedouin children.

If you are a woman traveling alone or in a group of women, be alert and street smart. You are likely to be heckled—just ignore it—or hit on in the coastal resorts.

THE SINAI PENINSULA

The Sinai Peninsula is a bridge between continents, and for ages travelers from Europe, Africa, and Asia have crossed and recrossed it. It's also one of history's hotbeds of conflict, where time and the elements have weighed in on the harsh terrain, leaving behind majestic landscapes cradled by the crystal blue waters of the Red Sea and the gulfs of Aqaba to the east and Suez to the west. On its desert sands more than 4,000 years ago, ancient Egyptian expeditions set out in search of copper and turquoise. Here, Moses led the Israelites across arid wastes before moving north to their promised land. Christian Europe's crusaders marched through the Sinai from the 11th through the 13th centuries, trying to take the Holy Land from the Muslims who ruled it. During the 20th century, Egypt and Israel traded the land back and forth in war as they fought for it in 1967 and 1973, launching the desert once again onto the world's strategic stage.

Forty million years ago, the Sinai was part of the African-Asian landmass. Then seismic activity began a process that split the landmass into two separate plates—Saudi Arabia and Yemen on one side and Egypt and Sudan on the other—each plate pulling equally in opposite directions. Further plate motion tore at and wrinkled the region, creating a protected underwater ecology, and leaving vast uninhabited areas of rugged mountain terrain and arid desert.

Three geological areas make up the Sinai. The first lies to the north and consists mainly of pure, shifting, soft sand dunes. Herein lie ancient *wadis* (dried-up riverbeds), where you can find fossils from the Mediterranean. The second area is in the central part of the peninsula, a flat elevated plateau broken occasionally by limestone outcroppings and water sources. Toward the south of the central massif, the landscape begins to change to a granite and volcanic rocky region—the beginnings of the third area, which forms a natural barrier between desert and sea. If you are driving into southern Sinai through the mountains, look out for that breathtaking view of the blue sea peeking out from behind the mountains.

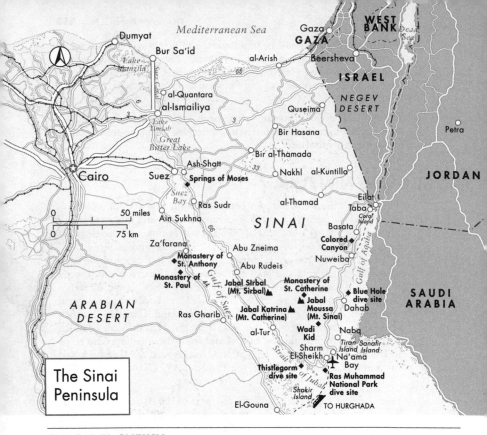

The Sinai Peninsula

SHARM EL-SHEIKH

510 km (320 mi) southeast of Cairo.

In the mid-1980s, Sharm El-Sheikh, at the Sinai's southern tip, had one hotel, two dive centers, and a snack bar. Today this bustling little town has more than 160 hotels, with respective dive centers, malls, casinos, and restaurants, and more Europeans than Egyptians. This exponential expansion marks the town as Egypt's key resort in what marketers call the Red Sea Riviera. Indeed, Sharm, as it is fondly called, is known for having some of Egypt's most lavish hotels, world-renowned dive centers, and nightlife galore. In many ways the town is more than a little schizophrenic. It's now a firm favorite for fun-in-the sun singles, couples, and families, but every so often this small corner of the Sinai takes to the world stage when political leaders gather for summit meetings or peace talks related to Middle East issues. The summit of May 2008 saw more than 150 world leaders—including President George W. Bush—and their associated entourages transform the town into a giant think tank.

Get rid of any preconceived notions of visiting a barren wasteland rich in archaeological sites and a simple desert lifestyle. If your aim is to dive, snorkel, enjoy outdoor and water activities, or simply to lounge before you hit the nightlife scene, you're in the right place. Sharm also makes a solid base for nearby desert sites, which can be visited on day trips.

There are four main areas within the vicinity of Sharm El-Sheikh. The most popular is known as Na'ama Bay, the central hub with the majority of the hotels, restaurants of various culinary merit, souvenir-filled shops, key nightspots, and excellent dive centers. North of Na'ama Bay is the new district of Nabq, which has a handful of large resort hotels. South of Na'ama Bay is Hadaba (the name means plateau), where the main highlight is the view of the surrounding area, and the number of hotels has been rising. South of Hadaba, Sharm al-Maya is often called downtown Sharm El-Sheikh. It's set on the more down-to-earth Sharm El-Sheikh harbor, where the dive boats dock at night. Here are more hotels, as well as typically Egyptian *ahwas* (cafés) where men smoke *shisha* (water pipes) and play backgammon.

Sharm isn't the place for sightseeing: the resorts don't have any sights to see. It's the seaside activities—windsurfing, parasailing, waterskiing, and diving and snorkeling—and side trips to the desert that make boredom an unknown quantity here.

> **DID YOU KNOW?**
>
> There are two theories regarding the origin of the name *Sinai*. The ancient inhabitants of this desert worshipped Sin, a moon goddess, therefore naming the land in her honor—perhaps. Or it could be that the Semitic word *sin* (tooth) gets the credit; the peninsula indeed has the shape of a tooth.

6

NEED A BREAK?

We know you don't need a full review of **Starbucks** (⊠ *King of Bahrain St., Old Market Area, Na'ama Bay* ☏ *069/360–2238*), but we have decided to make an exception for this branch, whose ever-willing staff happily takes nonstandard orders and serves the best coffee we've had at the chain. Plus the apple pie with cinnamon is delicious. A prime location means the whole gamut of visitors passes your table in the evenings.

WHERE TO EAT

The Na'ama Bay boardwalk is restaurant central. Grilled sea bass marinated in lemon juice, pepper, onions, and fresh garlic, served with french fries, is a local favorite. If you'd rather not bother with fish bones, look for flounder grilled or fried, served with lemon juice and a tasty garnish.

$$

MIDDLE EASTERN

★

✕ **Abou el Sid.** The best traditional Egyptian cuisine in the area is served here in an air-conditioned dining room or on an ample terrace. The number of Middle Eastern clients here tells you the food is authentic. Try a selection of mezze, which include excellent stuffed vine leaves and tabbouleh, or opt for an entrée of roast quail or slow-cooked lamb shank served with rice. Be prepared for massive portions; it's easy to order too much food and find yourself overwhelmed. The restaurant serves alcohol and has a good, if expensive, selection of Egyptian wines. Stay after your meal to enjoy a *shisha* and some mint tea. ⊠ *Sultan Qabous St., Na'ama Bay* ☏ *069/352–0320* ▭ *AE, MC, V* ◯ *No lunch.*

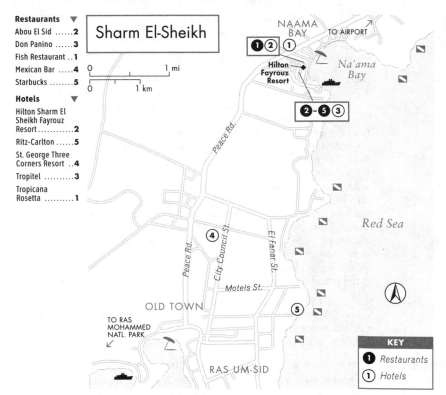

Sharm El-Sheikh

KEY
1 Restaurants
① Hotels

$ ✕**Don Panino.** Mouth-watering wraps, pizza slices, and sandwiches are
FAST FOOD   the backbone of this modern eatery with a terrace made for people-
watching on one of Na'ama Bay's busiest pedestrian thoroughfares. The
freshest, crispiest salad ingredients combine with Cajun beef or barbecue chicken in the wraps; these and the sandwiches are made to order
in a clean, open kitchen. Unlike many fast-food joints in town, you can
get chilled beer here, plus a selection of sodas. Don Panino's makes a
great pit stop any time of the day, but it's very popular for post-clubbing
refreshments since it stays open until 4 AM. ⊠*King of Bahrain St., Old
Market Area, Na'ama Bay* ☎*069/360–0601* ☐*AE, MC, V.*

$$$$ ✕**Fish Restaurant.** One of the most upscale restaurants in Sharm, Fish
SEAFOOD   Restaurant serves a short menu of nouvelle-style seafood, where your
food is like a picture on a plate. Popular choices include expertly prepared fillets, calamari, and lobster. The silver service and outdoor terrace out in the mature garden just off the beachfront boulevard let you
know that this restaurant is all about image and special occasions, and
accordingly, the dress code is casual-elegant. A splurge here is rewarded
with a better wine list and more attentive service than you'll find at
the more mainstream restaurants. ⊠*Hilton Sharm El-Sheikh Fayrouz
Resort, Peace Rd., Na'ama Bay* ☎*069/360–0136* ⟁*Reservations
essential* ☐*AE, DC, MC, V* ☾*No lunch.*

$$ ✗**Mexican Bar.** The decor and name suggest Tex-Mex, but the menu
ECLECTIC runs from Italy to the Alamo via the Far East. Despite the geographical stretch, the kitchen does a good job whether you order the spicy fajitas or the pasta carbonara, and there's a large terrace where you can enjoy your food in relative calm, somewhat removed from the throng of the Old Market area. Mexican Bar has a full range of international liquor brands including a selection of tequilas, and it's a popular pre-club meeting place as evening turns to night. ✉*Tropitel Na'ama Bay Hotel, Corner of Sultan Qabous St. and King of Bahrain St., Old Market Area, Na'ama Bay* ☎*069/360–0570* 🗖*AE, MC, V.*

WHERE TO STAY

$$$ 🏨**Hilton Sharm El Sheikh Fayrouz Resort.** Sitting across the boardwalk from the largest section of beachfront on Na'ama Bay, this hotel is a low-rise series of whitewashed bungalows within mature gardens. One of the town's oldest resorts, it certainly isn't showing its age, with crisp paintwork and clipped lawns indicating an all-around attention to detail. The resort provides a full range of water sports and a robust program of land-based activities and excursions that attract families and couples of all ages (though there are fewer singles here than at other resorts in this party town). **Pros:** Within walking distance of downtown Na'ama Bay and all its attractions; a good range of sports and activities available on-site; family rooms (limited number) mean kids aren't hidden behind a connecting door. **Cons:** Rooms at the very front of the property look out over the Na'ama Bay boardwalk and lack privacy; family atmosphere may not appeal to singles. ✉*Peace Rd., Na'ama Bay* ☎*069/360–0136* ⊕*www.hilton.com* ➶*206 rooms, 4 suites* ⅙*In-room: safe, Internet. In-hotel: 3 restaurants, room service, bars, tennis court, pools, beachfront, diving, water sports, children's programs (ages 4–11), laundry service, Wi-Fi, parking (free), some pets allowed, no-smoking rooms* 🗖*AE, DC, MC, V* ¶⃝*BP.*

$$$$ 🏨**Ritz-Carlton.** Combining the sensuality of ancient Egypt and the
★ breezy hush of a desert oasis, the Ritz offers its guests the definitive Red Sea resort experience. The Ritz has thought of everything, from aromatherapy and massage treatments in a tent overlooking the sea to childproof rooms and bathrooms. A maze of freshwater streams allows guests to float through lush gardens and waterfalls. In the evening, you can dine at one of five unique restaurants featuring Lebanese, Italian, and Asian cuisines. Finish your evening at the Cigar Divan, where tuxedo-clad waiters will serve you a perfect martini with your Cuban cigar. **Pros:** Excellent spa on-site; expansive, lush gardens and grounds. **Cons:** Away from the buzz of downtown. ✉*Om El-Sid, Hadaba* ⌖*Box 72, South Sinai* ☎*069/366–1919* ⊕*www.ritzcarlton.com* ➶*286 rooms, 35 suites* ⅙*In-room: safe, Internet. In-hotel: 5 restaurants, room service, bars, tennis courts, pools, gym, spa, beachfront, diving, water sports, laundry service, parking (free)* 🗖*AE, DC, MC, V* ¶⃝*BP.*

$$ 🏨**St. George Three Corners Resort.** High on the escarpment between Na'ama Bay and downtown Sharm El-Sheikh, this family-friendly hotel is highly regarded by the British visitors who frequent it. The kitchens cater to special dietary needs such as dishes for diabetics. Rooms are simply furnished but spacious enough to store the extra equipment

(strollers, etc.) that families might be toting. There are always organized activities around the busy pool, but the hotel balances this with a separate quiet pool. Enjoy the fully equipped gym and five-room spa. A shuttle bus provides access to the hotel's beach. **Pros:** Excellent range of amenities for the price point; very much a family hotel, so children will feel at home. **Cons:** Sunbeds around the pool are rather cheek by jowl; it's not on the beach; it's a taxi ride to restaurants and nightlife. ⊠*Magless El Madina St., Um El Sid* ☎*069/366–0888* ⊕*www.three corners.com* ⤏*262 rooms* ⚹*In-room: safe, refrigerator. In-hotel: 2 restaurants, room service, bars, gym, spa, diving, water sports, laundry service, Internet terminal, no-smoking rooms* �A|BP.

$$$ ⊡**Tropicana Rosetta.** This large hotel is on the mountain side off Peace Road, offering comfortable accommodation and good facilities without the frills—or price tag—of the typical four- or five-star Sharm resort. Budget-minded travelers will appreciate the three discrete pool areas (ask for a room at the very top of the resort for views across the largest pool). The dive center is one of the most respected in Na'ama Bay, and clients include dive trainees and dive aficionados in addition to couples and families with older children of many nationalities. It's a 3- to 5-minute walk to the nearest public beach. **Pros:** Excellent pool facilities for a hotel in this price range; within easy access of Na'ama Bay's downtown but away from the hubbub. **Cons:** Lack of a beach won't suit families with young children; the dining room has not been expanded as new rooms have been added, so breakfast can be very busy during prime hours. ⊠*Peace Rd., Na'ama Bay* ☎*069/360–1888* ⊕*www.tropicanahotels.com* ⤏*358 rooms* ⚹*In-room: safe, refrigerator. In-hotel: 3 restaurants, bars, pools, diving, laundry service, Internet terminal, parking (free)* ☰*AE, DC, MC, V* A|BP.

$$$$ ⊡**Tropitel Na'ama Bay Hotel.** Contributing to the heartbeat of Na'ama Bay with its restaurants and clubs, this hotel puts you where it all happens. To reach the hotel's beach you must cross the Na'ama Bay boardwalk and go through the Na'ama Bay Casino (a couple of minutes' walk), but the free-form pool offers ample compensation on-site. The five-story horseshoe-shaped building backs against a hillside, so most rooms have excellent sea views. Rooms are bright, with turquoise marine accents. The downtown location suits young singles and couples but also those who want to be one step from shopping and a range of eateries. **Pros:** Downtown location is great for fun-lovers; rooms on the upper floors have private balconies. **Cons:** Can be some noise from Na'ama Bay's clubs, which remain open until 3 or 4 AM; not a lot of room around the pool if the hotel is full. ⊠*Corner of Sultan Qabous St. and King of Bahrain St., Old Market Area, Na'ama Bay* ☎*069/360–0570* ⊕*www.tropitelhotels.com* ⤏*327 rooms, 10 suites* ⚹*In-room: safe, Wi-Fi. In-hotel: 3 restaurants, room service, bars, tennis court, gym, spa, diving, water sports, children's programs (ages 6– 14), laundry service, Wi-Fi, parking (paid), no-smoking rooms* ☰*AE, DC, MC, V* A|BP, MAP, FAP, AI.

SPORTS & THE OUTDOORS

DIVING Almost every hotel rents space to independent dive shops, most of which provide the same services for the same prices: PADI, NAUI, and CMAS courses from beginner to instructor levels; three- to seven-day safaris; and daily trips to Ras Muhammad, Tiran, and other local sites. What sets the dive centers apart is their degree of professionalism, quality of guides and boats, and levels of hospitality. Supervised introductory dives, local boat dives, and shore dives cost about €40 for two dives, weights included. Longer boat dives cost about €60; daily equipment rental costs €15; and a five-day, open-water certificate course costs about €350.

Tiran, one of Sharm's most-visited sites, is a one-hour drive east off the coast. It can be rough as you cross the Straits of Tiran, but it is well worth the trip. On a day of diving you cover two of the four reefs in this area; north to south they are Jackson, Woodhouse, Thomas, and Gordon. It is popular for its strong fly currents—there are drift dives only—and rich coral walls, and you may spot some big fish.

The *Thistlegorm* is a British World War II ship that the Germans sank in 1942 off the western shore of the Sinai. The ship was carrying, among other things, a train, cannons, jeeps, motorcycles, crates of guns, and boots. Now the *Thistlegorm* lies 100 feet down in the Gulf of Suez. The wreck is a diving-safari favorite, and some companies in Sharm will organize a day of diving that begins at 4 AM and returns you to Sharm, exhausted, at 5 PM. Strong currents and low visibility make this a hard dive, but it's a fantastic site.

Ras Nasrani is a favorite shore dive 18 km (11 mi) northeast of Na'ama Bay that is also often done by boat. From the shore you may get lucky and get a private tour of the reef with the resident napoleon fish. He will take you around and bring you right back to the entry point. Remember *not* to feed him, or any other fish.

★ **Ras Muhammad National Park,** the southernmost tip of the Sinai Peninsula, is considered one of the world's top dive sites. With great beaches and more than 10 reefs to choose from, the park is a great place for shore and boat diving. The yellow starkness of the desert contrasts wonderfully with the explosion of life and color under the water. The most popular boat-dive plan includes Shark's Reef and Jolanda Reef, where you can see hordes of great fish, beautiful coral, and some toilets and sinks deposited by the Cypriot freighter *Jolanda,* which sank here in 1980. ✉ *30 km (15 mi) south of Sharm El-Sheikh.*

If you want to be pampered, check in with **International Divers** (✉ *White House, Peace Rd., Na'ama Bay* ☎ *069/360–0865* ⊕ *www.diversintl. com*), one of the oldest centers in the area, which has other centers in the Sofitel Hotel and in two hotels in Hurghada. Managed by a team of professional divers who have been here for almost 20 years, International Divers owns its own boats, which means that even if you are the only diver booked, your excursion will not be canceled. The company also picks you up from your hotel and drops you off there at the end

6

of the day. Or you can return to the dive center for a comfortable chat and coffee with the dive guides and instructors.

Ocean College Dive Centre (✉ *Hilton Waterfalls Hotel, Ras Um El-Sid, Hadaba* ☎ *069/366–4305* ⊕ *www.ocean-college.com*) runs excellent courses but also offers a live-aboard diving option if you'd rather concentrate on enjoying the ocean depths than hit the bars in downtown Sharm. Other Ocean College centers can be found at the Ocean Club Hotel and the Na'ama Bay Hotel.

Red Sea Waterworld (✉ *Hyatt Regency Hotel, Gardens Bay, Na'ama Bay* ☎ *069/362–0315* ⊕ *www.redseawaterworld.com*), a five-star PADI dive center, works in collaboration with the National Geographic dive educator program. In addition to individual courses, it offers family dive training, including kid-friendly hours and supervision on boats so that parents don't have to worry if their children don't dive or don't stay down as long as they do.

The Swiss-run **SUBEX** (✉ *Maritim Jolie Ville Resort and Casino, Na'ama Bay* ☎ *069/360–0122* ⊕ *www.subex.org*) has an international reputation for being tightly run (if a bit stringent) and well equipped with staff, facilities, and gear. Guided dives go out with a maximum of four people, you must take a guide with you if you have fewer than 30 dives, and all divers have to go on an orientation dive to determine experience levels. There are good programs for junior divers.

SNORKELING   Snorkeling is quite popular on the Sinai coast. All dive centers rent snorkeling equipment, and some run specific snorkeling trips, though there's also good snorkeling from shore at most resorts. In addition, you can join diving trips as a nondiver with snorkeling gear; the downside is that you will be left to your own devices, snorkeling by yourself as the guide takes the divers into deeper waters. This could be disconcerting at best, dangerous at worst, especially if you are unfamiliar with the water conditions.

Unlike scuba diving, you do not need certification to rent and use snorkeling equipment. ■TIP➜ **Wherever you snorkel, wear a T-shirt or even a wet suit to protect your back from the sun. Sunscreen alone absolutely does not provide enough protection.**

Divers International (✉ *Sofitel, Na'ama Bay* ☎ *062/600–276*) has a one-day snorkeling excursion aboard one of three dive boats. You visit some of the area's most pristine locations, have lunch, and bask in the sun. The price including lunch and equipment is €38 to €43 per person.

Red Sea Waterworld (✉ *Hyatt Regency Hotel, Gardens Bay, Nabq* ☎ *069/362–0315* ⊕ *www.redseawaterworld.com*), alongside a recommendable dive operation, offers active help for its nondivers as well as a short introductory session to help you master the basics if you've never snorkeled before.

Sun 'n Fun (✉ *Beach Boardwalk, Hilton Sharm El Sheikh Fayrouz Resort, Peace Rd., Na'ama Bay* ☎ *069/360–0136 ext. 170* ⊕ *www.sunnfunsinai. com*) offers snorkeling trips that last from one hour to a full day.

GOLF What do California fan palms, Jerusalem thorns, Hong Kong orchids, and sand dunes have in common? They can all be found at the **Sharm El-Sheikh Golf Resort** (✉ *Maritim Jolie Ville Golf & Resort Sharm El Sheikh, Um Marikha Bay, Na'ama Bay* ☎ *069/600–200* ⊕ *www.jolieville-hotels.com*), which has Egypt's top golf course. Set along the Red Sea between Sharm El-Sheikh International Airport and the center of Na'ama Bay, this Sanford Associates–designed expanse of green is a well-watered oasis. The 18-hole course has 17 lakes, and PGA-qualified professionals are on hand to give lessons. Call ahead for tee times and to schedule lessons.

WATER There are so many water sports to choose from here—waterskiing (you
SPORTS can take lessons or barefoot ski), windsurfing, parasailing, and paddleboating. Another favorite, banana boating, is great fun, with a hint of danger: five or six people straddle a yellow, banana-shape boat and hold on for dear life as a speedboat pulls them around the bay. The driver will try to throw you off by taking sharp turns. Just hope you don't fall onto any fire coral.

Be prepared to pay for whatever you choose to do: about $15 for a 15-minute round of waterskiing; $15 for an hour of windsurfing; $36 for 10 minutes of parasailing for a single ($60 for two). Ask your hotel what activities it offers, or head to the beach at Na'ama Bay where several watersports companies operate right from the beach, offering a wide array of activities for hotel guests and nonguests. **Sun 'n Fun** (✉ *Beach Boardwalk, Hilton Sharm El-Sheikh Fayrouz Resort, Peace Rd., Na'ama Bay* ☎ *069/360–0136 ext 170* ⊕ *www.sunnfunsinai.com*) offers a wide selection of activities from its water sports center.

SHOPPING

For quality Egyptian-produced souvenirs, Sharm is disappointing, but it's brimming with shops selling mass-produced goods. Most hotels have their own shopping arcades, but their prices will be at least double what you would pay in Cairo. The only thing you might have an easier time finding in Sharm would be Red Sea or Sinai T-shirts. So if you plan to spend any time in Cairo at all, save your shopping for there.

Aladin (✉ *King of Bahrain St., Na'ama Bay* ☎ *069/360–0305* ⊕ *www.aladinsinai.com*) is the best place for genuine Egyptian handicrafts from small collectibles to fashion accessories to furniture. There are four branches in Sharm.

Mercato (✉ *Hadabet Um El Seed, Hadaba* ☎ *069/366–2204*) is a smart, open-air Italian Renaissance–style mall that opened in early 2008. Stores sell recognizable brand names, and cafés include Starbucks and Costa. Familiar names in the mall include Virgin Megastore, Timberland, and The Body Shop.

The **Sharm El-Sheikh Marketplace** (✉ *Na'ama Bay, across from Pacha nightclub*), has more than 20 stores that sell everything from carpets to expensive jewelry, from water pipes to T-shirts.

Sharm Old Market (✉ *At the end of Peace Rd., Downtown*) is the largest traditional shopping area in the Sharm El-Sheikh region. In addition to the usual kitsch souvenirs, you can find genuine handmade Bedouin carpets and leather goods fabricated in small family-owned workshops.

NIGHTLIFE

Sharm El-Sheikh may be hot, but the nightlife is super-cool. The resort is one of the must-play gigs on the international celebrity DJ circuit, and the clubs are thronged by the young and beautiful from around Europe. The town buzzes into the early hours of the morning; after a night of dancing, you can seek out one of the many *shisha* cafés, where you simply sink into a carpeted lounger and reflect on whatever comes to mind. If you feel lucky, head to the casino for slots or the gaming tables.

BARS **Ghazala Beach Bar** (⊠ *Beach Boardwalk, Ghazala Hotel, Na'ama Bay* ☎ *065/346–0150*) is where almost everyone makes their way at some point during a Sharm vacation. Big-screen sports, a three-hour happy hour, and the vocal talents of Zaki (who covers 1970s to '90s chart music) every evening between 9 PM and midnight, mean there's always something going on. It's fun and lighthearted enough for all ages.

Camel Bar (⊠ *Camel Hotel, King of Bahrain St., Na'ama Bay* ☎ *069/ 360–0700*) is Sharm's original "anything goes" dive bar and continues its run. Regulars love the down-at-the-heels main bar, with its scattering of ground nut shells on the floor, but if you head to the roof bar, you'll find a more comfortable area with plump cushions and rugs— ringside seats for the Na'ama Bay evening bustle.

Little Buddha (⊠ *Tropitel Na'ama Bay Hotel, Corner of Sultan Qabous St. and King of Bahrain St., Old Market Area, Na'ama Bay* ☎ *069/360– 1030* ⊕ *www.littlebuddha-sharm.com*), a sibling of the ultrasophisticated Buddha Bar in Paris, is a cool lounge offering great music and a laid-back vibe from the resident DJ (or the occasional special guest) along with a sushi bar and restaurant. The atmosphere suits couples and singles over 25.

CLUBS It's possible to turn day into night at **El Fanar** (⊠ *Ras Umm Sid, Hadaba* ☎ *069/366–2218* ⊕ *www.elfanar.net*). This beach club has an Italian restaurant and transforms itself into a buzzing, open-air dance club by night. The setting is particularly dramatic, with fantastic coastal vistas that can distract from the dance floor. Chill out away from the beat in various private, carpeted corners and on the rocks, which are stunningly lit by the varying hues of the disco floor.

Kamanga (⊠ *Peace Rd., Na'ama Bay* ☎ *069/360–0610*) is an ultra-contemporary restaurant, club, and lounge with a long cocktail list and innovative menu that aims to appeal to a more sophisticated clientele. It's one of the town's smaller open-air venues and just out of earshot of the clubs of central Na'ama Bay.

★ **Pacha** (⊠ *King of Bahrain St., Na'ama Bay* ☎ *069/360–0197* ⊕ *www. pachasharm.com*) is the queen of Sharm clubs because of its association with the famed Ministry of Sound London (the club that introduced house and trance music to Europe) and HedKandi (the house-music production label). This open-air venue hosts weekend sessions by alumni from the DJ Hall of Fame. When the house DJs are in residence, there's a rotating program of funk, house, or trance with regular chill-out sessions. It's a must-visit location for under-25's from around Europe.

CASINOS The dramatic lighting on the **Na'ama Bay Casino** (⊠ *Beachfront, Na'ama Boardwalk, Na'ama Bay* ☎*069/360–0705* ⊕*www.naamabaycasino. net*) makes it looks like a pirate ship docking in town. Perhaps if you lose a few dollars you might feel the analogy appropriate. Roulette, blackjack, and poker tables are available, plus lines of slots.

Sinai Grand Casino (⊠ *Peace Rd., Na'ama Bay* ☎*069/360–1050* ⊕*www. sinaigrandcasino.com*) became the Middle East's largest casino when it opened in 2008, and it's a veritable palace for the gaming tables. Blackjack and several styles of poker keep gamblers happy, plus there are hundreds of slots. Vegas-style shows and a restaurant put the icing on the cake.

ST. CATHERINE'S MONASTERY

★ *240 km (150 mi) northwest of Sharm El-Sheikh.*

The very image of the walled monasteries pictured in luxurious medieval tapestries, St. Catherine's rests at the foot of Mt. Sinai, nestled in a valley between jagged granite mountains. The monastery-cum-fortress was commissioned by the Byzantine emperor Justinian in AD 530 to protect those of Greek Orthodox faith. It also served as a strategic post on a bandit-ridden caravan route connecting Africa to Asia.

About 12 Greek Orthodox monks live and work here; the archbishop, who resides in Cairo, visits at Easter and other important holidays. Outside and around the monastery live the Christian Bedouin of the Jabaliyeh tribe, who have long served the monks by working in the gardens and orchards.

Buildings within the monastery have been erected and expanded upon throughout the centuries. The most important of these are the basilica, the Chapel of the Burning Bush, the monks' quarters, the Skull House, and the library, with its treasury of rare books that includes a 4th-century translation of the Hebrew Bible commissioned by Constantine the Great (the library is closed to the public). All buildings are enclosed by the fortress wall, which ranges in height and thickness as it adapts to the shape of the encompassing mountains.

Stepping through the modern-day north side entrance, you see the fountain of Moses to your left. It serves as the main source of fresh water. To the right, a minaret of a mosque was built in the 10th century in order to protect the church from the Fatimid Caliph's order to destroy all churches and monasteries. After passing the fountain, step through to the **basilica,** also known as the Church of the Transfiguration, in which the apse is adorned with an ancient mosaic of the Transfiguration of Jesus. Chandeliers and decorated ostrich eggs hang from the ceiling, and gilded icons from Crete decorate the walls. Take your time in here—there are treasured works of art all around. The basilica doors date to the 6th century.

6

The **Chapel of the Burning Bush,** behind the basilica, is the most sacred of the buildings in the monastery. Unfortunately, it's not always open to the public. Dating from the 4th century AD, the chapel is the oldest part of the church, and its walls are covered with icons, of which the monastery itself has 2,000. (You can see yet more icons in the hall next to the library; the rest are kept in secured rooms, closed to the public.) Outside the chapel, you can see the bush where it is believed that God spoke to Moses. Many attempts to transplant branches of the bush have failed.

The **Skull House** is a chamber to which the bones of deceased monks are transferred from the cemetery after five years of internment. (The burial plot is very small and must be constantly reused.) The skulls number around 1,500 and are lined up in neat rows. ☎069/347–0346 ⚄Free ☽ *Mon.–Thurs. and Sat. 9–noon.*

WHERE TO STAY

Better roads and improved journey times between St. Catherine's and the coastal resorts—not to mention the easy availability of day trips to the interior—have combined to cause accommodation close to the monastery (and Mt. Sinai) to suffer in quality. If you want a luxurious stay, book a hotel in Sharm El-Sheikh and make an early morning start to reach the monastery.

$$ ⛉Morganland Village. The stunning setting of this hotel is awe-inspiring—it is surrounded by the peaks of the Sinai range that are reflected throughout the day in the waters of the on-site swimming pool. The rooms, which are set around the pool, were completed in the late 1990s, but the interiors haven't fared as well as the exterior spaces, exhibiting careworn fittings and accessories. The Bedouin marketplace on-site has some atmosphere, selling a variety of local handicrafts as well as mass-produced souvenirs. **Pros:** Proximity to the start of the Mt. Sinai hike and St. Catherine's Monastery; excellent pool with stunning vistas. **Cons:** Careworn rooms; little atmosphere as most guests pass through on a one-night stay. ✉*3 km (2 mi) from St. Catherine's Monastery, just east of St. Catherine Rd., near the Zeituna area* ☎069/470–404 ⬦248 rooms ⚄In-hotel: restaurant, pool, parking (free) ☰No credit cards* ⍟MAP.

JABAL MOUSSA (MT. SINAI)

240 km (149 mi) northeast of Sharm El-Sheikh.

From the base of Mt. Sinai, any fellow hikers who have preceded you look like dots 7,504 feet ahead of you, and the prospect of reaching the top begins to assume biblical proportions. As you step up to the mountain, the serenity of the surrounding hills is disturbed only by passersby and the odd camel driver seeking your patronage. Stop every now and then to notice how the clean desert mountain air awakens your senses. The dusty rose tone of the granite mountains and the absolute peace makes it no surprise that this land has fostered so many religious expeditions and revelations. New Age advocates also believe there are ley

St. Catherine

Born in Alexandria to a ruling family in the 4th century, Catherine was a highly educated and erudite woman for her time. She presented herself at the court of Roman Emperor Maximinius to plead for the lives of Christians who were routinely put to death by his regime. Maximinius organized a caucus of learned men to refute and confound Catherine's arguments, but in fact the caucus was won over by her arguments. When they converted to Christianity, Maximinius had them put to death while Catherine was whipped and thrown into a cell. The Emperor's wife paid a visit, chaperoned by the head of the Roman army. They, too, heard Catherine's message and were converted—and were soon added to the list of Christian martyrs. After the conversion and martyrdom of the Emperor's wife, Catherine was put under sentence of death on the breaking (spiked) wheel. However, when she approached it, the apparatus fell to pieces under her touch. Undeterred, the Emperor had Catherine beheaded, but after her death it was said that angels carried her bones to the flanks of Mount Sinai where the monastery now sits.

In the centuries that followed, Catherine became a mainstream female saint, and virtuous maidens where especially devoted to her. She was included on the list of the "Fourteen Holy Helpers"; Joan of Arc said at her trial that she had been visited by the saint and was inspired to take on her crusade.

The spiked wheel that should have been the original means of her martyrdom—a popular form of torture in medieval times—became known as the Catherine wheel, and this name later transferred to the round firework that whirls at celebrations in modern times.

St. Catherine is still very much revered by Christians in the Orthodox and Catholic communities, but there is very little incontrovertible evidence that she actually existed. Some scholars have pondered whether Catherine had been a fictitious character whose story—the embodiment of maidenly Christian virtue—was meant to inspire medieval worshippers.

lines of gravitational energy running through the landscape here. Whatever you believe, it's truly a humbling place.

Mt. Sinai rises above St. Catherine's Monastery to the spot where Moses is supposed to have received the Ten Commandments. Scholars have debated the legitimacy of this claim for millennia now and have resolved nothing. Other locations have been suggested for the biblical Mt. Sinai, but the mountain's position on the chief ancient trade route and the accounts in the journals of pilgrims do seem to substantiate the claim for this mountain.

In 1934, a small chapel dedicated to the Trinity was built on the summit of Jabal Moussa, covering the ruins of a previous Justinian temple. Looking southeast from the peak, you'll have a crystal-clear view of the top of Mt. Catherine, which is the highest point on the Sinai Peninsula at 8,652 feet. With granite mountains in all directions, it may feel like you're at the center of the earth.

There are two routes up the mountain, and two essential times of day at which to start. The climb takes between 2½ and 3 hours. For a very steep climb, take the 3,750 steps that begin behind the monastery and lead directly to the summit. Please note that this is not exactly a proper staircase, and if you have knee problems, this will only exacerbate them. There is another route that is also a camel track; its last 230 feet consists of 700 steps. If you take this route, you can bet that drivers will ask—repeatedly—if you want a ride. If you opt for the camel, ask around for the going rate, then haggle. Expect to pay around £e60.

The climb is strenuous, and you'll need to take along water and a snack to eat at the top (bring a backpack if you can). Many visitors begin this climb around 2 AM to arrive at the summit at sunrise. If you are here during January, February, or March, it won't be too hot for a midday trip (which is much less crowded); at other times, it will be. If you're going to do the night hike, take long pants, because it gets cold, and a good flashlight, and wear layers that you can take off and put back on as you warm up and cool down. A solid pair of shoes (preferably hiking boots) is also essential.

DAHAB

100 km (55 mi) northeast of Na'ama Bay.

The drive from Sharm to Dahab snakes through the mountains of south Sinai offering you a peek at the precipitous peaks of the interior. Dahab itself is another world, still half-stuck in the 1960s, with New Age believers carrying on the original laid-back hippie philosophy that put this place on the international map. It's also a legendary location in the world of scuba. A new generation of dive students from Northern and Eastern Europe mix with seasoned veterans who return here year after year for the excellent conditions and unpretentious dive community. Many Bedouin have taken up the government's offer of permanent homes in the town, and they've brought along their goats and camels, which roam the streets blissfully uncaring of the 21st-century trucks and buses zipping by. All this adds to the slightly surreal but relaxed atmosphere. There's little more to do here than hang out and snorkel and dive.

Dahab stretches around a headland and now encompasses two flanking bays. Its four main areas are the **Assala**, where you find camps and independent dive resorts; the **Masbat**, a stretch of restaurants, shops, and Bedouin-style cafés that all look the same but blast different music, resulting in a strange cacophony; **Mashrab**, a combination of both the Assala and the Masbat; and **Dahab City**, the modern municipal district with a handful of larger hotels.

If the promise of resort holidays brought you to the Sinai, then Dahab probably isn't for you. Stray cats and dogs might snuggle up to you as you eat dinner. The resort seems to have eschewed large-scale tourist development, though, and it's working well in its own eclectic way.

Diving is the lifeblood of tourism in Dahab, and the waters here provide a top-flight training location. Water entry in Dahab is all done from the shore rather than from dive boats offshore, so entry does require balance and good footing but is much more convenient than it might otherwise be. The town is also known for windsurfing. And Dahab has easy access to some superb inland sights, including the Colored Canyon (*see* ⇨ *Nuweiba, below*). As with any off-the-beaten-path desert excursion, it is a good idea to go with a guide.

The trip to **Wadi Kid** (⊠ *approximately 20 km (12 mi) south of Dahab*) is a gorgeous trek that leads to Ain Kid. Ain in Arabic means "spring." As is often the case in the Sinai, the wadis lead to springs, where the fresh water gives life to luscious green trees and grazing areas. Your hotel can arrange a trip to the wadi. On the way you drive through a Bedouin village. Stop off for a tea in the shade of an acacia tree. This is a great photo op.

WHERE TO EAT

Restaurants and cafés in the Masbat all offer the same thing—pizza, pasta, fish, and chicken. The resorts offer typical breakfast and dinner buffets and have beach bars that serve sandwiches and salads; you might even find a theme lunch.

$ **✕ Al Capone Restaurant.** Al Capone's is one of a dozen Bedouin-style
ECLECTIC cushion-and-carpet outdoor restaurants in the Masbat. If you're not in the mood for pizza or fish, order a vegetable salad, tomatoes with Bulgarian cheese, and *shakshuka* (a spicy Middle Eastern omelette) with pita bread and play a game of backgammon while you wait. There's regular live music served up by a resident DJ. ⊠ *Beachfront Blvd., Masbat* ☎ *069/364–0181* ⊟ *No credit cards.*

WHERE TO STAY

If you don't mind roughing it, you can find inexpensive rooms at any of the camps in the Assala area. Be prudent about what you choose because cheap doesn't imply clean, and rarely does it include private bathrooms. If you must stay at any such establishments, wear flip-flops when you shower. At the hotels, although they are far from the mellow center of town, you can count on a higher quality of comfort and services.

$$ 🛏 **Bedouin Moon Hotel.** At this simple but clean hotel, you'll find the headquarters of Reef 2000, one of the best dive centers in Dahab. Some rooms have fridges, air-conditioning, and balconies, but not all have these features, so ask when you book. You'll stay here for the international client mix, mostly gregarious divers who are repeat customers, and for the pool area, which is excellent for hotels of this standard in the Sinai. The hotel has a resident yoga instructor and offers classes twice daily. **Pros:** Spacious, modern pool and sun terrace on the property; English-speaking management; lively atmosphere for divers. **Cons:** A taxi ride or 30-minute walk from the restaurants and cafés of Masbat; some rooms don't have balconies or a/c; hotel's beach is narrow and rocky. ⊠ *Blue Hole Rd., Assala* ☎ *069/364–0087* ⊕ *hosting.menanet.net/~bedouinmoon/bedouinmoon* 🛏 *29 rooms, 3*

dorm rooms ⚿ In-room: no a/c (some), no phone (some), refrigerator (some), no TV (some). In-hotel: restaurant, bar, pool, diving, water sports, Internet terminal ☰AE, MC, V ⑩BP.

$$$ ⌨ **Hilton Dahab.** The largest resort in Dahab, this Nubian-style, white-washed adobe village is set dramatically against the reddish hues of the Sinai Mountains. Saltwater lagoons and palm trees create a pleasant oasis feel. Rooms are airy and modern and have balconies or terraces. Waterskiing and snorkeling trips can be arranged, and the Club Mistral has a team of windsurfing experts here that teaches all levels. **Pros:** Styling is sympathetic to the local area; direct access to a private beach. **Cons:** A taxi ride away from the Masbat. ⊠ *Dahab City* ⌂ *Box 25* ☎ *069/364–0310* ⊕ *www.hilton.com* ⟿ *141 rooms* ⚿ *In-room: safe, Internet. In-hotel: 4 restaurants, room service, bars, tennis court, pools, beachfront, diving, water sports, laundry facilities, laundry service, parking (free)* ☰AE, D, MC, V ⑩BP.

$$$$ ⌨ **Le Méridien Dahab Resort.** This luxury resort designed by French architect and designer Alain Jaouen offers a 21st-century oasis in the Sinai. The public areas have a simple spacious feel right out of the late 1960s that are reminiscent of interiors from films like *The Thomas Crown Affair* or *Goldfinger* (minus the evil technological gadgets). Pale colors and straight lines dominate from the pool areas to the restaurants. The rooms line up side by side on two terraces below the main building allowing everyone a full view of the ocean. There's a contemporary cottage feel to the decor, and rooms open out onto spacious private balconies or patios. The resort's new spa is scheduled to open in 2009. **Pros:** Visually stunning property that's appeared in style magazines; sea views from all rooms; excellent cuisine at three on-site restaurants. **Cons:** A taxi ride away from the fun and nightlife scene of the Masbat area; there's nothing else in the immediate vicinity; expansion planned for early 2009 may mean some disruption on-site. ⊠ *Al Tahrir St., Dahab City* ⌂ *Box 2, Dahab* ☎ *069/364–0425* ⊕ *www.lemeridien. com* ⟿ *178 rooms, 4 suites* ⚿ *In-room: safe, DVD, Internet, Wi-Fi. In-hotel: 3 restaurants, room service, bars, pools, gym, spa, beachfront, diving, water sports, children's programs (ages 4–11), laundry service, Wi-Fi, parking (paid), no-smoking rooms* ☰AE, DC, MC, V ⑩BP.

NIGHTLIFE

Dahab has a reputation as a laid-back resort once known for its pot-smoking hippies. Things have changed, and today the hippies have been replaced by easygoing divers, while the nightlife scene, which is centered in Masbat, has evolved to include a line of bars and some nightclubs.

Black Prince (⊠ *Beachfront Blvd., Masbat* ☎ *012/412–9578)* is Dahab's major late-night clubbing venue, which attracts a varied mix of nationalities from Brits to Italians to Russians. The retro "Hits" parties are extra popular.

Tota Dance Bar (⊠ *Beachfront Blvd., Masbat* ☎ *069/364–0014)* is the social heart of Dahab for expats and vacationers. You'll recognize Tota by its pirate-ship facade, which takes pride of place on the waterfront walkway. Equal parts sports bar, Internet café, restaurant, and night-club, there's something going on here at all times.

SPORTS & THE OUTDOORS

DIVING The three sites below are about 30 minutes north of Dahab, so you might want to dive with one of the hotel dive centers, which can arrange transportation. Bring water with you, and plan to pass some time relaxing under the awning of a Bedouin cafeteria that provides basic refreshments. No toilet facilities are available, so follow the cardinal rule of the desert: women to the left, men to the right.

A phenomenal dive plan begins at the **Bells** and ends in the **Blue Hole.** This is one of Egypt's most spectacular underwater havens. Although you are unlikely to see sharks or big fish, the platelike coral formations, which run to nearly 1,000 feet below sea level, are gorgeous settings for other awesome marine life. The dive finishes at the mouth of the remarkable Blue Hole, a cone-shape coral enclave that seems to go on forever. Don't miss this dive.

The Canyon, right around the corner from the Blue Hole, is another great dive. You feel as if you're sky diving as you descend through 100 feet of coral cliffs on either side of you.

Poseidon Divers (⊠*Crazy Camel Camp, Mashraba* ☎*069/364–0091* ⊕*www.poseidondivers.com*) offers the PADI/National Geographic Open Water Course and diving Career Development Courses along with other programs, dive safaris, and live-aboards. They also have an office at the Le Méridien Hotel.

Reef 2000 (⊠*Blue Hole Rd., Assala* ☎*069/364–0087* ⊕*www.reef 2000.com*), a PADI Gold Palm resort close to the famed Blue Hole dive site, offers dive training and technical courses, plus guided dives for those already qualified. Their yoga/dive programs are certainly unique. You can also book camel/diving safaris (where the camels carry your equipment and you trek to the dive site, overnighting in a camp) and boat trips.

WATER Dahab is building a reputation as a windsurfing and kite-surfing cen-
SPORTS ter with ideal water and wind conditions. Most hotels have boards to rent, and there's an excellent school for both sports. Dahab Bay glistens with the colorful sails of windsurfers, which rent for €40 per half-day (minimum) or €190 to €210 per week from the **Harry Nass Surf & Action Center** (⊠*Novotel Coralia Dahab, Dahab City* ☎*069/364–0559* ⊕*www.harry-nass.com*).

NUWEIBA

70 km (44 mi) north of Dahab.

Nuweiba serves as both a crucial Gulf of Aqaba port and a resort with a couple of hotel areas and a quaint town center. Its name means "bubbling springs," and Nuweiba has long been an important oasis for Muslim pilgrims en route to Mecca. Sandy beaches and colorful coral reefs accessible from the shore have earned it a reputation as a dive center, though it hasn't thrived in the last decade in the same way as the rest of the Red Sea Riviera.

Maagana Bay, the main port area, sees constant traffic from trucks full of goods and equipment and travelers making their way to Mecca or Jordan. This is where you'll find a post office, telephone office, bus station, and beckoning taxi drivers. About 6 km (4 mi) north of the port lies the touristy city center, its simple stores filled with cheap local clothing, trinkets, souvenirs, and household goods. Inexpensive restaurants serve basic food, and supermarkets carry an adequate range of supplies. But you'll probably spend most of your time enjoying the beach, its coffeehouses, and the Sinai scenery.

> **MAN'S BEST FRIEND?**
>
> In the late 1990s a solitary dolphin, soon named Holly, made a home in the bay off Nuweiba el Muzeina. Though she was a sociable animal who became an international celebrity, she formed a special bond with Abdallah, a deaf fisherman. Over the years, Abdallah succeeded in developing limited language skills, his confidence swelled by this unusual relationship across the species divide. Holly stayed in the area until her death in 2006, and she's much missed by locals and visitors alike.

Nuweiba, which has a population of about 3,000, is the center for two tribes. Their members, once the outstanding fishermen of the Sinai coast, still inhabit the area in two communities: Nuweiba el Muzeina, south of Nuweiba's city center, and Nuweiba Tarabin, to the north.

Because of its central position on the Sinai coast, Nuweiba makes a good base for trekking into the Sinai interior to the Colored Canyon. Getting a glimpse of the Colored Canyon's red, yellow, rose, brown, and purple hues deep within the mountains northwest of Nuweiba is something that you can do only by camel or four-wheel-drive vehicle. The Abanoub Travel Agency *(see Tour Options in Sinai Peninsula Essentials, below)* or your hotel can arrange a trip to the canyon; you can also take tours from Sharm El-Sheikh or Dahab.

WHERE TO EAT

$$$$
MIDDLE
EASTERN

✕**Castle Zaman.** Probably the most unusual restaurant in the northern Sinai, this is to the eye a ruined medieval castle on a bluff above the Sinai coast; however, it was built from scratch starting in the late 1990s by architect Hany Roshdy. Eat in the stone-and-wood interior or on the terraces, which have magnificent views. The menu focuses on traditional slow-cooked dishes, including melt-in-your-mouth lamb shank or skirt steak. Since these dishes take a while to prepare, it's best to book at least a day in advance—to ensure the food is perfect. There's a pool on-site, and the set price includes time for lounging and swimming. ⊹ *On the coast, 25 km (14 mi) north of Nuweiba* ☎ *012/214–0591 or 069/350–1234* ⊕ *www.castlezaman.com* ⚭ *Reservations essential* ☰ *MC, V.*

WHERE TO STAY

$$$ ⊞ Hilton Nuweiba Coral Resort. This Hilton is only a five-minute taxi ride from Nuweiba's port, so it's ideally situated for trips into the Sinai interior as well as to Jordan, which stands directly across the Gulf of Aqaba. The Hilton's white-washed exterior is just about the brightest thing in Nuweiba. Rooms are spacious and clean, decorated with marine themes including underwater photographs. The clientele is a mixture of resort vacationers (predominately European and Eastern European) and short-stay tour groups. Wheelchair-accessible rooms are available, too. **Pros:** Well-maintained resort with mature, shady gardens; a comfortable base not far from most Sinai attractions, almost equidistant from Taba to the north or Sharm to the south; large balconies offer a great space for taking in cooling sea breezes. **Cons:** There's little to do in the immediate area, so it's a taxi ride if you want to eat out or browse for souvenirs. ⊠ *Maagana Bay* ☎ *069/352–0320* ⊕ *www.hilton.com* ⟿ *200 rooms* ⌕ *In-room: safe. In-hotel: 3 restaurants, room service, bar, tennis court, 2 pools, gym, beachfront, diving, water sports, laundry service, Internet terminal, parking (free)* ▤ *AE, DC, MC, V* ⏏︎*BP.*

> ### A CANINE COUSTEAU
>
> The latest Sinai celebrity is Moka, the chocolate Labrador at Castle Zaman who may have been a dolphin in a previous life. She dives to the bottom of the swimming pool at any opportunity to retrieve items thrown in by admiring fans.

$ ⊞ Nakhil Inn. This small, laid-back dive resort is on a wonderful, sandy
★ stretch of beach. Older rooms are spacious, while the newest wing (Nakhil Dreams) is made up of cute wooden bungalows, each with a mezzanine bedroom area. Both room categories have a contemporary style not found in other hotels at this price point along the coast. All have sea views, but you can also enjoy the views day or evening from Bedouin-style seating areas on the beach. The atmosphere is rather like a beachside country club. Owner Samer Aly is an underwater photographer, raconteur, and a great source of knowledge about the area. **Pros:** Neatly kept rooms offer excellent value for money; there's a broad sandy beach on-site; Wi-Fi works even on the beach, so you can surf by the surf. **Cons:** It's a 30-minute walk or a short taxi ride to what passes for downtown Nuweiba. ⊠ *Tarabeen Beach, 2 km (1 mi) north of downtown* ☎ *069/350–0879* ⊕ *www.nakhil-inn.com* ⟿ *28 rooms, 2 suites* ⌕ *In-room: no phone, refrigerator. In-hotel: restaurant, bar, beachfront, diving, Wi-Fi* ▤ *AE, MC, V* ⏏︎*BP.*

SPORTS & THE OUTDOORS

CAMEL   For a real Gertrude Bell or William Thesiger experience, head to the
TREKKING **Habiba Camel Training School** (⊠ *Downtown Nuweiba* ☎ *069/350– 0770* ✑ *habiba@sinai4you.com*), where you can learn about stewardship of this feisty ship of the desert during a three-day course that teaches you about camel characteristics, diet, riding techniques, and day-to-day care. After going through the training and receiving your license, you can choose to embark on a 3- to 10-day safari through the Sinai during which a Bedouin guide shows you the way but you are responsible for your designated animal. You'll live as the Bedouin did, finding kindling

6

for the campfire and sleeping under the stars. Camel School prices are €355 with half-board at Habiba Camp (though you can stay in other accommodation and still attend the course). A three-day trek to the Colored Canyon is €210 with meals, guide, and camel included.

TABA

48 km (30 mi) north of Nuweiba.

Taba borders Israel and is a sister city of the Israeli resort town of Eilat. It has been important since biblical times as a stopover for travelers entering or leaving Egypt.

Pharaoh's Island, so-called because it was first used during the reign of Ramesses III (1194–1163 BC), is a long, rocky island surrounded by reefs and the turquoise waters of the gulf. The best-known period in the island's occupation is marked by the dramatic remains visible from shore. These are the ruined walls of the Crusader outpost created here in 1115 by Baldwin I. For 55 years, the Crusaders controlled both the trade and pilgrimage routes that passed this way from the safety of the island. But in AD 1171, shortly after coming to power in Egypt, Salah al-Din attacked the fortress by surprise, having transported his dismantled ships secretly through the Sinai on camelback. Despite repeated attempts, the Crusaders never again regained control of the island. Most of what now remains dates from the Mamluk period (14th century).

Diving or snorkeling is good around the excellent reefs off the north end of the island (though currents are strong). With its ruined Crusader castle and Ottoman additions, Pharaoh's Island (also known as Coral Island) attracts many a roadside photographer. Boats to the island run from the Salah El-Deen Hotel; in high season the island can get quite crowded with travelers from Eilat and Aqaba. ⊠ *250 yards offshore* ⛴ *Castle $10, ferry $5* ⊙ *Daily 9–5 (boats run every 15 minutes).*

Taba Heights, the northern Sinai's largest new tourist venture, aims to develop into a self-contained settlement anchored by excellent tourist facilities including high-class accommodations, sports outfitters, shopping, and entertainment. This is a project that's still evolving, but already there are five hotels, an excellent dive center, an 18-hole golf course, a wide range of water sports, and a program of excursions, all set against the dramatic backdrop of the Sinai peaks and fronted by 3 miles of golden, sandy beaches. A village-style Old Town, with independent shops and eateries and served by shuttle buses from the hotels, adds interest and dining variety. ⊠ *20 km (12.5 mi) south of Taba.*

WHERE TO EAT

$$$ ✕ **El Mare.** The InterContinental's à la carte seafood restaurant has a quiet
SEAFOOD   beachfront location. You can eat under a canopy of fairy lights or in the circular templelike dining room. The entrees span the expected (an enticing seafood platter) to the imaginative (flaky grouper baked in a sea-salt crust or served in Provençale sauce), while the appetizers and desserts, including a formidable tiramisu, borrow influences from world cuisine.

A Day Trip to Petra

One of the most popular excursions from all Sinai resorts is a day trip to the rose-red city of Petra, in Jordan at the northern tip of the Red Sea. It's a long journey from Sharm El-Sheikh, but only a couple hours' travel from Nuweiba or Taba.

The capital of the Nabataean Empire, which grew rich on trade after the 4th century BC, the city thrived until the 4th century AD and is famed for its excellent collection of rock-cut buildings. The facade of the Treasury will be familiar to you if you have seen *Indiana Jones and the Last Crusade*.

While the trip into Petra is best done at dawn, it's still worth it to enter later in the day if this is likely to be your only chance to visit. Of course, some people simply choose to visit Petra for a two-day trip before their return home. Before you travel, find out from your travel agent if a day trip to a neighboring country is allowable with your Egyptian visa.

✉ *InterContinental Taba Heights Resort, Taba Heights* ☎ *069/358–0300* ♨ *Reservations essential* ▤ *AE, DC, MC, V* ◷ *No lunch.*

6

WHERE TO STAY

$$$$ ☷ **Hyatt Regency Taba Heights.** Looking as if it were designed by Dr. Seuss, the strong colors and off-the-wall lines and curves that characterize the "neo-Nubian" architecture of this resort do set the scene for vacation fun. Rooms with generous balconies or terraces line a seawater lagoon or overlook the golden beach. An immense pool fit for Olympic trainees as well as a spa offer other opportunities for relaxation. Although removed from the other resorts but still within Taba Heights, the Hyatt Regency gives you access to an excellent range of sports and activities for all ability levels. **Pros:** Dramatic architecture; excellent sports programs; access to the other hotels and downtown Taba Heights means you have ample off-resort dining opportunities. **Cons:** Taba Heights is a new tourism complex, so there's no old Sinai feel nearby. ✉ *Taba Heights* ☎ *069/358–0234* ⊕ *www.hyatt.com* ⇥ *426 rooms, 10 suites* ♨ *In-room: safe, Internet. In-hotel: 3 restaurants, room service, bars, golf, tennis courts, pools, gym, spa, beachfront, diving, water sports, children's programs (ages 4–10), laundry service, Wi-Fi, parking (free)* ▤ *AE, DC, MC, V* ◉ *BP.*

$$ ☷ **El Wekala.** Designed along the lines of a grand Arabian family living complex, the shady courtyard with its cooling fountain that greets your arrival at El Wekala draws you into its Moorish appeal while the decorated domes, curved arches, wooden fretwork, and traditional Cairene tiled floors in the rooms add to the atmosphere. In "Old Town" Taba Heights, the hotel's rooms intertwine with the rest of the village, with balconies overlooking verdant squares, restaurants, and cafés that fill with guests in the evenings. The main pool is surrounded by an expansive terrace with panoramic views over the rest of Taba Heights. **Pros:** Villagelike setting gives hotel a more authentic feel rather than a resort feel; excellent sports facilities of Taba Heights available to guests; all-inclusive but offers a dine-around option with other hotels in Taba Heights. **Cons:** The private beach area is remote from the hotel (access by shuttle bus only); corridors resonate sound if you have noisy fellow guests. ⊠ *Taba Heights* ☎ *069/358–0150* ⊕ *www. threecorners.com* ⚲ *178 rooms, 14 duplexes, 14 suites* ⚭ *In-room: safe, refrigerator, Wi-Fi. In-hotel: 2 restaurants, room service, bars, golf course, pools, diving, water sports, bicycles, children's programs (ages 4–12), laundry facilities, laundry service, Internet terminal* ☰ *MC, V* ⑪ *AI.*

SPORTS & THE OUTDOORS

DIVING &
WINDSURFING

The area has the coolest waters in the Egyptian Red Sea, but this does not mean that the diving is disappointing. On the contrary, there are protected reefs running all along the shelf just offshore. Conditions are also ideal for both sailing and windsurfing, and most of the dive centers offer these activities as well.

> **NATIONAL GEOGRAPHIC DIVER**
>
> National Geographic wanted to take dive training to a new level and got together with PADI to formulate its own diving certification program. In addition to the standard requirements for PADI openwater certification, the National Geographic course includes instruction on the marine environment and a module on marine conservation. Only dive centers with a proven track record and a commitment to sustainable diving are chosen by PADI/National Geographic to run these courses, so you can be guaranteed the highest-quality (and most environmentally sensitive) training.

★ **Red Sea Waterworld** (⊠ *Taba Heights* ☎ *069/358–0099* ⊕ *www.redsea waterworld.com*), a PADI five-star Gold Palm Resort and National Geographic Dive Center, has a professional team of managers and a multilingual staff with great modern equipment. It's also a recognized catamaran sailing school and windsurfing school.

GOLF   Warm winter temperatures and an excellent selection of resorts draw Northern European golfers to **Taba Heights Golf Resort** (⊠ *Taba Heights* ☎ *069/358–0073* ⊕ *www.tabaheights.com*) for an easily organized golf break with prearranged tee times. The undulating 18-hole, par-72 course with dramatic mountain- and seascapes was designed by John Sanford. There's PGA tuition, a driving range, and short practice area, plus a well-stocked golf shop.

THE RED SEA COAST

The Red Sea is one of the few seas on earth that is virtually closed, surrounded in this case by arid land: the Sinai to the north, the Eastern Sahara on the west, and the Arabian Peninsula to the east. The sea pours into the gulfs of Aqaba and Suez to the north; to the south, its mouth narrows into the strait of Bab al-Mandeb—The Gate of Tears. The Red Sea is 1,800 km (1,100 mi) long and 350 km (215 mi) wide. Along its central axis, depths reach 10,000 feet. The combination of minimal tidal changes, currents and wind, and almost year-round sunshine fosters the growth of a unique underwater ecology.

The Red Sea has been an important conduit for trade throughout human history. Along its coasts, archaeological sites currently being excavated date as far back as the earliest ancient Egyptian gold and turquoise expeditions, made more than 4,000 years ago. Ottoman outposts are being renovated and will reopen another chapter of life on the edge of the Eastern Sahara. Deeper in the mountains, Christian monastic life began at the Monastery of St. Paul, founded by the eastern church's first known hermit-priest.

Meanwhile the 21st century is very much in evidence as tourism increases in economic importance. Diving started the trend, and though this remains the paramount reason for spending a few days here, new resorts and activities are attracting visitors in ever-increasing numbers.

AIN SUKHNA

120 km (75 mi) southeast of Cairo; 45 km (29 mi) south of Suez.

The waters of Ain Sukhna (the name means "hot spring") originate at Jabal Ataka, a mountain on the Red Sea Coast. The turquoise water is clear and warm year-round. There is little to do here in the way of sightseeing, but it's a convenient day trip from Cairo or the Suez Canal zone if, like picnicking Cairenes, you're looking for a seaside day in the sun. The development along the coastline here has grown rapidly in the last decade, with villas and apartments bought up by wealthy residents of the capital.

6

WHERE TO STAY

$$ 🏨 **Palmera Resort.** On the sea with a beautiful private beach, the Palmera sprawls out into lush gardens. The rather boxy architecture and colorful tropical accents, including sunshine-yellow walls in the rooms, reveal the hotel's age as decidedly late 20th century. However, styling aside, the resort has a good variety of facilities that attract families from Cairo plus an increasing number of foreign (mostly European) vacationers looking for all-inclusive one- or two-week packages. The Egyptian food is good here; try the Pergola poolside restaurant for barbecue with a view of the sea. You can also smoke a shisha in the Arabic coffee shop. **Pros:** Wide, sandy beach; generous main pool; good choice of resort facilities for the price point. **Cons:** Mosquitoes can be a problem; some fixtures and fittings are a little careworn. ✉*30 km (20 mi) south of Suez, on the way to Ain Sukhna* ☎ *062/410–8124* ⊕*www.palmerabeachresort.com* ⇱*282 rooms, 18 suites* ⚓ *In room: safe, refrigerator. In-hotel: 6 restaurants, bars, pools, gym, beachfront, water sports, laundry service, Internet terminal, parking (free)* ▤*AE, MC, V* ⊙*BP.*

THE MONASTERIES OF ST. ANTHONY AND ST. PAUL

Egypt's oldest monasteries stand at the forefront of Christian monastic history. Isolated in the mountains near the Red Sea, they have spectacular settings and views of the coast. Getting to the monasteries isn't exactly a picnic, but their remoteness was the reason the saints chose these caves as their hermitages. The saints' endurance in the desert—against Bedouin raids, changing religious tides, and physical privation—give them an allure augmented by paintings and icons that add color to their otherwise stark appeal.

ARRIVING AND DEPARTING

To get to the monasteries you will need to rent a car or, preferably (because driving in Egypt is such a harrowing experience), hire a private taxi from Cairo (about £e500) or Hurghada (£e225). Note that Copts fast for 43 days in advance of Christmas, during which time most monasteries are closed to visitors. Call before you set out to confirm that the gates will be open.

Thomas Cook (✉ 8 Shar'a al-Sheraton, Hurghada ☎ 065/344–3338 ✉ 17 Mahmoud Bassiouny St., Cairo ☎ 02/2574–5191 ⊕ www.thomascook egypt.com) runs tours to the monasteries from Cairo and Hurghada.

THE MONASTERY OF ST. ANTHONY
110 km (69 mi) southwest of Ain Sukhna.

St. Anthony is a prominent figure in Coptic Christianity because of his influence on the monastic movement. And even though his contemporary Paul was the first hermit, Anthony was the more popular. He was born in the middle of the 3rd century AD to wealthy parents who left him with a hefty inheritance upon their death, when he was 18. Instead of reveling in his riches, he sold all his possessions, distributed the proceeds to the poor, sent his sister to a convent, and fled to dedicate his life to God as a hermit in the mountains overlooking the Red Sea.

Disciples flocked to Anthony, hoping to hear his preaching and to be healed. But the monk sought absolute solitude and retreated to a cave in the mountain range of South Qabala. After his death in the 4th century—the hermit lived to age 104—admirers built a chapel and refectory in his memory. St. Anthony's grew. In the 7th, 8th, and 11th centuries, periodic Bedouin predations severely damaged the structure. It was restored in the 12th century.

St. Anthony's is deep in the mountains. Its walls reach some 40 feet in height. Several watchtowers, as well as the bulky walls' catwalk, provide for sentries. The **Church of St. Anthony** was built over his grave, and it is renowned for its exquisite 13th-century wall paintings of St. George on horseback and the three Desert Fathers, restored in the 1990s.

Four other churches were built on the grounds of the monastery over the years. The most important of them is the 1766 **Church of St. Mark**, which is adorned with 12 domes and contains significant relics.

A 2-km (1-mi) trek—be sure to bring plenty of drinking water along—leads you to **St. Anthony's Cave**, 2,230 feet above sea level, where he spent his last days. Views of the Red Sea and the surrounding mountains are superb, and you're likely to encounter interesting local bird life on the hike to the cave. Inside the cave, among the rocks, pilgrims have left pieces of paper asking the saint for intervention. ☎*02/419–8560 monastery residence in Cairo* ⊕*www.stanthonymonastery.org.*

THE MONASTERY OF ST. PAUL
112 km (70 mi) south of Ain Sukhna.

St. Paul of Thebes (also known as St. Paul the Anchorite) made his way into the desert to live as a hermit in the 4th century, after a wealthy upbringing in Alexandria. It was his fellow penitent Anthony who revealed his sainthood to him. The monastery was built in the 5th century, after the saint's death. Following several raids about a thousand years later, the monastery was abandoned. Again Anthony came to Paul's aid: monks from the Monastery of St. Anthony eventually reopened St. Paul's.

A 7-km (4-mi) drive west from the Red Sea Coast highway twists through the rugged mountains and deposits you near the entrance of St. Paul's Monastery. The high walls of the monastery are surrounded by a village, which has a bakery, mills, and a few surrounding fields. The buildings of the monastery are believed to encompass the cave in which St. Paul lived for nearly 80 years. In the **Church of St. Paul**, paintings of the Holy Virgin cover the walls.

To experience the ascetic life of the monastery, you can overnight in guest houses here; women lodge outside the walls, men inside. For permission to lodge here, and for information on open days and hours, contact the monastery residence in Cairo. ☎*02/419–8560 monastery residence in Cairo.*

HURGHADA

410 km (255 mi) south of Ain Suhkna; 530 km (331 mi) south of Cairo.

Hurghada is an old fishing town that became a popular base for diving in the 1960s. As a result of the 1967 war between Egypt and Israel, Hurghada was closed to tourism and did not reopen until 1976. By this time, Sharm El-Sheikh, which was under Israeli occupation, was flourishing as a diving town. Hurghada had a lot of catching up to do.

Now, with a population of about 50,000, and some 75 hotels in and around town, Hurghada is definitely a Red Sea hot spot. Vacationers flock here in fall and winter specifically for its mild climate. But if it's sun, sand, and sea that you're after, other areas along Egypt's Red Sea Coast have more appealing beaches and desert diversions. Come to Hurghada if you're into scuba diving, however.

Hurghada has grown inexorably in the last decade, and almost all the development is tourism-related. The first hotels took the town beachfront. The oldest hotel here is the Sheraton, and it is often used as a landmark. The main boulevard, with its 15 car-splitting speed bumps, is called Shar'a Sheraton in the Sakalla district. Newer development stretches north along the road to Cairo and south through the newly gentrified Old Vic Village district, the 20 km (12 mi) to Sahl Hasheesh Bay where vast all-inclusive resort hotels are set in ample grounds.

This town is known for its strong north-northwesterly winds, so if you plan to lounge about, find a spot with a protective windbreak. From April to October, the hotter months, be prepared to battle the bugs: mosquitoes, light brown desert flies, and other flying insects have nasty bites. Bring bug repellent and spend your time in the sea.

WHERE TO EAT

Downtown Hurghada caters primarily to a European and Eastern European/Russian package-tour clientele, who are drawn to the abundance of Italian and fast-food eateries featuring kitsch decor. The town's newer hotels are often all-inclusive featuring international buffets of varying levels of quality. However, a few notable restaurants are worth seeking out.

$$$–$$$$ ✕**Zaafran.** With only 40 seats, Zaafran offers an intimate meal of fine
INDIAN Indian cuisine in a cozy room full of rich reds and golds and the dulcet
★ tones of live Egyptian guitar. The varied cuisine of the subcontinent is reflected in the menu with succulent *tandoori* chicken (roasted with a mint and spice marinade), a rich *rogan josh* (meat in a spiced tomato sauce), and fragrant *biryani* (saffron rice with meat and vegetables) as just some of the options. Top off your meal with a refreshing *kulfi* (dense Indian-style ice cream) for dessert. ⊠*Oberoi Sahl Hasheesh, Sahl Hasheesh Bay* ☎*065/344–0777* ⌂*Reservations essential* ☐*AE, DC, MC, V* ⊘*No lunch.*

$–$$ ✕**Felfela.** A sister of the Cairo-based Felfela, this is the best place in
MIDDLE town for a traditional Egyptian meal. The restaurant's four levels all
EASTERN have great harbor views. Sit down to a fresh lemonade and start choosing appetizers from the menu—tasty ful, the classic fava-bean dish, and koshary. From the grill dig into kebabs or wheat-stuffed pigeon. The grilled catch of the day is another delicious choice. Specialties here are the mezze: tahini, humus, *baba ghanouj* (eggplant dip), cumin-spiced tomatoes, *labne* (a yogurt-and-mint dip), and stuffed grape leaves. ⊠*Shar'a Sheraton, 2 km [1 mi] north of the Sheraton Hotel* ☎*065/344–2410* ☐*No credit cards* ⊘*No lunch.* .

$ ✕**Heaven Bistro.** Funky modern eatery full of bright colors, Heaven's
FAST FOOD a step beyond the standard Egyptian fast-food joint. You can make a pit stop here on the way back from the beach or before heading to a club for anything from a crisp salad to a burger, a bowl of chili, or beef stroganoff. It's just a shame there isn't any outside space where you could enjoy your meal al fresco. ⊠*Off El Arosa Square on the way to Ministry of Sound, Sekalla* ☎*012/104–2766* ☐*No credit cards.*

WHERE TO STAY

$$$$ ⊡**Oberoi Sahl Hasheesh.** The first boutique all-suites hotel along the Red
★ Sea Coast, the Oberoi is still the tops. You'll stay in a Moorish-style bungalow with a living room area and private courtyard complete with a dining table if you wish to take room service al fresco. Bathrooms are luxurious, with sunken baths and glass-sided showers that open onto a second small courtyard. Grand suites have their own private, heated

pools. The public areas give the impression of a 19th-century gentlemen's club with their dark wood and brass, but they are enhanced by 21st-century necessities that include a spa and spacious infinity pool. Service is discreet yet attentive. **Pros:** This is a genuine five-star luxury hotel, not a package-tour resort; 24-hour butler service; boutique size means you are never subjected to crowds of other guests. **Cons:** It's a 17-km (10-mi) journey to downtown Hurghada, though there is a strip mall within a mile of the hotel. ⊠ *Sahl Hasheesh Bay* ☎ *065/344–0777* ⊕ *www.oberoisahlhasheesh.com* ⟳ *100 suites* ⌂ *In-room: safe, Internet. In-hotel: 3 restaurants, room service, bars, pool, gym, spa, diving, laundry service, parking (free)* ▤ *AE, DC, MC, V* ⊚ *BP.*

$$$$ 🔲 **Steigenberger Al Dau Beach Hotel.** Close enough to town that you can enjoy the delights of Hurghada, yet offering a luxury retreat for relaxation, this resort offers the best of both worlds. The relaxed luxury is evident as soon as you enter the cathedral-like atrium of the reception area from where you can access restaurants and the Thalasso Spa. Rooms are a voluminous 50 square meters, with dark-wood furnishings set against white walls, plus deep balconies. Water is a major feature of the grounds—not just the oceanfront, but the massive free-form pools, with waterfalls and a lazy river ride, and the lagoon that forms the major feature of the golf course. **Pros:** Amenities are excellent, with a large 10-room Thalasso Spa, dive center, and golf course; close to the bars and nightlife of the town. **Cons:** Rooms are in one vast building rather then being scattered around the resort; atrium design could lead to possible noise if reception area is busy. ⊠ *Yossif Afifi Rd., Old Vic Village* ☎ *065/346–5400* ⊕ *www.steigenbergeraldaubeach.com* ⟳ *364 rooms, 16 suites* ⌂ *In-room: safe, refrigerator. In-hotel: 4 restaurants, room service, bars, golf course (9 holes), pools, gym, spa, beachfront, diving, water sports, bicycles, children's programs (ages 4–9), laundry service, Wi-Fi, parking (free), no-smoking rooms* ▤ *AE, DC, MC, V* ⊚ *BP.*

$$$$ 🔲 **Steigenberger Al Dau Club.** This good mid-sized Hurghada option is one block back from the waterfront, which means more reasonable prices. The hotel has its own private beach with dive center and beach bar. The design of the multi-story room blocks is rather lacking in imagination, but rooms are bright, and the pools and verdant gardens (with a mini-amphitheater) offer places to relax and enjoy the organized entertainment. For an extra fee, guests can play a round on the 9-hole golf course or visit the spa at sister hotel Steigenberger Al Dau Beach (a five-minute walk). **Pros:** You can take advantage of the golf course and gym facilities at the five-star sister hotel; good-size free-form pool; desert garden with hammocks offers a place to escape your fellow guests. **Cons:** All-inclusive pricing doesn't tempt you to try other options; standard rooms are too small and have no balconies, so we recommend only superior rooms. ⊠ *Youssif Alifi Rd., Old Vic Village* ☎ *065/346–5200* ⊕ *www.steigenbergeraldauclub.com* ⟳ *237 rooms, 9 suites* ⌂ *In-room: refrigerator. In-hotel: 2 restaurants, room service, bars, tennis courts, diving, bicycles, children's programs (ages 4–12), laundry service, Internet terminal, parking (free).* ▤ *AE, DC, MC, V* ⊚ *AI.*

6

$ ⊡ **Hotel White Albatros.** If you're looking for cheap, clean no-frills accommodation in the heart of Hurghada, then this is the best option. The green-and-white facade makes it easy to spot on Sheraton Road. Rooms are basic but have small balconies, and there's a cozy breakfast area on the ground floor as well as a well-situated plunge pool on the top floor, though it is currently in need of a little TLC. Most important, Amro, also known as Max, is a great host who's lived in both the U.S. and Canada. He's full of helpful tips on how to make the most of your stay. **Pros:** No price hike for foreigners, this is as inexpensive as it gets; near all the nightlife; balconies offer great bird's-eye views of downtown Hurghada. **Cons:** Traffic on the main thoroughfare can be noisy day and night. ⊠*Sheraton Rd., Sakalla* ☎*065/344–2519* ⊘*walbatros53@hotmail.com* ☞*45 rooms, 1 suite* ♻*In-room: refrigerator. In-hotel: restaurant, pool, Internet terminal* ▭*No credit cards* ¶⃝*CP.*

SPORTS & THE OUTDOORS

BEACHES Hurghada's beaches are simply not as good as those on the Sinai coast. Because public beach access is virtually nonexistent—and public beaches are not worth going to—it's best to stick with your hotel's beachfront. The newer hotel developments south of the downtown area have much better beaches but no public access at all.

DIVING **Giftun Drift,** on Small Giftun Island, is a beautiful, deep wall dive that is one hour offshore east of Hurghada. This is one of the deepest sites in the area, and the marine life here is beautiful. **Abu Ramada,** south of Small Giftun Island, has remarkable multicolored corals. **Shu'ab al-Erg** looks like a large crescent with big ergs (shifting dunes) at its tips. The site, two hours from Hurghada, has a gorgeous coral garden. You may also see dolphins here. One-day dives cost €50, including two tanks; full gear rental per day is €24. Inquire about diving packages of up to 10 days, which include 20 dives. An open-water course costs €315.

SUBEX (⊠*Aldahar* ☎*065/354–7593* ⊕*www.subex.org*) specializes in underwater safaris south of Hurghada. Ever in search of virgin reefs unpopulated by divers and boats, the guides offer weeklong liveaboard trips to the kinds of sites that make a splash in *National Geographic.*

Pioneers of technical diving in the Red Sea, **Divers' Lodge** (⊠*InterContinental Resort & Casino, Hurghada–Safaga Rd., Km 17* ☎*065/346–5100* ⊕*www.divers-lodge.com*) has its own jetty, fully equipped liveaboard boat, and several contracted daily boats. The company runs PADI courses from beginner to instructor levels and has night diving, technical diving, and NITROX and rebreather courses. The staff is warm and professional and includes divers from around the world. Divers' Lodge also has the only courses in Egypt in sign language for the hearing-impaired, conducted by a hearing-impaired instructor.

KITE-SURFING Kite-surfing is a growing sport in the Red Sea region, where the wind and water conditions are almost perfect year-round, offering tranquil shallows just offshore. You must take a tutorial in order to learn how to kite-surf. Prices for an introductory course are around €120; it helps to have some windsurfing experience, but these are very different sports.

Colona Watersports (⊠ *Magawish Resort, Youssif Alifi Rd., Old Vic Village* ☎ *010/344–1810* ⊕ *www.colonawatersports.com*) is the leading kite-surfing training center in Hurghada, with introductory courses for beginners and equipment rental for experienced riders (full day €75).

WATER
SPORTS
Waterskiing, windsurfing, parasailing, kayaking, and paddleboating are among the aquatic possibilities in Hurghada. Wave-runners, however, have been banned from the area. Inquire at your hotel about what activities it offers; the staff can point you in the right direction if your hotel doesn't offer the activity you're looking for.

NIGHTLIFE
With the arrival of the iconic Ministry of Sound–backed club, Hurghada has been transformed into one of the clubbing hot-spots for younger (teens to early twenties) European party-goers. This, in turn, has attracted branches of other well-known clubs and bars that keep the place rocking into the early hours.

BARS
Orange Café and Dutch Bar (⊠ *Opposite the Royal Palace Hotel, Old Vic Village Rd.* ☎ *012/247–3492*) is a Dutch/Egyptian-owned bar with a pub-style menu, great beer, music (from the 1970s to now), billiards, big-screen TV, karaoke, and occasional live bands. There's always a fun atmosphere.

CLUBS
Little Buddha (⊠ *Sinbad Resort, Old Vic Village Rd.* ☎ *065/345-00120* ⊕ *www.littlebuddha-hurghada.com*), a sibling of the famed Paris Buddha Bar, is a cool sushi bar and lounge in the evening that transforms into a progressive music club with resident and guest DJs after 11:30 PM.

★ **Ministry of Sound** (⊠ *Papas Beach Club, next to the public beach, Sakalla* ☎ *016/883-3551* ⊕ *www.ministryofsoundegypt.com*) launched house and trance music across Europe, and its celebrity DJs run regular sessions in conjunction with the HedKandi house record label at this iconic beach bar and club. Come to groove or to chill—but do make sure you come to feel the pulse of the current international nightlife scene.

EL-GOUNA

20 km (12 mi) north of Hurghada; 510 km (319 mi) south of Cairo.

El-Gouna is the dream of an Egyptian businessman who has utterly transformed a secluded bay and its surrounding resources. In 10 years, this virgin seacoast has been transformed into an established resort town and also a settlement for more than 10,000 full-time residents. Equipped with its own wells in the mountains, a hospital with a hyperbaric chamber for dealing with divers' decompression problems, four power plants, a school, a department of the American University in Egypt, and an impressive array of services, this environmentally friendly resort town is practically self-sustaining.

Designed around a series of seawater lagoons, the heart of El-Gouna is **al-Qafr,** a modern rendition of a traditional Egyptian settlement. To the north is **Abu Tig,** a majestic marina filled with multimillion-dollar yachts designed to recreate the atmosphere of the French or Italian Rivieras.

Ground has just broken on a second, larger marina that will accommodate the largest motor yachts on the market. South of al-Qafr is El-Gouna golf course, which is surrounded with lagoon-side villas and apartments, where Egyptians and foreign residents come to unwind from the hustle and bustle of Cairo. Visitors have the choice of 14 hotels and an excellent range of water sports activities.

DID YOU KNOW?

El-Gouna recycles 97% of its waste by using gray water on the golf course, composting what's natural, selling what's valuable, and transforming plastics into heavy-duty paving and Tetra Pak containers into heavy-duty paper bags.

WHERE TO EAT

El-Gouna has a wide range of international eateries spread across the village center and in the hotels. You'll find everything from snacks to silver-service dining.

$$–$$$ FRENCH **Deauville.** With its blue and white decor and pretty harborside terrace, Deauville takes its inspiration from the traditional French brasserie. The menu is certainly faithful to the Gallic spirit, as it's filled with French favorites such as *pâté de foie gras*, *veau* (veal), and *carré d'agneau* (rack of lamb). You can enjoy people-watching if you eat al fresco, and what could beat being surrounded by those fantastic yachts and cruisers? ✉ *Abu Tig* ☎ *065/354–9702 ext. 77902* ▭ *AE, DC, MC, V* ⏲ *No lunch.*

$$ SEAFOOD **El Sayadin.** What better place than a rustic waterfront shack to enjoy a lazy lunch or dinner? The weathered wooden deck of El Sayadin, overlooking the resort's main inlet, is the ideal place to take in the fantastic beaches and seascapes of El-Gouna. The menu combines excellent seafood with Egyptian specialities. Start with a mezze plate and then tuck into the grilled catch of the day, salmon served three ways, or *fritto misto* (crispy fried seafood). The restaurant's about 10 minutes by foot from Downtown. ✉ *Mövenpick Resort & Spa El Gouna, El-Gouna* ☎ *065/354–4501* ▭ *AE, DC, MC, V.*

$–$$ ITALIAN **Kiki's.** Not only is this a great Italian restaurant, serving arguably the best food in El-Gouna, but it's also a hip hangout. Kiki's opens at 8 PM to serve great plates of pasta plus grilled meats and seafood, but it really comes alive around 11—and keeps kickin' through the night until the last person leaves. ✉ *Museum Sq.* ☎ *065/354–9701* ✍ *Reservations essential* ▭ *No credit cards* ⏲ *No lunch.*

WHERE TO STAY

$$–$$$ **Dawar El Omda.** The name of this hotel within the Qafr means "the mayor's house," and that is its theme, with decorative touches depicting 19th-century Cairene styling. The small reception area is lighted by a massive old brass and copper lantern, and the tables in the dining room are made of heavy wood. The pool seems to spill over into the canal, and views are gorgeous. The rooms are cozy, and each has a balcony overlooking the canal and pool. Visit the Blue Bar for its exquisite decor of Iznik tiles, and be sure to check out El-Gouna's smallest restaurant, the seven-seat El Tablja. ✉ *Qafr* ☎ *065/358–0063* 🌐 *www.daware*

lomda-elgouna.com ⇥*62 rooms, 4 suites* ♿*In-room: safe, refrigerator, Wi-Fi. In-hotel: 2 restaurants, bar, pool, Internet terminal, Wi-Fi* ⊟*AE, DC, MC, V* ⦿*BP.*

GETTING AROUND
EL-GOUNA

Transportation within the resort is free, whether by microbus, tuff-tuff (topless bus), tok-tok (motor bike taxi), a funky multicolored Pakistani-style bus, or by boat.

$$$ 🏨**Mövenpick Resort and Spa El Gouna.** El-Gouna's oldest resort—it opened in 1995—has its longest beachfront, plus such a range of added features that it might be tempting not to leave the resort and explore the rest of El-Gouna. It's a large hotel, but rooms are set in well-spaced clusters around four swimming pools (plus three kids' pools), so it doesn't feel claustrophobic. The spacious rooms have a contemporary feel, with stone, mustard, and terracotta decor accented by cotton Bedouin rugs. All the restaurants in the hotel are no-smoking, which is, at the moment, rare in Egypt. There are 15 rooms designed for travelers with disabilities. **Pros:** Excellent selection of eateries and activities on-site; the extended facilities of El-Gouna are just a shuttle-bus ride away. **Cons:** The rather listless exterior paint scheme doesn't do the resort justice. ⊠*El-Gouna (southeast of Downtown, about 10 minutes by foot)* ☎*065/354–4501* ⊕*www.moevenpick-elgouna.com* ⇥*526 rooms, 28 suites* ♿*In-room: safe, Internet, Wi-Fi. In-hotel: 7 restaurants, room service, pools, gym, spa, beachfront, diving, water sports, bicycles, children's programs (ages 5–12), laundry service, Wi-Fi, parking (free), no-smoking rooms* ⊟*AE, DC, MC, V* ⦿*BP.*

$$$-$$$$ 🏨**Steigenberger Golf Resort.** In designing this resort, the innovative architect Michael Graves took cues from Egyptian and Bedouin influences, creating a style now known as neo-Nubian. The resort is housed in 10 separate terracotta-color buildings, which overlook the lagoon, pool, and the golf course, and the rooms and suites all have great views. In addition to the 18-hole championship golf course, the resort offers a variety of sports for both water and land. The hotel has lagoon beaches and offers a shuttle to a private area of seaside beach. **Pros:** Beautiful setting surrounded by lagoons and a golf course; lagoon beaches on-site offer a quiet place to relax; it's the closest El-Gouna hotel to the golf course. **Cons:** The sea and water sports are a shuttle-bus ride away; farthest hotel from downtown El-Gouna and the marina (about a 10-minute bus ride); no free bottled water in room. ⊠*El-Gouna (southeast of Downtown, about 10 minutes by bus)* ☎*065/358–0140* ⊕*www.steigenberger.com* ⇥*154 rooms, 45 suites* ♿*In-room: safe, Internet, Wi-Fi. In-hotel: 3 restaurants, room service, bars, pools, golf course, gym, spa, bicycles, children's programs (ages 5–12), Wi-Fi, parking (free), no-smoking rooms* ⊟*AE, DC, MC, V* ⦿*BP.*

$$ 🏨**Turtles Inn.** Usually booked up by the diving and kite-surfing crowd, Turtles Inn offers unpretentious accommodation in the heart of El-Gouna marina. The hotel acts as a meeting place as the day finishes with the roof bar being a popular place for a few beers. Rooms are modern and brightly but simply decorated, though not all have balconies. **Pros:** Location in the heart of the marina with direct access

6

to restaurants, bars, and shops; Orca Dive Center on-site; energetic, young vibe. **Cons:** Lack of on-site amenities won't suit families with young children; not on the beach (a shuttle takes you to Zeytouna Beach). ⊠*Abu Tig* ☎*065/358–0171* ⊕*www.turtles-inn.com* ⇆*28 rooms* ⚴*In-room: safe, Wi-Fi. In-hotel: restaurant, bar, diving, Wi-Fi* ▭ *AE, DC, MC, V* ⑩*EP.*

SPORTS & THE OUTDOORS

Water sports, desert excursions, and golf are available in El-Gouna. If you can't arrange these at your hotel, stop by the **Info-center** (⊠*al-Qafr* ☎*ext 2100 from any phone within El-Gouna* ⊕*www.elgouna.com*) for information.

BEACHES   Hotel beaches in El-Gouna are private and are reserved for the use of hotel guests only. **Zeytouna Beach** is an island—and the only public beach in El-Gouna—with a very popular beach bar. In high season there are enormous parties for everyone in El-Gouna, hotel guests as well as locals. To get here, hop on one of the boat buses that moor along the canals. **Mangroovy Beach** is a dedicated kite-surfing and water-sports beach with some great action.

DIVING   **Um Gamar** means "mother of the moon." Roughly 90 minutes offshore by speedboat, this is truly an amazing dive, with great walls and caves. The current here is light, making this one of the area's easier dives. **Abu Nahas** is a wreck diver's haven, with four large freighters sunk at reachable depths. About 25 years ago a ship carrying copper (*nahas* in Arabic) hit the reef and sank, hence the name of the site. The Tile Wreck carried Spanish tiles and sank in the same vicinity. And the Lentil Wreck became a smorgasbord for fish. You will encounter huge napoleons, groupers, schools of snappers, and catfish. *Giannis D.* hit the reef in 1983 and is a favorite; at 82 feet underwater you will find a large air pocket where you can speak to your buddy. Remember not to breathe the air, though, because it is stale and probably poisonous.

★ **The Dive Tribe** (⊠*Mövenpick Resort and Spa* ☎*065/358–0120* ⊕*www. divetribe.com*) is right on the beach at the Mövenpick Hotel. The young and international staff is passionate about diving and water sports. The impressive selection of dive courses includes all levels of PADI courses and technical diving, including the new Scubility diving course.

GOLF   **El-Gouna Golf Course** (☎*012/746–4712* ⊕*www.elgouna.com*) was designed by professional golfer Fred Couples and Gene Bates. The course has a sinuous design amongst the lagoons of El-Gouna. The par-74 course caters to many skill levels; there are an aqua driving range and practice putting green.

KITE-SURFING   The wide stretches of coastal shallows of El-Gouna offer ideal conditions for the sport, and several international competitions have been held here. Training courses for beginners cost €230, private lessons €55 per hour.

★ **Kitepower El-Gouna** (⊠*Mangroovy Beach* ☎*012/265–9596* ⊕*www. kitepower-elgouna.com*), with its own private expanse of El-Gouna shallows, has a great location and offers expert training.

★ Wellness is a mantra for the third millennium, and El-Gouna has a large facility run by one of the most respected names in the business. **Angsana Spa** (✉*Mövenpick Resort and Spa El Gouna, El-Gouna* ☎*065/354-4501* ⊕*www.angsana. com*) has 14 treatment rooms, a sauna, steam room, and Jacuzzi. The spa offers Asian-inspired treatments in a tranquil setting to ease tension or sooth the muscles you've strained on the golf course or under the kite board. There are also smaller Angsana spa outlets at El-Gouna Golf Club and Steigenberger Golf Resort.

WATER SPORTS **The Orange Concept** (✉*Abydos Marina* ☎*065/354-9702 ext. 77976* ⊕*www.theorangeconcept. com*) offers professional training in wakeboarding and has a talented, multilingual staff; the company offers such water sports as waterskiing, parasailing, and banana boat rides. Parasailing is €25 per single flight; wakeboard training sessions cost €25 each; banana boat rides are €6 per person.

SCUBILITY
Scubility is a revolutionary dive program specifically designed to allow divers with mobility issues to try diving and to undertake open-water certification. Scubility is designed to take into account and work around the varied challenges faced by divers with disabilities. The training also extends to the able-bodied with buddy training, which allows the dive-buddy to understand what is happening to the diver in the water and how they can offer the most appropriate assistance. Dive instructors can upgrade their expertise by undertaking a Scubility Instructor upgrade program.

6

NIGHTLIFE
The cream of Cairo society have second homes in El-Gouna (and often a yacht in the harbor); they visit on weekends and holidays, adding a touch of glamor to the nightlife venues.

BARS **Moods Bar** (✉*Abu Tig* ☎*065/354-9702*), at the mouth of Abu Tig Marina and flanked by motor cruisers and yachts, is the place to watch day turn to evening over a sunset cocktail. Everyone gathers here for aperitifs before moving on to dinner and then, perhaps, a club. It's a great location with beautiful people.

Peanuts Bar (✉*Ocean View Hotel, Abu Tig* ☎*065/358-0350*), a contemporary beer and ground-nuts bar, offers unpretentious fun with a mixed crowd of visitors and expats.

After finishing the day's activities, the dive crowd gathers to chat over beer at **Roof Bar** (✉*Turtles Inn, Abu Tig* ☎*065/358-0171*), which has a popular happy hour—but the divers tend to stay long after the cheap drinks dry up for the great conversation and convivial atmosphere.

CLUBS By night, **DuPort Pool Club** (✉*Ocean View Hotel, Abu Tig* ☎*065/358-0350*) transforms the classical templelike interior of the DuPort Lido into a cool lounge with views out across the marina.

BUR SAFAGA (PORT SAFAGA)

40 km (25 mi) south of Hurghada, approximately 200 km (124 mi) northeast of Luxor.

Like other cities on the Red Sea, this commercial town has been undergoing a transformation, slowly metamorphosing into a holiday resort. Like other cities on the Red Sea, the commercial port town sits close to great offshore dive sites. Unlike others, however, tourist development hasn't taken off in a meaningful way. But if the mass tourism in Hurghada is a turn-off, Safaga offers a small-scale and much more low-key alternative, though the best dive sites can still be seen on a day trip from Hurghada. Safaga is also the closest beach resort to Luxor and the Valley of the Kings, which lies 200 km (124 mi) to the southwest; when cruise ships offer land excursions to Luxor, they often do so through Safaga.

WHERE TO EAT

$$ ✕ **Taverna Barba Kiriakos.** The owner of the InterContinental Abu Soma
GREEK Resort was born in Greece, and this genuine taverna with its blue
★ and white decor and fishing boat outside is a little reminder of his homeland. Start with a crisp Greek salad or *dolmades* (stuffed vine leaves). Excellent slow-cooked *stifado* (beef stew in tomato sauce) and *moussaka* (a dish of eggplant, ground beef, and tomato sauce) make delicious entrées. Plate throwing is optional. ⊠ *InterContinental Abu Soma Resort, Abu Soma Bay, Hurghada–Safaga Hwy.* ☎ *065/326–0700* ⊟ *AE, DC, MC, V* ⊘ *No lunch.*

WHERE TO STAY

$$ ⊞ **InterContinental Abu Soma Resort.** Set on the finest stretch of beach
☾ along the entire Red Sea Coast, the InterContinental is the most imposing edifice in this low-key town. The decor in the main building is an over-the-top homage to the days when Egyptology was in its infancy, with gaudy Italianate styling and hand-painted panels depicting 19th-century scenes of Egyptian life. Thankfully, rooms are more sedate. The excellent sports programs here include a dedicated kite-surfing/windsurfing beach, and the sports center is run by the Mark Warner Company, which specializes in sports and children's programs. There's an excellent range of kids' club activities on-site. **Pros:** Excellent water sports offerings; lovely stretch of sand separate from the water sports area; extensive organized programs make it an excellent choice for families. **Cons:** There's little to do outside the hotel complex; prevailing winds may suit sports-minded guests but can get strong enough to disrupt sunbathing; children's programs must be booked separately through the Mark Warner Company (www.markwarner.co.uk). ⊠ *Abu Soma Bay, Hurghada–Safaga Hwy.* ☎ *065/326–0700* ⊕ *www.ichotels group.com* ↝ *378 rooms, 26 suites* ⅗ *In-room: safe, refrigerator, Internet. In-hotel: 5 restaurants, room service, bars, tennis courts, pools, gym, spa, beachfront, diving, water sports, children's programs (ages 2–17), laundry service, Wi-Fi, parking (no fee), no-smoking rooms* ⊟ *AE, DC, MC, V* ⦿*EP.*

AL-QUSEIR

85 km (53 mi) south of Bur Safaga.

Until the completion of the Suez Canal, Quseir was a crucial port, principally because of the *hajj* (pilgrimage to Mecca) and Middle East trade. With the canal in place, the port of Quseir was no longer needed as a stop for ships, laden with goods, passing from the Nile Valley across the Red Sea and beyond, and so it fell into decline. A development boom along the entire Red Sea Coast has started to transform Quseir into a resort town. Modern construction aims to be environmentally conscious, not only of marine life but also of land that is thought to be rich in artifacts, from bits of Roman-era glass to Mamluk archways.

Quseir Fort was one of many strategically located military posts that the Ottoman Turks built along the Red Sea Coast, and it was one of the chief posts that the Napoleonic Expedition in 1799 thoroughly bombed and then rebuilt. It is estimated that the fort was commissioned in the early 16th century during Ottoman rule by the sharifs of Mecca and Medina. They wanted to protect the hajj route and to maintain control of the passage of goods against the threat posed by the Portuguese fleet: the area around Quseir was a profitable granary for wheat and coffee from Yemen, and the most valuable spices of India and Persia were reloaded here. A small museum displays find uncovered during excavation work at the site. ✉*al-Quseir* ☎*No phone* 🎟*£e15* ☉*Daily 9–5.*

WHERE TO STAY

$$$
★ 🖵**Mövenpick al-Quseir Sirena Beach.** This is one of the more tranquil settings on the Red Sea Coast—even the buildings blend with the surrounding environment. One of Egypt's more prominent architects, Ramy Dahan, used the granite of the nearby mountains to create a Nubian-style village—and to give the bungalows the same rose tint found in the surrounding area. The resort is considered to be a green hotel development. **Pros:** Environmentally aware; traditional styling; extensive range of on-site activities. **Cons:** Isolated location. ✉*Sirena Beach, al-Quadim Bay, 7 km [4½ mi] north of al-Quseir* ☎*065/333–2100* ⊕*www.moevenpick.com* 💺*250 rooms* ⚐*In-room: Internet, Wi-Fi. In-hotel: 3 restaurants, room service, bars, tennis courts, pools, gym, spa, beachfront, diving, water sports, laundry service, parking (free), non-smoking rooms* ▤*AE, DC, MC, V* 🍽*BP.*

DIVING

The tightly run Swiss **SUBEX** (✉*Mövenpick al-Quseir Sirena Beach, al-Quadim Bay* ☎*065/333–2100*) is well equipped with staff, facilities, and gear. Guided dives go out with a maximum of four people; you must take a guide with you if you have fewer than 30 dives under your belt, and all divers must go on an orientation dive to ascertain experience levels.

MARSA ALAM

132 km (82 mi) south of al-Quseir.

The far southern enclave of the Egyptian Red Sea Coast, Marsa Alam, has flourished since the opening of an international airport in 2001. The **Port Ghalib** project plans a living community of nine Arabian- and Nubian-style villages along with beach resorts and a 1,000-vessel marina. Some hotels are now open, and the first villa owners took possession of their new homes in mid 2007, but the project is very much a work in progress at this writing.

THE SUEZ CANAL

The construction of the Suez Canal changed the nature of European trade by connecting the Red Sea to the Mediterranean. Ismailiya and Bur Sa'id were home to workers and leaders of the engineering team. Unfortunately, only a little of the colonial feel lingers in the old buildings that remain, raised on high wooden beams and decorated with French windows. National museums with small halls and a limited but interesting collection suffice as sources of historical information.

The Suez Canal was by no means the first attempt to bridge the short distance between the Mediterranean and the Red Sea. It is, however, the only canal that has bypassed the Nile. In 1855, after years of lobbying with Sa'id, the Egyptian khedive, French consul to Egypt Ferdinand de Lesseps received approval to incorporate the Suez Canal Company. After the sale of shares to raise the necessary cash, a contract was signed by the company and Sa'id, namesake of Bur Sa'id, that granted the French a 99-year concession to operate the canal. Construction began in 1859. And pressure was on, as the international demand for Egyptian cotton grew exponentially; the canal would facilitate the transfer of cotton to Europe and America.

Ten years later, on November 17, 1869, the world celebrated the inauguration of the Suez Canal. These weeks of lavish celebration nearly broke Khedive Isma'il, Sa'id's successor. No expense was spared to make this grand affair run as smoothly and elaborately as possible. To pay for his debts, Isma'il sold most of his shares in the Suez Canal Company to the British. From this point on, a French and British consortium managed the canal, ushering in the British influence that lasted until 1956, when President Gamal Abdel Nasser expelled them from the country.

In principle, the British agreed to let any nation at war or during peacetime use the canal. But in practice, during the two World Wars, they strategically positioned soldiers along the canal and permitted only Allied nations to pass. In 1950, because of the Arab-Israeli war, Egypt banned all Israeli vessels from the canal. After the British were expelled from the canal zone—and later the entire nation—they joined the United States in refusing to lend Egypt the funds with which to build the Aswan High Dam. In response, Nasser nationalized the canal and combined the income from the canal with loans from the former Soviet Union to construct the dam.

On October 29, 1956, after several border clashes, Israel invaded Egypt. Great Britain and France then attacked Egypt a week later in an attempt to restore international control over the canal. After United Nations interventions, the canal was reopened in 1957 under Egyptian management and was policed by the UN. It was closed again in 1967 during the Arab-Israeli war by sunken ships, and it didn't reopen again until 1975. Three years later Egypt lifted the ban on Israeli ships, and in 1980, a 10-mi-long tunnel was built under the canal to facilitate the passage of motor vehicles into and out of the Sinai.

> **DID YOU KNOW?**
>
> In the financial year 2006-07 the Suez Canal earned Egypt US$4.168 billion in income. That's the third-largest source of revenue for the country after tourism and money sent home by Egyptians working abroad.

ISMAILIYA

120 km (75 mi) east of Cairo; 87 km (54 mi) north of Suez.

Halfway between Bur Sa'id and Suez, this quaint city on Lake Timsah was founded by and named after Khedive Isma'il for those working on the canal. The director of the Suez Canal Company, Ferdinand de Lesseps, lived here until the completion of the canal, and his home still stands—off-limits, alas—to the public. Ismailiya's population is close to 700,000, and the city is known for its wide streets, expansive public gardens, and cleanliness.

There is a distinct colonial feel in the area known as Hay al-Afrangi (the foreign district), because of the French colonial architecture of the remaining buildings. A stroll down Shar'a Muhammad 'Ali leads you along the Sweetwater Canal and eventually to the house of Ferdinand de Lesseps.

Perpendicular to Shar'a Muhammad 'Ali, running away from the Sweetwater Canal, Shar'a Sultan Hussayn has a number of restaurants, stores, banks, and a Thomas Cook office. From here, if you turn left (southwest) onto Shar'a Saad Zaghloul and walk to Maydan al-Gummhurriya, you'll get a feel for the wide streets and calm pace.

The small **Ismailiya Regional Museum** has a modest collection of pharaonic and Greco-Roman artifacts. The majority of its collection consists of coins, pottery shards, and jewelry. The most impressive piece is a 4th-century Roman mosaic that has been cleverly laid in the floor of the hall. The picture shows Phaedra sending a love letter to her son Hippolyte. Other exhibits cover the ancient canals from the Nile to the Red Sea and contemporary canal history. ⊠*Shar'a Muhammad 'Ali, across from the Mallaha Gardens* ☎*064/291-2749* 🖃*@15* ⊙*Daily 9–5.*

6

WHERE TO EAT

$
MIDDLE
EASTERN

✕ **George's Restaurant.** This small, dark restaurant, with its English pub–like feel, seats no more than 30 people. Its full bar, an unusual facility in Ismailiya, is decorated with old signs for beer and liquor. The menu combines Egyptian and Greek staples. Dishes such as baba ghanouj and lightly sautéed calamari are hardly extravagant, but they are tasty. Beer and wine are available—or toss back a glass of ouzo. ✉ *Shar'a Sultan Hussayn* ☎ *No phone* ▤ *No credit cards.*

WHERE TO STAY

$$$

▤ **Mercure Forsan Island Ismailiya.** On the shores of Lake Timsah, the Mercure has a peaceful setting and a solid list of amenities. The lawns and beach add a leisured air, but lacquered wood furniture and floral-print bedding give a decidedly 1980s feel. Most rooms face the lake and have private balconies. **Pros:** Spacious gardens; lake views from most rooms; the closest thing you'll find to an international-standard hotel in the region. **Cons:** Hotel often draws large gatherings, which can disrupt the laid-back ambiance; fixtures and fittings are dated and worn. ✉ *Forsan Island* ☎ *064/391–6316* ⊕ *www.accorhotels.com* ⬦ *137 rooms, 15 suites* ⚘ *In-room: refrigerator. In-hotel: 2 restaurants, room service, bars, tennis court, pool, beachfront, water sports, laundry service, parking (free), no-smoking rooms* ▤ *AE, MC, V* ⦿ *BP.*

A TOWN IN LIMBO

The 19th-century governor of Ismailiya, Limbo Bey, was so unpopular during his tenure that after his death an effigy of the man was burned by the townsfolk. This one-off political statement developed into the annual Limbo Festival, but in modern times it's expanded scope beyond the hated Bey. A week after Coptic Easter, likenesses of almost any unpopular public figure, from a local soccer player going through a dry period to a soap opera character dishing the dirt, will be set alight after dark on the streets of Ismailiya.

BUR SA'ID (PORT SAID)

88 km (55 mi) north of Ismailiya.

Seaside Bur Sa'id is a charming and lively town with a decidedly European feel—and fading glamor from the era of the big ocean liners. Much of the architecture is French-colonial in style, giving the city a slight resemblance to the New Orleans French Quarter. It is a pleasant town to roam around in and to enjoy the seafront and canal-side promenades—think of it as a less-crowded, more tranquil alternative to Alexandria—but it isn't the kind of place that screams for a stop if you're in Egypt to see antiquities.

The city was founded in 1859 by Khedive Sa'id, in time for the start of excavation. Much of the area is built on sand fills from the digging of the canal. During the Arab-Israeli wars, most of the city was bombed, and parts of it still haven't been restored. At the north end of town, Bur Sa'id's Mediterranean beach has limited appeal, in part because of its unswimmable, polluted waters.

The small **Port Said National Museum** has an exquisite collection of artifacts spanning the history of Egypt from predynastic times until the 19th-century reign of Muhammed Ali. It's also the only place in Egypt to see finds from the Mamluk port of Teinis. The ground floor is dedicated to pharaonic history, the top floor to Roman, Coptic, and Islamic periods, including artifacts of the Khedival family. ⊠ *3 Shar'a 23 Julio, next to the Sonesta Hotel* ☎ *066/223–7419* ✉@15 ☉ *Daily 9–5.*

OFF THE BEATEN PATH

Port Fouad. Bur Sa'id's sister city is on the other side of the canal, which you can cross by free ferry. You can see large vessels and pretty homes from the slightly malodorous and run-down ferry. Port Fouad was built for the employees of the Suez Canal administration. With its English colonial-style houses and front gardens, it is a stark contrast to Bur Sa'id's bustling port-city/bazaar atmosphere.

> **THE HORUS ROAD**
>
> Egyptologists have pretty much ignored the northern Sinai in the rush to excavate the rich sites in the Nile Valley. The region was not well settled in ancient times, but it was the location of an arterial transport route, the Horus Road, that linked Egypt to the lands of the Levant and the Hittite Empire, which was a major power player at this time. Both Seti I and Ramesses II led armies up this route to do battle with the Hittites. In 2007, digs led by Dr. Mohamed Abdel-Maqsoud uncovered a large fort believed to be used as a staging ground for troops on these campaigns.

6

WHERE TO EAT

$$$
MIDDLE EASTERN

✕ **Canal Cruise Floating Restaurant.** The perfect way to combine sightseeing and dining, the glass-sided cruise launch glides along sections of the canal, offering arguably the best views of the historical buildings on both banks. You can get either soft drinks or a full buffet meal featuring a mix of Egyptian and international items. Cruise times during winter (October through May) are 4 PM, 6 PM, and 9 PM; summer cruises (June through September) are at 5 PM, 7 PM, and 10 PM. ⊠ *Port Said, in the port area* ☎ *066/334–5222* ▤ *No credit cards* ☉ *No lunch.*

WHERE TO STAY

$$$

▦ **Sonesta Hotel Port Said.** The modern decor lacks charm, and the boxy form fails to win any plaudits despite its jaunty yellow accents; nevertheless, this hotel is pleasant, and the sea, the canal, and the city center are all a stone's throw away. Indeed, on the corniche of the Suez Canal and surrounded by shopping arcades, the Sonesta is the best hotel in Bur Sa'id. **Pros:** Canal-view rooms allow you to watch the passage of ships from your window; you can enjoy the city on foot from the hotel; a range of eateries on-site means you don't have to venture into the city in the evening unless you want to. **Cons:** Swimming in the sea is not possible because of water quality. ⊠ *Shar'a Sultan Hussayn* ☎ *066/332–5511* ⊕ *www.sonesta.com* ⚲ *100 rooms* ♿ *In-room: safe, refrigerator. In-hotel: 4 restaurants, room service, bar, beachfront, water sports, laundry service, Internet terminal, parking (free)* ▤ *AE, MC, V* ⏐⦿⏐*AE.*

SINAI & RED SEA COAST ESSENTIALS

TRANSPORTATION

BY AIR

Regularly scheduled EgyptAir flights connect Sharm El-Sheikh to Cairo (a bit over an hour), Alexandria, Luxor, and Hurghada. Hurghada also has regularly scheduled EgyptAir flights from Cairo (less than an hour), Alexandria, and Aswan. Both Sharm and Hurghada have frequent service from many different European destinations on low-cost European airlines as well as on EgyptAir; some of this service is seasonal. You can also fly to the privately operated Marsa Alam airport from Cairo (three times weekly) or from Europe. *For information on international flights, see Air Travel in Egypt Essentials.*

Contacts **EgyptAir** (☎ *02/2267–7101 in Cairo, 069/360–3710 in Sharm El-Sheikh, 065/364–3034 in Hurghada, 065/364–3034 in Marsa Alam* ⊕ *www.egyptair.com).*

AIRPORTS & TRANSFERS
Hurghada International Airport is in the desert, 4 km (2½ mi) west of the Sheraton at the southern end of town. Most hotels offer airport transfers, but these will need to be prebooked; the taxi fare from the airport to the Sheraton Road, Sakalla, is around £e20.

Marsa Alam Airport is 20 km (12 mi) north of Marsa Alam town and 2½ km (1 mi) west of Port Ghalib. Taxi fare into Marsa Alam town is approx £e90.

In Sharm El-Sheikh, it's a £e40 fare into Na'ama Bay and a £e60 taxi fare to downtown Sharm; however, if you are light on luggage you could take the public minibus service that costs £e2 one way to Na'ama Bay or downtown (though these don't drop you directly at your hotel).

Contacts **Hurghada International Airport** (⊠ *Sheraton Rd., 4 km (2½ mi) west of the Sheraton* ☎ *065/344–2592).* **Marsa Alam Airport** (☎ *065/370–0021).* **Sharm El-Sheikh Airport** (⊠ *Airport Rd., Sharm El-Sheikh* ☎ *069/360–1141).*

BY BUS

The best way to get to the Suez Canal Zone is by bus from Cairo. You can take one early in the morning from Cairo to Bur Sa'id, walk around for a couple of hours, then hop on another bus to Ismailiya. Have lunch there, explore a bit, then head back to Cairo in the evening. Travel time on the buses will total around five hours.

However, long-distance bus travel to the Sinai or Red Sea Coast takes time and patience; obnoxious dramatic movies play for the duration, and despite NO SMOKING signs everywhere, even the driver lights up. El Gouna Bus Company offers frequent service between Cairo and Hurghada and El-Gouna. Frequent East Delta Bus Company buses run daily from Sinai Station in Abbasia to Sharm El-Sheikh, Nuweiba, and Taba. Super Jet has buses to Sharm El-Sheikh and Hurghada from Cairo's Maydan Tahrir station. The Upper Egypt Bus Company has several buses a day between Cairo and Hurghada, al-Quseir, and Marsa Alam; their company also operates routes to Luxor.

Super Jet and East Delta Bus Company buses run frequently from two stations in Cairo—from the Turgoman Bus Station in Bulaq, behind Shar'a Gala Downtown, and from Almaza Station in Heliopolis to Bur Sa'id. Buses also connect Bur Sa'id to Ismailiya. These buses vary in cleanliness. Be sure to book front seats, and get to the station ahead of time to book your ticket. And be aware that the ticket salespeople are not always helpful.

Contacts El Gouna Bus Company (☎ *065/355–6188*). **East Delta Bus Company** (☎ *02/2383–4753 in Cairo, 069/366–0660 in Sharm El-Sheikh, 069/364–0250 in Taba, 069/352–0371 in Nuweiba*). **Super Jet** (☎ *02/2290–9017 in Cairo, 065/355–3499 in Hurghada, 069/366–1622 in Sharm El-Sheikh, 02/2579–8181 in Bur Sa'id*). **Upper Egypt Bus Company** (☎ *02/2260–9279 in Cairo, 065/354–4582 in Hurghada, 065/325–1253 in Safaga, 065/333–0033 in al-Quseir*).

BY CAR

To cross the Suez Canal, you should take the Ahmed Hamdy Tunnel from the city of Suez on the southern end into the Sinai Peninsula; expect to pay tolls. Foreign travelers in vehicles who don't have a resident's permit will be expected to join a traveler's convoy. The times for these can vary, so if your hotel has a concierge, ask them to confirm times and the meeting place. If you employ a driver, he will organize your departure time to take into account convoy times, so you don't need to worry.

Roads in the Sinai are mostly single lane, though a two-lane highway is partly built along the west coast—and, at this writing, causing mayhem because drivers are unsure which sections are open. Turn-offs are not always marked. Though the main roads are in fine condition, you might want to take a taxi instead. Getting to remote sights requires some skill, and negotiating winding roads through the mountains requires extreme caution because local drivers usually don't stay in their own lanes.

The advantage of renting a car and driving to the Red Sea Coast is flexibility, but that might not outweigh the dangers posed by other drivers, including many trucks, and the hairpin turns before Ain Sukhna. If you don't have nerves of steel, fly to Hurghada or hire a taxi to take you to the monasteries. If you plan to stay in Hurghada or El-Gouna, you will not need a car. If you are going to travel south as far as al-Quseir or Marsa Alam, having a car will be helpful. The road there is well-marked and easy to drive.

Renting a car in Egypt is no different than it is in the U.S. You will need to bring both your domestic license and an international driver's license. Prices for a compact car are around $45 per day, hiring a driver is about $20 extra per day (with further charges if you want to keep the driver overnight). Cars in Egypt do not usually have unlimited mileage, so there may be a per-km charge if you exceed the daily allotment.

You do not need a car if you are staying in either Bur Sa'id or Ismailiya.

Car Rental Contacts Avis (✉ *Morgana Mall, off Peace Rd., Na'ama Bay, Sharm El-Sheikh* ☎ *069/360–2400* ✉ *Shar'a Sheraton, Hurghada* ☎ *065/344–7400*).

El Gouna Limousine (✉ *Tamr Henna, El-Gouna* ☎ *065/358–0061*). **Europcar** (✉ *Laguna Vista Hotel, Nabq Bay, Sharm El-Sheikh* ☎ *012/2267–2439*).

BY FERRY

The easiest way to get to Sharm El-Sheikh from the Red Sea Coast is by high-speed ferry. Sharm El-Sheikh–Hurghada ferries operate daily except for Friday and Sunday. The trip takes two to three hours, depending on sea conditions, and costs about £e270 per person one way, £e450 return.

Contacts Red Jet Company (☎ *02/257–61798 in Cairo, 012/822–9877 in Sharm El-Sheikh, 065/344–9481 in Hurghada*).

BY TAXI

Within Sharm El-Sheikh, Dahab, and Nuweiba, a taxi ride will cost about £e10. There are no meters, so be sure to agree on a price with your driver before you get into the car. You can also take a taxi between towns; here are some fare estimates: £e200 between Sharm El-Sheikh and Dahab; £e300 between Sharm and St. Catherine's Monastery; £e220 between Sharm and Nuweiba; and £e130 between Nuweiba and Taba. Taking the microbus in Sharm will be much cheaper.

In Hurghada, taxis are only available on the street (not by phoning a dispatcher). Taxis will cost at least £e10 for the shortest distance in Hurghada. A better, if more communal, option would be to flag down a microbus, which will cost only £e2 to £e5 per person. To travel between El-Gouna and Hurghada, a taxi will cost around £e90. Within El-Gouna, taxis are unnecessary since free microbuses and boats stop at all key hotels and hot spots.

In the Suez Canal Zone, taxis are everywhere. Just flag one down, and agree with the driver on a price before you get in. In Bur Sa'id, you should pay no more than £e5 for any local trip. In Ismailiya, you might pay up to £e10. The drivers are usually pleasant, and they will turn down the music if you ask them to. But brace yourself: they drive very fast.

CONTACTS AND RESOURCES

BANKS & EXCHANGE SERVICES

The coastal resorts of the Red Sea and the Sinai have a good number of ATMs and exchange bureaus. Most major hotels will have an ATM in the foyer, and you will be able to exchange foreign currency at reception (check exchange rates, which may not be advantageous when compared to commercial exchange bureaus). The towns in the canal area have fewer ATMs but a good supply of banks and commercial exchange agencies.

EMERGENCIES

If you have any security concerns, the Tourist Police will be able to assist. They patrol resort and town centers. For serious emergencies call the three-digit national numbers.

For minor health problems, if you are staying at a four- or five-star hotel, there should be a doctor on call. For more serious medical issues, the hospitals at Sharm El-Sheikh, Hurghada, and El-Gouna offer reasonable facilities and English-speaking staff. The best medical facilities are in the capital, Cairo, which may mean an expensive ambulance ride from the coast to transfer you to a suitable facility.

There are hyperbaric chambers in al-Quseir, Dahab, El-Gouna, Hurghada, Marsa Alam, Safaga, and Sharm El-Sheikh.

If you are in some remote area, it may be some time before assistance can reach you.

Emergency Services Ambulance (☎123). **Fire** (☎180). **Police** (☎122).

Dentists Dr. Nasser Mostafa (✉ *Sadek Poly Clinic, El Mashraba St., Dahab* ☎069/364-1322). **El-Gouna Hospital** (✉ *Downtown, El-Gouna* ☎065/358-0012). **Hadaba Dental Clinic** (✉ *Khazan Street, Umm El Sid Hill, Sharm El-Sheikh* ☎012/168-6603). **Hafaz Dental Center** (✉ *19 El Gomhoureya St., Bur Sa'id* ☎066/335-0033). **Moderne Dental Clinic** (✉ *Sheraton Rd., Sakalla, Hurghada* ☎010/582-0724).

Doctors El-Gouna Hospital (✉ *Downtown, El-Gouna* ☎065/358-0012). **1st Care Medical Services Poly Clinic** (✉ *Delta Sharm Resort, Hadaba, Sharm El-Sheikh* ☎069/366-0216). **Hassan Ahmed El Shahaly** (✉ *al-Horreya St., Ismailiya* ☎064/391-1500). **Ibrahim Fahim** (✉ *El Thalatheny St., Bur Sa'id* ☎066/333-7122). **Sedek Clinic** (✉ *El Mashraba St., Masbat, Dahab* ☎069/364-1322).

Hospitals Hurghada General Hospital (✉ *El Mostashfa St., Dahab Hurghada* ☎065/354-6740). **El-Gouna Hospital** (✉ *Downtown, El-Gouna* ☎065/358-0012). **El Kahrabaa Hospital** (✉ *Shabin El Koum St, El Salam, Ismailiya* ☎064/335-4125). **El Mabarra Hospital** (✉ *29 July St., Bur Sa'id* ☎066/324-5962).

Nuweiba Emergency Hospital (✉ *Downtown, Nuweiba* ☎069/350-0302). **Sharm El-Sheikh New Hospital** (✉ *Sharm al-Maya* ☎069/366-0425).

INTERNET, MAIL & SHIPPING
Internet cafés are popular and numerous, but they they come and go with surprising regularity, especially in the resort towns. Wi-Fi is growing in availability, with most major hotels and some bars and cafés offering services; however, free Wi-Fi is not common. Costs run around £e20 for 30 minutes but are cheaper per hour if you pay for blocks of time (more than five hours).

Mail services in Egypt are notoriously unreliable and slow, with delivery of even the smallest postcard taking around 14 days to arrive in the States. International courier services are available. Deliveries from Egypt to the United States take around three or four days but are very expensive. DHL has an office at the Tropicana Rosette Hotel in Sharm El-Sheikh; FedEx has offices in Bur Sa'id, Hurghada, and Ismailiya.

TOUR OPTIONS
In Sharm El-Sheikh, Abanoub Travel Agency runs camel, jeep, and trekking tours of varying durations to all parts of the Sinai and also offers overnight trips to Petra and Cairo.

In Dahab, Crazy Camel Desert Safaris organizes two- to six-day four-wheel-drive or camel excursions suited to your interests, be it Bedouin culture or bird-watching. Embah offers a full range of adventure activities, plus interesting options like a "Desert Dweller" tour to visit the Bedouin, and herb-gathering trips.

Desert Fox Safari offers exceptional Bedouin guides for multiday trips throughout the St. Catherine's Protectorate. Based in St. Catherine's Village, Fox guides also can arrange trips all over Sinai.

Contacts Abanoub Travel Agency (✉ *Aida Villas, Hadbet Om El-Said, Sharm El-Sheikh* ☎ *069/366–5731* ⊕ *www.abanoub.com*). **Crazy Camel Desert Safaris** (✉ *Masbat, Dahab* ☎ *0105–575161* ⊕ *www.crazy-camel.de*). **Desert Fox Safari** (✉ *St. Catherine's Village* ☎ *069/347–0344* ⊕ *www.desertfoxsafari.com*). **Embah** (✉ *Beachfront Boulevard, Masbat, Dahab* ☎ *069/364–1690* ⊕ *www.embah.com*).

Western Desert Oases

Dakhla oasis, marabouts in El Qasr

WORD OF MOUTH

"Siwa is great. It's in the Great Sand Sea, so you can go into the beautiful sandy desert and ride up and down the dunes. There are local guides who can take you out, or Cairo guides who will take you from Cairo. It has many of the old Berber traditions alive while you see lots of men with cell phones, and there's an internet café. Old buildings, tombs, some pharaonic ruins, etc."

—sunshine007

WELCOME TO WESTERN DESERT OASES

TOP REASONS TO GO

★ **Dune-Bashing in Siwa:** Set out in a four-wheel-drive vehicle to explore the monumental ridges of golden sand west of the town.

★ **Sunsets in the White Desert:** Watch the color of the chalk columns change and mellow as the sun drops over the desert.

★ **Swimming in Bir Wahed:** Take a refreshing dip in this natural spring near Siwa after a hot day of dune-bashing.

★ **The Golden Mummies:** Examine one of the famous gilded faces in the Mummy Museum in Bahariyya.

★ **The Qasr al-Dakhla:** Explore the heart of this historic Islamic citadel and the vibrant streets surrounding it.

1 Bahariyya Oasis. Rich in history, Bahariyya is the location of the Valley of the Golden Mummies. It's a friendly, laid-back place offering easy access to the Black Desert.

2 Farafra Oasis. With few ruins to occupy their time, most travelers use Farafra as a jumping-off point to visit the White Desert, an ancient sea floor with fascinating geological formations and fossils.

3 Dakhla Oasis. Dotted with Islamic fortress towns built on Roman foundations, Dakhla is one of the less-visited oases, but travelers may be drawn to Bashindi, a traditional village that seems to hark back to pharaonic times.

4 Kharga Oasis. Although more modernized than other oases, Kharga is justifiably famous for its Christian burial ground at Bagawat, as well as Roman ruins and a remarkable and mysterious underground aqueduct.

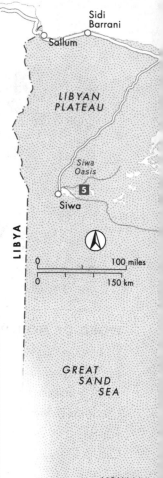

Bahariya Oasis, Valley of the Golden Mummies, Bahariya Museum, Clay statuettes of mourner

5 Siwa Oasis. Isolation has given Siwa much more of a Berber feel than the other oases, and tourism is more focused on the unique culture of the region. This is the best place to go if you want to buy authentic desert crafts.

Fortress of Shali, Siwa oasis.

GETTING ORIENTED

Whichever oasis you are bound for, all desert trips begin in Cairo. If you're driving to Siwa, head toward Alexandria. For the other oases head toward the pyramids in Giza. Check that your car is up to the trip, and make sure you have spare parts (especially a working jack), extra gasoline, water for you and the car, maps, guidebooks, and—if available—a good GPS. Always top off your tank when you come across a gas station because they're few and far between.

7

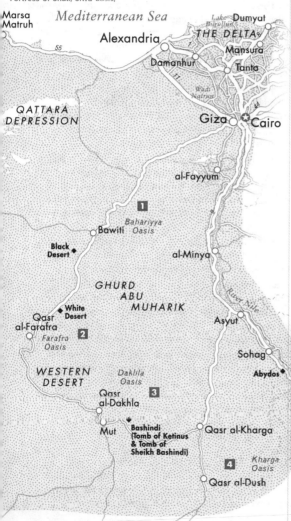

Marsa Matruh

Mediterranean Sea

55

Lake Biqullus

Dumyat

Alexandria

THE DELTA

Mansura

Damanhur

Tanta

QATTARA DEPRESSION

Wadi Natrun

Giza — Cairo

al-Fayyum

1

Bahariyya Oasis

Bawiti

Black Desert

al-Minya

GHURD ABU MUHARIK

White Desert

Qasr al-Farafra

Farafra Oasis

2

Asyut

WESTERN DESERT

Dakhla Oasis

River Nile

Sohag

Abydos

Qasr al-Dakhla

3

Mut

Bashindi (Tomb of Ketinus & Tomb of Sheikh Bashindi)

Qasr al-Kharga

4

Kharga Oasis

Qasr al-Dush

The White Desert

WESTERN DESERT OASES PLANNER

Transportation

By Air: Though there are airports at Dakhla and Kharga, there are no commercial flights linking the airports with Cairo at this writing.

By Bus: Buses provide cheap, reliable transportation to all the oases, but the travel is slow (4½ hours to Bahariyya, 7 hours to Farafra, 9 hours to Siwa, 12 hours to Kharga). To reach Siwa, you have to change in either Alexandria or Marsa Matruh. Super Jet buses are generally the most luxurious.

By Car: You can drive to the oases, and having a car affords the greatest freedom. All car rentals are in Alexandria or Cairo. Don't do any off-road exploring on your own; it's imperative to hire a local guide. Don't drive the Darb al-Siwa route linking Siwa to Bahariyya unless you have a four-wheel-drive vehicle.

Taxis: There are no taxis in Bahariyya, Farafra, or Siwa, though Siwa has small canopied donkey carts driven by teenage boys. In Kharga Oasis, a few taxis exist in the villages, and Dakhla also has a few. Most are available for hire by the day.

What's Great in the Western Desert

Camping: You can stay in a developed campground with shared facilities or out in the desert. You may be tempted to set up camp anywhere—on top of a dune, at a hot spring, near a ruined antiquity, or at some other beautiful spot—but you will need the permission of the local police, and they may require you to hire a local guide, which is a sensible precaution. Two rules: clean up after yourself, and don't take anything away with you.

Citadels: The immense Roman fortresses of Ain Om al-Dabadib, Deir al-Munira, and Qasr al-Labeka northeast of Kharga protected an ancient trade route. The Islamic citadel at Qasr al-Dhakla protected the local population inside its walls.

Desert Environments: The Great Sand Sea to the south and west of the oases is a mass of golden dunes, but in western Egypt you have the forest of chalk columns that's now called the White Desert (north of Farafra) and the dramatic black and terracotta hills of the Black Desert (around Bahariyya).

Mummies: The vast cache of well-preserved and intricately decorated Greco-Roman era mummies discovered near Bahariyya is a major find for Egyptologists.

Natural Springs: Artesian springs have given the oases their fertility. Cleopatra's Pool in Siwa is the most famous of the springs. However, the most beautiful—and normally less crowded because it's outside Siwa town and only reachable by a four-wheel drive vehicle—is Bir Wahed.

Off-Roading: Roads didn't exist much here until the 1970s, so everyone's pretty used to just taking off into the desert. Historically, trade caravans plied set routes, but today's desert trips are more for adventure. Desert safaris can last a morning, a day, or many weeks, and you can travel on foot or by four-wheel-drive vehicle. The deserts west of Siwa, around Bahariyya, or southwest of Dakhla all offer great opportunities for exploration. You can easily arrange a multiday trip right in Cairo, but you'll save significantly if you make your own way to the desert and make all your plans there. Whatever you do, don't go into the desert unescorted; always have a knowledgeable guide.

About the Restaurants

You can expect to dine on wholesome fare—mostly vegetable stews, grilled chicken, plenty of rice, and fresh fruit. Dining is generally al fresco, because the few restaurants that do exist are street-side affairs. Alcohol isn't usually available except at hotel restaurants. Finish off with tea made the Bedouin way.

Fresh fruit and vegetables from the locals stands are perfectly safe, though wash everything in bottled water. There's good locally produced cheese, too. Fresh whole=wheat flat bread is available each morning from local bakers.

Two musts: Don't miss out on oasis dates or Siwa's olive oil, which is rich and heady—gourmet without trying to be. Dates come in a number of varieties: sweet, firm, and yellow; sweet, mushy, and dark brown; or bitter, crunchy, and red. Try them all.

About the Hotels

There is a range of accommodations in the desert, from simple chalets or eco-camps to traditionally styled mud-brick hotels. Prices are generally lower than in the Nile Valley. Some hotels have air-conditioning, but you'll pay a premium for it. In the winter, a fan may be sufficient to keep the room cool enough for a good night's sleep. Although most hotels stay open throughout the year, the summer (May–September) is low season and a time for renovations and maintenance. Since restaurants are not numerous, most hotels offer a meal plan; some require it.

WHAT IT COSTS IN EGYPTIAN POUNDS, U.S. DOLLARS & EUROS			
$$$$	$$$	$$	$
Restaurants in Egyptian pounds			
over £e 150	£e100–£e 150	50 £e–100£e	under £e50
Hotels in dollars			
over $200	$130–$200	$70–$130	under $70
Hotels in euros			
over €130	€80–€130	€45-€80	under €45
Restaurant prices are per person for a main course at dinner. Hotel prices are for a double room in high season, excluding 10% tax and service charges (usually 10%).			

Planning Your Time

Bahariyya and Farafra, some 365 km (226 mi) southwest of Giza, make a good three-day trip. You'll need to spend at least one night in Bahariyya so you have a full day for the Black Desert. Another night in Farafra will give you time to see the al-Qasr district and the White Desert.

With another two days, you could add a trip to Siwa or Kharga and Dakhla. If you choose to go to Siwa, do that first and then drive east across the desert to Bahariyya. The road here, the Darb al-Siwa, is part asphalt and part sand, so it demands an experienced desert driver and a four-wheel-drive vehicle (and you need police permission). You could also spend a full five days in Siwa to get a better feel for Bedouin life.

When to Go

Traveling in the summer is possible if you're not bothered by the intense heat, but you must be very careful. Cover up (learn from the Bedouins), drink plenty of liquids with rehydration salts, and rest in the shade in the middle of the day, limiting sightseeing time to mornings and evenings. The desert's finest days fall between November and March. Avoid traveling in March and April, when the *khamaseen* (desert storms) blow. Light in the desert is best in October and November.

Updated by
Lindsay and
Pete Bennett

A FEW HUNDRED YEARS AGO the only outsiders interested in Egypt's oases were occasional desert raiders bent on stealing the fruits from the orchards, destroying water supplies, and abducting women. Generation after generation, life followed the seasons with little change. The most exciting events of the year were the autumn date harvest and the subsequent caravans that would assemble and trek to the Nile Valley to take the fruit to market.

In the 1970s, the government built an asphalt ring road joining Bahariyya, Farafra, Dakhla, and Kharga—the four southern oases—to the Nile Valley, and the tranquility of thousands of years of isolation met the hustle of 20th-century Egypt. Over the next few years, telephones, electricity, televisions, and elements of the modern world as we know it began to enter the traditional lives of the oases. Since the building of the road, increasing numbers of migrants from other parts of Egypt have settled with the native peoples, bringing new working practices and technologies.

Egypt's Western Desert makes up the northeastern third of the Libyan Desert, a 1-million-square-mi wasteland, nearly half of which is sand. Edged by the fertile soil of the Nile Valley, this desert joins its sister, the Sahara, in central Libya to make North Africa a most inhospitable land. In some places the desert has faulted and dropped, bringing subterranean water nearer the surface. This ancient water has slowly made its way north from central Africa, traveling downhill for centuries as it follows the African continental slope into the Mediterranean Sea. It bubbles to the surface in the depressions, creating the famed oases. Just as it sustains life today, it provided the necessary water for human beings at the dawn of history, but beyond the reassuring verdant and fertile oases lie inhospitable lands that beckon the human spirit. Today, the Western Desert remains one of the few places on earth where human beings can still taste total freedom and have a sense of genuine adventure.

For millennia the oases accommodated the permanent settlements of farmers and passing traders and nomads. The strict boundaries of today's nation states have all but ended nomadic desert life, and Bedouins and farmers mostly live together. Oasis dwellers possess qualities that seem to be vanishing from the societies of the modern world: honesty, integrity, respect for tradition and the law, and a high moral code.

There's always something interesting happening the minute you step into the desert. The setting changes constantly as you move from place to place—from mighty golden dunes, to high rocky escarpments, to chalk pillars, to dusty scrubland. You could discover that you're in a field of nummalites (small, coinlike fossils of sea creatures) and desert diamonds (small pieces of quartz that look like diamonds when polished). Man has also left a mark with huge ruins: Roman forts in Kharga, Islamic fortress towns in Dakhla and Siwa, ancient underground aqueducts, desert monasteries, and Roman watering stations. Most of the pharaonic monuments in the Western Desert were built during the 26th Dynasty (c. 664–525 BC). The rulers were Libyans; they regularly crossed through this otherwise isolated frontier from the Nile Valley, a frontier that's still a world apart from the rest of Egypt.

BAHARIYYA OASIS

Ancient travelers had to cross a dune belt several miles wide (and hundreds of miles long) to reach the Bahariyya Oasis from the Nile Valley. Then it took them an entire day to descend the cliffs that hem the oasis on all sides. These days you glide easily along the asphalt road at high speed, only slowing down to enjoy the descent that cuts through the cliffs and leads into the oasis. At this point, you must slow down in other ways, too, for you are stepping back into an older time. The mud-brick ruins of a Coptic monastery, on the right, is the first sign of civilization. This is where the ancient caravan roads from Cairo, al-Fayyum, and al-Minya once converged before reaching Bahariyya.

It's easy to adjust to the rural way of life here, not least because the people are so friendly and helpful. Bahariyya is the only one of the four southern oases that isn't part of the New Valley Governorate (Giza's governorate administers it), so it is the least modernized. As a result, you get a better idea of how people lived in the oases for thousands of years.

Bahariyya is rich in pharaonic, Greek, Roman, and Coptic history; however, the historical sights have pretty much been off-limits to the public. Things started to change in the mid-1990s, when a tomb-filled cemetery thought to contain hundreds of mummies was found south of Bawiti in what has been dubbed the Valley of the Mummies (also called the Valley of the Golden Mummies and the Valley of the 10,000 Mummies). More than 200 mummies have been uncovered in the area since 1999, and in 2000 archaeologists opened the long-sought tomb of an influential 26th-Dynasty ruler of Bahariyya nearby. The opening of this coffin, along with some others, was broadcast live on television in the United States, and the site is now open to the public. In addition, some of the mummies found in the Valley of the Mummies are on view in Bawiti.

7

BAWITI

About 365 km (226 mi) southwest of Giza.

In Bawiti, anybody's business is everybody's business. Donkeys, vegetables, and trucks are inspected and haggled over passionately in this small, bustling village while spectators sitting at the local cafés throw in their opinions for the crowd's entertainment. The town is the capital of Bahariyya, having usurped the position of the older capital, al-Qasr, a few generations ago. These days the two communities are blended together. The older village sections go back hundreds of years and are now being abandoned for newer homes. Don't miss the ancient Roman aqueduct that cuts underground through the heart of Bawiti, the gardens that cascade down the cliffside to the depression floor, or the now

CLOSE UP

The Golden Mummies

In 1999, an Egyptian Antiquities guard on a donkey fell through a hole in the ground and accidentally discovered the first of a series of important Greco-Roman era mummies (from the late 2nd century BC to early 4th century AD). The uncovered mummies were in excellent condition, providing archaeologists with a rich seam of evidence and information about life in the waning days of ancient Egyptian religious beliefs and practices. Particularly striking are the funerary masks of the mummies. Many have gilded faces—which inspired the popular name of the region, Valley of the Golden Mummies—with gold paint covering the skin of the face. Others have flesh-color clay masks, but all were sculpted to show an image of the person during life, with painted hair and differing facial expressions. Some masks have been made from actual life-casts of the individuals. The finest examples have gilded fingernails and toenails added to the bodies after mummification. They are encased in highly ornate sycamore-wood sarcophagi, usually depicting scenes from the Egyptian *Book of the Dead*. Archaeologists are particularly excited about studying the details of the mummification process and funerary rituals and how they differ from those used in earlier periods.

open temples and tombs. You can walk or drive through Bawiti (and al-Qasr), either on your own or with a guide.

The **Antiquities Office** (✉ *On the main street, in front of the Mummy Museum* ☎ *No phone*) sells a combination ticket that includes admission to the four major sights—the Mummy Museum; the mastabas of Bannentoiu, Zed Amun Ef Ankh, and Amenhotep Huy; the Temple of Alexander the Great; and the Ain Muftella Archaeological Site—for £e45. The office is open daily from 8 to 5.

A large 26th-Dynasty temple, now known as the **Ain Muftella Archaeological Site** was built by the mayor of Bawiti during the era (his tomb was among those uncovered in the Valley of the Golden Mummies). The sandstone complex has well-preserved colorful bas-reliefs and several sanctuaries dedicated to, among others, Horus and Bes. One panel depicts 12 of the panoply of Egyptian gods, allowing for a who's who of the ancient deities. The surrounding extensive mud-brick ruins are store rooms and living quarters. Pause at Ain Muftella for the breathtaking panoramic view of Bahariyya. ✉ *3 km (2 mi) south of Bawiti, at the end of the second main road in al-Qasr* ☎ *No phone* 🎟 *£e45, combination ticket for all local archaeological sites* ⊗ *Daily 8–5.*

If you've seen the mastabas of Saqqara or Luxor, the **Mastaba Tomb of Amenhotep Huy** is likely to disappoint; the few reliefs are in very poor condition, and you will need a car (preferably a guide) to find the tomb. Still, if you have come all the way to the oasis, it is usually included on guided tours. ✉ *1½ km (1 mi) east of Bawiti* ☎ *No phone* 🎟 *£e45, combination ticket for all local archaeological sites* ⊗ *Daily 8–5.*

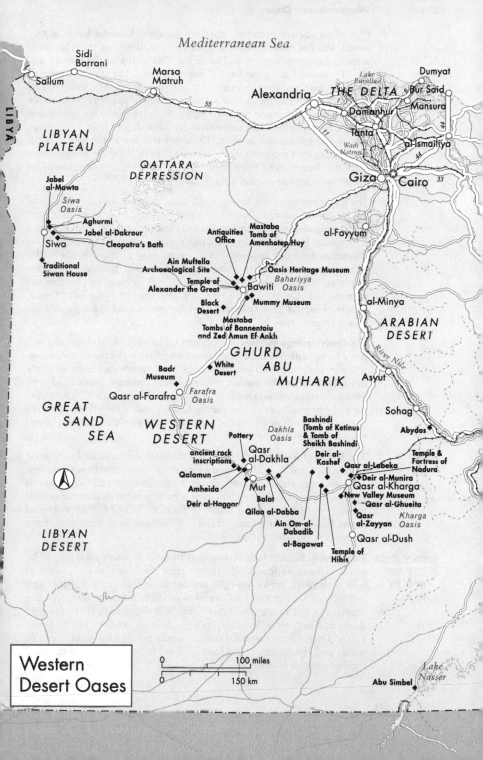

Mediterranean Sea

Sidi
Barrani

Sallum

Marsa
Matruh

Alexandria

THE DELTA

Dumyat

Bur Said

Mansura

Damanhur

Tanta

al-Ismailiya

LIBYA

LIBYAN
PLATEAU

QATTARA
DEPRESSION

Lake
Burullus

Wadi
Natrun

Giza   Cairo

Jabel
al-Mawta

Siwa
Oasis

Aghurmi

Jabel al-Dakrour

Siwa

Cleopatra's Bath

Traditional
Siwan House

Antiquities
Office

Mastaba
Tomb of
Amenhotep Huy

al-Fayyum

Ain Muftella
Archaeological Site

Oasis Heritage Museum

Bahariyya
Oasis

Temple of
Alexander the Great

Bawiti

Black
Desert

Mummy Museum

Mastaba
Tombs of Bannentoiu
and Zed Amun Ef-Ankh

al-Minya

ARABIAN
DESERT

GHURD
ABU
MUHARIK

River Nile

Badr
Museum

White
Desert

Qasr al-Farafra

Farafra
Oasis

Asyut

GREAT
SAND
SEA

WESTERN
DESERT

Dakhla
Oasis

Sohag

Abydos

Bashindi
(Tomb of Ketinus
& Tomb of
Sheikh Bashindi

Temple &
Fortress of
Nadura

Pottery

ancient rock
inscriptions

Qasr
al-Dakhla

Deir al-
Kashef

Qasr al-Labeka

Qalamun

Mut

Deir al-Munira

Qasr al-Kharga

Amheida

Balat

New Valley Museum

Qasr al-Ghueita

Deir al-Haggar

Qilaa al-Dabba

Ain Om-al-
Dabadib

Qasr
al-Zayyan

Kharga
Oasis

al-Bagawat

LIBYAN
DESERT

Temple of
Hibis

Qasr al-Dush

100 miles

150 km

Lake
Nasser

Abu Simbel

Western
Desert Oases

★ Part of an ancient cemetery, the 26th-Dynasty **Mastaba Tombs of Bannentoiu and Zed Amun Ef Ankh,** a father and son, illustrate the traditional scenes of mummification, including the "Weighing of the Heart" and the "Deceased Facing the Gods," among others. The style is charming and informal, and the colors are in superb condition. The tomb of Zed Amun Ef Ankh has the unique feature of painted papyrus columns, an element normally found only in temples. Both temples were reused during the Roman era, when side chambers were dug to hold sarcophagi, some of which are still in place. The descent down to the tombs is difficult because of the steep, narrow stairs. ⊠ *On the main street, across from the Antiquities Office* ☎ *No phone* 🎫 *£e45, combination ticket for all local archaeological sites* ۞ *Sat.–Thurs. 8–5.*

★ Ten mummies from the Valley of the Golden Mummies are on view at the **Mummy Museum,** including two children and a baboon. In a typically provincial style, the mummies are plastered, gilded, and decorated with scenes from the underworld in a native cartoonlike design. These mummies were not processed in the same way as those in the Valley of the Kings, resulting in some degradation. The heat and humidity in the rather makeshift museum is also not helping to preserve the mummies. ⊠ *On the main street, across from the Antiquities Office, near the hospital* ☎ *No phone* 🎫 *£e45, combination ticket for all local archaeological sites* ۞ *Daily 8–5.*

The **Oasis Heritage Museum** was opened by local artist Muhammed Eid. It is a large castlelike mud-brick structure filled with his naively expressive clay sculptures and sand paintings that capture the character of the oasis. Don't miss the garden in front of the museum that's filled with life-size statues whose simple charm makes them worth a look. ⊠ *On the right as you leave Bawiti on the Cairo road, 2 km (¾ mi) after the checkpoint at the north end of town* ☎ *012/710–7969* 🎫 *Free; donations welcome* ۞ *Hours vary.*

The **Temple of Alexander the Great** is a desolate ruin made of sandstone and surrounded by ruins of mud-brick store rooms and living quarters. The sanctuary shows pharaonic reliefs of Alexander the Great and his mother, Olympias. Alexander's rich legacy is what makes the temple appealing. ⊠ *5 km (3 mi) south of Bawiti* ✛ *Turn left after Ahmed Safari Camp* ☎ *No phone* 🎫 *£e45, combination ticket for all local archaeological sites* ۞ *Daily 8–5.*

**OFF THE
BEATEN
PATH**

★ **Black Desert.** Bahariyya is surrounded by golden desert sand topped by black rocks of various kinds. In one spot south of Bawiti, a string of hills with black peaks lines the ancient fault that created them. This is the Black Desert. Off-road travel is possible for short distances in a regular car, but a four-wheel-drive vehicle is required to climb the sand dunes and explore at length; so is a guide who can take you to places you will never find yourself. (You can easily arrange for a guide at area hotels and restaurants.) ⊠ *About 25 km (16 mi) south of Bawiti, on road to Farafra Oasis.*

WHERE TO EAT

$ ✕**Popular Restaurant.** People have
MIDDLE enjoyed this street-side café's tra-
EASTERN ditional food since its owner came
here from the Nile Valley not long
after the asphalt road was constructed. The wooden tables and
chairs and green-lattice walls make
for a rather basic atmosphere, but
most desert explorers, both foreign
and local, hang out here sooner or
later. The food is also very basic,
and there's no menu, so ask for
the price in advance to avoid sur-
prises. One special is prepared each
day. A typical meal includes one or
two vegetable stews, boiled meat
or grilled chicken, rice, potatoes,
bread, and tea. ✉ *Center of town,
near the police station on the al-
Qasr road, Bawati* ☎ *No phone* ▭ *No credit cards.*

DESERT BATHROOMS
Older hotels and two- or three-star properties in the oases will usually have a very small bathroom with a wet shower area. This means that the shower head is just on the wall in the corner, and the water usually drains through an outlet in the floor; if there is a shower basin, there may be no shower curtain. For both these options, water from your shower will certainly wet the whole bathroom area, so remove towels, toilet paper, and anything else you don't want to be drenched before you turn the shower on.

$ ✕**Rashid Restaurant.** This simple restaurant is a trustworthy option
MIDDLE that's frequented by many travelers. The owner specializes in grilled
EASTERN chicken and an array of Egyptian desserts made especially with foreigners in mind (locals seldom eat out). The cooking here is inventive
and varied. Both indoor and outdoor dining are available in a clean,
well-lighted, ceramic-tiled area shaded throughout the day. You can
also try the sisha here. ✉ *On the main road, Bawati* ☎ *02/384–7237*
▭ *No credit cards.*

WHERE TO STAY

$ ▦**El-Beshmo Lodge Hotel.** El-Beshmo is the ancient name of Bahariyya's
central hot springs, and the lodge's bungalows occupy a peaceful spot
at the mouth of the gorge. The hotel, built with local reddish stone
blended with ochre-painted walls, embraces a sloping courtyard with
a blossoming garden. The rooms have serviceable, if careworn, furnishings. Bathrooms are small with wet showers (shower basins but
no curtains). There's a relaxing indoor public area with local carpets
and comfy seats, but most people prefer to spend evenings in the warm
air of the cozy courtyard. **Pros:** The courtyard is a great place for conversations with fellow travelers, as it is cool in summer and sheltered
from the wind in winter; the restaurant serves simple but delicious local
cuisine; the hotel's plunge pool is very private. **Cons:** Room furnishings
and paint need some attention (everything is clean but worn); cracks in
some walls at the back of the property. ✉ *El-Beshmo Springs, Al Qasr*
☎ *012/174–0800* ⊕ *www.beshmolodge.com* ⇌ *23 rooms* ♿ *In-room:
no a/c (some), no phone, refrigerator, no TV. In-hotel: restaurant, pool,
parking (free)* |◎|*CP* ▭ *No credit cards.*

$ ▦**Nature Camp.** Get back to nature by staying in one of these sim-
ple thatch-and-palm cottages set in gardens and surrounded by farmland with the dunes beyond. The camp is in the far north of the oasis,

7

offering a real feel of the rural tranquility, which you can enjoy from your room terrace. Older cottages don't have electricity or bathrooms (there's a clean communal toilet/shower block), but at this writing, work has started on several that will include such amenities; plus, there's a pool in this new extended area. Rooms are clean and tidy with beds set on concrete plinths complete with mosquito nets. Walls are insulated against the wind, and, overall, the cottages have a cozy feel. **Pros:** You can explore this rural idyll and feel part of the community; the owner is a good host who is happy to share his experience with you; the hotel can organize overnight excursions and trips into the desert. **Cons:** Lack of private bathrooms; at present, no electricity. ⊠ *El Dist, 17km (10mi) north of Bawati* ☎*02/347–3643* ↩*12* ☌ *In-room: no a/c, no phone, no TV. In-hotel: restaurant, bicycles, parking (free)* ⊟*no credit cards* ❙◎❙*CP.*

$ ▦ **Oasis Panorama Hotel.** As the name suggests, you get magnificent views across Bahariyya Oasis from the lookout point at this hotel, which is set among dramatic black-sand outcrops. The rooms are in an arc behind the main reception building, overlooking a verdant garden cooled by fountains. Older rooms, which are in two-story blocks decorated with colorful naive frescoes, have simple but clean white-washed interiors; a more recently built block of single-story domed bungalows re-creates the traditional local building style. The restaurant serves alcohol. **Pros:** The gardens make a great place to relax in the evenings; you can walk into Bahariyya from here; there are three different environments for eating—the air-conditioned restaurant, a covered conservatory area, or outside on the terrace. **Cons:** No pool. ⊠*Bawati* ✛ *Turn left just beyond the city checkpoint as you leave Bawati on the Cairo Road* ☎*02/847-3354* ⊕*www.oasispanorama.net* ↩*32 rooms* ☌ *In-room: no a/c (some), refrigerator. In-hotel: restaurant, bar, parking (free).* ⊟*No credit cards* ❙◎❙*CP.*

$$ ▦ **Palma Village Hotel.** The grand classical entrance hall, with its columns and cornices, presents a curious first impression in the middle of the desert. The formal dining room with high-backed chairs perpetuates the feeling that you've stumbled upon the long-lost home of some turn-of-the-20th-century explorer. Rooms, which are set around the rear gardens, offer two options. Older single-story domed bungalows are well furnished and have small patios in front but have wet showers (no curtain); newer rooms in two-story buildings are much bigger and have matching metal-and-wood furniture. A new wing with a large pool was expected, at this writing, to open in early 2009. **Pros:** New rooms are spacious with modern styling; the pool is tiled and has a good seating area. **Cons:** Just a little too far out of town to walk. ⊠*El-Aguz, turn left off the Cairo road just after Oasis Heritage Museum* ☎*02/849-6272* ↩*40 rooms* ☌ *In-room: no phone (some), refrigerator (some). In-hotel: restaurant, pool, parking (free).* ⊟*No credit cards* ❙◎❙*MAP.*

$$ ▦ **Qasr El Bawity Hotel.** This stone complex makes a dramatic impression, looking like a modern Islamic citadel in the region's traditional form—there's no concrete in the construction, and only traditional mortar has been used. Rooms are beautifully styled, having natural stone

Hot and Cold Springs

The springs are a gift of the desert, and they can be enjoyed day or night. In other parts of the world people pay small fortunes for the medicinal effects of hot and cold springs, but here they're free. Don't expect a spa atmosphere, however; things are more primitive in the oases and can be as simple as a pipe gushing water into a cement enclosure in the open air. Not all the springs are open, but in every oasis, one or two have been set aside for travelers. Women should swim with their arms and legs covered if local people are around. Neither you nor they will be at ease if you expose too much. ⚠ **People with high blood pressure or heart conditions, and pregnant women, should avoid the hotter springs. Check with your doctor before leaving on your trip.**

and stucco interiors with locally produced rugs and other handicrafts surrounding the wrought-iron furniture. There's a small pool fed by a natural spring, a spacious cool pool, and a garden where you can relax or enjoy a shisha under the shade of a gazebo. **Pros:** Traditional styling that's well crafted; the restaurant serves excellent *tagines* (traditional stews); you can book desert adventures directly with the hotel. **Cons:** No a/c, though fans and domed ceilings keep the air cool; prices are high compared to other area accommodations. ✉ *Bawati* ☎ *012/258–2586* ⊕ *www.qasrelbawity.com* ⇆ *24 rooms, 4 suites* ᵭ *In-room: no a/c, no phone, no TV* ☐ *No credit cards* ❑ *MAP.*

7

NIGHTLIFE & THE ARTS

★ In the village of al-Aguz, 5 km (3 mi) north of Bawiti, Bahariyya's local star, Abdel Sadek, hosts nights of **Bedouin music** (☎ *011/802–677*) in a large straw tent. This is something that should not be missed; the intense emotions and romantic longings of the desert dwellers are expressed nowhere better than in their music. The song of the *simsimeya* (a harplike instrument), the quick beat of the *tabla* (drum), and the wailing and droning sound of the double flute will transport you. If you could understand the heartbreaking, witty, and sometimes improvised lyrics, you too would erupt spontaneously in loud praise as the locals do when they gather around their musicians for a night of song and dance. The tent is open almost every night; inquire at your hotel for details.

SPORTS & THE OUTDOORS

DESERT TOURS Despite the not-so-comfortable conditions, exploring the desert with a four-wheel-drive is like entering an enchanted kingdom, touching upon areas known only to Bedouins. Prices range from £e150 to £e250 per person for a full-day tour. Trips farther afield to almost any oasis or dune in the desert by four-wheel-drive vehicle, camel, or on foot are easily arranged at Bahariyya hotels. Independent operators' names change frequently, and some are not licensed. Either way, they're the same faces and vehicles you see when you book through the hotels, so it doesn't make much difference. Tours can be arranged for the Black

Desert, al-Hayez, and Gilf al-Kebir (home of the Cave of the Swimmers, which was featured in the hit 1996 film *The English Patient*). At this writing, Oasis Panorama, El-Beshmo Lodge Hotel, and Qasr El Bawity all offer packages of varying kinds, from day trips to overnight camping to expeditions lasting days or weeks.

HORSEBACK RIDING
Exploring the oasis and surrounding area on horseback puts you at the pace of the donkeys and carts of the farmers around you, and it's a worthwhile experience for an hour or two—or even for a whole day.

Palma Village Hotel (⊠ *Al-Aguz, turn left off the Cairo road just after Oasis Heritage Museum* ☎ 02/849–6272) has stables with 12 horses to rent at £e18 per hour, but you need to be an experienced rider since there's no instruction for beginners. There are no riding helmets available, either.

BIR AL-GHABA

15 km (9 mi) west of Bawiti.

Bir al-Ghaba (which means "the forest spring") is the hot spring traditionally reserved for visitors. It lies in a small forest of eucalyptus trees, which makes getting here a desert adventure. The drive—or hike—first passes through traditional oasis gardens where farmers plant, grow, and harvest a variety of crops interspersed with fruit trees—orange, apricot, mango, guava, olive, tangerine, banana, and, of course, date palms. Then the road meanders over a desert track between the many black-topped mountains of Bahariyya. On the way to Bir al-Ghaba, about 7 km (4½ mi) from Bahariyya is Bir al-Mattar, a cold spring; it's on the left of the road and is a great place for a quick, cooling swim. After covering more desert, you enter a garden and, suddenly, Bir al-Ghaba appears. Camping is welcome here. The terrain can be difficult but is navigable by regular car, though there is a lot of sand near Bir al-Mattar.

FARAFRA OASIS

Farafra is what most people picture when they imagine a desert oasis: bubbling springs, a lush garden, a little village, and a vast desert all around. The immense sky and endless desert add to the hushed atmosphere. People here are quiet, polite, and reserved. A local story tells of how the people of Farafra once lost track of time and had to send a rider to Dakhla to find out what day it was so they could perform the Friday prayer on the correct day. There are only a few ruins at Farafra, none of them interesting enough for the typical tourist to spend much time viewing, especially with the White Desert close at hand. A dynamic natural wonder that you can explore in numerous ways, the White Desert is the centerpiece of any trip to Farafra.

QASR AL-FARAFRA

About 180 km (112 mi) southwest of Bahariyya; 340 km (211 mi) northeast of Dakhla.

Ten years ago Qasr al-Farafra had a frontier atmosphere, and only a few timid one-story buildings spilled down from the fortress hill to meet the traffic on the Cairo road. These days, the village has spread to both sides of the road. The discovery of water has been changing the area's demographics, with people from the Nile Valley homesteading here in the many thousands (20,000 at the last count). The increase in population has helped to bring some measure of prosperity—enough to expand Qasr al-Farafra—but despite this rapid growth, it remains one of the most enchanting places in the desert. Sitting in the village is an experience in itself because the locals enjoy mingling with the travelers who come through (rarely are there more than 20 travelers here at a time).

The best way to savor the village and the surrounding desert is by walking. A meander through the maze of alleys in Qasr al-Farafra still gives you an idea of a time before the road linked the oases to the rest of Egypt, when this was an isolated fortress town weeks away from the Nile: giggling children play in the street, and old men in traditional clothing squat on the ground chatting as they make camel-wool yarn with homemade spindles. With luck you might even spot an old woman, complete with black embroidered dress, tattoos, and small gold nose ring, hurrying through a passageway. In the collapsing center of the village is a mound of Roman bricks, once a fortress but now conquered by goats. A walk in the ancient irrigated gardens on the gentle slope behind Qasr al-Farafra is a venture into the past; show respect and stay on the paths.

★ The small, constantly evolving **Badr Museum**, built of mud brick by the local artist Badr, is a multilevel castle of the imagination, where exterior and interior staircases and bridges connect terraces and courtyards to exhibition rooms. Badr's clay sculptures and paintings of the Farafra people, the desert, and his surreal dreams are displayed here. Carvings of Arabic calligraphy and desert scenes also adorn the walls. Around the building Badr is creating an almost grotesque-looking mini-desert, with tree trunks that resemble camels and stones fashioned to resemble old women. The museum doesn't have set hours; if it's closed, you can ask about the artist's whereabouts at the nearby Nice Time Coffee Shop. ✉*Next to the school, between the main road and old Qasr al-Farafra* ☎092/751–0091 ✉*Free; donations welcome* ✆*Hours vary.*

WHERE TO EAT & STAY

The inexpensive roadside restaurants cater mainly to truck drivers and visitors, and the menus are the same as everywhere else in the oases: rice; vegetables; chicken; *koshary* (a popular Egyptian meal of rice, lentils, and pasta served with browned onions and tomato sauce); *ful* (fava beans either stewed with tomatoes, with eggs, or even as a sandwich); and *ta'amiya* (Egyptian falafel consisting of fava beans ground with fresh herbs and spices and then deep fried). These small affairs close, reopen, and change names and owners often, but there's always a small handful of them strung along the main road.

$-$$
MIDDLE
EASTERN

✕ **El Badawiya Hotel Restaurant.** This large, air-conditioned dining hall offers a relaxing rest stop. You can eat out on the terrace on balmy evenings, but there's a fire inside to temper the chill in winter. The menu is predominantly local dishes—rice, chicken, omelettes, and *mezze* (small plates reminiscent of tapas) with ingredients sourced in the oasis and the surrounding area. There are different set menus each day. ⊠ *At the entrance to Qasr al-Farafra (from the direction of Bahariyya), before the gas station* ☎ *092/751–1163, 02/575–8076 in Cairo* ⊕ *www. badawiya.com* ⊟ *No credit cards.*

$

⊞ **El Badawiya Hotel.** Drawing inspiration from the traditional architectural style of the region, this hotel makes a comfortable base, and accommodation comes in three types. The hotel's 12 two-story, split-level rooms sit under domed ceilings; beds, covered with mosquito nets, are on the upper floors. There are also eight bungalows with the same facilities, and all these rooms have fans and heaters. The most recent additions are 13 air-conditioned suites furnished with local handicrafts. The restaurant–lobby is spread out under a series of white domes and arches opening onto gardens and courtyards. The hotel has the largest swimming pool in any of the oases. **Pros:** Nice styling throughout; suites are particularly well appointed and a good value for money; great pool. **Cons:** Only the suites are air-conditioned. ⊠ *At the entrance to Qasr al-Farafra (from the direction of Bahariyya), before the gas station* ☎ *092/751–1163, 02/575–8076 in Cairo* ⊕ *www.badawiya.com* ⇱ *20 rooms, 13 suites* ⚘ *In-room: no a/c (some), refrigerator (some). In-hotel: restaurant, pool, parking (free)* ⊟ *No credit cards* ¦⊙¦*BP.*

WHITE DESERT

★ *35 km (22 mi) north of Qasr al-Farafra.*

The White Desert is legendary. Covering most of the northeastern portion of the Farafra depression, it's a land of enchantment where everything is white: the ground, the cliffs, the mountains, even the horizon. This is an ancient ocean floor that erosion shaped into bizarre and comical outcroppings scattered about in small and large groupings. Some are a mere 2 feet tall and look like crickets. Others are 14 to 20 feet tall and look like elephants or whales or squirrels. Still others tower hundreds of feet into the air, true inselbergs (isolated mountains) housing seashells in their steep, straight sides. Two of the best have been named **The Monoliths** and are visible from a great distance. When the moon is full, the entire desert shimmers in pale light. You can stay an hour, a day, a week, or a year; it's endlessly enlightening. You can explore the White Desert on foot or by motorbike, car, or four-wheel-drive vehicle.

Two small springs, **Ain al-Wadi** and **Magic Spring,** are close to the White Desert. Both are visible at great distances as curious green mounds with palm trees stuck on top. They have made good rest stops for centuries, since the times when the Bedouin rested their caravans on their way to the Nile Valley.

One major reason to come to Farafra is to camp in the White Desert. All tour groups include the desert in their itineraries. While the vast majority of people visit on a guided tour, it is possible to go independently. If you do it on your own, you'll need to get permission from the police at either Farafra or Bahariyya. They may insist that you take an armed officer for security purposes (though the security risk is minimal). Stick close to the road, and be sure to bring food, fuel, sleeping bags, and water; then just pick a spot. Supplies, including warm camel blankets, are available in Qasr al-Farafra. A few rules: Keep tents and vehicles out of sight (hide them behind a white monolith) so others can enjoy the view; pick up all your debris before you leave; and don't take away any rocks or fossils.

DESERT TOURS
Three friendly brothers, Atef Ali, Hamdi, and Sa'ad, own the Badawiya Hotel in Qasr al-Farafra. Proud of their desert and its heritage, the brothers offer all types of desert tours through their **Badawiya Expedition Travel** (☎092/751–1163, 02/575–8076 in Cairo ⊕www.badawiya. com), with very good service as part of the bargain. Specialties are camel tours to the White Desert, Ain Della (a remote watering hole), and the Great Sand Sea (hundreds of square miles of constantly shifting sands to the west); four-wheel-drive trips also are available. Local tours include trips to Bir Setta and Cold Lake, or you can even try a 15-day expedition by jeep. Prices are about $120 to $150 per person per day, for a trip by camel or four-wheel-drive vehicle and meals. Some expeditions require governmental permits, which will be an extra daily charge.

DAKHLA OASIS

Dakhla remains a breadbasket, just as it was in Roman times. The rich patchwork of shifting yellow dunes, red earth, green farmland, and ancient mud-brick villages is like a mirage against a background of pink and white cliffs that rise up sharply to shelter the oasis. The people here wear straw hats, which give the place a South American feel. Although the oasis has a large number of ancient ruins—including the restored Egyptian temple at Deir al-Haggar, the ruins of an entire Roman community called Amheida, and an Old Kingdom site near Bashindi—the Islamic fortress towns remain its crowning glory.

Many of Dakhla's Islamic fortress towns are built on Roman foundations that probably overlay pharaonic structures; there's evidence that Dakhla has been inhabited constantly since Neolithic times. Sights are spread throughout the oasis, so if you visit, schedule two days for seeing them.

MUT

About 300 km (186 mi) southeast of Qasr al-Farafra; 147 km (91 mi) west of Kharga.

The central village of Mut (pronounced *moot*) has five main streets and five *maydans* (squares). Some have names, but most do not. Even if you ask directions from locals, they're not likely to know the newly adopted street names, but then the place is so small you can hardly get lost.

> ### DAKHLA HATS
>
> Look out for the hats worn by farmers in the countryside around Dakhla. These round, narrow-brimmed caps made of soft, hand-woven straw with a colored cotton trim are unique in the oases.

Along the base of a number of rocks near the south side of the road east of Tineida (50 km [30 mi] west of Mut) are **ancient rock inscriptions.** Rock art exists throughout North Africa, but much of it is found in places so remote that most of us will never see it. Here, the ancient art is a few feet from the modern road. It's an amazing hodgepodge of Bedouin giraffes, tribal brand markings, Coptic inscriptions, Islamic writing, and even a drawing of a pregnant woman. To preserve the inscriptions, do not add to them or take rubbings.

EN ROUTE From Mut you can take the secondary road west and north to Qasr al-Dakhla, making a left turn off the main road just north of the village of al-Dahuz. The secondary road takes you by a few old villages. You can see the Mamluk fortress-town of **Qalamun** appearing above the domes of an ancient Islamic cemetery against a dramatic background of palm trees and distant cliffs. Several kilometers to the north, the ruined arches and towers of **Amheida,** an ancient Roman town scattered over a large area close to the road, are impressive even today.

WHERE TO EAT

$ ✕**Abu Muhammed Restaurant.** The reputation of Abu Muhammed is as
MIDDLE big as the portions. While you eat the simple and delicious food—pri-
EASTERN marily rice, mezze, slow-cooked stews, and grilled meats—in the shade of vines on a tiny terrace, you may be shown a stack of guest books full of praise. This is also a good place to rent bicycles. ✉*Shar'a al-Thauwra al-Khadra* ☎*092/782–1431* ▭*No credit cards.*

$ ✕**Ahmed Hamdi Restaurant.** Restaurants run in Ahmed Hamdi's fam-
MIDDLE ily. Originally, his father operated a restaurant. His brother—they're
EASTERN friendly rivals—runs the Hamdi Restaurant on the same street; both are clean and friendly, practically side by side near the Mebarez Tourist Hotel. The food is good, and the prices modest. (A third brother runs tours that you can book at either restaurant.) You can dine inside or out. Meals are served from 6 AM to 11 PM. For breakfast, try the tomato omelette along with ful, the first national dish of Egypt, and ta'amiya. ✉*Third St. (the Farafra road)* ☎*092/794–0767* ▭*No credit cards.*

WHERE TO STAY

$ 🏨**Bedouin Oasis Village & Spa.** This kooky hilltop spot is part laid-back hippie village and part architectural experiment—with sand and seeds on the floors and crumpled brown paper adorning walls throughout the reception and communal areas. Accommodation is in small, domed Bedouin bungalows with simple furnishings and tiny bathrooms. The hotel has a natural spring pool and offers hot-sand spa treatments. The terrace restaurant and bar offer views over Mut town. The Oasis Village serves alcohol. **Pros:** Very individual styling unique in the oases; management style is laid-back; possibility of a cold beer after a day exploring in the heat. **Cons:** Rooms are very compact. ⊠*Mut, on the main road north to Farafra on the right, 1.5 km (1 mi) after the tourist office* ☎*016/335–8673* ⟿*30 rooms* ⚐*In-room: no a/c, no phone, no TV. In-hotel: restaurant, bar, pool, parking (free)* ▤*No credit cards* ⦿*MAP.*

$ ⌂**Mebarez Tourist Hotel.** What makes this four-story hotel noteworthy is that it brings the standard of mid-range interchangeable international hotels to the desert—where a nondescript hotel is in fact unique. The whole hotel is clean and well maintained, even though the fixtures are a few years old (this was the first hotel to open in town). There's an attention to detail and care here that's more noticeable than in other hotels in this price range. **Pros:** well-maintained three-star property; inviting pool and patio at the back of the hotel. **Cons:** Not all rooms have private bathrooms; all private baths have wet showers. ⊹*Take Shar'a al-Thauwra al-Khadra 1 km (½ mi) east of Mut* ☎*092/782–1524* ⟿*30 rooms* ⚐*In-room: no a/c (some), refrigerator, no TV. In-hotel: restaurant, pool* ▤*No credit cards* ⦿*CP.*

$$ ⌂**Sol Y Mar Mut Inn.** A curious two-part motel-style property that makes a good overnight stop is less inviting for a long stay. The main part of the property offers tiny bungalows around a natural hot spring, which has been formed into a swimming pool. There's a paved area for relaxation, but the young trees offer little shade. If you're tired of desert food, an international menu is served at the hotel restaurant, which is down the road (about 250 yards away) along with a few larger rooms, some without bathrooms. **Pros:** Restaurant offers more than just standard Egyptian fare; hot springs on-site are soothing, especially on chilly winter evenings or after a long dusty day on the road; alcohol is available. **Cons:** Rooms around the pool are small; beds in twin-bed rooms are very narrow. ⊹*Take Shar'a al-Thauwra al-Khadra 3 km (2 mi) east of Mut, in front of Wahat al-Khargha* ☎*092/792–7982* ⟿*21 rooms* ⚐*In-room: no a/c (some), no TV. In-hotel: restaurant, bar, pool, parking (free)* ▤*AE, MC, V* ⦿*MAP.*

DESERT TOURS

Tours to the desert and around Dakhla Oasis aren't as numerous as at Farafra and Bahariyya. They can be arranged through the **Ahmed Hamdi Restaurant** (⇨ *Where to Eat, above*), as well as through other restaurants in Dakhla, or through the tourist-information office in Mut (⇨ *Visitor Information in Western Desert Oases Essentials, below*). Most tours include the Islamic villages, but you can also go to the escarpment and various dune belts from here.

QASR AL-DAKHLA

32 km (20 mi) west of Mut on Farafra Road.

★ You approach Qasr al-Dakhla (*Qasr* means "castle") through a pine grove. Once you reach the old village, you must walk. Qasr al-Dakhla is still inhabited, though sparsely, and the entire village is now a protected historical site. The striking medieval village streets are really paths that lead past still-occupied mud-brick and stucco houses to a 12th-century Ayyubid mosque, its ancient minaret intact, and an Ayyubid *madrasa* (medieval school) used also as a courtroom and, until the late 20th century, a town hall meeting room. The most important antiquities in Dakhla are carved, wooden Islamic beams that were erected in medieval times over entrances to the houses of prominent citizens. There are a number of them here. In a few doorways, wooden door lintels rest on pharaonic temple stones reused as door frames, creating an unusual juxtaposition of Arabic writing against hieroglyphs. Admission is free, but a friendly guardian will lead you through the maze of dusty streets and narrow covered alleyways, so remember to give him a small tip.

At the edge of the village is a **pottery factory** where for centuries potters have made unique vessels, turning the ancient wheels with their feet. The pots are fired in hand-built kilns in the nearby potter's garden.

OFF THE
BEATEN
PATH

Al-Muzawaka. The two colorful tombs here—*muzawaka* actually contains the word for color—date to Roman times. The decorations combine stylized ancient Egyptian art with more realistic Roman figures and motifs. ✛ *Take the road to Farafra west from Qasr al-Dakhla for about 5 km (3 mi), then take the left (south) turnoff and continue for about 1 km (½ mi) to the tombs* 🕾 *No phone* 🎫 *£e25* ⊘ *Daily 9–5.*

Deir al-Haggar. Thanks to the shifting dunes, this small pharaonic temple (its Arabic name translates as "the stone monastery"), commissioned by the Roman emperor Nero and continued under Vespasian, Domitian, and Titus, is well preserved and well restored. It is dedicated to the Theban triad of Amun, Mut, and Khonsu, and some of the reliefs still have color. The interior shows images of the pharaoh making offerings to Horus. The carvings of two lions guarding the way into the inner sanctum—at the base of the two columns flanking the portal—have good detail. The inner sanctum shows Vespasian as pharaoh making offerings to Amun. The mud-brick ruins of a Byzantine monastery surrounding the temple have remains of frescoes. ✛ *Take the road to Farafra west from Qasr al-Dakhla for about 10 km (6 mi), then take the marked turnoff on the left (there are no signs in English) and follow this road until it ends (about 4 km [2½ mi]), then drive 2 km (1 mi) east, or toward the left, over the desert floor to the temple* 🕾 *No phone* 🎫 *£e25* ⊘ *Sat.–Thurs. dawn–dusk, Fri. until noon.*

WHERE TO STAY

$$$ 🏨 **Desert Lodge.** On a hill overlooking Qasr al-Dakhla, this hotel has
★ exceptional views over the town and the surrounding desert. Built of traditional mud bricks finished with a layer of mud and straw stucco,

the exterior design draws its inspiration from the old qasr. Only local products and local craftsmen were used during the construction, and the result is a triumph, offering one of the highest standards of service, not to mention the nicest rooms, in the desert. You'll find such unexpected luxuries as a public Internet terminal (albeit with a dial-up connection). The rooms are spacious, with turquoise the main accent on walls and furnishings. The historic citadel is just a 10-minute walk from the hotel, though it may be too hot to walk during the summer. The restaurant serves alcohol. **Pros:** Desert Lodge has an active eco policy, with filtered water that's suitable for drinking (to avoid use of plastic bottles) as well as a recycling program; the restaurant serves organic vegetables that are grown on the property's own nearby farm; the hotel can organize excursions and safaris. **Cons:** No a/c in rooms. ⊠ *Qasr al-Dakhla, on a hill above the town* ☎*092/772–7062, 02/690–5240 in Cairo* ⊕*www.desertlodge.net* ↩*32 rooms* ⌂*In-room: no a/c, no TV. In-hotel: restaurant, bar, pool, laundry service, Internet terminal, parking (free).* ⊟*AE, MC, V* ⦿*MAP.*

BALAT

35 km (21 mi) east of Mut.

Heading east from Mut toward al-Kharga you'll come upon a stretch of desert that separates the villages of Balat and Bashindi from the rest of Dakhla. On the edge of the desert, Balat, a tiny fortress village and site of an important Old Kingdom town, barely rises high enough to be called a hill fortress, but it's pretty enough to warrant a visit.

The small mastaba tomb of **Qilaa al-Dabba** is interesting in that it was the first evidence that Dakhla was known to the Old Kingdom. French archaeologists moved and reconstructed the mastaba, dedicated to Khentika, who was the governor of the oasis at the time, and unearthed the deep-lying tomb, now seen as a stone structure on the bottom of a huge pit. The colors of the scenes in the tomb chamber, which have been dated to the 6th Dynasty (2460–2200 BC), are intact. The desert around the site is full of mud-brick ruins. ✢*From the main road to Kharga, turn left onto the track on the eastern edge of Balat, and follow it into the desert for about 1 km (½ mi)* ☎*No phone* ⌸*£e20* ☉*Daily dawn–dusk.*

BASHINDI

5 km (3 mi) east of Balat; 40 km (24 mi) east of Mut.

Sometimes referred to as a *real* pharaonic village, Bashindi does have an unusual architectural style. Everything seems to be softly curving, bending, curling, and undulating in this tidy little place. Doors are oval and have "lips," corners are round, and stairs droop. The inhabitants are proud of their village and keep it clean; you might even be invited to see the inside of a house. If you do see such an interior, don't forget to tip.

Part of a small Roman cemetery, the **Tomb of Ketinus** is the only tomb in Bashindi that is still intact. Pharaonic reliefs show scenes of mummification and the deceased in front of the gods. Outside the tomb, several empty sandstone sarcophagi are scattered among the ruins. Ask in the village for the guard who can open the tomb. ✉ *Bashindi* ☎ *No phone* 🎫 *£e25, combined ticket with Tomb of Sheikh Bashindi* 🕐 *Daily dawn–dusk.*

The **Tomb of Sheikh Bashindi,** next to the Tomb of Ketinus, is an interesting architectural hybrid. It has an Egypto-Roman sandstone tomb as the square base and an Islamic mud-brick dome as a roof. The tomb may only be viewed from the outside. ☎ *No phone* 🎫 *£e25, combined ticket with Tomb of Ketinus.*

KHARGA OASIS

The dominant features of this oasis are its long lines of crescent dunes and mountains that rise up from the floor of the depression. The main town, Qasr al-Kharga, is the capital of the New Valley Governorate, and as such it has become very modernized—a concrete yawn conceived on the drawing board. To see that the Kharga Oasis possesses the best the desert has to offer, you have to move beyond its populated areas. Its major antiquities aren't the ancient Egypto-Roman ruins south of Qasr al-Kharga at Ghueita or Zayyan (Luxor's are far better), but rather the Christian burial ground at Bagawat, a remarkable array of remote Roman forts that present more mysteries than answers, and a growing number of even more mysterious underground aqueducts that keep being discovered throughout North Africa. Combined, these are the most spectacular man-made ruins in the Western Desert.

QASR AL-KHARGA

About 200 km (124 mi) east of Mut.

What was Kharga's main village is now a city. If it's your first stop in the desert, you'll likely be disappointed: Qasr al-Kharga is fairly average, and the antiquities pale in comparison to Nile Valley monuments. However, several magical Roman fortresses are on the outskirts of the city.

★ You need to travel by four-wheel-drive to reach **Ain Om al-Dabadib,** a Roman fortress 20 km (13 mi) west of Qasr al-Labeka via a desert track. Excavation at the settlement has been very limited, which adds to the magic of the place; the huge mud-brick fortress has four square towers that rise above two villages, a temple, a Coptic church from the 5th century AD, and four aqueducts (including one more than 13 km [8 mi] long). Unfortunately, looting by fortune-hunters is destroying the site. ⊕ *Take the Kharga–Asyut highway north from Qasr al-Kharga for 38 km (24 mi), turn left (west), and drive 10 km (6 mi) into the desert to Qasr al-Labeka; from there, take the desert track west for another 20 km (13 mi)* ☎ *No phone* 🎫 *Free* 🕐 *Daily dawn–dusk.*

★ Hundreds of brown-domed Coptic tombs line the crest of a hill in **al-Bagawat,** a Christian cemetery. They date from a time between the 4th and 7th centuries AD, when Nicaean and Arian Copts wrestled among themselves over the concept of God the Father, God the Son, and the Holy Spirit—was God one, or three in one?

Bagawat is probably the oldest Christian cemetery of such magnitude in the world, and it's certainly the oldest in this desert. Two tombs have ceilings painted with Biblical scenes. The Church of Peace is the best preserved, with scenes from the Bible, including depictions of Adam and Eve, Noah's Ark, and St. Paul. These date from the late 5th century AD. The Chapel of the Exodus at the summit of the complex dates from the 4th century, and the Biblical scenes and characters here are depicted in an earlier, more naive artistic style. The paintings are in better condition than those in the Church of Peace. There is also a mud-brick basilica. Behind the cemetery are a number of ruins that have yet to be excavated. They dot the plain like lonely sentinels in a place that once bustled with caravans. Bagawat is on the northern outskirts of Qasr al-Kharga, north of the Temple of Hibis. ⊠ *3 km (2 mi) north of Qasr al-Kharga, to the left of the Kharga–Asyut highway* ⊠ *£e30* ⊙ *Daily 8–5.*

The **Deir al-Kashef** (*Monastery of the Tax Collector*) overlooks one of the most important crossroads in the Western Desert. The imposing mud-brick ruin contains a honeycomb of monk cells and once stood five stories tall. Below it is the ruin of a small church. To get here, drive 1 km (½ mi) north on the desert track from al-Bagawat. ⊠ *About 4 km (2½ mi) north of Qasr al-Kharga, off to the left of the Kharga–Asyut highway* ⊠ *Free* ⊙ *Daily dawn–dusk.*

★ **Deir al-Munira,** also known simply as al-Deir (which means "the monastery"), is a Roman mud-brick fortress with 12 towers, and it is one of the must-sees in Kharga. Although it's in the desert, you can reach al-Deir without a four-wheel-drive vehicle if you have the help of an experienced guide. ⊹ *Take the Kharga–Asyut highway north from Qasr al-Kharga for 20 km (13 mi), turn right (east) at Azbet Ain al-Aal, and drive 10 km (6 mi) farther, into the desert* ☎ *No phone* ⊠ *Free* ⊙ *Daily dawn–dusk.*

The small, well-organized **New Valley Museum** is a perfect finale to a trip to the Western Desert oases. The collection spans more than 15,000 years of New Valley history. Finds are displayed from the Neolithic, pharaonic, Greco-Roman, Coptic, and Mamluk to Ottoman periods. The displays are presented in rather staid wood-and-glass cases, but the information in English is well put together. The ground floor concentrates on ancient finds, and pride of place must go to a small selection of Greco-Roman era mummies just beyond the entrance. One has the gilt face indicating it's one of the "Golden" mummies of the oases. The most rare objects are the nondescript Old Kingdom terracotta jars displayed in the hall to the right of the mummies, which are unique to the oases region. The second floor displays items from the Islamic era, including blue tiles, cut glass, and Mamluk clothing from Qasr al-Dakhla.

✉*Shar'a Jamal 'Abd al-Nasir, 2 km (1 mi) north of Qasr al-Kharga.*
🕿*No phone* 💳*£e30* 🕙*Sun.–Thurs. 9–5, Fri. 9–noon and 3–5.*

Rebuilt and restored by pharaonic, Ptolemaic, and Persian rulers, the well-preserved Ptolemaic **Qasr al-Ghueita** (*Palace of the Beautiful One*) is a sandstone temple dedicated to the Theban triad of Amun, Mut, and Khonsu. It's protected by a Roman mud-brick enclosure wall. ⚜ *Take the main road to Baris south from Qasr al-Kharga for 18 km (11 mi), take left (east) turnoff, and follow road for 2 km (1 mi)* 🕿*No phone* 💳*£e16* 🕙*Daily 8–5.*

★ The Roman mud-brick fortress of **Qasr al-Labeka**, built between the 3rd and 5th centuries AD, is accessible only with an all-terrain vehicle, but it's worth the effort. The site includes an aqueduct and two temples. The northern temple, surrounded by the fortress structure, is dedicated to Amun. Little information is available on the southern temple. Nearby, vaulted tombs show remains of color. ⚜ *Take the Kharga–Asyut highway north from Qasr al-Kharga for 38 km (24 mi), turn left (west), and drive 10 km (6 mi) into the desert* 🕿*No phone* 💳*Free* 🕙*Daily dawn–dusk.*

The temple at **Qasr al-Zayyan** is dedicated to the local deity Amon-Hebet, protector of Qasr al-Kharga. Next to the temple is a small Roman fortress. ⚜ *Take the main road to Baris south from Qasr al-Kharga for 18 km (11 mi), take left (east) turnoff, and follow road for 2 km (1 mi) to Qasr al-Ghueita; continue south along road for another 7 km (4½ mi)* 🕿*No phone* 💳*£e16* 🕙*Daily 8–5.*

On a desert hill east of the main road to Asyut is the **Temple and Fortress of Nadura** (*nadura* means "the lookout"). The mud-brick structure, built in AD 138 by Antonius Pius, is in ruins, but the view, which stretches across the surrounding area, is worth a look. ✉*2 km (1 mi) north of Qasr al-Kharga, off to the right of the Kharga–Asyut highway* 🕿*No phone* 💳*Free.*

The Persian **Temple of Hibis** is the pride of Kharga. It originally was dedicated to the god Amun and later was rebuilt during the reign of the emperor Darius I (510–490 BC). The temple has been the subject of intense activity during the last decade because rising groundwater has forced conservationists to move it a few hundred meters from its original site. It reopened to the public in late 2008. The pylon has fine bas-relief scenes, and some color remains. ✉*2 km (1 mi) north of Qasr al-Kharga, to the left of the Kharga–Asyut highway* 🕿*No phone* 💳*£e30* 🕙*Daily 8–5.*

▌ **OFF THE BEATEN PATH**

Qasr al-Dush. The legend that the temple here was covered in gold conveys the strategic importance of this hilltop fortress. As well as ruling over Darb al-Arbain—the southern gateway to Egypt on the ancient caravan trail to sub-Saharan Africa—the fortress probably controlled the Darb al-Dush route to Edfu and Esna in the Nile Valley. Built of sandstone by Domitian in the 1st century AD and dedicated to Osiris and Seraphis, the temple lies on the eastern side of the mud-brick fortress. Below are remains of Persian irrigation systems. A Roman gold crown and bracelets found here in 1987 are on display at the Egyptian Antiquities Museum in Cairo. ✉*115 km (75 mi) southeast of Qasr al-Kharga; 23 km (15 mi) southeast of Baris* ☎*No phone* 🎟️*£e25* ⊙*Daily 7–5.*

WHERE TO EAT & STAY

Good restaurants are conspicuously lacking in Kharga. For fair attempts at Western cooking and basic meals of ful, falafel, and chicken, try the restaurant at the Sol Y Mar Pioneer Hotel, which is also the only recommendable hotel in town. The owner of the Qasr El Bawity Hotel in Bahariyya (*see* ⇨ *Where to Stay, under Bahariyya, above*) is currently constructing a traditional-style property, the Qasr El Bagawat Hotel (at this writing, due to open in early 2009), which should improve competition.

> ### THE TEMPLE OF HIBIS
>
> This temple stands on the ancient, so-called 40-Day caravan route that linked Egypt with central Africa. It presents a dramatic statement of Egyptian power and influence—a sign of reassurance for Egyptians that they were close to home and a clear signal to any slaves or prisoners they were transporting that they were now subject to a mighty new rule of law.

$
MIDDLE
EASTERN
✕**Wemby Elb Sateen Restaurant.** With its marble walls and floors, including marble on the terrace outside, this restaurant has a more upmarket image than its neighbors. The menu, however, is the typical soup, rice, chicken, and salad offered everywhere. On the plus side, you can sit outside and watch everyday life happening on the square beyond. The tea shop next door will happily deliver to your table. ✉*Maydan Elb Sateen* ☎*092/793–7105* ▭*No credit cards* ⊙*No lunch Fri.*

$$$ 🏨**Sol Y Mar Pioneers Hotel.** The salmon-colored stucco Pioneers is the only truly international-style property in the region, offering amenities such as an ATM in the lobby, a comfortable lounge–bar where you can enjoy a drink, and a pool where it takes more than ten strokes to get from one end to the other. The styling and design is not sympathetic to the region, however; standards of decor and service are imported from the Nile Valley. Spacious rooms have sitting areas; some have balconies. The hotel offers desert tours of various durations that connect the oases to Luxor, Aswan, and Abu Simbel. **Pros:** facilities here are truly up to international standards; a good-size pool surrounded by manicured lawns. **Cons:** the hotel design and decor don't convey any sense of location. ✉*Shar'a Jamal 'Abd al-Nasir* ☎*092/792–9751* ⊕*www.solymar. com* ☞*96 rooms, 6 suites* ♿*In-room: safe. In-hotel: restaurant, bar, pool, laundry service, parking (free), no-smoking rooms* ▭*AE, V, MC* ❏◎*BP.*

7

DESERT TOURS

Despite the great number of sights around Qasr al-Kharga, visitors tend to stay away from the town, so arranging tours here isn't as easy as it is in the other oases—and much-needed all-terrain vehicles are difficult to get. The **Sol Y Mar Pioneers Hotel** (✉*Shar'a Jamal 'Abd al-Nasir*

CLOSE UP

The Toshka Project

Egypt's most ambitious civil engineering project since the building of the Aswan High Dam, the Toshka Project (or New Valley Project) will bring water to the desert via a new, 310-km-long canal from the Toshka Lakes (a westerly outcrop of Lake Nasser) to Paris Oasis just south of Kharga. A giant pumping station the size of 10 football stadiums will pump 25 million cubic meters of water every day into the canal—named after Sheikh Zayed of Saudi Arabia, who provided significant funds for the project—to irrigate 588,000 acres of desert. When the project is completed in 2020, the Egyptian government hopes to increase Egypt's stock of farmland by 10%, and by 2030 (when the irrigation scheme reaches full capacity), there will actually be a third more irrigated land here than at present, and the Nile Valley will have a sibling running parallel with it through the desert to the west.

☎092/792–9751 ⊕*www.solymar.com*) can arrange tours. You may also be able to find a tour guide at the bus station. If you do arrange a tour, visit at least one of the local forts.

SIWA OASIS

Siwa, the northernmost oasis in the Western Desert, and the smallest after Farafra, is leagues away from the loop road. Near the Libyan border, it has some of the most beautiful scenery you'll see in the Western Desert. Because of its location, Siwa's influences have come from North Africa rather than central Africa or the Nile Valley; it wasn't until the end of Ottoman rule in Egypt in 1820 that Siwa lost its status as an independent city–state (although locals say the oasis was independent until the 1980s, when the road connecting it to Marsa Matruh was built). The people here speak a Berber (an Afro-Asiatic language group) dialect, and some older people still wear exotic clothing and adornments; the Traditional Siwan House in the eponymous main town of the oasis is a good place to see how they live. Siwa was the home of the ancient Oracle that reportedly confirmed to Alexander the Great that he was the offspring of the gods.

Renting bicycles is a cheap and delightful way to explore the oasis. Main roads are paved, and the signposting is good.

SIWA

About 300 km (186 mi) southwest of Marsa Matruh; 783 km (485 mi) west of Cairo, via Marsa Matruh.

Siwans lived in the hilltop fortress village of **Shali**, founded in the 12th or 13th century, for hundreds of years, adding stories to their mud-brick homes as the population increased. The fortress enclave was occupied by two distinct groups—the westerners and the easterners—and they often broke into armed conflict over indiscretions. Today Shali is mostly in ruins, and the people live in more modern and convenient homes beneath its watchful eye. Still in use is the 17th-century Shali mosque, with its unique mud-brick minaret.

The main square below the ancient fortress village, which is illuminated at night, is the busy focal point of life in the oasis. Most hotels, shops, and restaurants are around it. From here, all explorations of Siwa begin.

The best places in the Western Desert to buy crafts, including jewelry, rugs, embroidery, and baskets, can be found around the foot of the crumbling Shali fortress. ⚠ There's only one bank in Siwa, so bring plenty of Egyptian cash with you.

THE DATE WINE FESTIVAL

The Date Wine Festival held at Jabel al-Dakrour has always traditionally marked the end of the date harvest. All the farming families in the surrounding area would get together and spend the night of the October full moon celebrating—each family bringing food to share with the others. Today, the harvest still takes place, but the party guest list has been widened to include anyone who wants to have fun. Visitors are invited, too. The event is now called the "Siwa Holiday."

Great leaders, artists, and thinkers of the ancient world—among them the Olympian poet Pindar, the Spartan general Lysander, the Greek geographer Strabo, and, of course, Alexander the Great—came to consult the Oracle at Siwa, in the hilltop village of **Aghurmi**. What remains of the ancient **Temple of the Oracle**, a 26th-Dynasty sandstone temple dedicated to Amun, stands at the heart of a later Islamic mud-brick fortress. There's little left of the temple itself, but the strong sandstone walls and monumental entrance portal stand in contrast to the disintegrating walls of the surrounding citadel, which was built in the 15th century. The original city gates are still in place; these were closed every night to keep the citizens safe against bandits. The mosque of the citadel has been restored with traditional date palm wood and mud stucco and is used for prayers. Below it, at the base of the rock hill on which Aghurmi was planted, are the ruins of the 30th-Dynasty **Temple of Amun**, which was built during the reign of King Nectambo II (360–343 BC). ✉ 4 km (2½ mi) east of the town of Siwa ✆ £e25, temple of Amun free ☉ Daily 9–5; Temple of Amun daily dawn–dusk.

Jabal al-Dakrour is known for its traditional rheumatism treatments, which include sitting in a hot sand bath. In addition, the traditional three-day Siwa Holiday, an ancient festival (formerly the Date Wine Festival) that takes place during the full moon in October, is held here. ✉ About 5 km (3 mi) southeast of the town of Siwa.

Jabal al-Mawta (the Mountain of the Dead), with its painted and inscribed 26th-Dynasty rock-cut tombs, is a highlight of the oasis. Two of the finest examples have wall paintings depicting Ptolemaic-era Egyptians with their curly hair and beards. This is currently an active archaeological site where tombs are still being documented and archived. More than 1,600 individual tombs have been identified, though most don't have such fine decor. ⊠ *About 1 km (½ mi) north of the town of Siwa, off to the right of the main road to Marsa Matruh* 🕾 *£e25* ⊙ *Daily 9–5.*

The **Traditional Siwan House** is the best place to learn about Siwan culture. It has a good collection of pottery, tools, and traditional clothing displayed in tableaux that depict the Siwan way of life. ⊠ *Behind main Siwa mosque, to your right as you face Shali from the main square* 🕾 *No phone* 🕾 *£e5* ⊙ *Oct.–Mar., daily 9–3; Apr.–Sept., Sun.–Thurs. 9–3.*

Ancient rumor has it that Cleopatra swam at the freshwater springs now known as **Cleopatra's Bath.** If she did, it can be assumed that either Julius Caesar or Mark Ant-

> ### HOT SAND DETOX
>
> The hot-sand bath has been a traditional remedy for rheumatism and many other ailments, but it has recently gained popularity as a detox treatment. It's not for the faint of heart: you'll be immersed in hot sand and left in the desert heat so that the toxins in the body leach out as you sweat. Some patients undertake several daily treatments to completely cleanse the system, ingesting only fruit, vegetables, and water during this time. The **Natural Hospital** in Siwa (🕾 10/128-7642) offers hot-sand treatments for around £e100 and rents bungalows if you'd like to take residential treatments.

ony did, too. Siwan springs are cooler than those at the southern oases. And while southern springs are contained in rectangular enclosures, the enclosures here are circular. ⊠ *3 km (2 mi) east of the town of Siwa* 🕾 *Free* ⊙ *Daily dawn–dusk.*

WHERE TO EAT

$ ✕ **Abdou's, Kelani & Sons.** Restaurants come and go here, but this one
MIDDLE   has been around for a while. That's probably because, of all the budget
EASTERN   eateries in town, this small, mud-brick restaurant in the main square
has the best food and the quickest service. Traditional desert fare served on plastic dishes is what you get, though the selection is more extensive compared with restaurants in the southern oases. ⊠ *On the main square* 🕾 *046/460–1243* ☰ *No credit cards.*

$ ✕ **Albabenshal Restaurant.** You can watch the activities of old Shali and
MIDDLE   modern Siwa from the terrace of this restaurant, making the most of
EASTERN   the cool evening air. The menu has typical oasis cuisine but also a few
unusual dishes, such as tagines (slow-cooked stews served with couscous), as well as couscous *khodar* (with vegetables) or *moza begui* (with a slow-cooked lamb shank); there's also a delicious *khodar masani* (grilled vegetable platter). If you prefer to eat indoors, there's a romantic dining room carved into the rock. ⊠ *Off the main square, Shali* 🕾 *046/460–2299* ☰ *No credit cards* ⊙ *No lunch.*

$ ✕ **Tanta Waa.** Set under lush palm trees beside Cleopatra's Pool, you can
MIDDLE   treat this as a café or restaurant—enjoying a post-swim soda or cup of
EASTERN   tea, or a full lunch of *kofta* (ground meat kebabs) or barbecue chicken.
In the evening the menu is a little more adventurous, though barbecuing is still the preferred form of cooking. Try the camel meat. ⊠ *At Cleopatra's Pool* 🕾 *010/472–9539* ☰ *No credit cards* ⊙ *May–Sept. opening times can be erratic.*

CLOSE UP

The Curse of Qara

The oasis village of Qara northwest of Siwa has no more then 300 residents. The number is precise because, after being refused the hospitality normally given to travelers, a local sheikh put a curse on the population saying that Qara could never have more then 300 people living there at any one time. If the population reached 301, than someone in the village would die (of an accident or natural causes), to bring the number down again. Even today, the people fear the curse, and when the birth of a baby raises the population count to 301, another resident in the village leaves, so as not to invoke the dire consequences. Qara has also developed a reputation for generosity to travelers who make their way to the oasis, hoping that this may in time lift the heavy burden they all bear.

WHERE TO STAY

Note that hotel rooms are scarce during Christmas, around the New Year, and at Ramadan. Reserve a room well in advance if you plan to come at these times.

$$$$ 🏨**Adrere Amellal Eco-Lodge.** Certainly the most expensive hotel in the oases—and the most unusual—eco-warriors have been watching Adrere Amellal (White Mountain) with great interest. Built from local materials incorporating desert stones and bricks, it's designed to look like an enchanted village. Everything is natural, from the *nummalites* (small coin-like fossils) on bathroom walls to the furniture made of salt pillars. The rooms look as if they have been pulled directly from the pages of *Architectural Digest*. There's no electrical power at the lodge: the chef cooks on a wood-burning stove, and beeswax candles and oil lamps light the lodge after sunset. The pool is a natural spring. Alcohol is served. **Pros:** You'll be staying in one of world's top eco-resorts; the rustic oasis design is impressive; complete privacy; desert sightseeing trips are included in the nightly rate; no electricity or a/c, which really transports you to a different era. **Cons:** Lighting levels are low at night, which means you may have difficulty reading the book you brought; location is remote, so it's difficult to explore on your own. ✉17 km (11 mi) west of town ☎046/460–1395, 02/736–7879 in Cairo ⊕www. adrereamellal.net ➾50 rooms ⏦In-room: no a/c, no phone, no TV. In-hotel: restaurant, pool, spa, laundry service, parking (free) ▤AE, MC, V ⏦FAP.

$ 🏨**Albabenshall Hotel.** Opened in 2008, this traditional-style mud-brick
★ hotel is built on the edge of Shali citadel, with "downtown" Siwa just outside the door. The whole complex offers traditional styling with natural stone and wood and a natural, traditional finish on the walls. Siwa-style carpets and basketry are used for decoration. The rooms are spread out across several levels and linked by staircases and small shady courtyards. Enjoy a drink or a meal on the terrace in the evening while watching the activities of the shops and street hawkers below. **Pros:** Traditional styling and architecture blend in with the surround-

ings; the location means you are only a couple of minutes from shops and eateries. **Cons:** No a/c; there's no outdoor space except the roof terrace and the small, high-sided courtyards, which can be a little stifling. ⊠*On the main square* ☎*046/460–2299* 📞*11 rooms* ♿*In-room: no a/c. In-hotel: restaurant* ▭*No credit cards* 🍴*BP.*

$ 🏨**Palm Trees Hotel.** This three-story concrete building's best assets are its beautiful, lush palm garden, friendly atmosphere, and central location. Happily, it's just far enough away from the square to be removed from most of the noise. The rooms are spartan; some have fans and a few have private baths. The six more recently constructed bungalows with small terraces offer the best accommodation, but there are no frills or pretty Bedouin touches here. This hotel has an Internet café. **Pros:** The hotel offers good value for money for budget travelers; friendly owners are happy to share their experience with you and offer a nice selection of tours. **Cons:** Rooms are basic and dated compared to other options available in Siwa for just a little more money. ⊠*Off the main square, on the road to Cleopatra's Bath* ☎*046/460–2304* 📞*21 rooms* ♿*In-room: no a/c (some), no phone, no TV. In-hotel: restaurant, bicycles, laundry facilities, Internet terminal* ▭*No credit cards* 🍴*BP.*

$ 🏨**Shali Lodge.** This traditionally styled hotel made from red stone, mud brick, and stucco has rooms leading off an internal courtyard. Rooms are simply yet stylishly furnished using Siwan handicrafts (carpets, baskets, and blankets). Fans are used to keep the interiors cool. Some rooms have terraces overlooking the gardens, for which there's no extra charge, so ask for one when you book. The interior communal lounge has palm trees growing out through the ceilings, and the canopies of these same trees provide shade for the upstairs terrace and café. It's a charming, comfortable place to stay. **Pros:** Traditional building and styling is in keeping with the location; the terrace café is a great place to while away an evening over cups of Bedouin tea; it's a couple of minutes' walk to the main square, so you can enjoy the atmosphere of the town. **Cons:** There are few amenities on-site; lack of outside space means most rooms lack private patios or balconies. ⊠*Midan El Souk, El Sebouka St.* ☎*046/460–1299, 02/736–7879 in Cairo* 📞*16 rooms* ♿*In-room: no a/c, no TV. In-hotel: restaurant* ▭*No credit cards* 🍴*BP.*

$–$$ 🏨**Siwa Safari Paradise.** The owner of one of the longest-established hotels in the oases continues to expand and improve the choice of rooms. The hotel is hidden in a quiet, shady palm garden just outside the center of town (on the way to Aghurmi). You can choose from simple fan-cooled older units, air-conditioned bungalows with domed ceilings and matching modern green wooden furniture, or the luxury El Khan suites complete with large bathrooms. There's a hot spring on-site for swimming. The resort offers a nightly Bedouin show and can arrange desert tours. **Pros:** Choice of rooms in several price ranges; with 100 rooms you should always find somewhere to sleep here, even in high season; El Khan rooms are some of the best outfitted in the oases. **Cons:** New buildings have taken over some of the gardens space, so when it's busy there's not much space to relax. ⊠*About ½ km (¼ mi) east of Siwa on the road to Aghurmi* ☎*046/460–1290* ⊕*www.*

siwaparadise.com 📶*100 rooms* ♿*In-room: no a/c (some), no phone (some), no TV (some). In-hotel: 2 restaurants, pool, bicycles, parking (free)* ▤*MC, V* ⏺*EP.*

$$$ 🏨**Siwa Shali Resort.** One of the prettiest and best-equipped hotels in the oases, the traditional styling of these single-story mud-brick buildings surrounded by maturing gardens helps make the resort a relaxing place to stay. Interior decor is simple, with natural local pigments and locally produced blankets and carpets. Bathrooms have walk-in showers and marble sinks. The resort pool is unusual: it's about 4 feet wide, and the narrow form snakes 600 feet through the gardens like a lazy river without the current. **Pros:** Rooms are spacious and have an oasis ambience in the decor; hotel facilities, such as massage and gym, attempt to emulate international hotels; both restaurants are attractive and inviting, with nice touches like pretty cotton chair covers that match the table linens. **Cons:** It's a long way from town along confusing roads, so you have no choice but to eat here at night. ✉*5 km (3 mi) east of town in the lee of Gabel Takrur Mountain* ☎*010/111–9730* ⊕*www.siwashali resort.com* 📶*30 rooms, 21 suites* ♿*In-room: refrigerator. In-hotel: 2 restaurants, pool, gym, laundry service, parking (free)* ▤*AE, MC, V* ⏺*MAP.*

DESERT TOURS

The Siwa Oasis is a good base from which to explore the surrounding desert; from here, you're close to the Qattara depression, the Great Sand Sea, and several isolated oases with fortresses and Roman tombs. However, the Egyptian military has been limiting tourist activity in this area, making overnight safaris difficult and time-consuming to organize. Most of the hotels in town can help you to arrange tours. Consult the management of these hotels about the current situation if you would like to spend one or more nights in the desert.

You need permission from the police (there's a station in the town of Siwa) in order to visit the sights and isolated oases south along the road to Bahariyya. Worth visiting in this direction are the tombs of al-Aareg (120 km [70 mi] south of the town of Siwa); al-Baharein (140 km [80 mi] south of Siwa); and Ain al-Sitra (160 km [90 mi] south of Siwa).

Bir Wahed, 15 km (9 mi) south of the town of Siwa, is a freshwater spring. Set in a surreal location among the dunes of the Great Sand Sea and next to a fish-filled lake, it's a favorite of visitors to the oasis. Permission from the police in Siwa and an all-terrain vehicle are necessary for you to make the trip.

SHOPPING

Siwa is renowned throughout Egypt for its handicrafts, particularly its carpets. Rugs made on desert looms follow the traditional designs and natural dye combinations of individual Bedouin tribes. Some motifs are amazingly similar to those of Native Americans. Most oases sell camel-hair products, including woolen gloves, hats, scarves, and blankets, at very reasonable prices. All oases have handwoven baskets, and each oasis has its own designs. Supplies of all crafts are limited, and the traditional dress and jewelry once worn by Siwan women are no longer found in the souvenir shops, having been bought out by collectors. Still, Siwa has the best and most abundant crafts of any of the desert oases.

Siwan shops also sell olive oil in hygienically sealed glass bottles and prepackaged dates. You won't make a dent in your credit card in the desert—you won't even be able to use it. There are few banks, and ATMs are beginning to make an appearance, but most banks don't change traveler's checks. ⚠ **Bring plenty of Egyptian cash with you just in case the ATMs are out of service and you wish to buy something.**

WESTERN DESERT OASES ESSENTIALS

TRANSPORTATION

BY BUS

The desert is backpacker heaven, and that means cheap transportation. But keep in mind that you lose flexibility—and time—when taking the bus. All bus travel to the Western oases starts at Cairo's Targoman Station, in downtown Bulaq, behind Shar'a Galaa and the *al-Ahram* newspaper building.

Cairo travel agencies have bus schedules, though they tend to be outdated. The only way to get reliable information is to go to the bus station, and even then you should take care in trusting what you are told about connections in other cities. You can reserve seats on air-conditioned buses only one day in advance.

Several bus lines go directly to the oases on the desert Loop Road, including the East Delta Bus Company and Upper Egyptian Bus Company. Super Jet buses generally are the most luxurious, and ticket prices are cheap; for example, the trip from Cairo to Dahkla is £e55 for a one-way ticket. Buses to the desert Loop Road oases stop in Giza on the way out of Cairo. The bus trip to Bahariyya takes 4½ hours; buses to Farafra take seven hours; and buses to Dakhla and Kharga take 10 and 12 hours, respectively.

For Siwa, you have to change either in Alexandria or Marsa Matruh. Buses to Alexandria (a 3-hour trip) leave every half-hour for Sidi Gaber Station; there's a connection to Siwa (a 9-hour trip). Bus trips from Cairo to Marsa Matruh take 7 hours. From Marsa Matruh you can catch a local service taxi to Siwa, a 4-hour trip.

Microbuses also serve the oases. They depart from different stops throughout sections of the city—such as the Bahariyya Café (Shar'a Qadri, off Shar'a Bur Sa'id in Sayida Zaynab), Maydan Tahrir, and Ramses Station—typically as soon as they fill up. There are seats for 12, but you can buy two or three seats to give yourself some extra room.

Contacts East Delta Bus Company (☎ *02/2577–8347*). **Super Jet** (☎ *02/2579–8181*). **Upper Egyptian Bus Company** (☎ *02/2431–6723*).

BY CAR

If you're fearless enough to make it through the streets of Cairo to get out of town, driving along the asphalt road in the desert is a relative breeze, and there is very little traffic. Off-road driving, however, requires skill and knowledge of local road conditions. Using a guide for all off-road jaunts is strongly recommended; driving off-road may violate the terms of your rental car contract in any case. Likewise, don't drive at night; some drivers don't use their headlights, and those who do will blink them on and off at you as you approach, which is blinding. It's illogical and dangerous, but it's the local custom.

There are gas stations within the oases, but always, always top off your gas tank whenever you see one—the next gas station you encounter may be out of fuel.

CAR RENTAL   Good car-rental agencies in Cairo offer a variety of vehicles. These rental companies have offices in all major hotels throughout Egypt and outlets all over Cairo but have no representation in the oases. To rent a car, you must have an International Driver's License. Ask for the car-rental office nearest you when you call to inquire about prices or make a reservation.

OFF-ROAD   If you want to do some off-road exploration, you can rent a four-
EXPLORING   wheel-drive vehicle to drive to the desert or come by bus or car and book a four-wheel-drive tour through many of the hotels or restaurants in the oases. Every oasis now has tours and safaris to exotic, awe-inspiring sights. If you do travel into the desert with your own four-wheel-drive vehicle, don't go off-road without a second vehicle and a guide. Between getting stuck and getting lost, the opportunities for fatal errors are abundant. If you're determined to sit behind the wheel yourself, you'll need to take some instruction and prove yourself competent before a desert tour agency will agree to put a guide in your vehicle or let your vehicle tag along on its tours. If in doubt, hire a driver and enjoy the adventure from the passenger seat.

Permission from the police is required for some of the more isolated destinations and is easily obtained with the help of the Tourist Information offices in the oases. Some destinations west of Siwa in the Great Sand Sea can be off-limits because they are controlled by the Egyptian military. Always take advice from the Tourist Office or police before venturing into these areas.

CONTACTS & RESOURCES

BANKS & EXCHANGE SERVICES

There are few banks or ATMs in the oases towns (both Siwa and Kharga have banks with ATMs, though they may not be working). Here, most of the economy still runs on cash that's kept at home (crime is very low here, so people have no fear of having their money stolen). Exchange services are nonexistent outside hotels, which may be willing to change your money or accept foreign currency in payment. The best advice is to change money in Cairo and bring plenty of Egyptian pounds with you.

7

Information Banque du Caire (✉ *On the road into town from Marsa Matruh, near the tourist office, Siwa*). **BNP Paribas** (✉ *Sol Y Mar Pioneers Hotel, Kharga*).

EMERGENCIES

Special tourist police patrol every oasis. They are so numerous—and the oases villages so small—that you will not have to search for them; indeed, if there's a problem, they'll find you. Their English is not always good, so they may have to take you to someone who speaks more English.

Medical facilities are rudimentary throughout the oases area, and there are only a few independent doctors and dentists. Every large village in the desert has a clinic with qualified staff, though services are not comprehensive. The nationwide emergency numbers aren't available throughout the oases, but anyone can direct you to these facilities. First-aid stations with ambulances have been put up at regular intervals all along the Loop Road through the southern oases. Most are at or near communications towers, about 45 km (30 mi) apart.

Hospitals Bawati City Hospital (✉ *Main street, close to the museum of the Golden Mummies, Bawati, Bahariyya* ☎ *02/3847–2390*). **Dakhla Hospital** (✉ *On the road to Kharga, 1 mi from Maydan Tahrir (the main square), Mut, Dakhla* ☎ *092/782–1555*). **Kharga Hospital** (✉ *On the main street, Qasr al-Kharga, Kharga* ☎ *092/792–0777*). **Siwa Military Hospital** (✉ *Close to the football stadium on the southern outskirts of town, Siwa* ☎ *046/460–0459*).

24-HOUR PHARMACIES There are no 24-hour pharmacies in the oases, but there is at least one pharmacy in each village and more in the major towns. Pharmacies open generally from 9 AM to 1 PM and from 6 PM to 11 PM. Look for a sign of a blue chalice with a red snake wrapped around it, which indicates a pharmacy.

Contacts Abdou Pharmacy (✉ *Shar'a Sadat, off the main square south in the direction of the hospital, Siwa* ☎ *010/472–5431*). **Hospital Pharmacy** (✉ *Opposite the hospital, Kharga* ☎ *092/792–6578*). **New Pharmacy** (✉ *Traveling south, make the first right after the Badawiyya Resort; the pharmacy is 100 yards farther on the right, Qasr al-Farafra* ☎ *010/546–2312*). **Siwa Pharmacy** (✉ *On the main square, opposite the Educational Department, Bawati, Bahariyya* ☎ *02/3847–3141*).

INTERNET CAFÉS

Internet access is still rare in the oases, even in hotels. You may find a couple of small Internet cafés in each town, but most are one-machine affairs in the backs of coffee shops. Many connections are still dial-up, so systems are slow and unreliable. Prices are around £e10 to £e15 for one hour.

Internet Cafés Abu Mohamed Restaurant (✉ *Shar'a al-Thauwra al-Khadra, Mut, Dakhla* ☎ *092/782–1431*). **Al Mannara Internet Café** (✉ *Shar'a Il Newabi el Mohandas, Kharga* ☎ *092/792–2760*). **MN Office/Photocopy** (✉ *On the main square, Bawati, Bahariyya* ☎ *023/847–2224*). **Palm Trees Hotel** (✉ *Off the main square on the road to Cleopatra's Pool, Siwa* ☎ *046/460–2304*).

TOUR OPTIONS

It's possible to arrange multiday sightseeing tours to the oases that include transportation, accommodations, meals, and desert tours. Prices per person for tours booked in Cairo range from $500 for three days to $800 for six. Locally booked oasis tours cost much less—about $100 per person per day—but then you have to make your own way out to the oases.

Cairo International has a number of itineraries to the oases, and you can design your own program. Mahmoud Marai specializes in organizing deep desert expeditions lasting from two weeks to six weeks. These are bespoke journeys for the last true explorers. Marzouk Desert Cruiser runs tours to all the oases, specializing in Fayyum-to-Bahariyya off-road tours. U.S.-based Tarot Tours Garranah can help you plan your oases tours and desert trips.

Contacts **Cairo International** (✉ *21 Shar'a Mokhtar Said, Heliopolis, Cairo* ☎ *02/2291–1491* ⊕ *www.cit-eg.com*). **Mahmoud Marai** (✉ *Building 56B, Apt 43, Nerco Buildings, Al Mazzra St., Ma'adi, Cairo* ☎ *010/951–1684* ⊕ *www.mahmoudmarai.com*). **Marzouk Desert Cruiser** (✉ *1 Maydan Ibn Sandar, Hamamat al-Kuba, Cairo* ☎ *02/258–8083* ⊕ *www.marzouk-dc.com*). **Tarot Tours Garranah** (✉ *378 Columbia Ave., Cliffside Park, NJ* ☎ *201/606–2255 or 201/450–1590* ⊕ *www.tarottoursusa.net*).

VISITOR INFORMATION

Apart from tiny Farafra, all oases have tourist information offices. All are usually open Saturday through Thursday from 8 to 2, often with additional evening hours; sometimes they're open Friday. They can help with hotels, tours, transportation, emergencies, and most anything else.

Contacts **Bahariyya Tourist Information Office** (✉ *On the main street, in the garden of the municipal building, Bawiti, Bahariyya* ☎ *018/802–222*). **Dakhla Tourist Information Office** (✉ *Shar'a al-Thauwra al-Khadra, Mut, Dakhla* ☎ *092/782–1686*). **Kharga Tourist Information Office** (✉ *Shar'a Jamal 'Abd al-Nasir, near Mabrouk Fountain, Qasr al-Kharga, Kharga* ☎ *092/790–1611*). **Siwa Tourist Information Office** (✉ *On the main road, next to the police station, Siwa* ☎ *046/460–2338*).

Nile & Lake Nasser Cruises

Cruising on the Nile River

WORD OF MOUTH

"We took a seven-day cruise and found it to be wonderful. No need to pack and unpack at various hotels. Each day took us to a new town or village. We always felt safe and welcomed."

—Baracuda2

Updated by
Lindsay and
Pete Bennett

CRUISING ALONG THE NILE WAS once the only form of travel in Egypt, and there is still nothing like it. Rural areas succeed one another on the banks of the river in a pattern of life that has not changed for thousands of years. As in ancient times, the Nile Valley farmer's life is adjusted to the predictable rhythm of the seasons. There's a timeless, almost biblical quality to the scene that unfolds as you follow the river. A Nile cruise affords the triple pleasure of enjoying comfortable relaxation on board, witnessing age-old ways of life on the riverbanks, and visiting some of the most famous and beautiful monuments in the world.

The Lake Nasser cruise is a different experience. "Lake" Nasser is actually a reservoir. Popularly known as the Nubian Sea, because of the land that surrounds it, the lake is 500 km (312 mi) long—370 km (230 mi) in Egypt and the rest in the Republic of Sudan. It takes its shape behind the Aswan High Dam, from the spread of water around sun-baked hills and into dry riverbeds.

The cruel irony of the "Nubian" Sea is that today the neat, domed houses of the Nubian people, their villages, their places of worship, and their burial grounds along the banks of the Nile are under water; in the 1960s the entire population of nearly 100,000 people was relocated to Kom Ombo in Egypt and to Kashm al-Girba in the Sudan before the completion of the dam.

For millennia, the Nile was the trade route into the continent, and ancient Egyptians called Nubia the "corridor to Africa." It is a barren land, rich in minerals, especially copper and gold, and its richness in ancient monuments attests to cultural links to Egypt from the earliest times. Here the Nile carved its way through the native sandstone, creating cliffs over which the river never rose in flood season to deposit its rich, silt-laden soil along the banks, as it did in Egypt. Ramesses II's Abu Simbel temple was carved into those cliffs—until the rising waters of Lake Nasser forced the government to cut the temple from its former location and move it 200 feet higher up the banks.

The High Dam—a vast rock-filled structure 11,790 feet long, 375 feet high, and with a base thickness of 3,200 feet—separates the reservoir from the upper reaches of the Nile. Cruisers do not have access from one to the other.

Note: The ancient temples are all easily accessible; some you can actually see while cruising on the Nile or Lake Nasser. (*The monuments are covered at length in Chapters 4 and 5.*)

CHOOSING A CRUISE

The traditional Nile cruise is recommended for first-time visitors to Egypt, not only because of the great diversity of monuments that you can view, but also because of the opportunity to see rural Egyptians, their villages, and, in places, local crafts. The Lake Nasser cruise is recommended if you have an archaeological bent, or if you simply want to get away from it all in the wide-open space of the lake.

You can travel the Nile on three-, four-, and seven-night cruises. The first two ply the river between Luxor and Aswan, taking in the towns and temples en route. The seven-night cruise extends north of Luxor to Dendera, the site of the Temple of Hathor, and then takes you on an overland day trip to that holiest of ancient cities, Abydos. An advantage of the seven-night cruise is that you sail along parts of the Nile that aren't so congested with cruise boats, past stretches of the valley that make for very impressive sightseeing.

Lake Nasser cruises usually start from Aswan on Monday, in which case they last four nights, or from Abu Simbel on Friday, in which case they last three nights. From north to south, sights viewed include the relocated temples of Kalabsha, Beit al-Wali, and Kertassi near the High Dam; the temples of Sebua, Dakka, and Meharakka reconstructed at Wadi al-Sebua; the temples of Amada, Derr, and the tomb of Penout reconstructed at Amada; Qasr Ibrim on its original site; and at Abu Simbel the famous temples of Ramesses II and his wife, Nefertari—hallmarks of the UNESCO-funded Nubian salvage operations. One decided advantage to seeing Abu Simbel as part of a Lake Nasser cruise itinerary is that you will have the opportunity to visit the site before or after the tourist hordes depart and will see it at night, when it is illuminated during the nightly Sound & Light Show.

If you are taking a Nile cruise and don't want to miss Abu Simbel, a flight can take you there and return you to Aswan the same day. Likewise, if you are taking a lake cruise, you can fly to Luxor for a day to see its famous East and West Bank monuments. The Aswan–Luxor flight lasts 30 minutes. Aswan–Abu Simbel takes 30 minutes; Luxor–Abu Simbel takes 90 minutes. Cruise costs do not include these flights.

If a week or more on the water is your goal, some travel agencies are now offering combined river and lake cruises.

TYPES OF SHIPS

FLOATING HOTELS

The so-called "floating hotel" is the standard Nile and Lake Nasser cruiser. These tiered boats look like boxes with windows stacked on low-slung hulls—the waters are calm enough not to require seagoing vessels—and they are essentially the same, differing only in size and decor. The craft are air-conditioned and have pools, hot tubs, exercise rooms, saunas, Turkish baths, restaurants, and panoramic halls for viewing the passing scenery. Most cruise ships have around 50 cabins. The newer luxury boats are of a smaller class and are more intimate.

There are some 350 cruise vessels on the Nile. For reasons of safety and security, we recommend that you use only vessels with solid reputations, which are generally more expensive. These also most closely meet American standards for hygiene and sanitation. Lake Nasser currently has five boats, and all these vessels are of a high standard.

DAHABIYYAS

Large Nile cruisers are a relatively modern invention. Historically, travelers would make the journey on smaller vessels, a little more luxurious than the *felucca* sailing craft used as ferries or fishing vessels. These elegant wooden houseboats with sails at bow and stern offered comfortable cabins for up to 12

DID YOU KNOW?

Pilots or captains of Nile cruise vessels traditionally come from only a few families, the skills of navigation, or "reading the river," being passed on from father to son.

people and a full kitchen offering the luxuries to which rich travelers of the early to mid-20th-century had become accustomed.

This style of travel is making a comeback in the form of the *dahabiyya*. These modern re-creations have six to eight individually decorated cabins plus a dining-room/lounge and a small shaded deck. They are generally designed in a retro style, with lots of polished wood and brass in addition to modern comforts like electric lighting, toilets, and showers (some may even have air-conditioning). They offer a more intimate approach to cruising—including the possibility of small-group charters—but don't offer amenities such as a pool or long, gourmet menus. Think of them as floating villas as opposed to the floating hotel that is the large Nile cruiser. Itineraries are also more flexible because these craft don't have engines, so speed depends entirely on the current and the prevailing breezes.

SANDALS

Traditional working boat of the Nile, the *sandal* has almost disappeared from the river, but a few of these double-masted craft have been converted into sailing cruisers with three or four cabins and a staff to captain, cook, and clean the vessel. Yes, there are toilets and showers, but these craft are more practical than luxurious.

FELUCCAS

Felucca is the name given to those single-masted sailboats that are the romantic symbol of Nile travel. They have cushioned benches along the sides, sometimes a table at the center, and are a pleasant way to spend an hour or two sailing along the Nile, especially at sunset. They are decidedly *not* the standard vessels for taking multiday cruises.

For adventurers, nature lovers, and those who want to sample a simpler life, larger feluccas can be hired for three or four days (depending on your interests) between Aswan and Luxor. The vessels always sail from south to north, with the flow of the river, and on such trips you sleep in the open, on deck, wrapped in blankets. This trip is recommended only for the hardiest travelers, to whom a lack of privacy is of little concern. Also keep in mind that food is bought locally, cooked by the sailors, and may not meet your normal standards of hygiene. Depending on the size and comfort of the felucca, the average cost is around £e70 to £e125 per person per day, inclusive of food and sightseeing. These prices are for a minimum of six people and a maximum of eight people. If you want to hire a felucca with fewer people, you'll need to haggle to achieve a suitable price. The felucca captain usually is responsible for obtaining the necessary police clearance to take a group on the Nile.

You can arrange for a felucca locally, but there are also now a few companies to help facilitate making your arrangements in advance. Sandal and dahabiyya charters should be made in advance since there are fewer of these sailing on the Nile.

Abd El Hakeem Hussein (✉ *Outside the Railway Station, Aswan* ☎ *097/231–2811 or 010/576–7594*), the general manager of the Tourist Office in Aswan, is happy to put you in contact with reliable felucca captains if you want to organize your own trip.

Responsible Travel (✉ *3rd Floor, Pavilion House, 6 Old Steine, Brighton, UK* ☎ *01273/600030* ⊕ *www.responsibletravel.com*) is a British-based company and Internet portal offering felucca cruises as part of its range of socially and environmentally aware tours.

Sail the Nile (✉ *Al Gezera Village, West Bank, Luxor* ☎ *010/356–4540* ⊕ *www.sailthenile.com*), an English/Egyptian company, offers felucca, sandal, and dahabiyya trips of varying lengths for groups of two to eight people.

THE CRUISE EXPERIENCE

Nothing is more relaxing than spending an afternoon on a boat's partially shaded upper deck sipping a beverage. Lie back on a chaise lounge and take in the wide valley of the Nile—its belts of palm groves and clusters of dun- and multicolored stucco houses passing in the foreground, its long ranges of limestone mountains stretching across the horizon. On a lake cruise, you'll look out on pristine deserts' tender, pale violet shadows patching ocher landscapes, the water turning to liquid gold from the reflection of the sunset.

Sailing, on river or lake, combines relaxation with sightseeing. Itineraries are structured around the time of the year and the hours that your boat reaches towns and monuments. In summer, shore excursions start before breakfast to avoid the heat and resume in the late afternoon, when a fair breeze often picks up and cools the heat of the day. In cooler winter months, tours start after breakfast and continue after the midday meal. Shore tours and admission to the monuments are almost always included, but verify that when you make your cruise arrangements.

CHECKING IN

Check-in usually takes place before lunch, checkout after breakfast. Passports are registered at the reception area, then returned to you. You'll often do some sightseeing before you depart, either in Aswan or Luxor.

ENTERTAINMENT

Entertainment is an important part of Nile cruises, and there is usually something different offered each evening: a cocktail party, a belly dancer, Nubian dancers (either a troupe from Aswan or the Nubian staff on board). One evening, guests arrange their own entertainment: a treasure hunt, a fancy dress party, a play, or a folkloric party in a tent-like setting where you sit on cushions and rugs, eat traditional food, smoke a *shisha* (water pipe) if you like, and men are encouraged to don *galabiyyas,* traditional full-length robes that *fellahin* (rural people) still wear. (It's kitschy but more fun in context that it sounds.) Group photographs are taken as souvenirs. A candlelight dinner overlooking Abu Simbel temples is a highlight of a Lake Nasser cruise.

The lounge is the best place to read or to enjoy a drink. The larger vessels generally afford a panoramic view, the smaller provide a cozy, drawing room–like atmosphere. Most boats have small libraries with a selection of books about Egypt, largely in English, as well as novels, magazines, and newspapers. Some of the boats now offer Internet access (for an extra charge) and perhaps even have a TV showing a movie, but there is no TV reception aboard the ships.

MEALS

Most meals on most boats are buffet style, with a wide variety of hot and cold food, as well as a selection of international, Egyptian, and vegetarian dishes. (There is plenty of choice if you follow a special diet.) Staff take professional pride in these buffets, and each is more like an excessive dinner celebration than an ordinary meal. However, the new generation of five-star boutique-style boats offer à la carte restaurant service. All three daily meals are served in a dining room unless a barbecue is set up on the sun deck; afternoon tea or coffee is generally served in the open air.

PRECAUTIONS

Water onboard is safe for bathing, because boats have their own purification systems built with the latest technology. However, tap water is not recommended for drinking, and bottled water is available.

The "gippy tummy" has its place in Nile cruise lore. Locals attribute it to excessive consumption of iced drinks immediately after touring in the hot sun, or sitting in direct sunlight for an extended time. The symptoms are diarrhea, sometimes severe, combined with feeling slightly queasy. It is almost certainly attributable to contaminated water, which makes drinking bottled water and not taking ice in drinks strongly advisable. *(For food-related and other health precautions, see the Health section in Egypt Essentials.)*

SECURITY

The security issues of the late 1990s caused the Egyptian government to stop all cruises between Cairo and Upper Egypt (Luxor and Aswan). Travel in Upper Egypt and Nubia is relatively safe, but the Egyptian government put in place a series of security measures in the aftermath of these problems that are still current. This security includes armed police strategically placed at popular tourist sites along the Nile, vessels manned by Egyptian security forces accompanying tourist vessels between Luxor and Qena on a Luxor–Dendera cruise, and armed Bedouin on the hills overlooking the monuments of Nubia. (Armed guards are not an uncommon sight in Egypt and should not cause alarm. They are also evident at the ancient sites, and outside embassies, museums, and the residences of foreign diplomats.)

TOUR GUIDES

Gone are the days when *dragomen* (a 19th-century term given to locally hired tour managers) conducted tourists to the monuments telling them tall tales of ancient kings. Today's guides are bi- or trilingual professionals who arc granted official licenses only after successfully passing an examination that covers pharaonic, Greco-Roman, Islamic, and modern history. They are personable young men and women with a sound knowledge of political and social events in Egypt, and they are informed about environmental matters and the flora and fauna of their country. Traveling with a cruise is a sought-after job, and cruise operators choose only top performers, whose professionalism is evaluated by the travelers themselves.

> **WORD OF MOUTH**
>
> "I was glad I had my running shoes—ended up wearing them most of the time. Not a fashion high-point but very good for walking in sand or gravel. My mom wore sandals a lot and was constantly dumping sand out of them." —Leslie_S

Most boats have a resident guide for small groups and for individuals who do not have their own accompanying guide. When there are different nationalities on board, more than one guide is provided. Guides speak English, French, Italian, Spanish, and German to accommodate travelers from around the world.

WHAT TO PACK

Travel light, and remember that Egypt is a conservative country. Egyptians dress modestly and respect those who observe their customs. When walking around Luxor and Aswan, it is wise to wear T-shirts with short sleeves rather than sleeveless tops, and trousers or skirts that come to the knee. (Sleeveless tops for women are entirely acceptable on board.) Swimwear should only be seen around the pool, and topless sunbathing is forbidden. Although the weather is sunny in winter, the evenings can be very cool, so bring clothing that you can layer, with at least one medium-weight woolen sweater for the nighttime chill of the after-dark Sound & Light performance at Karnak or Abu Simbel. You'll need a windbreaker in winter for the daytime. Proper walking shoes are a must—sandals are uncomfortable when walking in the sand, unless they're athletic sandals—and take hats, sunglasses, sunblock, tissues, and a small bottle of water on shore excursions. It doesn't rain, so rain gear is unnecessary.

Although casual wear is acceptable at meals during the day, four- and five-star vessels have a casual-but-elegant standard at night. This docs not necessarily mean jackets for men, merely long trousers and a collared shirt. Laundry service on boats is excellent; laundry bags are picked up in the morning and returned by the evening of the same day.

There is a great deal to photograph, so be sure to bring enough film or electronic storage for the images you take.

8

ITINERARIES

Daily itineraries are structured around visits to monuments. Bear in mind that cruise organizers, in order to maximize profits by running back-to-back cruises, tend to rush visits around Luxor and Aswan, the two cities with the heaviest concentration of ancient sights.

> **TOP TIP**
>
> Most short-duration Nile cruises sail during the night, which means you miss a lot of that wonderful river landscape. If you want to enjoy the river voyage as well as the ancient temples and tombs, book a longer tour.

On Nile cruises, for example, Luxor itineraries are necessarily rushed because there is enough to occupy even casual sightseers for several days. The monuments lie on both sides of the Nile and spread over a vast area—the two major Luxor and Karnak temples are on the East Bank, and the Theban Necropolis on the West Bank includes the mortuary temples (such as Deir al-Bahri and Madinet Habu), the Valley of the Kings, the Valley of the Queens, and Tombs of the Nobles. Guides are obliged to keep to schedules and might not give you as much time at sights as you would like. Consider spending one or two nights at a hotel in Luxor at either the beginning or end of your cruise to give you time to see sights not included on the boat's itinerary, or to revisit monuments that you want to see in greater depth.

On Lake Nasser cruises, although the boat docks at Kalabsha near Aswan, itineraries do not include most Aswan sights. You will see Nubian monuments reconstructed near the High Dam, but you should stay an additional night or two in Aswan to see the High Dam itself, the Nubia Museum, the Temple of Isis at Philae, the famous granite quarries, the tombs of the nobles on Qubbet al-Hawa, Elephantine Island, and the 5th-century St. Simeon's Monastery.

CRUISE COSTS

Each season, cruise companies determine their prices based on what they expect upcoming demand will be. Prices listed below are therefore guidelines. At this writing, prices per person per night, double occupancy, ranged from more than $100 to more than $1,000 in high season (October through April), depending on the boat. Note that prices increase 25% to 40% during Christmas and Easter, and they drop by as much as 50% during the hotter summer months. This wide disparity in cruise costs reflects the huge differences between vessels.

Transfers from airport to boat are not always included; round-trip transfers cost $30 to $50 per person. On board, a special gratuity box might be displayed at the reception area for the boat crew; tour guides might take it upon themselves to pass a separate envelope among members of their party, with a suggestion that $5 to $10 per passenger per day is appropriate, depending on the number of fellow passengers in your group. This is what the guide hopes to receive; tip whatever you feel is appropriate based on the service provided. The same applies for gratuities to the boat crew.

Payment for beverages and other services, such as laundry and outside phone calls, is not usually included in cruise prices, although some high-end cruises will occasionally offer some of these services as part of the package. The charge for drinks and laundry is reasonable, in line with any hotel, of any caliber, in Egypt. You sign bills when drinks are presented and services rendered, and you pay these at trip's end. Egyptian and some foreign currencies are accepted and most boats accept credit cards and traveler's checks. Banking facilities are not always available on board, but you will find them in Luxor and Aswan.

TOP TIP

With so many cruise vessels on the river, most ships have to dock side by side at Luxor, Aswan, and at temples along the route so that passengers can disembark. This means that at times all you can see out of your cabin window is the flank of the vessel moored alongside—a disappointment if you specifically booked a vessel with picture windows so you enjoy the views. Avoid this by booking a boat with private moorings—currently, only the *Zahra*, *St. George*, *Sun Boat III*, and *Sun Boat IV*.

WHAT IT COSTS IN U.S. DOLLARS AND EUROS			
$$$$	**$$$**	**$$**	**$**
Cruises in dollars	over $500	$350–$500	$200–$350	under $200
Cruises in euros	over €325	€225–€325	€130–€225	under €130

Average per diem per cabin, based on double occupancy, in high season (prices are 30% to 50% lower May–Sept.), excluding tips.

WHEN TO GO

The best time of year for a cruise is from the beginning of the winter season in October to the first half of April. Low water levels between late April and September may affect sailings north to Qena for the visit to Dendera, but very few boats make this trip. Sailings between Luxor and Aswan are not generally affected by water level. May is not recommended because of the likelihood of the *khamaseen*, sand-laden storms accompanied by scorching winds that make sightseeing all but impossible. Summer weather, especially in July and August, is dry. Temperatures in Upper Egypt and Nubia can soar to 108°F. Weather is ideal from November through February, when the mercury hovers between 75°F and 80°F. Temperatures drop at night, in both summer and winter.

BOOKING A CRUISE

USING A TRAVEL AGENT

If you intend to take a Nile cruise, make your bookings through a recognized international travel agency, preferably one that is a member of the American Society of Travel Agents (ASTA) or the Society of Incentive and Travel Executives (SITE). With more than 350 vessels in operation, the majority owned by small businesses, the choice of boats is vast, and standards among them vary considerably. The use of an established travel agent as a go-between is the best insurance that you will get what you think you are paying for.

Checklist: Get a printed itinerary with full details of communications, excursions, meals (whether included or not included), and availability of an English-speaking guide when you book your cruise.

RECOMMENDED AGENCIES IN EGYPT

There are hundreds of travel agencies in Egypt that can book Nile cruises. The following are among the most reliable.

Abercrombie & Kent (⊠ *18 Shar'a Youssef al-Guindy, Boustan Centre, Cairo* ☎ *02/2393–6255* ⊕ *www.akegypt.com*), apart from having good connections with many cruise companies, operates its own fleet of three five-star vessels on the Nile. The company also can combine Nile cruises with other sights throughout Egypt and the Middle East and Africa.

American Express (⊠ *Shar'a Abtel El Tahrir, El Corniche, Aswan* ☎ *097/230–6983* ⊠ *15 Qasr al-Nil, Cairo* ☎ *02/574–7991* ⊠ *33 Shar'a Nabil El Wakkad, Heliopolis, Cairo* ☎ *02/2413–0375* ⊠ *Winter Palace Hotel, Luxor* ☎ *095/237–8333*) is a major agency in Egypt.

Egypt Panorama Tours *(Ted Cookson)* (⊠ *4 Road 79, Ma'adi, Cairo* ⊕ *11728 Box 222, Ma'adi, Cairo* ☎ *02/2359–0200 or 02/2358–1301* ⊕ *www.eptours.com*) has a good reputation among expatriates for efficiency and reliability.

Emeco Travel (⊠ *2 Shar'a Tala'at Harb, Cairo* ☎ *02/2577–4646 or 02/2574–9360* ⊕ *www.emeco.com*) is a well-established company.

South Sinai Travel (⊠ *79 Shar'a Marghany, Heliopolis, Cairo* ☎ *02/2418–7310* ⊕ *www.southsinai.com*) is partnered with many U.S. travel agencies because of the company's expertise, efficiency, and reliability.

Thomas Cook (⊠ *17 Shar'a Mahmoud Bassiouny, Cairo* ☎ *02/2576–6982*) was the first company to run Nile cruises, and it owns two vessels. The Thomas Cook Offices at Luxor and Aswan offer a last-minute service that allows you to book and start your Nile cruise within one or two days. Visit their offices and let them know the level of luxury you want, and they will contact Nile cruise companies in that range to find out which boats have last-minute vacancies. Prices are advantageous at all times of year, but you can't guarantee a particular vessel.

Travcotels (⊠ *26th July Corridor, Sheikh Zayed City, Giza, Cairo* ☎ *02/3854–3222* ⊕ *www.travcotels.com*) owns a fleet of 16 cruisers, 15 on the Nile, the other on Lake Nasser.

CLOSE UP

Thomas Cook and the Birth of Mass Tourism

Born in 1808 in Derbyshire, England, Thomas Cook was a cabinet-maker, but he was also a Baptist and member of the Temperance Society. He began organizing day trips to local beauty spots for his fellow members, and in 1841 arranged for a local railway company to run a special train for his group, for which they charged a fixed fee that included passage and food—the first holiday package tour. By 1844 this had become an annual operation.

Cook quickly expanded this sideline. He organized trips for 165,000 people to attend the Great Exhibition in London in 1851, and four years later arranged his first tour outside Britain, when he sold packages to the Exposition Universelle in Paris. By the end of the decade, he was offering a European Grand Tour with travel, meals,

and hotels included. In the 1860s he added Egypt to his portfolio.

Cook went into partnership with his son, John Mason Cook, who had better business acumen than his father. John invested in the first Nile cruisers that were said to be the most luxurious seen on the river since Cleopatra's royal barge. When the British took control of Egypt in the 1880s, Thomas Cook Inc. became involved in military transport and postal services, and John became one of the most powerful men in Egypt.

Thomas Cook died in 1892, and John in 1898. The business stayed in the family until 1928, when it was sold by Cook's grandsons to Companie Internationale des Wagons-lits. However, the Thomas Cook name lives on in Egypt as the foremost tour operator.

IN THE U.S. A number of travel agents arrange special-interest and tailor-made cruises.

Abercrombie & Kent (⊠ *1520 Kensington Rd., Oak Brook, IL* ☎ *630/954–2944 or 800/554–7016* ⊕ *www.abercrombiekent.com*) tours range from family holidays to custom itineraries for couples and individuals. As part of the Nile Explorer tour, you take a four-day cruise from Aswan to Luxor that includes disembarkation for a flight to Abu Simbel and stops at Kom Ombo, Edfu, and Ensa. The Egypt and the Red Sea tour sails to Jordan and Israel and includes a four-day Nile cruise. Sections of mosques that are closed to the general public are often included in tours.

African Travel (⊠ *1100 E. Broadway, Glendale, CA* ☎ *818/507–7893 or 800/421–8907* ⊕ *www.africantravelinc.com*) offers an 11-day tour that hits major sights from Cairo to Aswan and includes five days cruising the Nile. The average tour group has 10 people.

American Express Travel Service (⊠ *822 Lexington Ave., New York, NY* ☎ *212/758–6510* ⊠ *605 North Michigan Ave., Suite 105, Chicago, IL* ☎ *312/943–7840* ⊠ *8493 W. 3rd St., Los Angeles, CA* ☎ *310/659–1682*) can book a wide range of tours.

Destinations & Adventures International (⊠ *2301 Twelfth Ave. South, Suite 202, Nashville, TN* ☎ *615/383–9050 or 800/659–4599* ⊕ *www.*

8

daitravel.com) offers an 11-day excursion through Egypt that includes a four-day cruise from Luxor to Aswan.

Geographic Expeditions (✉ *1008 General Kennedy Ave., San Francisco, CA* ☎ *415/922–0448 or 800/777–8183* ⊕ *www.geoex.com*) has tours of Egypt, including four-day Luxor–Aswan cruises.

Journeys of the Mind (✉ *221 N. Kenilworth Ave., No. 413, Oak Park, IL* ☎ *708/383–8739* ⊕ *www.journeysofthemind.com*) specializes in educational adventures that promote cultural understanding. The basic tour includes lectures, trips to archaeological digs, dinner in an Egyptian home, and a seven-day Luxor–Aswan cruise.

Lindblad Expeditions (✉ *96 Morton St., 9th Fl, New York, NY* ☎ *212/765–7740 or 800/397–3348* ⊕ *www.expeditions.com*) is an upscale adventure-oriented travel company with a good reputation; its Egypt cruises are on the MS *Triton*, a 20-cabin yacht. Tours may include talks with preservation specialists.

Misr Travel (✉ *630 Fifth Ave., Ste. 1460, New York, NY* ☎ *212/332–2600 or 800/223–4978* ⊕ *misrtravel.org*) specializes in Middle East tours and has been in business since 1934; it is based in Cairo and has a solid reputation in Egypt.

Tarot Tours Garranah (✉ *378 Columbia Ave., Cliffside Park, NJ* ☎ *201/606–2255 or 201/450–1590* ⊕ *www.tarottoursusa.net*) offers a choice of cruises and itineraries in different price ranges.

IN THE UNITED
KINGDOM

Abercrombie & Kent (✉ *St. George's House, Ambrose St., Cheltenham, UK* ☎ *0124/254–7700 or 0845/618–2203* ⊕ *www.abercrombiekent.co.uk*).

Bales Worldwide (✉ *Bales House, Junction Rd., Dorking, UK* ☎ *0845-057-1819* ⊕ *www.balesworldwide.com*) offers a range of cruises and is a booking agent for six different dahabiyyas.

Imaginative Traveller (☎ *0845/077–8802* ⊕ *www.imaginative-traveller.com*) arranges small-group and custom-designed trips throughout Egypt that include cruises on the Nile, but it is primarily a budget-oriented tour operator, so some trips include felucca sails.

Thomas Cook (✉ *Thomas Cook Business Park, Bretton Way, Peterborough, Cambridgeshire, UK* ☎ *0870/752–0049* ⊕ *www.thomascook.co.uk*).

Voyages Jules Verne (✉ *21 Dorset Sq., London, UK* ☎ *0845/166–7003 in the UK only or 0207/616–1000* ⊕ *www.vjv.com*) is a well-established company that offers 12 luxury Egypt voyages.

PAYMENT

You must pay the full cost of the cruise up front. If you have booked through a tour operator in Egypt, you may be asked to send payment via wire transfer; this is a common situation (and one reason why people often choose to book through a tour operator in their own country).

However, you may save considerably if you make your arrangements directly through the Egyptian operator of your cruise. On the whole, travelers are more than satisfied with their cruise experience, lauding it in glowing terms as a trip of a lifetime, an experience never to be forgotten. Of course, some customers go away more than dissatisfied. If that turns out to be you, and you feel that your experience was beyond atrocious, consider requesting a refund.

THE CRUISE FLEET

NILE CRUISE SHIPS

$$$ MS *Champollion.* Built in 1995, this vessel evokes the era of classical French decor and architecture. There's a grand central staircase rising from the foyer leading to a wood-paneled mezzanine area with a bar and good onboard shop. The pièce de résistance has to be the Sheherazade Bar, which re-creates a Bedouin tent with yards of ornate fabric covering the ceiling and low seating on traditional couches and pillows. Cabins are decorated with yew-wood furniture; unfortunately, bathrooms are a mish-mash of contrasts, with a period-style marble sink and a modern plastic shower tray. The ship is particularly popular with German passengers. *Pyramisa Hotels, Resorts and Nile Cruises, 60 Shar'a Giza, Dokki, Giza, Cairo* ☎02/336–0791 *or* 02/336–0792 ⊕*www.pyramisaegypt.com* 48 *cabins, 95 passengers, 4 decks In-room: safe, refrigerator, Wi-Fi. In-ship: dining room, buffet, pool, gym, hot tub, library, laundry service, Wi-Fi, no-smoking rooms.*

$ MS *Da Vinci.* Built in 1993 and operated by Mirotel, this five-star vessel, as the name suggests, takes its design elements from Renaissance Italy, with its wall-filling frescoes and marble columns supporting the wrought-iron twin staircases. Cabins have gold and pale green accents and light-colored wood furniture. The vessel has a large pool for its class. It also has a forward-facing bar-lounge, which means you don't have to be on deck to see where the ship is headed. Guests are primarily British and other Europeans. *15 Shar'a El Shaheed Mahmoud Talaat, Dokki, Cairo* ☎201/606-2255 *or* 201/450 1590 ⊕*www.tarottoursusa.net* 74 *rooms, 140 passengers, 4 decks In-ship: dining room, buffet, bar, pool, laundry service.*

$$ MS *Hamees.* Debuting on the Nile in late 2008, the Hamees is one of a trio of luxury vessels from the same stables. The styling is ultra contemporary, with a three-story atrium lobby area complete with white marble floors, black wrought-iron work, and red velvet banquettes. The lounge has accents of coffee, tan, and chocolate to complement the rich teak accents and tiger-print fabrics, while the bar offers more dramatic blacks and deep reds. In contrast, room decor is simple yet contemporary, making the most of the 71 square feet of space. *Tarot Tours Garranah, 378 Columbia Ave., Cliffside Park, NJ, 07010* ☎201/606–2255 *or* 201/450–1590 ⊕*www.tarottoursusa.net* 72 *cabins, 140 passengers, 5 decks In-cabin: safe. In-ship: Dining room, buffet, pool, laundry service, no-smoking cabins.*

8

$ ⛴MS *Nile Sovereign.* Travcotels operates nearly 20 vessels on the Nile, and this ship is one of their budget offerings. The spacious reception area is modern but motel-like. Well-presented but with few flourishes, cabins are compact—18 square meters—but are recently refurbished with burnt-orange and terracotta bed throws and curtains and slim, marble-topped desks/dressing tables. The accents are carried on into the dining area, brightening ebony-colored furniture. The restaurant serves buffet-style Egyptian and international cuisine. ⊠ *Travcotels, Travco Center, 26th July Corridor, Sheikh Zayed City, Giza, Cairo* ☎ *02/3854–2020* ⊕ *www.travcotels.com* ⛟ *30 cabins, 56 passengers, 3 decks* ⚓ *In-cabin: refrigerator. In-ship: dining room, buffet, bars, pool, laundry service, no-smoking cabins.*

$$$$ ⛴MS *Oberoi Zahra.* Currently the most luxurious craft on the Nile, *Zahra* is an all-suites vessel with an à la carte restaurant and a full-service spa on board. The decor is contemporary, with wooden floors, dark wood, and leather. All cabins have large picture windows that open, and panoramic mirrored windows in the bathrooms so you can shower while enjoying the landscape along the Nile. Service throughout is exemplary, including on guided tours of no more than six people. There's no organized entertainment program on board, and the atmosphere is more adult house-party than on other boats. ⊠ *Mena House Oberoi, Pyramids Rd., Giza, Cairo* ☎ *02/3377–3222 or 02/3376–6644* ⊕ *www.oberoihotels.com* ⛟ *27 cabins, 54 passengers, 3 decks* ⚓ *In-cabin: safe, refrigerator, DVD, Wi-Fi. In-ship: dining room, bars, pool, gym, spa, laundry service, no-smoking rooms.*

$$$$ ⛴MS *Philae.* Elegant interiors invoke the era of the late-19th century English country mansion. Public areas are decorated with teak wainscoting and have parquet floors covered by hand-woven rugs; furnishings are antiques and period-style pieces. Cabins have distinctive wrought-iron balconies decorated with ornate flourishes. The interiors have plain beige walls and drapes, with finely chiseled, slim-legged teak furniture that adds to the feeling of spaciousness. On the top deck the circular pool is surrounded by artificial turf to absorb the heat. Some deck areas are shaded. The Oberoi-managed boat offers excellent standards of service. ⌂ *Hotel Mena House Oberoi, Pyramids Rd., Giza, Cairo* ☎ *02/3377–3222 or 02/3376–6644* ⊕ *www.oberoihotels. com* ⛟ *58 cabins, 120 passengers, 4 decks* ⚓ *In-cabin: safe. In-ship: dining room, buffet, bars, pool, gym, library, laundry service, no-smoking rooms.*

$$$ ⛴MS *Radamis II.* One of the largest boats on the Nile, the style of this ship is fairly conservative, appealing to a range of international tastes, though the upper deck has been fitted out with the modern plastic rattan-style furniture that's so fashionable in 2008. Golds, blues, and dark-wood veneers predominate in the public areas. The lounge tables are set in booths around a circular dance floor, while the main dining room offers an ambience of an Italian trattoria or French brasserie. Cabins have gold- and fern-colored drapes; the blue in the carpet is carried through into details in the modular bathrooms. ⌂ *Mövenpick Hotels and Resorts, 67 Shar'a al-Horreya, Heliopolis, Cairo* ☎ *02/690–1797* ⊕ *www.moevenpick-radamis.com* ⛟ *75 cabins, 150 passengers,*

4 decks ⚓ In-cabin: safe. In-ship: dining room, buffet, bars, pool, gym, laundry service, no-smoking cabins.

$$$$ ⌖**MS Royal Lily.** The Mövenpick Hotels group's most contemporary vessel has decor inspired by Asia and Japan, with black wood furniture contrasting with strong reds and metal accents (gilt and silver). The cavernous, minimalist reception area sets the scene with single bamboo stalks in glass vases. In the spacious cabins, the frosted glass between the bedroom and the bathroom mimics Japanese rice-paper screens. Royal Lily has a great pool with a large shallow area, where you can soak in six or seven inches of water to keep cool. It also has a roof-deck hot tub. ⌂67 Shar'al-Horreya, Heliopolis, Cairo ☏02/690–1797 ⊕www.moevenpick-hotels.com ⇥60 cabins, 120 passengers, 5 decks ⚓ In-cabin: safe, DVD (some). In-ship: dining room, buffet, bar, pool, gym, laundry service, Internet, no-smoking rooms.

$$$$ ⌖**MS St. George.** The flagship of the four-ship Sonesta Nile fleet, the *St. George* is designed with an exterior reminiscent of an old Mississippi River steamer, but inside it's a veritable Italianate palace on the water—with the advantage of all modern conveniences. The grand foyer makes a perfect first impression with its crystal chandelier and inlaid marble flooring and painted frescoes. The cabins are richly furnished with inlaid wood, marble, and hand-painted artwork matched by sumptuous drapes; each has a full-length window for views of the water. Public areas are blanketed with marble or gracefully sculpted mouldings offset with gilt. The panoramic lounge has views out over the direction of travel, and the leather club chairs make the perfect place to sip a drink while you cruise. ⌂120 Shar'a al-Thauwra, Heliopolis, Cairo ☏02/2481–3540 ⊕www.sonesta.com ⇥59 cabins, 118 passengers, 4 decks ⚓ In-cabin: Wi-Fi. In-ship: dining room, buffet, pool, gym, spa, bars, laundry service, Wi-Fi, no-smoking cabins.

$$$$ ⌖**MS Sudan.** For a touch of real Nile history, take a trip on the river on one of Egypt's last remaining steam ships. Built in 1885, *Sudan* really looks the part—a forest of varnished wood clads its facades, and a black funnel rises through its heart. The ship has been modernized for its return to service, but it has retained the original period decor. Each room is individually furnished with 19th-century pieces, including wrought-iron beds and sepia-tone photographs; original sketches and watercolors on the walls add a human touch. You could almost imagine Agatha Christie sitting in a quiet corner planning the next sequence for *Death on the Nile.* ⌂55 rue Sainte-Anne, Paris, 75002, France ☏01 73/00–81–88 in France ⊕www.vdm.com ⇥23 cabins, 46 passengers, 3 decks ⚓ In-cabin: no phone, no TV. In-ship: dining room, buffet, bar, library, laundry service, no kids under 7, no-smoking cabins.

$$$$ ⌖**MS Sun Boat III.** The latest metamorphosis of this Abercrombie & Kent vessel transformed it in 2005 into a floating Arabian oasis— the swimming pool is styled as a natural spring and cotton tents surround the top deck's sun beds and banquettes to provide travelers with shade and privacy. The ship has an "Out of Africa" feel. Cabins have teak four-poster beds covered with yards of natural linen, while public areas are decorated with plump cushions on rattan sofas and textiles in natural hues that offset tribal-style decorative elements. A&K enforces

8

no-cell-phone and no-smoking policies. The boat has private docks at Aswan and Luxor. ⌂*18 Yousef al-Gindi St., 10th fl, Boustan Center, Cairo* ☎*02/2393–6255* ⊕*www.akegypt.com* ⌐*18 cabins, 36 passengers, 3 decks* ⌂*In cabin: safe, Wi-Fi. In-ship: dining room, buffet, bar, pool, gym, library, laundry service, Wi-Fi, no-smoking rooms.*

$$$$ ⌐**MS Sun Boat IV.** Launched in 1996, *Sun Boat IV* underwent a multi-million-dollar makeover in 2006 to create a vessel that combines classical and contemporary decor, from the sleek lines of the Venetian-style pool on the sundeck to the Manhattan-loft feel of the main lounge. The restaurant offers buffet and à la carte meals among life-size frescoes of Egyptian life on the Nile. Cabins have full-length windows with sumptuous satin drapes; dark woods, particularly teak, are the main decor elements. A&K enforces no-cell-phone and no-smoking policies. The boat has private docks at Aswan and Luxor. ⌂*18 Yousef al-Gindi St., 10th fl, Boustan Center, Cairo* ☎*02/2393–6255* ⊕*www.akegypt.com* ⌐*40 cabins, 80 passengers, 4 decks* ⌂*In-cabin: safe, Wi-Fi. In-ship: dining room, buffet, bar, pool, gym, library, laundry service, Wi-Fi, no-smoking rooms.*

DAHABIYYAS

$$ ⌐**MS Princess Donia.** This is about as luxurious as you can get on smaller-scale dahabiyyas. The captain's cabin—which is now reserved for guests—takes up the full width of the boat, while the four standard cabins are more compact, though still well furnished. The company that runs *Princess Donia* prefers to charter the whole vessel rather than take individual bookings, so get together with your like-minded family or friends. A six-man crew is there to cater to your every whim. ☎*010/686–1688 in Cairo, 0781/123256 in the UK* ⊕*www.princess donia.com* ⌐*5 cabins, 10 passengers, 2 decks* ⌂*In-cabin: no phone, no TV. In-ship: dining room, bar, no-smoking cabins.*

$$$ ⌐**MS Zahra.** This all-wooden twin-sail craft offers a genteel journey along the river, taking its rhythm from the river's flow. The six cabins are individually furnished, and each is named after an indigenous flower. They are air-conditioned and have en-suite bathrooms. There's a cozy paneled lounge and a shady terrace on the upper deck. The vessel doesn't serve alcohol, but passengers are welcome to bring their own supplies—the boat has a range of soft drinks to make excellent cocktails. This craft is one of six operated by the El Gendy brothers, who pioneered Lake Nasser cruises. ✉*17 Shar'a Tunis, New Ma'adi, Cairo* ☎*02/518–9649* ⊕*www.dahabiya.com* ⌐*6 cabins, 12 passengers, 2 decks* ⌂*In-cabin: no TV. In-ship: dining room, no-smoking cabins.*

LAKE NASSER CRUISE SHIPS

$$$ ⌐**MS Eugenie.** This three-deck vessel was the first boat to be built above the High Dam to carry passengers on lake cruises. The work of the El Gendy brothers, the *Eugenie* is the last word in taste and refinement, with an attentive crew and decor reminiscent of colonial-era elegance. Public areas have excellent design touches, including

wood paneling and deep velour upholstery in gold and scarlet. Cabins are more simply decorated, but those on the upper decks have small private balconies. There's ample room on the sun decks, both shaded and open. *Eugenie Investment Group, 17 Shar'a Tunis, New Ma'adi, Cairo* 02/516–9649 or 02/516–9653 *www.eugenie.com. eg* 52 suites, 104 passengers, 3 decks *In-room: no TV. In-ship: dining room, buffet, pool, sauna, steam room, bars, laundry service, no-smoking cabins.*

$$$$ **MS Prince Abbas.** Just like the classic cruisers of old, *Prince Abbas* has exterior wooden walkways around the decks, and you enter the cabins from the outside. But styling is the only hint of those days almost a century ago—mirrored glass in the cabin windows ensuring your privacy is only one of a range of contemporary design features. Throughout, the interiors mix simple modern styles with colors designed to maximize the space. The spacious main lounge has ample tables for all passengers, but the ship also has other bars and lounges, and a cozy library where you can often find some quiet alone time. The pool is the best on Lake Nasser. *Mövenpick Hotels and Resorts, 67 Shar'a al-Horreya, Heliopolis, Cairo* 02/2690–1797 or 02/2690–8325 *www.moevenpick-prince-abbas.com* 65 suites, 130 passengers, 4 decks *In-room: refrigerator, DVD (some). In-ship: dining room, buffet, café, pool, gym, bars, library, laundry service, Internet terminal, no-smoking cabins.*

$$$ **MS Qasr Ibrim.** The riot of art nouveau details aboard this vessel transports you back to the early-20th-century heyday of Nile cruising. The vast lounge is particularly stunning, with its low-backed sofas and mirrored bar, but the ship also stands out in the reception area with its sensuous curved metal staircase and in the wood-paneled cabins, which have black-and-white tile bathrooms. Cabins on the upper decks have private balconies. The pool on the top deck is a good size, and there's lots of deck space for relaxation. *Eugenie Investment Group, 17 Shar'a Tunis, New Ma'adi, Cairo* 02/516–9649 or 02/516–9653 *www.eugenie.com.eg* 65 cabins, 120 passengers, 4 decks *In-cabin: no TV. In-ship: dining room, buffet pool, sauna, steam room, bars, laundry service, no-smoking rooms.*

$ **MS Tania.** This is the most longstanding member of the considerable Travcotels fleet on Lake Nasser. The overall decor has an art deco feel. The restaurant suggests a smart French dining room, with black high-backed chairs contrasting with white table linens; architectural prints grace the walls. The spacious lounge area has panoramic windows and is decorated with comfortable, terracotta-colored sofas and hand-woven Egyptian carpets. Elegant cabins have large windows that open. There's a two-level sundeck; the pool, on the lower deck, also has a bar. *Travcotels, 26th July Corridor, Sheikh Zayed City, Giza, Cairo* 02/3854–3222 *www.travcotels.com* 28 cabins, 55 passengers, 3 decks *In-cabin: refrigerator. In-ship: dining room, buffet, pool, bars, library, laundry service, no-smoking cabins.*

8

Egypt Essentials

PLANNING TOOLS, EXPERT INSIGHT, GREAT CONTACTS

There are planners and there are those who, excuse the pun, fly by the seat of their pants. We happily place ourselves among the planners. Our writers and editors try to anticipate all the issues you may face before and during any journey, and then they do their research. This section is the product of their efforts. Use it to get excited about your trip to Egypt, to inform your travel planning, or to guide you on the road should the seat of your pants start to feel threadbare.

GETTING STARTED

We're proud of our Web site: Fodors. com. It is a great place to begin any journey. Scan Travel Wire for suggested itineraries, travel deals, restaurant and hotel openings, and other up-to-the-minute info. Check out Booking to research prices and book plane tickets, hotel rooms, rental cars, and vacation packages. Head to Talk for on-the-ground pointers from travelers who frequent our message boards. You can also link to loads of other travel-related resources.

▌RESOURCES

ONLINE TRAVEL TOOLS
All About Egypt Egypt Today (⊕www.egypt today.com) is an English-language current affairs and culture magazine covering a range of issues. **Go Red Sea** (⊕www.goredsea.com) has useful background information about the main Red Sea resorts and a booking engine for hotels and travel packages.

Guardian's Egypt (⊕www.guardians.net) brings together information and news about Egypt and Egyptology. **History for Kids** (⊕www.historyforkids.org) has helpful, simple information to help your kids understand what they'll see on their trip. **State Information Service** (⊕www.sis.gov.eg) has information about a range of issues from politics to travel to culture, issued by the Egyptian government.

Safety Transportation Security Administration (TSA; ⊕www.tsa.gov)

Time Zones Timeanddate.com (⊕www.time anddate.com/worldclock) can help you figure out the correct time anywhere.

Weather Accuweather.com (⊕www. accuweather.com) is an independent weather-forecasting service with good coverage of hurricanes. **Weather.com** (⊕www.weather.com) is the Web site for the Weather Channel.

WORD OF MOUTH

After your trip, be sure to rate the places you visited and share your experiences and travel tips with us and other Fodorites in Travel Ratings and Talk on www.fodors.com.

VISITOR INFORMATION
Before You Leave Egyptian Tourist Authority (☎212/332–2570 in New York City, 323/653–8961 in Los Angeles, 312/280–4666 in Chicago ⊕www.egypt.travel).

In Egypt Ministry of Tourism (✉Misr Travel Tower, Maydan Abbassiya, Downtown, Cairo ☎02/285–4509).

▌THINGS TO CONSIDER

GOVERNMENT ADVISORIES
Egypt has suffered a number of terrorist attacks in the past two decades; a spate of attacks in Luxor and Cairo in the mid-1990s, as well as bombings in the Sinai and in Cairo in 2004 and 2005. These attacks appear to have been undertaken by domestic terrorists whose purpose is to unsettle the government by hitting the tourist market (the country's biggest money-earner) rather than part of a wider terrorist network.

The U.S. State Department advisory on Egypt gives clear advice on travel to these regions.

Security measures are in place to protect foreign travelers in Egypt. These include providing armed officers to travel with tourists, arranging visitors traveling by road into convoys, and ensuring that all hotels have guards and x-ray machines to check all incoming bags.

That said, the atmosphere in the streets and at attractions, cafés, and hotels is generally relaxed, with no threatening overtones. Most Egyptians are very welcoming of foreign visitors, and if you get a chance to chat with any Egyptians, they are usually very interested in finding out about you.

■ **TIP**→ Consider registering online with the State Department (https://travelregis tration.state.gov/ibrs/), so the government will know to look for you should a crisis occur in the country you're visiting.

General Information & Warnings Aus-tralian Department of Foreign Affairs & Trade (⊕ www.smartraveller.gov.au). **Consular Affairs Bureau of Canada** (⊕ www.voyage. gc.ca). **U.K. Foreign & Commonwealth Office** (⊕ www.fco.gov.uk/travel). **U.S. Department of State** (⊕ www.travel.state.gov).

GEAR

The key to packing for a trip to Egypt is to focus on lightweight and practical items for daytime sightseeing. Cottons, linens, and moisture-wicking fabrics make the most sensible choices for the heat. Egypt is an Islamic country, albeit a more open society than some in the Middle East, but attitudes toward dress are still more conservative than in the U.S, particularly with regard to women's attire. The clientele in Cairo's upmarket hotels and night-clubs tend to dress up.

It's important that all travelers—but particularly women—not to expose too much flesh. Pack T-shirts with sleeves that end between shoulder and elbow rather than tank-tops or those with spaghetti straps. Long shorts and capri pants are fine for women, but full-length pants are better. Skirts should be at least knee length. Short shorts and short skirts will cause stares; moreover, to visit churches and mosques in Egypt women must have shoulders and knees covered. In mosques you'll also need to cover your hair, so if you don't want to use a scarf supplied by the mosque, carry your own lightweight scarf.

For men, long shorts are acceptable when you're traveling on tours, but full-length lightweight pants are preferable and are especially recommended in Cairo and in the desert, where they offer more protec-tion from the sun. Regular T-shirts are fine, but lightweight collared shirts help protect your neck and arms from the sun better. Only a few hotels require a jacket and tie (most notably the Sofitel Winter Palace in Luxor), but men will be expected to wear long pants, collared shirts, and shoes (not sandals) in the evenings.

WORD OF MOUTH

You'll notice more security around than we're used to in the U.S. They take the position in Egypt (and Jordan) that a good offense is the best defense. Every hotel has screening devices for your luggage and bags. Some are more professionally staffed than others. Every tourist site has a number of armed Tourist Police and x-ray machines for your backpacks and camera bags. But you don't feel oppressed. It's a business as usual approach.—AZEBS

If you travel in winter, pack a fleece or a jacket for the cool evening air. This is especially true if you intend to overnight in the desert.

Beachwear is appropriate only around the pool, even in the coastal resorts. Although you may find visitors of other nationalities scantily dressed in hotel lobbies and even around town, be assured that this is not respectful to local sensibilities.

Must packs: comfortable shoes, because you'll be walking a lot and climbing up and down rickety or badly set stairs into tombs; a hat, because the sun is hot at all times of year; sunglasses, because temple facades and rock faces are extremely bright in the daylight; and sunscreen to protect any exposed skin. Pharmacies in Egypt are well stocked. ■ **TIP**→ Don't bother bringing expensive prescription medicine for intestinal upsets. Instead, buy Antinal, a locally available intestinal antibi-otic that is commonly used to treat diarrhea, when you arrive in Egypt and take a course the moment you feel any problems. It's cheap (about $1), available in every pharmacy, and very effective. In more serious cases, a doctor or pharmacist can prescribe a stronger antibiotic, which will cost much less than at home.

Extra stuff that will be helpful includes: a small flashlight for visiting dimly lit tombs and temples; lightweight binoculars, to allow you a clearer view of monumental temple facades, and for bird-watching on the Nile; anti-bacterial gel, so that you can clean your hands before eating no matter where you are.

Except in the Western Desert, you can buy almost anything you need in the cities and main towns, from baby formula to feminine hygiene products and contact lens supplies, but prices may be more expensive than at home.

PASSPORTS & VISAS

U.S. and EU citizens can buy tourist visas on arrival in Egypt at any Egyptian international airport; the process takes only a few minutes, and the windows selling visas are immediately before immigration (look to the left in Cairo). The current cost of a single-entry visa is $15 (payable in U.S. dollars, euros, or pounds sterling), and it is valid for a period not exceeding three months. The visa is often more expensive if you buy it in advance in your home country. You'll find a kiosk immediately before immigration in every major airport. All visitors must have at least six months validity on their passports to enter Egypt.

If you have booked through a tour operator or have arranged a transfer with your hotel, the representative will be waiting for you in the arrivals hall and will help with this process, but it's not complicated.

If you arrive in Egypt via Israel at Taba you will not be able to buy a full tourist visa at the border crossing. They will only issue a visa limiting you to the Sinai region; to get a tourist visa that allows you to travel to other parts of Egypt, you must visit the Egyptian Consulate in Eilat.

U.S. Passport Information U.S. Department of State (☎877/487–2778 ⊕ http://travel.state.gov/passport).

GENERAL REQUIREMENTS FOR EGYPT	
Passport	Must be valid for 6 months after date of arrival
Visa	Required for Americans ($15)
Vaccinations	None required; Hep A and B recommended
Driving	International driver's license required.
Departure Tax	None

HEALTH ISSUES

The CDC recommends vaccination against Hepatitis A; it's also wise to have a vaccination against Hepatitis B. The risk of typhoid is generally low, but if you plan to visit the Western Desert oases or stay in the countryside you should discuss this risk with your doctor; get a typhoid vaccination if you intend to take a multi-day felucca trip on the Nile.

Otherwise, the main health risks are for intestinal upsets from contaminated food and water; you can usually treat these conditions with widely available over-the-counter medications purchased in Egypt. *For more information see Health under On the Ground in Egypt, below.*

■ TIP→ If you travel a lot internationally—particularly to developing nations—refer to the CDC's *Health Information for International Travel* (aka Traveler's Health Yellow Book). Info from it is posted on the CDC Web site (www.cdc.gov/travel/yb), or you can buy a copy from your local bookstore for $24.95.

Health Warnings National Centers for Disease Control & Prevention (CDC ☎877/394–8747 international travelers' health line ⊕ www.cdc.gov/travel). **World Health Organization** (WHO ⊕ www.who.int).

TRIP INSURANCE

We believe that comprehensive trip insurance is especially valuable if you're booking a very expensive or complicated trip (particularly to an isolated region) or if you're booking far in advance.

A comprehensive travel policy will cover trip-cancellation and interruption, letting you cancel or cut your trip short because of a personal emergency, illness, or, in some cases, acts of terrorism in your destination. Such policies also cover evacuation and medical care. Another type of coverage to look for is financial default—that is, when your trip is disrupted because a tour operator, airline, or cruise line goes out of business. Generally you must buy this when you book your trip or shortly thereafter, and it's only available to you if your operator isn't on a list of excluded companies.

Everyone traveling to Egypt—but particularly travelers on Medicare—should have a travel medical or evacuation plan. Medicare—as well as some HMOs—will not cover your medical expenses outside of the United States (including time aboard a cruise ship, even if it leaves from a U.S. port). Medical-only policies typically reimburse you for medical care (excluding that related to pre-existing conditions) and hospitalization abroad, and provide for evacuation. You still have to pay the bills and await reimbursement from the insurer, though.

Expect comprehensive travel insurance policies to cost about 4% to 7% or 8% of the total price of your trip (it's more like 8%–12% if you're over age 70). A medical-only policy may or may not be cheaper than a comprehensive policy. Always read the fine print of your policy to make sure that you are covered for the risks that are of most concern to you. Compare several policies to make sure you're getting the best price and range of coverage available.

TRIP INSURANCE RESOURCES

Insurance Comparison Sites Insure My Trip. com (☎800/487-4722 ⊕www.insuremytrip. com). Square Mouth.com (☎800/240-0369 or 727/490-5803 ⊕www.squaremouth.com).

Comprehensive Travel Insurers Access America (☎800/729-6021 ⊕www.acces-samerica.com). CSA Travel Protection (☎800/873-9855 ⊕www.csatravelprotection. com). HTH Worldwide (☎610/254-8700 ⊕www.hthworldwide.com). Travelex Insurance (☎800/228-9792 ⊕www.travelex-insurance. com). AIG Travel Guard (☎800/826-4919 ⊕www.travelguard.com). Travel Insured International (☎800/243-3174 ⊕www.travel insured.com).

Medical-Only Insurers International Medical Group (☎800/628-4664 ⊕www.imglobal. com). International SOS (⊕www.international sos.com). Wallach & Company (☎800/237-6615 or 540/687-3166 ⊕www.wallach.com).

▮ BOOKING YOUR TRIP

Because of the complexities of booking an independent trip in Egypt, this is one destination where it still pays to use a knowledgeable travel agent. Many agents specialize in travel to Egypt and the Middle East and have direct contact with reliable local tour operators and agents. Even if these travel agents can't offer you a cheaper trip, they will often offer you a smoother trip. However, an independently planned and booked trip to Egypt is still within reach of almost any traveler.

ACCOMMODATIONS

The Egyptian government awards star-ratings to all hotels, with five-star being the highest rating. The star-rating of a hotel or cruise ship also dictates the price range the management can charge. However, Egyptian star-ratings don't quite equate to international standards. You may notice a difference in service and standards of fixtures and fitting when compared to an equivalent hotel at home.

Egypt has a huge range of choice in the five-star and one- or two-star categories, but relatively little choice in the middle range. Under three stars, properties are basic but usually clean. Most will have a small basic en-suite shower-only bathroom.

Five-star hotels have a wide range of facilities. Those in Cairo also cater to business clients, so they tend to have smaller pools and fewer or no sports facilities, whereas hotels on the Red Sea Coast and in the Sinai have large pools and more expansive leisure facilities. More expensive hotels generally have Web sites that allow you to book online, but large tour operators often book huge blocks of rooms far in advance, so don't be surprised if you don't initially find a vacancy even in the off-season. It's sometimes easier to book upscale hotels through travel agents and tour operators for this reason.

Smaller and more inexpensive hotels don't always accept credit cards. Enquire before you book. It's not uncommon for cheaper properties to require an electronic wire transfer for payment, which they will usually ask for in advance.

■ TIP→ Assume that hotels operate on the European Plan (EP, no meals) unless we specify that they use the Breakfast Plan (BP, with full breakfast), Continental Plan (CP, Continental breakfast), Full American Plan (FAP, all meals), Modified American Plan (MAP, breakfast and dinner) or are all-inclusive (AI, all meals and most activities).

AIRLINE TICKETS

All domestic air travel in Egypt is on EgyptAir. It is possible—but can be difficult—to book these flights directly; many travelers find it easier to work with a travel agent or tour operator with contacts in Egypt.

CHARTER FLIGHTS

There are a large number of charter flights from Europe to Egypt (a lot of these are from the U.K. to the beach resorts in the Sinai and on the Red Sea coast, though some also go direct to Luxor). These flights can be booked only through U.K.-based tour operators and travel agents.

RENTAL CARS

Egypt is one destination where renting a car is not generally recommended. There are several reasons for this. First, the level of driving skill in Egypt is generally erratic; there's little adherence to laws and safety guidelines, and driving at dangerous speeds for the conditions is the norm. Second, major towns and cities have poor signage, making navigation next to impossible; parking is almost nonexistent. Finally, for security reasons, the government organizes all tourist traffic along the Nile Valley into convoys, which run a certain fixed hours. Even if you self-drive, you must join a convoy, making it impossible to travel on your own timetable.

Because of all these difficulties, you'll find numerous tour operators on the ground, all of which provide inexpensive, reliable tours to all major sights, making the need to rent a car redundant. In addition, you may be able to book private tours and guides for little more than the cost of renting a car.

The one area where it may be sensible to rent a vehicle is in the Sinai or for trips along the Red Sea coast from a base in Hurghada or El-Gouna—roads here are less busy.

Since the late 1990s the number of international car rental companies in Egypt has dropped dramatically. You cannot rent a car in Luxor or Aswan, for instance, though you can rent in Cairo or Alexandria, on the Red Sea coast, and in the Sinai, though even those offices with an international brand-name will be franchises.

Most companies have minimum age limits (normally 21 or 23). You'll also need an international driving license. Unlimited mileage is generally not offered in Egypt; most car-rental deals only offer 100 km per day in the basic rental price. The average rate for each kilometer (0.62 mi) after that is around $0.25. This can add greatly to your bill when you return the vehicle. Most car-rental agency agreements prohibit off-road driving, so avoid dirt roads in the Sinai or desert tracks away from the Nile Valley.

Make sure that the car you receive is in good condition; it is wise to specify that you want a new car. Many vehicles are at least two years old and most have dents and scrapes. Make sure you receive an emergency number you can call 24 hours a day in case of mechanical problems or accident.

With so little demand you should have no problem finding car rentals at any time of the year. If you decide to rent in a resort, visit the rental office a couple of days before you need the car. If you want to rent from the time of your arrival, book from home.

If you rent and intend to park at your hotel between journeys, you'll be asked to hand in the car registration document and your driving license at the security gate during your time in the hotel complex. The documents will be returned when you leave. Don't forget the registration card because if you don't return it with the car at the end of your rental period, there's a huge penalty of $300 to $500 to cover the time and cost for the rental company to get a replacement.

If you intend to return your rental car to Cairo airport during the day (except on Friday), add an extra 60 minutes to your travel time in case of traffic delays.

Major Agencies Avis (☎800/331-1084 in the U.S., 02/265-2429 in Cairo ⊕www. avis.com). **Budget** (✉Cairo International Airport, Heliopolis, Cairo ☎02/265-2395 ✉22 Shar'a El Mathaf El Ziraee, Dokki, Cairo ☎02/726-0518 ☎800/472-3325 In the U.S. ⊕www.budget.com). **Europcar** (✉6m Maydan 1226, Heliopolis Sheraton Buildings, Heliopolis, Cairo ☎02/2267-1815 ✉Cairo International

Airport, Heliopolis, Cairo ☎02/2267-2439 ⊕www.europcar.com). **Hertz** (✉Ramses Hilton, 1115 Corniche al-Nil, Cairo ☎02/575-8914 ✉Cairo International Airport, Heliopolis, Cairo ☎02/265-2430 ✉Le Méridien Pyramids Hotel, Giza, Cairo ☎02/3377-3388 ✉InterContinental Pyramids Hotel & Resort, Giza, Cairo ☎02/3838-8300 ☎800/654-3001 or 02/347-2238 for central reservations office in Egypt ⊕www.hertz.com).

Local Agencies Smart Rental (✉Corniche El-Nil, Ma'adi, Cairo ☎02/524-3006 ⊕www. smartlimo.com).

CAR-RENTAL INSURANCE

Most rental companies in Egypt include full insurance in the quoted rental price, but do check the fine print to make sure you're getting on paper what was agreed to verbally. Insurance does not cover the loss of the car registration document; if you don't return this with the car, you'll be liable for at least $300 for a replacement (including loss of income as the vehicle stands idle as the rental agency waits for the replacement document).

■ TIP→ You can decline the insurance from the rental company and purchase it through a third-party provider such as Travel Guard (www.travelguard.com)—$9 per day for $35,000 of coverage. That's sometimes just under half the price of the CDW offered by some car-rental companies.

VACATION PACKAGES

Many people travel to Egypt after buying a package and this can work out well pricewise. Remember to ask what's included in your package in order to decide what's the most suitable package for you. For example, are excursions included on your Nile cruise? Is an English-speaking guide included?

The disadvantage of buying a package is that many operators are tied into certain hotel and boat chains in Egypt, so this substantially limits your options. Most operators only include the main sights and resorts as part of their packages, so if you want to go off the beaten track—

the desert oases, for example—or if you want to stay longer in a certain town than normal, you'll need to think about a private trip.

■ TIP→ **Some packages and cruises are sold only through travel agents. Don't always assume that you can get the best deal by booking everything yourself.**

Each year consumers are stranded or lose their money when packagers—even large ones with excellent reputations—go out of business. How can you protect yourself?

First, always pay with a credit card; if you have a problem, your credit-card company may help you resolve it. Second, buy trip insurance that covers default.

Third, choose a company that belongs to the United States Tour Operators Association, whose members must set aside funds to cover defaults. Finally, choose a company that also participates in the Tour Operator Program of the American Society of Travel Agents (ASTA), which will act as mediator in any disputes.

You can also check on the tour operator's reputation among travelers by posting an inquiry on one of the Fodors.com forums.

Organizations American Society of Travel Agents (ASTA ☎ 703/739-2782 or 800/965-2782 ⊕ www.astanet.com). **United States Tour Operators Association** (USTOA ☎ 212/599-6599 ⊕ www.ustoa.com).

TRANSPORTATION

Egypt has always been ruled by the close relationship between the Nile and the desert. Nile waters make the land fertile and even today the vast majority of Egyptians live within a mile or so of the river. The river was also the major conduit for transport until the arrival of the railways just over 100 years ago. The country's major rail line follows the river as does a modern highway.

Since ancient times, the country has geographically been divided into two regions, Upper Egypt and Lower Egypt. Lower Egypt is the northernmost section of the Nile Valley (closest to the Mediterranean Sea), incorporating the oldest Egyptian capital of Memphis, the modern capital Cairo, and the Nile Delta. It's called Lower Egypt because it refers to the lower reaches of the river. Upper Egypt covers the southern stretches of the country and the ancient capital of Thebes (modern Luxor). The name refers to the fact that this part of the country lies around the most upstream sections of the Nile that lay within the boundaries of Egypt.

Cairo, the capital since the end of the first millennium AD, is still the country's main hub for transport connections. Domestic air flights will offer the fastest connections anywhere, and a 2-hour flight will get you almost anywhere in the country. Overland, the train trip from Cairo to Luxor takes around 12 hours, 15 hours to Aswan, and 2 or 3 hours to Alexandria.

The Red Sea and the Sinai Peninsula are east of Cairo. The two main towns, Hurghada on the Red Sea and Sharm El-Sheikh in the Sinai, can both be reached by road and by air from Cairo. Road surfaces are generally good. Flights take around one hour with the overland journey being around seven hours to Hurghada and six hours to Sharm.

Until the 1970s, the only way to reach the Western Desert oases was by camel train.

Today, there are paved highways, dropping the journey time from Cairo to Bahariyya from many days to a half-day. The road is in good condition. Siwa is considerably more remote, a 15-hour nonstop journey from Cairo on a circuitous route with road conditions that vary from excellent to poor (though it's certainly passable with a standard vehicle). You'll need permission and a four-wheel-drive vehicle to use the cross-country route from Siwa to Bahariyya. Sand has swallowed up much of the old asphalt road, making navigation difficult. The journey takes around 6 hours. Bear in mind that although road surfaces are generally in good condition, signage is poor, and there are numerous hazards, from slow-moving animal carts to people walking on the highway. You may prefer not to undertake long journeys by public bus.

TRAVEL TIMES FROM CAIRO TO:	BY AIR	BY BUS	BY TRAIN
Alexandria	30 min.	2.5 hours	2–3 hours
Sharm El-Sheikh	1 hour	6 hours	n/a
Hurghada	1 hour	7 hours	n/a
Luxor	1.5 hours	n/a	9.5 hours
Aswan	n/a	2–3 hours	12.5 hours
Baharriya	n/a	5–6 hours	n/a

▌BY AIR

Flying time to Cairo from New York is 10 hours on a nonstop flight; from the West Coast, the minimum flying time is 17 hours (you'll need to make at least one stop). Cairo is 4 hours from Paris, Amsterdam, and Frankfurt, and 5 hours from London.

If you need to book domestic flights after you have arrived in Egypt, you'll need to visit an EgyptAir office (or book online) or a reputable travel agent at least one day before you fly—but don't expect there to be seats available that late, especially in peak season. Book flights to Abu Simbel as early as possible as these flights fill up fast at all times of year.

Airlines & Airports Airline and Airport Links.com (⊕www.airlineandairportlinks.com) has links to many of the world's airlines and airports.

Airline Security Issues Transportation Security Administration (⊕www.tsa.gov) has answers for almost every question that might come up.

AIRPORTS

Cairo International Airport is the country's primary international airport and the only one that has nonstop flights from the U.S. Terminal 3, which opened in late 2008, is devoted solely to EgyptAir, both international and domestic flights, and EgyptAir's Star Alliance partner airlines that fly to Egypt (at this writing, Austrian Airlines, BMI, Lufthansa, Singapore Airlines, and Turkish Airlines). Small numbers of scheduled flights from Europe also land at Sharm El-Sheikh, Hurghada, and Luxor.

If you book a package through a travel agent or have prearranged a tour, your airport transfers will almost certainly be included in the price. Look for your company's sign as you exit baggage claim. If you book independently, then you may have to take a taxi. Ask your hotel if it has a limo transfer service; most hotels do, and though the vehicle is not a true limousine, it will be a vehicle in good condition. You will be charged more than the normal taxi fare for this service (some hotels include transfers if you book an executive-floor room), but after a long flight, the stress-free transfer may be worth the extra money.

Cairo airport also offers fixed-rate limo service to all hotels. This costs more than a private taxi, but there's no need to haggle a fee and the vehicles are in good condition.

Anticipate long lines and be sure to give yourself a full two hours for international check-in.

Information Cairo International Airport (CAI ⊠Cairo ☎02/265–3308). **Hurghada** (HRG ⊠Hurghada ☎065/344–2592). **Luxor International Airport** (LXR ⊠Luxor ☎095/237–4655). **Sharm El-Sheikh International Airport** (SSH ⊠Sharm El-Sheikh ☎069/360–1141).

FLIGHTS TO AND FROM EGYPT

Only EgyptAir and Delta Airlines offer nonstop flights to Egypt from the U.S. Both fly from New York's JFK into Cairo. Most European airlines offer flights to Egypt, and the majority of Americans must connect in Europe to reach Cairo. Some European budget airlines also fly to Egypt, though few of these airlines have telephone numbers in the country, relying instead on their Web sites.

Nonstops to Egypt Delta (☎02/736–2030 in Cairo, 800/241–4141 in the U.S. ⊕www.delta. com). **EgyptAir** (☎0900/70000 (national call center) in Egypt, 212/581–5600 in New York, 310/215–3900 in Los Angeles ⊕www. egyptair.com).

Major European Airlines Air France (☎800/237–2747 ⊕www.airfrance.us). **Alitalia** (☎800/223–5730 ⊕www.alitaliausa.com). **Austrian Airlines** (☎800/843–0002 ⊕www. aua.com). **British Airways** (☎800/247–9297 ⊕www.britishairways.com). **Finnair** (☎800/950–5000 ⊕www.finnair.com). **KLM Royal Dutch Airlines** (☎800/225–2525 ⊕www.nwa.com). **Lufthansa** (☎800/399–5838 ⊕www.lufthansa.com). **SAS Scandinavian Airlines** (☎800/221–2350 ⊕www. flysas.com). **Swiss International Airlines** (☎877/359–7947 ⊕www.swiss.com).

European Budget Airlines Air Berlin (⊕www.airberlin.com). **Astreaus** (⊕www. flystar.com). **Condor Airlines** (⊕www. condor.com). **Easyjet** (⊕www.easyjet.com).

Jet Air Fly (⊕www.jetairfly.com). **Thomas Cook Belgium** (⊕www.thomascookairlines. com). **Thomsonfly** (⊕www.thomsonfly.com). **Transavia** (⊕www.transavia.com). **XL Airways** (⊕www.xl.com).

FLIGHTS WITHIN EGYPT

EgyptAir is the only provider of scheduled domestic flights in Egypt. In addition to Cairo, Aswan, Luxor, Hurghada, and Sharm El-Sheikh, Egyptair flies to Abu Simbel, Alexandria, Assuit, and Marsa Alam.

Domestic Egyptian Airlines Egyptair (☎0900/70000 (national call center) in Egypt, 212/581-5600 in New York, 310/215-3900 in Los Angeles ⊕www.egyptair.com).

▮ BY BUS

Privately owned buses are the cheapest way to get around Egypt, but because of security concerns, the Egyptian authorities dissuade independent travelers from using them on certain routes, specifically from Cairo down the Nile to Luxor and from Luxor east to Hurghada.

Bus transport in Egypt is divided geographically, usually with one major company providing services in each region, except in the Sinai and Red Sea coast areas, where there is some competition. Fares are cheap, and buses are generally modern and in good condition, though the stream of video entertainment played at high volume and overzealous air-conditioning can make the journey slightly unpleasant. Driving standards are poor.

The East Delta Travel Company runs from Cairo to the Suez Canal and the Sinai; El Gouna Transportation runs from Cairo down the Red Sea Coast; Super Jet offers services from Cairo to the Sinai and the Red Sea; the Upper Egyptian Bus Company has service from Cairo down the Nile to Luxor and Aswan and east from Luxor to Hurghada; the West and Middle Delta Company covers routes to Alexandria, and along the Mediterranean Coast to the Libyan border and Siwa Oasis.

Bus Information East Delta Travel Company (☎02/2577-9347 or 02/262-3128 ⊕www. eastdeltatravel.com). **El Gouna Transportation** (☎19567 (in Egypt only) or 02/2201-9941). **Superjet** (☎809/682-9670). **Upper Egypt Company** (☎809/682-9670 ⊕www.bus. com.eg). **West and Middle Delta Company** (☎809/682-9670 ⊕www.bus.com.eg).

▮ BY CAR

Driving in Egypt can be a stressful and harrowing experience. Egyptian drivers usually ignore speed limits on open roads and drive vehicles that are dangerous from a structural and mechanical point of view. Out in the countryside, there are no pedestrian walkways, and the road shoulders are not well defined. You'll need to watch out for little children, goats, camels, and oxen—constant vigilance is required. At night these same animals can still be problems, but worse is the fact that few Egyptian drivers use their headlights after dark, so it's not always easy to see oncoming traffic.

In the city, you'll need to watch constantly for other traffic and for pedestrians who cross the street anywhere. They can and do appear from behind stationary vehicles, and they cross in the gaps between moving traffic.

Wherever you travel by road in Egypt you meet police checkpoints. The authorities control all traffic but particularly vehicles carrying foreign tourists. If you are traveling along the Nile Valley in Upper Egypt by car, you should travel with a guarded traffic convoy. Visit the tourist office to find out where the convoy meets and at what time; if you don't join the convoy, you'll be stopped at the first checkpoint out of town and either turned back or told to wait for the next convoy or for a guard to be assigned to your vehicle. Waiting for a guard can take well over an hour and could ruin any carefully prepared itinerary.

GASOLINE

Gas stations and rest areas are plentiful on major highways, and credit cards are widely accepted. In areas that see fewer travelers, such as the Western Desert, they are less so. Carrying cash is a good idea, and always be sure to take extra gas with you when traveling in the Western Desert. Most gas stations in Egypt are full-service, and it's customary to tip the attendant who fills up your car a pound or two. All gas is unleaded and is sold by the liter. Plain unleaded is called *tamanin*, or 80, denoting the level of purity. Higher-quality gasoline is available as *tisa'in*, or 90, and occasionally *khamsa wa tisa'in*, or 95.

Prices are reasonable by U.S. standards—£e1.10 per liter (around $0.78 per gallon)—but are in flux with rapidly rising oil prices. Most pumps show amounts in Roman numerals but you still may find some in Arabic. Watch as the attendant starts the pump to see that it reads 000.

ROAD CONDITIONS

Road conditions are generally good, especially in the Sinai and along the Red Sea coast. There are very few maps available, and signposting—although in Arabic and English—is generally poor.

ROADSIDE EMERGENCIES

Make sure that your car rental company provides you with the contact details or a 24-hour emergency number to call in case of any problems.

Any traffic accidents will be dealt with by police.

Always take extra water when traveling long distances, especially on the desert roads. If at all possible, carry a cell phone with you as well the telephone numbers of police stations and hotels along your route. If you have car trouble on the highway, get your car off the road as soon as possible, then wait and flag down any passing vehicle. Even remote areas are served by daily buses, and they will stop for you if they see you. More worrisome are accidents. Many Egyptian car owners don't carry insurance, and disputes tend to be resolved on the scene with more or less fanfare depending on the seriousness of the accident. Insist on getting a policeman who speaks English, and take down the license number of the other driver. For serious accidents in which people have been injured, get emergency help first and then immediately contact or drive to your embassy. In all situations, insist on having present a senior police officer who speaks English.

Emergency Services Police (☎122).

RULES OF THE ROAD

Speed limits are 60 kph in built-up areas and 90 kph on the open road (these should be posted at regular intervals at the side of the highway), but most local drivers ignore these and drive as fast as they can. Lane discipline is nonexistent, and drivers will try to pass even on bends and up hills when they cannot see if there's traffic coming in the other direction. There are restrictions against using cell phones while driving, and seat belts are compulsory. However, drivers regularly flout these laws. There are numerous traffic officers in the main towns, but enforcement is patchy. Fines of £e100 are the norm, but officers can confiscate your license if they feel you have been driving dangerously.

Drunk driving is a serious offense, and perpetrators can be arrested, fined (around £e500), and have their vehicles confiscated. The legal blood alcohol level above which it is an offense to drive is 0.05%. However, breath tests are not common because most Egyptians don't drink alcohol. There is no legislation relating to children. Car rental companies do not supply car seats for infants; if you have small children, consider bringing a car seat from home.

Around Egypt, there are police checkpoints every 30 km or so along every highway, and also at all major intersections and river crossings. You may need to show your passport to the officers manning the barrier.

Right turns are permitted on red at some intersections—indicated by a flashing light above or to the side of the traffic lane. But not all drivers waiting in this lane want to turn right.

You are not allowed to take cars rented in Egypt out of the country.

In Cairo many traffic lights at intersections do not work, and these areas are manned by traffic officers who control traffic with hand movements.

If you are traveling in one direction on a main highway but want to turn around—or if you merge onto a highway but cannot initially travel in the direction you want, you need to look ahead for a midstream turning area on the left-hand side of the highway. You should see a sign on the overhead gantry, but these are not always well signposted. Be very careful as these feeder lanes lead you directly into the flow of the fastest traffic.

In Upper Egypt, tourist traffic is organized into guarded convoys that follow set routes at set times each day. Whether you self-drive, have a driver, book a day tour, or travel in an organized itinerary, you'll have to work within the convoy system and travel at prescribed times.

▌ BY TAXI

Taxis are the backbone of transport in Egypt. Fares are cheap and, in theory, regulated, but in practice you'll need to haggle. Ask your guide or hotel concierge what are realistic fares between destinations before you depart. And always make sure you agree to a fare with the driver before you enter the taxi.

In Cairo, blue-and-white taxis have meters, but they never work. The yellow taxis are part of a newer fleet with working meters (plus working windows and air-conditioning), but the prices are more expensive than the blue cab fares.

In Sharm El-Sheikh, taxi fares are posted at major taxi stands, but visitors rarely make it to these places to check out the prices. Hikes in fuel prices in 2008 have also played havoc with well-established fares.

Information **City Cabs** (☎16516 or 19195) in Cairo only.

▌ BY TRAIN

Between Alexandria and Cairo, Turbo trains are the fastest form of transport (average journey time is 2 hours), and tickets for these services cost £e46 for first class and £e29 for second class. Speed Trains take a few minutes longer, and tickets cost £e41 for first class and £e25 for second class. Tickets for the slower Express train services (average journey time is 3 hours) are £e35 for first class and £e19 for second class.

Currently, Turbo trains depart Alexandria at 7 AM, 8 AM, 2 PM, 3 PM, 7 PM, and 7:30 PM. Speed trains depart at 8:15 AM, 11 AM, 4:30 PM, and 10:15 PM; Express trains depart at 5.50 AM, 7:15 AM, 10 AM, 12:30 PM, 1 PM, 3:30 PM and 8 PM.

Trains also travel between Cairo and Upper Egypt. From Cairo to Luxor, a one-way ticket is £e90 in first class and £e46 in second class; from Cairo to Aswan it's £e109 in first class and £e55 in second. First class offers you more space, and you have a choice of traveling during the day or at night. Considerably more comfortable sleeper cars run by private company Abela make the daily trip to and from Luxor and Aswan. Buy your tickets far in advance (at least 10 days). Fares are in U.S. dollars, and the price is $60 per person each way in a double compartment.

For exact schedules and ticket prices, inquire and purchase tickets a few days before departing at the main Ramses train station in Cairo.

Information **Abela** (✉Ramses Train Station, Cairo ☎02/2574-9474 ⊕www.sleepingtrains. com).

ON THE GROUND

▮ COMMUNICATIONS

INTERNET

Paid Internet access of some kind is available in almost every hotel, though you may sometimes have access to only one slow and old terminal in the lobby. Most of the five-star hotels in Cairo have paid access in the rooms, though free Internet access is usually one of the privileges of booking an executive-floor room. In remote areas of the country, Internet access may still be via a dial-up connection.

Wi-Fi is becoming more prevalent in the better hotels, particularly in Cairo; it is usually free but generally exists only in the lobby and some public areas, rather than in your room. Free Wi-Fi is also available in dozens of modern coffeehouses in the main downtown districts. There are dozens of Internet cafés in Cairo, and usually one or two in each of the major towns and resorts. Access prices vary from £e5 per hour in internet cafés in the capital to £e30 per 30 minutes in hotels.

Contacts **Cybercafes** (⊕www.cybercafes. com) lists over 4,000 Internet cafés worldwide.

PHONES

To call Egypt from the United States, dial 00, then the country code 20 and the local number.

CALLING WITHIN EGYPT

To make a local call, you must dial the regional code plus the 7-digit or 8-digit number. Directory assistance for calls within Egypt is 140; its operators are known to speak English well.

City codes within Egypt include: Cairo 02; Alexandria 03; Luxor 095; Aswan 097; Sharm al-Sheikh 069; and Hurghada 065.

Rates for calling within Egypt vary by the hotel, but local calls are sometimes only a few piastres per minute.

CALLING OUTSIDE EGYPT

From Egypt, just dial 00–1 plus the area code and number to call the U.S. or Canada. For the international operator dial 120. It's cheaper to call after 8 PM in the evening.

The AT&T USA Direct and MCI calling cards can be used in Egypt. Simply dial the access number and follow the instructions. If you use a pay phone to call, you may require a coin or card deposit. Some hotels block the use of these numbers. If this is the case, try contacting the telephone company operator for a connection.

Access Codes **AT&T** (☎02/2510–0200). **MCI** (☎02/279–5570).

CALLING CARDS

Phone cards, which are sold at gift shops and supermarkets, can usually give you considerable savings if you're calling the United States or Canada.

MOBILE PHONES

The mobile phone network is well established in Egypt—you'll often see rural farmers riding home on their donkey while deep in conversation on their mobiles. Vodafone, Mobinil, and Etisalat are the three major companies in Egypt, and they have offices all across the country. If you have a tri-band GSM phone, it will probably work in Egypt, but you can also bring an old phone from home (get the phone company to unlock the phone for you) and by a SIM card once you get to Egypt so that you can receive calls and texts on a local number. With Vodafone, handsets start at £e180, SIM cards cost around £e25, and you can buy top-up minutes from £e10 to £e200 at one time. To call the U.S., the cost is £e0.08 per minute between midnight and 8 AM.

Contacts **Cellular Abroad** (☎800/287–5072 ⊕www.cellularabroad.com) rents and sells GMS phones and sells SIM cards that work in many countries. **Mobal** (☎888/888–9162 ⊕www.mobalrental.com) rents mobiles and sells GSM phones (starting at $49) that will operate in 140 countries. Per-call rates vary throughout the world. **Planet Fone** (☎888/988–4777 ⊕www.planetfone.com) rents cell phones, but the per-minute rates are expensive.

■ CUSTOMS & DUTIES

When entering Egypt, there are few restricted items, beyond the normal prohibited goods, such as firearms, narcotics, etc. Customs officers will be concerned if you bring in goods in large amounts to sell for a profit—for instance, large numbers of cameras or mobile phones—but most visitors have no problems.

The Egyptian authorities are very keen to keep control of their historical heritage, so you'll need official paperwork to allow you to export anything regarded as an antique or antiquity.

If you want to bring your pet, you'll need a certificate of origin and a health certificate. The certificate of origin should be from the breeder or store where you bought your pet. The certificate of health need to be dated and stamped by your vet.

When you arrive in Egypt you can bring in alcohol and tobacco duty-free. You can also buy further supplies at accredited duty-free shops during the first 48 hours after you arrive. In Cairo, you'll find shops at the airport and at City Stars Mall. There are also shops in El-Gouna and Sharm El-Sheikh.

U.S. Information U.S. Customs and Border Protection (⊕www.cbp.gov).

■ EATING OUT

Traditional Egyptian food generally consists of *ful* a bean stew, roasted meat or chicken, rice, unleavened bread, and Middle Eastern salads such as *hummus*

WORD OF MOUTH

Was the service stellar or not up to snuff? Did the food give you shivers of delight or leave you cold? Did the prices and portions make you happy or sad? Rate restaurants and write your own reviews in Travel Ratings or start a discussion about your favorite places in Travel Talk on www.fodors.com. Your comments might even appear in our books. Yes, you, too, can be a correspondent!

(chick-pea dip) and tomato-and-cucumber salad. Local eateries are no more than street kitchens with a couple of tables, though you can find better restaurants serving local food in Cairo and the major tourist towns.

Cairo and Alexandria are both well known for their *ahwas* (coffee shops). Today these traditional cafés are being joined by U.S.-style joints, offering caffeine in a range of flavors and styles.

In all major towns you'll find a range of international cuisines including Thai, Chinese, and Italian. The best restaurants are usually found in upscale hotels. Vegetarians will always be able to find local salads, hummus, and rice to sustain them; however, finding variety during a trip may be a problem (pizza is available in most tourist destinations, as are delicious soups, just be aware that some of these soups are made with meat-based stocks). Typically, hot and cold *mezze* (starter dishes) are offered at the beginning of every meal, including stuffed vine leaves, lentil soup, and *tahini* (sesame paste).

For information on food-related health issues, see Health below.

MEALS & MEALTIMES
Unless otherwise noted, the restaurants listed in this guide are open daily for lunch and dinner.

The main meal of the day is lunch (*ghada*). It starts with a soup, such as *shorbat'ads* (lentil), for which Egypt is famous throughout the Middle East, or *molukhiyya,* a thick green-leaf soup. A wide range of *mezze* (appetizers) follows, and this can make a meal in itself. You'll taste dips like *tahini* (sesame-seed paste) or *baba ghanouj* (mashed roasted eggplant), *wara einab* (stuffed grape leaves), a crispy local *ta'amiya* (Egyptian felafel), and *ful* (stewed fava beans). The main course is invariably grilled chicken, often roasted whole in a rotisserie oven, lamb shish kebab (skewered in chunks), or *kofta* (minced lamb on skewers). Beef is expensive and rarely served in Egyptian restaurants, but *hamam mahshi* (stuffed pigeon) is immensely popular. Fresh vegetables are hard to come by, except in the rather generic cucumber salad, but stewed vegetables such as *bamia* (okra) are common. Every meal comes with round loaves of pita-style bread, either *'aish baladi* (coarse-grain wheat) or *'aish shami* (white). *'Asha,* or dinner, is composed of a similar menu, although many Egyptian families partake in only a light meal at night, consisting of fruit and sandwiches.

For *fitar* (breakfast), you can do as Egyptians do and indulge in a steaming plate of ful, accompanied by fried eggs, bread, and pickles. Lighter fare includes croissants and other savory pastries, bought fresh from the local bakery and topped with cheese or jam. In Cairo, there are a few American-style breakfast restaurants, but these are by no means widespread. Certain places like El Fishawy Café in the Khan El Khalili stay open for 24-hours.

In the countryside, few Egyptians eat out and so restaurants there tend to be rudimentary affairs. In cities and resorts you'll find a range of restaurants, from street kitchens to gourmet spots with silver service. Most restaurants stay open throughout the day, so you'll always be able to find somewhere when you get hungry.

PAYING

Credit cards are widely accepted in hotel restaurants; less so in private establishments. More private establishments in Cairo and the Red Sea resorts accept cards than in the rest of the country.

For guidelines on tipping see Tipping below.

RESERVATIONS & DRESS

Make reservations when planning to dine in upscale hotel restaurants, particularly if you are not a guest. Restaurants requiring a jacket and tie for men are rare, with the notable exception of several restaurants in the Sofitel Winter Garden Hotel in Luxor. Diners in upscale Cairo restaurants tend to dress up, however.

WINES, BEER & SPIRITS

Although Egypt is an Islamic country and many Egyptians do not drink alcohol, the country does produce its own beer and wine. Local beers are very thirst-quenching, especially if drunk cold. Look for the trade names Luxor, Saqqara, and Heineken (brewed under license in Egypt). The wine industry isn't competition for the French or Californian vineyards but does supply acceptable table wine—look for the labels Grand Marquis, Sheherazade, or Omar Khayam.

Many local restaurants don't serve alcohol, so ask before you order your food if this is important to you. Any hotel above a two-star should by law serve alcohol, but outside the tourist hot-spots there may not be enough demand for hotels to hold a stock. Imported alcohol and wine are very expensive, so expect to pay a premium for these when they are available.

▌ ELECTRICITY

The electrical current in Egypt is 220 volts, 50 cycles alternating current (AC). Most wall outlets take rounded plugs, so North American travelers will need both a converter and an adapter.

If your appliances are dual-voltage, you'll need only an adapter. Don't use 110-volt outlets marked FOR SHAVERS ONLY for high-wattage appliances such as blow-dryers. Most laptops operate equally well on 110 and 220 volts and so require only an adapter.

■ EMERGENCIES

Violence against foreign tourists is very rare in Egypt; pick-pocketing and theft can be a problem in busy markets and at popular tourist sights. Tourist police patrol all main tourist areas and have brown uniforms with TOURIST POLICE on their armbands. They are helpful, but not all of the street officers speak English well.

If you are a victim of theft, you'll need to report it to the regular police and get a case number in order to make a claim on your insurance policy. This can be a time-consuming exercise (two or three hours).

If you are ever threatened on the street or in a public place, do not hesitate to scream for help or make a scene—it will not go unheard, and you'll find more than one person coming to your defense. Whatever the emergency, expect Egyptians to go out of their way to help.

Medical personal generally speak some English, and almost all doctors are English-speakers . Medical facilities are not as good as at home. Pharmacists are well-qualified and able to give advice on common low-risk ailments; they can also prescribe many medications (including antibiotics and even Viagra) that are available only by prescription in the U.S. Each town or district has at least one late-night pharmacy but these open in rotation—so ask your hotel concierge to find out which one is open when you need it. Pharmacies normally stay open until 10 PM. In major cities you'll also find 24-hour pharmacies; these are listed at the end of each chapter.

If you are the victim of a serious crime or accident, contact the U.S. Embassy in Cairo for assistance.

Emergencies Ambulance (☎123). **Fire Brigade** (☎125). **Police** (☎122). **Tourist Police** (☎126).

U.S. Embassy United States Embassy (✉8 Shar'a Kamel El Din Salah, Garden City, Cairo ☎02/2797–3300).

■ ETIQUETTE & BEHAVIOR

Dress is a very important part of respect in Egypt. Wearing shorts, short skirts, and halter tops in the streets is considered inappropriate, despite the fact that many tourists persist in being inappropriately attired. Cover shoulders and knees when you enter mosques and churches.

Beyond this, the relationship between the sexes is very different compared to a non-Muslim country. Profuse shows of affection between couples is not normal in Egypt. This is a country where kissing and cuddling is considered private behavior. Public drunkenness is also frowned upon.

Sexuality is not widely discussed in Egypt, and homosexuality remains taboo. Therefore an open gay population is hard to come by, and a general acceptance also isn't prevalent. However, there is a large gay and lesbian population that remains underground. While there's no law against homosexuality, gay men in particular can be jailed and/or prosecuted under Egypt's wide-ranging and ill-defined indecency laws. With discretion, gay travelers can expect to get along fine, as most Egyptians will assume that the relationship is simply a friendship, and public shows of affection amongst men (holding hands and walking arm in arm) is a normal show of masculine brotherhood in Egypt and many other Muslim countries.

▌ HEALTH

There are several minor hazards in Egypt that you need to bear in mind. First, never underestimate the power of the sun. Even in the coolest months, there's a risk of sunburn and sunstroke. Stay out of the sun as much as possible, wear a hat when you are out and about, apply high-SPF sun cream regularly (international brands are available in pharmacies and supermarkets), and keep hydrated by drinking plenty of fluids (not alcohol).

Water quality is a concern. Never drink water from the tap water or from public fountains. Local people drink this water but it may contain microbes that your body isn't used to. Ice in five-star hotels should be produced using purified water, but if in doubt ask for drinks without ice (*min gheir talg*). Bottled water (*mayya ma'daniya*) is inexpensive and readily available. Remember to check that the seal on the bottle is intact before you open it.

If you are traveling with children, all this advice goes double. Children may not be aware that they are beginning to suffer from dehydration or sunstroke. Give them plenty to drink even if they don't complain of being thirsty, and keep their heads and skin covered.

Most people get some form of intestinal disturbance in Egypt. This can be a minor change in regularity put down to a change in water supply or the hot weather, but it's sometimes more serious and may be related to the ingestion of contaminated food or water. To minimize your risk, make sure the meat you eat is well cooked, avoid unpeeled fruits and vegetables, and avoid dairy products, as these may not be pasteurized. Ask about whether the salad in your hotel has been washed in purified water. Antinal is a locally produced remedy for traveler's diarrhea that's inexpensive and effective, but if symptoms become severe call a doctor immediately. The main danger here is dehydration, so if you cannot keep down liquids, don't hesitate to call for a doctor immediately.

Do not swim in the Nile, and don't drink the river water because of the risk of picking up waterborne parasites. Avoid all standing fresh water as there is the risk of bilharzia (schistosomiasis).

There's no risk of malaria in Egypt—so there's no need to take anti-malarial tablets—but it's worth protecting yourself from insect bites as some of these little critters do carry dengue fever or West Nile virus. You can buy anti-insect skin creams and sprays in pharmacies and tourist shops. It's easy to buy the anti-mosquito coils that burn to give off fumes that repel the insects.

OVER-THE-COUNTER REMEDIES

Pharmacies in Egypt are well stocked—you can even buy antibiotics over the counter—and medications are quite inexpensive by U.S. standards, but not all product names will be the same as in the U.S. Pharmacists are trained to help and will be able to offer you the generic drug you need or one that will deal with your symptoms.

▌ HOURS OF OPERATION

Banks are open for business 9 to 2 Sunday through Thursday. In addition, you can withdraw money from your home bank using ATMs found outside major banks and inside hotels. Businesses are usually open by 8 AM and close by 4 or 5 PM Sunday through Thursday.

Egypt's postal offices are open from 8:30 to 3. The larger post offices in Cairo—Muhammad Farid (Downtown), Ataba Square (next to the Postal Museum), and the Ma'adi offices—are open until 6 PM daily.

Shops are open 9 AM until 10 PM. Most close for a short time for Friday prayers and some close on Sundays, though in the tourist towns, souvenir shops are open daily. In the coastal resorts shops sometimes close during the afternoons.

HOLIDAYS

Egypt's fixed national holidays include New Years Day (January 1) Sinai Liberation Day (April 25), Labor Day (May 1), Evacuation Day (June 18), and Revolution Day (July 23).

The Muslim lunar calendar is normally 10 to 11 days earlier than the Gregorian year. The month of Ramadan lasts for anywhere from 28 to 30 days and entails fasting—no food, water, or smoking—from dawn to sunset. It's followed by Ead al-Fetr, known as the "small feast" in English. The "big feast" is Eid al-Adha, which occurs at the end of the Pilgrimage Period. The other two main Muslim holidays are the Muslim New Year (in late March or early April), and the Prophet Muhammad's birthday (falling anywhere between late May to late June). Coptic holidays are observed by Coptic citizens only. They are Christmas (January 7), Baptism (January 20), Palm Sunday (the Sunday before Easter), and Easter.

▌ LANGUAGE

Arabic is the national language in Egypt, but English is a widely spoken second language—even if the English is not fluent. Staff at major tourist attractions and front-desk personnel in most major hotels speak good English, and it is widely spoken in the tourist regions; only in remote regions may you have difficulty making yourself understood. Having said that, you may be surprised to find the owner of a tiny hotel in a far-off oasis studied for a PhD in the U.S. Egypt is just that way.

Outside popular tourist establishments, using smiles and gestures will help, and though you can manage with just English, people are even more courteous if you try to speak their language. Buy one of those skinny phrase books, and just try.

There seem to be innumerable ways to transliterate Arabic into the Roman alphabet. The aim here has been for the closest approximation of correct pronunciations. One example is the name al-Husayn, which is often spelled el-Hussein. Considering that it's pronounced hu-*sayn*, not hus-*ayn*, this book doesn't double the *s*. In that spirit consonants generally aren't doubled in this book unless correct pronunciation demands it. Along that vein, *ayn* is thought to be more akin to the Arabic sound of the word than is *ein*. This system of transliteration is one that many scholars, among them Albert Hourani, author of *A History of the Arab Peoples,* use.

▌ MAIL

Egypt Post maintains post offices in all large villages and towns and in every city district. Postcards to countries outside the Middle East cost £e1.50 and take a minimum of seven days to reach their destination. A more costly express-mail service is also available with arrival within 48 hours. Note that these are expected delivery times, as advised by the postal service; they don't reflect how long mail actually takes to arrive. If in doubt, double these times. If you need to send a package home, it's more reliable to use FedEx or DHL, which are very expensive.

▌ MONEY

All-inclusive travel packages to Egypt that include flights, transfers, hotels, guides, and fully catered Nile cruises begin at $3,500 for a 14-day package, but you can pay far more. Independent travelers should budget around £e300 ($55) per day for food and short taxi rides. Half-day tours with a reputable company with transportation, guide, and lunch cost around $55, full-day tours around $80.

It's fine to tip tour guides in U.S. dollars, but for small tips (restroom attendants especially) local currency is better since

£e1 is worth far less than US$1. Some stores will even accept U.S. dollars, so you may not need to exchange a large amount of currency unless you plan to eat in many upscale restaurants outside of hotels.

ATMs (*makinat al-flus*) are plentiful in major tourist areas, and you can rely on them to restock your wallet with Egyptian pounds. You'll certainly need cash to purchase locally produced souvenirs, cheap snacks and beverages, and for taxi, *felucca* (sailboat), and carriage rides. All restrooms in Egypt are attended, and the staff expect a small tip of £e1 or at least 50 piastres. Be prepared to tip a few pounds for all kinds of service. Small-denomination notes are in short supply in Egypt, so you'll really oil the wheels of your trip if you keep stocks of £e1 and £e5 for short taxi rides, small purchases, and for tipping. Bring plenty of one-dollar bills because these will be accepted as readily as the domestic currency. All major hotels, cruise ships, and leading restaurants take payment by credit cards. In shops and *souks,* cash is still king. Far fewer establishments outside hotels take credit cards, and paying by credit card can incur 2% to 3% surcharges.

ITEM	AVERAGE COST
Cup of coffee	£e25 for American coffee
Glass of wine	£e30–£e60, though wine is not commonly available
Glass of beer	£e22
Sandwich	£e20
One-mile taxi ride in capital city	£e5
Museum admission	£e30–£e50

Prices throughout this guide are given for adults. Substantially reduced fees are almost always available for children, students, and senior citizens.

ATMS & BANKS

Your own bank will probably charge a fee for using ATMs abroad; the foreign bank you use may also charge a fee. Nevertheless, you'll usually get a better rate of exchange at an ATM than you will at a currency-exchange office or even when changing money in a bank. And extracting funds as you need them is a safer option than carrying around a large amount of cash.

ATMs that accept international cards (Cirrus and Plus) are numerous in Cairo, Luxor, Aswan, and in the coastal resorts of Hurghada, El-Gouna, and Sharm El-Sheikh. You can find them at bank branches, in shopping malls, and in the lobbies of major hotels. Major providers include the National Bank of Egypt, HSBC, Credit Agricole Egypt, and National Societe General Bank (NSGB). Screen commands are in Arabic and English.

In the oases of the Western Desert, the banking system still lags behind the rest of Egypt. Bring enough cash with you to fully fund your trip.

CREDIT CARDS

Throughout this guide, the following abbreviations are used: **AE,** American Express; **DC,** Diners Club; **MC,** Master-Card; and **V,** Visa.

It's a good idea to inform your credit-card company before you travel, especially if you're going abroad and don't travel internationally very often. Otherwise, the credit-card company might put a hold on your card owing to unusual activity—not a good thing halfway through your trip. Record all your credit-card numbers—as well as the phone numbers to call if your cards are lost or stolen—in a safe place, so you're prepared should something go wrong. Both MasterCard and Visa have general numbers you can call (collect if you're abroad) if your card is lost, but you're better off calling the number of your issuing bank, since MasterCard and

Visa usually just transfer you to your bank; your bank's number is usually printed on your card.

Major credit cards (American Express not as often) are accepted at most hotels, large stores, and restaurants.

Reporting Lost Cards American Express (☎202/5672–404 in Cairo, or 336/393–1111 collect from abroad ⊕www.americanexpress.com). **Diners Club** (☎800/234–6377 in the U.S. or 303/799–1504 collect from abroad ⊕www.dinersclub.com). **MasterCard** (☎800/627–8372 in the U.S. or 636/722–7111 collect from abroad ⊕www.mastercard.com). **Visa** (☎800/847–2911 in the U.S. or 410/581–9994 collect from abroad ⊕www.visa.com).

CURRENCY & EXCHANGE

The Egyptian pound (£e) is divided into 100 piasters (pt). Bank notes currently in circulation are the following: 10pt, 25pt, and 50pt notes; £e1, £e5, £e10, £e20, £e50, and £e100 notes. There are also 5pt, 10pt, 20pt, 25pt, and £e1 coins. Don't accept any dog-eared bills, as many vendors will refuse to take them. Just politely give it back and ask for a newer bill.

You may need to change some money, though U.S. dollars are widely accepted. At this writing, the exchange rate was approximately £e5.30 to US$1.

Independent merchants willingly accept U.S. dollars; however, change will be in Egyptian pounds. Always make certain you know in which currency any transaction is taking place. Carry a pocket calculator if your mental arithmetic isn't too hot.

You can find currency-exchange offices at all airports, as well as on the street, and in major shopping areas throughout the island. A passport is usually required to cash traveler's checks. Save some of the official receipts you are given with your transaction. If you end up with too many Egyptian pounds when you are ready to leave the country, you may need to show the receipts when you exchange the pounds for dollars since they are not convertible outside of Egypt. Hotels provide exchange services, but, as a rule, offer less favorable exchange rates.

TRAVELER'S CHECKS

Traveler's checks can still be converted into local currency; since American Express is one of the world's largest providers of traveler's checks and has offices in all major tourist destinations, it is the company of choice for most travelers. You can exchange traveler's checks in banks, but it's not easy; outside of major upscale hotels, traveler's checks are not accepted for payment in most establishments.

Contacts American Express (☎888/412–6945 in the U.S., 801/945–9450 collect outside of the U.S. to add value or speak to customer service ⊕www.americanexpress.com).

∎ SAFETY

Violent crime against tourists in Egypt is very rare and even petty theft is at a low level compared to other international destinations. While robbery is unlikely, you are more likely to be ripped off by a taxi driver or a vendor who makes easy money from tourists who are poor hagglers. However, in Red Sea and Sinai resort areas where there are a lot of tourists, crime (particularly theft) is rising, and you should exhibit the same caution you would in any unfamiliar destination. Never leave items on the beach when you go for a swim. If you have a safe in your hotel room, use it.

You'll be approached for *buksheesh* (tip money) for almost anything (⇨ *Tipping*). Young kids will feel happy to say hello as you pass, then as you reply immediately open their hands for money. At major attractions, men may engage you in conversation as you cross a road then stop the traffic to ease your crossing— then demand a cash reward. One should always be mindful of the poverty of many households, but on the other hand, should you pay out for services that you did not specifically demand or even want? Don't feel obliged to hand over money if you don't feel that it has been earned.

Beware a young Egyptian male who attaches himself to your party as you explore the markets. He'll notice your interest and produce samples of bread or dates for you to try, then eventually will ask for "guiding" money. Another scam is to encourage you into a local shop in the pretence that it's only for tea and a chat, only to press a sale once you're seated and relaxed. But, remember too that these individuals are mixed in with hundreds of very genuine Egyptians who are willing to help for no reward except a chance to chat with a visitor and practice their English, so don't treat everyone with suspicion, just be aware that these approaches do happen.

Women may find themselves on the receiving end of attention from teenage boys and men. This attention is mainly blatant staring and some kind of opening gambit to engage you in conversation, but it can also include very inappropriate comments. This sort of behavior is best ignored. Assault is not common, but occasionally men will attempt to touch women. If this happens to you, do not stay silent. Shout "Leave me alone" or "Stop that" loudly, and this should result in a chastened offender. Make it very clear you find this behavior offensive.

■TIP➜ **Distribute your cash, credit cards, I.D.s, and other valuables between a deep front pocket, an inside jacket or vest pocket, and a hidden money pouch. Don't reach for the money pouch once you're in public.**

▮ TAXES

There is no departure tax when you leave the country. On services such as hotel rooms, group travel, and car rental, a 10% tax is levied. Imported goods are highly taxed, but this is included in the ticketed sale price.

▮ TIME

Egypt is two hours ahead of GMT. The country observes daylight saving time between the last Friday in April and the last Thursday in September.

▮ TIPPING

Tipping, or *baksheesh,* is a way of life in Egypt. Everyone who performs some kind of service for you will expect some kind of monetary reward. This has become so engrained into Egyptian society that small children may come up and simply ask for money. Adults may engage you in conversation and then ask for a little *baksheesh* as you part company. Another ploy is to offer you a free gift, a small piece of alabaster or a scarab, then ask for a monetary "gift" in return. The amounts are small—£e1 is sufficient for restroom attendants, £e2 or £e3 is sufficient for most other small services—but it is up to you whether you feel obliged to hand over cash for such "services." Lots of households live very close to the poverty line in Egypt, and the dollar you hand over will have far more spending power in Luxor than in Los Angeles.

Generally, a 10% service charge is included in all hotel and higher-class restaurant bills. When in doubt, ask. Even then it's still expected that you will tip an extra 5% to 10% in cash (especially if you are using a credit card) if the service was to your liking. In hotels, it's customary to leave at least a dollar per day for the hotel maid. Taxi drivers don't expect a tip for short journeys around town, but you should tip if you engage a driver to take you to several attractions with waiting time, or book a driver for a day (add 10% to the agreed fee). Hotel porters expect at least $1.

INDEX

Photo Credits: Chapter 1: Experience Egypt: 7, *Luis Orteo/Hemis.fr/Aurora Photos.* 8, *Sylvain Grandadam/age fotostock.* 9 (left), *Petr Bonek/Alamy.* 9 (right), *Oberoi Hotels & Resorts.* 10, *Franck Guiziou/age fotostock.* 11 (left), *Christian Delbert/Shutterstock.* 11 (right), *J.D. Dallet/age fotostock.* 12, *Kevin O'Hara/age fotostock.* 13 (left), *Olivier Asselin/Alamy.* 13 (right), *Jose Fuste Raga/age fotostock.* 14 (left), *James Steidl/Shutterstock.* 14 (top center), *Sylvain Grandadam/age fotostock.* 14 (top right), *Bertrand Gardel /Hemis.fr/Egyptian Tourist Authority.* 14 (bottom right), *Holger Mette/Shutterstock.* 15 (top left), *Dainis Derics/Shutterstock.* 15 (bottom left), *frantisekhojdysz/Shutterstock.* 15 (bottom center), *Ramzi Hachicho/Shutterstock.* 15 (right), *Bertrand Gardel /Hemis.fr/Egyptian Tourist Authority.* 16, *Danita Delimont/Alamy.* 17, *Samuel Zuder/laif/Alamy.* 18, *Bertrand Rieger/ Hemis.fr/Egyptian Tourist Authority.* 19 (left), *Middle East/Alamy.* 19 (right), *simo/Alamy.* 24, *Keith Schengili-Roberts.* 25 (left), *Alvin Empalmado.* 25 (right), *Pierdelune/Shutterstock.* 27 (left), *Henryk Kaiser/eStock Photo.* 27 (right), *Helene Rogers/Alamy.* Chapter 2: Cairo: 29, *Miguel Carminati/age fotostock.* Chapter 3: Alexandria: 119, *Elvele Images/Alamy.* 120 (top), *Worldwide Picture Library/ Alamy.* 120 (bottom) and 121 (bottom), *Bertrand Gardel /Hemis.fr/Egyptian Tourist Authority.* 121 (top), *SCPhotos/Alamy.* Chapter 4: The Nile Valley and Luxor: 151, *J.D. Dallet/age fotostock.* 152 (top), *Mika Stock/eStock Photo.* 152 (center), *Picture Finders Ltd./eStock Photo.* 152 (bottom), *Mirek Hejnicki/Shutterstock.* Chapter 5: Aswan & Lake Nasser: 209 and 210 (bottom), *Sylvain Grandadam/age fotostock.* 210 (top) and 211 (bottom), *Bertrand Rieger/Hemis.fr/Egyptian Tourist Authority.* 211 (top), *Dmytro Korolov/Shutterstock.* Chapter 6: The Sinai Peninsula & Red Sea Coast: 247, *Jon Spaull/age fotostock.* 248 (top), *Sylvain Grandadam/age fotostock.* 248 (bottom), *SIME s.a.s/eStock Photo.* 249 (top), *Nick Hanna/Alamy.* 249 (bottom), *simo/Alamy.* Chapter 7: Western Desert Oases: 297, *Franck Guiziou/age fotostock.* 298, *Danita Delimont/Alamy.* 299 (top), *Ariadne Van Zandbergen/Alamy.* 299 (bottom), *Bruno Perousse/age fotostock.* Chapter 8: Nile & Lake Nasser Cruises: 333, *Hemis.fr/SuperStock/age fotostock.*

NOTES

NOTES

NOTES

NOTES

NOTES

ABOUT OUR WRITERS

Lindsay Bennett discovered her love of travel while backpacking around the world in between studies that led to a degree in politics. Today, she's written more than 40 travel guides on destinations worldwide, from the little-explored wilderness destination to the fashionable urban metropolis, and her passion for setting out to far horizons is as fresh as ever.

Despite shrinking journey times and the development of the information superhighway, she believes there's still a big world out there to be experienced, savored, and described in print. Lindsay often works in tandem with her husband, Pete Bennett, who is also a renowned destination and lifestyle photographer. The synergy of words and images they produce is appreciated by an international client list.

Egypt is an enduring favorite assignment. Though still entranced by the majesty of the ancient monuments, the couple are also happy relaxing over a glass of tea or two at a street-side café in Cairo, Alexandria, or Siwa and soaking up the rich atmosphere of 21st-century Egyptian life.

Lindsay and Pete divide their time between their homes in the UK and France, hotel rooms around the world, and journeys in their 34-foot-long Winnebago—a vehicle that's traveled a long way, from a factory in Indiana to European destinations ranging from the Baltic coast to Turkey's eastern border with Syria.